Java: An Introduction to Computing

D0217793

Joel Adams

Larry R. Nyhoff

and

Jeffrey Nyhoff

Calvin College, Grand Rapids, MI

An Alan R. Apt Book

Prentice Hall

PRENTICE HALL
Upper Saddle River, NJ 07458

Library of Congress Cataloging-in-Publication Data on file

Publisher: Alan R. Apt
Associate Editor: Toni D. Holm
Vice President and Editorial Director, ECS: Marcia Horton
Vice President and Director of Production and Manufacturing: David W. Riccardi
Executive Managing Editor: Vince O'Brien
Managing Editor: David A. George
Production Editor: Scott Disanno
Manufacturing Manager: Trudy Pisciotti
Manufacturing Buyer: Pat Brown
Art Director: Heather Scott
Director, Creative Services: Paul Belfanti
Creative Director: Carole Anson
Art Management: Xiaohong Zhu
Assistant to Art Director: John Christiana
Cover Designer: Marjory Dressler
Cover Image: Leonardo Da Vinci's Horse, Nina Akamu, Courtesy of Frederic Meijer Gardens, Grand Rapids
MI.
Interior Design: Elm Street Publishing Services

Prentice
Hall

© 2001 by Prentice Hall, Inc.
Prentice-Hall, Inc.
Upper Saddle River, NJ 07458

Printed in the United States of America
10 9 8 7 6 5 4 3 2

ISBN 0-13-014251-4

Prentice-Hall International (UK) Limited, *London*
Prentice-Hall of Australia Pty. Limited, *Sydney*
Prentice-Hall Canada, Inc., *Toronto*
Prentice-Hall Hispanoamericano, S.A., *Mexico*
Prentice-Hall of India Private Limited, *New Delhi*
Prentice-Hall of Japan, Inc., *Tokyo*
Pearson Education Asia Pte. Ltd., *Singapore*
Editora Prentice-Hall do Brasil, Ltda., *Rio de Janeiro*

ABOUT THE COVER

of the horse, I shall say nothing because I know the times. . . .

Leonardo da Vinci: circa 1497
(expressing his regret at not being
able to complete the horse statue)

In 1482, the duke of Milan, Italy, commissioned Leonardo da Vinci to create a horse statue that was to be 24 feet tall. In *designing* this statue, da Vinci filled notebook pages with sketches of this great charger like that shown on the cover. Eventually, based on his sketches, he sculpted a full-sized clay *model* and recorded notes about how to cast it in bronze. Before it could be realized as the 80-ton *object* he envisioned, da Vinci's model was destroyed—French archers used it for target practice after taking over Milan. Il Cavallo was lost to history for more than four centuries.

Then, in 1977, a story entitled "The Horse That Never Was" appeared in the September *National Geographic* describing the rediscovery in Spain of some of da Vinci's sketches and notes about the statue. After seeing this story, airline pilot Charles Dent became fascinated with the prospect of building the bronze statue as a gift from the American people to the people of Italy. He founded an organization, Leonardo da Vinci's Horse, Inc., to raise funds for this effort and devoted his life to the project until his death in 1994.

A few years later, Frederick Meijer, a well-known businessman and long time arts patron in Grand Rapids, Michigan, became involved with the project and agreed to become a key financial backer, provided that two identical statues would be built, one for Milan, Italy, and one for Grand Rapids, Michigan. Also at this time, American sculptor Nina Akamu was brought in to resolve some problems with the models that had been built. Eventually, she was asked to create her own original version. Work progressed rapidly and in 1999, the two 24-foot statues were completed at the Tallix Art Foundry in New York.

The magnificent American Horse is shown on the cover. This regal steed, the largest equestrian bronze sculpture in the Western Hemisphere, was unveiled in Grand Rapids on October 7, 1999 and towers over the botanical gardens and sculpture park of the Frederik Meijer Gardens.

(See www.meijergardens.org and www.leonardoshorse.org for more information.)

PREFACE

To properly introduce students to computing, we believe that the first computing course should accomplish two goals:

1. Introduce students to the breadth of the discipline of computing, so that they come to understand the role of programming in the broader context of computing.
2. Introduce the methodologies and techniques of computer programming using a modern programming language, providing a (fairly) complete introduction to the language.

The aim of this textbook is to accomplish both of these goals, the latter using Java.

THE BREADTH OF COMPUTING

The first goal grows out of an important theme of curriculum recommendations of the Association of Computing Machinery (ACM) that an introductory course in computing should introduce the various knowledge areas of the discipline:

❑ Architecture
❑ Artificial Intelligence and Robotics
❑ Database and Information Retrieval
❑ Human-Computer Communication
❑ Numerical and Symbolic Computation
❑ Operating Systems
❑ Programming Languages
❑ Software Methodology and Engineering
❑ Social, Ethical, and Professional Context

To accomplish the first goal, we include the Part of the Picture sections, several of which are written by experts in various areas of computing. These sections introduce these areas, trying to capture the spirit of these curriculum guidelines in a natural, unobtrusive way. They have been carefully selected to provide an overview of the discipline of computer science and to provide a foundation for further study in theoretical and/or applied computer science. Titles include:

What is Computer Science?

The History of Computing

Introduction to Computer Systems

Ethics and Issues (by Anne Marchant)

Data Representation

Computability Theory

Boolean Logic and Digital Design

Computer Architecture (by William Stallings)

Introduction to Algorithm Analysis

Numerical Methods

Database Systems (by Keith VanderLinden)

Artificial Intelligence (by Keith VanderLinden)

The TCP/IP Communications Architecture (by William Stallings)

Data Structures

A solid base is thus established for later courses in theoretical and/or applied computer science.

CS1 & CS2

To help with accomplishing the second goal, a sequel to this book is planned. This first text will introduce the essential ideas of Java programming and the breadth of the discipline of computing, making it ideal for a one-semester course in computer science. The second text will be available in two flavors:

- ❏ *C++: An Introduction to Data Structures* (already available) for those who wish to change to C++ in the CS2 course
- ❏ *Java: An Introduction to Data Structures*, for those who wish to continue with the same language in the CS2 course.

Both will introduce elementary data structures and their implementations as well as other topics that are traditionally taught in the second course including sorting, searching, and algorithm analysis. Together, this text followed by one of those listed above will provide a solid introduction to the discipline of computer science.

PEDAGOGICAL APPROACHES

A popular feature of other texts we have written is to use a problem at the beginning of each chapter to introduce the subject of that chapter (e.g., methods, control, structures, inheritance, and so on). Following this example, the concepts and theory behind those ideas are explored, and other examples given to reinforce the ideas. In this approach, students see the *practice* of a new topic before the *abstract* definitions and theory that underlie that topic, providing them with a framework in which those abstract aspects can be organized and understood.

We also continue the "use it, then build it" approach with respect to the more difficult topics for beginning programmers—e.g., *methods, classes*, and *graphical programming*—a kind of **spiral approach** that revisits topics in increasingly greater detail. For example, to show students how methods are used, predefined methods are used in Chapters 2 and 3 as components of expressions. Once students have experience using (predefined) methods, Chapters 4 and 5 teach them to build simple methods, and subsequent chapters show how to build increasingly sophisticated methods. Similarly, students are introduced to classes in Chapter 1, with more practice following in subsequent chapters. Once students are firmly grounded in building and using classes, they explore inheritance and polymorphism in detail in Chapter 11. Through this "use it, then build it" approach, students receive extensive exposure to the concepts underlying each of these constructs, reducing the learning curve when the time comes to actually build those constructs.

We have added chapter objectives and expanded the end-of-chapter features to include a chapter summary that contains key terms and concepts along with documentation for some of the key Java classes used in the chapter. These augment the popular programming pointers used in others of our texts to provide students with good program design and style guidelines as well as warn of potential pitfalls.

This text also exposes the introductory student to object-oriented programming early and consistently. We have included many examples of developing a program to solve a problem, all of which use a design strategy that we have termed **object-centered design** (OCD). This gives the students a problem-solving methodology to follow. The example programs all model good documentation techniques and habits to help students learn the importance of writing maintainable programs.

New to this text are the Graphical/Internet Java sections designed to introduce students to graphics programming. The approach here also is a spiral one. Chapter 1 contains a simple greeting applet, Chapter 2 gives a simple GUI greeting application. In each chapter thereafter, the applet and/or GUI application being built is increasingly more sophisticated—for example, event-driven programming is introduced in Chapter 7 and using threads in animations in Chapter 13. The examples all make use of Java's Swing components. There is one such section per chapter, but if desired, they can be passed over in a first look at "text-based" Java programming and then covered later.

CONTENT AND ORGANIZATION

❑ The background and introductory information has been consolidated into a Chapter 0, which instructors can cover in lecture, assign as reading, or omit as preferred. The presentation of computing history has been updated with more events and photos in a *timeline* of important people and events in the history of computing.

❑ Chapter 1 introduces Java applications and applets with a very simple example. It also introduces the design methodology, called *object-centered design*, a four-phase graduated methodology that novice programmers can use as an aid in designing software solutions. This methodology is used consistently to solve the problems presented throughout the remainder of the text. As the reader learns new language constructs in subsequent chapters, the methodology is expanded to incorporate these new constructs—for example, use methods to create new *operations* not provided in the language and classes to create new types for *objects* needed in a problem. A superb new presentation of the major ethical issues in computing has been contributed by Ann Marchant of George Mason University.

❑ Chapters 2 and 3 introduce the fundamental ideas of types, operations and expressions, including predefined methods.

❑ Chapters 4 and 5 introduce reusability, using methods as a way to encapsulate program statements that can be reused. Object-centered design is expanded (phase II) to incorporate this new idea.

❑ Chapter 6 builds on the ideas introduced in Chapters 1–3, presenting classes and instance methods. Object-centered design is again expanded (phase III) to incorporate this new idea. Our colleague Keith VanderLinden has contributed a Part of the Picture section on artificial intelligence for this chapter.

❑ Chapters 7 and 8 expand on the introduction in Chapter 5 to control structures for selection and repetition. These control structures are used to build increasingly sophisticated functions. Recursion is also introduced in Chapter 8. These chapters also include a concise but thorough summary of computer architecture contributed by William Stallings.

❏ Chapter 9 introduced arrays and illustrates their use with several examples. The important topics of sorting and searching are also introduced as well as multidimensional arrays. A Class `Matrix` is constructed in detail.

❏ Chapter 10 introduces file input and output, along with the important concept of exceptions in Java. Our colleague Keith VanderLinden kindly contributed a Part of the Picture section on databases.

❏ Chapter 11 builds on earlier chapters, reinforcing the idea of *reusability* through class *extension* and *inheritance*, showing how one class can reuse the work of another. Object-centered design is expanded a final time (phase IV), resulting in **object-oriented design**.

❏ Chapter 12 introduces Java's `ArrayList` and `LinkedList` classes and uses them to implement stacks and queues. A modified structure is used in a polygon-sketching GUI. Binary search trees are also introduced in this chapter.

❏ Chapter 13 introduces the more advanced capabilities of Java: multithreading and client-server networking. An animation of moon phases demonstrates the use of threads in graphical programming.

STANDARD JAVA

We have used the specification of Java 2 published by Sun as our primary reference in preparing this text. This language specification along with the API documentation can be found at Sun's website (`java.sun.com/docs`).

OTHER FEATURES

❏ The websites `cs.calvin.edu/books/java/intro/1e/` will be maintained by the authors and will include corrections, additions, reference materials, Internet exercises, and other supplementary materials. These and additional items, including an on-line study guide, will also be available at the Companion Website (`www.prenhall.com/adams`) for this text.

❏ Chapter objectives and summaries consisting of key words and notes help the student identify the main concepts of each chapter

❏ Programming Pointers at chapter ends highlight important points, including:

  ❏ Proper techniques of design and style

  ❏ Common programming pitfalls

❏ Approximately 450 Quick Quiz questions provide a quick check of understanding the material being studied. The answers to all of the quick-quiz questions are given in the text.

❏ Nearly 500 written exercises extend the quick quizzes and apply the material of the preceding section(s). No answers for these are provided in the text and they can therefore be used for written assignments.

❏ The Programming Problems sections at the end of the chapters contain more than 300 programming problems drawn from a wide range of application areas.

❏ An attractive new design makes the text attractive and readable.

❏ Color is used to emphasize and highlight important features.

❑ Boxed displays make it easy to find descriptions of the basic Java statements and constructs.

❑ Icons serve as markers to point out key parts of the text.

	Object-Centered Design		Object-Oriented Design
	Note		Warning, potential pitfall
REFERENCE	Documentation		Quick Quiz
	Exercises		Part of the Picture
	Graphical/Internet Java		Chapter Summary
	Key Terms and Notes		Programming Pointers
	Program Style and Design		Programming Problems

SUPPLEMENTARY MATERIALS

❑ Websites at www.prenhall.com/adams and cs.calvin.edu/books/java/intro/1e will contain source code, color screen snaps of graphical output produced by programs, an online study guide, links to important sites that correspond to items in the text, and many other supplementary materials.

❑ The CD-ROM accompanying this text also contains most of the above items along with a Java compiler (JBuilder), an HTML reference guide, and a lab manual containing laboratory exercises and projects coordinated with the text.

❑ The Instructor's Resource CD-ROM contains the preceding materials along with PowerPoint slides along with solutions to the exercises and many of the programming problems.

❑ A lab manual contains laboratory exercises and projects coordinated with the text.

SUGGESTIONS

The authors welcome feedback, both positive and negative. Comments on features of the text that work especially well as well as those that could be improved will aid us in the preparation of subsequent editions. We would also appreciate being notified of errors. Such comments can be directed to any of the authors at `adams@calvin.edu`, `nyhl@calvin.edu`, or `jnyhoff@calvin.edu` via the Internet, or at the following address:

> Department of Computer Science
> Calvin College
> 3201 Burton SE
> Grand Rapids, MI 49546
> USA

ACKNOWLEDGMENTS

We express our sincere appreciation to all who helped in any way in the preparation of this text, especially Alan Apt, Scott Disanno, Toni Holm, Nick Murray, Heather Scott, Ana Terry, and Jake Warde. We also appreciate the valuable comments and suggestions made by the following reviewers: Donald Cooley (Utah State Univ.), Mike Davarpanah (Cal Poly Pomona), Brian Durney (Brigham Young Univ., Hawaii), Henry A. Etlinger (Rochester Institute of Technology), Pedro Larios (Metrowerks), Ralph Sanford (Bristol Community College), and Pam Vermeer (Washington and Lee Univ.) We also thank Ann Marchant, William Stallings, and Keith VanderLinden for contributing Part of the Picture sections. And, of course, we must also thank our families—Barb, Roy, and Ian; Shar, Jeff, Jim, Greg, Julie, Joshua, Derek, Tom, Joni, and Abigail; Dawn, Rebecca, Megan, and Sara— for encouraging and supporting us, and for being understanding and patient when we slighted their needs and wants. Above all, we give thanks to God for giving us the opportunity, ability, and stamina to prepare this text.

JOEL ADAMS
LARRY NYHOFF
JEFFREY NYHOFF

CONTENTS

BEGINNING SNAPSHOTS

Is computer science a science? An engineering discipline? Or merely a technology, an inventor and purveyor of computing commodities? What is the intellectual substance of the discipline? Is it lasting, or will it fade within a generation?
From the 1989 report of the Task Force on the Core of Computer Science

I wish these calculations had been executed by steam. *Charles Babbage*

Where a computer like the ENIAC is equipped with 18,000 vacuum tubes and weighs 30 tons, computers in the future may have only 1,000 vacuum tubes and weigh only 1½ tons. *Popular Mechanics, March 1949*

640K ought to be enough for anyone. *Bill Gates, 1981*

So IBM has equipped all XTs with what it considers to be the minimum gear for a serious personal computer. Now the 10-megabyte disk and the 128K of memory are naturals for a serious machine. *Peter Norton, 1983*

Chapter Contents

Chapter Objectives

- (Optional) Give an overview of computer science to show its breadth
- (Optional) Provide a context for many fundamental concepts of computing by pointing out some of the events from the past that have led to modern-day computing.
- (Optional) Describe basic components and organization of computer systems to better understand programming methods and features.

A first course in computing should help students develop an accurate and balanced picture of computer science as a discipline. This is important to students majoring in computer science, for whom this introduction to the discipline will be fleshed out in later courses, as well as to students majoring in other disciplines, for whom the portrayal of computing should be a realistic one. Thus, although most of this text is devoted to developing problem-solving and programming skills, we attempt to give a more complete picture of computer science by including special "Part of the Picture" sections throughout the text that introduce topics from various areas of computer science. They may be omitted without loss of continuity, but *we encourage you to read these Part of the Picture sections to better understand this young discipline called computer science.*

0.1 | PART OF THE PICTURE: WHAT IS COMPUTER SCIENCE?

The term *computer science* has been a source of confusion. Although there are sciences called physics and biology, there are no disciplines called telescope science or microscope science. How can there be a computer science if a computer is simply another scientific tool or instrument?

Let us begin with what computer science is not. It is not simply writing computer programs. Although problem solving and programming are indeed the primary focus of this text, the discipline of computing consists of much more. The breadth of the discipline is evidenced by the following list of the main areas of computer science given curriculum recommendations from the professional societies ACM (Association of Computing Machinery) and IEEE (Institute of Electrical and Electronics Engineers).[1] This list contains some terms that you may not understand, but most of them will be explained later. In our attempt to portray computer science as a discipline, the Part of the Picture sections that follow will focus on many of these areas and help you to better understand them.

Area of Computer Science	What This Area Deals with
Algorithms and Data Structures	Specific classes of problems and their efficient solutions
	Performance characteristics of algorithms
	Organization of data relative to different access requirements
Architecture	Methods of organizing efficient, reliable computing systems
	Implementation of processors, memory, communications, and software interfaces
	Design and control of large, reliable computational systems
Artificial Intelligence and Robotics	Basic models of behavior
	Building (virtual or actual) machines to simulate animal and human behavior

[1] Allen B. Tucker, ed., Computing Curricula 1991: Report of the ACM/IEEE-CS Joint Curriculum Task Force (ACM Press and IEEE Computer Society Press, 1991).

Area of Computer Science	What This Area Deals with
	Inference, deduction, pattern recognition, and knowledge representation
Database and Information Retrieval	Organizing information and designing algorithms for the efficient access and update of stored information
	Modeling data relationships
	Security and protection of information in a shared environment
	Characteristics of external storage devices
Human–Computer Communication	Efficient transfer of information between humans and machines
	Graphics
	Human factors that affect efficient interaction
	Organization and display of information for effective utilization by humans
Numerical and Symbolic Computation	General methods for efficiently and accurately using computers to solve equations from mathematical models
	Effectiveness and efficiency of various approaches to the solution of equations
	Development of high-quality mathematical software packages
Operating Systems	Control mechanisms that allow multiple resources to be efficiently coordinated during execution of programs
	Appropriate service of user requests
	Effective strategies for resource control
	Effective organization to support distributed computation
Programming Languages	Notations for defining virtual machines that execute algorithms
	Efficient translation from high-level languages to machine codes
	Extension mechanisms that can be provided in programming languages
Software Methodology and Engineering	Specification, design, and production of large software systems

Area of Computer Science	What This Area Deals with
	Principles of programming and software development, verification, and validation of software
	Specification and production of software systems that are safe, secure, reliable, and dependable
Social and Professional Context	Cultural, social, legal, and ethical issues related to computing

Because to some people the term *computer science* seems inadequate to describe such a broad range of areas, the Computing Curricula 1991 Report suggests that *computing* is a more appropriate term than *computer science*. However, we will use the two terms interchangeably throughout this text.

0.2 PART OF THE PICTURE: THE HISTORY OF COMPUTING[2]

The computer is one of the most important inventions in history. It has evolved into an essential component of many areas of human culture, including business, industry, government, science, and education; indeed, it has touched nearly every aspect of our lives. The impact of the twentieth-century information technology has already been nearly as widespread as the impact of the printing press and the Industrial Revolution. As part of the picture of computing, it is necessary to be aware of some of the events that led to modern-day computing, not only for the purpose of contextualizing the present-day computer within its own history but also because an examination of the history of the computer serves as a superb introduction to the fundamental concepts of computing.

Four important concepts have shaped the history of computing:

- ❏ The **mechanization of arithmetic**
- ❏ The **stored program**
- ❏ The **graphical user interface**
- ❏ The computer **network**.

The following timeline of the history of computing shows some of the important events and devices that have implemented these concepts, especially the first two. Additional information about these and the other two important concepts follow the timeline.

---

[2] The videotape series entitled "The Machine That Changed The World" is highly recommended by the authors. For information about it, see http://ei.cs.vt.edu/~history/TMTCTW.html. A Jacquard Loom, Hollerith's tabulator, the ENIAC, UNIVAC, early chips, and other computer artifacts can also be viewed at the National Museum of American History of the Smithsonian Institution in Washington, D.C. Also see this book's website for more information about the history of computing.

MACHINES TO DO ARITHMETIC

The term *computer* dates back to the 1600s. However, until the 1950s, the term referred almost exclusively to a *human* who performed computations.

For human beings, the task of performing large amounts of computation is one that is laborious, time-consuming, and error-prone. Thus, the human desire to mechanize arithmetic is an ancient one. One of the earliest "personal calculators" was the abacus. It has movable beads strung on rods to count and to do calculations. Although its exact origin is unknown, the abacus was used by the Chinese perhaps 3000 to 4000 years ago and is still used today throughout Asia. Early merchants used the abacus in trading transactions.

The ancient British stone monument Stonehenge, located near Salisbury, England, was built between 1900 and 1600 B.C. and, evidently, was used to predict the changes of the seasons.

In the twelfth century, a Persian teacher of mathematics in Baghdad, Muhammad ibn-Musa al-Khowarizm, developed some of the first step-by-step procedures for doing computations. The word *algorithm* used for such procedures is derived from his name.

In Western Europe, the Scottish mathematician John Napier (1550–1617) designed a set of ivory rods (called Napier's bones) to assist with doing multiplications. Napier also developed tables of logarithms and other multiplication machines.

National Museum of American History of the Smithsonian Institution in Washington, D.C.

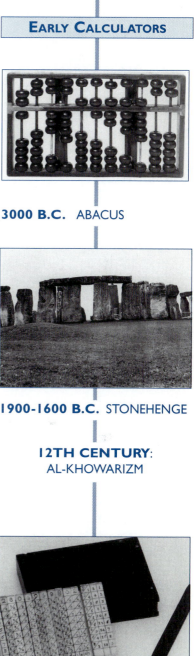

EARLY CALCULATORS

3000 B.C. ABACUS

1900-1600 B.C. STONEHENGE

12TH CENTURY: AL-KHOWARIZM

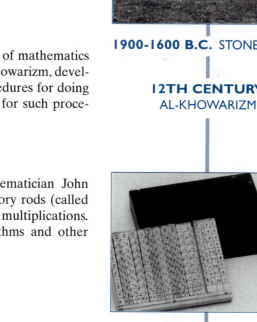

1612 NAPIER'S BONES

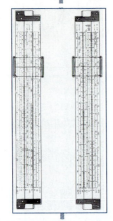

1630 SLIDE RULE

The English mathematician William Oughtred invented a circular slide rule in the early 1600s. Slide rules were based on Napier's logarithms and more modern ones like that shown here were used by engineers and scientists through the 1950s and into the 1960s to do rapid approximate computations.

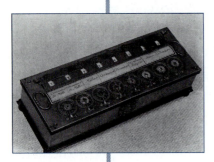

1642 PASCALINE

The young French mathematician Blaise Pascal (1623–1662) invented one of the first mechanical adding machines to help his father with calculating taxes. It used a series of eight ten-toothed wheels (one tooth for each decimal digit), which were connected so that numbers could be added or subtracted by moving the wheels.

The "Pascaline" was a **digital** calculator, because it represented numerical information as discrete digits, as opposed to a graduated scale like that used in *analog* instruments of measurement such as non-digital clocks and thermometers. Each digit was represented by a gear that had ten different positions (a *ten-state device*) so that it could "count" from 0 through 9 and, upon reaching 10, would reset to 0 and advance the gear in the next column so as to represent the action of "carrying" to the next digit.

Although Pascal built more than 50 of his adding machines, his commercial venture failed because the devices could not be built with sufficient precision for practical use.

1673 LEIBNIZ' CALCULATOR

The German mathematician Gottfried Wilhelm von Leibniz invented an improved mechanical calculator that, like the Pascaline, used a system of gears and dials to do calculations. However, it was more reliable and accurate than the Pascaline and could perform all four of the basic arithmetic operations of addition, subtraction, multiplication, and division.

A number of other mechanical calculators followed that further refined Pascal's and Leibniz's designs, and by the end of the nineteenth century, these calculators had become important tools in science, business, and commerce.

THE STORED PROGRAM

The fundamental idea that distinguishes computers from calculators is the concept of a stored program that controls the computation. A **program** is a sequence of instructions that the computer follows to solve some problem. An income tax form is a good analogy. While a calculator can be a useful tool in the process, computing taxes involves much more than arithmetic. To produce the correct result, one must execute the form's precise sequence of steps of writing numbers down (storage), looking numbers up (retrieval), and computation to produce the correct result. Likewise, a computer program is a precise sequence of steps designed to accomplish some human task.

The stored program concept also gives the computer its amazing versatility. Unlike most other machines, which are engineered to mechanize a single task, a computer can be programmed to do many different tasks—that is, the choice of task is deferred to the user. This is the fascinating paradox of the computer: although its **hardware** is designed for a very specific task—the mechanization of arithmetic—computer software programs enable the computer to perform a dizzying array of human tasks, from navigational control of the space shuttle to word processing to musical composition. For this reason, the computer is sometimes called the **universal machine**.

1801 JACQUARD LOOM

An early example of a stored program automatically controlling a hardware device can be found in the weaving loom invented in 1801 by the Frenchman **Joseph Marie Jacquard**. Holes punched in metal cards directed the action of this loom: A hole punched in one of the cards would enable its corresponding thread to come through and be incorporated into the weave at a given point in the process; the absence of a hole would exclude an undesired thread. To change to a different weaving pattern, the operator of this loom would simply switch to another set of cards. Jacquard's loom is thus one of the first examples of a programmable machine, and many later computers would make similar use of punched cards.

The punched card's present-or-absent hole also marks the early occurrence of another key concept in the history of computing: the **two-state device**, which refers to any mechanism for which there are only two possible conditions. Within a decade, thousands of automated looms were being used in Europe, threatening the traditional weaver's way of life. In protest, English weavers who called themselves *Luddites* rioted and destroyed several of the new looms and cards. Some of the Luddites were hanged for their actions. (The term Luddite is still used today to refer to someone who is skeptical of new technology.)

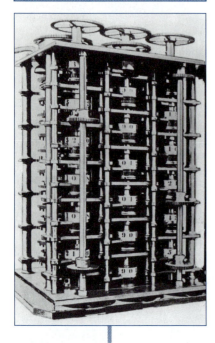

1822 BABBAGE'S DIFFERENCE ENGINE

1833 BABBAGE'S ANALYTICAL ENGINE

The two fundamental concepts of mechanized calculation and stored program control were combined by the English mathematician **Charles Babbage** (1792–1871). In Babbage's lifetime, humans involved in almost any form of computation relied heavily upon books of mathematical tables that contained the results of calculations that had already been performed by others. However, such mathematical tables took far too long for humans to produce and were typically rife with errors. Moreover, world travel, the Industrial Revolution, and other new scientific and economic realities had produced an explosion in the need for mathematical computations. It was clear to Babbage that "human computers" were simply not up to the task of supplying the demand.

In 1822, supported by the British government, Babbage began work on a machine that he called the *Difference Engine*. Comprised of a system of gears, the Difference Engine was designed to compute polynomials for preparing mathematical tables. Babbage continued this work until 1833, when he abandoned this effort having completed only part of the machine. According to Doron Swade, curator of the London Science Museum, the cantankerous Babbage argued with his engineer, ran out of money, and was beset by personal rivalry.

In 1833, Babbage began the design of a much more sophisticated machine that he called his **Analytical Engine**, which was to have over 50,000 components. The operation of this machine was to be far more versatile and fully automatic, controlled by programs stored on punched cards, an idea based on Jacquard's earlier work. In fact, as Babbage himself observed: "The analogy of the Analytical Engine with this well-known process is nearly perfect."

The basic design of Babbage's Analytical Engine corresponded remarkably to that of modern computers in that it involved the four primary operations of a computer system: **processing**, **storage**, **input**, and **output**. It included a mill for carrying out the arithmetic computations according to a sequence of instructions (like the central processing unit in modern machines); the store was the machine's memory for storing up to 1,000 50-digit numbers and intermediate results; input was to be by means of punched cards; output was to be printed; and other components were designed for the transfer of information between components. When completed, it would have been as large as a locomotive, been powered by steam, been able to calculate to six decimal places of accuracy very rapidly and print out results, all controlled by a stored program.

Babbage's machine was not built during his lifetime, but it is nevertheless an important part of the history of computing because many of the concepts of its design are used in modern computers. For this reason, Babbage is sometimes called the "Father of Computing."

Ada Augusta, Lord Byron's daughter, was one of the few people other than Babbage who understood the Analytical Engine's design. This enabled her to develop "programs" for the machine, and for this reason she is sometimes called "the first programmer." She described the similarity of Jacquard's and Babbage's inventions: "The Analytical Engine weaves algebraic patterns just as the Jacquard loom weaves flowers and leaves." In the 1980s, the programming language Ada was named in her honor.

During the next 100 years, little progress was made in realizing Babbage's dream. About the only noteworthy event during this time was the invention by **Herman Hollerith** of an electric tabulating machine that could tally census statistics that had been stored on punched cards. There was a fear that, because of growing population, it would not be possible to complete processing of the 1890 census before the next one was to be taken. Hollerith's machine enabled the United States Census Bureau to complete the 1890 census in 2 1/2 years. The Hollerith Tabulating Company later merged with other companies to form the International Business Machines (IBM) Corporation.

Much of Babbage's dream was finally realized in the "Z" series of computers developed by the young German engineer **Konrad Zuse** in the 1930s. Ingeniously, Zuse designed his computers to mechanize arithmetic of **binary** numbers rather than that of decimal numbers. Because there are only two binary digits, 0 and 1, Zuse could construct his machine from two-state devices instead of ten-state devices, thus greatly simplifying the engineering of his computer. The two-state device Zuse deployed was the electro-mechanical relay, a two-position switch that would either complete or break the circuit connecting two phone lines. This mechanism was in wide use in the telephone industry to automate connections previously managed by human operators.

However, Zuse ultimately grew dissatisfied with the slow speed at which the relay switched from one state to the other. His assistant, **Helmut Schreyer**, made the brilliant suggestion of using vacuum tubes, which could switch between states—on and off—electronically, thousands of times faster than any mechanical device involving moving parts. In the middle of World War II, however, Adolf Hitler was convinced that victory was near and refused to fund Zuse's proposal to build the first fully **electronic** computer.

1842 ADA AUGUSTA

ELECTROMECHANICAL COMPUTERS

1890 HOLLERITH'S TABULATING MACHINE

1935-1938 KONRAD ZUSE

EARLY ELECTRONIC COMPUTERS

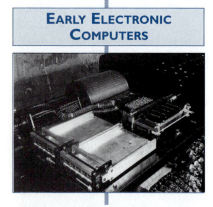

In addition to building electro-mechanical computers, Konrad Zuse in 1945 designed a high-level programming language that he named Plankalkül. Although Zuse wrote programs using this language, it was never actually implemented due to a lack of funding. As a result, it lay in obscurity until 1972 when Zuse's manuscripts were discovered. This language was amazingly sophisticated for its time—over 15 years passed before its features began to appear in other languages. Zuse designed programs to perform tasks as diverse as integer and floating-point arithmetic, sorting lists of numbers, and playing chess.

World War II also spurred the development of computing devices in the United States, Britain, and Europe. In Britain, **Alan Turing** developed the universal machine concept, forming the basis of **computability theory** (see Chapter 5). During World War II, he was part of a team whose task was to decrypt intercepted messages of the German forces. Several machines resulted from this British war effort, one of which was the Collosus, finished in 1943.

The best-known computer built before 1945 was the Harvard **Mark I** (whose full name was the Harvard-IBM Automatic Sequence Controlled Calculator). Like Zuse's "Z" machines, it was driven by electromechanical relay technology. Repeating much of the work of Babbage, Howard Aiken and others at IBM constructed this large, automatic, general purpose, electromechanical calculator. It was sponsored by the U.S. Navy and (like Babbage's machines) was intended to compute mathematical and navigational tables.

The first fully electronic binary computer, the **ABC** (Atanasoff-Berry Computer), was developed by **John Atanasoff** at Iowa State University to do long mathematical calculations in physics. With the help of his assistant, **Clifford Berry**, he built a prototype in 1939 and completed the first working model in 1942.

Unfortunately, because the ABC was never patented and because others failed at the time to see its utility, it took three decades before Atanasoff and Berry received recognition for this remarkable technology. Although the ENIAC (1943–1946) bore the title of the first fully electronic computer for many years, a historic 1973 court decision ruled that Atanasoff was the legal inventor of the first electronic digital computer.

Grace Murray Hopper (1907-1992) began work as a coder—what we today would call a programmer—for the Mark I. In the late 1950s, "Grandma COBOL," as she has affectionately been called, led the effort to develop the COBOL programming language for business applications.

The actual physical components that make up a computer system are its **hardware**. Several generations of computers can be identified by their type of hardware. **First-generation** computers are characterized by their extensive use of **vacuum tubes**. Although they could do calculations much more rapidly than mechanical and electro-mechanical computers, the heat generated by large numbers of vacuum tubes and their short lifetimes led to frequent failures.

The **ENIAC** is arguably the best-known of the early electronic computers (and long thought to be the first). It was designed by **J. Presper Eckert** and **John Mauchly**, who began work on it in 1943 at the Moore School of Engineering at the University of Pennsylvania. When it was completed in 1946, this 30-ton machine had 18,000 vacuum tubes, 70,000 resistors, 5 million soldered joints, and consumed 160 kilowatts of electrical power. Stories are told of how the lights in Philadelphia dimmed when the ENIAC was operating.

This extremely large machine could multiply numbers approximately 1000 times faster than the Mark I, but it was quite limited in its applications and was used primarily by the Army Ordnance Department to calculate firing tables and trajectories for various types of artillery shells.

The instructions that controlled the ENIAC's operation were entered into the machine by rewiring some of the computer's circuits. This complicated process was very time-consuming, sometimes taking a number of people several days; during this time, the computer was idle. In other early computers, the instructions were stored outside the machine on punched cards or some other medium and were transferred into the machine one at a time for interpretation and execution. Unfortunately, because of the relative slowness of the moving parts of mechanical input devices in comparison to the electronic parts of the computer dedicated to processing, such computers would always finish executing the instruction long before the next instruction was finished loading. Thus, again, the processing portion of the computer was sitting idle too much of the time.

1944 GRACE HOPPER

FIRST-GENERATION COMPUTERS

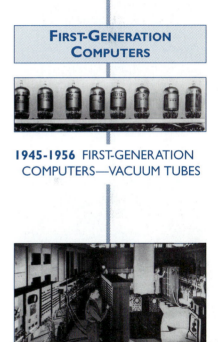

1945-1956 FIRST-GENERATION COMPUTERS—VACUUM TUBES

1943-1946 ENIAC

1945 JOHN VON NEUMANN'S "FIRST DRAFT OF A REPORT ON THE EDVAC"

In 1945, John von Neumann wrote "First Draft of a Report on the EDVAC" computer in which he described a scheme that required program instructions to be stored internally before execution. This led to his being credited as the inventor of the stored-program concept. The architectural design he described is still known as the **von Neumann architecture** (although there is evidence that others including Eckert and Mauchly and Zuse had similar ideas several years before this).

The advantage of executing instructions from a computer's memory rather than directly from a mechanical input device is that it eliminates time that the computer must spend waiting for instructions. Instructions can be processed more rapidly and more importantly, they can be modified by the computer itself while computations are taking place. The introduction of this scheme to computer **architecture** was crucial to the development of general-purpose computers.

1945 COMPUTER BUG

While working on the Mark II computer, Grace Hopper found one of the first computer "**bugs**"—an actual bug stuck in one of the thousands of relays that has been preserved in the National Museum of American History of the Smithsonian Institution. She glued it into the logbook, and subsequent efforts to find the cause of machine stoppage were reported to Aiken as debugging the computer.

1951 UNIVAC

Eckert and Mauchly left the University of Pennsylvania to form the Eckert-Mauchly Computer Corporation, which built the **UNIVAC** (Universal Automatic Computer). Started in 1946 and completed in 1951, it was the first commercially available computer designed for both scientific and business applications. The UNIVAC achieved instant fame partly due to its correct (albeit unbelieved) prediction on national television of the election of President Eisenhower in the 1952 U.S. presidential election, based upon 5% of the returns. UNIVAC soon became the common name for computers.

Soon afterward, because of various setbacks, Eckert and Mauchly sold their company to the Remington-Rand Corporation, who sold the first **UNIVAC** to the Census Bureau in 1951.

Second-generation computers, built between 1959 and 1965, used **transistors** in place of the large, cumbersome vacuum tubes, marking the beginning of the great computer shrinkage. These computers were smaller, faster, required less power, generated far less heat, and were more reliable than their predecessors. They were also less expensive.

Early computers were difficult to use because of the complex coding schemes used to represent programs and data. A key development during the late 1950s and early 1960s was the development of programming languages that made it much easier to develop programs.

In 1957, after 3 years of work, John Backus and his colleagues delivered the first **FORTRAN** (FORmula TRANslation) compiler for the IBM 704. Their first report commented that a programmer was able to write and debug in 4 to 5 hours a program that would have taken several days to do before. FORTRAN has undergone several revisions and remains a powerful language for scientific computing.

In 1958, IBM introduced the first of the second-generation computers (the 7090 and other computers in their 7000 series) vaulting IBM from computer obscurity to first place in the computer industry.

Also in 1958, as part of his work in developing artificial intelligence, John McCarthy developed the programming language **LISP** (LISt Processing) for manipulating strings of symbols, a non-numeric processing language.

Since 1952, Grace Hopper had been developing a series of natural-language-like programming languages for use in business data processing. This culminated in 1960 with the development of **COBOL** (Common Business Oriented Language) by an industry-wide team. Since then, more programs have been written in COBOL than in any other programming language.

Another language that appeared in 1960 was **ALGOL 60** (ALGOrithmic Language), which became the basis of many programming languages that followed, such as **Pascal**.

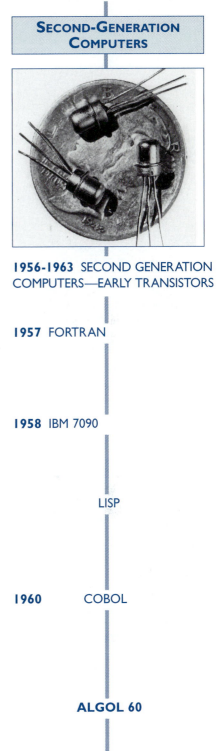

SECOND-GENERATION COMPUTERS

1956-1963 SECOND GENERATION COMPUTERS—EARLY TRANSISTORS

1957 FORTRAN

1958 IBM 7090

LISP

1960   COBOL

ALGOL 60

1964-1971 THIRD-GENERATION COMPUTERS—CHIPS AND INTEGRATED CIRCUITS

Third-generation computers used **integrated circuits** (chips), which first became commercially available from the Fairchild Corporation. These ICs were based on the pioneering work of **Jack Kilby** and **Robert Noyce**.

It was also during this period that, in addition to improved hardware, computer manufacturers began to develop collections of programs known as **system software**, which made computers easier to use. One of the more important advances in this area was the third-generation development of **operating systems**. Two important early operating systems still used today are Unix (1971) and MS-DOS (1981).

1964 THE IBM SYSTEM/360

The **IBM System/360**, introduced in 1964, is commonly accepted as the first of the third generation of computers. Orders for this family of mutually compatible computers and peripherals climbed to 1000 per month within 2 years

1965 PDP-8

In 1965, Digital Equipment Corporation introduced the **PDP-8**, the first commercially successful **minicomputer**. Because of its speed, small size, and reasonable cost—$18,000, less than 20% of the six-digit price tag for an IBM 360 mainframe—it became a popular computer in many scientific establishments, small businesses, and manufacturing plants.

In 1968, **Douglas Engelbart** and his research team worked at developing a more user-friendly form of computing, usable by average persons and for purposes other than numerical computation. Engelbart's inventions anticipated many of the attributes of personal computing, including the **mouse**, word processor, windowed interfaces, integrated "Help," and linked text that would later be termed "hypertext."

1968 DOUGLAS ENGELBART: COMPUTER MOUSE, 2-DIMENSIONAL DISPLAY, EDITING, HYPERMEDIA

Disillusioned by how work on the multiuser operating system Multics was proceeding, **Ken Thompson** of Bell Telephone Laboratories began work in 1969 on a simpler OS aimed at the single user. His first implementation of Unix was written in the assembly language of a spare Digital Equipment Corporation PDP-7 computer. In a pun on the name Multics, the new operating system was named Unix.

Unix is still undergoing development today and has become one of the most popular operating systems. It is the only operating system that has been implemented on computers ranging from microcomputers to supercomputers. (See §1.1 for more details.)

1969 KEN THOMPSON: UNIX

Another noteworthy event began in 1969 when the Advanced Research Projects Agency (ARPA) of the U.S. Department of Defense introduced the **ARPANET**, a network linking computers at some of the department's university research centers. Transmissions between the ARPANET computers traveled in the form of **packets**, each of which was addressed so that it could be routed to its destination. As more and more hosts were added to the ARPANET backbone, it became known as the **Internet**.

ARPANET— THE BEGINNING OF THE INTERNET

Computers from the 1980s on, commonly called **fourth-generation computers**, use very large-scale integrated (VLSI) circuits on silicon chips and other microelectronic advances to shrink their size and cost still more while enlarging their capabilities. A typical chip is equivalent to millions of transistors, is smaller than a baby's fingernail, weighs a small fraction of an ounce, requires only a trickle of power, and costs but a few dollars.

The first chip was the 4004 chip designed by Intel's **Ted Hoff**, giving birth to the microprocessor, which marked the beginning of the fourth-generation of computers. This, along with the first use of an 8-inch floppy disk at IBM, ushered in the era of the personal computer.

Robert Noyce, one of the cofounders of the Intel Corporation, which introduced the 4004 microprocessor in 1971. contrasted microcomputers with the ENIAC as follows:

> An individual integrated circuit on a chip perhaps a quarter of an inch square now can embrace more electronic elements than the most complex piece of electronic equipment that could be built in 1950. Today's microcomputer, at a cost of perhaps $300, has more computing capacity than the first electronic computer, ENIAC. It is twenty times faster, has a larger memory, consumes the power of a light bulb rather than that of a locomotive, occupies 1/30,000 the volume and costs 1/10,000 as much. It is available by mail order or at your local hobby shop.

To simplify the task of transferring the Unix operating system to other computers, Ken Thompson began to search for a high-level language in which to rewrite Unix. None of the languages in existence at the time were appropriate; therefore, in 1970, Thompson began designing a new language called B. By 1972, it had become apparent that B was not adequate for implementing Unix. At that time, Dennis Ritchie, also at Bell Labs, designed a successor language to B that he called C, and approximately 90 percent of Unix was rewritten in C. (See §1.1 for more details.)

Other noteworthy events in 1973 included:

- **Ethernet**. the basis for LANs (Local Area Networks) was developed at Xerox Parc by Robert Metcalf
- A district court in Minneapolis ruled that John Atanasoff was the legal inventor of the first electronic digital computer, thus invalidating Eckert's and Mauchly's patent.

Noteworthy in 1974

● The MITS **Altair 8800** hobby-kit computer was invented by Edward Roberts (who coined the term **personal computer**), William Yates, and Jim Bybee. It was driven by the 8-bit Intel **8080** chip, had 256 bytes of memory, but no keyboard, no display, and no external storage. It sold for $300-400.

● **Bill Gates** and **Paul Allen** wrote a BASIC compiler for the Altair.

● Working in a garage, **Steven Jobs** and **Steve Wozniak** developed the Apple I.

One of the most popular early personal computers was the **Apple II**, introduced in 1976 by Steven Jobs and Steve Wozniak. Because of its affordability and the availability of basic software applications, it was an immediate success, especially in schools and colleges.

The first **supercomputer** and the fastest machine of its day, the **Cray I**, developed by Seymour Cray, was also introduced in 1976. It was built in the shape of a C so components would be close together, reducing the time for electronic signals to travel between them.

Also in 1976, **Apple** Corporation and **Microsoft** Corporation were founded.

1974

ALTAIR

BASIC

JOBS & WOZNIAK: APPLE I

1976 APPLE II

CRAY I

APPLE CORP.
MICROSOFT CORP.

1981 IBM PC

In 1981, IBM entered the personal computer market with the IBM PC, originally called the Acorn. Driven by the Intel 8-bit 8088 chip, it used Microsoft's **DOS** operating system under an agreement that gave Microsoft all the profits in exchange for their having borne the development costs. MS-DOS thus became the most popular operating system for personal computers, and the PC established a microcomputer standard adopted by many other manufacturers of personal computers.

The IBM XT debuted the following year, sporting a 10-megabyte hard disk drive. The IBM AT followed in 1983, driven by the 16-bit Intel 80286 microprocessor, the first in the line of Intel's "80x86" chips.

1983 BJARNE STROUSTRUP: C++

By the late 1970s, a new approach to programming appeared on the scene—**object-oriented programming (OOP)**—that emphasized the modeling of objects through classes and inheritance (see Chapters 3, 4, 6, and 11). A research group at Xerox' Palo Alto Research Center (PARC) created the first truly object-oriented language, named **Smalltalk-80**.

Another Bell Labs researcher, **Bjarne Stroustrup**, began the work of extending C with object-oriented features. In 1983 the redesigned and extended programming language C With Classes was introduced with the new name C++. (See §1.1 for more details.)

NOVELL
ANNOUNCES NETWARE

TCP/IP

Also in 1983:

● **Novell** Data Systems introduced NetWare, a network operating system (NOS), which made possible the construction of a **Local Area Network** (**LAN**) of IBM PC-compatible microcomputers.

● **Transmission Control Protocol/Internet Protocol** (**TCP/IP**) became the official protocol governing transmitting and receiving of data via the ARPANET. Later that year, Berkeley released a new version of BSD (also known as Berkeley UNIX), which included TCP/IP, thus providing academic computing systems nationwide with the technology to tie into the ARPANET. Explosive growth in the ARPANET resulted.

Using a renowned Orwellian advertisement parodying the downtrodden masses subservient to the IBM PC, Apple announced in 1984 the **Macintosh**, a new personal computer driven by the 32-bit Motorola 68000 microprocessor. Inspired by Steve Jobs' visit to Xerox PARC in 1979, the "Mac" brought the graphical user interface (GUI) to personal computing.

1984 MACINTOSH

In 1985, Microsoft introduced **Windows 1.0**, its graphical user interface for IBM-PC-compatibles. It was not until the release of Windows 3.0 in 1990, however, that it gained widespread acceptance.

1985 WINDOWS

In 1986, **Intel** released the 32-bit **80386 chip** (better known as the "386" chip), which became the best-selling microprocessor in history. It contained 275,000 transistors. The **80486**, released in 1989, had more than a million.

1986 INTEL 386 CHIP

In 1991, CERN (European Laboratory for Particle Physics) introduced the **World Wide Web**, developed by **Tim Berners-Lee**.

1991 TIM BERNERS-LEE: WWW

Linux, a free version of the Unix operating system for PCs, was introduced in 1992.

1992 LINUX

1993 PENTIUM CHIPS

POWER PC CHIP

MOSAIC

APPLE NEWTON

1994 NETSCAPE NAVIGATOR 1.0

YAHOO!

1995 JAMES GOSLING: JAVA

WINDOWS 95
INTERNET EXPLORER

INTERNET GOES COMMERCIAL

Several noteworthy things happened in 1993:

● Intel introduced the 64-bit **Pentium chip** containing more than 3 million transistors. The Pentium Pro released in 1995 had more than 5.5 million. The Pentium II followed in 1997 with 7.5 million transistors, and the Pentium III in 1999 with more than 10 million.

● Motorola shipped the first PowerPC chip.

● The National Center for Supercomputing Applications (NCSA) at the University of Illinois released a first version of **Mosaic**, the first graphical web browser.

● Apple introduced the Newton, the first "palmtop" computer.

In 1994:

● **Netscape Navigator 1.0** was released.

● **Yahoo!**, the first major web index, went online. It was started in April 1994 by Electrical Engineering Ph.D. candidates at Stanford University, David Filo and Jerry Yang, as a way to keep track of their personal interests on the Internet.

In 1995, the new C++-based object-oriented programming language Oak, developed at Sun Microsystems by **James Gosling**, was renamed **Java** and burst onto the computer scene. Applications created in Java can be deployed without modification to any computing platform, thus making versions for different platforms unnecessary. (See §1.1 for more details.)

Other important events in 1995:

● Microsoft introduces **Windows 95**.
● Microsoft releases **Microsoft Internet Explorer 1.0** to compete with the unforeseen popularity of Netscape.

● The U.S. Government turns the maintenance of the Internet backbone over to commercial networking companies. Commercial traffic was now allowed on the Internet. America Online, Compuserve, and Prodigy brought the Internet to the public.

In 1998:

● Microsoft announced **Windows 98**, the last version of Windows that will be separate from Windows NT, Microsoft's high-end operating system. Plans are to merge Windows and Windows NT into Windows 2000.

● Apple released the **iMac**.

● The U.S. Justice Department takes Microsoft to court over alleged anti-trust violations. In 1999, a federal judge finds it to be monopolistic.

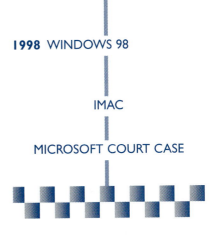

1998 WINDOWS 98

IMAC

MICROSOFT COURT CASE

This summary of the history of computing has dealt mainly with the first two important concepts that have shaped the history of computers: the mechanization of arithmetic and the stored program concept. Looking back, we marvel at the advances in technology that have, in barely 50 years, led from ENIAC to today's large array of computer systems, ranging from portable palmtop, laptop, and notebook computers to powerful desktop machines known as workstations, to supercomputers capable of performing billions of operations each second, and to massively parallel computers, which use thousands of microprocessors working together in parallel to solve large problems. Someone once noted that if progress in the automotive industry had been as rapid as in computer technology since 1960, today's automobile would have an engine that is less than 0.1 inch in length, would get 120,000 miles to a gallon of gas, have a top speed of 240,000 miles per hour, and would cost $4.

We have also seen how the stored program concept has led to the development of large collections of programs that make computers easier to use. Chief among these is the development of operating systems, such as UNIX, Linux, MS-DOS, Windows 95, and Mac OS, that allocate memory for programs and data and carry out many other supervisory functions. They also act as an interface between the user and the machine, interpreting commands given by the user from the keyboard, by a mouse click, or by a spoken command and then directing the appropriate system software and hardware to carry them out.

The Graphical User Interface

The third key concept that has produced revolutionary change in the evolution of the computer is the graphical user interface (GUI). A user interface is the portion of a software program that responds to commands from the user. User interfaces have evolved greatly in the past two decades, in direct correlation to equally dramatic changes in the typical computer user.

In the early 1980s, the personal computer burst onto the scene. However, at the outset the personal computer did not suit the average person very well. The explosion in the amount of commercially available application software spared computer users the task of learning to program in order to compose their own software; for example, the mere availability of the Lotus 1-2-3 spreadsheet software was enough to convince many to buy a PC. Even so, using a computer still required learning many precise and cryptic commands, if not outright programming skills.

In the early 1980s, the Apple Corporation decided to take steps to remedy this situation. The Apple II, like its new competitor, the IBM PC, employed a command-line interface, requiring users to learn difficult commands. In the late 1970s, Steve Jobs had visited Xerox PARC and had viewed several technologies that amazed him: the laser printer, Ethernet, and the graphical user interface. It was the last of these that excited Jobs the most, for it offered the prospect of software that computer users could understand almost intuitively.

Drawing upon child development theories, Xerox PARC had developed the graphical user interface for a prototype computer called the Alto that had been realized in 1972. The Alto featured a new device that had been dubbed a "mouse" by its inventor, PARC research scientist Douglas Engelbart. The mouse allowed the user to operate the computer by pointing to icons and selecting options from menus. At the time, however, the cost of the hardware the Alto required made it unfeasible to market, and the brilliant concept went unused. Steve Jobs saw, however, that the same remarkable change in the computer hardware market that had made the personal computer feasible also made the graphical user interface a reasonable possibility. In 1984, in a famous commercial first run during half-time of the Super Bowl, Apple introduced the first GUI personal computer to the world: the Macintosh. In 1985, Microsoft responded with a competing product, the Windows operating system, but until Windows version 3.0 was released in 1990, Macintosh reigned unchallenged in the world of GUI microcomputing. Researchers at the Massachusetts Institute of Technology also brought GUI to the UNIX platform with the release of the X Window system in 1984.

The graphical user interface has made computers easy to use and has produced many new computer users. At the same time, it has greatly changed the character of computing: computers are now expected to be "user-friendly." The personal computer, especially, must indeed be "personal" for the average person and not just for computer programmers.

Networks

The computer network is a fourth key concept that has greatly influenced the nature of modern computing. Defined simply, a computer network consists of two or more computers that have been connected in order to exchange resources. This could be hardware resources such as processing power, storage, or access to a printer; software resources such as a data file or access to a computer program; or messages between humans such as electronic mail or multimedia World Wide Web pages.

As computers became smaller, cheaper, more common, more versatile, and easier to use, computer use rose and with it, the number of computer users. Thus, computers had to be shared. In the early 1960s, timesharing was introduced, in which several persons make simultaneous use of a single computer called a host by way of a collection of terminals, each of which consists of a keyboard for input and either a printer or a monitor to display output. With a modem (short for "modulator/demodulator," because it both modulates binary digits into sounds that can travel over a phone line and, at the other end, demodulates such sounds back into bits), such a terminal connection could be over long distances.

Users, however, began to wish for the ability for one host computer to communicate with another. For example, transferring files from one host to another typically meant transporting tapes from one location to the other. In the late 1960s, the Department of Defense began exploring the development of a computer network by which its research centers at various universities could share their computer resources with each other. In 1969, the ARPANET began by connecting research center computers, enabling them to share software and data and to perform another kind of exchange that surprised everyone in terms of its popularity: electronic mail. Hosts were added to the ARPANET backbone in the 1970s, 1980s, and 1990s at an exponential rate, producing a global digital infrastructure that came to be known as the Internet.

Likewise, with the introduction of microcomputers in the late 1970s and early 1980s, users began to desire the ability for PCs to share resources. The invention of Ethernet network hardware and such network operating systems as Novell NetWare produced the Local Area Network, or LAN, enabling PC users to share printers and other peripherals, disk storage, software programs, and more. Microsoft also included networking capability as a major feature of its Windows NT.

The growth of computer connectivity continues today at a surprising rate. Computers are becoming more and more common, and they are used in isolation less and less. With the advent of affordable and widely available Internet Service Providers (ISPs), even home computers are now "wired" into a growing global digital infrastructure.

EXERCISES

1. What are four important concepts in the early history of computation?

2. Match each item in the first column with the associated item in the second column

_____ John von Neumann	A. early high-level language
_____ Charles Babbage	B. first commercially available computer
_____ Blaise Pascal	C. developed first fully electronic computer
_____ Herman Hollerith	D. stored program concept
_____ Grace Murray Hopper	E. Difference Engine
_____ Konrad Zuse	F. designer of FORTRAN language
_____ Alan Turing	G. Harvard Mark I
_____ Howard Aiken	H. an early electronic computer
_____ John Backus	I. integrated circuits (chips)
_____ Joseph Jacquard	J. vacuum tubes
_____ Ada Augusta	K. transistors
_____ John Atanasoff and Clifford Berry	L. Apple Computer
_____ Bjarne Stroustrup	M. automatic loom
_____ Steven Jobs and Steve Wozniak	N. developed the UNIX operating system

_____ Ken Thompson	O. developed the World Wide Web
_____ Dennis Ritchie	P. developed the C language
_____ James Gosling	Q. developed the C++ language
_____ Tim Berners-Lee	R. developed the Java language
_____ FORTRAN	S. first programmer
_____ ARPANET	T. adding machine
_____ first-generation computers	U. punched card
_____ second-generation computers	V. minicomputer
_____ third-generation computers	W. universal machine concept
_____ ENIAC	X. precursor of the Internet
_____ PDP-8	Y. the first computer bug; COBOL
_____ UNIVAC	Z. developed pre-World-War-II computers that used binary arithmetic

For Questions 3–24, describe the importance of the person to the history of computing:

3. al-Khowarizm	4. William Oughtred
5. Charles Babbage	6. Blaise Pascal
7. John von Neumann	8. Herman Hollerith
9. Joseph Jacquard	10. Gottfried Wilhelm von Leibniz
11. John Atanasoff	12. Steven Jobs and Steve Wozniak
13. Robert Noyce	14. J. Prespert Eckert
15. John Backu	16. Alan Turing
17. Konrad Zuse	18. Grace Murray Hopper
19. Ken Thompson	20. Dennis Ritchie
21. Bjarne Stroustrup	22. James Gosling
23. Tim Berners-Lee	24. Bill Gates

For Exercises 25–35, describe the importance of each item to the history of computing.

25. ENIAC	26. Analytical Engine
27. Jacquard loom	28. UNIVAC
29. Mark I	30. MITS Altair 8800
31. Apple II	32. Cray I
33. DOS	34. ARPANET
35. Java	

36. Distinguish the four different generations of computers.

0.3   PART OF THE PICTURE: INTRODUCTION TO COMPUTER SYSTEMS

Babbage's Analytical Engine (described in the history timeline of the preceding section) was a system of several separate subsystems, each with its own particular function: processing, storage, input, and output. This general scheme was incorporated in many later computers and is, in fact, a common feature of most modern computers. In this section we briefly describe the major components of a modern computing system and how program instructions and data are stored and processed. For a more complete description see the Part of the Picture: Computer Architecture in Chapter 7.

Processing

Most present-day computers exhibit a structure that is often referred to as the von Neumann architecture after Hungarian mathematician John von Neumann (see the entries for 1945 in the history timeline of the preceding section), whose theories defined many key features of the modern computer. According to the von Neumann architecture, the heart of the computing system is its central processing unit (CPU). The CPU controls the operation of the entire system, performs the arithmetic and logic operations, and stores and retrieves instructions and data. Every task that a computer performs ultimately comes down to instructions and data that can be operated upon by the CPU. The instructions and data are stored in a high-speed memory unit, and the control unit fetches these instructions from memory, decodes them,

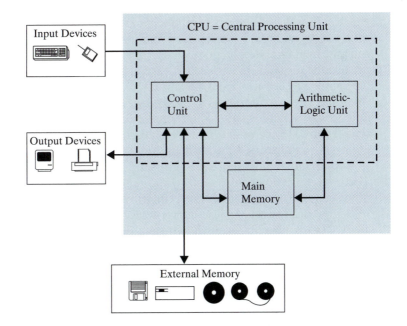

Figure 1. Major components of a computing system.

and directs the system to execute the operations indicated by the instructions. Those operations that are arithmetical or logical in nature are carried out using the circuits of the arithmetic-logic unit (ALU) of the CPU. These operations of the CPU are known as processing.

In contrast to the one-instruction-at-a-time operation by the CPU in the von Neumann architecture, parallel processing computers improve performance by employing two or more CPUs. The world's fastest supercomputers employ thousands of CPU chips and for this reason are termed massively parallel processing computers. Parallel computing, however, requires a very different programming strategy in order to make use of the power of systems with thousands of processors.

Storage

The memory unit of a computer system serves several purposes. Main memory is also known as internal, primary, or random access memory (RAM), and its main function is to store the instructions and data of the programs being executed. Most modern computers also have a smaller amount of high-speed memory called cache memory that is usually on the same chip as the CPU. It is used to speed up execution by storing a set of recent or current instructions being executed so they need not be fetched from main memory. Also, as part of the CPU's processing, it may need to temporarily write down (store) a number and read (retrieve) it later. Main memory can be used by the CPU in this manner, but there is also a set of special high-speed memory locations within the CPU called registers. Values that are stored in registers can typically be accessed thousands of times faster than values that are stored in RAM.

One problem with RAM and registers is that they are volatile: that is, if the power to the computing system is shut off (either intentionally or accidentally), values that are stored in these memory components are lost. To provide long-term storage of software programs and data, most computing systems also have components that are called secondary, external, or auxiliary storage. Common forms of this type of storage include magnetic media such as hard disks, floppy disks, and magnetic tapes and optical media such as CD-ROM and DVD, which make use of laser technology to store and retrieve information. These devices are non-volatile, in that they provide long-term storage for large collections of data, even if power is lost. However, the time required to access data that is stored on such devices can be thousands of times greater than the access time for data stored in RAM.

Both main memory and secondary storage are collections of two-state devices. There are only two possible digits, 0 and 1, in the binary number system. Thus, if one of the states of a two-state device is interpreted as 0 and the other as 1, then a two-state device can be said to be a one-bit device, since it is capable of representing a single binary digit (or "bit"). Such two-state devices are organized into groups called bytes, with one byte consisting of eight bits.

To indicate larger amounts of storage, some of the prefixes of the metric system are used; for example, kilobyte. However, there is an important difference. The metric system is convenient precisely because it is a decimal system, based on powers of ten, but modern computers are binary computers, based upon powers of two. Thus, in computing, the prefix kilo usually is not used for 1000 but, rather, is equal to 2^{10} or 1024. Thus, a kilobyte (KB) is 1024 bytes, not 1000 bytes; one megabyte (MB) is 1024

KB or 1,048,576 bytes. not one million bytes; and one gigabyte (GB) is 1024 MB or 1,073,741,824 bytes, not one billion bytes.

Bytes are typically grouped together into words. The number of bits in a word is equal to the number of bits in a CPU data register. The word size thus varies on different computers, but common word sizes are 16 bits (= 2 bytes), 32 bits (= 4 bytes) and 64 bits (= 8 bytes). Associated with each word or byte is an address that can be used to directly access that word or byte. This makes possible random access (direct access): the ability to store information in a specific memory location and then to directly retrieve it later from that same location.

The details of how various types of data are represented in a binary form and stored are described in Part of the Picture: Data Representation in Chapter 3.

Input and Output

For instructions and data to be processed by a computer's CPU, they must be digitized—that is, they must be encoded in binary form and transmitted to the CPU. This is the main function of input devices. The keyboard is the most common input device, followed by such pointing devices as the mouse, trackball, and joystick. Similarly, scanners convert and input graphics as binary information, and audio and video capture boards can encode and input sounds and video.

Once a CPU has completed a process, in order for that binary result to be meaningful to a human, it needs to converted to another form. This is the main function of output devices. Two of the more common types of output device are terminals (monitors) and printers. However, the varieties of output that can be generated by a computer are of a growing and surprising variety. Computers can output information as graphics, sound, video, and as motion in the case of robotics.

The communication between the CPU and input and output devices often happens by way of a port, a point of connection between the computer system's internal components and its peripherals (external components). Some ports, such as a monitor port, are designed for a single and specific use. Others, such as parallel and serial ports, are more flexible and can accommodate a variety of types of peripherals. Ports in turn connect to the computer system's bus, a kind of highway running through the computer system. By way of the bus, the computer systems components can send instructions and data to and from the CPU and memory.

Operating Systems

In order for a computer to be a general-purpose computer, it must first load a system software program called an operating system (OS). In very general terms, this software program performs two main functions:

1. It serves as an interface between the computer user(s) and the system hardware.
2. It serves as an environment in which other software programs can run.

The OS and the computer system hardware together comprise a platform upon which additional functionality can be built. Some operating systems can run only on a single type of hardware. For example, the DOS and Windows operating systems run only on PC hardware. In contrast, the UNIX operating system will operate on several types of computer hardware.

Programming

Program instructions for the CPU must be stored in memory. They must be instructions that the machine can execute, and they must be expressed in a form that the machine can understand—that is, they must be written in the machine language for that machine. These instructions consist of two parts: (1) a numeric opcode, which represents a basic machine operation, such as load, multiply, add, and store; and (2) the address of the operand. Like all information stored in memory, these instructions must be represented in a binary form.

As an example, suppose that values have been stored in three memory locations with addresses 1024, 1025, and 1026 and that we want to multiply the first two values, add the third, and store the result in a fourth memory location 1027. To perform this computation, the following instructions must be executed:

1. Fetch the contents of memory location 1024 and load it into a register in the ALU.
2. Fetch the contents of memory location 1025 and compute the product of this value and the value in the register.
3. Fetch the contents of memory location 1026 and add this value to the value in the register.
4. Store the contents of the register in memory location 1027.

If the opcodes for load, store, add, and multiply are 16, 17, 35, and 36, respectively, these four instructions might be written in machine language as follows[3]:

1. 00010000000000000000010000000000
2. 00100100000000000000010000000001
3. 00100011000000000000010000000010
4. 00010001000000000000010000000011

    opcode   operand

These instructions can then be stored in four (consecutive) memory locations. When the program is executed, the control unit will fetch each of these instructions, decode it to determine the operation and the address of the operand, fetch the operand, and then perform the required operation, using the ALU if necessary.

Programming in the machine language of an early computer was obviously a very difficult and time-consuming task in which errors were common. Only later did it become possible to write programs in assembly language, which uses mnemonics (names) in place of numeric opcodes and variable names in place of numeric ad-

---

[3] In binary notation, the opcodes 16, 17, 35, and 36 are 10000, 10001, 100011, and 100100, respectively, and the addresses 1024, 1025, 1026, 1027, are 10000000000, 10000000001, 10000000010, and 10000000011, respectively. See Section 12.3 and Appendix F for more information about non-decimal number systems, including methods for converting base-10 numbers to base-2 (binary).

dresses. For example, the preceding sequence of instructions might be written in assembly language as

1. LOAD A, ACC
2. MULT B, ACC
3. ADD C, ACC
4. STOR ACC, X

An assembler, which is part of the system software, translates such assembly language instructions into machine language.

Today, most programs are written in a high-level languages such as C++ and Java. Such programs are known as source programs. The instructions that make up a source program must be translated into machine language before they can be executed. For some languages (e.g., C++), this is carried out by a compiler that translates the source program into an object program. For example, for the preceding problem, a programmer might write the C++ statement

$$X = A * B + C;$$

which instructs the computer to multiply the values of A and B, add the value of C, and assign the value to X. A C++ compiler would translate this statement into a sequence of machine language instructions like those considered earlier. (For programs that use libraries, a linker will also be used to connect items that are defined outside of the object file with their definitions to produce an executable program.)

For most high-level languages, programs are written for a particular computer platform and must be translated into the machine language of that computer. A compiler for that language is a system program for that platform that produces an executable program that is specific to that machine. Some languages, however, (e.g., some versions of BASIC) are interpreted rather than compiled. Like a compiler, an interpreter translates source program statements into machine language, but after each statement is translated, the resulting machine language instruction is immediately executed before other source program statements are translated. The method used to translate Java programs is described in Section 1.1.

EXERCISES

1. Match each item in the first column with the associated item in the second column.

_____ peripheral devices	A. high-speed memory used by the CPU
_____ bit	B. central processing unit
_____ byte	C. 1024
_____ megabyte	D. terminals, scanners, printers
_____ object program	E. binary digit
_____ source program	F. group of binary digits
_____ CPU	G. 1024 K bytes
_____ K	H. written in machine language
_____ RAM	I. written in high-level language
_____ cache	J. language translator

Briefly define each of the terms in Exercises 2–16.

2. ALU
3. CPU
4. peripheral devices
5. bit
6. byte
7. word
8. K
9. megabyte
10. source program
11. object program
12. machine language
13. assembly language
14. compiler
15. assembler
16. interpreter

PROBLEM SOLVING AND SOFTWARE ENGINEERING

If we really understand the problem, the answer will come out of it, because the answer is not separate from the problem. *Jiddu Krishnamurti (1895–1986)*

People always get what they ask for; the only trouble is that they never know, until they get it, what it actually is that they have asked for. *Aldous Huxley (1894–1963)*

It's the only job I can think of where I get to be both an engineer and an artist. There's an incredible, rigorous, technical element to it, which I like because you have to do very precise thinking. On the other hand, it has a wildly creative side where the boundaries of imagination are the only real limitation. *Andy Hertzfeld (circa 1992)*

■ Chapter Contents

Chapter Objectives

- Indicate the many and varied uses of computers
- Give a brief historical background of how Java developed
- Describe the platform-independent scheme for translating a Java program
- Take a first look at a Java application
- Take a first look at a Java applet and compare/contrast it with an application
- Illustrate the basic phases of the software life cycle, including object-centered design
- Highlight issues that computing professionals face and give some ethical principles

The computer has become indispensable in many areas of human endeavor. Its applications are far too many to enumerate, and those in the following list and those pictured in Figure 1.1 are intended only to show the diverse use of computers. These

1

FIGURE 1.1   (a) **CAD design of an automobile. (b) Student(s) / Teacher finding information on the Internet. (c) Robot-controlled Chrysler automobile assembly plant. (d) National Weather Service satellite imagery. (e) Oil-drilling computerized tracking model. (f) Flight deck of the space shuttle *Columbia*.(g) Northern Arizona University observatory.**

and many other applications all require the development of *software,* and the focus of this text is on how Java can be used to write such software.

❑ Business and Finance

Mailing lists and billings

Payroll, accounts receivable, accounts payable

Inventory control

Reservations systems (airlines, car rentals, etc.)

Word processing

Data management

Spreadsheets

EFT (electronic funds transfer)

ATMs (automatic teller machines)

Electronic mail

Home banking

Financial planning

Processing of insurance claims

❑ Industry

Robots in assembly lines

CAD (computer-aided design)

CAM (computer-aided manufacturing)

CIM (computer-integrated manufacturing)

Market analysis

Project management and control

Production scheduling

❑ Government

Defense systems

Space programs

Compilation of census data

Weather forecasting by NOAA (National Oceanic and Atmospheric Administration)

Automated traffic-control systems

State and local lotteries

The FBI's NCIS (national crime information system)

❑ Medicine

CAT (computerized axial tomography) and MR (magnetic resonance) scans

Online access to patients' medical records

Monitoring life-support systems

Expert diagnosis systems

❑ Entertainment

Animation, colorization, and creation of special effects in the film industry

Video games

❑ Science

Analysis of molecules

Study of crystal structures

Testing food quality

Simulation of large dynamical systems

❑ Information Technology

Digital libraries

Multimedia reference works

Online art galleries

Developing programs to solve problems is a complex process that is both an art and a science. It requires imagination, creativity, and ingenuity, but it also makes use of techniques and methodologies. **Software engineering** is the application of these techniques and methodologies to produce software solutions to problems. In this chapter, we describe some of these methodologies and phases of the software development process and illustrate them with examples.

1.1   A BRIEF HISTORY OF OOP AND JAVA

As noted in the summary of the history of computing in the preceding chapter, one of the important advances in system software was the development of **high-level languages**. Early computers were very difficult to program. In fact, programming some of the earliest computers consisted of designing and building circuits to carry out the computations required to solve each new problem. Computers capable of reading in and storing programs soon followed. However, these programs were difficult to write because they had to be written entirely using **machine language**, in which all instructions are represented as strings of 0s and 1s. Later, computer instructions could be expressed using **assembly language**, in which short abbreviations for instructions and more readable numbers could be used. But these programs were still very cryptic, and programming remained very tedious and error-prone. High-level languages made it possible to enter instructions using an English-like syntax.

The first high-level languages to gain widespread acceptance were FORTRAN, COBOL, and LISP, but these were followed in the 1960s and 70s by more than 200 different programming languages. Some of the more popular high-level languages that developed are BASIC, Pascal, C, Ada, Smalltalk, C++, and Java. Computers would not have gained widespread use had it not been for the development of such high-level programming languages.

One of these languages, C, has had a profound effect on computing. It has its origins in 1969, when a researcher named **Ken Thompson** was beginning the design and implementation of the **Unix operating system** at AT&T's Bell Laboratories. His first implementation of Unix was written in the assembly language of a spare PDP-7 mini-computer, but it was not long before it became necessary to implement Unix on a more powerful machine, a DEC PDP-11. However, because Unix had been written in PDP-7 assembly language, it was not directly portable to the PDP-11. The prospect of rewriting the thousands of lines of Unix in a different assembly language was distinctly unpleasant, particularly because it was obvious that this problem would recur each time Thompson wanted to implement Unix on a new machine. To simplify the task of transferring Unix to other computers, Thompson began to search for a high-level language in which to rewrite Unix.

None of the high-level languages in existence at the time were appropriate; therefore, in 1970, Thompson began designing a new language called B that was based on an existing language BCPL. By 1972, it had become apparent that B was not adequate for implementing Unix. At that time, **Dennis Ritchie**, also at Bell Labs, designed a successor language to B that he called **C**, and approximately 90 percent of Unix was rewritten in C. This new language quickly became very popular in colleges and universities across the country and eventually spread to the business world as well. With the availability of inexpensive C compilers for microcomputers, C has become the language in which many microcomputer applications are written.

Although C is a very powerful language, it has two characteristics that make it inappropriate for a modern introduction to programming. First, C requires a level of sophistication in its users beyond that of the typical beginning programmer. Second, C was designed in the early 1970s, and the nature of programming has changed significantly since that time.

In 1967, the researchers Kristen Nygaard and Ole-Johan Dahl introduced a new language for creating real-world simulations named **Simula-67**. To facilitate the modeling of real-world objects, Simula provided a new language feature called the **class**, which could be extended through an inheritance mechanism. These capabilities laid the groundwork for **object-oriented programming** (**OOP**), a new approach to programming that emphasized the modeling of objects through classes and inheritance. By the late 1970s, it became apparent that this new approach held great promise for reducing the cost of upgrading and maintaining software. A research group at Xerox' Palo Alto Research Center (PARC) built upon these ideas and created the first truly object-oriented language, named **Smalltalk-80**.

Across the country at Bell Labs, another researcher named Bjarne Stroustrup undertook the project of extending C with object-oriented features. Stroustrup also added new features that eliminated many of the difficulties C posed for beginning programmers. The resulting language, first called C with Classes, was renamed **C++** in 1983 after more improvements were added. By blending the power of its parent C with the benefits of object-oriented programming, it has grown rapidly from obscurity to popularity.

The **Java** programming language was developed at Sun Microsystems in 1991. It was the invention of **James Gosling**, a top-notch programmer working on an exciting new project. In the "Green" project, as it was called, Gosling and his colleagues sought to develop a technology for programming the many electronic devices and appliances found in the home and office so that they could be controlled from a central location. Gosling had initially attempted the project using C++, but it was proving ill-suited to the task, so Gosling decided to develop a new programming language instead, one which he dubbed "Oak." Since the program code would need to be deployed in a large variety of small but important devices, Gosling designed Oak to be efficient, stable, and of maximum portability. But the Green project ultimately proved too expensive to be feasible, and Sun shelved the project.

However, Sun soon discovered a use for Gosling's programming language, which it renamed Java. One of the problematic aspects of the Internet is that it is comprised of computers of a variety of platforms. Java, however, was designed to be **platform independent**. Thus, in 1994, Sun demonstrated World Wide Web pages containing small software programs called **applets** that had been written in Java. The browser Sun used for the demonstration, **HotJava**, had also been written in Java, illustrating the fact that Java was a full-fledged programming language, well-suited also to applications programming. When Netscape browsers began supporting Java applets in 1995, Java was firmly established as a major programming language.

For most high-level languages, programs are written for a particular computer platform and must be translated into the machine language of that computer. A **compiler** for that language is a system program for that platform that produces an executable program that is specific to that machine. In some cases (but not all), a program can be **ported** to a different platform by recompiling it using a compiler that will generate a different binary executable for that platform:

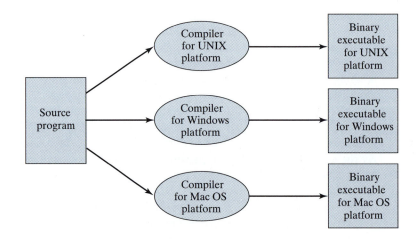

Some languages (e.g., some versions of BASIC) are interpreted rather than compiled. Like a compiler, an **interpreter** translates source program statements into machine language, but after each statement is translated, the resulting machine language instruction is immediately executed before other source program statements are translated.

Still another approach for translating source code into executable binary code is, in a sense, a combination of these two. In this method, which is the one used for Java, the source program is compiled into a machine-independent **intermediate code** format, called **bytecode** for Java. This bytecode is then executed by a special interpreter, which for Java, is called the **Java virtual machine (JVM)**.

The resulting **platform independence** is one of the most attractive features of Java.

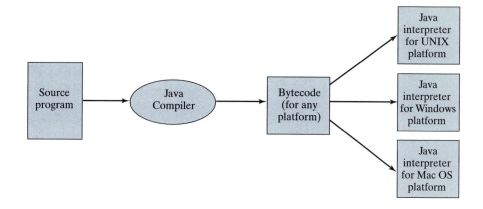

It is possible because Java interpreters exist for a wide variety of computer platforms. Thus, regardless of the platform upon which the Java source program was compiled, the bytecode that was produced will be executable on any platform for which a Java interpreter exists.

✔ Quick Quiz 1.1

1. _____ is the application of techniques and methodologies to produce software solutions to problems.

2. What three high-level languages were the first to gain widespread acceptance?

3. Match each item in the first column with the associated item in the second column

_____ Designed the Unix operating system	A. applet
_____ small software program that can be put in a web page and executed by a browser	B. bytecode
	C. compiler
_____ system program that translates a program into executable code for a specific machine	D. Dennis Ritchie
	E. Ken Thompson
	F. Bjarne Stroustrup
_____ Designed the C language	G. JVM
_____ Designed the C++ language	H. James Gosling
_____ Designed the Java language	I. Simula-67
_____ first language to have classes	J. Smalltalk-80
_____ first truly object-oriented language	
_____ machine-independent intermediate code for Java	
_____ special interpreter used with Java	

1.2   INTRODUCTION TO JAVA APPLICATION PROGRAMS

A **program** can be thought of as a collection of statements written in a programming language. Since most programs are written to solve problems, a program's statements usually specify exactly what steps must be taken to solve the problem.

```
1.Start
2.Repeatedly do the following:
     2.1. This
     2.2. That
     2.3. The Next Thing
     2.4. If it's time to quit,
          Stop this repetition
3.Output the results of This and That
4.Stop
```

Java is only one of many programming languages in which a program can be written. Just as there are *grammar rules* that specify the structure of a correct sentence in English and other human languages, there are Java grammar rules that specify how Java statements are formed and how they can be combined into more complex statements and into programs. Much of this text is devoted to learning how to write Java statements and how to assemble them into a program.

In an *object-oriented programming language* like Java, a program constructs **objects** that carry out tasks needed to solve the problem and then sends **messages** to these objects to perform these tasks. These objects thus interact with each other in a way that solves the problem.

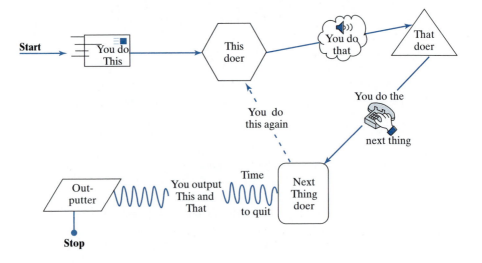

Objects are created from **classes** and are thus also called **instances** of those classes. Stated differently, classes are *blueprints* or *patterns* for building objects. In this text you will learn about the classes that Java provides and also learn how to build other classes.

There are therefore two different, but equally correct, ways to think about an object-oriented program:

1. A collection of statements that solve a problem
2. A collection of object interactions that solve a problem

Example: A Java Application that Displays a Greeting

Figure 1.2 shows a simple Java program that displays a greeting that includes the current time and date. The program constructs three objects: one to represent the user's screen, another to represent the time and date, and a third object that is a string containing the time and date information. It sends one message to the time-date object that instructs it to convert itself to a form that the string object can store and then another message to a screen object instructing it to display this string containing the time-date information along with a greeting to the user.

FIGURE 1.2 JAVA APPLICATION TO DISPLAY A GREETING.

```java
/* Greeter1.java is a simple first Java program that displays
 *    a greeting to a user.
 * Output: A greeting that includes the current date and time.
 */

import ann.easyio.*;        // Screen class
import java.util.*;          // Date class

class Greeter1 extends Object
{
  public static void main(String [] args)
  {
    Date currentDate = new Date();
    String today = currentDate.toString();

    Screen theScreen = new Screen();
    theScreen.println("Welcome! Today, " + today
                    + ", you begin your study of Java!");
  }
}
```

Sample run:

```
Welcome! Today, Mon Jan 10 10:07:16 EDT 2000, you begin your study of Java!
```

Some lines in the preceding program are quite understandable, but others are probably quite bewildering. Let's walk through the program and take a first look at what is happening; that is, a first look at the Java programming language.

The first line of the program begins with the pair of characters / *, and the fourth line ends with the pair * /. In a Java program, anything contained between these character pairs is a **comment**. In Figure 1.2, the multiline comment in the first four lines of the program is **opening documentation** that describes what the program does. Multiline comments may also be used at other places in the program to provide additional documentation.

As we noted earlier, this program uses three objects:

1. The user's *screen*
2. The current *time and date*
3. A *string* to store the time and date information

Objects are constructed from classes, and for the preceding objects we need three classes that are provided in three different **packages**, which are collections of related classes:

Class name	Package name	Package description
Screen	ann.easyio	A collection of input/output classes developed by the authors to simplify input and output in Java. (It is provided on the CD distributed with this text.)
Date	java.util	A collection of utility classes provided in Java.
String	java.lang	A collection of classes that are fundamental parts of the Java language

The **fully-qualified name** of one of these classes consists of the package name followed by a period and then the *simple name* of the class. Thus, our program needs the following classes:

1. ann.easyio.Screen
2. java.util.Date
3. java.lang.String

Using such long names is prone to typing errors and soon becomes wearisome. This is why Java provides **import statements** like those in the two lines following the opening documentation of our example program. The first import statement

```
import ann.easyio.*;
```

allows us to use in a program the simple names (e.g., Screen) of the classes from the ann.easyio package instead of the preceding long names (ann.easyio. Screen).[1] Similarly,

```
import java.util.*;
```

---

[1] The asterisk (*) is a *wildcard* character that represents any class in this package. Since we are using only one of these classes, we could have used the statement import ann.easyio.Screen; instead.

lets us use simple names (e.g., `Date`) of classes in the `java.util` package instead of their long names (`java.util.Date`). We could also have added `import java.lang.*` to the program, but this is not necessary because Java automatically imports the classes such as `String` from the `java.lang` package into every program.

At the ends of these lines are **single-line comment**s that begin with the characters `//` and continue to the end of the line. Here, the comments tell which classes from the packages are being used in the program: `Date` from `java.util` and `Screen` from `ann.easyio`. Like multiline comments, these single-line comments may be used anywhere in the program.

The rest of the program in Figure 1.2 is a **class declaration** of the form

```
class ClassName extends Object
{
    Declarations of class members
}
```

The name of the class in our application is `Greeter1`. The `extends Object` clause that follows indicates that `Greeter1` is built using a more general definition of a class that already exists in the Java language: the `Object` **class**.[2] This `extends` **clause** specifies that the class `Greeter1` *inherits* the attributes and behaviors (methods) of the `Object` class and *extends* it by adding new attributes and behaviors, which define the class more specifically. In the terminology of object-oriented programming, the class `Greeter1` is a **subclass**, related to a **superclass** (the `Object` class) by the principle of **inheritance**. These important concepts will be studied in detail in subsequent chapters.

Between the outermost set of curly braces (`{` and `}`) are declarations of the class' **members**, which may be **variables** (called *attribute variables* or *instance variables*) that store data values or **methods** that perform operations on these values. In Figure 1.2, class `Greeter1` has no variable members and has only one method. The method's name is `main`, and every Java application must have such a method, because *this is where execution starts when the application begins running*. The form of this method, called the **main method**, is:

```
public static void main(String [] args)
{
    A list of Java statements
}
```

You can see the name `main` in the method's heading. The role of the other items will be explained in later chapters. For now, you need only remember that every Java main method begins this way.

Execution of a Java program begins with the first statement enclosed between the curly braces of this main method and proceeds through the statements that follow it.

---

[2] The `extends Object` clause may, in fact, be omitted because it will be assumed that the class extends Java's `Object` class. We will use it in this text, however, to emphasize that every class we build extends some other class.

Note in Figure 1.2 that each statement ends with a semicolon. Execution terminates when it reaches the end of the main method.

In our example, the first statement is

```
Date currentDate = new Date();
```

This statement does the following:

1. `Date currentDate`, to the left of the = symbol, declares that `currentDate` is a variable that can refer to a `Date` *object* (i.e., an *instance* of the class `Date`).
2. This `Date` object is created by the expression on the right of the = symbol; the `new` operation provided in Java is used to construct objects.

For the next line

```
String today = currentDate.toString();
```

the following occur:

1. `String today` declares a `String` *variable* named `today` that can refer to a `String` object (i.e., an instance of the class `String`) that stores a string of characters.
2. This `String` object is created by the expression on the right of the = symbol. It sends a message to the `Date` object referred to by `currentDate` instructing it to use its `toString()` method (provided in the class `Date`) to convert itself to a `String` object that contains the time-date information.

The third statement in the main method,

```
Screen theScreen = new Screen();
```

is similar to the `Date` declaration two lines above it. It declares a `Screen` variable named `theScreen` that refers to the `Screen` object created by the `new` operation. This object is an instance of class `Screen`, which was imported into the program from the `ann.easyio` package.

The next two lines contain a statement that sends a message to `theScreen` to use its `println()` method to display the string enclosed between the parentheses:

```
"Welcome! Today, " + today
+ ", you begin your study of Java!"
```

This string is called an **argument** of the `println()` method and is said to be *passed to* this method. Sending a message to an object to use one of its methods is also referred to as **calling** or **invoking** a method.

Several items in these statements require explanation:

❑ Characters enclosed between double quotes will be displayed exactly as shown (except for certain special characters described in the next chapter).

❑ Values referred to by variables such as the `String` variable `today` will be displayed. Their names are not enclosed between quotes.

❑ + is the **concatenation** operator that joins strings together.

❑ The `println()` method causes an automatic advance to a new line after the string passed to it is displayed.

This message to `theScreen` will thus cause its `println()` method to display on the screen a greeting of the form

```
Welcome! Today, _____, you begin your study of Java!
```

with the blank filled in with the current date and time, and the screen's cursor then advances to a new line. Subsequent output produced by another `println()` message to `theScreen` would appear on this line.

The last two lines in the program in Figure 1.2 each contain a closing curly brace (`}`). The first one matches the opening curly brace (`{`) for the main method and thus marks the end of this method. The last one matches the opening curly brace for the class `Greeter1` and thus marks the end of this application class.

This concludes our walk-through of the Java program in Figure 1.2. We have taken a first look at several important Java features, including:

- ❑ use of comments for documentation
- ❑ use of `import` statements to allow us to use short names of classes in packages
- ❑ declaring variables and constructing objects (i.e., instances of classes)
- ❑ methods—in particular, the main method in a Java program
- ❑ sending messages to an object, instructing it to use methods provided in the class of which it is an instance

These important concepts will be studied in detail in the chapters that follow.

✔ Quick Quiz 1.2

1. A(n) _____ is a collection of statements written in a programming language.
2. An object-oriented programming language like Java constructs _____ that perform tasks needed to solve a problem and then sends _____ to them to do these tasks.
3. Objects are created from _____, which are _____ for building objects
4. What are the two ways to think about an object-oriented program?
5. In a Java program, anything contained between `/*` and `*/` is a(n) _____.
6. In a Java program, anything following `//` to the end of the line is a(n) _____.
7. _____ statements make it possible to use short names of classes from packages instead of their longer fully-qualified names.
8. `java.util` is a(n) _____.
9. Two kinds of class members are _____ and _____.
10. Every Java application must have a(n) _____ where execution begins.
11. `+` is the _____ operator for strings.

1.3 INTRODUCTION TO JAVA APPLET PROGRAMS

As we noted in Section 1.1, Java's emergence as a major programming language is directly related to the invention of the World Wide Web and graphical web browser software. In fact, many programmers learn Java specifically for the purpose of authoring programs for the World Wide Web.

Programs like that in the preceding section are called **applications**. These are stand-alone programs that can be executed with a Java interpreter. In contrast, an **applet** is a small program that can be placed in a World Wide Web page and will be executed by the web browser when that web page is retrieved and opened.

Java applets have become extremely popular on the World Wide Web because they make it possible to add "dynamic content" to a web page—audio, video, animation, interactive elements such as buttons and forms, and even complete software programs such as calculators, spreadsheets, and games. *Because Java is a full-fledged programming language, almost any kind of task that can be accomplished by an application program can potentially be implemented as a Java applet running inside a World Wide Web page.* In fact, as Java and web browsers continue to develop, the distinction between *application* and *applet* may eventually disappear altogether.

Example: A Java Applet That Displays a Greeting

In the preceding section we described an application program `Greeter1` (see Figure 1.2) that displayed a welcome greeting along with the current time and date. The program `Greeter2` in Figure 1.3 is an applet version of this greeting program. We will examine the differences between these two versions because they illustrate several key concepts of applet programming.

FIGURE 1.3   JAVA APPLET TO DISPLAY A GREETING.

```java
/* Greeter2.java is a simple Java applet that displays
 *    a greeting to a user.
 * Output: A greeting that includes the current date and time.
 */

import javax.swing.*;             // JApplet, JLabel
import java.util.*;               // Date

public class Greeter2 extends JApplet
{
  public void init()
  {
    Date currentDate = new Date();
    String today = currentDate.toString();

    JLabel greeting = new JLabel("Welcome! Today, " + today
                            + ", you begin your study of Java!");

    getContentPane().add(greeting);
  }
}
```

Like an application, a Java applet is a class. However, unlike an application class like that in Figure 1.2, which is built from Java's `Object` class, applets are built using one of the general definitions of applets that already exist in the Java language: the `Applet` class or the `JApplet` class.

Most Java applets are graphical in that they operate by drawing graphics in a defined screen area and in that they typically enable users to interact with the applet program by means of **graphical user interface (GUI)** elements inside that area. Earlier versions of Java (1.0 and 1.1) provided the **AWT (Abstract Windowing Toolkit)**, a collection of classes designed for building these user interfaces. The `Applet` class is one of the AWT components. However, in 1997 a new collection of classes known as the **JFC (Java Foundation Classes)**, was announced as an extension to Java and is now an integral part of Java 2. One of the exciting features of the JFC is the collection of **Swing components** that greatly enhance a programmer's ability to build GUIs. Although Java 2 still supports AWT, Swing components should be used instead because they have far greater capabilities. You can easily distinguish Swing components from their AWT counterparts because their names start with J. Thus, the `JApplet` class that we will use in this text is the Swing component for building applets. It extends the `Applet` class by enabling applets to use other Swing components.

Although the Swing collection is very large, most programs use only a few of its packages. In particular, most of the Swing classes that we need for this text are contained in the `javax.swing` package. Thus our applet begins (after the opening documentation) with the import statement

```
import javax.swing.*;
```

so that we can use the short names of the classes `JApplet` and `JLabel` that we need from this package. It also imports the `java.util` package so that we can use the short name for the `Date` class as in the program in Figure 1.2.

Like the `Greeter1` application program, the remainder of the code defines the `Greeter2` class. However, the declaration of `Greeter2` differs from the application version in several ways, beginning with the header. For a **Swing applet** (i.e., one that uses Swing components), it must have the form[3]

---

[3] Because `JApplet` extends `Applet`, this form is also okay for *regular applets* (i.e., those with no Swing components). In this case, however, it is also permissible to use a heading of the form

```
public class ClassName extends Applet
```

```
public class ClassName extends JApplet
```

Since `Greeter2` will use Swing components, it's heading is

```
public class Greeter2 extends JApplet
```

The `extends` clause specifies that `Greeter2` is a subclass of Java's `JApplet` class, rather than the `Object` class used for applications. This means that it inherits the attributes and behaviors of `JApplet` (and thus also those of the `Applet` class) and builds upon this general definition of applets by adding more specific attributes and behaviors. (Notice also the addition of the keyword `public`. This is a necessary consequence of inheriting from the `JApplet` superclass, which is a public class. Such modifiers in class definitions will be discussed in Chapter 6.)

Next we examine the body of the `Greeter2` class declaration. First, notice that unlike applications, there is no `main()` method in an applet. This is because Java's `JApplet` class provides several other methods that are called instead of a main method to handle the execution of an applet.

The `init()` method is the first method called when an applet is executed. This method is called only once in the course of the execution of an applet.[4] In our example, it is the only method in the class `Greeter2`.

The two statements in `init()` that involve the `Date` object are the same as in the `Greeter1` application, but the remaining statements are different. In graphical user interfaces, freestanding strings of text (as opposed to text that is part of a button or menu) are called **labels**. Thus, in our applet program, we construct the message as an instance of `JLabel`, which is a Swing class for displaying short labels (and images).

In Swing, graphical user interfaces are constructed by adding GUI objects such as buttons, labels, and menus to **containers**, which serve to group and position GUI elements. *Top-level containers* define the overall window (or frame) in which the user interface as a whole operates. The portion of such a window (frame) to which GUI objects can be added is called the **content pane**, which consists of all of the window area except for any title bar or menu bar. The content pane can in turn be divided into smaller panes called **panels**.

In the case of an applet, the `JApplet` object is the top-level container. Thus we add elements to the applet window by adding them to the `JApplet` object's content pane. The `getContentPane()` method gives us access to this content pane. Specifically, we want to send a message to the content pane to use its `add()` method to add our `greeting` label to the content pane. The statement

```
getContentPane().add(greeting);
```

does exactly this.

---

[4] Interestingly, the Java `JApplet` class has a default definition of the `init()` method (which it inherits from `Applet`), but it an empty one—it does nothing. Thus, the definition of `init()` in the `Greeter2` class does not declare a new method, but, rather, it **overrides** the do-nothing definition of `init()` from the `JApplet` superclass.

Applets and Web Pages—HTML

As noted earlier, a Java applet can be embedded in a web page and will be executed when that web page is loaded by the web browser. World Wide Web pages are structured from special formatting codes called **HTML (Hypertext Mark-up Language)** tags. The basic structure of a web page is defined by the following tags:

```
<HTML>

<HEAD>

    . . .

</HEAD>

<BODY>

    . . .

</BODY>

</HTML>
```

HTML tags are set off by angled brackets and usually appear in pairs: one tag to turn on a particular format and another, consisting of the same tag with a forward slash added, to turn the format off.

A Java applet is embedded into a web page by inserting the `<APPLET>` and `</APPLET>` tags. For example, the output displayed in the sample run in Figure 1.3 can be generated by inserting the following statement into a web page:

```
<APPLET CODE="Greeter2.class" WIDTH=500 HEIGHT=100>
</APPLET>
```

The `CODE` argument in the `<APPLET>` tag defines the class containing the desired applet. The `WIDTH` and `HEIGHT` arguments in the `<APPLET>` tag define the width and height of the applet window in pixels. The entire code of the web page used in the sample run is as follows:

```
<HTML>

<HEAD>
</HEAD>

<BODY>

<APPLET CODE="Greeter2.class" WIDTH=500 HEIGHT=100>
</APPLET>

</BODY>

</HTML>
```

This file was created using a simple text editor and saved as `Greeter2.html`. To execute the applet, you simply open the HTML file in the **appletviewer** utility that Sun provides as part of Java's Standard Development Kit (SDK) or in a web browser that supports Java.[5]

This file is a minimal HTML file that contains an applet. There are several other HTML features that can be used to modify what the applet produces. As an example, see Programming Problems 6 and 7 at the end of this chapter to see how parameters can be passed into an applet to set or modify fonts and colors. The CD and the websites for this book (see the preface) also contain additional information about HTML files.

Web pages are exchanged over the Internet according to a **server** and **client** scheme: a computer running a web browser (client) requests the receipt of a web page that is stored on another computer (server) somewhere else on the Internet. Embedding Java applets in web pages makes it possible for Internet computers to exchange pages that contain not only text and graphics but also software programs. Unlike most software, which is composed for a specific hardware platform, Java is designed to be **platform-independent**. This makes it an ideal programming technology for the Internet, which is comprised of computers of many different platforms.

At the same time, running a software program on your computer that was sent from another computer carries certain risks. For this reason, applets are restricted from performing certain functions that might cause breaches of security.

✔ Quick Quiz 1.3

1. Applications extend Java's `Object` class. What do applets extend?
2. GUI is an acronym for _____ .
3. AWT is an acronym for _____ .
4. JFC is an acronym for _____ .
5. (True or false) An applet is a superclass of the `JApplet` class.
6. (True or false) Every applet must have a `main()` method.
7. (True or false) Swing components are preferred over AWT components for building GUIs.
8. Complete the following heading of an applet class:
   `public class MyApplet` _____
9. What are two ways that an applet can be executed?
10. Special _____ formatting codes are used to structure web pages.
11. A(n) _____ and _____ scheme is used to exchange web pages over the Internet.

---

[5] At the time this text was prepared, some web browsers did not fully support applets prepared with Swing elements. Others require downloading a special plug-in. We will use appletviewer, therefore, to execute the examples in this text.

1.4   PROBLEM SOLVING THROUGH SOFTWARE ENGINEERING

As we noted in the introduction to this chapter, software engineering uses certain basic methodologies to obtain software solutions to problems. Although the problems themselves vary, several **phases** or **steps** are common in software development:

1. **Design**: The problem is analyzed and a solution is designed, resulting in an *algorithm* to solve the problem.

2. **Coding**: The solution is written in the syntax of a high-level language (e.g., Java), resulting in a *program*.

3. **Testing, Execution and Debugging**: The program is rigorously tested and errors (called *bugs*) are removed.

4. **Maintenance**: The program is updated and modified, as necessary, to meet the changing needs of its users.

In this section, we examine each of these stages in the **software life cycle** and illustrate them with an example. This is a rather simple example, so that we can emphasize the main ideas in each stage without getting lost in a maze of details.

PROBLEM

Sarah O'Sprinter is a student at Somewhere University in the United States and is a member of the track team. Although she runs the 100-meter, 200-meter, and 400-meter races, her favorite event is the 100-meter race, for which her best time is 11.2 seconds. To impress her friends and relatives back home in Ireland, Sarah would like to be able to tell them how fast she runs. So she wants to write a program that will compute her average speed in kilometers per hour.

 OBJECT-CENTERED DESIGN

Problems to be solved are usually expressed in a natural language, such as English, and often are stated imprecisely, making it necessary to analyze the problem and formulate it more precisely. For the preceding problem, this is quite easy:

> *Given a distance of 100 meters traveled in a time of 11.2 seconds, compute the average speed in kilometers per hour.*

For many problems, however, this may be considerably more difficult, because the initial descriptions may be quite vague and imprecise. People who pose the problems often do not understand them well. Neither do they understand how to solve them nor what the computer's capabilities and limitations are.

We will call the approach we use in designing a software solution to a problem **object-centered design** (**OCD**). In its simplest form, it consists of the following steps:

1. *Behavior:*   State how you want the program to behave, as precisely as possible.

2. *Objects:*   Identify the real-world objects in your problem description, and categorize them. If some of these cannot be directly represented using the types

provided in Java —*primitive types* such as `int` and `double,` or one of Java's classes such as `String`—write a class to represent them, thus *modeling a real-world object with a software object.*[6]

3. *Operations:*   Identify the operations that are needed to solve the problem.

4. *Algorithm:*   Arrange the problem's objects and their operations in an order that solves the problem.

The arrangement of a problem's objects and operations that results from step 4 is called an **algorithm** for the problem, and this algorithm serves as a blueprint for writing the main method of our application.

BEHAVIOR. We begin by writing out exactly what we want our program to do (i.e., how we want it to behave). The remainder of our design depends on this step, so we must make it as precise as possible:

> *Behavior:* The program should display on the screen a prompt for a distance in meters. The user should enter this distance at the keyboard, from which the program should read it. The program should then display on the screen a prompt for a time in seconds. The user should enter this time at the keyboard, from which the program should read it. The program should then compute the speed in kilometers per hour and display it on the screen.

Note that we have generalized the problem from calculating the speed for running 100 meters in 11.2 seconds to calculating the speed for an arbitrary distance and time. This **generalization** is an important aspect of analyzing a problem. The effort involved in later phases of solving a problem demands that the program to be developed should be flexible enough to solve not only the given specific problem but also any related problem of the same kind with little, if any, modification required.

THE PROBLEM'S OBJECTS. Once we have decided exactly what should happen, we are ready for the next step, which is to identify the real-world objects in the problem. One approach is to begin by identifying all of the *nouns* in our behavioral description, ignoring pronouns and nouns that refer to the *user*.

> *Behavior:* The program should display on the screen a prompt for a distance in meters. The user should enter this distance at the keyboard, from which the program should read it. The program should then display on the screen a prompt for a time in seconds. The user should enter this time at the keyboard, from which the program should read it. The program should then compute the speed in kilometers per hour and display it on the screen.

Note that nouns that give measurement units of other nouns (e.g., meters, seconds, kilometers, hour) are included as a part of them, and that nouns like *user* and pronouns like *it* are ignored. This gives us the following list:

---

[6] As we saw in Section 1.2, the term *object* has a precise meaning in Java—an instance of a class. To avoid confusion, we will refer to objects (i.e., things) in a problem's description as *real-world objects* or as *problem objects* and use the term *software objects* for those things used to represent the real-world objects in a programming language. Some of these software objects will be Java objects and others will be variables, constants, or literals whose values are one of Java's primitive types.

Problem's Objects: program
screen
prompt for a distance in meters
distance
keyboard
prompt for a time in seconds
time
speed in kilometers per hour

Next, it is useful to identify the type of each object, and whether the value of that object will vary or remain constant as the program executes. Objects whose values will vary are called variables and must be named, while objects whose values remain constant may or may not be named. In our example, we can classify our objects as follows:

Description of problem's object	Type	Kind	Name
The program	??	??	??
Screen	Screen	variable	*theScreen*
Prompt for distance (meters)	String	constant	none
Distance in meters	double	variable	*meters*
Keyboard	Keyboard	variable	*theKeyboard*
Prompt for time (seconds)	String	constant	none
Time in seconds	double	variable	*seconds*
Speed (kilometers/hour)	double	variable	*kilometersPerHour*

Because there is no existing type from which the program can be created, object-centered design tells us to build a class for it. Because this program is to calculate the speed for a given distance and time, we will call the class *Speeder*.

As we saw in Section 1.1, the ann.easyio package provides a Screen class that we can use to represent a screen object. It also provides a Keyboard class for representing keyboard objects. Our program will import the ann.easyio package so that these short class names can be used.

User prompts are just strings of characters, so we can use Java's String class for them. We will not name these prompt objects because their values do not change during execution of the program and are unlikely to change in the future.

We chose the names *meters* and *seconds* for the distance-in-meters and time-in-seconds problem objects, respectively, rather than *distance* and *time*, for example, because they convey both what is being measured and the units of measurement. Both of these values will vary, because the user will enter them from the keyboard. Variables that can store real values (i.e., numbers with decimal points) can be represented by the type double in Java.

Finally, we chose the name *kilometersPerHour* for the speed we are computing. Its type can be `double` because it will store a real value. It is a variable because its value will be computed by the program.

OPERATIONS.   Once we have identified and classified the problem's objects, we can proceed to the next step, which is to identify the operations needed to solve the problem. To identify the objects, we identified the nouns in our behavioral description; to identify the operations, we can begin by identifying the *verbs* (ignoring verbs that are actions by the user):

> *Behavior:* The program should <u>display</u> on the screen a prompt for a distance in meters. The user should enter this distance at the keyboard, from which the program should <u>read</u> it. The program should then <u>display</u> on the screen a prompt for a time in seconds. The user should enter this time at the keyboard, from which the program should read it. The program should then <u>compute</u> the speed in kilometers per hour and <u>display</u> it on the screen.

Using the problem objects we have identified, we can describe these operations as follows:

> **Operations**: Display on *theScreen* a prompt for a distance in meters
> Read a real value from *theKeyboard* and store it in *meters*
> Display on *theScreen* a prompt for a time in seconds
> Read a real value from *theKeyboard* and store it in *seconds*
> Compute *kilometersPerHour*
> Display *kilometersPerHour* on *theScreen*

As we described in Section 1.2, the `Screen` class in the package `ann.easyio` provides a `println()` method for displaying `String` values on the screen and then advancing to a new line. It also provides a `print()` method that also displays `String` values but does not follow this with a line advance. We can use one of these methods to display the prompts for the distance and time. The `Screen` class also provides other `print()` and `println()` methods that display `double` values, so we can use them to display *kilometersPerHour*.

One of the methods provided in the `Keyboard` class is a `readDouble()` method that reads a number from the keyboard and returns it as a Java `double` value. We can use this method to read the *meters* and *seconds* values.

Computing the speed requires some additional work. Average speed is given by the formula

$$speed = distance \mathbin{/} time$$

In terms of the variables in our program, this formula can be written as

$$metersPerSecond = meters \mathbin{/} seconds$$

However, we need the speed in kilometers per hour. There are 1000 meters in a kilometer, so dividing by 1000 gives us the speed in kilometers per second:

$$kilometersPerSecond = metersPerSecond / 1000$$

There are 3600 seconds in an hour, so multiplying our *kilometersPerSecond* value by 3600 gives us the speed in kilometers per hour:

$$kilometersPerHour = kilometersPerSecond \times 3600$$

This implies that we need to expand our list of objects:

Description of problem's object	Type	Kind	Name
The program	??	??	??
Screen	Screen	variable	*theScreen*
Prompt for distance (meters)	String	constant	none
Distance in meters	double	variable	*meters*
Keyboard	Keyboard	variable	*theKeyboard*
Prompt for time (seconds)	String	constant	none
Time in seconds	double	variable	*seconds*
Speed (kilometers/hour)	double	variable	*kilometersPerHour*
Speed (meters/second)	double	variable	*metersPerSecond*
Speed (kilometers/second)	double	variable	*kilometersPerSecond*
1000	int	constant	*METERS_PER_KILOMETER*
3600	int	constant	*SECONDS_PER_HOUR*

We also must expand our list of operations:

Operations: Display on *theScreen* a prompt for a distance in meters

Read a real value from *theKeyboard* and store it in *meters*

Display on *theScreen* a prompt for a time in seconds

Read a real value from *theKeyboard* and store it in *seconds*

Compute *kilometersPerHour*

—divide reals (*meters* by *seconds*, *metersPerSecond* by *METERS_PER_KILOMETER*)
—multiply reals (*kilometersPerSecond* and *SECONDS_PER_HOUR*)

Display *kilometersPerHour* on *theScreen*

As in most languages, real values can be multiplied in Java using the * operator and can be divided using the / operator. Thus, all of the operations needed to solve our problem are readily available.

ALGORITHM. Once we have identified all of the objects and operations, we are ready to arrange those operations into an algorithm. If we have done the preceding steps correctly, this is usually straightforward:

Algorithm for Computing Speed

1. Construct *theScreen*.
2. Ask *theScreen* to display a prompt for a distance in meters.
3. Construct *theKeyboard*.
4. Ask *theKeyboard* to read a `double` value and store it in *meters*.
5. Ask *theScreen* to display a prompt for a time in seconds.
6. Ask *theKeyboard* to read a `double` value and store it in *seconds*.
7. Compute *metersPerSecond = meters / seconds*.
8. Compute *kilometersPerSecond = metersPerSecond / METERS_PER_KILOMETER*.
9. Compute *kilometersPerHour = kilometersPerSecond * SECONDS_PER_HOUR*.
10. Ask *theScreen* to display *kilometersPerHour* along with some descriptive text.

This sequence of instructions is sometimes called a **pseudocode** algorithm, because it is not written in any particular programming language, and yet it bears some similarity to a program's code. This algorithm becomes our blueprint for the next stage of the process.

Coding

Once we have designed an algorithm for our problem, we are ready to translate that algorithm into a high-level language like Java. The program that results is given in Figure 1.4.

FIGURE 1.4 COMPUTING SPEED

```
/* Speeder.java computes an object's speed, given its distance and time.
 * Input:  The distance (meters) and the time (seconds)
 * Output: The speed (km/hr)
 */

import ann.easyio.*;                  // Keyboard, Screen

class Speeder
{
  public static void main(String [] args)
  {
    final int METERS_PER_KILOMETER = 1000;
    final int SECONDS_PER_HOUR     = 3600;

    Screen theScreen = new Screen();
    theScreen.print("To compute the speed for a distance traveled" +
                    "\n enter the distance (in meters): ");
    Keyboard theKeyboard = new Keyboard();
    double meters = theKeyboard.readDouble();

    theScreen.print(" enter the time (seconds): ");
    double seconds = theKeyboard.readDouble();
```

```
    double metersPerSecond = meters / seconds;
    double kilometersPerSecond = metersPerSecond / METERS_PER_KILOMETER;
    double kilometersPerHour = kilometersPerSecond * SECONDS_PER_HOUR;

    theScreen.println("\nThe speed is " + kilometersPerHour +
                      " km/hour.");
  }
}
```

Sample run:

```
To compute the speed for a distance traveled
 enter the distance (in meters): 100
 enter the time (seconds): 11.2

The speed is 32.14285714285714 km/hour.
```

Most of the features in this program should be understandable to you after our walk-through of the program in Figure 1.2, but there are a few items that require some explanation. The first two statements are declarations of integer constants named METERS_PER_KILOMETER and SECONDS_PER_HOUR. These constants are of type int, one of the **primitive types** provided in Java for processing integers, and their values are 1000 and 3600, respectively. The keyword final specifies that these values cannot be changed during program execution and thus METERS_PER_KILO-METER and SECONDS_PER_HOUR are *constants* and not *variables*.

As we noted earlier, the print() and println() methods in the Screen class can be used to display strings on a screen and that the only difference between them is that println() causes an automatic advance to a new line after displaying the string sent to it, but print() does not. In our program we used print() to display the prompts so the user can enter the values on the same line as the prompt (as shown in the sample run).

Keyboard is another class provided in the ann.easyio package. It represents the keyboard and contains several methods to facilitate input of various kinds of values from the user's keyboard. One of these is readDouble(), which converts the string of characters entered from the keyboard to a double value (if possible) and stores it in a variable of type double. Thus, the statement

```
    double meters = theKeyboard.readDouble();
```

gets a double value from the keyboard and stores it in the variable meters. Similarly, the statement

```
    double seconds = theKeyboard.readDouble();
```

gets a double value from the keyboard and stores it in the variable seconds.

The next three statements illustrate how Java's division (/) and multiplication (*) are used. The first statement

```
    double metersPerSecond = meters / seconds;
```

retrieves the values entered by the user and stored in meters and seconds, divides the first by the second, and stores the result in the double variable metersPer-Second. The next two statements are similar and calculate the values of double variables kilometersPerSecond and kilometersPerHour:

```
double kilometersPerSecond =
        metersPerSecond / METERS_PER_KILOMETER;

double kilometersPerHour =
        kilometersPerSecond * SECONDS_PER_HOUR;
```

Note that we could have saved several variables by computing `kilome-tersPerHour` using a single formula:

```
double kilometersPerHour =
        meters / seconds / METERS_PER_KILOMETER * SECONDS_PER_HOUR;
```

Both approaches work equally well; the former is more readable, but the latter requires less space.

A software program called a *text editor* can be used to enter this program into a computer.[7] The text editor is also used in the next stage of software development to correct errors in the program.

Testing, Execution, and Debugging

There are a number of different points at which errors can be introduced into a program. Two of the most common are:

1. Violations of the grammar rules of the high-level language in which the program is written
2. Errors in the design of the algorithm on which the program is based

The process of finding such errors is called **debugging** the program.

The first kind of error is called a **syntax error**, because the program violates the syntax (i.e., the grammar rules) of the language. As the compiler translates a program, it checks the program's syntax.[8] If it detects a syntax violation, the compiler will generate an *error* (or *diagnostic*) message that explains the (apparent) problem. For example, if we forgot to type the semicolon at the end of the line

```
import ann.easyio.*;
```

---

[7] Common text editors include: *vi*, *emacs*, and *pico* (for Unix); *edit* (for MS-DOS); *TextPad*, *WordPad*, and *WinEdit* (Windows); *TeachText* and *SimpleText* (Macintosh). Also, any word processing program (e.g., *MS-Word*, *WordPerfect*) can be used as a text editor by saving one's document in text-only format. Java integrated development environments (IDEs) such as *CodeWarrior*, *JBuilder*, *Symantec Café*, and *Visual J++* provide an integrated text editor. The free/shareware editors *TextPad* and *WinEdit* have been customized to provide built-in commands including commands to compile a Java program, to interpret and execute the resulting `.class` file for an application, or to generate a minimal HTML page and launch appletviewer for an applet.

[8] Sun's Java compiler (`javac`) is bundled with the Java 2 Software Development Kit (SDK). The most recent version is always freely available for download from `www.javasoft.com`. On command-line systems (e.g., Unix, MS-DOS), a Java program can be compiled from the command line by typing a line of the form

```
javac ProgramName.java
```

(The system's PATH environment variable must include the SDK directory.) Users of the `emacs` text editor can compile from within the editor by using the `M-x compile` command. `emacs` will respond with `make-k` which can be replaced with a compile command like that above. Java IDEs (see Footnote 7) provide a `Compile` (or `Project`) menu that includes a `Compile` choice that uses the IDE's compiler.

in the program in Figure 1.4, and instead entered

```
import ann.easyio.*
```

the compiler might display diagnostic messages like the following:

```
Speeder.java:6: ';' expected.
  import ann.easyio.* // Keyboard, Screen
                     ^

Speeder.java:15: Class Screen not found in type declaration.
  Screen theScreen = new Screen();
         ^

Speeder.java:15: Class Screen not found in type declaration.
  Screen theScreen = new Screen();
                         ^

Speeder.java:18: Class Keyboard not found in type declaration.
  Keyboard theKeyboard = new Keyboard();
           ^

Speeder.java:18: Class Keyboard not found in type declaration.
  Keyboard theKeyboard = new Keyboard();
                             ^

5 errors
```

Notice how a single mistake can produce multiple errors. Because the compiler is unable to complete the `import` statement, it never learns about the `Screen` and `Keyboard` classes in `ann.easyio`, so that subsequent references to these classes generate additional errors. On the positive side, making one change (i.e., adding the missing semicolon) fixes all five of these errors.

NOTE   What can we learn from this? When fixing the syntax errors in a program, fix the mistakes *in the order listed by the compiler.* If you try to fix "later" errors without fixing the "earlier" ones, you may waste a great deal of time trying to find a mistake whose cause is somewhere else. Also, learning to understand the messages that a compiler produces is an important skill. One way to study these messages is to intentionally introduce errors into a working program in order to see how the compiler responds.

The second kind of error is called a **logic error**, because such errors represent programmer mistakes in the design of the algorithm. For example, the program in Figure 1.4 contains the statement

```
double kilometersPerHour = kilometersPerSecond * SECONDS_PER_HOUR;
```

But suppose we accidentally typed a + in place of the * operator:

```
double kilometersPerHour = kilometersPerSecond + SECONDS_PER_HOUR;
```

Because the resulting program violates none of the grammatical rules of Java, *the compiler* will not detect the error. It has no basis for identifying this statement as erroneous, because it is a valid Java statement. Consequently, the program will compile and execute, but it will produce incorrect values because the formula used to compute `kilometersPerHour` is not correct.

To determine whether a program contains a logic error, it must be run using sample data and the output produced checked for correctness. This **testing** of a program should be done several times using a variety of inputs, ideally prepared by people other than the programmer, who may be making non-obvious assumptions in the choice of test data. If *any* combination of inputs produces incorrect output, then the program contains a logic error.

Once it has been determined that a program contains a logic error, finding the error is one of the most difficult parts of programming. Execution must be traced step by step until the point at which a computed value differs from an expected value is located. To simplify this tracing, most implementations of Java provide a **debugger** program[9] that allows a programmer to execute a program one statement at a time, and observe how the values of the program's variables change in response to statement execution. Once the error has been located, the text editor can be used to correct it.

Thorough testing of a program will increase one's confidence in its correctness, but it must be realized that it is almost never possible to test a program with every possible set of test data. There are cases in which apparently correct programs have been in use for more than ten years before a particular combination of inputs produced an incorrect output caused by a logic error. The particular data set that caused the program to execute the erroneous statement(s) had never been input in all that time!

As programs grow in size and complexity, the problem of testing them becomes increasingly more difficult. No matter how much testing is done, more could always be done. Testing is never finished; it is only stopped, and there is no guarantee that all the errors in a program have been found and corrected. Testing can only show the presence of errors, not their absence. It cannot prove that a program is correct; it can only show that it is incorrect.

Maintenance

Student programs are often run once or twice and then discarded. By contrast, real-world programs often represent a significant investment of a company's resources and may be used for many years. During this time, it may be necessary to add new features or enhancements to the program. This process of upgrading a program is called **software maintenance**.

To illustrate, suppose that for the program in Figure 1.4, Sarah O'Sprinter decides that the program would be more useful if it displayed her speed in both kilometers per hour and miles per hour. So we would add another variable *milesPerHour* of type `double` to our list of problem objects. Since 1 kilometer is (approximately) .621 miles, we can compute *milesPerHour* by multiplying *kilometersPerHour* by 0.621:

$$milesPerHour = kilometersPerHour \times 0.621$$

The program in Figure 1.4 might be modified by making the changes (shown in color) in the program in Figure 1.5. It declares a new `double` conversion constant

---

[9] Sun distributes its freeware *jdb* debugger with SDK. Java IDEs integrate the debugger with the compiler and editor, and usually provide a `Debug` menu choice to enable debugging.

MILES_PER_KILOMETER and a new `double` variable `milesPerHour` whose value is assigned using the above formula. The message sent to `theScreen` to display the computed speeds is modified to output the speed in both kilometers per hour and miles per hour.

FIGURE 1.5   COMPUTING SPEED—REVISED

```
/* Speeder2.java computes an object's speed, given its distance and time.
 * Input:   The distance (meters) and the time (seconds)
 * Output: The speed (km/hr amd mph)
 */

import ann.easyio.*;                    // Keyboard, Screen

class Speeder2
{
  public static void main(String [] args)
  {
     final int METERS_PER_KILOMETER   = 1000;
     final int SECONDS_PER_HOUR       = 3600;
     final double MILES_PER_KILOMETER = 0.621;

     Screen theScreen = new Screen();
     theScreen.print("\nTo compute the speed for a distance traveled" +
                     "\n enter the distance (in meters): ");
     Keyboard theKeyboard = new Keyboard();
     double meters = theKeyboard.readDouble();

     theScreen.print(" enter the time (seconds): ");
     double seconds = theKeyboard.readDouble();

     double metersPerSecond = meters / seconds;
     double kilometersPerSecond = metersPerSecond / METERS_PER_KILOMETER;
     double kilometersPerHour = kilometersPerSecond * SECONDS_PER_HOUR;
     double milesPerHour = kilometersPerHour * MILES_PER_KILOMETER;

     theScreen.println("\nThe speed is " + kilometersPerHour +
                       " km/hour, \n which is " + milesPerHour +
                       " miles/hr.");
  }
}
```

```
Sample run:

To compute the speed for a distance traveled
 enter the distance (in meters): 100
 enter the time (seconds): 11.2

The speed is 32.14285714285714 km/hour,
 which is 19.960714285714282 miles/hr
```

In other problems, it may be necessary to compute speeds whose distances and times are measured very precisely. When we execute the program, we find that it produces imprecise answers. This imprecision might be caused by the fact that the value for MILES_PER_KILOMETER (0.621) only uses three decimal places of precision, so we might increase the precision:

```
     final double MILES_PER_KILOMETER = 0.62137119223733;
```

On the other hand, some users might prefer that the program "cleaned up" the numbers it displays, by showing just one or two decimal digits. For this kind of formatting problem, our `ann.easyio` package provides `printFormatted` methods for the `Screen` class. These methods will be described in the next chapter.

✔ Quick Quiz 1.4

1. Name the four stages of the software life cycle.
2. List the four steps in object-centered design.
3. The _____ in a problem can be identified by finding the nouns in the behavioral description of the problem.
4. The _____ in a problem can be identified by finding the verbs in the behavioral description of the problem.
5. Objects whose values may change during program execution are called _____.
6. Objects whose values cannot change during program execution are called _____.
7. `int` and `double` are _____ types in Java.
8. _____ is Java's multiplication and _____ is its division operator.
9. Finding the errors in a program is called _____.
10. What are two types of errors that can occur in developing a program?

PART OF THE PICTURE: ETHICS AND ISSUES

by Anne Marchant, George Mason University

To be good is noble, but to show others how to be good is nobler, and no trouble.   *Mark Twain*

ETHICS AND SOCIETY

What will the future bring? Will we live a life of leisure with all our tedious chores performed by intelligent machines? Perhaps we will live instead in an "information prison" with all the details of our lives recorded and analyzed by government or by corporations that exist solely to buy and sell information. To a large extent, the future will be driven by the choices we make now.

Computers permeate every aspect of our lives. In addition to making businesses more productive, they also perform many life-critical tasks such as air-traffic control, medical diagnosis and treatment, and emergency communication. The field of computer science is largely unregulated. Programmers are not required to pass proficiency exams or obtain state licenses to practice their art. In an effort to protect society from the obvious dangers, the field is regulating itself. It does this by encouraging the study of ethics and by demanding the highest level of integrity from its members. Some companies are instituting ethics training for their employees and ethics web sites are appearing where professionals can debate ethical concerns. Professional organizations such as the Association for Computing Machinery (ACM) and the IEEE (Institute of Electrical and Electronics Engineers) have adopted and instituted a Code of Ethics.[10] Students are encouraged to join these organizations and familiarize themselves with these codes. Most colleges and universities also have policies governing the responsible use of computers. Students are encouraged to read these carefully and to develop their own personal standards.

COMPUTER CRIME AND SECURITY

Some computer crimes are old crimes that simply make use of computer technology. These include harassment, stalking, child pornography, fraud and embezzlement. Other crimes, such as the release of rogue programs, are new forms of crime. "Rogue software" is a class of software designed with some malicious intent. "Viruses" are programs that "infect" software in order to replicate. They usually do something harmful as well. A virus may corrupt or erase information on your disks. "Worms" are self-replicating programs that repeatedly propagate until they overwhelm the computer's resources. Although they may be spread across a network, viruses tend to create problems on PCs. In general, worms create problems on networks. "Trojan horses" can occur anywhere. These are programs that appear to do something useful while secretly doing something malicious. An example might be a program that appears to be a space war game that secretly transmits the user's login, password, and user privileges to someone else.

In recent years, macro viruses and email viruses have become a more serious threat. Macro viruses attack macros in office documents. A macro is a short program used to automate frequently performed tasks. If your office software has a "macro virus protection" option, you may wish to enable it. Viruses may also be sent as attachments to email. Be wary of mails sent from anyone unknown to you. Instead of double clicking on an attached document, save it to disk and scan it before opening it.

"Denial of service attacks" are becoming a serious problem on networks. A denial of service attack occurs when there are so many requests for a network service that the targeted machine becomes overwhelmed and service to others is effectively denied. Coordinated attacks by groups of hackers can be especially difficult to thwart.

The term "hacker" has undergone a semantic shift in recent years. Originally the term meant someone who wrote poor programs (a "hack"). It then came to mean a computer enthusiast. Now it has come to mean a computer criminal (sometimes also called "crackers"). Hackers often justify their actions by claiming that they are just trying to learn about computers. Would-be hackers might consider that computer security is a rapidly expanding field. There is a tremendous need for "computer enthusiasts" with creative ideas. Recently, "happy hacker" web sites are starting to appear. These are groups that encourage constructive and legal ways of learning. If you are looking for a challenge, creating a secure system is a much more challenging problem than breaking security. Students who put their

---

[10] For more information, see the book's website. The URL is given in the preface.

energy into learning about computer security may well be on the way to a rewarding career!

How can we protect ourselves against (destructive) hackers and rogue programs? The first line of defense is to use passwords that are not dictionary words and to change passwords frequently. Better means of user authentication are starting to appear. These include biometrics (e.g., fingerprint or retinal scans) and the use of encryption certificates. Backups should be kept of any information that is precious. It is very important to have at least two copies of every file at all times. It is also wise to keep backups at separate locations and in different media.

Users should keep antiviral software on their computers and be sure that they are familiar with how it works. Antiviral software needs to be updated periodically, at least every several months or so. Encryption should be used when transmitting any information that needs to be kept secure, including passwords, credit card numbers, or other confidential information.

Firewalls are systems that monitor traffic between networks to ensure that all network traffic is legitimate. Every network connecting to the Internet should have a firewall in place. System administrators should keep operating system and network security patches up to date, watch for security advisories, keep detailed logs, and use software tools (port scanners) designed to uncover system weaknesses.

Traditional security is especially important. Physically restricting access to computer systems can prevent many problems. The majority of computer crimes are not committed by hackers, but rather by employees or former employees of organizations. This means that employers need to screen applicants carefully, monitor employees' behavior, encourage a positive work ethic, and reward integrity. Grievance procedures should be in place to resolve work-related problems and diffuse hostilities when they arise. Secure audit systems should be in place to track fraud.

In 1996, President Clinton established a Commission on Critical Infrastructure Protection. The mission of this commission was to identify weaknesses in critical systems, such as communications, banking, energy, etc., and to propose defensive strategies. Cyberterrorism and cyberwarfare were identified among the potential threats. In response to these concerns, the National Infrastructure Protection Center was formed within the FBI. No doubt both defensive and offensive information warfare capabilities are being developed by governments and organizations around the world. A discussion of warfare is beyond the scope of this chapter, but the ethical implications of this new form of warfare are profound. Will civilian casualties be increased or reduced? As information warfare develops, will the world be a safer place or a more dangerous place? Finally, can information technology be used in such a way as to increase the socio-economic bonds between peoples around the world, making the need for such tactics less likely?

HEALTH CONCERNS AND THE ENVIRONMENT

Today, our economy is based largely on information-related jobs. This means that many of us spend long hours behind the computer staring at monitors. The most obvious problem this creates is lack of exercise. We need to remember to make exercise a regular part of our lifestyle. A more insidious problem is a class of injuries known as repetitive stress injuries (RSIs) that result from performing the same actions repeatedly without taking breaks. Carpal tunnel syndrome is one such injury that may result from typing for many hours. These injuries can be incapacitating and may require surgery.

Questions have been raised as to whether computer use can cause problems such as miscarriages, birth defects, and cancer. These are still controversial. Some have suggested that stress and lack of exercise may be more harmful than electromagnetic radiation.

Staring at monitors for long periods of time may cause one to lose the ability to focus prematurely ("farsightedness"). One should reduce glare when possible and use the highest resolution screen possible. It is also advisable to look away from the screen and focus on distant objects periodically.

The ethical employer will insist on ergonomic work station design, encourage employees to take regular breaks and exercise, and watch for signs of excessive stress in fast-paced information-related jobs.

"Internet addiction" is now a recognized obsessive-compulsive disorder. This is the inability to leave the computer for any length of time especially to the extent that it interferes with personal relationships, academic or job performance. Individuals may use "chat rooms" or news groups as a way to escape other problems. Or they may develop obsessions with on-line gambling, web surfing, or pornography. Parents may want to limit their children's access time to the Internet, just as they set limits on TV or other activities.

We think of the computer industry as being relatively friendly to the environment, but there are a number of serious concerns. The manufacture of computer chips can involve some chemicals that need to be carefully managed and disposed of. The ethical manager will see to it that paper and laser printer toner cartridges are recycled. Beyond that, each programmer and engineer needs to address the question: "Will my contributions make the world a better place or will my work cause harm?"

INFORMATION OWNERSHIP

Congress is granted the authority to "promote the Progress of Science and useful Art, by securing for limited Times to Authors and Inventors the exclusive Right to their respective Writings and Discoveries." *U.S. Constitution, art. I, section 8, cl. 8*

Copyrights protect the original expression of ideas. You can't copyright a fact or the idea itself, but you can copyright the expression of an idea once it is fixed in a tangible medium. (This may be written text, recorded sound, or software stored on a disk.) A phone call can not be copyrighted (unless taped), but email or on-line chat may be copyrighted if it is saved to disk. (Note that some company contracts co-opt their employees' email copyrights.) Under today's laws, a copyright notice © is not required to secure a copyright, nor need it be registered with the Library of Congress. However, these precautions will help to protect your work and support your case should you try to prove infringement. In 1989, the United States signed the Berne Convention, an international copyright agreement. With the growth of the Internet, international protection for intellectual property is a rising concern. The 1997 NET (No Electronic Theft Act) specifies harsh penalties for both commercial and non-commercial infringement of the copyright of electronic materials. This law does not specify "fair use" of a limited portion of copyrighted materials for educational, research or journalistic purposes. Therefore, unless work is specifically identified as being in the public domain, it's safest to get permission of the copyright holder before using someone else's work.

A copyright grants the copyright holder exclusive rights to the work's duplication, any derivative work, and the right of distribution or display. The integrity of the work must be maintained and the work must be properly attributed to the copyright holder. Copyrights may last up to 100 years depending on the date and nature of the work.

Students should be aware that it is an infringement to copy pictures or text from other web sites onto your own web page unless the copyright holder has granted permission. Creating a link to another page is legal (although this too has been challenged in court!). Similarly, it is illegal to scan in images to use on your web page without permission. You are essentially "publishing" someone else's work. Note that this is different from quoting something in a written paper that you submit as class work. As long as you include only a small portion of the work and properly attribute it to the author, this is considered "fair use."

Software is usually copyrighted. The holder of the copyright does not sell the software itself, but rather sells licenses to use the software. It is worth taking a minute to read the license that comes with software you purchase commercially. In general, it is illegal to make copies of commercial software except for the purposes of making a backup. As a rule, you must purchase a legal copy of the software for every machine you intend to install it on (although there are exceptions in some cases). Large companies and educational institutions will often purchase "site licenses" that allow them to install the software on a network file server. Duplicating software without paying for it is called "software piracy" or "bootlegging."

Sometimes software may be distributed as "shareware." Usually, shareware may be freely duplicated and distributed, but the author will require you to register the software and pay a fee if you decide to keep the software. Freeware is software that the author has placed in the public domain and may be duplicated freely.

Inventions, processes, and algorithms may be patented. An idea must pass a rigorous set of tests in order to be patented. The concept must be a new idea, it must be useful, and it must be "non-obvious" to other professionals working in the field. A patent may be held for 20 years and grants the patent holder the right to control sale of the invention and the right to royalties.

The legal system is struggling to manage the protection of electronic intellectual property. Does it make sense to grant an individual exclusive rights to an idea for 20 years in the rapidly changing field of computer science? As the use of computerized information continues to increase, society will need to adapt by making new laws and by changing existing laws. Exciting careers await those who combine the study of law and the study of computer science!

"NETIQUETTE" AND HOAXES

On-line "chat," newsgroups, and email create a new realm for social interaction. In one sense, the lack of face-to-face interaction has a leveling effect on society. We make judgments based on a person's ideas instead of on their age, race, social standing, religion, ethnicity, or appearance. On the other hand, there is a disturbing lack of accountability that leads people to engage in inflammatory exchanges. These "flame wars" are usually viewed by more experienced users as a sign of immaturity and inexperience.

Chain mail is disallowed by many institutions and may be illegal in some instances. Be suspicious of mail that encourages you to forward the message to many other users. These messages may try to play on your emotions with such statements as: "Little Johnny is dying of cancer and would like your email messages before he dies. . . ." or "Forward this mail to as many people as you can and it will bring you luck. If you don't, some serious harm will come to you." Such "chain mail" propagates quickly and overwhelms network resources. Don't be taken in!

Virus warnings are often hoaxes. Be especially leery of email viruses such as the "Good Times" virus. (This is a very old hoax!) Check with CERT (the Computer Emergency Response Team) to verify virus alerts (see CERT's web address provided at the end of this section).

Should anonymous email be permitted? Should we be accountable for the things that we say? On the one hand, we instinctively want to have the ability to "blow the whistle" anonymously—especially in cases where negative repercussions are likely. Anonymity may also protect such people as AIDS patients, abuse victims, and other folks who need to get information or support. On the other hand, anonymous email makes it easy to harass other users or make libelous statements. Before sending anonymous email, ask yourself why you need to send it anonymously. Is it really because you may be unfairly punished or is it really just a way to say something you are not brave enough to take responsibility for?

While most folks feel that free speech is an important right, few are willing to support "spam." Spam is unsolicited, bulk email, usually selling a product or service. While spam may just be a nuisance for the average user, spam can cause a serious loss of productivity to large corporations. There have been attempts to legislate against spam, and a number of court cases have not supported the idea that spam is a protected form of speech. We are beginning to see a whole line of anti-spam products and services appear.

INTERNET CONTENT AND FREE SPEECH

The vast quantity of information now available world-wide is bound to have profound, long term ramifications. Information that was formerly only available within the walls of academia or published in obscure journals is now easily accessible to people of all classes, as long as they are computer literate and have access to the Internet. The problem is that the Internet is a reflection of society at large. The information on the Internet includes hate, doctrines of violence, a lot of information that is wrong, and information that may be harmful to children.

Should Internet content be regulated? If so, how do we effectively regulate an international medium? Whose standards do we implement? There have been two major attempts at legislation, the Communications Decency Act (CDA), struck down by the Supreme Court in 1997 as a violation of the First Amendment, and the Child Online Protection Act (COPA), which is currently facing challenges in court.

Some argue that filtering software may provide a solution. Such software can be used by schools and libraries to prevent children from gaining access to undesirable material. Others argue that this is censorship and question the standards used in setting up filtering guidelines.

This is a topic that will continue to be hotly debated. What seems to be lost in the debate is a realization that with freedom comes responsibility—a responsibility to use the Internet appropriately, a responsibility to teach children to use the Internet in a constructive manner, and a responsibility borne by all of us to make judgments about the information we use and the sites that we patronize.

Students will need to make judgments about the web sites that they use as source material for course work and research. Is a given page from a reliable, unbiased source? Is the author selling a product or service? Is the author knowledgeable? Then too, there are web sites that offer students papers and homework solutions. What effect will these have on the development of each student? What will be the effect on society in general?

PRIVACY

While the US Constitution does not specifically guarantee a right to privacy, several of the Amendments have been interpreted as implying a right to privacy. (One example is the Fourth Amendment, which protects citizens against unreasonable search and seizure.) Do you feel that a right to privacy is important in a free society?

Database technology and the Internet make it very easy to store and transmit large quantities of information. Everything from our medical histories to our driving records are routinely bought and sold. As a society we need to come to terms with what information should be stored, how its accuracy can be verified, how it should be protected, and when it should be destroyed.

Ask yourself how you would feel if you were turned down for a loan because your credit history had been accidentally (or deliberately!) swapped with someone else's. When it is your word against the computer's, where is the burden of proof? Now imagine a worse scenario. Imagine that your name and social security number is very close to that of a convicted felon. Might this affect your ability to get a government job? On the other hand, law enforcement needs to maintain extensive databases to assist them in preventing and solving crimes.

Recently, there has been discussion about the implementation of routine "profiling" of airline passengers and subjecting those with suspicious profiles to extra searches. Profiles are generated by matching information in different databases to try to identify "suspicious" persons. Is safety more important than civil liberty? Should you have the right to know what information about you is being stored?

Concerns have been raised about information that is gathered about us online. Be aware of the information you supply to online retailers or when filling out online petitions or other forms. Imagine how this information might be used. Children should be cautioned against giving out personal information over the Internet. Many businesses publish a privacy policy that clearly indicates how information about clients will be used. A non-profit organization, TRUSTe, certifies that online businesses are adhering to fair information practices. If this sort of self-regulation is unsuccessful, congress may be forced to regulate business practices that infringe on consumer privacy.

Does your employer have the right to monitor your email and Internet usage? As long as this is disclosed, they probably do. How does this make you feel about your work? If you know that you are being monitored, are you likely to change the way you behave at work? Should all employees be monitored or only those in particularly sensitive jobs?

With world populations continuing to rise, governments and economies become increasingly dependent on computerized systems to function. The danger is that if we do not make careful choices, we will be ever defined and controlled by data files. Worse, in the wrong hands, information systems can become the tools of oppressors.

As computer professionals, you can do your part to protect privacy by observing security precautions, restricting access to information, and by encouraging professional behavior among your colleagues. When information is gathered, procedures and policies must be in place to define how it will be used, to ensure its integrity, and to determine how and when it will be destroyed. Remember that email should be treated as if it were a "post card," and not a sealed letter. Information that needs to be kept private should be encrypted and important documents should be digitally "signed." You should become familiar with the Electronic Communications Privacy Act (ECPA) of 1986 that protects private communications.

QUALITY CONTROL AND RISK REDUCTION

As you are beginning to learn, writing good software is extremely difficult. Software needs to be carefully designed, carefully developed, and tested as thoroughly as possible. Commercial software is routinely put through in-house testing ("alpha" testing) and then testing by select clients ("beta" testing). Some managers will even plant bugs in their products knowing that in the process of finding these bugs, their programmers will uncover other errors. Standards for software in life-critical applications need to be extremely high. Interfaces must be easy to learn and must be "bullet proof." They must anticipate user errors and safeguard against potentially serious mistakes. Documentation and user training need to be part of the overall product plan, not afterthoughts. If serious flaws are detected, there should be some mechanism in place to report problems, correct them quickly, and notify users.

Computers are powerful tools. This means that when we make mistakes with computers, they tend to be large scale! As students you should learn to do "back of the envelope" approximations to develop a sense when results are wrong. You should develop a style of coding that is readable. Remember that the person writing the code may well not be the one to maintain it! Even when code appears to work, make use of debuggers, assertion checking, or simply print out the values of variables to make sure that code is correct. Finally, document your code thoroughly with comments, "help" or "readme" files, manuals, or whatever system is required by the application.

The recent Y2K issue has drawn attention to our increasing dependence upon computer technology. (This problem occurred because historically, programmers used only the last two places to store a date. In other words, 1999 would have been stored as 99. This meant that computers could not differentiate between 1900 and 2000.) While there was a great deal of hype, and a certain amount of fraud, many experts feel that forcing society to implement a thorough testing of systems and to develop backup systems and procedures has had many benefits and prevented many problems. The lesson to be learned from Y2K is to plan ahead!

THE FUTURE

Advances in technology are creating many admirable improvements in the quality of many lives. "Telecommuting" enables new parents to work, improves access for the disabled, and helps the environment by cutting down on traffic. "Distance learning" is making educational opportunities available throughout the world. All sorts of new economic possibilities are being created. Improvements in the speed of world-wide communication and the vast amount of information now readily available has profound implications we are only just beginning to imagine. Yet there are dangerous hazards to be negotiated. Choices we make now will determine how well we will meet these challenges.

✍ EXERCISES

Briefly define each of the terms in Exercises 1–16.

1. ACM
2. chain mail
3. copyright
4. fair use
5. firewall
6. hacker
7. IEEE
8. patent
9. piracy
10. rogue software
11. RSI
12. site license
13. telecommuting

14.   Trojan horse

15.   virus

16.   worm

17.   Examine recent issues of the *New York Times, Time, Newsweek,* or other newspapers and news magazines to find an article that describe one of the following:

(a) A new application of computing.

(b) A problem caused by a computer error, either in hardware or software.

(c) Difficulties caused by a new computer virus, worm, or Trojan horse.

(d) A break-in by a hacker or a group of hackers to databases containing sensitive information.

Write a report that summarizes the article and your reaction to it, especially to any ethical and moral issues that are involved.

18.   Many of the publications of the professional computing societies contain articles that are of interest to students. Select one or several of the publications in the following list, locate an article dealing with some current ethical issue, and prepare a written summary of the article, the ethical or moral problem involved, suggestions for dealing with the problem, and your reaction.

Communications of the ACM

Computers and Society, a publication of the ACM Special Interest Group on Computers & Society

COMPUTERWORLD

IEEE Computer

IEEE Software

IEEE Spectrum

New Scientist

SIGCAPH Newsletter, a publication of the ACM Special Interest Group on Computers and the Physically Handicapped

SIGCHI Bulletin, a publication of the ACM Special Interest Group on Computer & Human Interaction

Software Engineering Notes, an informal newsletter of the ACM Special Interest Group on Software Engineering

19.   Create your own "Code of Ethics" for an imaginary company. A good way to start is to think about school or workplace behavior that you find objectionable. Try to think of a code to address these problems.

20.   Discuss freedom of speech and the Internet. Should any form of expression be permitted? Should individuals be free to post child pornography, hate, violent material, or materials that might incite others to commit crimes? What happens when different cultural standards collide? Are there technological solutions to these problems?

21. Discuss the gender gap in computer science academic programs. Men outnumber women roughly 3 to 1. Why is this, when parity has been achieved in other top professional fields? A recent study has shown that 95% of hackers are male. Why is this?

22. Create a web page on one of the topics below and include links to related pages:

CFAA (1986 Computer Fraud and Abuse Act)

ECPA (1986 Electronic Communications Privacy Act)

COPA (1998 Child Online Protection Act)

FBI NCCS (National Computer Crime Squad. (See http://www.fbi.gov)

encryption

software piracy

viruses

FOR FURTHER READING

Baase, S. *A Gift of Fire.* Prentice Hall, 1997.

Bowyer, K. *Ethics and Computing.* IEEE Computer Society Press, 1996.

Cavazos, E. & Morin, G. *Cyberspace and the Law.* MIT Press, 1995.

Cheswick, R. & Bellowin, S. *Firewalls and Internet Security.* Addison Wesley, 1994 (2000 edition due out).

Denning, D. *Information Warfare and Security.* ACM Press/Addison Wesley, 1999.

Hoffman, L. *Rogue Programs, Viruses, Worms, and Trojan Horses.* Van Nostrand Reinhold, 1990.

Icove, D.J. *Computer Crime: A Crime-fighter's Handbook.* O'Reilly Associates, 1995.

Johnson, D.G. & Nissenbaum, H. *Computer Ethics & Social Values.* Prentice Hall, 1995.

Neumann, P. *Computer Related Risks.* Addison Wesley, 1995.

Parker, D.B. *Fighting Computer Crime.* J. Wiley and Sons, 1998.

Schneier, B. *Applied Cryptography.* J. Wiley and Sons, 1995.

CERT Coordination Center http://www.cert.org

Computer Professionals for Social Responsibility http://www.cpsr.org

Ethics References http://www.cs.gmu.edu/~amarchan/cs105/ethics.html

Electronic Frontier Foundation http://www.eff.org

The Online Ethics Center for Engineering and Science http://onlineethics.org/text/index.html

CHAPTER SUMMARY

KEY TERMS AND NOTES

algorithm	interpreter
applet	invoking a method
appletviewer	James Gosling
application	`JApplet` class
argument	Java virtual machine (JVM)
Abstract Windowing Kit (AWT)	Ken Thompson
Bjarne Stroustrup	labels
bytecode	logic error
C	main method
C++	method
calling a method	object
class declaration	`Object` class
client	object-centered design (OCD)
comment	object-oriented programming (OOP)
compiler	package
concatenation operator	panels
containers	platform independence
content pane	program
debugger	server
debugging	Smalltalk-80
Dennis Ritchie	software engineering
`extends` clause	software life cycle
fully-qualified name	software maintenance
graphical user interface (GUI)	subclass
high-level languages	superclass
HTML (Hypertext Mark-up Language)	Swing
import statement	syntax error
intermediate code	Unix

◎ Java is designed to be platform-independent. Java code is compiled into bytecode that can be executed by a Java Virtual Machine (JVM).

◎ In an *object-oriented programming language* like Java, a program constructs *objects* that carry out tasks needed to solve the problem and then sends *messages* to these objects to perform these tasks.

◎ Objects are created from *classes* and are also called *instances* of those classes.

◎ Multiline comments are enclosed between /* and */; single-line comments are preceded by // and run to the end of the line.

◎ Import statements allow a programmer to use simple names of classes—*className*—in a package instead of their fully-qualified names—*packageName.className*.

◎ Form of Java applications:

```
class ClassName extends Object
{
 Declarations of class members
}
```

◎ Form of Java applets:

```
public class ClassName extends JApplet
{
 Declarations of class members
}
```

◎ Applications extend the `Object` class; applets extend the `JAppplet` (or `Applet`) class.

◎ Members of a class may be *variables* that store values that determine an object's attributes or *methods* that operate on these values and determine an object's behavior.

◎ If class *A* extends class *B*, then *A* inherits the members of *B* and can add new ones.

◎ Every Java application must have a main method, whose heading has the form

```
public static void main(String [] args)
```

This is where execution of the application begins.

◎ The statements of a method are enclosed between curly braces { and }.

◎ Applications are standalone programs that can be executed with a Java interpreter. Applets can be placed in a web page and will be executed by the web browser when that web page is opened. They can also be executed by the appletviewer utility provided as part of Java's Software Development Kit (SDK).

◎ Java's AWT and its collection of Swing components can both be used to build GUIs but the Swing collection should be used because of its more powerful and flexible capabilities.

◎ Swing components are distinguishable from their AWT counterparts by the fact that they begin with `J`.

◎ The `javax.swing` package contains most of the Swing classes needed by beginning programmers.

◎ For Swing components, GUI objects are *not* added directly to the top-level container (unlike AWT containers). Instead, they are added to its content pane which is accessed using the container's `getContentPane()` method.

◎ Applets that contain Swing components must extend `JApplet`.

◎ Applications begin execution with their `main()` method; applets begin execution with their `init()` method. They should override the empty `init()` method they inherit from `JApplet` with their own `init()` method.

◎ Applets are added to web pages by using the `<APPLET>` and `</APPLET>` tags:

```
<APPLET CODE = "Name.class", WIDTH = xxx, HEIGHT = yyy>
</APPLET>
```

◎ Software development involves several phases: design; coding; testing, execution, and debugging; and maintenance.

◎ The object-centered design (OCD) methodology used in this text consists of 4 steps: (1) Describe the behavior of the program. (2) Identify the real-world objects in your problem description, and categorize them according to their types. (3) Identify the operations needed to solve the problem. (4) Arrange the problem's objects and operations in an algorithm that solves the problem.

◎ When fixing the syntax errors in a program, fix the mistakes in the order listed by the compiler.

◎ Programs should be tested several times using a variety of inputs.

Documentation

REFERENCE ■ The `print()` and `println()` methods in the `ann.easyio` package return the `Screen` object to which the message was sent. For example,

```
theScreen.println("Hello.");
```

not only displays `"Hello"` but also returns `theScreen` as a value. This means that we can *chain* calls to `print()` and `println()` together as in

```
theScreen.println("Hello.").println("How are you?");
```

The first message to `theScreen` outputs `"Hello"` and returns `theScreen`, so the preceding chain of messages becomes

```
theScreen.println("How are you?");
```

which will output `"How are you?"` on a new line. The output produced by this statement is, therefore,

```
Hello.
How are you?
```

This chained message is therefore equivalent to the two separate messages

```
theScreen.println("Hello.");
theScreen.println("How are you?");
```

It can also be written as a single message

```
theScreen.println("Hello.\nHow are you?");
```

which can be split over several lines (which may be necessary for longer strings):

```
theScreen.println("Hello."
                  + "\nHow are you?");
```

Here \n is a special character called an **escape sequence**. When it is encountered in any output statement, it causes an advance to a new line.

■ The following HTML code can be used to make a simple web page for testing an applet:

```
<HTML>

<HEAD>
</HEAD>

<BODY>
```

```
<APPLET CODE = "applet_name.class"
    WIDTH = number1 HEIGHT = number2>

</APPLET>

</BODY>

</HTML>
```

PROGRAMMING PROBLEMS

SECTION 1.2

1. Modify the program in Figure 1.2 so that it displays a message like the following with the date and time replaced with the current date and time and with John Doe replaced with your name:

   ```
   Welcome! Today, Mon Jan 10 10:07:16 EDT 2000,
   you begin your study of Java, John Doe!
   ```

2. Enter and execute the following Java program on your computer system:

   ```
   /* This program adds the values of variables x and y.
    *
    * Output (screen): The value x + y
    */

   import ann.easyio.*;

   class Adder
   {
     public static void main(String [] args)
     {
       int x = 214,          // the first value
           y = 2057,         // the second value
           sum = x + y;

       // output the resulting value
       Screen theScreen = new Screen();
       theScreen.println(x + " + " + y + " = " + sum);
     }
   }
   ```

3. Make the following changes in the program in Problem 2 and execute the modified program:

   (a) Change 214 to 1723 in the statement that gives x a value.

   (b) Change the variable names x and y to alpha and beta throughout.

   (c) Add the comment

   ```
   // find their sum
   ```

   to the declaration of sum.

   (d) Change the variable declarations to

```
int alpha = 214,            // the first value
    beta = 2057,            // the second value
    difference = alpha - beta,  // find their difference
    sum = alpha + beta;     // find their sum
```

and add the statement

```
theScreen.println(x + " - " + y + " = " + difference);
```

after the output statement that displays the sum of x and y.

SECTION 1.3

4. Proceed as in Problem 1, but modify the applet in Figure 1.3.

5. Modify the applet in Figure 1.3 to specify a font type and color by making the following changes:

(a) Add the line

```
import.java.awt.*;     // Font, Color
```

at the end of the list of `import` statements.

(b) Add the following lines before the last statement of the `init()` method:

```
Font screenFont = new Font("Arial", Font.BOLD, 12);
greeting.setFont(screenFont);
greeting.setForeground(Color.red);
```

Execute the modified applet.

6. Applets can receive parameters from the HTML files that launch them. Make the following modifications to the applet in Figure 1.3 so that it can receive a parameter named `day` from an HTML file.

(a) Delete the lines

```
import.java.awt.*;     // Font, Color
```

and

```
Date currentDate = new Date();
```

(b) Change the line

```
String today = currentDate.toString();
```

to:

```
String today;
```

(c) Immediately after this line, add the following line:

```
today = getParameter("day");
```

(d) Then, add a `<PARAM>` tag to the `<APPLET>` tag in the HTML file that launches this applet:

```
<APPLET CODE="Greeter2.class" WIDTH=500 HEIGHT=100>
<PARAM NAME=day VALUE="a simply glorious day!">
</APPLET>
```

Execute the modified applet.

7. Modify the result of Problem 6 so that it passes the font name "Courier" to the applet.

   (a) After the line

   ```
   String today;
   ```

   add this line:

   ```
   String fontName;
   ```

   (b) After the line

   ```
   today = getParameter("day");
   ```

   add this line:

   ```
   fontName = getParameter("font") ;
   ```

   (c) Then, change the line

   ```
   Font screenFont = new Font("Arial", Font.BOLD, 12);
   ```

   to

   ```
   Font screenFont = new Font(fontName, Font.BOLD, 12);
   ```

   (d) Finally, add another <PARAM> tag to the <APPLET> tag in the HTML file that calls this applet so that it reads:

   ```
   <APPLET CODE="Greeter.class" WIDTH=500 HEIGHT=100>
   <PARAM NAME=day VALUE="a simply glorious day!">
   <PARAM NAME=font VALUE="Courier">
   </APPLET>
   ```

   Execute the modified applet.

SECTION 1.4

For each of the problems described in Problems 8–10, give a precise description of how a program to solve that problem must behave. Then describe the problem's objects and the operations needed to solve the problem, and design an algorithm for it.

8. Calculate and display the perimeter and the area of a square with a given side.

9. Calculate and display the diameter, circumference, and the area of a circle with a given radius. (The diameter is twice the radius. For radius r, the circumference is $2\pi r$ and the area is πr^2 where π is the mathematical constant pi whose value is approximately 3.14159.)

10. Sam Splicer installs coaxial cable for the Metro City Cable Company. For each installation, there is a basic service charge of $25.00 and an additional charge of $2.00 for each foot of cable. The president of the cable company would like a program to compute the revenue generated by Sam in any given month. For example, if during the month of January, Sam installs a total of 263 yards of cable at 27 different locations, he generates $2253.00 in revenue.

11. Proceed as in Problem 1, but have the user input his or her name. Use a statement of the form

```
String name = theKeyboard.readline();
```

to read a string and store it in a variable named *name*.

12. Using the programs in this chapter as a guide, write a Java program to solve the problem in Problem 8.

13. Using the programs in this chapter as a guide, write a Java program to solve the problem in Problem 9. For the value π, you can use the constant `Math.PI` provided in Java.

14. Using the programs in this chapter as a guide, write a Java program to solve the problem in Problem 10. You can use a statement of the form

```
int number = theKeyboard.readInt();
```

to read an integer and store it in a variable named *number*.

SOME JAVA FUNDAMENTALS

Kindly enter them in your notebook.
And, in order to refer to them conveniently,
let's call them A, B, and Z. *The Tortoise in Lewis Carroll's What the Tortoise Said to Achilles*

". . . The name of the song is called 'Haddocks' Eyes.'"

"Oh, that's the name of the song, is it?" Alice said, trying to feel interested.

"No, you don't understand," the Knight said, looking a little vexed. "That's what the name is called.
The name really is 'The Aged Aged Man.'"

"Then I ought to have said 'That's what the song is called'?" Alice corrected herself.

*"No, you oughtn't: that's quite another thing! The song is called 'Ways and Means': but that's only
what it's called, you know!"*

"Well, what is the song, then?" said Alice, who was by this time completely bewildered.

*"I was coming to that," the Knight said. "The song really is 'A-sitting on a Gate': and the tune's my
own invention."* Lewis Carroll

*For, contrary to the unreasoned opinion of the ignorant, the choice of a system of numeration is a
mere matter of convention.* Blaise Pascal

■ Chapter Contents

Chapter Objectives

- See what primitive types Java provides and some literals of these types
- Explain Java's syntax rules for forming identifiers and naming conventions for them
- Take a first look at the difference between primitive types and reference types
- Study variables and constants—what they are, how they differ, how they are declared, and how they are used

- (Optional) Investigate how values of the various primitive types are represented internally in a computer and some of the advantages and limitations of these representations
- Take a first look at the structure of classes and how they are declared
- See why import statements are used
- Take another look at methods and how to use them—sending messages to objects, passing arguments, returning values
- Study the organization of the Java API and learn how to use the extremely valuable web-based documentation for it to find information about the large number of classes it contains
- Take a first look at how to design and build a simple GUI application

The preceding chapter focused on the software development process and it included three simple Java programs. However, because we had not yet undertaken a systematic study of the Java programming language, our walkthroughs of these programs were considerably simplified. We ignored many language details in the hope that you would gain some understanding—albeit incomplete—of what was going on in these programs. In this chapter, we will present some of these fundamental features of Java more precisely and in more detail.

2.1 EXAMPLE: A PAYROLL PROGRAM

In the opening section of the preceding chapter we looked at a simple program that displayed a welcome greeting. In the last section, we developed a program to calculate speed from a given distance and time. In this section, we will consider a simple payroll program and use it to illustrate some of the features of the Java language studied in the next two sections.

PROBLEM

Chuck Controller is the sole employee in Cawker City Candy Company's accounting department and is finding it increasingly difficult to keep up with his duties. As a first step in computerizing some of the department's tasks, he would like a program to calculate employee wages. Currently, each employee is paid a fixed hourly rate for any number of hours—no overtime is paid.

 ### OBJECT-CENTERED DESIGN

In developing this program, we will use the OCD method described in the previous chapter:

1. Describe the program's behavior
2. Identify the problem's objects
3. Identify the problem's operations
4 Organize these objects and operations in an algorithm

BEHAVIOR. Our program should display on the screen a prompt for the number of hours worked and the hourly rate. The user will enter these real values at the keyboard. The program should read these numbers and compute the wages. It should display wages along with a descriptive label.

THE PROBLEM'S OBJECTS. From our behavioral description of what the program is to do, we can identify the following objects in this problem:

Description of problem's object	Type	Kind	Name
The program	??	??	??
Screen	Screen	variable	*theScreen*
Prompt for hours and rate	String	constant	none
Number of hours worked	double	variable	*hoursWorked*
Hourly pay rate	double	variable	*hourlyRate*
Keyboard	Keyboard	variable	*theKeyboard*
Wages	double	variable	*wages*
Descriptive label	String	constant	none

OPERATIONS. Again, using our behavioral description, we can identify the operations needed to solve this problem:

   i. Display strings (the prompts) on the screen

  ii. Read nonnegative real numbers (*hoursWorked* and *hourlyRate*) from the keyboard

 iii. Compute *wages*

 iv. Display a real value (*wages*) and a string on the screen

As we saw in Section 1.3, input and output operations (i, ii, and iv) are provided by the `ann.easyio` package. The wages are calculated by

$$wages = hoursWorked \times hourlyRate$$

which requires the following operations

iii-a. Multiplication of reals

iii-b. Store a real value in a variable

ALGORITHM. Organizing these objects and operations into an algorithm gives:

   1. Construct `Screen` object *theScreen* and `Keyboard` object *theKeyboard*.

   2. Ask object *theScreen* to display a prompt for the hours worked by the employee.

   3. Ask object *theKeyboard* to read a real value and store it in *hoursWorked*.

   4. Ask object *theScreen* to display a prompt for the employee's hourly pay rate.

5. Ask object *theKeyboard* to read a real value and store it in *hourlyRate*.

6. Compute *wages = hoursWorked × hourlyRate*.

7. Ask object *theScreen* to display *wages* and a descriptive label.

Coding, Execution, and Testing

Figure 2.1 shows one way to implement the preceding algorithm as a program. Also shown is a sample run with test data for which the output can be easily verified and a second execution with some more realistic data values.

FIGURE 2.1   PAYROLL PROGRAM

```
/* Payroll1.java computes an employee's wages.
 * Input:  Hours worked by the employee and his/her hourly rate
 * Output: Employee's wages (no overtime pay)
 */

import ann.easyio.*;               // Keyboard, Screen

class Payroll1 extends Object
{
  public static void main(String [] args)
  {
    Screen theScreen = new Screen();
    Keyboard theKeyboard = new Keyboard();

    theScreen.print("Enter the number of hours worked by employee: ");
    double hoursWorked = theKeyboard.readDouble();
    theScreen.print("Enter the employee's hourly pay rate: ");
    double hourlyRate = theKeyboard.readDouble();

    double wages = hoursWorked * rate;
    theScreen.println("\nEmployee's wages are $" + wages);
  }
}
```

Sample runs:

```
Enter the number of hours worked by employee: 3
Enter the employee's hourly pay rate: 1.25

Employee's wages: $3.75


Enter the number of hours worked by employee: 39
Enter the employee's hourly pay rate: 8.75

Employee's wages: $341.25
```

Maintenance

One obvious enhancement to the program would be to design it to process both regular and overtime wages. But this requires a selection structure, which we will describe and study in Chapters 5 and 7. Another improvement would be to design the program to process any number of employees without having to re-execute it each time. But this requires using a repetition structure, which will be studied in Chapters 5 and 8.

Another way the program could be improved is not revealed by the sample runs. However, if we execute it with 39 hours worked and a pay rate of $8.11, the output produced is

```
Enter the number of hours worked by employee: 39
Enter the employee's hourly pay rate: 8.11

Employee's wages: $316.28999999999996
```

Obviously, the format of the value for wages is not good. It would be better to display wages as $316.29, with two decimal places. Similarly, for 39 hours worked and a pay rate of $8.10, the output produced is

```
Enter the number of hours worked by employee: 39
Enter the employee's hourly pay rate: 8.10

Employee's wages: $315.9
```

This isn't as bad as the preceding sample run, but it would be preferable to display the wages with two decimal places—$315.90.

For this kind of formatting problem, we have included a printFormatted() method in the ann.easyio package. It can be used in several different forms, which are described in the Documentation section of the chapter summary. Figure 2.2 shows a modified version of the program in Figure 2.1; it uses one of these forms to display the value of wages with two decimal digits.

FIGURE 2.2   PAYROLL PROGRAM—REVISED

```java
/* Payroll2.java computes an employee's wages.
 * Input:  Hours worked by the employee and his/her hourly rate
 * Output: Employee's wages (no overtime pay)
 */

import ann.easyio.*;                    // Keyboard, Screen

class Payroll2
{
  public static void main(String [] args)
  {
    Screen theScreen = new Screen();
    Keyboard theKeyboard = new Keyboard();

    theScreen.print("Enter the number of hours worked by employee: ");
    double hoursWorked = theKeyboard.readDouble();
    theScreen.print("Enter the employee's hourly pay rate: ");
    double hourlyRate = theKeyboard.readDouble();

    double wages = hoursWorked * hourlyRate;
    theScreen.print("\nEmployee's wages: $");
    theScreen.printFormatted(wages, 2);
    theScreen.println();
    // or as a chain of messages:
    // theScreen.print("\nEmployee's wages: $")
    //          .printFormatted(wages, 2).println();
  }
}
```

Sample runs:

```
Enter the number of hours worked by employee: 39
Enter the employee's hourly pay rate: 8.11

Employee's wages: $316.29


Enter the number of hours worked by employee: 39
Enter the employee's hourly pay rate: 8.10

Employee's wages: $315.90
```

As the comment indicates, the `printFormatted()` method can be chained together with `println()` and `print()` methods. (See the Documentation section at the end of Chapter 1 for an explanation of how this works.) The call to `println()` with no argument at the end of the chained messages simply causes subsequent output to appear on a new line.

In the next two sections we examine in detail several basic Java features. We will use the preceding program along with those in the preceding chapter to illustrate these features.

2.2   TYPES, VARIABLES, AND CONSTANTS

As we discussed in Chapter 1, object-centered design involves identifying the real-world objects in a problem, identifying what operations on them are needed, and then developing and encoding an algorithm that manipulates these objects and operations. To allow the Java compiler to check that the corresponding software objects within a program are being used properly, Java requires that the types of these objects be specified, or **declared**, before they are used. In this section, we take a first look at the types that Java provides, the values in these types, and some of the basic syntax rules for choosing names for and declaring variables, constants, and objects to store these values. The Part of the Picture section that follows shows how values of various types are stored in memory and the next chapter describes these types in more detail.

Types

Before the name of a variable, constant, or method can be used in a program, its name must be associated with a **type**, which informs the Java compiler how much space in memory must be allocated for each kind of value. The program in Figure 2.2 uses several types:

❑ `void`, the type associated with the `main()` method, denotes the absence of any type

❑ `String []`, the type associated with an argument (`args`) that can be passed to the main method (and, in general, the type associated with arrays of strings)

❏ `Keyboard`, the type associated with `theKeyboard`

❏ `Screen`, the type associated with `theScreen`

❏ `double`, the type associated with real values such as `hoursWorked`, `hourlyRate`, and `wages`

Java divides types into two categories:

1. Primitive types

2. Reference types

The **primitive types** include `int`, `double`, and `char` and can be thought of as the basic building blocks in Java. Table 2.1 gives a listing of Java's primitive types and shows their memory requirements.

TABLE 2.1   JAVA'S PRIMITIVE TYPES

Type	Kind of Values	Number of Bits
byte	very small integers	8
short	small integers	16
int	integers	32
long	large integers	64
float	small reals	32
double	reals	64
boolean	logical (true/false) values	1
char	individual characters	16

Reference types, such as `String`, `Screen`, and `Keyboard`, on the other hand, are built out of other types. Most often these other types are *classes*, and so we will use the term *reference type* for now as a synonym for *class type*. A particular instance of a class is called an **object**.[1] For example, `String` values are objects, `Keyboard` values are objects, and `Screen` values are objects; but `int` values and `double` values are not objects. The type of an object must be a reference type.

Notice that the names of primitive types begin with a lowercase letter—e.g., `int` and `double`. The names of reference types (e.g., `String`, `Keyboard`, and `Screen`) usually begin with an uppercase letter.

Another difference between the two kinds of types is that primitive-type names are Java **keywords** but reference-type names are not. That is, the names of primitive types have predefined meanings in the Java language, which are thus known to the Java compiler, while the meanings of reference-type names must be explained to the compiler. Definitions of reference types must appear either within the file that uses them (as in the case of our `Payroll1` and `Payroll2` classes) or in a package (e.g.,

---

[1] Other reference types are *interface types* (see Section 7.5) and *array* types (see Chapter 9). There are no instances of interfaces, but instances of arrays are also called *objects*.

`ann.easyio`) from which a program can access them. Primitive and reference types are discussed in more detail in Chapter 3.

Literals. A value of a given type is known as a **literal**.[2] Table 2.2 gives some examples of literals for a few of Java's standard types.

TABLE 2.2   SOME LITERALS

Type	Example literals
`int`	`-3, -1, 0, 1, 100, 1000`
`double`	`-2.5, 0.0, 0.001, 3.0e8, 1.0E-4`
`String`	`"Hi", "Bye", "Enter your name: "`
`char`	`'A', 'B', 'a', 'b', '0', '1', '$', '+', '\n'`
`boolean`	`true, false`

From this list, it should be evident that integers and whole numbers are `int` (or `byte`, or `short`, or `long`) literals; real numbers are `double` (or `float`) literals; sequences of characters enclosed in double quotes are `String` literals; individual characters enclosed in single quotes are `char` literals; and the keywords `true` and `false` are `boolean` literals.

Identifiers

In the program in Figure 2.1, we chose the name `theKeyboard` to refer to a `Keyboard` object, the name `theScreen` to refer to a `Screen` object, and the names `hoursWorked`, `hourlyRate`, and `wages` for variables that could store `double` values. Such names are called **identifiers**. They may not be keywords such as `import`, `double`, `public`, `class`, and `extends`, because these words already have predefined meanings in Java. A complete list of the Java keywords is given in Appendix B.

In Java, an identifier may begin with a letter or _ (underscore), which may be followed by any number of these characters or digits.[3] This allows a programmer to use meaningful names that describes what that they represent. For example, the identifier

        `hoursWorked`

is more meaningful than the shortened identifier

        `h`

---

[2] This usage of the word *literal* in computing refers to any value typed in by the programmer that does not change during the program execution—the string of characters you type is (literally) the value you get.

[3] A letter is any of the symbols A–Z, a–z, or a Unicode character that is a letter in another language. Also, a dollar sign ($) is allowed, but it is used for special purposes.

which might refer to *height, hard-drive, henrys, hertz,* or *hackers,* or anything else beginning with the letter 'h'. One should resist the temptation to use a short identifier simply to save a few keystrokes. *Complete words are preferable to abbreviations. It is good programming practice to use meaningful identifiers that suggest what they represent, because such names make a program easier to read and understand. They serve, therefore, as part of the program's documentation and thus facilitate program maintenance.*

It is important to remember that *Java is case sensitive—that is, it distinguishes between uppercase and lowercase.* For example, `hourlyRate` and `hourlyrate` are different identifiers in Java. Similarly, the main method must be named `main`, not `Main`. One must be very careful to use the same names consistently.

Although different programmers have different programming styles, there are certain naming conventions that are commonly practiced because they are recommended in the *Java Language Specification.* We will follow these guidelines in this text.

Classes: Names are given in lowercase, except for the first letter of each word in the name. For example: `Payroll`, `Screen`, `Keyboard`, `StringBuffer`, and `JOptionPane`.

Variables: Names of storage locations for values that can change are given names like class names, except that the first letter of the name is in lowercase. For example: `wages`, `hourlyRate`, and `theKeyboard`.

Constants: Names of storage locations for values that do not change are in uppercase. If a name consists of several words, these words are separated by underscore (_) characters. For example: `PI`, `METERS_PER_KILOMETER`, and `SECONDS_PER_HOUR` (see Figure 1.4).

Methods: Method names are like variable names, but are followed by parentheses. For example: `main()`, `readDouble()`, `print()`, and `println()`.

These naming conventions make it easy to determine what role a name plays in a program: whether it is the name of a class, a variable, a constant, or a method.

Declaration Statements

Any name in a program that is not a Java keyword is an identifier, and while keywords have predefined meanings to the Java compiler, identifiers do not. To use an identifier in a program, we must provide the compiler with the meaning of that identifier before its first use. This is accomplished by using a **declaration statement**. For example, in the program in Figure 2.1, the lines

```
class Payroll extends Object
{
    . . .
}
```

declare the identifier `Payroll` as the name of a class. Similarly, the lines

```
public static void main(String [] args)
{
    . . .
}
```

declare the identifier `main` as the name of a method within the `Payroll1` class. The package `ann.easyio` contains the declarations of `Keyboard` and `Screen` as names of classes and the statement

```
import ann.easyio.*;
```

informs the compiler that these identifiers `Keyboard` and `Screen` are the short names for the classes `ann.easyio.Keyboard` and `ann.easyio.Screen`, respectively.

Variable Declarations. Most programs store data values in memory locations from which these values can be retrieved and processed. Locations whose contents may change because new values are stored in them are called **variables** and are declared for the Java compiler with **variable declaration statements**. For example, the declaration statement

```
double hoursWorked = theKeyboard.readDouble();
```

in the main method in Figure 2.1 declares that `hoursWorked` is of type `double` and is to be initialized with the value returned by the `readDouble()` method from the `Keyboard` class. If the value 38.5 is entered by the user, we might picture the result of this declaration as follows:

```
hoursWorked  38.5
```

If we replaced the declaration with

```
double hoursWorked;
```

the memory location associated with `hourWorked` would contain zero, because this is the *default value* used to initialize `doubles`:

```
hoursWorked  0.0
```

The statement

```
hoursWorked = theKeyboard.readDouble();
```

could then be used to give `hoursWorked` a new value.

Whereas the memory allocated to a primitive-type variable stores a *value* of that type, the memory for a reference-type variable stores the *address* of a memory location where a value of that type can be stored.[4] To illustrate, consider the statement

```
String anAnimal = "three-horned unicorn";
```

---

[4] It may help to remember that in computing, the word *reference* is commonly used as a synonym for *address*.

It declares the name `anAnimal` as a variable and allocates memory to `anAnimal`: for example, a memory location with address `0x123abc`:

This memory location is one that can store another address of a memory location where the string of characters "`three-horned unicorn`" is stored:[5]

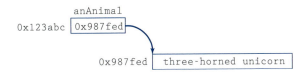

A reference-type variable like `anAnimal` is said to be a **handle** for the `String` object that stores the string of characters.

As another example, consider the first statement in the main method in Figure 2.1:

```
Screen theScreen = new Screen();
```

The first part of this declaration,

```
Screen theScreen
```

declares the name `theScreen` as a variable and allocates memory to `theScreen` that can be used to store a memory address. Ignoring the actual memory addresses, we might picture this as follows:

theScreen   [   ]

---

[5] This sounds like a modern-day version of the second Lewis Carroll quote at the beginning of this chapter:
"... The name of the animal is called `anAnimal`."
"Oh, that's the name of the animal, is it?" Alice said, trying to feel interested.
"No, you don't understand," the Knight said, looking a little vexed. "That's what the name is called. The name really is memory location `0x123abc`.
"Then I ought to have said 'That's what the animal is called'?" Alice corrected herself.
"No, you oughtn't: that's quite another thing! The animal is called memory location `0x987fed`: but that's only what it's called, you know!"
"Well, what is the animal, then?" said Alice, who was by this time completely bewildered.
"I was coming to that," the Knight said. "The animal really is a '`three-horned unicorn`': and it's my own invention."

The `new` operation finds a location in memory where this `Screen` object will be stored and stores its address in the memory location allocated to `theScreen`. which we might picture as follows:

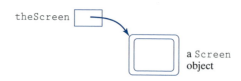

The variable `theScreen` is a handle for this `Screen` object. We will study reference types in more detail in Chapters 3 and 6.

The general form of a variable declaration is:

Variable Declaration

Form:

```
type variable_name;
```
or
```
type variable_name = expression;
```
where:

  type may be any type that is known to the compiler;
  variable_name is a valid identifier; and
  expression is any expression (as described in later sections) producing a value
    whose type is *type*.

Purpose:

Instructs the compiler to associate a memory location with *variable_name* and initialize it with a value of that type. For the first form, this value is a **default value**:

  • zero for primitive numeric types
  • `false` for `boolean` type
  • `null` for reference types

For the second form, the value will be the value of *expression*, which, for a reference type, will be an address of a memory location where a value of type *type* can be stored.

For additional documentation, some programmers also add brief comments after each variable declaration to indicate what the variable represents, how it is to be used, its valid values, and so on. The following examples illustrate this style:

```
int     idNumber;            // Student Id-Number

double  cumulativeHours,      // Total credits to date
        hoursThisTerm,        // Credits this semester
        gradePointAverage;    // Cumulative GPA: 0.0 - 4.0

char    letterGrade;          // 'A', 'B', 'C', 'D', 'F'

byte    year;                 // 1 - freshman, 2 - sophomore
                              // 3 - junior, 4 - senior,
                              // 5 - continuing
```

Constant Declarations. Whereas the values of variables may change as a program runs, the values of **constants** do not change. Java provides many different constants in its various classes; for example, PI is a constant in the java.lang.Math class that represents the mathematical constant π. This and other constants are discussed in Chapter 3. But the programmer can also define a constant by using the final **modifier** to specify that the value stored in a memory location cannot be changed. For example, the program in Figure 1.4 of the preceding chapter contained the constant declarations

```
final int METERS_PER_KILOMETER = 1000;
final int SECONDS_PER_HOUR = 3600;
```

The general form of a constant declaration is:

Constant Declaration

Form:

final *type CONSTANT_NAME = expression*;
where:
final is a Java keyword;
type may be any type that is known to the compiler;
CONSTANT_NAME is a valid Java identifier; and
expression is any valid expression (as described in later sections) producing a value
   whose type is *type*.

Purpose:

Associates a memory location with *CONSTANT_NAME* and initializes it with the value of *expression*; the modifier final specifies that it cannot be changed. Any attempt to modify the value of *CONSTANT_NAME* during execution is an error.

There are two important reasons for using constants instead of the literals they represent. One reason is *improved readability*. To illustrate, compare the readability of the statement

```
populationChange = (0.1758 - 0.1257) * population;
```

with the statement

```
populationChange = (BIRTH_RATE - DEATH_RATE) * population;
```

If we define BIRTH_RATE and DEATH_RATE to be constants by

```
final double
        BIRTH_RATE = 0.1758, // rate at which people are born
        DEATH_RATE = 0.1257; // rate at which people die
```

we can use the second statement, and that part of the program becomes more readable.

A second benefit of using constants is that they *facilitate program maintenance.* To illustrate, suppose that new values are published for the birth and death rates of the population you are studying. If we used the birth-rate and death-rate literals 0.1758 and 0.1257 throughout the program, we would have to find each occurrence of the old values and replace them with the new values. Not only is this a time-consuming task, but we might miss some occurrences so that some of the values get changed and some do not.

To modify a program using constants, however, we need only change their declarations:

```
final double
        BIRTH_RATE = 0.1761, // rate at which people are born
        DEATH_RATE = 0.1252; // rate at which people die
```

NOTE Changing the values of BIRTH_RATE and DEATH_RATE in these declarations will change their values throughout the program without any further effort on our part. It is considered good programming practice to *place all constant declarations at the beginning of the class or method in which they are used.* This makes it easy to locate these declarations when it is necessary to modify them. If a constant is used in more than one method, it can be declared in the class containing those methods.

✔ Quick Quiz 2.2

1. What are the two categories of types in Java?
2. List the four primitive integer types.
3. List the two primitive real types.
4. Name two nonnumeric primitive types.
5. Tell what default values are used in variable declarations for the primitive types and for reference types.
6. (True or false) A primitive type is a class.
7. A value of a particular type is called a(n) _____.

For Questions 8–11, tell whether each is a legal identifier. If is it not legal, indicate the reason.

8. 55MPH   9. W_D_4_0   10. N/4   11. First Name

12. Write a declaration for a variable distanceTraveled of type int.

13. Write declarations for variables idNumber of type long, salary of type float, and employeeCode of type char.

14. Repeat Question 12, but initialize `distanceTraveled` to zero.

15. Repeat Question 13, but initialize `idNumber` to 12346, `salary` to zero, `employeeCode` to a blank.

16. Write a constant declaration to associate `GRAVITY` with the integer 32.

17. Write constant declarations to associate `EARTH` with 1.5E10 and `MARS` with 1.2E12.

✍ Exercises 2.2

For Exercises 1–16, determine if each is a valid Java identifier. If it is not, give a reason.

1. `XRay`	2. `X-Ray`	3. `Jeremiah`	4. `R2_D2`
5. `3M`	6. `PDQ123`	7. `PS.175`	8. `x`
9. `4`	10. `N/4`	11. `M&M`	12. `Z_Z_Z_Z_Z_Z`
13. `night`	14. `ngiht`	15. `nite`	16. `to day`

For Exercises 17–21, write declarations for each variable.

17. `item`, `number`, and `job` of type `double`

18. `shoeSize` of type `int`

19. `mileage` of type `double`, `cost` and `distance` of type `short`

20. `alpha` and `beta` of type `long` and `root` of type `double`

21. `name` of type `String` and `isAStudent` of type `boolean`

22–26. For each variable in Exercises 17–21, tell what default value will be used to initialize it.

For Exercises 27–28, write declarations for each variable so that it has the specified type and initial value.

27. `numberOfDeposits` and `numberOfChecks` to be of type `int`, each with an initial value of 0; `totalDeposits` and `totalChecks` to be of type `double`, each with an initial value of `0.0`; and `serviceCharge` to be of type `double` with an inital value of `0.25`

28. `symbol_1` and `symbol_2` to be of type `char` and with a blank character and a semicolon for an initial value, respectively; and `debug` to be of type `boolean` with an initial value of `true`

For Exercises 29–32, write constant declarations to associate each name with the specified literal:

29. `1.25` with the name `RATE`

30. `40.0` with the name `REGULAR_HOURS` and `1.5` with the name `OVERTIME_FACTOR`

31. `1776` with the name `YEAR`, the letter F with `FEMALE`, and a blank character with `BLANK`

32. 0 with `ZERO`, * with `ASTERISK`, and an apostrophe with `APOSTROPHE`

33. Write constant declarations that associate the current year with the name `YEAR` and 99999.99 with `MAXIMUM_SALARY` and variable declarations that declare `number` and `prime` to be of type `int` and `initial` to be of type `char`.

PART OF THE PICTURE: DATA REPRESENTATION

The third Part of the Picture section in Chapter 0—Introduction to Computer Systems—noted that a binary scheme having only the two binary digits 0 and 1 is used to represent information in a computer. It also described how instructions can be represented in base-two and stored in memory. We now look at how literals of the primitive types can be represented in base two and stored in memory.

REPRESENTING INTEGERS

In Section 2.2 we noted that in Java, values of the various integer types are stored in 8, 16, 32, or 64 bits of memory. This is done by storing their binary representations in the required number of bits. To illustrate, suppose that the integer 58 is to be stored in 32 bits. The base-two representation of 58 is[6]

$$111010_2$$

The six bits in this binary representation of 58 can be stored in the rightmost bits of the memory word and the remaining bits filled with zeros:

sign

0 0 0 0 0 0 0 0 0 0 0 0 0 0 0 0 0 0 0 0 0 0 0 0 0 0 1 1 1 0 1 0

As the diagram indicates, one of the bits is reserved for the sign of the integer.

There are several ways to represent negative integers, but one of the most common methods is the **two's complement** representation. In this scheme, nonnegative integers are represented in binary form as just described, with the leftmost bit set to 0 to indicate that the value is nonnegative. The two's complement representation of a negative integer $-n$ is obtained by first finding the binary representation of n, complementing it—that is, changing each 0 to 1 and each 1 to

---

[6] To distinguish decimal numerals from those in other bases, it is common practice to attach the base of a non-decimal system as a subscript of the numeral. One method for finding the base-b representation of a whole number given in base-ten notation is to divide the number repeatedly by b until a quotient of zero results. The successive remainders are the digits from right to left of the base-b representation. For example, the binary representation of 26 is 11010_2, as the following computation shows:

$$
\begin{array}{r}
0 \ R \ 1 \\
2\overline{)1} \ R \ 1 \\
2\overline{)3} \ R \ 0 \\
2\overline{)6} \ R \ 1 \\
2\overline{)13} \ R \ 0 \\
2\overline{)26}
\end{array}
$$

Appendix E gives additional information about nondecimal number systems (binary, octal, and hexadecimal).

0—and then adding 1 to the result. For example, the two's complement representation of -58 using a string of 32 bits is obtained as follows:

1. Represent 58 by a 32-bit binary numeral:

$$00000000000000000000000000111010$$

2. Complement this bit string:

$$11111111111111111111111111000101$$

3. Add 1:

$$11111111111111111111111111000110$$

This string of bits is then stored:

sign

Note that the sign bit in this two's complement representation of a negative integer is always 1, indicating that the number is negative.

The number of bits used to store an integer value determines the range of the integers that can be stored internally. For example, the range of integers that can be represented using 32 bits is

$$10000000000000000000000000000000_2 = -2^{31} = -2147483648$$

through

$$01111111111111111111111111111111_2 = 2^{31} - 1 = 2147483647$$

Representation of an integer outside the allowed range would require more bits than can be stored, a phenomenon known as **overflow.** Using more bits to store an integer (e.g., as in Java's `BigInteger` class described in the next chapter) will enlarge the range of integers that can be stored, but it does not solve the problem of overflow; the range of representable integers is still finite since a computer's memory is finite.

REPRESENTING REALS
Digits to the left of the binary point in the binary representation of a real number are coefficients of nonnegative powers of two, and those to the right are coefficients of negative powers of two. For example, the expanded form of 10110.101_2 is

$$(1 \times 2^4) + (0 \times 2^3) + (1 \times 2^2) + (1 \times 2^1) + (0 \times 2^0) +$$
$$(1 \times 2^{-1}) + (0 \times 2^{-2}) + (1 \times 2^{-3})$$

which has the decimal value

$$16 + 0 + 4 + 2 + \frac{1}{2} + 0 + \frac{1}{8} = 22.625$$

To store real numbers in computer memory, Java uses a floating-point representation that was standardized in 1985 by the Institute for Electrical and Electronics Engineers (IEEE). This **IEEE Floating Point Format (754)** specifies two formats for representing real values: *single precision*, which uses 32 bits, and *double precision*, which uses 64 bits. Java's `float` type uses the 32-bit format, and its `double` type uses the 64-bit format. The latter format is just a wider version of the single precision format, so to save space we will consider only the single precision format.

We begin by writing the binary representation of the number in **floating-point form**, which is like scientific notation except that the base is two rather than ten:

$$b_1.b_2b_3\cdots \times 2^k$$

where each b_i is 0 or 1, and $b_1 = 1$ (unless the number is 0). $b_1.b_2b_3 \ldots$ is called the **mantissa** (or **fractional part** or **significand**) and k is the **exponent** (or **characteristic**). To illustrate, consider the real number 22.625, which we have seen can be written in binary as

$$10110.101_2$$

(See the exercises for a method for converting decimals to binary.) Rewriting this in floating-point form,

$$1.0110101_2 \times 2^4$$

is easy since multiplying (dividing) a base-two number by 2 is the same as moving the binary point to the right (left). 1.0110101_2 is the mantissa and 4 is the exponent.

In the IEEE format for single precision real values,

❑ the leftmost bit stores the sign of the mantissa, 0 for positive, 1 for negative

❑ the next 8 bits store the binary representation of the exponent + 127; 127 is called a **bias**

❑ the rightmost 23 bits store the bits to the right of the binary point in the mantissa (the bit to the left need not be stored since it is always 1)

For 22.625, the stored exponent would be $4 + 127 = 10000011_2$ and the stored mantissa would be $01101010000000000000000_2$:

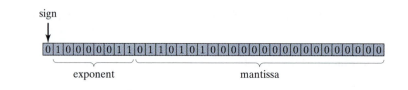

sign

exponent   mantissa

The IEEE representation for double precision uses an 11-bit exponent with a bias of 1023 and 53 bits for the signed mantissa.

Because the binary representation of the exponent may require more than the available number of bits, we see that the **overflow** problem discussed in connection with integers also occurs in storing a real number whose exponent is too large. An 8-bit exponent restricts the range of real values to approximately -10^{38} to 10^{38}, and overflow occurs for values outside this range. A negative exponent that is too small to be stored causes an **underflow**. Small real values represented using an 8-bit exponent must be greater than approximately 10^{-38} or less than -10^{-38}, and underflow occurs between these values:

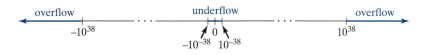

Also, there obviously are some real numbers whose mantissas have more than the allotted number of bits; consequently, some of these bits will be lost when such numbers are stored. In fact, most real numbers do not have finite binary representations and thus cannot be stored exactly in any computer. For example, the binary representation of the real number 0.7 is

$$(0.101100110011001100110011001100110 \ldots)_2$$

where the block 0110 is repeated indefinitely. Because only a finite number of these bits can be stored, the stored representation of 0.7 will not be exact (e.g., 0.6999999284744263). This error in the stored representation of a real value, called **roundoff error**, can be reduced, but not eliminated, by storing a larger number of bits, as with the `BigDecimal` class described in the next chapter. A 24-bit mantissa gives approximately 7 significant decimal digits for real values and a 53-bit mantissa gives approximately 14 significant digits.

REPRESENTING CHARACTERS

The schemes used for the internal representation of character data are based on the assignment of a numeric code to each symbol to be represented. ASCII (American Standard Code for Information Interchange), which uses 8 bits to represent characters, has been the standard coding scheme in programming languages for years. Java, however, uses a newer scheme called **Unicode**, which uses 16 bits to represent each character.[7] Thus, whereas ASCII can encode only 128 characters, Unicode can represent $2^{16} = 65,536$ different symbols. This is important for **global computing**, because it makes it possible to represent the symbols of non-Latin languages such as Arabic, Cyrillic, Greek, Hebrew, and Thai.

A character is represented internally using the binary representation of its numeric code. For example, the Unicode representation of c is 99 (same as in ASCII),

---

[7] See www.unicode.org for more information about the aims and goals of Unicode.

whose 16-bit representation is 00000000011000011_2 which can be stored in two bytes:

$$\boxed{0}\boxed{0}\boxed{0}\boxed{0}\boxed{0}\boxed{0}\boxed{0}\boxed{0}\boxed{0}\boxed{1}\boxed{1}\boxed{0}\boxed{0}\boxed{0}\boxed{1}\boxed{1}$$

c

The code for the non-Latin character π (Greek pi) is 960, whose 16-bit representation is 0000001111000000_2. Unicode thus represents the character π in two bytes as follows:

$$\boxed{0}\boxed{0}\boxed{0}\boxed{0}\boxed{0}\boxed{0}\boxed{1}\boxed{1}\boxed{1}\boxed{1}\boxed{0}\boxed{0}\boxed{0}\boxed{0}\boxed{0}\boxed{0}$$

π

REPRESENTING BOOLEANS

There are only two boolean values: `false` and `true`. If `false` is encoded as 0 and `true` as 1, then a single bit is all that is needed to store a `boolean` value.

✍ Exercises

Find the 32-bit two's complement representation of each of the integers in Exercises 1–6.

1. 255
2. 1024
3. −255
4. −256
5. −345678
6. $−3ABC_{16}$

The decimal value of an integer given in two's complement representation can be found as follows:

(1) Flip the bits
(2) Add 1
(3) Convert the resulting binary number to base-ten, making it positive or negative according as the sign bit of the given number is 0 or 1.

Find the decimal representation of each of the 32-bit integers in Exercises 7–12.

7. 00000000000000000000000001000000
8. 11111111111111111111111111111110
9. 11111111111111111111111110111111
10. 00000000000000000000000011111111
11. 11111111111111111111111100000000
12. 10000000000000000000000000000001

To convert a decimal fraction to its base-*b* equivalent, repeatedly multiply the fractional part of the number by *b*. The integer parts are the digits from left to right of the base-*b* representation. For example, the decimal numeral 0.6875 corresponds to the binary numeral 0.1011_2, as the following computation shows:

$$
\begin{array}{r|l}
 & .6875 \\
 & \times\ 2 \\
\hline
1 & .375 \\
 & \times\ 2 \\
\hline
0 & .75 \\
 & \times\ 2 \\
\hline
1 & .5 \\
 & \times\ 2 \\
\hline
1 & .0 \\
\end{array}
$$

Assuming IEEE floating point representation of real numbers, indicate how each of the single-precision real numbers in exercises 13–18 would be stored.

13. 0.375   14. 37.375   15. 0.03125

16. 63.84375   17. 0.1   18. 0.01

2.3   SOME BASIC PROGRAM FEATURES

The preceding section described some of the fundamental features of Java programs—how variables and constants are declared and Java's syntax rules for identifiers. The programs that we have seen, however, obviously involve much more than simply declarations of variables and constants. We previewed some of these other features in our walkthroughs of the programs in the preceding chapter. In this section, we will take a closer look at them, using the programs in Section 2.1 as illustrations.

Comments and Opening Documentation

The first four lines of the payroll program in Figure 2.1 comprise **opening documentation**, which should be included in every program. Although we will keep this opening documentation rather brief in this text to save space, in practice it should include items like the following:

- ❏ A description of what the program does
- ❏ What is input to the program and what output the program produces
- ❏ Special techniques, algorithms, etc. used in the program
- ❏ Special instructions for using the program
- ❏ The programmer's name, the date the program was written, a history of its modification

This documentation can be incorporated into a Java program as a **multiline comment**, which begins with the pair of characters /* and ends with the pair */. All comments will be ignored by the Java compiler.[8]

Java also allows **inline comments** that begin with a pair of slashes (//) and run to the end of the line. They are useful in `import` statements for listing the classes that are used in the program (see the `import` statement in Figure 2.1), for adding additional information about a variable or constant declaration, to identify key program statements, to provide additional explanations about some more difficult or obscure sections of code, and so on.

Classes

In Section 2.2, we saw that Java has two kinds of types: primitive types—`byte`, `short`, `int`, `long`, `float`, `double`, `char`, and `boolean`—and reference types, which are classes. We also observed in Section 1.3 that in the second step of OCD (object-centered design),

> *identify the real-world objects in your problem description, and categorize them*

some real-world objects cannot be directly represented using the available types. In this case, we

> *build a class to represent them.*

Such classes can thus be thought of as *extensions* to Java; by building a class, a programmer can add new types to Java.

But what exactly is a class? The word *class* is often used to describe a group or category of things that have a set of attributes in common. For example, students at some colleges are described as being in one of the following classes:

- ❑ *freshman class*, if they have earned fewer than 30 credits
- ❑ *sophomore class*, if they have earned more than 30 but fewer than 60 credits
- ❑ *junior class*, if they have earned more than 60 but fewer than 90 credits
- ❑ *senior class*, if they have earned more than 90 credits

In programming, a **class** is a pattern (or blueprint or template) that is used to model real-world objects that have similar attributes. A value whose type is a class—i.e., a *reference* type—is called an **object** or **instance** of that class. *Classes are thus used to create software objects that can model real-world objects.*

A simplified form of a class declaration is:

---

[8] Java provides a another kind of multiline comment called a **javadoc comment** that begins with /** and ends with */ that can be used to automatically generate the documentation for a class in HTML format for the World Wide Web. Such documentation is described in more detail in Chapter 4. The Java documentation generator `javadoc` can read these comments and generate a documentation file.

> ### Class Declaration (Simplified)
>
> **Form:**
>
> ```
> class className extends existingClassName
> {
>     // Attributes (variables and constants)
>     // and behaviors (methods)
> }
> ```
> where:
> > *className* is the name of a new reference type, and
> > *existingClassName* is any class whose name is known to the Java compiler.
>
> **Purpose:**
>
> This creates a new type that the compiler can use to create objects. This type *inherits* all of the attributes and behaviors of *existingClassName*. The Java `Object` **class** is often used for *existingClassName*, and in this case, the `extends` clause may be omitted.

The curly braces { and } mark the boundaries of the class declaration. It can contain variables (and constants), called **attribute variables** or **instance variables**, which determine the class' **attributes** or **state**. Changing the value in one of these variables changes the state of that class object by changing the corresponding attribute for that object.

A class also has **methods** that determine the class's **behavior**—how an object of that class will respond when other objects *send it messages* to do something. Methods are like functions, procedures, subprograms in other languages. They are groups of Java statements that perform specific tasks. We will say more about methods later in this section and in the next three chapters.

An example of a class is the `Payroll1` class in Figure 2.1, which has the form

```
class Payroll1 extends Object
{
    . . .
}
```

The phrase `extends Object` informs the Java compiler that the `Payroll1` class is a specialized kind of Java `Object`. `Object` is the name of a class declared in the `java.lang` package, which contains many basic Java classes. As noted above, this `extends Object` clause may, in fact, be omitted because it will be assumed that the class extends Java's `Object` class. We will use it in our examples, however, to emphasize that every class we build extends some other class.

The `Payroll1` class has no data members, and it has only one method, the **main method**. As we observed in Section 1.1, every Java application must have a main method because this is where execution begins. In our examples in this and the preceding chapter, we have used other classes that have several methods. The `String` class provided as part of Java, for example, has more than 50 methods that perform various operations on strings such as `toLowerCase()`, which converts all of the characters in the string to lower case, and `toUpperCase()`, which converts them all to upper case. The `Keyboard` and `Screen` classes that we designed to simplify input and output for programs each have several methods; for example, we have used the `print()`, `println()`, and `printFormatted()` methods from `Screen` in several programs.

We will learn more about classes and objects and how to build our own classes in later chapters. For now, the only classes we build ourselves will be program classes such as `Payroll1`. We will be *users* of other classes such as `String`, `Keyboard`, `Screen`, and `JApplet`.

Importing Packages

In Java, classes that are related in some way can be grouped together and stored in a container called a **package**. A program wishing to use one of these classes must supply the compiler with information about where to find that class. One way is to use a class' **fully-qualified name**, which has the form

```
package_name1.ClassName
```

If the package is contained in another package, we add it to this chain, using this same *dot notation*,

```
package_name2.package_name1.ClassName
```

and so on. For example, in Figure 2.1, if we had omitted the `import` statement we would have needed statements like the following to construct the objects `theKeyboard` and `theScreen`:

```
ann.easyio.Screen theScreen = new ann.easyio.Screen();
ann.easyio.Keyboard theKeyboard = new ann.easyio.Keyboard();
```

Using fully-qualified names of classes obviously can become clumsy. An easier way is to use an `import` **statement** that allows one to leave off the package names and just use a class' *simple name*, which consists of a single identifier. For example, the statement

```
import ann.easyio.*;       // Keyboard, Screen
```

in Figure 2.1 imports the classes in the `ann.easyio` package into the program, which means that the short names of the classes in this package—e.g., `Keyboard` and `Screen`—can be used in the program. The asterisk (*) indicates that *all* of the classes from this package are imported. This is what allowed us to use the more concise statements

```
Screen theScreen = new Screen();
Keyboard theKeyboard = new Keyboard();
```

to construct the objects `theKeyboard` and `theScreen`.

NOTE

Note the comment at the end of this `import` statement. *If an `import` statement imports all of the classes in a package (using `*`), it is good programming practice to add a comment to the `import` statement to indicate which classes from the package will actually be used.* This helps explain to a reader why that particular package is needed by the program.

We could also have imported the `Keyboard` and `Screen` classes with the statements

```
import ann.easyio.Keyboard;
import ann.easyio.Screen;
```

These would allow us to use short names only for the two classes `Keyboard` and `Screen` but not for the other classes in the `ann.eaysio` package.

The general form of the `import` statement is as follows:

Import Statement

Form:

```
import package_name.*;
```
or
```
import package_name.ClassName;
```
where:

`package_name` is the name of a package accessible to the Java compiler; and `className` is any class stored within `package_name`.

Purpose:

The first form allows any class in `package_name` to be referred to by its simple name—the single identifier used in the package for the class' name. The second form allows this only for the class whose fully-qualified name is listed.

The most basic classes of the Java language (e.g., `Object` and `String`) are stored in the package `java.lang`. These classes are used so often that the Java compiler automatically imports them; we can thus use those classes without writing

```
import java.lang.*; // Don't bother
```

Using Methods

To activate one of the methods in an object, we must **send a message** to that object instructing it to perform that method. This is also referred to as **calling** (or **invoking**) **the method** in that object. A message is constructed by attaching the object name to the method name with a dot, as illustrated by the following statement in the program in Figure 2.1:

```
theScreen.print("Enter the number of hours worked by employee: ");
```

Here the program sends a message to the `Screen` object `theScreen` instructing it to use its `print()` method to display a prompt to the user. The `String` literal `"Enter the number of hours worked by employee:  "` is passed to this method; it is called an **argument** for the method. When `theScreen` receives this message, it's `print()` method displays this literal on the computer's screen,

```
Enter the number of hours worked by employee:
```

which serves as a prompt to the user to enter a value.

Some methods **return** a value when they are called. In this case, the message to an object telling it to use such a method must also say what is to be done with the value returned. For example, to get the number of hours worked by an employee, the program in Figure 2.1 sends the `Keyboard` object `theKeyboard` a message to use its `readDouble()` method to read a `double` value from the computer's keyboard:

```
double hoursWorked = theKeyboard.readDouble();
```

When `theKeyboard` receives this message, it waits until the user enters a value at the keyboard, which it then reads and returns as a `double` value. The preceding statement, called an **assignment statement**, then stores this value returned by `readDouble()` in the variable `hoursWorked`, which is of type `double`.

In general, messages to objects to perform one of their methods have the following form:

Message to an Object

Form:

  objectName.*methodName(arguments)*

where:

  objectName is a Java object whose type, therefore, is a reference type
  methodName is the name of a method provided in the class of which this object is
     an instance; and
  arguments is a list (possibly empty) of comma-separated values that the method
     requires to perform its task.

Purpose:

Sends *objectName* a message instructing it to use *methodName()* and passing it the values given in *arguments*. If *methodName()* returns no value, appending a semicolon makes this expression a statement

  objectName.*methodName(arguments)*;

If *methodName()* returns a value, then this expression must be used in some statement that uses this value appropriately, for example, by storing it in a variable of a matching type:

  variable_name = *objectName*.*methodName(arguments)*;

✔ Quick Quiz 2.3

1. What are two kinds of comments in Java and how are they written in a Java program?
2. A(n) _____ is a pattern that is used to model real-world objects that have similar attributes.
3. _____ are values whose type is a class.
4. Instance variables in a class determine its _____.
5. Methods in a class determine its _____.
6. Every Java application must have a(n) _____ method .
7. A group of related classes can be stored in a(n) _____.
8. A(n) _____ statement can be used to make simple names of classes in a package available to a program.
9. Calling a method in an object is also known as sending a(n) _____ to the object.

2.4   JAVA DOCUMENTATION—API

REFERENCE   In the `Greeter1.java` program of Figure 1.2 we saw how to display a date and time by constructing a `Date` object and then sending it a message to use its `toString()` method to convert it to a `String` object and return this string so that it could be output. In the `Payroll1.java` program in Figure 2.1 we saw how to input a real number by sending a `Keyboard` object a message to use its `readDouble()` method to get user input from the keyboard and return it as a `double` value. In the revised payroll program of Figure 2.2 we saw how to display a `double` with a specified number of decimal places by sending a `Screen` object a message along with a `double` value and an `int` value telling it to use its `printFormatted()` method to display that `double` value with the specified number of decimal digits.

It may seem that every time we face a problem, we can find a Java method to solve it, like a magician pulling a rabbit out of a hat. Although this is not always the case— e.g., *we* wrote the `Keyboard` and `Screen` classes and the methods they provide to facilitate input and output in this text—Java's designers have done an amazing job of providing standard classes and methods that give "off-the-shelf" solutions to a wide variety of common problems.

Java 2 provides a collection of *over 1600 classes* known as the Java **Application Programmer's Interface** or **API**. Each of these classes provides many different methods, each of which performs some useful operation. It should be obvious that with so many different classes, it is impossible for any textbook to provide detailed and complete coverage of *all* of them. Moreover, Java is continuously evolving, so that any book that tried to provide comprehensive coverage of Java might easily be outdated before it was published!

To organize all of these classes, the Java API stores each class in a package whose name describes the kind of classes the package contains. For example, the `java.lang` package contains the most basic classes of the Java language; the `java.util` package is a collection of useful utility classes; the `java.math` package contains classes that extend Java's normal mathematical capabilities; the `java.io` package contains Java classes to facilitate input and output. The package names thus group Java's classes into broad categories, according to the kind of functionality they provide.

So how does one go about finding information about a particular class in the API? Fortunately, Java's designers anticipated this problem and have provided an extremely useful and extensive hypertext-based documentation system for the Java API specification that is accessible on the World Wide Web via your favorite web browser. It uses the organization described above to simplify the problem of locating a particular class or method. The first page of the API documentation has 3 frames:

Java Platform		
All Classes	**Java® 2 Platform API Specification**	
Packages java.applet java.awt java.awt.color java.awt.datatransfe	This document is the specification for the Java® 2 Platform API. **See:** Description	
All Classes AbstractAction AbstractBorder AbstractButton AbstractCollection AbstractColorChoo	**Java Platform Packages**	
	java.applet	Provides the classes necessary to create an applet and the classes an applet uses to communicate with its applet context.
	java.awt	Contains all of the classes for creating user interfaces and for painting graphics and images.

- One that contains an alphabetical list of the packages available in Java
- Another that contains an alphabetical list of all of Java's classes
- A "main" frame that initially lists the Java packages

Clicking on the name of a package in the "main" frame produces a list of the classes in that package; for example:

Package java.lang

Provides classes that are fundamental to the design of the Java programming language.

. . .

Class Summary

Boolean	The Boolean class wraps a value of the primitive type boolean in an object.
Byte	The Byte class is the standard wrapper for byte values.
Character	The Character class wraps a value of the primitive type char in an object.

. . .

Clicking on the name of a class will display information about that class. For example, the first part of the frame displayed when we click on class `Math` is:

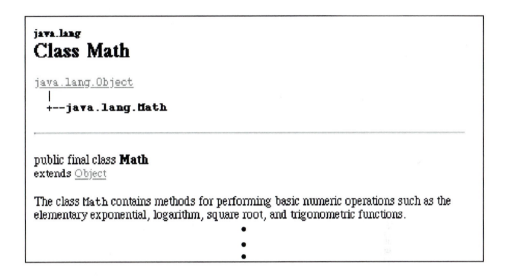

The diagram at the top of the frame and the lines that follow it show that `Math` extends the class `Object`. This is followed by a description of the contents of the class including a list of the fields (attribute variables and constants) and methods of that class:

---

java.lang
Class Math

java.lang.Object
   |
   +--java.lang.Math

---

public final class **Math**
extends Object

The class Math contains methods for performing basic numeric operations such as the elementary exponential, logarithm, square root, and trigonometric functions.

.
.
.

Field Summary

static double	**E** The double value that is closer than any other to e, the base of the natural logarithms.
static double	**PI** The double value that is closer than any other to π, the ratio of the circumference of a circle to its diameter.

Method Summary

static double	**abs**(double a) Returns the absolute value of a double value.
static float	**abs**(float a) Returns the absolute value of a float value.

.
.
.

If you click on the name of one of the methods or fields, you will see a detailed description of that method or field; for example:

max

```
public static double max(double a,
                         double b)
```

Returns the greater of two double values. If either value is NaN, then the result is NaN. Unlike the the numerical comparison operators, this method considers negative zero to be strictly smaller than positive zero.
Parameters:
   a - a double value.
   b - a double value.
Returns:
   the larger of a and b.

If we look at the description of the class JApplet, we see a **class hierarchy**, from Object at the top (called the *root*) down to JApplet:

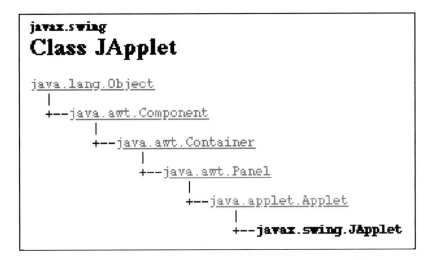

This diagram tells us that the class JApplet (from the package javax.swing) extends the class Applet (from the package java.applet), or stated differently, Applet is a **superclass** of class JApplet. The class Applet extends the class Panel, which, in turn, extends the class Container, which extends the class Component (with all three classes from the package java.awt). Finally, at the top of this **class hierarchy**, we see that the class Component extends the class Object, which is a superclass of every class.

From the preceding section, we know that a class that extends another class *inherits* the attributes (fields) and behaviors (methods) of that class. This means, that the class JApplet inherits the attributes and behaviors of *all* of the classes Applet, Panel, Container, Component, and Object. Thus, in addition to the fields and methods that are listed in the description of class JApplet, one should also look at those listed in the classes above it in Java's class hierarchy.

The Java API documentation is an important reference source and it is important that you learn to use it to find information about Java's classes and methods. Although we are using the latest version of Java available at the time of writing this text (Java 2), this version will be superseded by a new version all too soon. The most up-to-date and comprehensive information about Java (including announcements of new features) is always available at the Sun website.[9]

---

[9]The most recent Java API documentation can be found at *java.sun.com/docs/*. It can be downloaded for faster access by reducing the time spent waiting for web-pages to load.

✔ **Quick Quiz 2.4**

1. (True or false) The Java language as presented in this text is in its final form.
2. (True or false) Java provides fewer than 100 classes.
3. The Java _____ is where the most up-to-date information on Java can be found.
4. The java. _____ package contains the most basic classes of the Java language.
5. The java. _____ package contains several useful utility classes.
6. Classes are grouped together into _____ .
7. The class _____ is at the very top of the class hierarchy.
8. If class C extends class D, then C _____ the attributes and behaviors of D.

✍ **Exercises 2.4**

You are to use the Java API documentation to find the information asked for in the following exercises.

1. How many Java packages are described in the Java API documentation?

Exercises 2–8 pertain to the package java x . swing. Find the requested information about this package in the Java API documentation.

2. What are the names of the tables labeled summaries?
3. Name 5 of the classes in the java x . swing package.
4. The class used in Section 2.5 is JOptionPane. What description is given for this class in the class-summary table?
5. What class does JOptionPane extend?
6. List the classes in the Java class hierarchy from the class Object to JOptionPane.
7. What interface does JOptionPane implement?[10]
8. The program in Figure 2.3 in the next section uses the showMessageDialog() method. How many forms of this method are there?

Exercises 9–14 pertain to the class BigInteger described in the next chapter. Find the requested information about this package in the Java API documentation.

9. To what package does BigInteger belong?
10. Find another class in the package from Exercise 9.
11. What description is given for the package in Exercises 9 and 10?
12. What interface does BigInteger implement?
13. List the classes in the Java class hierarchy from the class Object to BigInteger.
14. What method in BigInteger can be used to determine if an integer is probably a prime number?

---

[10] Interfaces are discussed in Section 7.5.

2.5 INTRODUCTION TO GUIS: A GUI GREETER

In the preceding chapter, we looked at two programs that displayed a welcome greeting to the user, one an application program and the other an applet program. In this section, we will look at a modified version of this program that has a **graphical user interface (GUI)**. However, rather than simply give the program and then walk through it, we will design and build the program. In doing so, we will see that the design steps for building a GUI program differ slightly from those for building a non-GUI program like that in Section 1.4, especially in the description of how the program is to behave.

PROBLEM

Write a program with a graphical user interface that displays a window containing an appropriate prompt for the user to enter her first name, a box where the name will be entered, and buttons to click when finished. A personalized greeting will then be displayed in another window.

OBJECT-CENTERED DESIGN

Using object-centered design, we will describe the behavior of the program, identify the problem's objects and operations, and then organize them in an algorithm. However, the keyboard and screen objects are usually omitted when building GUI programs.

BEHAVIOR. The program should display a window containing a prompt for a user's name, a textbox in which the user can enter her name, and one or more suitably labeled option buttons—e.g., OK and Cancel buttons. The user should click in the textbox and enter her name. When the user presses *Enter* or clicks an OK button, the program should read the name from the box, hide the window, and display a second window containing a greeting personalized with the user's name. Clicking the Cancel button will cause the window to disappear. The second window should also contain a suitably labeled button that the user can click to terminate the program.

When building a graphical user interface, it is usually helpful in the design process to draw sketches of the different ways the screen will look, what changes can occur, and what user action causes these changes. The resulting series of sketches can be thought of as a graphical description of the program's behavior. For this problem, we might use the following sequence of diagrams:

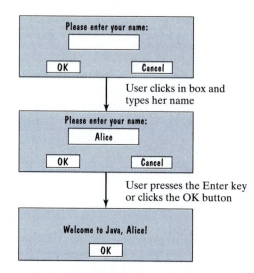

These simple diagrams show different windows that the program might display and the user actions that cause the transitions between them. For this reason, such sketches are called **transition diagrams**. They are a commonly-used tool in the design of GUI programs.

PROBLEM'S OBJECTS. Once we know what the program is to do, we create a list of problem objects from the behavioral description and the transition diagrams. Since there is no predefined type to build this particular program, we must define a class to do this. We will call it *GUIGreeter*.

In graphical user interface programming, a graphical object that can be used as an object in a program is called a **widget**. For example, windows, menus, buttons, and dialog boxes are all examples of GUI widgets. In this problem we need a widget to get textual input from a user and another widget to display information to a user.

After a bit of searching through the Java API, we find that one of the simplest ways to construct the widgets needed in this problem is to use a Java **input-dialog** for the window to display a prompt and get the user's input, and a Java **message-dialog** for the window to display the program's personalized greeting. Such dialogs can be created using the `JOptionPane` class from the `javax.swing` package. The user's name and the personalized greeting can be represented using `String` values. This results in the following list of objects for this problem:

Description of problem's objects	Type	Kind	Name
The program	??	—	*GUIGreeter*
A window to display a prompt	input-dialog	—	none
A prompt for the user's name	`String`	constant	none
A window to display the greeting	message-dialog	—	none
The user's name	`String`	varying	*userName*
A personalized greeting	`String`	varying	none

Our dialogs have no names because the API documentation for `java.swing` tells us that dialogs can be created simply by sending appropriate messages to Java's `JOptionPane` class.

OPERATIONS. From our behavioral description, we identify the following operations to perform:

i. Display a window containing a prompt and a textbox (i.e., an input-dialog)

ii. Read a `String` from the window's textbox

iii. Hide the window

iv. Display a second window containing a personalized greeting (i.e., a message-dialog)

v. Terminate the program

The Java API description of class `JOptionPane` indicates that its `showInputDialog()` method can be used for operations i-iii and the `showMessageDialog()` method for operation iv. Operation v is provided by the `exit()` method in the `System` class.

More precisely, `showInputDialog()` causes a window to appear that contains the following:

❑ A small picture called an **icon** (by default a question mark but other options are described in Table 2.1)

❑ A prompt string that was sent to this method

❑ A text field where the user can enter a response

❑ A button labeled *Ok* and another button labeled *Cancel*. When the user clicks the *Ok* button, any contents of the dialog's text field are returned to the user as a `String`. If the *Cancel* button is clicked, a special value `null` is returned. The *Ok* button is the *default button*, meaning that clicking it and pressing the *Enter* key are equivalent actions.

When the user enters text and clicks *Ok* or presses *Enter*, the `showInputDialog()` method returns the text entered as a `String` and hides that dialog window.

The `showMessageDialog()` method is similar. It causes a titled window to appear containing

❑ A (platform-dependent) information icon

❑ A `String` sent to it

❑ A button labeled *OK*

The `exit()` **method** of Java's `System` class terminates the program that sends the `System` class this message. It takes a single integer argument that indicates the termination status, with 0 being used to indicate normal termination and 1 usually used to indicate abnormal termination.

ALGORITHM. We can organize these problem objects and operations into the following algorithm:

Algorithm for GUI Greeter

1. Display an input-dialog asking the user for her name; store the `String` value returned by the dialog in *userName*.

2. Using *userName*, display a message-dialog containing a personalized greeting for the user.

3. Terminate the program.

Coding in Java

Once we have an algorithm to serve as our blueprint, we can consult the class and method descriptions in Java's API documentation to identify the precise syntax of the statements needed to encode it in Java. Figure 2.3 presents the program that results. More information about the input and message dialogs that it uses can be found at the end of this section.

FIGURE 2.3   APPLICATION `GUIGreeter`

```
/** GUIGreeter.java greets its user using Swing dialogs.
 *   Input:  userName, a String
 *   Output: a personalized greeting.
 */

import javax.swing.*;                           // JOptionPane

public class GUIGreeter
{
 public static void main(String [] args)
  {
    String userName = JOptionPane.showInputDialog("Please enter your name:")

    JOptionPane.showMessageDialog(null,
                        "Welcome to Java, " + userName + "!");
    System.exit(0);
  }
}
```

Executing this program produces the following window:

Once a user clicks within the text-box and types her name, we have

but as soon as the user clicks the OK button or presses the *Enter* key, its appearance changes as follows:

   This program is sufficiently simple that a few more executions are probably sufficient to check its correctness. More complex programs will require many more sample inputs to test them.

Program Maintenance

Suppose that sometime after the program in Figure 2.3 was written, you decide that it would be better if the window of the personalized greeting in the last snapshot had the title `Greetings!` instead of `Message`. To do this, our program must be modified, or *maintained*. If we search the Java API documentation for the `JOptionPane` class again, we find that there is another version of the `showMessageDialog()` method that can be used to solve our problem. Figure 2.4 shows the necessary changes in color:

FIGURE 2.4 `GUIGreeter2`

```
/** GUIGreeter2.java greets its user using Swing dialogs.
 *  Input: userName, a String
 *  Output: a personalized greeting.
 */

import javax.swing.*;                               // JOptionPane
public class GUIGreeter2
{
 public static void main(String [] args)
 {
   String userName = JOptionPane.showInputDialog("Please enter your name:")

   JOptionPane.showMessageDialog(null,
                          "Welcome to Java, " + userName + "!",
                          "Greetings!",
                          JOptionPane.INFORMATION_MESSAGE);
   System.exit(0);
 }
}
```

When executed, this program displays the same input dialog as before, but its message dialog now has a different title:

Input and Message Dialog Widgets

Java's dialogs provide a reasonably simple, yet powerful, means of getting information to and from the user in a GUI environment. The following brief descriptions show how various forms of the dialog methods can be used.

Input Dialogs. Input dialogs are GUI widgets used to get textual input from a user. Figures 2.3 and 2.4 used a simple form of the `showInputDialog()` method to construct an input dialog,

> `showInputDialog(`*prompt*`)`

where *prompt* can be a `String`, a graphic image, or other Java `Object`. The Documentation section in the chapter summary describes other forms provided in the `JOptionPane` class for constructing input dialogs.

Message Dialogs. Message dialogs are GUI widgets used to display information to a user. Figure 2.3 used a simple form of the `showMessageDialog()` method to construct an message dialog,

>   `showMessageDialog(null, message)`

and Figure 2.4 used the extended form

>   `showMessageDialog(null, message, title, messageKind)`

The `null` argument causes the dialog containing the specified message to be centered on the screen. The second form specifies a title to be used instead of "Message" and the kind of message to be displayed (as described below). Other forms of the `showMessageDialog()` method provided in the `JOptionPane` class are described in the Documentation section of the chapter summary.

The Message Kind Parameter. The more complicated forms of the `showInput-Dialog()` and `showMessageDialog()` methods require an argument that describes the *kind* of message being displayed. Table 2.1 shows the five categories provided in the `JOptionPane` class for the kinds of messages. The program in Figure 2.4 uses the second constant, `INFORMATION_MESSAGE`.

REFERENCE

TABLE 2.1   KINDS OF DIALOG MESSAGES

Category	JOptionPane **constant**
Tell the user an error has occurred	ERROR_MESSAGE
Tell the user something they need to know	INFORMATION_MESSAGE
Tell the user they are doing something risky	WARNING_MESSAGE
Ask the user a question	QUESTION_MESSAGE
Tell the user anything else	PLAIN_MESSAGE

The Java run-time environment provides a **user-interface manager** that determines the "look and feel" of an application. The `messageKind` constants are hints as to how the program intends to use the dialog, so that the user-interface manager can construct the dialog appropriately. For example, on the Windows platform, for an `INFORMATION_MESSAGE`, the user-interface manager will automatically display the following icon:

Others are shown in the Documentation section of the chapter summary.

✔ Quick Quiz 2.5

1. Programs in which the user interacts with windows and buttons have a(n) _____.
2. _____ diagrams trace the execution of a GUI program by showing the sequence of windows it will display and what user action causes a change from one to the next.
3. A graphical object that can be used as an object in a program is called a(n) _____ .
4. In Java, a(n) _____ is a widget that can be used for inputting text from a user.
5. In Java, a(n) _____ is a widget that can be used to display text to a user.
6. What items are displayed in an input dialog?
7. What items are displayed in a message dialog?

CHAPTER SUMMARY

KEY TERMS AND NOTES

Application Programmer's Interface (API)	invoke a method
argument	keyword
assignment statement	literal
attribute variable	method
call a method	`Object` class
class	package
class hierarchy	primitive type
declaration statement	reference type
default value	return value
`final` modifier	send a message
fully-qualified name	superclass
graphical user interface (GUI)	transition diagram
handle	type
identifier	variable
`import` statement	widget
instance variable	

◎ There are two kinds of types in Java: primitive types and reference types. The primitive types are: `byte`, `short`, `int`, and `long` for integers; `float` and `double` for real values; `boolean` for logical values; and `char` for individual characters. Reference types are (usually) class types.

◎ The type of an object must be a reference type.

◎ An identifier may begin with a letter or _ (underscore), which may be followed by any number of these characters or digits; it may not be a Java keyword.

◎ Use meaningful identifiers that suggest what they represent, because such names make a program easier to read and understand.

◎ Java is case sensitive.

◎ Any name in a program that is not a Java keyword is an identifier and must be declared before it can be used.

◎ The value of a primitive-type variable is a value of that type; the value of a reference-type variable is an address of a memory location where a value of that type can be stored.

◎ If no initial value is specified in a variable declaration, a *default value* will be used. This is zero for numeric types, `false` for `boolean`, and `null` for reference types.

◎ The `final` modifier is used to declare that a value stored in a memory location cannot be changed during program execution.

◎ Using named constants instead of the literals they represent improves code readability and facilitates program maintenance.

◎ Placing constant declarations at the beginning of the class or method in which they are used is good programming practice because it makes it easy to locate them when modifications are necessary.

◎ Every program should contain opening documentation that describes what the program does, its input and output, special techniques and algorithms it uses, special instructions for using program, the programmer's name, the date the program was written, and a history of its modification. A multiline comment enclosed between / * and * / can be used for this.

◎ Inline comments begin with / / and run to the end of the line. They are useful to list imported classes, to add information about a variable or constant declaration, to identify key program statements, and to explain difficult or obscure sections of code.

◎ A class is a pattern or blueprint that is used to model real-world objects that have similar attributes. The form of a class is:

```
class className extends existingClassName
{
  // Variables (and constants)
  // They determine an object's attributes / state
  // Methods
  // They determine an object's behavior
}
```

◎ Every Java application must have a main method because this is where execution begins.

◎ Import statements allow one to refer to classes in a package by their simple names—the single identifiers used in the package—instead of using their fully-qualified names of the form *package_name.ClassName*.

◎ The classes in `java.lang` are imported automatically; no import statement is needed.

◎ The Java Application Programming Interface (API) is a collection of more than 1600 classes organized into packages. Hypertext-based documentation accessible via a web browser is an extremely valuable tool for finding information about these classes.

◎ Java's `Object` class is at the root (top) of the API class hierarchy and is thus a super-class of every class.

◎ A class that extends another class *inherits* the attributes (fields) and behaviors (methods) of that class. Thus in searching the API documentation for information about classes, one should also look at what they inherit from superclasses.

◎ In designing GUI applications, it is helpful to draw transition diagrams to describe the program's behavior—different windows that can appear and the user actions that cause changes from one to another.

◎ The `exit()` method in Java's `System` class can be used to terminate execution of a program.

◎ Input- and output-dialogs provided by Java's Swing `JOptionPane` class provide a fairly simple, yet powerful, way to get information from and to the user in a GUI environment.

Documentation

REFERENCE ■ Storage requirements for primitive types:

Type	Number of bits
byte	8
short	16
int	32
long	64
float	32
double	64
void	0
boolean	1
char	16

■ To assist with formatting output of numeric values, a `printFormatted()` method is included in the `ann.easyio` package. In can be used in any of the following forms, where `numDecDigits` and `numIntDigits` are integers and `fillChar` is of type `char`:

```
printFormatted(doubleValue)
```
Displays *doubleValue* using a default format

```
printFormatted(doubleValue, numDecDigits)
```
Displays *doubleValue* rounded to *numDecDigits* digits

```
printFormatted(doubleValue, numIntDigits, numDecDigits)
```

Displays *doubleValue* with *numIntDigits* to the left of the decimal point and rounded to *numDecDigits* digits to the right of the decimal point

`printFormatted(doubleValue, numIntDigits, numDecDigits, fillChar)`

Displays *doubleValue* with *numIntDigits* to the left of the decimal point, rounded to *numDecDigits* digits to the right of the decimal point, and with empty positions filled with *fillChar*

Like the `print()` and `println()`, `printFormatted` returns the `Screen` object to which the message is sent, so that these three methods can be used in a chain of messages.

■ JOptionPane's showInputDialog() FORMS

Method	Description
`showInputDialog(Object prompt)`	Construct an input dialog in the center of the screen with title "Input", and in it display *prompt*, a text field for user input, and buttons labeled *OK* and *Cancel*. The *prompt* can be a String, graphic image, or other Java Object. Clicking *Ok* returns the contents of the text field as a String; clicking *Cancel* returns the special value `null`.

`showInputDialog(`
  `Component parent,`
  `Object prompt)`
	Construct an input dialog as above, with position relative to *parent*, which may be a window, frame, panel, or other Java GUI Component. If *parent* is null, the dialog is centered on the screen as above.

`showInputDialog(`
  `Component parent,`
  `prompt,`
  `String title,`
  `int messageKind)`
	Construct an input dialog as above, but with specified *title*, and whose message is described by *messageKind*, which determines the appearance of the dialog (see Table 2.1).

`showInputDialog(`
  `Component parent,`
  `Object prompt,`
  `String title,`
  `int messageKind,`
  `Icon icon,`
  `Object [] selectionValues,`
  `Object initialSelectionValue)`
	Construct an input dialog as above, but with specified *icon*, whose valid values are given by *selectionValues*, and whose default selection is *initialSelectionValue*.

■ `JOptionPane`'s `showMessageDialog()` FORMS

Method	Description

`showMessageDialog(`
`  Component parent,`
`  Object message)`
	Construct a message dialog positioned relative to `parent` with title "Message" and displaying `message`. The parent may be a window, frame, panel, or other Java GUI `Component`. If `parent` is `null`, the dialog is centered on the screen. The `message` may be any Java `Object`.

`showMessageDialog(`
`  Component parent,`
`  Object message,`
`  String title,`
`  int messageKind)`
	Construct a message dialog as above, but with `title` and `messageKind` as described for `showInputDialog()`.

`showMessageDialog(`
`  Component parent,`
`  Object message,`
`  String title,`
`  int messageKind)`
`  Icon icon)`
	Construct a message dialog as above, but with `icon` as described for `showInputDialog()`.

■ **WINDOWS MESSAGE-KIND ICONS**

JOptionPane constant	Windows user-interface default icon
`ERROR_MESSAGE`	
`INFORMATION_MESSAGE`	
`WARNING_MESSAGE`	
`QUESTION_MESSAGE`	
`PLAIN_MESSAGE`	No icon

PROGRAMMING PROBLEMS

SECTION 2.1

1. Modify the program in Figure 2.1 so that it also reads the employee's number from the keyboard and displays it on the screen.

2. Proceed as in Problem 1 but read the employee's name from the keyboard and display it on the screen.

SECTIONS 2.2 & 2.3

For each of the problems described in Problems 3–5, give a precise description of how a program to solve the problem must behave, describe the problem's objects and operations. and design an algorithm for it. Then write and test a program to implement the algorithm.

3. Read the lengths of the two legs of a right triangle, and then calculate and display its area (one-half the product of the legs).

4. Proceed as in Problem 3, but also calculate the length of the hypotenuse of the right triangle (square root of the sum of the squares of the legs). The square root of a `double` value in a Java program can be calculated using `Math.sqrt(`*double_value*`)`.

5. A manufacturing company maintains a fleet of trucks to deliver its products. On each trip, the driver records the distance traveled in miles, the number of gallons of fuel used, the cost of the fuel, and other costs of operating the truck. As part of the accounting process, the controller needs to calculate and record for each truck and for each trip the miles per gallon, the total cost of that trip, and the cost per mile. A simple program is to be designed to assist the controller in performing these calculations for a given trip.

SECTION 2.5

6. Modify the program in Figure 2.3 so that the prompt is "What is your favorite color?" and the greeting is replaced by a message like "I like _____ also, but I really love burnt sienna!" where the blank is replaced by the color entered by the user.

7. Modify the program in Figure 2.3 so after a user enters her first name, a window prompts for and reads the user's last name. The welcome greeting should contain both the user's first name and last name.

8. Modify the program in Figure 2.4 so that the title of the message dialog is "WARNING," the icon is the warning icon (an exclamation mark), and the message is "Watch out" followed by the user's name.

TYPES AND EXPRESSIONS

There are three types of people in this world: Those who can count,
and those who can't. *Seen on a bumper sticker*

```
<>!*''#
^"`$$-
!*=@$_
%*<>~#4
&[]../
|{,,SYSTEM HALTED
```
The WakaWaka Poem[1]
Fred Bremmer and Steve Kroeze
(while students at Calvin College)

Arithmetic is being able to count up to twenty without taking off your shoes. *Mickey Mouse*

A little inaccuracy sometimes saves tons of explanation. *Saki (H.H. Munroe)*

■ Chapter Contents

---

[1] Several years ago, a magazine poll established "waka" as the proper pronunciation for the angle-bracket characters < and >. Here is a phonetic version of this poem:

Waka waka bang splat tick tick hash,
Caret quote back-tick dollar dollar dash,
Bang splat equal at dollar underscore,
Percent splat waka waka tilde number four,
Ampersand bracket bracket dot dot slash,
Vertical-bar curly-bracket comma comma CRASH.

Chapter Objectives

- Study another example of software development using OCD
- Review the difference between primitive types and reference types
- Take a detailed look at numeric types—both integer and real—together with operations and methods for these types, focusing mainly on primitive types but also looking at the corresponding wrapper classes as well as those for processing very large numbers
- Study the assignment operator and the related increment and decrement operators along with the shortcut assignment operators
- Examine the `boolean` data type and operators for building expressions—both simple and compound—along with short-circuit evaluation of these expressions
- Look at Java's character-related types: `char`, `Character`, and `String`
- Study another example of a GUI application and another example of a GUI applet

The concept of **type** plays a central role in object-oriented programming. As we have seen, Java provides two different kinds of types: *primitive types* for representing numbers, individual characters, and true/false values; and *reference types* for representing more complex kinds of objects. Since the majority of real-world objects cannot be represented using predefined types, object-oriented programming is largely about creating reference types to represent such objects efficiently and conveniently.

In this chapter, we study these two kinds of types. Our main focus will be on primitive types, but some special reference types that expand the capabilities of the primitive types will also be considered.

3.1   INTRODUCTORY EXAMPLE: EINSTEIN'S EQUATION

PROBLEM

For his physics course, Albert Onemug has a large problem set that is due by the next class meeting. Many of the problems require (among other things) using Einstein's equation to calculate the amount of energy released by a quantity of matter for a mass given in the problem. Because the deadline is near, Albert asks for our help. Our task, therefore, is to write a program to do these calculations.

 OBJECT-CENTERED DESIGN

In developing this program, we will apply the steps of object-centered design.

BEHAVIOR. The program should display on the screen a prompt for the quantity of matter (i.e., its mass). The user will enter a nonnegative real value at the keyboard. The program should read this number and use Einstein's equation to compute the energy that can be produced by that quantity of matter. It should display this amount of energy along with a descriptive label.

PROBLEM'S OBJECTS. From our behavioral description, we can identify the following objects in the problem:

Description of problem's object	Type	Kind	Name
Screen	Screen	varying	*theScreen*
Prompt	String	constant	none
Quantity of matter	double	varying	*mass*
Keyboard	Keyboard	varying	*theKeyboard*
Quantity of energy	double	varying	*energy*
Descriptive label	String	constant	none

OPERATIONS. From our behavioral description, we see that the following operations will be needed:

i. Display a string (the prompt) on the screen

ii. Read a nonnegative number *(mass)* from the keyboard

iii. Compute *energy* from *mass*

iv. Display a number *(energy)* and a string on the screen

Each of these operations is provided for us by the `ann.easyio` package, with the exception of operation iii. It requires the use of Einstein's equation,

$$e = m \times c^2$$

where *m* is the mass, *c* is the speed-of-light constant, and *e* is the energy produced. Performing this operation thus requires the following operations:

Exponentiation (c^2)
Multiplication of reals $(m \times c^2)$
Storage of a real $(e = m \times c^2)$

This refinement to Step 3 adds two additional objects to our object list:

Description of problem's object	Type	Kind	Name
Screen	Screen	varying	*theScreen*
Prompt	String	constant	none
Quantity of matter	double	varying	*mass*
Keyboard	Keyboard	varying	*theKeyboard*
Quantity of energy	double	varying	*energy*
Descriptive label	String	varying	none
c	double	constant	*SPEED_OF_LIGHT*
2	int	constant	none

ALGORITHM. Organizing these objects and operations into an algorithm gives:

1. Ask *theScreen* to display a prompt for the mass to be converted into energy.

2. Ask *theKeyboard* to read a number and store it in *mass*.

3. Compute *energy = mass* × *SPEED_OF_LIGHT*².

4. Ask *theScreen* to display *energy* and a descriptive label.

Coding, Execution, and Testing

Figure 3.1 shows one way to implement the preceding algorithm as a program. Also shown are two sample runs with test data for which the output can be easily verified and a third execution showing the amount of energy released if the mass of one of the authors were converted to energy.

FIGURE 3.1   MASS-TO-ENERGY CONVERSION

```
/* EinsteinConverter.java computes energy from a given mass using
 * Einstein's mass-to-energy conversion equation.
 *
 * Input:        The mass (in kilograms) being converted to energy
 * Precondition: mass >= 0
 * Output:       The energy (in kilojoules) corresponding to mass
 */

import ann.easyio.*;                              // Keyboard, Screen

class EinsteinConverter extends Object
{
  public static void main(String [] args)
  {
    final double SPEED_OF_LIGHT = 2.997925e8;  // meters/sec

    Screen theScreen = new Screen();
       theScreen.print("To find the amount of energy obtained from a " +
                  " given mass,\nenter a mass (in kilograms): ");

    Keyboard theKeyboard = new Keyboard();
    double mass = theKeyboard.readDouble();    // get mass

                                               // compute energy
    double energy = mass * Math.pow(SPEED_OF_LIGHT, 2.0);

                                               // display energy
    theScreen.println("-> " + mass + " kg of matter will release\n"
                  + energy + " kilojoules of energy");
  }
}
```

Sample runs:

```
To find the amount of energy obtained from a given mass,
enter a mass (in kilograms): 1
-> 1.0 kg of matter will release
8.987554305625E16 kilojoules of energy

To find the amount of energy obtained from a given mass,
enter a mass (in kilograms): 2
-> 2.0 kg of matter will release
1.797510861125E17 kilojoules of energy

To find the amount of energy obtained from a given mass,
enter a mass (in kilograms): 100
-> 100.0 kg of matter will release
8.9875543056249999E18 kilojoules of energy.
```

This program uses both primitive and reference types. We will review the differences between these two kinds of types in the next section.

3.2 PRIMITIVE TYPES AND REFERENCE TYPES

As we saw in the preceding chapter, each data value in Java has a type and any variable (or constant) that stores this value must be *declared* to have that type before it can be used. The compiler uses this information about the type to:

1. Allocate memory for the variable (or constant)
2. Check that the variable (or constant) is being used correctly

We also saw that Java has two different kinds of types: *primitive types* and *reference types*. In this section, we will review these two kinds of types. Subsequent sections will focus on the primitive types, but some related reference types will also be considered. Classes, which are used to construct reference types, will be studied in detail in Chapter 6.

The Primitive Types

Java's primitive types are used to represent "simple" values. These types are:[2]

- ❑ `int`, `byte`, `short`, and `long` for integer values (whole numbers and their negatives)
- ❑ `float` and `double` for real values (fractional numbers)
- ❑ `char` for characters (letters, digits, symbols, and punctuation)
- ❑ `boolean` for logical values (`true` and `false`)

A value of one of these types is called a **literal.**[3] For example, `123` is an `int` literal, `-45.678` is a `double` literal, `'A'` is a `char` literal, and `true` is a `boolean` literal.

Java provides this diversity so that different kinds of data can be processed and memory can be used most efficiently. For example, it would be wasteful to store integers in 128 bits when 32 or 64 bits are sufficient. Types thus allow the Java compiler to allocate an amount of memory for a variable (or constant) that is appropriate for the kind of values it is to store.

Reference Types

Although the primitive types are adequate to represent simple values, using them to represent objects such as windows, buttons, menus, students, employees, and so on is clumsy at best. To make it more convenient to represent such objects, Java allows a

---

[2] The keyword `void` is sometimes considered to be one of Java's primitive types, but it is, in actuality, simply a keyword that denotes *the absence of any type*. There are no literals of (and no operators or methods for) type `void`. Its primary use is to provide a return type for *methods that do not return anything to their caller* (e.g., the main method of an application). See Chapter 4 for more details.

[3] See Footnote 1 in Chapter 2 re use of the term *literal*.

programmer to create new types (e.g., *Window, Button, Menu, Student, Employee,* and so on), and this is done by creating classes:

Create a class and you have created a new type whose name is the name of the class.

Types created from classes are called **reference types**.[4]

As we noted in Section 2.4, Java 2 provides over 1600 reference types. Some that we have used or that will be considered in this chapter are:

❑ String: a class to represent *constant* sequences of characters
❑ StringBuffer: a class to represent *variable* sequences of characters
❑ BigInteger: a class to represent integers of *unlimited* size
❑ BigDecimal: a class to represent real numbers of unlimited size

In the next section, we will also consider some classes related to the primitive types that provide operations beyond those available for the primitive types, including converting values between the primitive types:

❑ Character: a class to represent individual characters
❑ Boolean: a class to represent boolean values
❑ Integer: a class to represent integers
❑ Double: a class to represent real numbers

Because each of these classes (and the classes Byte, Short, Long, and Float) essentially "wraps" a primitive type with a set of extended capabilities for that type, they are called **wrapper classes.**

Creating Reference Type Values—Constructors

Reference types differ from primitive types in several ways. One difference is in how values are created for each type. Because primitive types use *literals* for their values and the meanings of literals are built into the Java compiler, primitive type values are predefined in Java. For example, a programmer can write:

```
int intValue = 321;
char charValue = 'A';
```

The first statement uses the int literal 321, the second statement uses the char literal 'A'. As we noted in the preceding chapter, these declarations will cause mem-

---

[4] Other reference types in Java are arrays and interfaces, but we will wait with considering them until later.

ory locations to be associated with the variables `intValue` and `charValue` and will store the value `321` in `intValue`'s location and `'A'` in `charValue`'s location:

intValue ┃ 321 ┃   charvalue ┃ A ┃

(Actually, the integer 65, the Unicode representation of the letter "A", will be stored in `charValue`'s location. See the Part of the Picture section in the preceding chapter for more information.)

By contrast, there are no pre-existent values for reference types. Instead, reference-type values must be created using the new **operation.**[5] For example, we might write

```
Screen theScreen = new Screen();

Integer integerValue = new Integer(321);

Character characterValue = new Character('A');
```

Each statement uses the `new` operation to create a new object: the first statement to create a new `Screen` object; the second to create an `Integer` object whose value is `321`; and the third to create a `Character` object whose value is `'A'`. As we noted in Chapter 2, the `Screen` variable `theScreen`, the `Integer` variable `integerValue`, and the `Character` variable `characterValue` will store the addresses of where these objects are located, which we might picture as follows:

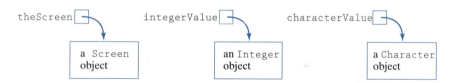

Each of these variables is said to be a **handle** for the object to which it refers: `theScreen` is a handle for the `Screen` object; `integerValue` is a handle for the `Integer` object; and `characterValue` is a handle for the `Character` object.

Such reference-type variables can also be initialized with a special `null` **value** to indicate that they do not yet refer to a value of that type; for example,

```
Screen theScreen = null;
```

This is also the *default value for reference types,* that is, the initial value used if none is given in a declaration; for example,

```
Screen theScreen;
```

This null value is commonly represented by a *ground symbol* instead of an arrow:

---

[5] The `String` class is an exception to the rule since it has literals and `String` objects can be created either with the new operation or by initializing it with a literal; for example, `String name = "John Doe";`.

theScreen

They can later be assigned values created with `new`; for example,

```
theScreen = new Screen();
```

Using `new` to create a reference-type value is called **constructing an object.** To facilitate object construction, a class provides one or more special methods called **constructor methods,** or just **constructors.** For example, the `Integer` class has two constructors:

```
Integer(int value)   // constructs a new Integer representing value

Integer(String str) // constructs a new Integer representing str
```

The statement

```
Integer integerValue = new Integer(321);
```

uses the first constructor, but we could have used the second constructor

```
Integer integerValue = new Integer("321");
```

to accomplish exactly the same thing using a `String` instead of an `int`. The Java API documentation for a class includes descriptions of the class' constructors in a special Constructor Summary section.

In general, expressions that construct objects have the following form:

Object Construction

Form:

```
new ClassName(arguments)
```

where:
`ClassName` is the name of a class; and
`arguments` is a sequence of zero or more values separated by commas, whose types match those permitted by a `ClassName` constructor method.

Purpose:

Create an object of type `ClassName`, initialized as specified by `arguments`, and returns the address of the memory location where this object is stored.

The address of the constructed object returned by `new` is normally stored in a variable whose type is `ClassName`:

```
ClassName variable = new ClassName(arguments);
```

This makes *variable* a handle for that object that can be used to access and use that object in a program.

✔ Quick Quiz 3.2

Classify each of the types in Questions 1–12 as a primitive type or a reference type.

1. `int` _____
2. `Integer` _____
3. `BigInteger` _____
4. `char` _____
5. `double` _____
6. `byte` _____
7. `Character` _____
8. `Double` _____
9. `short` _____
10. `StringBuffer` _____
11. `boolean` _____
12. `float` _____
13. A value of a particular primitive type is called a(n) _____.
14. _____ denotes the absence of any type.
15. _____ types are formed from classes.
16. (True or false) `Integer` is an example of a wrapper class.
17. (True or false) `String` is an example of a wrapper class.
18. Values of a reference type must be created using the _____ operation.
19. A variable whose value is a reference type is called a(n) _____ for an object of that type.

3.3   NUMERIC TYPES AND EXPRESSIONS

Java provides six primitive types for representing numbers. Two of these types are used for real values:

Real type	Bits used to store value	Range of values (approximate)
float	32	$\pm 3.4028235 \times 10^{38}$
double	64	$\pm 1.7976931348623157 \times 10^{308}$

There are four types for representing integer values and one for characters:

Integer type	Bits used to store value	Range of values
byte	8	$-128 \ (= -2^7)$ through $127 \ (= 2^7 - 1)$
short	16	$-32768 \ (= -2^{15})$ through $32767 \ (= 2^{15} - 1)$
int	32	$-2147483648 \ (= -2^{31})$ through $2147483647 \ (= 2^{31} - 1)$
long	64	$-9223372036854775808L \ (= -2^{63})$ through $9223372036854775807L \ (= 2^{63} - 1)$
char	16	0 through $65535 \ (= 2^{16} - 1)$, the Unicode representations of characters

Java classifies char as an integer type because characters are represented in memory by numeric codes, and in Java, values of type char are stored using their numeric Unicode representations. (See the Part of the Picture section in Chapter 2 and Appendix A for more information about Unicode.) This mixing of integer and character values can be confusing (see Potential Pitfall 2 in the Programming Pointers at the end of this chapter).

As we saw in the preceding section and will describe later in this section, Java also provides a wrapper class for each of these primitive types to provide additional capabilities: Float, Double, Byte, Short, Integer, Long, and Character. In the java.math package, Java also provides the classes BigInteger and BigDecimal for processing integer and real values whose size is bounded only by the amount of available memory.

In theory, Java provides this many types for representing numeric values so that programmers can choose the type that most closely matches the range of values that a variable is expected to store. In practice, numeric computations are usually performed using the primitive types int and double. As we will see later, a major use of the wrapper classes is to perform type conversions. The BigInteger and BigDecimal classes are used when a computation involves numbers too large to be represented by the long and double types, respectively.

Numeric Literals

Integer Literals. By default, positive or negative whole numbers (e.g., $-30, 0, 1, 12,365$) are treated as literals of type int by the Java compiler. This is the primary reason that the types byte, short, and long are not often used.

Appending the letter L or l to a literal (e.g., $-30L, 0L, 1L, 12L, 365L$) instructs the compiler to treat a literal value as a long instead of as an int. *An uppercase* L *should be used because the lowercase* l *is easily confused with the digit 1.*

Base-8 and base-16 representations of numbers are important in computing. Thus, most modern programming languages such as Java allow integers to be represented **WATCH** in base 10, 8, or 16. *In Java, integer literals are taken to be base-10 (decimal) integers unless they begin with* 0. In this case:

OUT

❏ A sequence of digits that begins with 0 is interpreted as an **octal** (i.e., base-8) integer, provided that the digits are octal digits $0, 1, \ldots, 7$.

❏ A sequence of digits preceded by 0x is interpreted as a **hexadecimal** (i.e., base-16) integer; the hexadecimal digits for ten, eleven, . . . , fifteen are A, B, . . . , F, respectively, or their lowercase equivalents a, b, . . . , f.

❏ Any other digit sequence is a decimal (base-ten) integer.

For example, the integer literal

```
12
```

has the decimal value $12_{10} = 1 \times 10^1 + 2 \times 10^0$, but the integer literal

```
012
```

has the octal value $12_8 = 1 \times 8^1 + 2 \times 8^0 = 10_{10}$, while the integer literal

```
0x12
```

has the hexadecimal value $12_{16} = 1 \times 16^1 + 2 \times 16^0 = 18_{10}$. Table 3.1 is a quick guide to the Java representation of integer values in the three bases. (See Appendix E for additional details about binary, octal, and hexadecimal number systems.)

Real Literals. Like most programming languages, Java provides two ways to represent real values: fixed-point notation and floating-point notation. A **fixed-point** real literal has the form

```
m.n
```

where either the integer part m or the decimal part n (but not both) can be omitted. For example,

```
5.0      0.5      5.      .5
```

are all valid fixed-point real literals in Java.

Scientists often write very large or very small real numbers using a special notation called *exponential, scientific,* or *floating-point* notation. For example, a scientist might write the number 12 billion (12,000,000,000) as:

$$0.12 \times 10^{11}$$

TABLE 3.1   JAVA INTEGER CONSTANTS

Decimal	Octal	Hexadecimal
0	0	0x0
1	01	0x1
2	02	0x2
3	03	0x3
4	04	0x4
5	05	0x5
6	06	0x6
7	07	0x7
8	010	0x8
9	011	0x9
10	012	0xA
11	013	0xB
12	014	0xC
13	015	0xD
14	016	0xE
15	017	0xF
16	020	0x10
17	021	0x11
18	022	0x12
19	023	0x13
20	024	0x14

In Java, a **floating-point** real literal has one of the forms

> *xEn*   or   *xen*

where *x* is an integer or fixed-point real literal and *n* is an integer exponent (that can be positive or negative). For example, 12 billion = 0.12×10^{11} can be written in any of the following forms:

> 0.12e11   1.2E10   12.0E9   12.e9   12E9

Java compilers treat all real literals (whether fixed- or floating-point) as being of type double. *This means that if a value is computed using real literals and assigned to a* float *variable, then the Java compiler will generate an error because the (32-bit) variable does not have sufficient space to store the (64-bit) computed value. For this reason, many programmers never use the type* float, *and instead always use the type* double *for real values because real literals are by default given the type* double *and stored as 64-bit values.*

NOTE

To instruct the compiler to process a real literal as a float, an F or f can be appended to it. For example, 1.0F, 3.1416F, and 2.998e8F are real literals of type float.

Numeric Expressions

A **primitive expression** is a sequence of one or more primitive-type objects called *operands* and zero or more *operators* that combine to produce a value. Thus 12 is a primitive expression consisting of one operand (12) and no operators, producing the int value twelve. Similarly, 2.2 + 3.3 is a primitive expression with two operands (2.2 and 3.3), one operator (+), and produces the double value 5.5. The type of the value produced by an expression is called the **type of the expression.** Expressions that produce an int value are called int expressions, expressions that produce a double value are called double expressions, and so on.

Numeric Operators. In Java, addition and subtraction are denoted by the usual + and − signs. Multiplication is denoted by *, which must be used for every multiplication. That is, to multiply n by 2, we can write 2*n or n*2 but not 2n. Division is denoted by /, which is used for both real and integer division. Another operation closely related to integer division is the **modulus** or **remainder** operation, denoted by %, which gives the remainder in an integer division. The following table summarizes these operators.

Operator	Operation
+	Addition, unary plus
−	Subtraction, unary minus
*	Multiplication
/	Real and integer division
%	Modulus (remainder in integer division)

For the operators +, −, *, and /, the operands may be of any primitive integer or real type. If both are integer, the result is integer, but if either is real, the result is real. For example,

$$2 + 3 = 5 \qquad\qquad 2 + 3.0 = 5.0$$

$$2.0 + 3 = 5.0 \qquad\qquad 2.0 + 3.0 = 5.0$$

$$7.0 / 2.0 = 3.5 \qquad\qquad 7 / 2 = 3$$

It is important to understand the difference between integer and real division. In the expression

$$3/4$$

both operands (3 and 4) are integers, so integer division is performed producing the integer quotient 0. By contrast, in the similar expression

$$3.0/4$$

a real operand (3.0) is present, so real division is performed producing the real result 0.75. One of the common problems for beginning programmers is to *remember that the value of*

WATCH

OUT

$$1/n$$

is 0 if n *is an integer different from* −1, 0, *or* 1.

Integer division produces both a quotient and a remainder and Java uses one operator (/) to give the integer quotient and another operator (%) to give the remainder from an integer division[6]. The following are some examples:

$$9 / 3 = 3 \qquad\qquad 9 \% 3 = 0$$

$$86 / 10 = 8 \qquad\qquad 86 \% 10 = 6$$

$$197 / 10 = 19 \qquad\qquad 197 \% 10 = 7$$

Bitwise Operators. Java also provides other numeric operators, including operations that can be applied to integer data at the individual bit level. In the following descriptions, b, b_1, and b_2 denote binary digits (0 or 1); x and y are integers.

---

[6] Neither i / j nor i % j is defined if j is zero.

BITWISE OPERATORS

Operator	Operation	Description
~	bitwise negation	$\sim b$ is 0 if b is 1; $\sim b$ is 1 if b is 0
&	bitwise and	b_1 & b_2 is 1 if both b_1 and b_2 are 1; it is 0 otherwise
|	bitwise or	b_1 | b_2 is 1 if either b_1 or b_2 or both are 1; it is 0 otherwise
^	bitwise exclusive or	b_1 ^ b_2 is 1 if exactly one of b_1 or b_2 is 1; it is 0 otherwise
<<	bitshift left	x << y is the value obtained by shifting the bits in x y positions to the left
>>	bitshift right	x >> y is the value obtained by shifting the bits in x y positions to the right*

*Note: There is also an *unsigned right shift operator* >>> that fills the vacated bit positions at the left with 0s. >> is a *signed* right-shift operator that fills these positions with the sign bit of the integer being shifted.

To illustrate the behavior of these operators, if theScreen is a Screen object, then the statements

```
byte i = 6;                      // 00000110
theScreen.println(i | 5);   // 00000110 OR   00000101 = 00000111
theScreen.println(i & 5);   // 00000110 AND 00000101 = 00000100
theScreen.println(i ^ 5);   // 00000110 XOR 00000101 = 00000011
theScreen.println(i << 1);  // 00000110 LS   1          = 00001100
theScreen.println(i >> 1);  // 00000110 RS   1          = 00000011
theScreen.println(~i);       // NEG 00000110           = 11111001
```

produce this output:

```
7
4
3
12
3
-7
```

In practice, such operations are used by methods that must inspect memory or interact directly with a computer's hardware, such as low-level graphics methods or operating system methods. See the exercises at the end of this section for some examples.

Operator Precedence. The order in which operators in an expression are applied is determined by a characteristic known as **operator precedence** (or **priority**): *In an expression involving several operators the operators* *, /, and % *have higher precedence than (i.e., are applied before) the operators* + *and* −. Thus, in the expression

NOTE

$$2 + 3 * 5$$

`*` has higher precedence than `+`, so the multiplication is performed before the addition; therefore, the value of the expression is 17.

Operator Associativity. In Java the binary operators +, −, *, /, and % are all **left-associative** operators, which means that in an expression containing operators with the same priority, the left operator is applied first. Thus,

$$9 - 5 - 1$$

is evaluated as

$$(9 - 5) - 1 = 4 - 1 = 3$$

Associativity is also used in more complex expressions containing different operators of the same priority. For example, consider

$$7 * 10 - 5 \% 3 * 4 + 9$$

There are three high-priority operations, *, %, and *, and so left associativity causes the leftmost multiplication to be performed first, giving the intermediate result

$$70 - 5 \% 3 * 4 + 9$$

% is performed next, giving

$$70 - 2 * 4 + 9$$

and the second multiplication is performed last, yielding

$$70 - 8 + 9$$

The two remaining operations, − and +, are equal in priority, and so left associativity causes the subtraction to be performed first, giving

$$62 + 9$$

and then the addition is carried out, giving the final result

$$71$$

Unary Operators. The operators + and − can also be used as **unary operators** (i.e., they can be applied to a single operand); for example, −x and +34 are allowed. Similarly, the expression 3 * −4 is a valid Java expression, producing the value −12. Unary operations have higher priority than *, /, and %. Thus, the integer expression:

$$-6 * +2 / -3$$

produces the value +4.

Using Parentheses. Parentheses can be used to change the usual order of evaluation of an expression as determined by precedence and associativity. Parenthesized subexpressions are first evaluated in the standard manner, and the results are then combined to evaluate the complete expression. If the parentheses are "nested"—that is, if one set of parentheses is contained within another—the computations in the innermost parentheses are performed first.

To illustrate, consider the expression

$$(7 * (10 - 5) \% 3) * 4 + 9$$

The subexpression $(10 - 5)$ is evaluated first, producing

$$(7 * 5 \% 3) * 4 + 9$$

Next, the subexpression $(7 * 5 \% 3)$ is evaluated left to right, giving

$$(35 \% 3) * 4 + 9$$

followed by

$$2 * 4 + 9$$

Now the multiplication is performed, giving

$$8 + 9$$

and the addition produces the final result

$$17$$

**WATCH
OUT**

Care must be taken in writing expressions containing two or more operations to ensure that they are evaluated in the order intended. Even though parentheses may not be required, they should be used freely to clarify the intended order of evaluation and to write complicated expressions in terms of simpler expressions. It is important, however, that the parentheses balance—*for each left parenthesis, a matching right parenthesis must appear later in the expression*—since an unpaired parenthesis will result in a compilation error.

Numeric Methods

We noted in Chapter 1 that invoking a method in an object can be thought of as **sending a message** to that object. For example, the program in Figure 3.1 sends its Keyboard object theKeyboard the readDouble() message to get a double value entered at the keyboard and store this value in the double variable mass:

```
double mass = theKeyboard.readDouble();
```

The program then computes the value of energy using the statement

```
double energy = mass * Math.pow(SPEED_OF_LIGHT, 2.0);
```

As this example demonstrates, in addition to simple objects like literals, constants, and variables, an operand in an expression may also be a value computed by a method. In this case, we used the method pow() from Java's Math class (in package java.lang) to perform exponentiation. However, we sent the readDouble() message to an *object* (i.e., theKeyboard), but we sent the pow() message to a class (i.e., Math). Why is there a difference?

For maximum flexibility, Java supports two different kinds of methods:

❑ A method that is invoked by sending a message to a *class* is called a **static method** or a **class method.**

❑ A method that is invoked by sending a message to an *object* is called an **instance method** (or simply a **method**).

For example, `readDouble()` is an instance method and so a message invoking it must be sent to an *object* (i.e., an *instance* of a class):

```
double mass = theKeyboard.readDouble();
```

By contrast, the `pow()` method is a static method in Java's `Math` class. To use it, therefore, we send the message directly to the `Math` class,

```
double energy = mass * Math.pow(SPEED_OF_LIGHT, 2.0);
```

instead of creating a `Math` object and sending a message to it.

The keyword **static** is used inside the definition of a class to distinguish static methods from instance methods—*a method not preceded by* `static` *is an instance method, a method preceded by* `static` *is a static method.* We will use the terms *static method* and *class method* interchangeably.

NOTE

Java's `Math` Class. Java's `Math` class contains a variety of class constants and methods that can be used to solve various kinds of mathematical problems. Table 3.2 lists the two mathematical constants defined in this class: E and PI. Each is a `double` value that best approximates the specified mathematical constant. (*Note:* Java also has a *package* `java.math`. It must not be confused with Java's `Math` class in the package `java.lang`.)

TABLE 3.2   Math **CLASS CONSTANTS**

REFERENCE

Math.	Description
E	e (2.71828 . . .), the base of natural logarithms
PI	π (3.14159 . . .), the ratio of a circle's circumference to its diameter

To use one of these constants, we would use its qualified name as, for example, in the statement

```
double circumference = 2.0 * Math.PI * radius;
```

Table 3.3 lists the more commonly used `Math` class methods. Others, including the trig functions and a random number generator, are described in the Documentation section of the chapter summary. Unless noted otherwise, each of these methods takes arguments of type `double` and returns a value of type `double`. Thus, to calculate the square root of 5, we can write

```
Math.sqrt(5.0)
```

As a more complicated example, if we wish to calculate $\sqrt{b^2 - 4ac}$, we could write

```
Math.sqrt(Math.pow(b, 2) - 4.0 * a * c)
```

TABLE 3.3   SOME Math CLASS METHODS

Method	Description
abs(*v*)	Absolute value of *v* (double, float, long, or int)
pow(*x*,*y*)	x^y
sqrt(*x*)	Square root of *x*
ceil(*x*)	Smallest double $\geq x$ that is equal to an integer
floor(*x*)	Largest double $\leq x$ that is equal to an integer
rint(*x*)	int value closest to *x*
round(*x*)	long value closest to *x* (an int if *x* is float)
max(*v*,*w*) min(*v*,*w*)	Maximum / minimum of *v*, *w* (double, float, long, or int)
exp(*x*)	e^x
log(*x*)	Natural logarithm of *x*

Note that if the value of the expression

```
Math.pow(b, 2) - 4.0 * a * c
```

is negative, then an error results because the square root of a negative number is not defined.

Wrapper Classes. The basic operations such as addition, subtraction, multiplication, and division are carried out efficiently by the primitive types. There are some operations, however, such as converting values between primitive types, that are not provided by the primitive types. It is for this reason that in addition to the Math class, the java.lang package also contains the **wrapper classes** Byte, Short, Integer, Long, Float, and Double (as well as Boolean and Character). These classes are so named because each of them extends the capabilities of the corresponding primitive type essentially by wrapping it with an assortment of useful constants and methods.

To illustrate, each of these classes provides static constants that define the maximum and minimum values for their respective primitive types. For example, the expression

```
Integer.MAX_VALUE
```

can be used to access the maximum int value (i.e., 2147483647);

```
Integer.MIN_VALUE
```

can be used to access the minimum int value (i.e., −2147483648). The other wrapper classes provide similar constants—see the API documentation for the particular constants of each class.

One example of the additional operations provided is the parseInt() **method** in the Integer class. This method converts a String of digits into the corresponding int value. For example, the statement

```
int number = Integer.parseInt("4321");
```

converts the string "4321" to the int value 4321 and uses it to initalize the int variable number. Conversely, the toString() **method** in the Integer class converts an int value into its corresponding String of digit characters. For example, if number is the int variable defined above, then the statement

```
String digits = Integer.toString(number);
```

will initialize variable digits to the String value "4321".

Each of these classes also provides other methods for manipulating their respective primitive types. Table 3.4 lists some of the methods provided by the Integer class. (The Documentation section of the chapter summary lists some others; also see Java's API documentation for additional Integer methods and those of the other wrapper classes.) The *receiver* in the second column referred to by some of the methods is the Integer object to which the message is sent.

REFERENCE

TABLE 3.4   SOME Integer METHODS

Method	Description
Integer(*is*)	Construct an Integer object equivalent to *is* (of type int or String)
compareTo(*valInt*)	Return zero, a negative int value, or a positive int value, according to whether the receiver is equal to, less than, or greater than *valInt* (of type Integer or Object)
byteValue(), shortValue(), intValue(), longValue(), floatValue(), doubleValue()	Return the byte, short, int, long, float, or double value equivalent of the receiver
equals(*obj*)	Return true if the receiver equals object *obj* and false otherwise
toString()	Return a String equivalent to the receiver
Static Methods	
parseInt(*str*) parseInt (*str, b*)	Return the int equivalent of String *str*; in the second form, *str* is interpreted as a base-*b* numeral
toBinaryString(*i*) toOctalString(*i*) toHexString(*i*)	Return the base-2, base-8, or base-16 representation of int *i*
toString(*i*) toString(*i, b*)	Return a String equivalent to *i*; in the second form, *str* is interpreted as a base-*b* numeral
valueOf(*str*) valueOf(*str, b*)	Return an Integer equivalent to *str*; in the second form, *str* is interpreted as a base-*b* numeral

Many of these and similar methods provide operations to convert `int` and `Integer` values between the `byte`, `short`, `long`, `int`, `float`, `double`, and `String` types. Since some methods are static methods and others are not, you should check a method's description in Java's API documentation to ensure that you use it properly. To illustrate, suppose we have constructed an `Integer` object such as

```
Integer integerValue = new Integer(4321);
```

and we want to convert it to its corresponding `String` of digits. For this, we should use the instance method `toString()` with no arguments:

```
String integerDigits = integerValue.toString();
```

By contrast, suppose we have input an `int`, say with

```
int intValue = theKeyboard.readInt();
```

and we want to convert it to its corresponding `String` of digits. Then the most efficient way is to use the static method `toString()` that receives the int to be converted as an argument:

```
String intDigits = Integer.toString(intValue);
```

Someone who was not aware of this second form of the `toString()` method might write

```
int intValue = theKeyboard.readInt();          // Ok, but
Integer integerValue = new Integer(intValue); // inefficient
String intDigits = integerValue.toString();
```

This would accomplish the required conversion, but it is not a good solution because of its inefficiency. Creating the object `integerValue` requires extra time and space.

The `BigInteger` and `BigDecimal` Classes. For those situations where the numbers being used are too large to be represented by the `int`, `long`, or `double` types, Java provides the predefined `BigInteger` and `BigDecimal` classes in the package `java.math`. Since `BigInteger` and `BigDecimal` are reference types, values of these types must be constructed using the `new` operation and the classes' constructor methods. Each class has several constructors that construct an object out of some other value. To illustrate, the `BigDecimal` class has one constructor to build a `BigDecimal` value from a `double` value, another to build a `BigDecimal` from the `String` representation of a real value, and two constructors to build `BigDecimal` values from `BigInteger` values. To construct a `BigDecimal` variable whose initial value is 0.98765432109876543210987654321, for example, we use the second constructor as follows:

```
BigDecimal fraction =
            new BigDecimal("0.98765432109876543210987654321");
```

`BigInteger` also has several constructors. One of these is shown in Table 3.5, which describes some of the operations for the `BigInteger` class. (See the Java API

TABLE 3.5   SOME `BigInteger` METHODS

REFERENCE

Method	Description
`BigInteger(str)`	Construct `BigInteger` object equivalent to `String` `str`
`abs()`	Return the `BigInteger` object that is the absolute value of the receiver

`add(bv)`
`divide(bv)`
`gcd(bv)`
`max(bv)`
`min(bv)`
`mod(bv)`
`multiply(bv)`
`remainder(bv)`
`subtract(bv)`
	Return a `BigInteger` object equivalent to the
	sum
	quotient
	greatest common divisor
	maximum
	minimum
	modulus (receiver mod bv)
	product
	remainder
	difference
	of the receiver and `BigInteger` object bv

`pow(n)`	Return a `BigInteger` object equivalent to the receiver raised to the `int` exponent n
`compareTo(bv)`	Return zero, a negative `int` value, or a positive `int` value, according to whether the receiver is equal to, less than, or greater than `BigInteger` object bv
`equals(obj)`	Return true if the receiver equals object obj and false otherwise
`doubleValue()`,`floatValue()`,`intValue()`,`longValue()`	Return the `double`, `float`, `int`, or `long` value that is equivalent to the receiver
`toString()`	Return the base-10 `String` representation of the receiver
Static Methods	
`toString(b)`	Return the base-b `String` representation of the receiver
`valueOf(lv)`	Return a `BigInteger` object equivalent to `long` value lv

documentation for complete descriptions of the two classes `BigInteger` and `BigDecimal`.) The *receiver* in the second column referred to by some of the methods is the `BigInteger` object to which the message is sent.

As a simple illustration, suppose we want to multiply two arbitrarily big integers entered from the keyboard. To accomplish this, we could write:

```
theScreen.println("Enter two integers, each on a separate line:");
```

```
String valueString = theKeyboard.readWord();
BigInteger value1 = new BigInteger(valueString);

valueString = theKeyboard.readWord();
BigInteger value2 = new BigInteger(valueString);

BigInteger theirProduct = value1.multiply(value2);

theScreen.println(value1 + "\n *\n" + value2
                 + "\n =\n" + theirProduct);
```

Note that `BigInteger` and `BigDecimal` values can be displayed in the usual manner. However, the `Keyboard` class does not provide a method for reading `BigInteger` or `BigDouble` values. Instead, to input a `BigInteger` or `BigDecimal` value, it should be read as a `String`, and the constructor in the `BigInteger` or `BigDecimal` class that accepts a `String` can then be used to build an object whose value is represented by that `String`.

Implicit Type Conversion—Promotion

We have seen that the division operation in the expression

$$3.0 \ / \ 4$$

performs real division and produces a real value as its result, even though only one of the operands is a real value. Some programming languages do not allow integer and real values to be intermixed within an expression in this manner. By contrast, Java will automatically *widen* integer values to real values as needed. For example, in the expression

$$3.0 \ / \ 4$$

the `double` value `3.0` is stored in 64 bits and the `int` value `4` is stored in 32 bits. Java will automatically widen the 32-bit integer value to a 64-bit real value, so that the division can be performed on two 64-bit real values, producing a 64-bit real as the result. No information or precision is lost, as would happen if the wider `double` were narrowed to the size of the `int`. This automatic widening of a narrower value to the size of a wider value in an expression is often described as **promotion** of the narrower value. The promotions allowed in Java are shown in the following diagram in which the arrows denote "can be promoted to:"

```
byte → short → int → long → float → double
                ↑
               char
```

As a result of promotion, `byte`, `short`, `int`, and `long` (and `char`) integer values and `float` and `double` real values can be freely intermixed in Java numeric expressions, which is a great convenience for the programmer. However, promotion does have its limits. It is a *one-way* relationship as the arrows in the preceding diagram suggest. This means that we can write

```
double sum = 1;
```

and the 32-bit `int` value 1 will be widened and stored in the 64 bits associated with `sum`. But the Java compiler prevents us from writing either of the statements

```
int count = 1.0; // ERROR: cannot promote double to int

int intVal = 1L; // ERROR: cannot promote long to int
```

because a larger (i.e., 64-bit) representation of a number cannot in general be stored in a smaller (i.e., 32-bit) variable without loss of information.

Compatibility. If the type of one expression is the same as or can be promoted to the type of another expression, then the first expression is described as **type-compatible** (or simply **compatible**) with the second expression. That is, the "can be promoted to" arrows in the preceding diagram also denote the "is compatible with" relationship. The one-way property of the arrows means that although an `int` is compatible with a `double`, a `double` is not compatible with an `int`. Also, the `boolean` type is not shown in the diagram because it is not compatible with any of the other primitive types.

Explicit Type Conversion—Casting

Sometimes it is necessary to mix incompatible types in an expression. For such situations, Java provides two ways that a programmer can explicitly perform a type conversion. The first mechanism is to use the type-conversion methods in the wrapper classes. To illustrate, suppose that we need to *round* a `double` value named `doubleVal` to an `int`. We can do this using the `Double` wrapper class as follows:[7]

```
Double roundedDoubleVal = new Double(doubleVal + 0.5);
int intVal = roundedDoubleVal.intValue();
```

Because the wrapper classes do not contain a *static* method to convert a `double` to an `int`, this approach requires creating a `Double` object and then sending it the `intValue()` message. Since creating intermediate objects like `roundedDouble-Val` is not efficient, Java also provides a second, more direct, mechanism to perform explicit type conversions. Using it, we can round `doubleVal` to an `int` very easily:

```
int intValue = (int) (doubleVal + 0.5);
```

This expression adds `0.5` to `doubleVal`, after which the `(int)` operation converts the resulting sum to an `int`, truncating the decimal portion of the sum. The `(int)` operation that performs the explicit type conversion is called a **type-cast,** or simply **cast.**

More generally, if `doubleExpr` is a `double` expression, then the cast expression

```
(int) doubleExpr
```

will truncate the fractional part and produce the integer part of `doubleExpr` as its value, while

---

[7] Note that neither of the rounding methods in Java's `Math` class (see Table 3.3) round a `double` to an `int`.

```
(float) doubleExpr
```

will *narrow* `doubleVal` to a 32-bit real value. Similarly,

```
(int) longExpr
```

will narrow a `long` expression `longExpr` to a 32-bit integer value.
In general, explicit type casting can be done as follows:

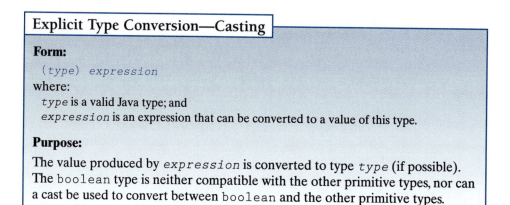

Explicit Type Conversion—Casting

Form:

`(type) expression`
where:
   `type` is a valid Java type; and
   `expression` is an expression that can be converted to a value of this type.

Purpose:

The value produced by `expression` is converted to type `type` (if possible).
The `boolean` type is neither compatible with the other primitive types, nor can
a cast be used to convert between `boolean` and the other primitive types.

WATCH

!

OUT

The cast mechanism should be used with restraint, because it can result in a loss of information. If losing information is necessary in solving a problem (e.g., rounding a `double` to an `int`), then casting is an efficient way to do so. It should not be used, however, as a "quick fix" for compilation errors.

✔ Quick Quiz 3.3

1. Name the two Java primitive types used for real values and give the memory requirements for each.
2. Name the four Java primitive types used for integer values and give the memory requirements for each.
3. (True or false) All real literals are treated as being of type `double`.
4. (True or false) `0123` and `123` represent the same integer value.
5. (True or false) `0xA` and `10` represent the same integer value.
6. _____ refers to automatic widening of a narrower value to the size of a wider value in an expression.
7. Distinguish between instance methods and static methods.

For Questions 8–15, tell whether each is an integer literal, a real literal, or neither.

8. `1234`	9. `1,234`	10. `1.234`	11. `123e4`
12. `123-4`	13. `0.123E-4`	14. `0x123E4`	15. `0199`

Find the value of each of the expressions in Questions 16–27, or explain why it is not a valid expression.

16. `3 - 2 - 1`
17. `2.0 + 3.0 / 5.0`
18. `2 + 3 / 5`
19. `5 / 2 + 3`
20. `7 + 6 % 5`
21. `(7 + 6) % 5`
22. `(2 + 3 * 4) / (8 - 2 + 1)`
23. `12.0 / 1.0 * 3.0`
24. `Math.sqrt(6.0 + 3.0)`
25. `Math.pow(2.0, 3)`
26. `Math.floor(2.34)`
27. `Math.ceil(2.34)`

Questions 28–39 assume that `two`, `three`, and `four` are reals with values 2.0, 3.0, and 4.0, respectively, and `intFive`, `intEight`, and `intTwelve` are integers with values 5, 8, and 12, respectively. Find the value of each expression.

28. `two + three * three`
29. `intFive / 3`
30. `(three + two / four) * 2`
31. `intEight / intFive * 5.1`
32. `four * 2 / two * 2`
33. `intFive * 2 / two * 2`
34. `Math.sqrt(two + three + four)`
35. `Math.pow(two, intFive)`
36. `intTwelve & intFive`
37. `intTwelve | intFive`
38. `intTwelve << 3`
39. `intTwelve >> 3`
40. Write a Java expression equivalent to $10 + 5B - 4AC$.
41. Write a Java expression equivalent to the square root of $A + 3B^2$.

✍ EXERCISES 3.3

For Exercises 1–20, classify each as an integer literal, a real literal, or neither. If it is neither, give a reason.

1. `12`
2. `12.`
3. `12.0`
4. `"12"`
5. `8 + 4`
6. `-3.7`
7. `3.7-`
8. `1,024`
9. `+1`
10. `$3.98`
11. `0.357E4`
12. `24E0`
13. `E3`
14. `five`
15. `3E.5`
16. `.000001`
17. `1.2 - 10`
18. `-(-1)`
19. `0E0`
20. `1/2`

Find the value of each of the expressions in Exercises 21–52, or explain why it is not a valid expression.

21. `9 - 5 - 3`
22. `2 / 3 + 3 / 5`
23. `9.0 / 2 / 5`
24. `9 / 2 / 5`
25. `2.0 / 4`
26. `(2 + 3) % 2`
27. `7 % 5 % 3`
28. `(7 % 5) % 3`
29. `7 % (5 % 3)`
30. `(7 % 5 % 3)`
31. `25 * 1 / 2`
32. `25 * 1.0 / 2`
33. `25 * (1 / 2)`
34. `-3.0 * 5.0`

35. `5.0 * -3.0`   36. `12 / 2 * 3`

37. `((12 + 3) / 2) / (8 - (5 + 1))`   38. `((12 + 3) / 2) / (8 - 5 + 1)`

39. `(12 + 3 / 2) / (8 - 5 + 1)`   40. `13 & 9`

41. `13 | 9`   42. `13 ^ 9`

43. `13 >> 2`   44. `13 << 2`

45. `Math.sqrt(Math.pow(4.0, 2))`   46. `Math.pow(Math.sqrt(-4.0), 2)`

47. `Math.sqrt(Math.pow(-4.0, 2))`   48. `Math.floor(8.0 / 5.0)`

49. `Math.ceil(8.0 / 5.0)`   50. `Math.rint(1.234)`

51. `(int) 1.234`   52. `(double) 7`

Questions 53–60 assume that `r1` and `r2` are reals with values 2.0 and 3.0, respectively, and `i1`, `i2`, and `i3` are integers with values 4, 5, and 8, respectively. Find the value of each expression.

53. `r1 + r2 + r2`   54. `i3 / 3`

55. `i3 / 3.0`   56. `(r2 + r1) * i1`

57. `i3 / i2 * 5.1`   58. `Math.pow(i1, 2) / Math.pow(r1, 2)`

59. `Math.pow(i2, 2) / Math.pow(r1, 2)`

60. `Math.sqrt(r1 + r2 + i1)`

Write Java expressions to compute each of the quantities in Exercises 61–67.

61. $10 + 5B - 4AC$

62. Three times the difference $4 - n$ divided by twice the quantity $m^2 + n^2$

63. The square root of $a + 3b^2$

64. The square root of the average of m and n

65. $|A / (m + n)|$ (where $|x|$ denotes the absolute value of x)

66. a^x, computed as $e^{x \ln a}$ (where ln is the natural logarithm function)

67. The real quantity *amount* rounded to the nearest hundredth

68. Using the given values of `cost`, verify that the expression

```
(int)(cost * 100.0 + 0.5) / 100.0
```

can be used to convert a real value `cost` to dollars, rounded to the nearest cent.

(a) 12.342   (b) 12.348   (c) 12.345   (d) 12.340   (e) 13.0

69. Write an expression similar to that in Exercise 68 that rounds a real amount `x` to the nearest tenth.

70. Write an expression similar to that in Exercise 68 that rounds a real amount `x` to the nearest thousandth.

For each of Exercises 71–73, give values for the integer variables a, b, and c for which the two given expressions have different values:

71. `a * (b / c)` and `a * b / c`   71. `a / b` and `a * (1 / b)`

73. `(a + b) / c` and `a / c + b / c`

3.4 ASSIGNMENT EXPRESSIONS

An **assignment expression** uses the assignment operator (=) to change the value of a variable:

Assignment Expression

Form:

```
variable = expression
```

where:

    `variable` is a valid Java identifier, declared as a variable; and

    `expression` is a valid Java expression whose type is compatible with that of `variable`.

Behavior:

1. `expression` is evaluated to produce some value *v*;
2. The value of `variable` is changed to *v*; and
3. *v* is the value of the complete assignment expression.

For example, if `xValue` and `yValue` are `double` variables declared by

```
double xValue, yValue;
```

then 64-bit memory locations are allocated to `xValue` and `yValue` and they are defined with default value zero. We might picture this as follows:

Now consider the assignment statements:

```
xValue = 25.0;
yValue = Math.sqrt(xValue);
```

The first statement changes the value of `xValue` to 25.0,

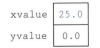

and then (using the value of `xValue`), the second statement changes the value of `yValue` to 5.0:

It is important to remember that for the *primitive* types, an assignment statement is a *replacement* statement. Some beginning programmers forget this and write an assignment statement like

    a = b;

when the statement

    b = a;

is intended. These two statements produce very different results: The first assigns the value of b to a, leaving b unchanged, and the second assigns the value of a to b, leaving a unchanged.

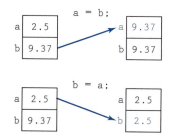

To illustrate further the replacement property of an assignment, suppose that the integer variables alpha and beta have values 357 and 59, respectively, and that we wish to interchange these values. For this, we use a third integer variable temp to store the value of alpha while we assign beta's value to alpha; then we can assign this stored value to beta.

    temp = alpha;
    alpha = beta;
    beta = temp;

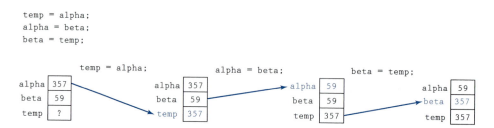

In a valid assignment statement, *the variable whose value is to be changed must appear to the left of the assignment operator (=), and a type-compatible expression must appear on the right.* The following table shows several *invalid* Java assignments along with explanations of why they are not valid. The variables x, y, number, and grade have the following declarations:

```
double x, y;
int number;
char grade;
```

Statement	Error
`5 = number;`	The left operand of an assignment must be a variable.
`x + 3.5 = y;`	The left operand of an assignment cannot be an expression.
`grade = "ABC";`	Type `String` is not compatible with type `char`.
`number = x;`	Type `double` is not compatible with type `int`.
`number = false;`	Type `boolean` is not compatible with any other type.

Assignment as an Operation

We have seen that an assignment

> *variable* = *expression*

produces three actions:

1. *expression* is evaluated, producing a value *v*.
2. The value of *variable* is changed to *v*.
3. The = operator produces the value *v*.

Thus far in our discussion, we have concentrated on actions (1) and (2), but we now turn our attention to action (3) in this description.

In the expression

$$2 + 3$$

+ is the operator, its operands are 2 and 3, and it produces the value 5. Similarly, in the assignment

```
number = 4
```

= is the operator, its operands are `number` and 4, and it produces the value 4; as a "side effect" it also stores the value 4 in `number`'s memory location.

As another example, suppose the value of `number` is 4 and consider the expression

```
number = number * 2
```

The * is applied first because it has higher precedence (the priority of the = operator is lower than almost all other operators),

```
number = (number * 2)
```

producing the result 8. The assignment thus becomes

```
number = 8
```

which changes the value of `number` to 8 and produces the result 8. Although we are usually most interested in the side effect of the assignment—of changing the value of

NOTE   number to 8—*it is important to remember that the assignment operator = is a value-producing binary operator whose result is the value assigned to the left operand.*

Chaining Assignment Operators

Because = is a value-producing operator, several assignment operators can be chained together in a single statement such as

```
x = y = 2.5;
```

which is equivalent to the two separate statements

```
y = 2.5;
x = y;
```

Unlike most of the arithmetic operators, the assignment operator = is **right-associative,** so that in the statement

```
x = y = 2.5;
```

the rightmost = is applied first,

```
x = (y = 2.5);
```

which changes the value of y to 2.5, and produces the value assigned to y (i.e., 2.5). The assignment thus becomes

```
x = (2.5);
```

which changes the value of x to 2.5. It also produces the assigned value 2.5 as its result so the statement becomes

```
2.5;
```

which is a valid Java statement; it just doesn't do anything.

Because of right-associativity and the value-producing property of =, chained assignments can be used to assign the same value to a group of variables; for example,

```
a = b = c = d = 1;
```

will set each of d, c, b, and a to 1.

The Increment and Decrement Operations

Algorithms often contain instructions of the form

"Increment *counter* by 1."

One way to encode this instruction in Java is

```
counter = counter + 1;
```

Such a statement in which the same variable appears on both sides of the assignment operator often confuses beginning programmers. Although we read English sentences from left to right, execution of this statement goes from right to left because + has higher priority than =:

1. `counter + 1` is evaluated
2. This value is assigned to `counter` (overwriting its previous value).

For example, if `counter` has the value `16`, then

1. The value of `counter + 1` `(16 + 1 = 17)`, is computed; and
2. This value is assigned as the new value for `counter`:

As we have seen, the old value of the variable is lost because it is replaced with a new value.

This kind of assignment (i.e., incrementing a variable) occurs so often that Java provides a special unary **increment operator ++** for this operation. It can be used as a postfix operator,

        variableName++

or as a prefix operator,

        ++*variableName*

where *variableName* is an integer variable whose value is to be incremented by 1. Thus, the assignment statement

        counter = counter + 1;

can also be written

        counter++;

or

        ++counter;

The difference between the postfix and prefix use of the operator is subtle. To explain the difference, consider the following program segments where `counter`, `number1`, and `number2` are `int` variables:

```
//POSTFIX: Use first, then increment          Output
counter = 10;
theKeyboard.println("counter = " + counter);  counter = 10

number1 = counter++;
theKeyboard.println("number1 = " + number1);  number1 = 10
theKeyboard.println("counter = " + counter);  counter = 11
```

and

```
//PREFIX: Increment first, then use                  Output
counter = 10;
theKeyboard.println("counter = " + counter);      counter = 10

number2 = ++counter;
theKeyboard.println("number2 = " + number2);      number2 = 11
theKeyboard.println("counter = " + counter);      counter = 11
```

Note that after execution of both sets of statements, the value of `counter` is 11. However, in the first set of assignments, the value assigned to `number1` is 10, whereas in the second set of assignments, the value assigned to `number2` is 11.

To understand this difference, we must remember that increment expressions are "shortcut" assignment expressions and thus produce values. If `counter` has the value 10, then in the *prefix* expression

```
++counter
```

`counter` is incremented (to 11) and *the value produced by the expression is the incremented value* (11). By contrast, if `counter` again has the value 10, then in the *postfix* expression

```
counter++
```

`counter` is still incremented (to 11), but *the value produced by the expression is the original value* (10). Put differently, the assignment

```
number2 = ++counter;
```

is equivalent to

```
counter = counter + 1;
number2 = counter;
```

while the assignment

```
number1 = counter++;
```

is equivalent to

```
number1 = counter;
counter = counter + 1;
```

It does not matter whether the prefix or postfix form is used if the increment operator is being used simply to increment a variable as a stand-alone statement:

```
counter++;
```

or

```
++counter;
```

Both of these statements produce exactly the same result; namely, the value of counter is incremented by 1.

Just as you can increment a variable's value with the ++ operator, you can decrement the value of a variable (i.e., subtract 1 from it) using the **decrement operator (− −),** For example, the assignment statement

```
counter = counter - 1;
```

can be written more compactly as

```
counter--;
```

(or −−counter;). The prefix and postfix versions of the decrement operator behave in a manner similar to the prefix and postfix versions of the increment operator.

Other Assignment Shortcuts

The increment and decrement operations are special cases of a more general assignment that changes the value of a variable using some expression that involves its original value. For example, the pseudocode statement

"Add *counter* to *sum*"

implicitly changes the value of *sum* to the value of *sum* + *counter.* This can be encoded in Java as

```
sum = sum + counter;
```

The following diagram illustrates this for the case in which the integer variables sum and counter have the values 120 and 16, respectively.

This operation occurs so frequently that Java provides special operators for it. Instead of writing

```
sum = sum + counter;
```

we can write

```
sum += counter;
```

to accomplish the same thing.

A similar shortcut is provided for each of the other arithmetic operators. For example,

```
number = number / 2;
```

can be written

```
number /= 2;
```

In general, a statement of the form

```
alpha = alpha Δ beta;
```

can be written :

```
alpha Δ= beta;
```

where Δ is any of the arithmetic operators +, −, *, /, or %, or one of the bitwise operators &, |, ^, <<, >>, or >>>. Each of the following is, therefore, an acceptable variation of the assignment operator:

```
+=,  −=,  *=,  /=,  %=,  &=,  |=,  ^=,  <<=,  >>=,  >>>=
```

Like the regular assignment operator, each of these is right-associative and produces the value assigned as its result, which means that they can be chained together. This is not good programming practice, however, because it produces expressions for which it can be difficult to follow how they are evaluated. For example, if x has the value 4.0 and and y the value 2.5, then the statement

```
x *= y += 0.5;        // poor programming style
```

is evaluated as follows:

1. Evaluate `y + 0.5 = 2.5 + 0.5 = 3.0` and assign this value to `y`.
2. Now evaluate `x * 3.0 = 4.0 * 3.0 = 12.0` and assign this value to `x`.

NOTE

Chaining such operators together should normally be avoided so that the readability of the program does not suffer. Programs that are cleverly written but difficult to read are of little use because they are too costly to maintain.

✔ Quick Quiz 3.4

Questions 1–15 assume that the following declarations have been made:

```
int m, n;
double d;
```

Tell whether each is a valid Java statement. If it is not valid, explain why it is not.

1. d = 3.0;
2. 0 = n;
3. n = n + n;
4. n+n = n;
5. m = 1;
6. m = "1";
7. m = n = 1;
8. m = m;
9. d = m;
10. m = d;
11. m++;
12. m + n;
13. ++d;
14. d += 1;
15. d += d;

For Questions 16–25, assume that the following declarations have been made:

```
int intEight = 8, intFive1 = 5, intFive2 = 5, jobId;
double two = 2.0, three = 3.0, four = 4.0, xValue;
```

Find the value assigned to the given variable or indicate why the statement is not valid.

16. `xValue = three + two / four;`
17. `xValue = intEight / intFive1 + 5.1;`
18. `jobId = intEight / intFive1 + 5.1;`
19. `xValue = Math.sqrt(three * three + four * four);`
20. `jobId = Math.abs(three - 4.5);`
21. `jobId = intFive1++;`
22. `jobId = ++intFive2;`
23. `intEight *= 8;`
24. `intEight &= 9;`
25. `intEight <<= 2;`

For each of Questions 26–27, write a Java assignment statement that calculates the given expression and assigns the result to the specified variable.

26. *rate* times *time* to *distance*   27. $\sqrt{a^2 + b^2}$ to *c*
28. Assuming that *x* is an integer variable, write three different statements that increment *x* by 1.

✍ EXERCISES 3.4

Exercises 1–14 assume that `number` is an integer variable, `xValue` and `yValue` are real variables. Tell whether each is a valid Java statement. If it is not valid, explain why it is not.

1. `xValue = 2.71828;`   2. `3 = number;`
3. `number = number + number;`   4. `xValue = 1;`
5. `number + 1 = number;`   6. `xValue = "1.23";`
7. `xValue = yValue = 3.2;`   8. `yValue = yValue;`
9. `xValue = 'A';`   10. `xValue /= yValue;`
11. `xValue = number;`   12. `number = yValue;`
13. `xValue = yValue++;`   14. `number += number++;`

For Exercises 15–27, assume that the following declarations have been made:

```
int int1 = 16, int2 = 10, int3;
double real1 = 4.0, real2 = 6.0, real3 = 8.0, xValue;
```

Find the value assigned to the given variable or indicate why the statement is not valid.

15. `xValue = (real1 + real2) * real2;`
16. `xValue =(real2 + real1 / real3) * 2;`
17. `xValue = int1 / int2 + 5;`
18. `int3 = int1 / int2 + 5;`

19. `xValue = Math.pow(int2, 2) / Math.pow(int1, 2);`

20. `int3 = Math.pow(int2, 2) / Math.pow(int1, 2);`

21. `real1 = 2;`

22. `real1 = "1.2E3";`

23. `int1 = int1 + 2;`

24. `int1 |= int1;`

25. `int1 &= 24;`

26. `int1 <<= 2;`

27. `int3 = Math.ceil(Math.pow(int1 % int2, 2) / real3);`

For each of Exercises 28–32, write an assignment statement that changes the value of the integer variable `number` by the specified amount.

28. Increment `number` by 77.

29. Decrement `number` by 3.

30. Increment `number` by twice its value.

31. Add the rightmost digit of `number` to `number`.

32. Decrement `number` by the integer part of the real value `xValue`.

For each of Exercises 33–38, write a Java assignment statement that calculates the given expression and assigns the result to the specified variable. Assume that all variables are of type `double`, except where otherwise noted.

33. `rate` times `time` to `distance`

34. `xValue` incremented by an amount `deltaX` to `xValue`

35. $$\dfrac{1}{\dfrac{1}{res1} + \dfrac{1}{res2} + \dfrac{1}{res3}} \quad \text{to } \texttt{resistance}$$

36. Area of a triangle with a given `base` and `height` (one-half base times height) to `area`

37. The last three digits of the integer `stockNumber` with a decimal point before the last two digits to `price` (e.g., if `stockNumber` is 1758316, `price` is assigned the value 3.16)

38. `tax` rounded to the nearest dollar to `tax`.

3.5   JAVA'S `boolean` TYPE AND EXPRESSIONS

In the mid-1800s, a self-taught British mathematician George Boole (1815–1864) developed an algebra for building expressions representing logic. Such logical expressions produce either the value `true` or the value `false`, and have come to be known as **boolean expressions.** They are also often called **conditions,** and we will use the two terms interchangeably.

Every modern programming language provides some means for constructing boolean expressions, and in this section we consider how they are constructed in Java.

We look first at simple boolean expressions and then at how logical operators can be used to combine boolean expressions to form compound boolean expressions.

The `boolean` Primitive Type

In Java, the primitive type `boolean` has two literals: `false` and `true`. A boolean expression is thus a sequence of operands and operators that combine to produce one of the boolean values, `false` or `true`.

The operators that are used in the simplest boolean expressions test some *relationship* between their operands. For example, the boolean expression

```
mass >= 0
```

which compares the (variable) operand `mass` and the (literal) operand `0` using the greater-than-or-equal-to relationship, produces the value `true` if the value of `mass` is nonnegative, but produces the value `false` if the value of `mass` is negative. Similarly, the Java boolean expression

```
count == 5
```

tests the equality relationship between the operands `count` and `5`, producing the value `true` if the value of `count` is 5 and the value `false` otherwise.

WATCH

OUT

Note: Be sure to use the == operator for equality comparisons, and not = (assignment). Trying to compare two values using the = operator will produce a compiler error.

Operators like `>=` and `==` that test a relationship between two operands are called **relational operators,** and they are used in boolean expressions of the form

```
expression₁ RelationalOperator expression₂
```

where *expression₁* and *expression₂* are two compatible expressions, and the *RelationalOperator* may be any of the following:

Relational operator	Relation tested
<	Is less than
>	Is greater than
==	Is equal to
!=	Is not equal to
<=	Is less than or equal to
>=	Is greater than or equal to

These relational operators can be applied to operands of any of the primitive types: `char`, `int`, `float`, `double`, and so on. For example, if `x`, `a`, `b`, and `c` are of type `double`, and `number` and `demoninator` are of type `int`, then the following are valid boolean expressions formed using these relational operators:

```
x < 5.2

b * b >= 4.0 * a * c

number == 500

denominator != 0
```

Compound `boolean` Expressions

Many relationships are too complicated to be expressed using only the relational operators. For example, a typical test score is governed by the mathematical relationship

$$0 \le \text{test score} \le 100$$

WATCH

OUT

which is true if the test score is between 0 and 100 (inclusive), and is false otherwise. However, this relationship *cannot* be correctly represented in Java by the expression

```
0 <= testScore <= 100
```

The reason is that these relational operators are left-associative, and so the preceding expression is processed by the Java compiler as

```
(0 <= testScore) <= 100
```

The Java compiler determines that the subexpression

```
(0 <= testScore)
```

produces a `boolean` value, which it then tries to use as an operand for the second `<=` operator, giving the expression

```
(aBooleanValue <= 100)
```

At this point, the compiler generates an error, because `boolean` and `int` values are not compatible and thus cannot be compared (even with a cast).

To avoid this difficulty, we must rewrite the mathematical expression

$$0 \le \text{test score} \le 100$$

in a different form:

$$(0 \le \text{test score}) \text{ and } (\text{test score} \le 100)$$

This expression can be correctly coded in Java, because Java provides **logical operators** that combine boolean expressions to form **compound boolean expressions.** These operators are defined as follows:

Logical operator	Logical expression	Name of operation	Description
!	! p	*Not* *(Negation)*	! p is false if p is true; ! p is true if p is false.
&&	p && q	*And* *(Conjunction)*	p && q is true if both p and q are true; it is false otherwise.
||	p || q	*Or* *(Disjunction)*	p || q is true if either p or q or both are true; it is false otherwise.

These definitions are summarized by the following **truth tables,** which display all possible values for two conditions p and q and the corresponding values of the logical expression:

p	$!p$
true	false
false	true

p	q	p && q	p || q
true	true	true	true
true	false	false	true
false	true	false	true
false	false	false	false

We can thus use the && operator to represent the mathematical expression

$$(0 \le \text{test score}) \text{ and } (\text{test score} \le 100)$$

by the compound boolean expression

```
(0 <= testScore) && (testScore <= 100)
```

This expression will correctly evaluate the relationship between 0, testScore, and 100, for all possible values of testScore.

Short-Circuit Evaluation

An important feature of the && and || operators is that they do not always evaluate their second operand. For example, if p is false, then the condition

```
p && q
```

is false, regardless of the value of q, and so Java does not evaluate q. Similarly, if p is true, then the condition

```
p || q
```

is true, regardless of the value of q, and so Java does not evaluate q. This approach is called **short-circuit evaluation,** and has two important benefits:

1. One boolean expression can be used to *guard* a potentially unsafe operation in a second boolean expression.
2. A considerable amount of time can be saved in the evaluation of complex conditions.

As an illustration of the first benefit, consider the boolean expression

```
(n != 0) && (x < 1.0 / n)
```

No division-by-zero error can occur in this expression, because if n is 0, then the first expression

```
(n != 0)
```

is false and the second expression

```
(x < 1.0 / n)
```

is not evaluated. Similarly, no division-by-zero error will occur in evaluating the condition

```
(n == 0) || (x >= 1.0 / n)
```

because if n is 0, the first expression

```
(n == 0)
```

is true and the second expression is not evaluated.

Operator Precedence. A boolean expression that contains an assortment of arithmetic operators, relational operators, and logical operators is evaluated using the following precedence (or priority) and associativity rules:[8]

Operator	Priority	Associativity
()	10	Left
!, ++, −−, − (unary), + (unary) (*type-cast*), new	9	Right
/, *, %	8	Left
+, −	7	Left
<, >, <=, >=	6	Left
==, !=	5	Left
&&	4	Left
||	3	Left
=, +=, *=, . . .	1	Right

An operator with a higher priority number has higher precedence and is applied before an operator with a lower priority number.

To illustrate, consider the boolean expression

```
x - (y + z) > a / b + c
```

where x, y, z, a, b, and c are all of type double. Because parentheses have the highest priority, the subexpression (y + z) is evaluated first, producing an intermediate real value $r1$ and the expression

```
x - r1 > a / b + c
```

Of the remaining operators, / has the highest priority, so it is applied next producing some intermediate value $r2$:

```
x - r1 > r2 + c
```

---

[8] The "gap" between priorities 1 and 3 in this table is because the table lists only the Java operators we have seen thus far. A complete table is given in Appendix C.

In the resulting expression, − and + have the highest priority, so these operators are applied next, from left to right (because of left-associativity). The − operator produces an intermediate value `r3`,

```
r3 > r2 + c
```

and the + operator produces some other intermediate value `r4`:

```
r3 > r4
```

Finally, the > operator is used to compare the last two (real) intermediate values and produces the value of the expression (`false` or `true`).

Because it is difficult to remember so many precedence levels, it is helpful to remember the following:

- ❑ Parenthesized subexpressions are evaluated first.
- ❑ `*`, `/`, and `%` have higher precedence than + and −.
- ❑ `!` is the highest-precedence logical operator.
- ❑ Every relational operator has higher precedence than the logical operators `&&` and `||`.
- ❑ Numeric operators have higher precedence than relational and/or logical operators (except `!`).
- ❑ Use parentheses for all the other operators to clarify the order in which they are applied.

The Boolean Class

The `java.lang` package contains a `Boolean` wrapper class that provides a few additional methods for manipulating boolean values. We will not be using them, however, and so will not describe them here. Details about them can be found in the Java API documentation.

✔ Quick Quiz 3.5

1. The two `boolean` literals are _____ and _____.
2. List the six relational operators.
3. List the three logical operators.

For Questions 4–8, assume that p, q, and r are boolean expressions with the values `true`, `true`, and `false`, respectively. Find the value of each boolean expression.

4. `p && !q`
5. `p && q || !r`
6. `p && !(q || r)`
7. `!p && q`
8. `p || q && r`

Questions 9–16 assume that `number`, `count`, and `sum` are integer variables with values 3, 4, and 5, respectively, and that `check` is of type `boolean`.

In Questions 9–13, find the value of each boolean expression, or indicate why it is not valid.

9. `sum — number <= 4`

10. `number*number + count*count == sum*sum`

11. `number < count || count < sum`

12. `0 <= count <= 5`

13. `(number + 1 < sum) && !(count + 1 < sum)`

In Questions 14–16, Find the value assigned to `check` or indicate why the statement is not valid.

14. `check = number == 3;`

15. `check = (1 < sum < 10);`

16. `check = (count > 0) || (count > 10);`

17. Write a boolean expression to express that x is nonzero.

18. Write a boolean expression to express that x is strictly between −10 and 10.

19. Write a boolean expression to express that both x and y are positive or both x and y are negative.

✍ EXERCISES 3.5

For Exercises 1–10, assume that m and n are integer variables with the values −5 and 8, respectively, and that x, y, and z are real variables with the values −3.56, 0.0, and 44.7, respectively. Find the value of the boolean expression.

1. `m <= n`

2. `2 * Math.abs(m) <= 8`

3. `x * x < Math.sqrt(z)`

4. `(int) z == (6 * n − 4)`

5. `(x <= y) && (y <= z)`

6. `!(x < y)`

7. `!((m <= n) && (x + z > y))`

8. `!(m <= n) || !(x + z > y)`

9. `!((m <= n) || (x + z > y))`

10. `!((m > n) && !(x < z))`

For Exercises 11–16, use truth tables to display the value of the boolean expression for all possible (boolean) values of a, b, and c:

11. `a || !b`

12. `!(a && b)`

13. `!a || !b`

14. `(a && b) || c`

15. `a && (b || c)`

16. `(a && b) || (a && c)`

For Exercises 17–25, write Java boolean expressions to express the following conditions:

17. x is greater that 3

18. y is strictly between 2 and 5

19. r is negative and z is positive

20. Both `alpha` and `beta` are positive

21. `alpha` and `beta` have the same sign (both are negative or both are positive)

22. $-5 < x < 5$

23. `a` is less than 6 or is greater than 10

24. `p` is equal to `q`, which is equal to `r`

25. `x` is less than 3, or `y` is less than 3, but not both

Exercises 26–28 assume that `a`, `b`, and `c` are boolean values.

26. Write a boolean expression that is true if and only if `a` and `b` are true and `c` is false.

27. Write a boolean expression that is true if and only if `a` is true and at least one of `b` or `c` is true.

28. Write a boolean expression that is true if and only if exactly one of `a` and `b` is true.

3.6   JAVA'S CHARACTER-RELATED TYPES AND EXPRESSIONS

Java provides four character-related types:

- ❑ `char`, the primitive type for representing single characters
- ❑ `Character`, a class for representing single characters
- ❑ `String`, a class for representing constant sequences of characters
- ❑ `StringBuffer`, a class for representing variable sequences of characters

In this section, we introduce the first three types. A more detailed discussion of the `String` and `StringBuffer` classes will be given later.

The `char` Primitive Type

As we have seen, Java uses the type `char` to represent *individual characters*. This includes the uppercase letters `A` through `Z`; lowercase `a` through `z`; common punctuation symbols such as the semicolon (`;`), comma (`,`), and period (`.`); and special symbols such as +, =, and >.

We have also seen that `char` *literals* are usually written in Java as single character symbols enclosed in apostrophes (or single quotes). For example,

```
'A', '@', '3', '+'
```

are all examples of Java `char` literals. The apostrophe is thus used to **delimit** (i.e., surround and distinguish) `char` literals from other items in a Java program.

Using an apostrophe as a delimiter raises the question, *What is the character literal for an apostrophe?* A similar question arises for characters such as the newline character, for which there is no corresponding symbol. For such characters that have a special purpose and cannot be described using the normal approach, Java provides **escape sequences,** comprised of a backslash and another character. For example, the character literal for an apostrophe can be written as

```
'\''
```

and the newline character by

```
'\n'
```

Table 3.6 lists the escape sequences provided in Java.

TABLE 3.6   JAVA CHARACTER ESCAPE SEQUENCES

Character	Escape sequence
Backspace (BS)	\b
Horizontal tab (HT)	\t
Newline or Linefeed (NL or LF)	\n
Carriage return (CR)	\r
Double quote (")	\"
Single quote (')	\'
Backslash (\)	\\
With Unicode hexadecimal code hhhh	\uhhhh

As the last escape sequence indicates, Java represents characters using the **Unicode** encoding scheme (see below) and any Unicode character can be generated from its hexadecimal code.[9]

`char` **Expressions.** Compared to the other primitive types, there are very few predefined operations for objects of type `char`. Such objects can be defined and initialized in a manner similar to `int` and `double` objects; for example,

```
final char MIDDLE_INITIAL = 'C';

char       direction = 'N';       // N, S, E or W
```

Character values can be assigned in the usual manner,

```
direction = 'E';
```

but there are no shortcuts for `char` assignments comparable to those for numbers.

Values of type `char` can be compared using the relational operators. Such comparisons are performed using the Unicode numeric codes, so the expression

```
'A' < 'B'
```

produces `true` because the Unicode value for A (65) is less than the Unicode value for B (66). Similarly, the expression

```
'a' < 'b'
```

produces the value `true`, because the Unicode value for a (97) is less than the Unicode value for b (98). The boolean expression

```
'a' < 'A'
```

---

[9] The most up-to-date list of Unicode hexadecimal codes is available at www.unicode.org.

is `false`, because the Unicode value for a (97) is not less than the Unicode value for A (65).

Compound boolean expressions can also be used to compare non-numeric values. For example, suppose we are solving a problem whose solution requires that a character variable *letter* must have an uppercase value. Such a condition might be expressed in Java using a compound boolean expression:

```
('A' <= letter) && (letter <= 'Z')
```

The `Character` Reference Type

In addition to the `char` primitive type, Java also provides the `Character` wrapper class. This class provides a variety of convenient operations, some of which are given in Table 3.7. (See Java's API documentation for the `Character` class for the complete list.) The *receiver* in the second column referred to by some of the methods is the `Character` object to which the message is sent.

REFERENCE

TABLE 3.7   SOME `Character` METHODS

Method	Description
`Character(`*ch*`)`	Construct a `Character` object equivalent to *ch* of type `char`
`charValue()`	Return the `char` value equivalent to the receiver
`toString()`	Return a `String` equivalent to the receiver
Static Methods	
`digit(`*ch*`, `*b*`)`	Return the `int` for `char` symbol *ch* in base *b*
`forDigit(`*i*`, `*b*`)`	Return the `char` symbol for `int` *i* in base *b*
`getNumericValue(`*ch*`)`	Return the Unicode `int` for `char` *ch*
	Return true if `char` *ch* is:
`isDigit(`*ch*`)`	a digit character
`isISOControl(char `*ch*`)`	a control character
`isLetter(`*ch*`)`	a letter character
`isLowerCase(`*ch*`)`	a lowercase letter
`isUpperCase(`*ch*`)`	an uppercase letter
`isWhitespace(`*ch*`)`	a white-space character (space, tab, line feed, carriage return, etc.)
	and return false otherwise
	Return the
`toLowerCase(`*ch*`)`	lowercase equivalent of `char` *ch* if *ch* is uppercase; otherwise return *ch*
`toUpperCase(`*ch*`)`	uppercase equivalent of `char` *ch* if *ch* is lowercase; otherwise return *ch*

As this table shows, the `Character` class provides several useful methods, ranging from `boolean` methods to test a `char` value (e.g., `isLetter()`, `isWhiteSpace()`, etc.) to methods that convert within the `char` type (e.g., `toLowerCase()`, `toUpperCase()`), to methods that convert between the `char` type and other types (e.g., `getNumericValue()`). Notice that although the `getNumericValue()` method serves to convert a char to its corresponding integer representation,

```
char ch = theKeyboard.readChar();
int itsCode = Character.getNumericValue(ch);
```

a cast must be used to convert an `int` to the corresponding `char` it represents:

```
int i = theKeyboard.readInt();
char ch = (char) i;
```

If the `int` to be converted is a literal, then the Unicode escape sequence can be used:

```
final char CAPITAL_A = '\u0041'; // hex for decimal 65
```

The `String` Reference Type

The `String` type plays a very important role in Java, in that most input and output are (by default) accomplished through `String` values. As a result, it is important to become familiar with Java's `String` class and its capabilities. We introduce the `String` type here, and will study it in more detail in subsequent chapters.

String Literals. We have seen that the `String` reference type allows a sequence of characters to be represented as a single object. As such, `String` literals consist of zero or more characters (including `char` escape sequences) surrounded by double-quotes. The following are thus valid `String` literals:

```
""

"123"

"\n\tEnter the mass: "

"\u0048\u0069\u0021"
```

The `String` class (and its cousin, the `StringBuffer` class) are unusual among Java's reference types, in three ways:

1. The Java compiler provides built-in support for `String` literals.
2. String variables can be initialized in the same way as the primitive types.
3. The Java compiler supports the + operator for operating on `String` values.

As we saw earlier, most reference type values must be constructed using the `new` operator and a *constructor* method. We can use this syntax to initialize a `String` variable,

```
String firstName = new String("Jane");
```

but Java also allows a `String` to be initialized directly from a `String` literal:

```
String lastName = "Doe";
```

String Operations. Java's `String` class provides a rich set of operations for manipulating `String` values. Perhaps the most frequently used is the `String` **concatenation (+) operator** which, given two `String` operands, produces a `String` consisting of the left operand followed by the right operand. For example, given the declarations:

```
String state = "Michigan",
       greatLake;
```

the assignment statement

```
greatLake = "Lake " + state;
```

concatenates the `String` literal "Lake " and the `String` associated with `String` variable `state`, and stores a reference to the resulting `String` in the `String` variable `greatLake`, which we can picture as follows:

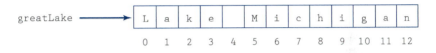

If one of the operands of the + operator is a `String` and the other is one of the primitive types, then the non-`String` operand is automatically converted to a `String` and + is treated as the concatenation operator. Thus, the statements

```
int two = 2;
String robot = "R" + two + "D" + two;
```

build a `String` referred to by `robot` as follows:

As these pictures indicate, a `String` is an **indexed** variable, which means that the individual characters within the `String` can be accessed via an integer index. In Java, `String`'s `charAt()` method is used for this. The first character in a `String` always has index 0, so the expression

```
greatLake.charAt(0)
```

produces the `char` value `'L'`, the expression

```
greatLake.charAt(1)
```

produces the `char` value `'a'`, and so on.

In addition to the concatenation operator and `charAt()` method, the Java `String` class provides many `String`-related methods. Because the class contains too many methods to list here—there are eleven different constructor methods alone—Table 3.8 provides a sample of what is available. (See the `String` class API

TABLE 3.8   String CLASS METHODS

Method	Description
String(*str*)	Construct a String object that is a copy of String *str*
charAt(*i*)	Return the char at index *i* in the receiver
compareTo(*strobj*)	Return zero, a negative value, or a positive value according to whether the receiver is equal to, less than, or greater than *strobj* (of type String or Object)
compareToIgnoreCase(*str*)	Compare the receiver to String *str* (as above) ignoring uppercase/lowercase differences
endsWith(*str*)	Return true if the receiver ends with String *str* and false otherwise
equals(*obj*)	Return true if the receiver and object *obj* have the same characters and false otherwise
equalsIgnoreCase(*str*)	Compare the receiver and String *str* (as above) ignoring uppercase/lowercase differences
indexOf(*chstr*) indexOf(*chstr, startAt*)	Return the index of *chstr* (of type char or String) within the receiver; in the second form, the search begins at index *startAt*
lastIndexOf(*chstr*) lastIndexOf(*chstr, startAt*)	Like indexOf(), but finds the index of the last occurrence of *chstr*
length()	Return the number of characters in the receiver
replace(*old, new*)	Return a copy of the receiver, in which all occurrences of char *old* are replaced by char *new*
startsWith(*str*)	Return true if the receiver begins with String *str* and false otherwise
substring(*start, stop*)	Return the substring of the receiver beginning at int index start and ending at int index stop

toLowerCase()
 	
toUpperCase()
	Return a copy of the receiver in which:
	    all uppercase letters are converted to lowercase
	    all lowercase letters are converted to uppercase

Static Methods	
valueOf(*val*)	Return the String representation of *val* (of type boolean, char, int, or double)

documentation for the complete list.) The *receiver* in the second column referred to by some of the methods is the `String` object to which the message is sent.

✔ Quick Quiz 3.6

1. A `char` literal must be enclosed in _____.
2. A `String` literal must be enclosed in _____.
3. `'\n'` is an example of a(n) _____ sequence.
4. (True or false) `char x = '1/2';` is a valid initialization declaration.
5. (True or false) `char x = '\u0012';` is a valid initialization declaration.
6. (True or false) `String x = "1a2b";` is a valid initialization declaration.
7. (True or false) `String x = new String("1a2b");` is a valid initialization declaration.
8. Write a boolean expression to test the condition that the value of the `char` variable `c` is one of the digits `'0'`, `'1'`, `'2'`, . . . `'9'`.
9. Repeat Question 8 but use a method from the `Character` class.
10. Write a statement that checks if the value of the `char` variable `c` is an uppercase letter, and if so, converts it to lower case.

In Questions 11–16, assume that `s1`, `s2`, and `s3` are of type `String` and have values `"list"`, `"en"`, and `"dear"`, respectively. Find the value of the given expression

11. `s1 + s2`	12. `s2 + s1`	13. `s1 + s2 + " " + s3`
14. `s1.charAt(2)`	15. `s2.charAt(0)`	16. `s1.length()`

3.7 GRAPHICAL/INTERNET JAVA: EINSTEIN'S EQUATION

In Section 3.1, we built a Java application that, given a quantity of mass, used Einstein's equation to compute the quantity of energy that could be obtained from it. In this section, we will rewrite this program to obtain the (numeric) quantity of mass using a Java input dialog and to display the output using a Java message dialog.

GUI: An Einstein Calculator

OBJECT-CENTERED DESIGN.

Our object-centered design for this problem is quite similar to what we derived in Section 3.1. The main differences are that we are using dialog widgets to perform the input and output. Since an input dialog widget only returns a `String` and a message dialog only displays a `String`, the program will have to convert between the `String` and `double` types.

BEHAVIOR.   The program should display an input dialog box that prompts the user for the quantity of matter (i.e., its mass). The user will enter a real value in the dialog box's text field. The program should read this quantity of matter as a `String`, convert it to a real number, and then use Einstein's equation to compute the energy that can be produced by that quantity of matter. It should then build a `String` consisting of the energy and a descriptive label, and then display this string using a message dialog box. When the user clicks the *Ok* button on the message dialog box, the program should terminate.

Since we are building a GUI, we next sketch its different appearances, linked by the events that cause it to change from one appearance to another. The following transition diagram pictures the program's behavior:

```
Mass-to-Energy Conversion

?   To computer energy,
please enter mass in
kilograms

┌──────────────────────────┐
│                          │
└──────────────────────────┘

        ┌──────┐  ┌────────┐
        │  OK  │  │ Cancel │
        └──────┘  └────────┘
```

          │
          ▼ User enters mass *m*

```
Mass-to-Energy Conversion

?   To computer energy,
please enter mass in
kilograms

┌──────────────────────────┐
│ m                        │
└──────────────────────────┘

        ┌──────┐  ┌────────┐
        │  OK  │  │ Cancel │
        └──────┘  └────────┘
```

          │
          ▼ User presses *Enter* key or clicks *OK*;
             (program computes energy e)

```
Mass-to-Energy Conversion

m kgs of nass will release
e kilojoules of energy

        ┌──────┐
        │  OK  │
        └──────┘
```

OBJECTS. From our behavioral description, we can identify the following objects:

Description of problem's object	Type	Kind	Name
The program	?		—
An input dialog	—	?	none
Dialog widget titles	String	constant	*TITLE*
Prompt	String	constant	none

Dialog box's text field	—	—	none
Quantity of matter as a `String`	`String`	varying	*massString*
Real number	`double`	varying	*mass*
Quantity of energy	`double`	varying	*energy*
Descriptive label	`String`	constant	none
Energy and label as a `String`	`String`	varying	*energyString*
Message dialog	—	—	none
OK and *Cancel* buttons	—	—	none

No names of types were given for the input and message dialogs or for the buttons because, as we saw in the GUI example in Section 2.5, these are created automatically by methods of the `JOptionPane` class

OPERATIONS AND ALGORITHM. From our behavioral description, we have the following operations:

1. Display an input box
2. Read a `String` *(massString)* from the input box
3. Convert a `String` *(massString)* to a `double` *(mass)*
4. Compute *energy* from *mass*
5. Convert a `double` *(energy)* to a `String` *(energyString)*
6. Display a message box showing *energyString*
7. Terminate the program when the user presses its *OK* button

Step 1 is provided for us by the `showInputDialog()` method from the `JOption-Pane` class. Since it is a static method, we can accomplish this operation by sending a message directly to the `JOptionPane` class. This method returns the `String` entered by the user, providing Step 2 for us. For Step 3, the Java API documentation for the `Double` class describes a class method named `parseDouble()` that converts a `String` to a `double`. Step 4 is exactly as it was before in our earlier version of this program. To perform Step 5, we could use the `Double` class method `toString()`, but since we must concatenate a descriptive label anyway, we will let the concatenation operator perform the conversion for us. Step 6 can be performed using the `showMessageDialog()` method, and Step 7 can be accomplished using the `System` class method `exit()`.

The preceding operations are already arranged in the order they are to be performed, so they actually comprise an algorithm for our problem. Thus we can proceed directly to encoding it in Java.

Coding, Execution, and Testing. Figure 3.2 shows a Java implementation of our algorithm.

FIGURE 3.2   GUI MASS-TO-ENERGY CONVERSION

```
/* GUIEinsteinConverter1.java computes energy from a given mass using
 *  dialog boxes and Einstein's mass-to-energy conversion equation.
 *
 * Input:        The mass (in kilograms) being converted to energy
 * Precondition: mass >= 0
 * Output:       The energy (in kilojoules) corresponding to mass
 */

import javax.swing.*;               // JOptionPane

class GUIEinsteinConverter1 extends Object
{
  public static void main(String [] args)
  {
    final String TITLE = "Mass-to-Energy Conversion"; // title for dialogs
    final double SPEED_OF_LIGHT = 2.997925e8;         // meters/sec

    String massString = JOptionPane.showInputDialog(null,
                            "To compute energy, enter mass in kilograms",
                            TITLE,
                            JOptionPane.QUESTION_MESSAGE);

    double mass = Double.parseDouble(massString);
    double energy = mass * Math.pow(SPEED_OF_LIGHT, 2.0);
    String energyString = mass + " kg of matter will release "
                        + energy + " kilojoules of energy.";
    JOptionPane.showMessageDialog(null,
                            energyString,
                            TITLE,
                            JOptionPane.PLAIN_MESSAGE);
    System.exit(1);
  }
}
```

Sample run:

Applet: An Einstein Calculator

In Chapter 1 we considered two kinds of Java programs, **applications** and **applets,** and described the differences between them. An application is a standalone program that can be executed by a Java interpreter. In contrast, an applet is a small program that can be loaded as part of a World Wide Web page and executed by a web browser. We have given two application programs that solved the Einstein-converter problem: a text-based version in Section 3.1 and a GUI version in this section. We look now at an applet version of this program.

Figure 3.3 gives our applet version of the program from Figure 3.2. The main changes are highlighted in color.

FIGURE 3.3   GUI MASS-TO-ENERGY CONVERSION—APPLET VERSION

```
/* GUIEinsteinConverter2.java computes energy from a given mass using
 *   dialog boxes and Einstein's mass-to-energy conversion equation.
 *
 * Input:        The mass (in kilograms) being converted to energy
 * Precondition: mass >= 0
 * Output:       The energy (in kilojoules) corresponding to mass
 */

import javax.swing.*;             // JOptionPane, JApplet

public class GUIEinsteinConverter2 extends JApplet
{
  public void init()
  {
    final String TITLE = "Mass-to-Energy Conversion"; // title for dialogs
    final double SPEED_OF_LIGHT = 2.997925e8;         // meters/sec

    String massString = JOptionPane.showInputDialog(null,
                          "To compute energy, enter mass in kilograms",
                          TITLE,
                          JOptionPane.QUESTION_MESSAGE);

    double mass = Double.parseDouble(massString);
    double energy = mass * Math.pow(SPEED_OF_LIGHT, 2.0);
    String energyString = mass + " kg of matter will release\n"
                          + energy + " kilojoules of energy.";
    JOptionPane.showMessageDialog(null,
                          energyString,
                          TITLE,
                          JOptionPane.PLAIN_MESSAGE);

  }
}
```

Sample run:

As we can see, this applet version is very similar to the GUI application in Figure 3.2., but there are a few significant differences. One is that in the application, the `GUIEinsteinConverter1` class extends the `Object` class, but the `GUIEinsteinConverter2` class in the applet version extends Java's `JApplet` class.[10] Also, here the `GUIEinsteinConverter2` class is declared to be `public`. This makes the class accessible to the other classes and in particular, makes it possible for a web browser to execute the applet. The `JApplet` class is a public class, and all applets that extend it must also be public.

The other difference is that the applet has no `main()` method. As we noted in the introduction to applets in Section 1.3, this is because the `JApplet` class contains several other methods that are called instead of `main()` to handle the execution of an applet program. The first of these is the `init()` method. This is where execution of the applet begin and replaces, therefore, the `main()` method of an application.

Notice also that unlike the `main()` method, `init()` is not declared with the `static` keyword. As we saw in Section 3.3, this makes `init()` an instance method rather than a static (or class) method. Because the `init()` method inherited from `JApplet` is an instance method and we are overriding it here, this definition of `init()` also must be.

Finally, we have removed the `System.exit(1)` statement, because it is not needed in the applet version of the program.

The windows shown in the sample run of this applet (and for all or our applet examples in thie text) were produced by using Java's appletviewer utility. Applet frames produced by a web browser may have a slightly different appearance such as the following:[11]

[10] In our description of the API in Section 2.4, we saw that `JApplet` extends `Applet`, which extends `Panel`, which extends `Container`, which extends `Component`, which extends `Object`, which means that `JApplet` extends `Object` indirectly, and therefore, so also does the `GUIConverter2` class in Figure 3.3.
[11] As we noted in the preceding chapter, at the time this text was prepared, some web browsers did not fully support applets prepared with Swing elements and may require downloading a special Java plug-in.

The message `Warning: Applet Window` is intended to call the user's attention to the fact that this frame has been generated by an applet running within a web browser so that the user will not mistake the applet window for another kind of software window. Unfortunately, the potential exists for an unscrupulous programmer to write an applet that mimics another software program in the hope of tricking the user into entering information (e.g. the user's password) that could be used for ill purposes. This type of software hazard is called a *Trojan Horse*. (See the section *Part of the Picture: Ethics and Computing* in the preceding chapter for more information about Trojan horses and other malicious software.)

CHAPTER SUMMARY

KEY TERMS AND NOTES

applet	left-associative
application	modulus
assignment operator (=)	`new` operation
bitwise operations	`null` value
cast	octal
class constant	operator precedence
class method	operator priority
compatible (or type-compatible)	`parseInt()` method
compound `boolean` expression	primitive expression
concatenation (+) operator	primitive types
condition	promotion
constructor	reference types
decrement operator (−−)	right-associative
delimit	sending a message
escape sequence	short-circuit evaluation
fixed-point	static constant
floating-point	static method
handle	Trojan horse
hexadecimal	type-cast
increment operator (++)	unary operator
indexed variable	wrapper class
instance method	

- ◎ The compiler uses information about the type of a variable to determine how much memory to allocate for the variable and to check that it is being used correctly,
- ◎ Creating a class creates a new type whose name is the name of the class.
- ◎ The `new` operation is used to create reference-type variables.
- ◎ Classes have special methods called constructors used to construct objects.

◎ An expression of the form new `ClassName(arguments)` constructs a `ClassName` object, using the specified `arguments` to initialize it, and returns the address of this object. Storing this address in a variable of type `ClassName` as in

```
ClassName variable = new ClassName(arguments);
```

makes `variable` a handle for this object by which it can be accessed and used.

◎ Integer literals that begin with 0 are interpreted as hexadecimal (base-16) integers if they begin with 0x and otherwise as octal (base-8) values.

◎ In Java, real values can be represented in fixed-point notation—*m.n*—or in floating-point notation—*xEn* or *xen* where *x* is in fixed-point form and *n* is an integer.

◎ All real literals are treated as of type `double`.

◎ If *a* and *b* are both integers with *b* ≠ 0, *a* / *b* gives the integer quotient when *a* is divided by *b*, and *a* % *b* gives the remainder. If *a* or *b* is real, real division is used for *a* / *b* and *a* % *b* results in an error.

◎ In an expression, *, /, and % have higher precedence than (i.e., are applied before) + and −.

◎ Associativity determines whether equal-priority operators are applied from left to right or from right to left.

◎ Parentheses can be used to change the usual order of evaluation in an expression.

◎ *Static* (or *class*) methods are invoked by sending a message to a *class; instance methods* are invoked by sending a message to an *object* (i.e., an *instance* of a class).

◎ Inside a class definition, a method not preceded by the keyword `static` is an instance method; a method preceded by `static` is a static (or class) method.

◎ Java's `Math` class (in its `java.lang` package) contains constants and methods for several of the familiar mathematical constants and functions.

◎ `Float`, `Double`, `Byte`, `Short`, `Integer`, `Long`, and `Character` are wrapper classes that provide added capabilities for the corresponding primitive types; one important use is for type conversion. For example, two useful type-conversion methods in the `Integer` class are `toString()` and `parseInt()`.

◎ Classes `BigInteger` and `BigDecimal` in the `java.math` package are useful for processing values too large to be represented by the `long` and `double` types, respectively,

◎ In numeric expressions that contain mixed types, narrower numeric values are promoted automatically to wider ones and integers to reals.

◎ Type-casting can be used to convert one numeric primitive type to another.

◎ An assignment statement is a replacement statement: a = b replaces the value of a with the value of b; b = a replaces the value of b with the value of a.

◎ Like other binary operators, the assignment operator = produces a value. In an assignment expression a = b, = is an operator with operands a and b. In addition to replacing the value of a with the value of b, it also produces this value as a result.

◎ A prefix increment expression ++*variable* increments the value of the variable by 1 and produces this new value as the result. A postfix increment expression *variable*++ increments the value of the variable by 1 but produces its original value as the result. Decrement expressions behave similarly.

◎ In an expression of the form a + b, where a or b is of type `String` and the other is of a primitive type, the non-`String` operand will be converted to type `String` and + treated as concatenation.

◎ For str of type String and i an integer, str.charAt(i) is the character in position i of str (counting from 0).

Documentation

REFERENCE ■ Operator Priorities:

Operator	Priority
( )	10
!, ++, − −, − (unary), + (unary) (*type-cast*), new	9
/, *, %	8
+, −	7
<, >, <=, >=	6
==, !=	5
&&	4
||	3
=, +=, *=, . . .	1

■ The following tables describe some of the more commonly used items in the Math, Integer, BigInteger, and Character classes. For Math, unless noted otherwise, the type of the arguments is double and the return type is the same as the argument type. See the Java API documentation for more complete descriptions of these classes along with the other wrapper classes Byte, Short, Long, Float, Decimal, and Boolean, and the class BigDecimal.

Math **CLASS**

Math.	Description
Static Constants	
E	The `double` value that best approximates the base (2.71828. . .) of natural logarithms
PI	The `double` value that best approximates the value of π (3.14159. . .), the ratio of a circle's circumference to its diameter
Static Methods	
abs(v)	Absolute value of v, which may be a `double`, `float`, `long`, or `int`
pow(x,y)	x raised to the power y
sqrt(x)	The square root of x
ceil(x)	Least `double` greater than or equal to x that is an integer
floor(x)	Greatest `double` less than or equal to x that is an integer
rint(x)	The nearest `int` to x
round(x)	The nearest `long` to x (of type `double`)
round(f)	The nearest `int` to f (of type `float`)
max(v,w)	Maximum of v, w, which may be `double`, `float`, `long`, or `int` values
min(v,w)	Minimum of v, w, which may be `double`, `float`, `long`, or `int` values
random()	A random number r such that $0 \le r < 1$
expx)	Exponential function e^x
log(x)	Natural logarithm of x
acos(x),asin(x),atan(x)	Inverse cosine, sine, tangent of x
atan2(x,y)	The θ component of the point (r, θ) in polar coordinates that corresponds to the point (y, x) in Cartesian coordinates
cos(x),sin(x),tan(x)	Cosine, sine, tangent of x
toDegrees(x)	Convert x from radians to degrees
toRadians(x)	Convert x from degrees to radians

Note: Only the `IEEERemainder()` method is omitted from this table. See the Java API documentation for information about it and for more details about the methods listed here.

Integer CLASS

Method	Description
`Integer(int value)`	Construct an `Integer` object equivalent to `value`
`Integer(String str)`	Construct an `Integer` object equivalent to `str`
`byte byteValue()`	Return the `byte` equivalent of the receiver
`int compareTo(Integer value)`	Return zero, a negative value, or a positive value according to whether the receiver is equal to, less than, or greater than `value`
`int compareTo(Object obj)`	Compare the receiver to `obj`—see preceding form
`static Integer decode(String str)`	Return an `Integer` object equivalent to `str`
`double doubleValue()`	Return the `double` equivalent of the receiver
`boolean equals(Object obj)`	Return `true` if the receiver equals `obj` and false otherwise
`float floatValue()`	Return the `float` equivalent of the receiver
`int intValue()`	Return the `int` equivalent of the receiver
`long longValue()`	Return the `long` equivalent of the receiver
`static int parseInt(String str)`	Return the `int` equivalent of `str`
`static int parseInt(String str, int b)`	Return the `int` equivalent of `str`, which is given in base `b`
`short shortValue()`	Return the `short` equivalent of the receiver
`static String toBinary String(int i)`	Return the base-2 representation of `i`
`static String toHexString(int i)`	Return the base-16 representation of `i`
`static String toOctalString(int i)`	Return the base-8 representation of `i`
`String toString()`	Return a `String` equivalent to the receiver
`static String toString(int i)`	Return a `String` equivalent to `i`
`static String toString(int i, int b)`	Return a `String` equivalent to `i` expressed in base `b`
`static Integer valueOf(String str)`	Return an `Integer` equivalent to `str`
`static Integer valueOf(String str, int b)`	Return an `Integer` equivalent of `str`, which is given in base `b`

BigInteger CLASS

Method	Description
BigInteger(String *str*)	Construct BigInteger object equivalent to *str*
BigInteger abs()	Return the BigInteger object that is the absolute value of the receiver
BigInteger add(BigInteger *value*)	Return a BigInteger object equivalent to the sum of the receiver and *value*
int compareTo(BigInteger *value*)	Return zero, a negative value, or a positive value according to whether the receiver is equal to, less than, or greater than *value*
BigInteger divide(BigInteger *value*)	Return a BigInteger object equivalent to the quotient of the receiver and *value*
double doubleValue()	Return the double equivalent of the receiver
boolean equals(Object *obj*)	Return true if and only if *obj* equals the receiver
float floatValue()	Return the float equivalent of the receiver
BigInteger gcd(BigInteger *value*)	Return a BigInteger object that is the greatest common divisor of abs(the receiver) and abs(*value*)
int intValue()	Return the int equivalent of the receiver
long longValue()	Return the long equivalent of the receiver
BigInteger max(BigInteger *value*)	Return a BigInteger object that is the maximum of the receiver and *value*
BigInteger min(BigInteger *value*)	Return a BigInteger object that is the minimum of the receiver and *value*
BigInteger mod(BigInteger *value*)	Return a BigInteger object equivalent to the receiver mod *value*
BigInteger multiply(BigInteger *value*)	Return a BigInteger object equivalent to the product of the receiver and *value*
BigInteger pow(int *exponent*)	Return a BigInteger object equivalent to the receiver raised to the power *exponent*
BigInteger remainder(BigInteger *value*)	Return a BigInteger object equivalent to the remainder when the receiver is divided by *value*
BigInteger subtract(BigInteger *value*)	Return a BigInteger object equivalent to the difference of the receiver and *value*
String toString()	Return the base-10 String representation of the receiver
static String toString(int *b*)	Return the base-*b* String representation of the receiver
static BigInteger valueOf(long *value*)	Return a BigInteger object equivalent to *value*

Character **CLASS**

Method	Description
Character(char *ch*)	Construct a Character object equivalent to *ch*
char charValue()	Return the char equivalent to the receiver
static int digit(char *ch*, int *b*)	Return the int for symbol *ch* in base *b*
static char forDigit(int *i*, int *b*)	Return the char symbol for *i* in base *b*
static int getNumericValue(char *ch*)	Return the Unicode int for *ch*
static boolean isDigit(char *ch*)	Return true if and only if *ch* is a digit character
static boolean isISOControl(char *ch*)	Return true if and only if *ch* is a control character
static boolean isLetter(char *ch*)	Return true if and only if *ch* is a letter character
static boolean isLowerCase(char *ch*)	Return true if and only if *ch* is a lowercase letter
static boolean isUpperCase(char *ch*)	Return true if and only if *ch* is a uppercase letter
static boolean isWhitespace(char *ch*)	Return true if and only if *ch* is a whitespace character (space, tab, line feed, carriage return, etc.)
static char toLowerCase(char *ch*)	Return the lowercase equivalent of *ch* (if *ch* is uppercase; otherwise return *ch*)
static char toUpperCase(char *ch*)	Return the uppercase equivalent of *ch* (if *ch* is lowercase; otherwise return *ch*)
String toString()	Return a String equivalent to the receiver

 PROGRAMMING POINTERS

In these sections at chapter ends we consider some aspects of program design and suggest guidelines for good programming style. We also point out some errors that may occur in writing Java programs.

PROGRAM STYLE AND DESIGN

1. In the examples in this text, we adopt certain stylistic guidelines for Java programs, and you should write your programs in a similar style. In this text we use the following; others are described in the Programming Pointers of subsequent chapters.

❏ *Put each statement of the program on a separate line.*

❏ *Use uppercase and lowercase letters in a way that contributes to program readability,* In this text we will use the following guidelines, which are suggested in the Java language specification:

—Class names are in lowercase, but capitalize the first letter of each word in them.

—Variables are in lowercase, but capitalize the first letter of each word after the first.

—Constants are all uppercase, with words in them usually separated by underscores.

—Method names are like variable names but are followed by parentheses.

❏ *Put each { and } on a separate line.*

❏ *Align each { and its corresponding }. Indent the statements enclosed by { and }.*

❏ *When a statement is continued from one line to another, indent the continued line(s).*

❏ *Align the identifiers in each constant and variable declaration, placing each on a separate line;* for example,

```
const double taxRate = 0.1963,
              interestRate = 0.185;

int empNumber;

double hours,
       rate,
       wages;
```

❏ *Insert blank lines between declarations and statements and between blocks of statements to make clear the structure of the program.*

❏ *Separate the operators and operands in an expression with spaces to make the expression easy to read.*

2. *Programs cannot be considered to be correct if they have not been tested.* Test all programs with data for which the results are known or can be checked by hand calculations. This, or course, does not guarantee their correctness, but it does increase one's confidence in them.

3. *Programs should be readable and understandable.*

❏ *Use meaningful identifiers. For example,*

```
wages = hours * rate;
```

is more meaningful than

```
w = h * r;
```

or

```
z7 = alpha * x;
```

Also, avoid "cute" identifiers, as in

```
baconBroughtHome = hoursWasted * pittance;
```

❑ *Use comments to describe the purpose of a program or other key program segments.* However, do not clutter the program with needless comments; for example, the comment in the statement

```
counter++;    // add 1 to counter
```

is not helpful and should not be used.

❑ *Label all output produced by a program.* For example,

```
theScreen.println("Employee #" + empNumber
               +" Wages = $" + wages);
```

produces more informative output than

```
theScreen.println(empNumber + " " + wages);
```

4. *Programs should be general and flexible.* They should solve a collection of problems rather than one specific problem. It should be relatively easy to modify a program to solve a related problem without changing much of the program. Using named constants instead of "magic numbers" as described in Section 2.2 is helpful in this regard.

WATCH

OUT

POTENTIAL PITFALLS

1. *Character constants must be enclosed in single quotes.* In particular,

❑ `String` *literals cannot be assigned to variables of type* `char`. For example, the declaration

```
char ch = "x";
```

is not valid.

2. *Values of type* `char` *are stored as their (integer) numeric codes.* This can be confusing, since strange things like the following are allowed in Java:

```
char letterGrade = 65;
```

This causes `letterGrade` to have exactly the same value as if it had been initialized to `'A'` (since 65 is the decimal Unicode representation of `'A'`). Such mixing of integer and character values within an expression should normally be avoided.

3. `String` *literals must be enclosed within double quotes.* If either the beginning or the ending double quote is missing, an error will result. Escape sequences, such as `\n`, are used to represent newlines, tabs, double quotes, single quotes, etc.

4. *The type of value stored in a variable should be the same as or promotable to the type of that variable.*

5. *If an integer value is to be stored in a real variable, Java will automatically promote the integer to a real type. If a real value is to be assigned to an integer variable, a type-cast should be used to convert it to an integer value (by truncating its decimal part) before assigning it.*

6. *Parentheses in expressions must be paired.* That is, for each left parenthesis, there must be exactly one matching right parenthesis that occurs later in the expression.

7. *Both real and integer division are denoted by* `/`; *which operation is performed is determined by the type of the operands.* Thus, `8 / 5 = 1`, but `8.0 / 5.0 = 1.6`.

8. *All multiplications must be indicated by* `*`. For example, `2*n` is valid, but `2n` is not.

9. *A semicolon must appear at the end of each programming statement.*

10. *Comments are enclosed within* `/*` *and* `*/` *or between* `//` *and the end of the line.* Be sure that:

❑ *Each beginning delimiter* `/*` *has a matching end delimiter* `*/`. Failure to use these in pairs can produce strange results. For example, in the program segment

```
/* Read employee's hours and rate
hours = theKeyboard.readDouble();
rate = theKeyboard.readDouble();
/* Calculate wages */
wages = hours * rate;
```

everything from "Read employee's hours . . ." through "Calculate wages," including the two input messages to `theKeyboard`, is a single comment. No values are read for `hours` and `rate`, and so they have the default value zero when the statement `wages = hours * rate;` is executed.

❑ *There is no space between the* `/` *and the* `*` *or between the two slashes.* Otherwise these pairs will not be considered to be comment delimiters.

11. *Every* `{` *must be matched by a* `}`. Failure to include either one produces a compilation error.

12. *All identifiers must be declared.* Attempting to use an identifier that has not been declared will produce a compilation error. In this connection, remember that:

❑ *Java distinguishes between uppercase and lowercase letters.* For example, declaring

```
double sumOfXValues;
```

and then later in the program writing

```
sumOfXvalues += x;
```

causes a compile-time error since the identifier `sumOfXvalues` has not been declared.

13. *Keywords, identifiers, and literals may not be broken at the end of a line, nor may they contain blanks (except, of course, a* `String` *literal may contain blanks).* Thus, the statement

```
String output = "The number of the current employee is: "
                + empNumber;
```

is valid, whereas the statement

```
String output = "The number of the current employee
                is: " + empNumber;
```

is not. If it is necessary to split a string over two lines, as in the second statement, the string should be split into two separate strings, each enclosed in double quotes, and concatenated:

```
String output = "The number of the current employee " +
                "is " + empNumber;
```

14. *Use parentheses in complex expressions to indicate those subexpressions that are to be evaluated first.* (See the preceding Documentation section for a table of the priorities of operators we have considered thus far.) There are so many operators in Java (the table lists only a few of them) that remembering their precedence levels is difficult. For this reason, we recommend using parentheses in complex expressions to specify clearly the order in which the operators are to be applied.

15. *When real quantities that are algebraically equal are compared with ==, the result may be a false boolean expression, because most real numbers are not stored exactly.* For example, even though the two real expressions x * (1/x) and 1.0 are algebraically equal, the boolean expression x * (1/x) == 1.0 may be false for some real numbers x. (See the Part of the Picture in Chapter 2 for more details.)

16. *A common error in writing boolean expressions is to use an assignment operator (=) when an equality operator (==) is intended.*

PROGRAMMING PROBLEMS

1. Write a program that reads two three-digit integers, and then calculates and displays their product and the quotient and the remainder that result when the first is divided by the second. The output should be formatted to appear as follows:

```
      739
  x    12
  --------
     8888
```

```
          61 R 7
      12) 739
```

2. Write a program to read the lengths of the three sides of a triangle, and to calculate and display its perimeter and its area. (The area can be calculated using *Hero's formula:* area $= \sqrt{s(s - a)(s - b)(s - c)}$ where *a, b,* and *c* are the three sides and *s* is one-half the perimeter.)

3. Write a program to read values for the coefficients *a, b,* and *c* of the quadratic equation $ax^2 + bx + c = 0$, and then find the two roots of this equation by using the quadratic formula

$$\frac{-b \pm \sqrt{b^2 - 4ac}}{2a}$$

Execute the program with several values of *a, b,* and *c* for which the quantity $b^2 - 4ac$ is nonnegative, including $a = 4, b = 0, c = -36$; $a = 1, b = 5, c = -36$; and $a = 2, b = 7.5, c = 6.25$.

4. Write a program to convert a measurement given in feet to the equivalent number of (**a**) yards, (**b**) inches, (**c**) centimeters, and (**d**) meters (1 ft = 12 in, 1 yd = 3 ft, 1 in = 2.54 cm, 1 m = 100 cm). Read the number of feet, number of inches, number of centimeters, and number of meters.

5. Write a program to read a student's number, his or her old grade point average, and the old number of course credits (e.g., 31479, 3.25, 66), and then display these with appropriate labels. Next, read the course credit and grade for each of four courses—for example, course1Credits = 5.0, course1Grade = 3.7, course2Credits = 3.0, course2Grade = 4.0, and so on. Calculate:

old # of honor points = (old # of course credits) * (old GPA)

new # of honor points = course1Credits * course1Grade +
course2Credits * course2Grade + ···

total # of new course credits = course1Credits + course2Credits + ···

$$\text{current GPA} = \frac{\text{\# of new honor points}}{\text{\# of new course credits}}$$

Display the current GPA with an appropriate label. Finally, calculate

$$\text{cumulative GPA} = \frac{(\text{\# of old honor points}) + (\text{\# of new honor points})}{(\text{\# of old course credits}) + (\text{\# of new course credits})}$$

and display this with a label.

6. The shipping clerk at the Rinky Dooflingy Company is faced with the following problem: Dooflingies are very delicate and must be shipped in special containers. These containers are available in four sizes: huge, large, medium, and small, which can hold 50, 20, 5, and 1 dooflingy, respectively. Write a program that reads the number of dooflingies to be shipped and displays the number of huge, large, medium, and small containers needed to send the shipment in the minimum number of containers, and with no wasted space in any container. Use constant definitions for the number of dooflingies each type of container can hold. The output for 1098 dooflingies should be similar to the following:

```
Container       Number
=========       ======
Huge              21
Large              2
Medium             1
Small              3
```

Execute the program for 3, 18, 48, 78, and 10,598 dooflingies.

7. Write a program that reads the amount of a purchase, the amount received in payment (both amounts in cents), and then computes and displays the change in dollars, half-dollars, quarters, dimes, nickels, and pennies.

8. Angles are often measured in degrees (°), minutes ('), and seconds ("). There are 360 degrees in a circle, 60 minutes in one degree, and 60 seconds in one minute. Write a program that reads two angular measurements given in degrees, minutes, and seconds, and then calculates and displays their sum. Use the program to verify each of the following:

$$74°29'13" + 105°8'16" = 179°37'29"$$

$$7°14'55" + 5°24'55" = 12°39'50"$$

$$20°31'19" + 0°31'30" = 21°2'49"$$

$$122°17'48" + 237°42'12" = 0°0'0"$$

9. Write a program that reads two three-digit integers and then displays their product in the following format:

```
          7 4 9
  x ____  3 8 1
  _ _ _ _ _ _ _
          7 4 9
        5 9 9 2
      2 2 4 7
  _ _ _ _ _ _ _
      2 8 5 3 6 9
```

Execute the program with the following values: 749 and 381; −749 and 381; 749 and −381; −749 and −381; 999 and 999.

10. In a certain region, pesticide can be sprayed from an airplane only if the temperature is at least 70°, the relative humidity is between 15 and 35%, and the wind speed is at most 10 miles per hour. Write a program that accepts three numbers representing temperature, relative humidity, and wind speed; assigns the value true or false to the boolean variable okToSpray according to these criteria; and displays this value.

11. The Cawker City Credit Company will approve a loan application if the applicant's income is at least $25,000 or the value of his or her assets is at least $100,000; in addition, total liabilities must be less than $50,000. Write a program that accepts three numbers representing income, assets, and liabilities; assigns the value true or false to the boolean variable creditOK according to these criteria; and displays this value.

12. Write a program that reads three real numbers, assigns the appropriate boolean value to the following boolean variables, and displays this value.

triangle: true if the real numbers can represent lengths of the sides of a triangle (the sum of any two of the numbers must be greater than the third); false otherwise.

equilateral: true if triangle is true and the triangle is equilateral (the three sides are equal); false otherwise.

isosceles: true if triangle is true and the triangle is isosceles (at least two sides are equal); false otherwise.

scalene: true if triangle is true and the triangle is scalene (no two sides are equal); false otherwise.

13. Proceed as in Problem 2, but make it a GUI program.

14. Proceed as in Problem 3, but make it a GUI program.

13. Proceed as in Problem 8, but make it a GUI program.

METHODS

It is common sense to take a method and try it; if it fails, admit it frankly and try another. But above all, try something." *Franklin Delano Roosevelt*

Though this be madness, yet there is method in't. *William Shakespeare, "Hamlet"*

A child on a farm sees a plane fly overhead and dreams of a faraway place. A traveler on the plane sees the farmhouse . . . and dreams of home. *Carl Burns*

Chapter Contents

Chapter Objectives

- Take a first look at how to build static (or class) methods
- Study how a method is called, how arguments and parameters are used to pass values to the method, and how the method can return a value to the calling method
- Investigate how a method is executed and how execution returns to the calling method
- Explain parameter passing and how it is different for reference types than for primitive types
- Show how the design process for methods is virtually identical to that for programs

163

- Give an example of how the Swing class `JApplet` can be used as a container in building applets

Most people dislike unnecessary work. One way to avoid unnecessary work in programming is to write code that is *reusable*. One technique for writing reusable code is to store the code to be reused in a method. An object can then reuse the code by invoking the method. This chapter takes a first look at how to write Java methods. We will deliberately keep our examples quite simple so that we can focus on the form of a method, how values are passed to the method, how it is executed, how values are passed back to the calling method, and how execution returns to the calling method. In the next chapter, we will look at how to design and implement methods with more complicated control structures, and in Chapter 6 we will look at a different kind of method.

4.1   INTRODUCTORY EXAMPLE: *OLD MACDONALD HAD A FARM . . .*[1]

The children's song *Old MacDonald* consists of a series of verses like the following:

Old MacDonald had a farm, E-I-E-I-O
And on this farm he had a cow, E-I-E-I-O
With a moo-moo here and moo-moo there
Here a moo there a moo everywhere a moo-moo
Old MacDonald had a farm, E-I-E-I-O

Old MacDonald had a farm, E-I-E-I-O
And on this farm he had a sheep, E-I-E-I-O
With a baa-baa here and baa-baa there
Here a baa there a baa everywhere a baa-baa
Old MacDonald had a farm, E-I-E-I-O

Old MacDonald had a farm, E-I-E-I-O
And on this farm he had a duck, E-I-E-I-O
With a quack-quack here and quack-quack there
Here a quack there a quack everywhere a quack-quack
Old MacDonald had a farm, E-I-E-I-O

and so on. Our problem is to write a program to generate the verses of this song.

---

[1] Special thanks to Owen Astrachan for this problem. A C++ solution is given in his book *C++ A Computer Science Tapestry* (McGraw-Hill, 1996).

PROBLEM: *Old MacDonald . . .*

Write a program that displays the lyrics of *Old MacDonald*.

One Approach

Before we begin, it should be apparent that we could write a program that does nothing more than display a very long `String` containing the song's lyrics:

```java
// ...
class SimpleOldMacDonald extends Object
{
  public static void main(String [] args)
  {
    Screen theScreen = new Screen();
    theScreen.println("\nOld MacDonald had a farm, E-I-E-I-O"
        + "\nAnd on his farm he had a cow, E-I-E-I-O"
        + "\nWith a moo-moo here and a moo-moo there"
        + "\nHere a moo there a moo everywhere a moo-moo"
        + "\nOld MacDonald had a farm, E-I-E-I-O\n"
        + "\nOld MacDonald had a farm, E-I-E-I-O"
        + "\nAnd on his farm he had a sheep, E-I-E-I-O"
        + "\nWith a baa-baa here and a baa-baa there"
        + "\nHere a baa there a baa everywhere a baa-baa"
        + "\nOld MacDonald had a farm, E-I-E-I-O\n"
        + "\nOld MacDonald had a farm, E-I-E-I-O"
        + "\nAnd on his farm he had a duck, E-I-E-I-O"
        + "\nWith a quack-quack here and a quack-quack there"
        + "\nHere a quack there a quack everywhere a quack-quack"
        + "\nOld MacDonald had a farm, E-I-E-I-O\n"
        // plus any additional verses
              );
  }
}
```

While this would be a correct program, it ignores the structure of the song, which consists of similar verses. Ignoring this structure leads to a great deal of redundant coding effort—of the roughly 40 words in each verse, 32 of them are the same from verse to verse.

Eliminating Redundant Code

The key to eliminating redundant code is to take time at the outset to study the structure of the song and build the lyrics in such a way so as to "factor out" the words that are common to each verse. As we study the verses, we see that each follows a consistent pattern:

```
Old MacDonald had a farm, E-I-E-I-O
And on his farm he had a creature, E-I-E-I-O
```

```
        With a sound-sound here and a sound-sound there
        Here a sound there a sound everywhere a sound-sound
        Old MacDonald had a farm, E-I-E-I-O
```

That is, everything is the same from one verse to another except for two "variables"—
the verse's *creature,* and the *sound* the creature makes. These items that vary from one
verse to another are the *parameters* of the verse. Since each word can be represented as a String, we can devise a "verse-building" method that has two String parameter variables, one named creature and one named sound. The basic form of
the method will be as follows:

```
        private static String buildVerse(String creature, String sound)
        {
            // … statements to build a verse from creature and sound
        }
```

To actually build a verse, the words that each verse has in common can be "hard-
wired" into the method as String literals. The String concatenation operator + can
be used to combine these String literals and the parameters into verses, as shown
in Figure 4.1.

FIGURE 4.1   OLD MACDONALD HAD A FARM . . .

```
/** OldMacDonald.java displays the lyrics to "Old MacDonald."
 *  Output: The lyrics of the song.
 */

import ann.easyio.*;          // Screen

class OldMacDonald extends Object
{
 /** utility method to simplify verse-building
  *  Receive: creature, a String; sound, a String
  *  Return:  a verse of "Old MacDonald" using creature and sound
  */

 private static String buildVerse(String creature, String sound)
 {
   return "\nOld MacDonald had a farm, E-I-E-I-O"
       + "\nAnd on this farm he had a " + creature + ", E-I-E-I-O"
       + "\nWith a " + sound + "-" + sound + " here and a " +
       sound + "-" + sound + " there"
       + "\nHere a " + sound + " there a " + sound +
           " everywhere a " + sound + "-" + sound
       + "\nOld MacDonald had a farm, E-I-E-I-O\n";
 }

 public static void main(String [] args)
 {
   String lyrics = buildVerse("cow", "moo")
                 + buildVerse("sheep", "baa")
                 + buildVerse("duck", "quack")
                 // plus any other verses
                 ;
   Screen theScreen = new Screen();
   theScreen.println(lyrics);
 }
}
```

Sample run:

```
Old MacDonald had a farm, E-I-E-I-O
And on his farm he had a cow, E-I-E-I-O
With a moo-moo here and a moo-moo there
Here a moo there a moo everywhere a moo-moo
Old MacDonald had a farm, E-I-E-I-O

Old MacDonald had a farm, E-I-E-I-O
And on his farm he had a sheep, E-I-E-I-O
With a baa-baa here and a baa-baa there
Here a baa there a baa everywhere a baa-baa
Old MacDonald had a farm, E-I-E-I-O

Old MacDonald had a farm, E-I-E-I-O
And on his farm he had a duck, E-I-E-I-O
With a quack-quack here and a quack-quack there
Here a quack there a quack everywhere a quack-quack
Old MacDonald had a farm, E-I-E-I-O
```

The main method builds its `lyrics` by concatenating together the `String` values returned by each of the `buildVerse()` messages. Because it invokes the `build-Verse()` method, the main method is sometimes described as the **caller** of the `buildVerse()` method or the **sender** of the `buildVerse()` message. We will use these phrases interchangeably.

The words that are different from one verse to another are the *arguments* that our main method passes to the `buildVerse()` method, in order for it to build a particular verse. That is, the message

```
buildVerse("sheep", "baa")
```

passes the arguments `"sheep"` and `"baa"` to our method. During the execution of this call to the method, the parameter `creature` refers to the argument `"sheep"` and the parameter `sound` refers to the argument `"baa"`. By contrast, the message

```
buildVerse("duck", "quack")
```

passes the arguments `"duck"` and `"quack"` to our method. During the execution of this call to the method, parameters `creature` and `sound` refer to the arguments `"duck"` and `"quack"`, respectively.

Because it "factors out" the code that is common to each verse, our `build-Verse()` method makes it easy to add new verses to the song. For example, the expression

```
buildVerse("horse", "neigh")
```

builds and returns the verse:

```
Old MacDonald had a farm, E-I-E-I-O
And on this farm he had a horse, E-I-E-I-O
With a neigh-neigh here and a neigh-neigh there
Here a neigh there a neigh everywhere a neigh-neigh
Old MacDonald had a farm, E-I-E-I-O
```

When different parts of a program contain the same code, a **method** provides a way to extract the common code and *encapsulate* it in one place, so that code need not be written more than once. A method's **parameters** provide a means by which different values (called **arguments**) can be passed into the method.

Methods are the first of several techniques Java provides for writing reusable code. In the following sections, we will learn how to design and build methods.

4.2   GETTING STARTED WITH METHODS

Computing with Formulas

There are many problems whose solutions involve the use of one or more formulas. For example, the speed-calculation problem in Section 1.4 used the formula *speed = distance / time;* the wage-calculation problem in Section 2.1 used the formula *wages = hoursWorked × hourlyRate;* the problem in Section 3.1 of computing the amount of energy released by a quantity of matter, used Einstein's equation $e = m \times c^2$. As these examples demonstrate, writing programs to solve such problems is usually straightforward if we know how to write Java expressions for the formulas.

Computing with Methods

Programs that simply use a formula to compute a value may solve the problem at hand, but the code representing the formula cannot be reused by another program. For example, if some program besides that in Figure 3.1 needed to use Einstein's equation, the equation would have to be recalled and retyped because the equation given in Figure 3.1 cannot be reused by another program (except by physically copying and pasting it, which doesn't count).

Methods provide a way to make such equations reusable. Computing with methods is thus to plan for the future—to take a long-term strategic approach—presuming that the method is sufficiently useful to be needed again someday.

Method Design And Coding

As we saw in the previous section, code can be made reusable by defining a method containing that code, with appropriate parameters for those parts of the code that can vary from one use to the next. Definitions of Java methods have the following general form:

method by following the steps of OCD. We begin by noting that since the radius is the only varying value in the formula, the caller should pass this value to the method.

Behavior. This method should receive from its caller a radius value. It should then compute and return to the caller the result of multiplying 4 times π times the cube of the radius, all divided by 3.

Objects in the Volume Problem. From the behavioral description and the volume formula, our method must implement the following problem objects (ignoring nouns like *caller* and *method*). As we saw earlier, we include a column in the object list to describe the *movement* of values with respect to our method:

Description of problem object	Type	Kind	Movement	Name
Radius	double	variable	received	*radius*
Result	double	varying	returned	none
4.0	double	constant	local	none
π	double	constant	local	Math.PI
3	integer	constant	local	none
3.0	double	constant	local	none

Writing the specification and stub for this method is left as an exercise.

Operations. From our behavioral description and formula, we see that our method needs these operations:

   i. Receive a real value from the caller *(radius)*
   ii. Cube a real value ($radius^3$)
   iii. Multiply real values ($4 \times \pi \times radius^3$)
   iv. Divide real values ($4 \times \pi \times radius^3 / 3$)
   v. Return a real value ($4 \times \pi \times radius^3 / 3$)

All of these operations are predefined in Java. The return statement (described previously) can be used by a method to return a value to the method's caller.

Algorithm. Our method's algorithm is thus quite simple:

ALGORITHM FOR VOLUME METHOD

   1. Receive radius from the caller.
   2. Return 4.0 * π * $radius^3$ / 3.0 to the caller.

Method Coding. Since this is a sphere operation, we first create an empty *Sphere* class

```
class Sphere
{
}
```

and then define the volume() method within the class:

```
class Sphere extends Object
{
   /** compute a sphere's volume, given its radius
    *  Receive:       radius, a double.
    *  Precondition:  radius > 0
    *  Return:        the volume of a sphere of the given radius
    */
   public static double volume(double radius)
   {
      return 4.0 * Math.PI * Math.pow(radius, 3) / 3.0;
   }
}
```

We define the method as `public` so that other classes can use it. We make it a static method so that main methods (which *must* be `static`) can use it without creating a `Sphere` object. We define the return type of the method as `double` because it computes a real value. We name the method `volume` to describe accurately the value it returns. The parentheses inform the compiler that this is a method being defined, and that it has one parameter, a `double` named `radius`. The body of the method then specifies the steps it takes when invoked. In this case, the body consists of a single `return` statement that computes and returns the volume of a sphere with the given radius.

Once our `Sphere` class has a `volume()` method, we can test it by constructing a driver program as described in Section 4.2. Once `volume()` has been thoroughly tested, we can move on to design and implement the `mass()` method for class `Sphere`.

The Mass Method

Given a method for computing a sphere's volume from its radius *r*, the mass of a sphere of density *d* can be computed from the formula:

$$mass = d \times volume(r)$$

We can design a method to compute the mass by following the steps of OCD. Since there are two variables in the formula, the caller should pass two arguments: a *density* and a *radius*.

Behavior. The method should receive from its caller a *radius* value and a *density* value. It should compute and return to the caller the result of multiplying the *density* by the volume (computed using the *radius* value).

Objects in the Mass Problem. From the behavioral description and formula, the method must implement the following objects (again ignoring nouns like *caller* and *method*):

Description of problem's object	Type	Kind	Movement	Name
Radius	double	variable	received	*radius*
Density	double	variable	received	*density*
Volume	double	variable	local	*volume(radius)*
Result	double	variable	returned	none

Operations. Again, from our behavioral description and formula, the method needs these operations:

    i. Receive real values from the caller *(radius, density)*

    ii. Compute volume of a sphere (given its radius)

    iii. Multiple real values *(density × volume(radius))*

    iv. Return a real value *(density × volume(radius))*

Since the `Sphere` class contains a `volume()` method and the other operations are provided in Java, all of these operations are available.

Algorithm. We can now build the following algorithm for our method.

    ALGORITHM FOR MASS METHOD

    1. Receive *radius, density* from the caller.

    2. Return *density × volume(radius)* to the caller.

Method Coding. Since this is an operation on a sphere, we define method `mass()` within the `Sphere` class, as shown in Figure 4.4.

FIGURE 4.4   A Sphere CLASS: STATIC METHODS

```
/** Sphere.java provides a class to represent Sphere objects.
 *  Contains static methods volume() and mass().
 */

class Sphere extends Object
{
 /** class method to compute sphere's volume
  *  Receive:       radius, a double
  *  PRECONDITION: radius >= 0.
  *  Return;        the volume of a sphere of given radius
  */
 public static double volume(double radius)
 {
   return 4.0 * Math.PI * Math.pow(radius, 3) / 3.0;
 }

  /** class method to compute sphere's mass
   *  Receive:        radius, a double; density, a double
   *  PRECONDITION: radius >= 0 && density >= 0.
   *  Return:         the mass of a sphere of given radius and density
   */
  public static double mass(double radius, double density)
  {
    return density * volume(radius);
  }
}
```

Once we have finished coding the `mass()` method, we would write a simple driver program to test and verify that `mass()` behaves correctly. Doing so is left as an exercise.

Coding and Testing the `SphereWeigher` Class

Given the `Sphere` class shown in Figure 4.4, our `SphereWeigher` class can now be written. Here is the algorithm used by its main method:

ALGORITHM FOR MAIN METHOD

1. Construct *theKeyboard* and *theScreen*.
2. Ask *theScreen* to display a prompt for the radius of a spherical ball.
3. Ask *theKeyboard* to read a `double` value and store it in *radius*.
4. Ask *theScreen* to display a prompt for the density of a spherical ball.
5. Ask *theKeyboard* to read a `double` value and store it in *density*.
6. Compute *weight* using *mass()* method from class `Sphere`.
7. Ask *theScreen* to display *weight* (along with the usual descriptive text).

The Java program in Figure 4.5 implements this algorithm.

FIGURE 4.5   `SphereWeigher` USING STATIC METHODS

```
/** SphereWeigher.java computes the weight of an arbitrary sphere.
 *   Input: radius and density, both doubles.
 *   Output: the weight of the sphere.
 */

import ann.easyio.*;        // Keyboard, Screen, ...
import Sphere;

class SphereWeigher extends Object
{
 public static void main(String [] args)
  {
    Screen theScreen = new Screen();
    theScreen.print("\nTo compute the weight of a sphere,"
                  + "\n enter its radius (in feet): ");

    Keyboard theKeyboard = new Keyboard();
    double radius = theKeyboard.readDouble();

    theScreen.print(" enter its density (in pounds/cubic foot): ");
    double density = theKeyboard.readDouble();

    double weight = Sphere.mass(radius, density);

    theScreen.print("\nThe sphere's weight is approximately ")
            .printFormatted(weight).println(" pounds.");
  }
}
```

Sample runs:

```
To compute the weight of a sphere,
 enter its radius (in feet): 6.5
 enter its density (in pounds/cubic foot): 14.6

The sphere's weight is approximately 16,795.059 pounds.
```

4.4   METHODS: A SUMMARY

Methods are an essential part of Java, because they are used to write program components that are reusable. Because they are so fundamental to Java programming, we summarize some of the important ideas about methods considered in this chapter.

❑ *For each value that a method must receive from its caller, a variable to hold that value must be declared within the parentheses of the method's heading.* Such variables are called the *parameters* of the method. For example, in the definition of the method mass() of class Sphere,

```
public static double mass(double radius, double density)
{
    return density * volume(radius);
}
```

the variables radius and density are the method's parameters.

❑ *A value that is supplied to a method when it is sent is an argument to that method. Each argument is evaluated and its value is copied to the corresponding parameter of the method.* For example, suppose that a program sends Sphere the following message to invoke its mass() method,

```
double w = Sphere.mass(1.0, d);
```

1.0 and d are the arguments of the message. When execution reaches this call, the values of the arguments 1.0 and d are *passed* (i.e., copied) from the caller to the parameters radius and density in method mass():

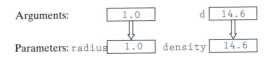

❑ *When a method is called, the list of arguments is matched against the list of parameters from left to right, with the leftmost argument associated with the leftmost parameter, the next argument associated with the next parameter, and so on. The number of arguments must be the same as the number of parameters in the method heading, and the type of each argument must be compatible with the type of the corresponding parameter.*

❑ *For an argument whose type is a reference type, the address of the object referred to by that argument will be copied to the corresponding parameter so that both will refer to the same object.* This means that if the object referred to by that parameter is modified by the method, the object referred to by the corresponding argument in the calling method will also be changed.

❏ Static (*or* class) *methods are defined as* `static`; *messages that invoke them are sent to a class.*Thus, we can send the `mass()` message to class `Sphere` if we provide arguments for both the radius and the density:

```
double w = Sphere.mass(1.0, d);
```

❏ Instance (*or* object) methods are defined without `static`; *messages that invoke them are sent to an instance of the class (i.e., to an object).*Instance methods are described in more detail in Chapter 6.

❏ *When one method* `m()` *calls another method* `n()`, *the flow of execution is from* `m()` *to* `n()` *and then back to* `m()`. To illustrate, consider again the main method's call of method `mass()` in Figure 4.5:

```
         .
         .
         .
public static void main(String [] args)
{
         .
         .
         .
   double weight = Sphere.mass(diameter/2, density);
         .
         .
         .
}
```

When the call to `mass()` is encountered, execution proceeds as follows:

1. The values of the arguments `diameter/2` and `density` are determined.
2. These values are passed from the main method to `mass()` in class `Sphere`, and copied into the parameters `radius` and `density`.
3. Execution then transfers from the statement sending the message (in `main()`) to the first statement of `mass()`, which begins execution using the values of its parameters.
4. When a `return` statement (or the final statement of the method) is executed, execution switches back to the caller (i.e., the main method). If the `return` statement specifies a value to be returned by the method, that value will be made available to the caller.

❏ *Local objects are defined only while the method containing them is executing.*They can be accessed only within the method, and any attempt to use them outside the method is an error.

❏ `void` *is used to specify the return type of a method that returns no values.* Such methods are called with statements of the form

```
methodName(argument_list);
```

❏ *A value is returned from a method to the calling method via a* `return` *statement of the form* `return expression;`. *For a method that returns no value (and whose return*

type is thus `void`), *execution transfers back to the calling method when a* `return;`
statement (with no expression) is encountered or the end of the method is reached.

The ability to define methods is a powerful tool in object-oriented programming.
If the solution of some problem requires an operation not provided in Java (as an operator or as a predefined method), we can simply define a method to perform that operation.

4.5 GRAPHIC/INTERNET JAVA: *OLD MACDONALD . . .* APPLET

In the opening section of this chapter, we developed a Java application to display
verses of the familiar children's song *Old MacDonald Had a Farm.* In that program
(see Figure 4.1), each verse was produced by sending the method `buildVerse()` the
name of an animal and the sound it makes, and the method displayed the appropriate verse of the song. In this section we will show how to convert this application into
an applet. Our applet will display several verses of the song along with a picture of
Mr. MacDonald himself. Once again we will use the powerful new tools for graphics
programming provided by Java's Swing classes.

We know that in an applet, an `init()` method replaces the `main()` method used
in applications. Also, we can use the same method `buildVerse()` from Figure 4.1
to generate each verse and store it in a `String` variable `lyrics.` What we must
change is the output. In the application program, output is produced simply by sending a message to a `Screen` object to display the `String lyrics` that we send to
it. Here, however, we must figure out how to specify a part of the screen to be used
for the graphical output and then how to get the verses of the song and the picture
of Old MacDonald **painted** (i.e., *drawn*) in some area of the screen specified for the
graphical output.

Java's Swing classes provide a variety of **containers** and other components for this.
Some of the containers are *top-level containers,* such as `JApplet` and `JFrame,` that
create an area of the screen, called a **window** or a **frame,** where the graphical output
is to take place. These top-level containers contain *intermediate containers* known as
panes (or **panels**), the most important of which is the **content pane.**[4]

The content pane is used to group and position the components that do the painting (or perform some other action such as accepting user input). The sizes of these
components and how they are arranged depends upon the container's **layout manager.**
These layout schemes allow for the placement of components relative to each other,
regardless of the specific video settings (e.g. resolution) of the computer running the
program.

---

[4] This containment is usually *indirect*—the top-level container contains some intermediate container which
contains some other intermediate container . . . which contains a content pane. In most cases, one need
not be concerned with what intermediate containers there are between a top-level container and its content pane.

The default layout for the content pane of a `JApplet` is the `Borderlayout,` in which items can be positioned in any of five areas of the pane, which are designated `NORTH`, `SOUTH`, `EAST`, `WEST`, and `CENTER`:

```
                    N O R T H


    W                                        E
    E                                        A
    S              C E N T E R               S
    T                                        T



                   S O U T H
```

All extra space goes in the center region. (Other layout managers will be covered in more detail in later chapters.) In the applet in Figure 4.6, the verses of the song are displayed in the west region and the picture of Old MacDonald in the east region:

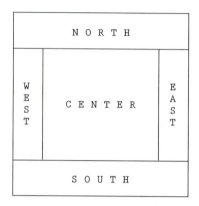

The `add()` method is used to place a component in one of these specific areas in the content pane. For example, in the program in Figure 4.6, the statement

```
getContentPane().add(song, "West");
```

adds `song` to the leftmost (west) region. Here, `song` is a `JTextArea` component, which can be used to display lines of text. It was created by the statement

```
JTextArea song = new JTextArea(lyrics);
```

The right side of this statement invokes a constructor method of the form `JTextArea(`*str*`),` where *str* is of type `String.`

The picture of the farmer is added to the rightmost (east) region with the statement

```
getContentPane().add(farmerPicture, "East");
```

Here `farmerPicture` is an object of type `JLabel,` constructed by the statement

```
JLabel farmerPicture = new JLabel(new ImageIcon("farmer.gif"));
```

`JLabel` is a container that is intended to be used for short strings or images. The location of this text or image can be specified, but the default, which is used here, is to center it in the specified region. One of the constructors from the `ImageIcon` class is used to convert the image stored in the file `farmer.gif` to an icon and paint it on the screen.

The complete program is shown in Figure 4.6. For some of the other methods provided in the `swing` classes `JTextArea, JLabel,` and `ImageIcon,` see the Documentation section in the chapter summary and Java's API documentation.

FIGURE 4.6   `OldMacDonald` APPLET

```
/** OldMacDonaldApplet.java displays the lyrics to "Old MacDonald."
 *  Output: The lyrics of the song.
 *
 *  HTML note -- include the following in your web page:
 *     <APPLET CODE="OldMacDonaldApplet.class" WIDTH=500 HEIGHT=350>
 *                                                         </APPLET>
 */

import javax.swing.*;          // JApplet


public class OldMacDonaldApplet extends JApplet
{

/**  utility method to simplify verse-building
  *  Receive: creature, a String; sound, a String
  *  Return:  a verse of "Old MacDonald" using creature and sound
  */

 private static String buildVerse(String creature, String sound)
 {
   return "\nOld MacDonald had a farm, E-I-E-I-O"
          + "\nAnd on this farm he had a " + creature + ", E-I-E-I-O"
          + "\nWith a " + sound + "-" + sound + " here and a " +
                sound + "-" + sound + " there"
          + "\nHere a " + sound + " there a " + sound +
               " everywhere a " + sound + "-" + sound
          + "\nOld MacDonald had a farm, E-I-E-I-O\n";
 }
```

```
public void init()
{
   String lyrics = buildVerse("cow", "moo")
                   + buildVerse("sheep", "baa")
                   + buildVerse("duck", "quack");
                   // plus any other verses

   JTextArea song = new JTextArea(lyrics);
   getContentPane().add(song, "West");

   JLabel farmerPicture = new JLabel(new ImageIcon("farmer.gif"));
   getContentPane().add(farmerPicture, "East");
}
}
```

CHAPTER SUMMARY

KEY TERMS AND NOTES

`add()` method	paint
alias problem	pane
class method	panel
container	postcondition
content pane	precondition
encapsulate	public method
frame	`return` statement
instance method	specification
layout manager	static method
locals	stub
method	`void`
method body	window
method heading	

◉ A method provides a way to encapsulate code in one place so that it can be reused. It's general form is:

> *Method Heading*
> *Method Body*

where the heading has the general form

> *modifiers returnType methodName(parameterDeclarations)*

and the body is a sequence of statements enclosed in curly braces ({ and }):

```
    {
        statements
    }
```

◎ Values (called arguments) can be passed into a method via parameters.

◎ Execution transfers from a method back to the caller when a `return` statement is encountered or the end of the method is reached.

◎ No `return` statement is required for methods whose return type is `void`.

◎ A specification for a method should include descriptions of values it receives—parameters and their types; values input to the method; the value it returns; values it outputs; preconditions; and postconditions.

◎ A method's documentation should include a comment that describes its specification.

◎ Locals exist only while a method is executing and thus can be accessed only within the method. This means that other methods may reuse the name of a local for some other purpose without causing a conflict.

◎ When a method is called within the class in which it is defined, its name can be used without qualification.

◎ When a method is called, the arguments are associated with the parameters from left to right—the first argument with the first parameter, the second argument with the next parameter, and so on, until the matching is complete. There must be the same number of arguments as parameters and each argument's type must be compatible with the type of the corresponding parameter.

REFERENCE

Documentation

SOME `JTextArea` METHODS

Method	Description
`JTextArea()`	Constructs a new empty text area
`JTextArea(String text)`	Constructs a new text area containing the specified `text`
`JTextArea(String text,` `        int rows, int columns)`	Like the preceding, but with the specified number of rows and columns
`void append(String str)`	Appends `String str` to the text
`void insert(String str, pos)`	Inserts `String str` into the text at the specified `int` position `pos`
`void replaceRange(String str,` `          int start, int end)`	Replaces the part of the text from position `start` to position `end` with `str`
`int getRows()` `int getColumns()`	Returns the number of rows (columns) in the text area
`void setRows(n)` `void setColumns(n)`	Sets the number of rows (columns) in the text area to n

SOME JLabel METHODS

Method	Description
`JLabel(String text, int align)`	Constructs a new label using `text`. It will be centered vertically in its display area and with horizontal alignment specified by `align`, whose value is one of the following constants (defined in `Swing-Constants`): LEFT, CENTER, RIGHT, LEADING, TRAILING. If `align` is omitted, the default alignment is LEADING.
`JLabel(Icon icon, int align)`	Like the preceding, but with `icon` in place of `text`
`JLabel(String text, Icon icon, int align)`	Like the preceding but using both `text` and `icon`; `text` will be placed on the trailing edge of `icon`
`int getHorizontalAlignment()`	Returns the horizontal alignment in the label as one of the Swing constants listed above
`void setHorizontalAlignment (int align)`	Sets the horizontal alignment in the label to `align`, whose value is one of the Swing constants listed above
`int getVerticalAlignment()`	Returns the vertical alignment in the label as one of the Swing constants (defined in `SwingConstants`): TOP, CENTER, BOTTOM
`void setVerticalAlignment (int align)`	Sets the vertical alignment in the label to `align`, whose value is one of the Swing constants listed above
`int getHorizontalTextPosition()`	Like `getHorizontalAlignment()`, but returns the horizontal position of the label's text relative to its image
`void setHorizontalTextPosition (int align)`	Like `setHorizontalAlignment()`, but sets the horizontal position of the label's text relative to its image
`int getVerticalTextPosition()`	Like `getVerticalAlignment()`, but returns the vertical position of the label's text relative to its image

`void setVerticalTextPosition` `        (int align)`	Like `setVerticalAlignment()`, but sets the vertical position of the label's text relative to its image
`Icon getIcon()`	Returns the label's icon
`void setIcon(Icon icon)`	Sets the label's icon to `icon`
`String getText()`	Returns the label's text
`void setText(String text)`	Sets the label's text to `text`
`int getIconTextGap()`	Returns the space (in pixels) between the label's icon and text
`voie setIconTextGap(int n)`	Sets the space between the label's image and icon to n (pixels)

SOME `ImageIcon` STATIC METHODS

Method	Description
`ImageIcon(String filename)`	Creates an `ImageIcon` from the specified file. (Other constructors create it from a `URL` object, an `Image` object, or a `byte` array)
`int getIconHeight()` `int getIconWidth()`	Returns the height (width) of the icon

`void paintIcon(Component c,`
`    Graphics g, int x,`
`        int y)`
	Paints the icon on component c, using `Graphics` object g, at the position specified by x and y

☞ PROGRAMMING POINTERS

PROGRAM STYLE AND DESIGN

1. *Methods should be documented.* The documentation should include:

- ❏ A statement of what it does
- ❏ its *specification,* which consists of those of the following that apply:

  —What it *receives*—i.e., its *parameters*
  —What is *input* to the method
  —*Preconditions:* restrictions or limitations on the parameters' values in order for the method to work properly
  —What it *returns*
  —What it *outputs*
  —*Postconditions:* effects produced by the method

2. *Methods are separate components, and the white space in a program should reflect this.* In this text, we

- ❏ Insert appropriate documentation before each method defined in the main method's file, to separate it from other program components.
- ❏ Indent the declarations and statements within each method.

3. *Guidelines for programming style also apply to methods.*

4. *Once a problem has been analyzed to identify its objects and the operations needed to solve it, an algorithm should be constructed that specifies the order in which the operations are applied to the data objects.*

5. *Operations that are not predefined (or are nontrivial) in Java should be encoded as methods.*

6. *A method that encodes an operation should be designed in the same manner as the main method.*

7. *A method that returns no values should have return type* `void`.

8 *A method that receives no values should have no parameters.*

WATCH

OUT

POTENTIAL PITFALLS

1. *When a method is called, the list of arguments is matched against the list of parameters from left to right, with the leftmost argument associated with the leftmost parameter, the next argument associated with the next parameter, and so on. The number of arguments must be the same as the number of parameters in the method heading, and the type of each argument must be compatible with the type of the corresponding parameter.* For example, consider a method with the heading

```
public static int f(int number1, int number2)
```

The statements

```
int y = f(x);
```

and

```
int y = f(2, 3.75);
```

are incorrect. In the first case, the number of arguments (1) does not agree with the number of parameters (2). In the second case, the real value `3.75` should not be passed to the integer parameter `number2`.

2. *Identifiers defined within a method (e.g., parameters, local variables, and local constants) are defined only during the execution of that method; they are undefined both before and after its execution.* Any attempt to use such identifiers outside the method (without redeclaring them) is an error. For example, in the method

```
public static void f(int x, float y)
{
    int a, b;
        .
        .
        .
}
```

neither the local variables a and b nor the parameters x and y can be accessed outside of method f().

3. *Changing the value of a primitive-type parameter does not change the value of the corresponding argument; however, modifying the object referred to by a reference-type parameter (but not its address) does change the value of the object referred to by the corresponding argument, because both refer to the same object.* For example, if a method m() is defined as

```
public static int m(int x)
{
   x = 4;
   return 0;
}
```

and then called by

```
        .
        .
        .

int y = 12345,
    z;

z = m(y);

        .
        .
        .
```

z will be assigned the value 0 following the call to method m(), and the value of y will still be 12345. If, however, the method f() were defined by

```
public static int m(Point x)
{
   x.setLocation(0, 0);
   return 0;
}
```

and called by

```
        .
        .
        .

Point y = Point(1,2);
int z;

z = m(y);
```

then, after the call to method m(), z would be assigned the value 0, but the Point object referred to by y would be changed; instead of representing the point with coordinates $(1, 2)$, it would represent the point with coordinates $(0, 0)$.

4. *Each { must have a matching }.* To make it easier to find matching braces, we align each { with its corresponding }.

PROGRAMMING PROBLEMS

SECTION 4.1

The lyrics of the songs in the following problems can be found on the Internet using a search engine. You can also check the website for this book for links to where they can be found (see the preface).

1. Write and test a program to display a verse of "Happy Birthday to You" with the name of some person you know inserted at the appropriate place in the lyrics.
2. Write and test a program to display some of the verses of "The Farmer in the Dell."
3. Write and test a program to display some of the verses of "This Old Man."
4. Write and test a program to display some of the verses of "The Hokey Pokey."

SECTION 4.2

5. Write a driver program to test the method `range()` of Exercise 4.
6. Write a driver program to test the method `wages()` of Exercise 5.
7. Write a driver program to test the circle-processing methods of Exercises 6 and 7.
8. Write a driver program to test the rectangle-processing methods of Exercises 8 and 9.
9. Write a driver program to test the triangle-processing methods of Exercises 10 and 11.
10. Write a driver program to test the culture-of-bacteria method of Exercise 12.
11. Write a driver program to test the time-conversion methods of Exercises 13–16.
12. Write a driver program to test the phone-number method of Exercise 17.
13. Write a driver program to test the wind-chill method of Exercise 18.
14. Write a driver program to test the heat-index method of Exercise 19.
15. Write a driver program to test the stick-number methods of Exercise 20.
16. Complete Problem 15 by writing and testing the additional methods needed to display all digits.

SECTION 4.3

17. Add and test a `density()` method to the `Sphere` class to calculate the density of a sphere given its weight and volume as described in Section 4.3.
18. Consider the program developed in Section 4.3 to solve part of the ball-of-twine problem. Add a method to the program in Figure 4.5 to convert pounds to tons and use it to find the weight of the twine ball in tons.
19. There is also a second part to the twine-ball problem (see Problem 18): How many miles would the twine reach if it were unrolled?
    (a) Extend the statement of the behavior of the problem in Section 4.3 to include this.
    (b) Extend the list of objects as necessary for this modified problem.
    (c) Extend the list of operations to include those needed to solve this modified problem. Assume that approximately 350 feet of twine must be wound to form a ball that weighs 1 pound and there are 5280 feet in a mile, so the total length of the twine in the ball is 350 *weight* / 5280 miles.

(d) Modify the algorithm so that it will solve this modified problem.

(e) Modify the program in Figure 4.5 so that it will solve this modified problem.

20. Extend the program in Problem 19 to calculate the length of the twine in both feet and miles.

SECTION 4.5

21. Write and test an applet for the "Happy Birthday to You" song in Problem 1, adding one or more appropriate pictures (e.g., a birthday cake or a photo of some person being honored).

22. Write and test an applet for the "The Farmer in the Dell" song in Problem 2, adding one or more appropriate pictures (e.g., the farmer, wife, child, nurse, cow, dog, cat, rat, cheese),

23. Write and test an applet for the "This Old Man" song in Problem 3, adding one or more appropriate pictures.

24. Write and test an applet for the "The Hokey Pokey" song in Problem 4, adding one or more appropriate pictures.

USING CONTROL STRUCTURES IN METHODS

Progress might be a circle, rather than a straight line. *Eberhard Zeidler*

If you don't know where you're going, you'll wind up somewhere else. *Yogi Berra (1925–)*

If you can keep your head, when all about are losing theirs . . . *Rudyard Kipling*

Those who do not learn from history are doomed to repeat its mistakes. *Unknown*

Chapter Contents

Chapter Objectives

- Give an example of a problem that requires new control structures for its solution
- Take a first look at the three basic control structures—sequential, selection, and repetition
- Study one of the statements provided in Java to implement selective execution—the `if` statement
- See how Java's `for` statement can be used for counter-controlled repetitions
- See how Java's `for` statement can be used to construct forever loops and how they can be used to build input loops

- Give an example of an applet that uses a loop to generate output
- (Optional) Give a brief indication of the area of computability theory
- (Optional) Describe the kinds of problems in which numerical methods are used, give an example from calculus (approximating areas), and apply it to a real-world problem

The preceding chapter emphasized the use of *methods* for writing reusable code. The examples were necessarily very simple because we had not yet studied many of the features of the Java programming language. In particular, the flow of execution through our methods was strictly *sequential* or *straight-line,* starting with the first statement and proceeding to the last, with each statement being executed exactly once.

There are many problems, however, for which sequential processing is not adequate. In such cases, their solutions require other ways to control execution. One of these control mechanisms is called *selection;* in which there are various paths that execution may follow, and exactly one of these paths must be selected. Another common control mechanism is *repetition* or *looping,* in which a collection of instructions are executed repeatedly, until some termination condition causes the repetition to stop.

This chapter will introduce one of the selection structures (the `if` statement) and one of the repetition structures (the `for` statement) provided in Java. Selection will be considered in more detail in Chapter 7 and repetition in Chapter 8.[1]

5.1   EXAMPLE: AN IMPROVED PAYROLL PROGRAM

In Chapter 2 we developed a program for calculating payroll. It was deliberately kept simple because we had few Java features available. In this section we will revise this payroll program to make it more practical—in particular, to calculate overtime pay and to process more than one employee. (In Chapter 11 we will revisit this problem and further enhance it to process different kinds of employees—salaried, hourly, and salespersons paid on commission—by representing each of these kinds of employees as classes that are extensions of an employee class.)

PROBLEM

Sales of Cawker City Candy Company's confections have increased over the past several months to the point that more employees have been hired and many employees are working overtime to help the company meet demand. This means that the payroll supervisor, Chuck Controller, must upgrade his program for calculating employee wages to include overtime pay. Also, because his current program (see Figure 2.1) calculates pay for only one employee at a time and the number of employees

---

[1] This chapter provides only an introduction to selection and repetition. Chapters 7 and 8 give complete presentations of selection and repetition structures.

has increased considerably, he would like to have it calculate the payroll for all employees.

OBJECT-CENTERED DESIGN

BEHAVIOR. Our program should begin by displaying a prompt on the screen for the number of employees and reading this value from the keyboard. For each employee, it should then display on the screen a prompt for the name, the number of hours worked, and the hourly rate for that employee. The user will enter these values at the keyboard. For each set of values it should calculate and display the wages for that employee, with time and a half paid for overtime. It should do this for all employees.

THE PROBLEM'S OBJECTS. From our behavioral description of what the program is to do, we can identify the following objects in this problem:

Description of problem's object	Type	Kind	Name
The program	??	??	??
Screen	Screen	variable	*theScreen*
Number of employees	int	variable	*numEmployees*
Prompt for hours and rate	String	constant	none
Number of hours worked	double	variable	*hoursWorked*
Hourly pay rate	double	variable	*hourlyRate*
Keyboard	Keyboard	variable	*theKeyboard*
Regular wages	double	variable	*regularPay*
Overtime pay factor	double	constant	*OVERTIME_FACTOR*
Overtime wages	double	variable	*overtimePay*
Wages (regular + overtime)	double	variable	*wages*

OPERATIONS. Again, using our behavioral description, we can identify the operations needed to solve this problem:

   i. Display strings (prompts and output labels) on the screen

   ii. Read nonnegative integer *(numEmployees)* and real numbers *(hoursWorked* and *hourlyRate)* from the keyboard

   iii. Compute *regularPay, overtimePay,* and *wages*

   iv. Display real values *(wages)* on the screen

   v. Repeat steps i–iv for each employee

From our earlier version of this problem, we know that i, ii, and iv are provided by the ann.easyio package. Operation iii is more complicated than our earlier formula for calculating wages because the calculations are done in two different ways:

If *hoursWorked* $\leq$ 40, calculate:
  regularPay = hoursWorked $\times$ *hourlyRate,*
  overtimePay = 0

Otherwise, calculate:
  regularPay = 40 $\times$ *hourlyRate,*
  overtimePay = OVERTIME_FACTOR $\times$ *(hoursWorkd* − 40) $\times$ *hourlyRate*

Then, calculate:
  wages = regularPay + overtimePay

So we see that the operations required by the formulas are

iii-a. Comparison of reals with $\leq$

iii-b. Multiplication of reals

iii-c. Addition of reals

iii-d. Store a real value in a variable

But we don't yet have a *selection* mechanism for choosing which set of formulas to use for *regularPay* and *overtimePay*. Several selection mechanisms are, in fact, provided in Java, and in this chapter we will look at one of these: the `if` *statement*. Others are considered in Chapter 7.

The other mechanism for controlling execution we need is for the repetition in (v). Java also provides several repetition structures, commonly called *loops,* the most popular of which is the `for` *statement* introduced in this chapter. The form of the `for` statement that we will use for this problem requires a counter variable to count the repetitions so we know when to stop. Thus, we must add one more problem object to our list:

Description of problem's object	Type	Kind	Name
. . .	. . .	. . .	. . .
Loop counter	`int`	variable	*count*

ALGORITHM. We now organize these objects and operations into an algorithm:

Algorithm for Improved Payroll Problem

1. Construct `Screen` object *theScreen* and `Keyboard` object *theKeyboard*.
2. Ask *theScreen* to display a prompt for the number of employees.
3. Ask *theKeyboard* to read an integer value and store it in *numEmployees.*
4. For *count* ranging from 1 through *numEmployees,* do the following:

   a. Ask *theScreen* to display prompts for the hours worked and the hourly pay rate for an employee.

   b. Ask *theKeyboard* to read a real value and store it in *hoursWorked,* and then read another real value and store it in *hourlyRate.*

c. If *hoursWorked* ≤ 40, calculate
   i. *regularPay = hoursWorked × hourlyRate,*
   ii. *overtimePay = 0*

Otherwise calculate:
   i. *regularPay = 40 × hourlyRate,*
   ii. *overtimePay = OVERTIME_FACTOR × (hoursWorked − 40) × hourlyRate*

d. Calculate *wages = regularPay + overtimePay.*
e. Ask *theScreen* to display a message containing *wages.*

Coding, Execution, and Testing

The program in Figure 5.1 implements the preceding algorithm. The `if` statement and the `for` statement are highlighted in color. Also shown is a sample run with a small data set.

FIGURE 5.1   PAYROLL PROGRAM—UPGRADED

```
/** Payroll1.java computes wages for several employees, with overtime paid
 *  for all hours above 40.
 *
 *  Input:  Hours worked and hourly rate for each employee
 *  Output: Each employee's wages
 */

import ann.easyio.*;                    // Keyboard, Screen

class Payroll1 extends Object
{
  public static void main(String [] args)
  {
    final double OVERTIME_FACTOR = 1.5;

    Screen theScreen = new Screen();
    Keyboard theKeyboard = new Keyboard();

    theScreen.print("\nEnter the number of employees: ");
    int numEmployees = theKeyboard.readInt();
    double hoursWorked, hourlyRate,
           regularPay, overtimePay, wages;

    // Loop to calculate wages for all employees
    for (int count = 1; count <= numEmployees; count++)
    {
      theScreen.print("\nFor employee #" + count + ", Enter: "
                      + "\n  hours worked: ");
      hoursWorked = theKeyboard.readDouble();
      theScreen.print("  hourly pay rate: ");
      hourlyRate = theKeyboard.readDouble();
```

```
// Calculate regular pay and overtime pay
if (hoursWorked <= 40)
{
  regularPay = hoursWorked * hourlyRate;
  overtimePay = 0;
}
else
{
  regularPay = 40 * hourlyRate;
  overtimePay = OVERTIME_FACTOR * (hoursWorked - 40) * hourlyRate;
}

wages = regularPay + overtimePay;
theScreen.print("\nEmployee's wages are $");
theScreen.printFormatted(wages, 2);
theScreen.println();
}
}
}
```

Sample run:

```
Enter the number of employees: 4
For employee #1, enter:
  hours worked: 40
  hourly pay rate: 10.00

Employee's wages are $400.00

For employee #2, enter:
  hours worked: 41
  hourly pay rate: 10.00

Employee's wages are $415.00

For employee #3, enter:
  hours worked: 38.5
  hourly pay rate: 8.25

Employee's wages are $317.62

For employee #4, enter:
  hours worked: 44
  hourly pay rate: 9.35

Employee's wages are $430.10
```

5.2   METHODS THAT USE SELECTION

As we noted in the introduction to this chapter, some problems cannot be solved using only sequential execution. They require more powerful mechanisms such as selection and repetition, both of which were used in the program in Figure 5.1. We will look at another problem in this section to illustrate one of the selection structures provided in Java.

PROBLEM: FINDING THE MINIMUM OF TWO VALUES

Write a method that, given two real values, returns the minimum of the two values.

OBJECT-CENTERED DESIGN

BEHAVIOR. Our method should receive two real values from its caller. If the first is less than the second, the method should return the first; otherwise, it should return the second.

THE PROBLEM'S OBJECTS. From the behavioral description, we can identify the following objects in this problem:

Description of problem's object	Type	Kind	Movement	Name
The first value	double	variable	received	*first*
The second value	double	variable	received	*second*
The minimum value	double	variable	returned	none

We can thus specify this problem as follows:

   Receive: *first* and *second,* two real values

   Return: the minimum of *first* and *second*

From this information, we can write the following stub for our method:

```
public static double minimum(double first, double second)
{
}
```

To fill in the body of the stub, we must look at what operations are needed to solve the problem.

OPERATIONS. Once again, from the problem's behavioral description, we can identify the following operations:

   i. Receive two real values from the method's caller
   ii. Compare two real values to see if one is less than the other
   iii. Return the first value
   iv. Return the second value
   v. Select either iii or iv (but not both), based on the result of ii

Operation (i) will occur automatically through the normal method-call mechanism, because we are providing two parameters to hold the values received:

```
double minimum(double first, double second)
```

Operation (ii) can be performed using the relational operator $<$ described in Section 3.5:

```
first < second
```

We have also seen that `return` statements can be used to perform the third and fourth operations:

```
return first;

return second;
```

Our difficulty is with the last operation. How can we select one and only one of these two `return` statements? The answer is to use Java's `if` **statement,** which allows the selection of either of a pair of statements.

ALGORITHM.   We can use a pseudocode version of an `if` statement to express the logic of our solution as follows:

> **Algorithm for Minimum of two numbers**
> 1. Receive first, second.
> 2. If *first < second*
>   return *first;*
>   otherwise
>   return *second.*

Coding.   In Java, this algorithm can be expressed as shown in Figure 5.2:

FIGURE 5.2.   A `minimum()` METHOD

```
/** minimum() finds the minimum of two doubles.
 * Receive: first and second, two double values
 * Return: the minimum of first and second
 */

public static double minimum(double first, double second)
{
   if (first < second)
      return first;
   else
      return second;
}
```

Testing.   To verify that our method is correct, we can test it with a simple driver program like that in Figure 5.3 that calls `minimum()`. We use a variety of input combinations to exercise it. As described earlier, once we have verified that `minimum()` behaves correctly, it can be stored in a class so that any program needing its functionality can reuse it easily.

FIGURE 5.3.   DRIVER PROGRAM TO TEST `minimum()`

```
// MinimumDriver.java tests the minimum() method.

import ann.easyio.*;                    // Keyboard, Screen

class MinimumDriver
{
  // Insert definition of minimum() from Figure 5.2 here

 public static void main(String [] args)
 {
   Keyboard theKeyboard = new Keyboard();
   Screen theScreen = new Screen();
   theScreen.print("Enter two numbers: ");
   double num1 = theKeyboard.readDouble();
   double num2 = theKeyboard.readDouble();
   theScreen.println("Minimum is " + minimum(num1, num2));
 }
}
```

Sample runs:

```
Enter two numbers: -2 -5
Minimum is -5

Enter two numbers: 3 -2
Minimum is -2

Enter two numbers: 3 3
Minimum is 3

Enter two numbers: 3 5
Minimum is 3
```

Sequential Execution

If we think of the flow of execution through a program as traveling along a roadway, then **sequential execution** is like traveling down a straight road from one place to another:

A **flow diagram** is a chart that uses arrows to indicate the order in which the statements in the diagram are executed. The following flow diagram shows the *straight line* pattern of execution that characterizes **sequential execution.**

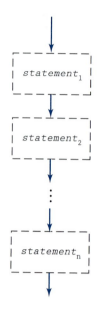

Some programmers prefer to use **box diagrams** instead of flow diagrams. A box diagram for sequential flow has the following form:

As these diagrams indicate, sequential execution refers to the execution of a sequence of statements in the order in which they given, so that each statement is executed exactly once. All of the methods of earlier chapters and sections were methods that used only sequential control.

Selective Execution

For situations where statements must be executed **selectively,** Java provides the `if` **statement** (and other selection statements described in Chapter 7). If we think of the flow of execution through a program as traveling along a roadway, we might visualize an `if` statement as a *fork* in the road:

In a flow diagram the fork is usually indicated by a diamond-shaped box that contains the boolean expression with one corner labeled true and one labeled false:

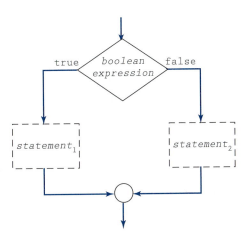

Based on the value of a boolean expression, execution will pass either through *statement₁* or through *statement₂, but not both,* before proceeding to the next statement. The corresponding box diagram for selection is

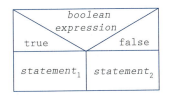

When execution reaches an `if` statement, its boolean expression is evaluated.

```
if (first < second)
    return first;
else
    return second;
```

If the boolean expression evaluates to true, then the statement in the `if` part is executed, and the `else` part is skipped:

```
if (first < second)
   return first;
else
   return second;
```

However, if the boolean expression evaluates to `false`, then the `if` part is skipped, and the statement in the `else` part is executed:

```
if (first < second)
   return first;
else
   return second;
```

In general, the form of the `if` statement can be summarized as follows:

`if` Statement (General Form)

Forms:

```
if (boolean_expression)
   statement
```
or
```
if (boolean_expression)
   statement₁
else
   statement₂
```
or
```
if (boolean_expression₁)
   statement₁
else if (boolean_expression₂)
   statement₂
      .
      .
      .
else if (boolean_expressionₙ)
   statementₙ
else
   statementₙ₊₁
```
where:
   `if` and `else` are keywords;
   each `statement`, `statement₁`, `statement₂`, . . . is a Java statement
   (and may be a *block* statement).

Purpose:

In the first form, if the `boolean_expression` is true, then `statement` is executed; otherwise `statement` is bypassed.

In the second form, if the `boolean_expression` is true, then `statement₁` is executed and `statement₂` is bypassed; otherwise `statement₁` is bypassed and `statement₂` is executed.

In the last form, if `boolean_expression`$_1$ is true, then `statement`$_1$ is executed and the remainder of the statement is bypassed; otherwise if `boolean_expression`$_2$ is true, then `statement`$_2$ is executed and the remainder of the statement is bypassed; and so on. If none of the `boolean_`
`expression`$_i$ is true, then `statement`$_{n+1}$ (if present) is executed.

Blocks

When a group of statements must be selected for execution, we enclose them between curly braces { and } to form a single statement. This is called a **block,** or a **compound statement:**

Block (Compound Statement)

Form

```
{
    statement₁
    statement₂
        .

        .

    statementₙ
}
```

where:
   each `statement`$_i$ is a Java statement.

Purpose

The sequence of statements is treated as a single statement, in which `statement`$_1$, `statement`$_2$, . . . , `statement`$_n$ are executed in order, with each statement being executed exactly once.

Note that the block does not require a semicolon after the final curly brace; a block is a complete statement by itself.

We have already seen examples of blocks: the body of a method is a block. Thus, the general form of a method definition can be described by

```
modifiers returnType methodName(parameterDeclarations)
block
```

A block is also used when more than one statement must be selected in an `if` statement. For example, the wage-calculation program in Figure 5.1 uses

```
if (hoursWorked <= 40)
{
   regularPay = hoursWorked * hourlyRate;
   overtimePay = 0;
}
else
{
   regularPay = 40 * hourlyRate;
   overtimePay = OVERTIME_FACTOR * (hoursWorked - 40) * hourlyRate;
}

wages = regularPay + overtimePay;
```

If the value of hoursWorked is 40.0 or less, the two statements in the first block are executed and the second block is bypassed. If the value of hoursWorked is greater than 40.0, the first block is bypassed and the second block is executed.

Checking Preconditions

In Section 4.3, we built the following methods to encode sphere-related formulas:

```
class Sphere
{
   public static double volume(double radius)
   {
      return 4.0 * Math.PI * Math.pow(radius, 3) / 3.0;
   }

   public static double mass(double radius, double density)
   {
      return density * volume(radius);
   }
}
```

These methods work correctly so long as the arguments passed by the caller satisfy the methods' preconditions, namely, that the arguments must be non-negative. But what happens if the caller violates a method's precondition by passing it a negative argument?

NOTE   In order for a method to work correctly when it receives arguments that violate a precondition, it should *check each precondition* and only proceed with the computation if that precondition is true. If the precondition is false (i.e., the arguments are invalid), the method can display an error message or throw an exception (see Chapter 10).

The if statement provides a way to check preconditions within a Java method. To illustrate, we might revise the body of the volume() method as follows:

```
public static double volume(double radius)
{
   if (radius >= 0)
      return 4.0 * Math.PI * Math.pow(radius, 3) / 3.0;
```

```
    else
    {
        System.err.println("\n*** Sphere.volume(): invalid radius "
                            + radius + " received.");
        return 0.0; // default return-value
    }
}
```

This new definition uses the if-else (second) form to test our precondition: if it is true, the method proceeds with the computation of the sphere's volume. Otherwise, the method displays a diagnostic message and returns a default value. To display this message, we have used the object err from Java's System **class** (in package java.lang), which is commonly used to display such error messages on the screen.

Since our mass() method has a more complicated precondition, we might use the if-else-if (third) form of the if statement to test each part of its precondition separately:

```
public static double mass(double radius, double density)
{
  if (radius < 0)          // if first precondition violated
  {
    System.err.println("\n*** Sphere.mass(): invalid radius "
                        + radius + " received.");
    return 0.0;
  }
  else if (density < 0)  // if second precondition violated
  {
    System.err.println("\n*** Sphere.mass(): invalid density "
                        + density + " received.");
    return 0.0;
  }
  else                       // both preconditions satisified
    return density * volume(radius);
}
```

By doing so, our diagnostic messages can describe what is wrong more precisely.

Style

There are a variety of styles used by programmers to write if statements. They differ in the placement of the statements in relation to the if and else keywords, the location of a block's curly braces, and so on. In our opinion, the key issue is *readability:*

Use a form that is easy to read.

Accordingly, we will

1. Align the if and the else, and
2. Use white space and indentation to clearly mark the statements that are being selected by the if and else.

When a single statement is being selected, we will usually indent that statement on the line below the `if` or the `else`; for example,

```
if (first < second)
    return first;
else
    return second;
```

When a block of statements is involved, we will place the curly braces on separate lines, aligned with the `if` and `else`, and indent the statements they enclose; for example:

```
if (hours > 40.0)
{
    overtime = hours - 40.0;
    overtimePay = 1.5 * overtime * rate;
    regularPay = 40.0 * rate;
}
else
{
    regularPay = hours * rate;
    overtimePay = 0.0;
}
```

In our opinion, consistent alignment of curly braces produces more readable code, and it reduces the chance of omitting the closing curly brace, a common problem for beginning programmers.

When writing `if-else-if` statements (the third form), we will place the `else` and the following `if` on the same line, and indent the statements in each part; for example:

```
if (percentage >= 90)
    grade = 'A';
else if (percentage >= 80)
    grade = 'B';
else if (percentage >= 70)
    grade = 'C';
else if (percentage >= 60)
    grade = 'D';
else
    grade = 'F';
```

Occasionally, when an `if` selects a single statement and has no associated `else`, we will place the statement on the same line as the `if`; for example:

```
if (x == 0) break;
```

To improve readability, we will usually put blank lines above and below such statements.

Nested ifs

The statements selected by if and else may be any Java statements; in particular, they may be other if statements. In this case, an inner if statement is said to be **nested** within the outer if statement.

When one if statement is nested within another, it may not be clear which ifs and elses are associated. (See Potential Pitfall 6 in the Programming Pointers at the end of this chapter.) The following important rule in Java resolves this ambiguity:

NOTE

In a nested if *statement, an* else *is matched with the nearest preceding unmatched* if.

Aligning each else with its corresponding if helps make this clear.

It should be noted that the if-else if form we considered earlier is really a nested if statement—we are simply reformatting

```
if (boolean_expression₁)
    statement₁
else
    if (boolean_expression₂)
        statement₂
    else
        if (boolean_expression₃)
            statement₃
          .
           .
            .

              else
                  if (boolean_expressionₙ)
                      statementₙ
                  else
                      statementₙ₊₁
```

by putting an if on the same line as the else that precedes it:

```
if (boolean_expression₁)
    statement₁
else if (boolean_expression₂)
    statement₂
else if (boolean_expression₃)
    statement₃
    .
    .
    .

else if (boolean_expressionₙ)
    statementₙ
else
    statementₙ₊₁
```

Not only is this more compact, but it also shows more clearly the *multi-alternative* nature of this structure in which exactly one of the *statementᵢ* will be selected for execution.

Method Signatures and Overloading

Earlier in this section, we considered a method `minimum()` for finding the minimum of two `double` values:

```
public static double minimum(double first, double second)
{
   if (first < second)
      return first;
   else
      return second;
}
```

It is likely that we will also need a method to find the minimum of two `int` values:

```
public static int minimum(int first, int second)
{
   if (first < second)
      return first;
   else
      return second;
}
```

Is it possible to use both of these methods in the same program?

It would seem that the answer to this question should be "no"—that using the same name for two different methods in the same program should generate an error. However, no name conflict occurs because the Java compiler is in fact able to distinguish these methods from one another without ambiguity by checking the methods' *signatures.*

The **signature** of a method consists of the name of the method and a list of the types of its parameters. For example, the signature of the `buildVerse()` method in Figure 4.1 is

```
buildVerse(String, String)
```

and the signature of the `volume()` method in Section 4.3 is

```
volume(double)
```

while the signature of the `mass()` method in this same program is

```
mass(double, double)
```

If two different methods have the same name, that method name is said to be **overloaded.** For example, when we use the same name for both of the preceding methods for finding the minimum of two values, we are overloading the name `minimum` with two different methods. The compiler is able to distinguish the methods from one another because they have different signatures. If we call `mimimum()` with two `int` values,

```
theScreen.println("Minimum is " + minimum(intVal1, intVal2));
```

the compiler associates this call with the first definition of the method `minimum()`, whose signature has two `int` types. However, if we call it with two `double` values,

```
theScreen.println("Minimum is " + minimum(dubVal1, dubVal2));
```

the compiler associates this call with the second definition of the method `minimum()`, whose signature has two `double` types.

Signatures thus allow the Java compiler to distinguish calls to different methods with the same name. As a result, we have the following rule governing overloading:

NOTE

> *The name of a method can be overloaded, provided no two definitions of the method have the same signature.*

Note that the return type of a method is not a part of its signature. Thus, two methods with identical signatures but with different return types cannot have the same name.

✔ Quick Quiz 5.2

In Questions 1–11, `theScreen` is a `Screen` object.
Questions 1–3 refer to the following `if` statement:

```
if (x >= y)
    theScreen.println(x);
else
    theScreen.println(y);
```

1. Describe the output produced if x = 6 and y = 5.
2. Describe the output produced if x = 5 and y = 5.
3. Describe the output produced if x = 5 and y = 6.

Questions 4–6 refer to the following `if` statement:

```
if (x >= 0)
    if (y >= 0)
        theScreen.println(x + y);
    else
        theScreen.println(x - y);
else
    theScreen.println(y - x);
```

4. Describe the output produced for x = 5 and y = 5.
5. Describe the output produced for x = 5 and y = –5.
6. Describe the output produced for x = –5 and y = 5.

Questions 7–11 refer to the following `if` statement:

```
if (n >= 90)
    theScreen.println("excellent");
else if (n >= 80)
    theScreen.println("good");
else if (n >= 70)
    theScreen.println("fair");
else
    theScreen.println("bad");
```

7. Describe the output produced for n = 100.

8. Describe the output produced for n = 90.

9. Describe the output produced for n = 89.

10. Describe the output produced for n = 70.

11. Describe the output produced for n = 0.

12. Write a statement that displays "Out of range" if number is negative or is greater than 100.

13. Write an efficient `if` statement to assign n the value 1 if $x \leq 1.5$, the value 2 if $1.5 < x < 2.5$, and the value 3 otherwise.

✎ EXERCISES 5.2

In Exercises 1–7, theScreen is a Screen object.
Exercises 1–4 refer to the following `if` statement:

```
if (x * y >= 0)
    theScreen.println("yes");
else
    theScreen.println("no");
```

1. Describe the output produced for x = 5 and y = 6.

2. Describe the output produced for x = 5 and y = −6.

3. Describe the output produced for x = −5 and y = 6.

4. Describe the output produced for x = −5 and y = −6.

Exercises 5–7 refer to the following `if` statement:

```
if (Math.abs(n) <= 4)
    if (n > 0)
        theScreen.println(2*n + 1);
    else
        theScreen.println(2*n);
else
    theScreen.println(n + " out of range");
```

5. Describe the output produced for n = 2.

6. Describe the output produced for n = −7.

7. Describe the output produced for n = 0.

For Exercises 8–10, write `if` statements that will do what is required.

8. If `taxCode` is 'T', increase `price` by adding `taxRate` percentage of `price` to it.

9. If `code` is 1, input values for x and y and calculate and display the sum of x and y.

10. If a is strictly between 0 and 5, set b equal to $1/a^2$; otherwise set b equal to a^2.

For Exercises 11–14, write methods that will do what is required. To test these methods, you should write driver programs as instructed in Programming Problems 1–5 at the end of this chapter.

11. Calculate a cost for a given distance, according to the following table:

Distance	Cost
0 through 100	5.00
More than 100 but not more than 500	8.00
More than 500 but less than 1000	10.00
1000 or more	12.00

12. A quadratic equation of the form $ax^2 + bx + c = 0$ has real roots if the discriminant $b^2 - 4ac$ is nonnegative. Write a method that receives the coefficients $a, b,$ and c of a quadratic equation, and returns true if the equation has real roots and false otherwise.

13. A certain city classifies a pollution index less than 35 as "pleasant," 35 through 60 as "unpleasant," and above 60 as "hazardous." Write a method that returns the appropriate classification for a pollution index.

14. A wind chill of 10° F or above is not considered dangerous or unpleasant; a wind chill of −10° F or higher but less than 10° F is considered unpleasant; if it is −30° F or above but less than −10° F, frostbite is possible; if it is −70° F or higher but below −30° F, frostbite is likely and outdoor activity becomes dangerous; if the wind chill is less than −70° F, exposed flesh will usually freeze within half a minute. Write a method that returns the appropriate weather condition for a wind chill index. (See Exercise 18 of Section 4.2 for a definition of wind chill.)

5.3   METHODS THAT USE REPETITION

We have seen that some problems can be solved with *sequential* execution. In the last section, we saw that there are problems whose solutions require *selection.* In this section we consider *repetition,* a different form of control that is needed to solve many problems.

PROBLEM: COMPUTING FACTORIALS

The **factorial** of a nonnegative integer n, denoted by **$n!$,** is defined by:

$$n! = \begin{cases} 1 \ if \ n = 0 \\ 1 \times 2 \times \cdots n \quad if \ n > 0 \end{cases}$$

Write a method that, given an integer $n \geq 0$, computes n factorial.

OBJECT-CENTERED DESIGN

BEHAVIOR. To describe how the method should behave, we might begin by looking at how to solve the problem by hand. We would probably begin with 1, multiply it by 2, multiply that product by 3, and so on, until we multiply it by n. For example, to find $5!$, we might do the following computation:

$$
\begin{array}{r}
1 \\
\times\, 2 \\
\hline
2 \\
\times\, 3 \\
\hline
6 \\
\times\, 4 \\
\hline
24 \\
\times\, 5 \\
\hline
120
\end{array}
$$

In order for our method to imitate this approach, we need to identify its various objects and the roles they play. It should be clear that we are keeping a running product and a counter:

$$
\begin{array}{rl}
1 & \leftarrow \quad \text{inital running product} \\
\times\, 2 & \leftarrow \quad \text{inital count} \\
\hline
2 & \leftarrow \quad \text{new running product} \\
\times\, 3 & \leftarrow \quad \text{new count} \\
\hline
6 & \leftarrow \quad \text{new running product} \\
\times\, 4 & \leftarrow \quad \text{new count} \\
\hline
24 & \leftarrow \quad \text{new running product} \\
\times\, 5 & \leftarrow \quad \text{new count} \\
\hline
120 & \leftarrow \quad \text{new running product}
\end{array}
$$

THE PROBLEM'S OBJECTS. This gives us the following list of problem objects:

Description of problem's object	Type	Kind	Movement	Name
A nonnegative integer	int	variable	received	*n*
The running product	int	variable	returned	*product*
The counter	int	variable	none (local)	*count*

This list allows us to specify the problem as follows:

Receive: n, an integer

Precondition: $n \geq 0$

Return: $product = n!$, an integer

From this information, we can write a stub for the method:

```
public static int factorial(int n)
{
}
```

To fill in the body of this stub, we must consider the operations required in the computation.

OPERATIONS.   Analysis of the operations performed in this approach gives the following list (in addition to receive/return operations):

i. Check the precondition ($n \geq 0$)

ii. Define and initialize two integer variables (*product* and *count*)

iii. Multiply two integers (*product* and *count*) and assign the result to an integer (*product*)

iv. Increment an integer variable (*count*)

v. Repeat operations iii and iv so long as *count* is less than or equal to *n*

In the previous section, we saw how the `if` statement can be used for the first operation. The second operation is also familiar:

```
int product = 1;
int count = 2;
```

We have also seen how to perform operation iii,

```
product *= count;
```

and operation iv:

```
count++;
```

The difficulty lies with operation v. *How can statements be executed more than once?* One way is to use a `for` **loop** to execute a statement once for each number in a given range.

ALGORITHM.   The idea of the `for` loop can be captured in pseudocode as shown in the following algorithm for our problem:

Algorithm for Factorial Computation

1. Receive a number *n* from the caller; check the precondition.

2. Initialize *product* to 1.

3. Repeat the following for each value of *count* in the range 2 through *n*:
   Multiply *product* by *count*

4. Return *product*.

CODING.   The method given in Figure 5.4 implements this algorithm:

FIGURE 5.4 METHOD factorial()

```
/** factorial() computes the factorial of a nonnegative integer.
 * Receive:       n, an integer
 * Precondition:  n >= 0
 * Return:        n! = 1 * 2 * ... * (n-1) * n
 */

public static int factorial(int n)
{
  if (n < 0)                             // check precondition
  {
    System.err.println("\n*** factorial(n): n must be non-negative");
    System.exit(1);
  }

  int product = 1;

  for (int count = 2; count <= n; count++)
    product *= count;

  return product;
}
```

TESTING. To test this method, we can write a simple driver program like that in Figure 5.5 to display the values returned by the method for some easy-to-check inputs.

FIGURE 5.5 DRIVER FOR METHOD factorial()

```
// FactorialDriver.java tests the factorial() method

import ann.easyio.*;

class FactorialDriver
{
 // Insert definition of factorial() from Figure 5.4 here

 public static void main(String [] args)
 {
   Screen theScreen = new Screen();
   theScreen.print("To compute n!, enter n: ");
   Keyboard theKeyboard = new Keyboard();
   int number = theKeyboard.readInt();
   theScreen.println(number + "! = " + factorial(number));
 }
}
```

Sample runs:

```
To compute n!, enter n: 0
0! = 1

To compute n!, enter n: 1
1! = 1

To compute n!, enter n: 5
5! = 120

To compute n!, enter n: 12
12! = 479001600

To compute n!, enter n: -1

*** factorial(n): invalid argument -1 received
```

Note that both valid and invalid input values are used in the sample runs, to ensure that our precondition-testing code is working correctly. These results indicate that our `factorial()` method performs as expected for values of n through 12. Further testing of this method is discussed at the end of this section.

Repeated Execution: The `for` Statement

If we once again think of executing a program as being analogous to driving on a roadway, then a repeated execution of a portion of the program is analogous to driving onto a race track, circling it for a certain number of laps, and then leaving the track to resume traveling on the roadway:

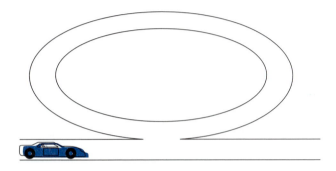

Notice that there are three parts to this **repetition mechanism** (also called a **loop**):

1. *Initialization* ("entering the track")
2. *Repeated execution* ("circling the track")
3. *Termination* ("leaving the track")

For algorithms like our factorial algorithm in which a statement must be executed more than once, Java provides the `for` **statement** (and other repetition statements described in Chapter 8), which executes a statement *repeatedly,* so long as a boolean expression is true.

To illustrate, consider the `for` statement from Figure 5.4:

```
for (int count = 2; count <= n; count++)
    product *= count;
```

When it is executed, this `for` statement behaves as shown in the following flow-graph,

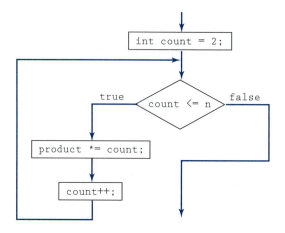

or as a box diagram:

```
int count = 2;

while count <= n

        product *= count;

        count **;
```

When execution reaches the loop, the variable count is created and initialized to 2. The value of count is then tested against n. If count exceeds n, control passes immediately to the next statement. However, if count is less than or equal to n, then the statement controlled by the loop is executed, which multiplies product by count. The value of count is then incremented by 1, after which control returns to the top of the loop where the boolean expression count <= n is re-evaluated and the cycle starts again. This cyclical behavior continues as long as the boolean expression count <= n evaluates to true.

Another way to understand the execution of a loop is with a **trace table,** which traces the execution of the loop's statements, one at a time. The following is a trace table for the execution of factorial(5):

Time	Statement Executed	product	count	Comment
0	`int count = 2;`	1	2	loop initialization
1	`count <= n`	1	2	`true`, loop executes
2	`product *= count;`	2	2	`product` updated
3	`count++;`	2	3	`count` incremented
4	`count <= n`	2	3	`true`, loop executes
5	`product *= count;`	6	3	`product` updated
6	`count++;`	6	4	`count` incremented
7	`count <= n`	6	4	`true`, loop executes
8	`product *= count;`	24	4	`product` updated
9	`count++;`	24	5	`count` incremented
10	`count <= n`	24	5	`true`, loop executes
11	`product *= count;`	120	5	`product` updated
12	`count++;`	120	6	`count` incremented
13	`count <= n`	120	6	`false`, repetition ceases

The `for` statement has the following general form:

`for` Statement

Form:
```
for (initExpression; booleanExpression; stepExpression)
    statement
```
where:
  `for` is a keyword;
  `initExpression`, `booleanExpression`, and `stepExpression`
    are Java expressions; and
  `statement` is a Java statement (individual or block).

Purpose:
When execution reaches a `for` statement, the following actions occur:
  (1) `initExpression` is evaluated.
  (2) `booleanExpression` is evaluated.
  (3) If `booleanExpression` is true, then
      a. `statement` is executed.
      b. `stepExpression` is evaluated.
      c. Control returns to Step (2).
    Otherwise
      Control passes to the statement immediately following the `for` statement.

Note that, like the `if` statement, a `for` loop controls access to a *statement*, called the **body** of the loop, which can be either a single statement, as in

```
for (int count = 2; count <= n; count++)
    product *= count;
```

or a block of statements:

```
theScreen.print("How many values? ");
int numValues = theKeyboard.readInt();
int newValue,
    sum = 0,
    sumOfSquares = 0;
for (int count = 1; count <= numValues; count++)
{
    newValue = theKeyboard.readDouble();
    sum += newValue;
    sumOfSquares += newValue * newValue;
}
```

Note also that allowing the *stepExpression* to be an arbitrary expression makes the `for` loop very flexible. For example, to count downwards from 10 to 1, we could write

```
for (int value = 10; value >= 1; value--)
    theScreen.print(" " + value);
```

which will display

```
10 9 8 7 6 5 4 3 2 1
```

Similarly, to count from 0 to 2 by 0.5, we could write

```
for (double counter = 0.0; counter <= 2.0; counter += 0.5)
    theScreen.print(" " + counter);
```

which will display

```
0.0 0.5 1.0 1.5 2.0
```

Finally, note that when the `for` statement is being used to count by ones, either the prefix or the postfix form of the increment (or decrement) operator can be used. That is, to count from 1 to 10, we can write either

```
for (int count = 1; count <= 10; count++)
    statement
```

or

```
for (int count = 1; count <= 10; ++count)
    statement
```

The two are equivalent because each adds 1 to `count`, as described in Section 3.4.

Processing Several Input Values

The driver program in Figure 5.5 for computing factorials suffers from one major drawback: It processes only one value of n. To compute factorials for other values, the program must be re-executed, which is very inconvenient.

A more user-friendly program would permit the user to process any number of values before it terminated. One way to do this is to have the user specify in advance how many values are to be processed and then wrap the body of the program in a for loop that counts from 1 to that number, as shown in the following main method:

```
public static void main(String [] args)
{
    Screen theScreen = new Screen();
    theScreen.print("This program computes n! for n >= 0.\n"
            + "How many factorials do you wish to compute? ");
    Keyboard theKeyboard = new Keyboard();
    int numValues = theKeyboard.readInt();
    int n;
    for (int count = 1; count <= numValues; count++)
    {
      theScreen.print("\nEnter n: ");
      n = theKeyboard.readInt();
      theScreen.println(n + "! = " + factorial(n));
    }
}
```

A sample run might appear as follows:

```
This program computes n! for n >= 0.
How many factorials do you wish to compute? 3

Enter n: 5
5! = 120

Enter n: 2
2! = 2

Enter n: 1
1! = 1
```

By enclosing the critical portion of a driver program within a loop, we can process several input data values without having to re-execute the program. This was the approach used in the payroll problem in Section 5.1, where the number of employees was entered and a loop repeated the wage calculation for that many employees.

The drawback to this approach is that it requires knowing the number of input values in advance, which may be difficult to determine. Moreover, when testing a program, one usually does not know in advance how many data values will be used.

Fortunately, the for loop provides a better approach. Figure 5.6 illustrates.

FIGURE 5.6 COMPUTING SEVERAL FACTORIALS

```
// FactorialLoopDriver.java computes any number of factorials.

import ann.easyio.*;

class FactorialLoopDriver
{
 // Insert the definition of factorial() from Figure 5.4 here

 public static void main(String [] args)
 {
    Screen theScreen = new Screen();
    Keyboard theKeyboard = new Keyboard();
    int theNumber;

  for (;;)
  {
    theScreen.print("To compute n!, enter n (-1 to quit): ");
    theNumber = theKeyboard.readInt();

    if (theNumber < 0) break;

    theScreen.println(theNumber + "! = "
                      + factorial(theNumber) + "\n");
  }
 }
}
```

Sample run:

```
To compute n!, enter n (-1 to quit): 1
1! = 1

To compute n!, enter n (-1 to quit): 2
2! = 2

To compute n!, enter n (-1 to quit): 5
5! = 120

To compute n!, enter n (-1 to quit): 6
6! = 720

To compute n!, enter n (-1 to quit): -1
```

We call the special kind of loop used in this program a **forever loop** because it repeats its body an unspecified number of times. More precisely, if the *initExpression*, *booleanExpression*, and *stepExpression* are omitted from a `for` loop as in the main method of Figure 5.6, the statements in the loop body will be repeated *indefinitely*. For this reason, such loops are sometimes referred to as **indefinite loops.**[2]

Since the boolean expression that normally controls repetition is omitted in a forever loop, some other means of terminating repetition must be provided. This is typically accomplished with an `if-break` **combination**—an `if` statement that selects a `break` **statement** when its boolean expression is true:

---

[2] Almost all modern programming languages provide indefinite loops. For example, C++ provides the same `for` statement as Java, *Ada* and *Turing* provide the `loop` statement, *Modula-2* and *Modula-3* the LOOP statement, and *Fortran 90* the DO loop. Many *Fortran 90* programmers use only indefinite input loops, and *Turing* provides *only* an indefinite loop.

```
for (;;)
{
    theScreen.print("To compute n!, enter n (-1 to quit): ");
    theNumber = theKeyboard.readInt();

    if (theNumber < 0) break;

    theScreen.println(theNumber + "! = "
                    + factorial(theNumber) + "\n");
}
```

When it is executed, the `break` statement immediately transfers control to the first statement that follows the loop (in this case, the end of the main method).[3] Since the `break` statement is selected only when the boolean expression `theNumber < 0` evaluates to true, repetition will stop only when a negative value is entered for `theNumber`. Such a boolean expression is called a **termination condition** or **exit condition.**

In a similar manner, we could have used an indefinite loop in the payroll program in Figure 5.1:

```
int count = 1;
for (;;)
{
    theScreen.print("\nFor employee #" + count + ", Enter: "
                  + "\n hours worked (-1 to quit): ");
    hoursWorked = theKeyboard.readDouble();
    if (hoursWorked < 0) break;
    . . .
    // calculate and display employee's pay
    count++;
}
```

In these examples, the user is instructed to enter an invalid value called a **sentinel** when there are no more values to process. (Here, any negative value can serve as a sentinel, because factorials are defined only for nonnegative integers and `hoursWorked` must be a nonnegative value.) This general pattern

```
for (;;)
{
    // prompt for a value
    // input a value

    if (the value is the sentinel) break;

    // if execution gets here, then the value is not the sentinel,
    // so process it as a normal value.
}
```

---

[3] An alternative form of the break statement,

```
break label;
```

can be used to transfer control to a statement with the specified label. See Section 8.2 for more information.

is called **sentinel-based input processing,** and can be used for a wide variety of problems that involve processing lists of data.[4]

A general form for the forever loop is as follows:[5]

The Forever Loop

Form:

```
for (;;)
{
    statementList₁

    if (booleanExpression) break;
    // or if (booleanExpression) return;

    statementList₂
}
```

where:
for, if, and break are Java keywords;
booleanExpression is a termination condition, and
statementList₁ and statementList₂ are sequences of zero or more Java statements.

Purpose:

statementList₁ is executed and the booleanExpression is then evaluated. If it is true, repetition terminates; otherwise statementList₂ is executed, statementList₁ is executed, and the booleanExpression is evaluated again. This continues until the booleanExpression becomes true.

In the case of an if-break combination, execution of the loop will terminate, and execution will continue with the statement immediately following the loop.

In the case of an if-return combination, the loop and the method containing it are terminated, and control returns to the calling method.

---

[4] Some programmers whose experience is with earlier programming languages prefer using a while loop (described in Chapter 8) for sentinel-based processing:

```
// prompt for a value
// input a value
while (the value is not the sentinel)
{
    // process the value
    // prompt for a value
    // input a value
}
```

However, this approach requires prompting for and inputting values before the loop is entered, and again at the bottom of the loop body. Such duplication of code is eliminated in a forever loop approach. The preceding form of input loop also seems to be less intuitive for a beginning programmer.

[5] Some programmers prefer to write forever loops using a while loop of the form

```
while(true)
    body of loop
```

The two forms are completely equivalent. We use the for-loop version in this text because this has been the "standard" way to write such loops in C and C++, the ancestral languages of Java. If desired, for(;;) may be replaced everywhere with while(true) and the programs will work.

Note that *statementList*$_1$ and *statementList*$_2$ are optional. If *statementList*$_2$ is omitted,

```
for (;;)
{
  statementList₁
  if (booleanExpression) break;
}
```

the resulting loop is called a **posttest** (or **test-at-the-bottom**) **loop.** Posttest loops have special uses, because testing the exit condition at the end of the loop guarantees that *the loop body is executed at least once.*

By contrast, if *statementList*$_1$ is omitted,

```
for (;;)
{
    if (booleanExpression) break;
    statementList₂
}
```

then the loop is called a **pretest** (or **test-at-the-top**) **loop**. Pretest loops also have special uses, because testing the exit condition at the top means that *if the exit condition is initially true, statementList$_2$ will not be executed at all.* As we will see in Chapter 8, Java provides other statements that provide a more convenient way to write pretest and posttest loops.

Testing and Maintaining `factorial()`

Testing `factorial()` More Carefully. In the sample runs given in Figure 5.6, we saw that the `factorial()` method behaves correctly for the values 1 through 12. If we enter the value 13, the program executes as follows:

```
To compute n!, enter n: 13
13! = 1932053504
```

However, 13! = 6227020800 and not 1932053504; thus, for n = 13, and in fact, for all n ≥ 13, the values returned by our `factorial()` method are not valid. This illustrates the importance of **exhaustive testing:** just because a method works correctly for a few easily-checked values does not mean it works correctly for all values!

Maintaining the `factorial()` Method. There is nothing wrong with the *algorithm* our method uses. The problem is our use of the int type for the value our method computes and returns—the factorial function grows too rapidly for the int type to represent most of its values. (See the *Part of the Picture: Data Representation* section in Chapter 2 for a discussion of the limitations of representing integers in a fixed amount of memory.)

To address this problem, we can use the same algorithm, but we must find a different way to represent the values our method computes. One approach is to use the BigInteger reference type described in Sections 3.2 and 3.3, since it allows the representation of integer values bounded only by the amount of available memory. Converting our method to use `BigInteger` values instead of `int` values is straightforward, provided we consult the Java `BigInteger` API to see how to perform the operations our method needs. For example, when `product` and `count` are `int` variables, we can write

```
product *= count;
```

but when `product` and `count` are `BigInteger` variables, we must write

```
product = product.multiply(count);
```

because shortcut operators that work for the primitive numeric types do not work for reference numeric types like `BigInteger`. Figure 5.7 shows the complete method and driver, with the differences from the previous version highlighted in color.

FIGURE 5.7   DRIVER FOR `BigInteger` METHOD `factorial()`

```java
// BigIntegerFactorialDriver.java tests the factorial() method.

import ann.easyio.*;                              // Screen, Keyboard
import java.math.BigInteger;

class BigIntegerFactorialDriver
{
  final static BigInteger ZERO = new BigInteger("0");

 /** factorial() computes n!, given a nonnegative BigInteger
  * Receive:      n, a BigInteger
  * Precondition: n >= 0
  * Return:       n! = 1 * 2 * ... * (n-1) * n
  */
 public static BigInteger factorial(BigInteger n)
 {
   if(n.compareTo(ZERO) < 0)                       // check precondition
   {
     System.err.println("\n*** factorial(n): invalid argument "
                        + n + "received");
     System.exit(1);
   }
   final BigInteger ONE = new BigInteger("1");   // constant 1
   BigInteger product = new BigInteger("1");

   for (BigInteger count = new BigInteger("2");  // initExpression
                   count.compareTo(n) <= 0;       // booleanExpression
                   count = count.add(ONE))        // stepExpression
      product = product.multiply(count);          // statement

   return product;
 }
```

```
public static void main(String [] args)
{
  Screen theScreen = new Screen();
  Keyboard theKeyboard = new Keyboard();
  String numberString;
  BigInteger theNumber;
  for (;;)
  {
    theScreen.print("To compute n!, enter n (-1 to quit): ");
    numberString = theKeyboard.readWord();
    theNumber = new BigInteger(numberString);

    if (theNumber.compareTo(ZERO) < 0) break;

    theScreen.println(theNumber + "! = "
        + factorial(theNumber) + "\n");
  }
}
}
```

Sample runs:

```
To compute n!, enter n: 12
12! = 479001600

To compute n!, enter n: 13
13! = 6227020800

To compute n!, enter n: 20
20! = 2432902008176640000

To compute n!, enter n: 40
40! = 815915283247897734345611269596115894272000000000

To compute n!, enter n: 69
69! = 17112245242814131137246833888127283909227054489
520369939364804092325727975414064742400000000000000000

To compute n!, enter n: 70
70! = 11978571669969891796072783721689098736458938142
5464258575553628646280095827898453196800000000000000000

To compute n!, enter n: 100
100! = 9332621544394415268169923885626670049071596826438
16214685929638952175999932299156089414639761565182862586
36979208272237582511852109168640000000000000000000000000
```

As indicated by the sample runs, this version of the method computes and returns correct values for 13 (the point at which our `int` version failed), for 70 (the point at which our hand calculator failed), and beyond.

Once it is thoroughly tested, `factorial()` should be moved to a separate class (e.g., `MyMath`) so that any program needing to use this method can do so conveniently.

✔ Quick Quiz 5.3

In the following questions, `theScreen` is a `Screen` object and `theKeyboard` is a `Keyboard` object. For Questions 1–8, describe the output produced.

```
1. for (int i = 1; i <= 5; i++)
     theScreen.println("Hello");
```

```
2. for (int i = 1; i < 4; i++)
     theScreen.print("Hello");
```

```
3. for (int i = 1; i <= 5; i += 2)
     theScreen.println("Hello");
```

```
4. for (int i = 1; i < 7; i++)
     theScreen.println(i + "  " + (i + 1));
```

```
5. for (int i = 6; i > 0; i--)
     theScreen.println("\n" + i*i);
```

```
6. for (int i = 6; i <= 6; i++)
     theScreen.println("Hello");
```

```
7. for (int i = 6; i <= 5; i++)
     theScreen.println("Hello);
```

```
8. for (int i = 1; i <= 10; i++)
   {
     theScreen.println(i);
     i++;
   }
```

9. How many lines of output are produced by the following?

```
      for (int i = 1; i < 6; i++)
      {
          theScreen.println(i);
          for (int j = 0; j <= 3; j++)
             theScreen.println(i + j);
      }
```

10. What is the difference between a pretest and a posttest loop?

11. (True or false) A pretest loop is always executed at least once.

12. (True or false) A posttest loop is always executed at least once.

13. Assuming that `number` is an `int` variable, describe the output produced by the following loop:

```
      for (;;)
      {
          if (number > 100) break;
          theScreen.println(number);
          number *= 2;
      }
```

14. Assume that `number` and `limit` are `int` variables in the following code segment:

```
limit = theKeyboard.readInt();
number = 0;
for (;;)
{
    if (number > limit) break;
    theScreen.println(number);
    number++;
}
```

Describe the output produced for the following inputs:

(a) 4   (b) −2

15. Assume that `number` and `limit` are `int` variables in the following code segment:

```
limit = theKeyboard.readInt();
number = 0;
for (;;)
{
    theScreen.println(number);
    number++;
    if (number > limit) break;
}
```

Describe the output produced for the following inputs:

(a) 4   (b) −2

✍ EXERCISES 5.3

For Exercises 1–5, describe the output produced.

1.
```
for (int i = −2; i <= 3; i++)
    theScreen.println(i + " squared = " + i*i);
```

2.
```
for (int i = 1; i <= 5; i++)
{
    theScreen.println(i);
    for (int j = i; j >= 1; j--)
        theScreen.println(j);
}
```

3.
```
int k = 5;
for (int i = −2; i <= 3; i++)
{
    theScreen.println(i + k);
    k = 1;
}
```

4.
```
for (int i = 1; i <= 3; i++)
    for (int j = 1; j <= 3; j++)
        for (int k = 1; k <= j; k++)
            theScreen.print(i + " " + j + " " + k);
```

5.
```
for (int i = 1; i <= 3; i++)
    for (int j = 1; j <= 3; j++)
    {
        for (int k = i; k <= j; k++)
            theScreen.print(i + " " + j + " " + k);
        theScreen.println();
    }
```

6.
```
int i = 0, j = 0, k;
for (;;)
{
    k = 2 * i * j;
    if (k > 10)  break;
    theScreen.print(i + " " + j + " " + k);
    i++;
    j++;
}
theScreen.println(k);
```

7.
```
int i = 0, j = 0, k;
for (;;)
{
    k = 2 * i * j;
    if (k > 10) break;
    theScreen.print(i + " " + j + " " + k);
    if (i + j > 5) break;
    i++;
    j++;
}
theScreen.println(k);
```

8.
```
int i = 5, j;
for (;;)
{
    theScreen.println(i);
    i -= 2;
    if (i < 1) break;
    j = 0;
    for (;;)
    {
        j++;
        theScreen.println(j);
        if (j >= i) break;
    }
    theScreen.println("###");
}
theScreen.println("****");
```

Each of the program segments in Exercises 9–11 is intended to find the smallest integer number for which the sum $1 + 2 + \cdots + $ number is greater than limit. For each exercise, make three trace tables that display the values of number and sum, one table for each of the following values of limit:

(a) 10   (b) 1   (c) 0

9.
```
/* Using a pretest loop */
number = 0;
sum = 0;
for (;;)
{
    if (sum > limit) break;
    number++;
    sum += number;
}
```

10.
```
/* Using a posttest loop */
number = 0;
sum = 0;
for (;;)
{
    number++;
    sum += number;
    if (sum > limit) break;
}
```

11.
```
/* Using a test-in-the middle loop */
number = 0;
sum = 0;
for (;;)
{
    number++;
    if (sum > limit) break;
    sum += number;
}
```

For Exercises 12 and 13, write methods that will do what is required. To test these methods, you should write driver programs as instructed in Programming Problems 7 and 8 at the end of this chapter.

12. For a positive integer n, use a for loop to find the sum $1 + 2 + \cdots + n$ and return this sum.

13. For two integers m and n with $m \leq n$, use a for loop to find the sum $m + m+1 + \cdots + n$ and return this sum.

For Exercises 14–20, write a loop to do what is asked for.

14. Display the squares of the first 100 positive integers in increasing order.

15. Display the cubes of the first 50 positive integers in decreasing order.

16. Display the square roots of the first 25 odd positive integers.

17. Display a list of points (x, y) on the graph of $y = x^3 - 3x + 1$ for x ranging from -2 to 2 in steps of 0.1.

18. Display the value of x and decrease x by 0.5 as long as x is positive.

19. Read values for a, b, and c and display their sum, repeating this as long as none of a, b, or c is negative.

20. Calculate and display the squares of consecutive positive integers until the difference between a square and the preceding one is greater than 50.

5.4 GRAPHICAL/INTERNET JAVA: *OLD MACDONALD . . .* APPLET REVISITED

In the Graphical/Internet Java section of the last chapter, we gave an applet that displayed a few verses of the song *Old MacDonald Had a Farm* and a picture of Mr. MacDonald. Since this was our first introduction to using frames, layout managers, and content panes, we deliberately kept the example quite simple so we could focus on the widgets provided in Java's Swing classes to produce graphical output.

To generate the verses, we simply concatenated three verses generated by the `buildVerse()` method from Section 4.1, but with animal names and sounds that were "hard-coded" into the program:

```
String lyrics = buildVerse("cow", "moo")
         + buildVerse("sheep", "baa")
         + buildVerse("duck", "quack");
         // plus any other verses
```

We created a `JTextArea` named `song` that contained these verses and put it in the leftmost (west) region of the content pane:

```
JTextArea song = new JTextArea(lyrics);
getContentPane().add(song, "West");
```

Recall that a `JTextArea` is a container that can hold several lines of text.

Finally, we created a `JLabel` named `farmerPicture` that contained the picture of Mr. MacDonald and placed it in the rightmost (east) region of the content pane:

```
JLabel farmerPicture = new JLabel(new ImageIcon("farmer.gif"));
getContentPane().add(farmerPicture, "East");
```

The `JLabel` container is intended for use with short strings or images.

Now that we have more control structures, we can write versions of this applet whose structure is more flexible. We give one example in this section; others are suggested in the exercises. In this version we will allow the user to enter the names of several animals, and, for each animal, the sound it makes. As we saw in Section 2.5, an easy way to do this is with an input dialog created by the `showInputDialog()` method in the `JOptionPane` class. We can invoke this method in a statement of the form

```
String users_input = JOptionPane.showInputDialog(prompt);
```

which will:

1. Construct an input dialog in the center of the screen

2. Display the prompt in it along with a text field for user input and buttons labeled *OK* and *Cancel*

3. Return the string entered by the user (when the *OK* button is clicked or the Enter key pressed) and assign it to the `String` variable *users_input*

For example, the applet in Figure 5.8 uses the statement

```
String animalName
    = JOptionPane.showInputDialog("Animal #" + count + " name:");
```

to construct an input dialog for the user to enter the name of an animal. When it is executed, a window like the following is displayed:

Here the user entered "horse" for the animal's name and this string was assigned to `animalName`. A similar statement,

```
String animalSound
    = JOptionPane.showInputDialog("Animal #" + count + " sound:");
```

is used to create an input dialog in which the user can enter the sound for that animal:

The animal's name and sound can now be passed to the `buildVerse()` method we have used before to generate a verse of the *Old MacDonald* song.

We have one problem remaining, however, and that is how to generate several verses with different animals and sounds and have them appear in the `JTextArea` container `song`. But this is easy. We simply start by inserting an empty `song` in the leftmost region of our content pane,

```
JTextArea song = new JTextArea();
getContentPane().add(song, "West");
```

A `for` loop can then be used to carry out the repetition:

For a counter ranging from 1 to the number of verses desired do the following:

    a. Have the user input an animal's name and sound.

    b. Call the `buildVerse()` method to generate a verse of the song.

    c. Append this verse to the song already placed in the content pane.

The `append()` method provided in the `JTextArea` class can be used to carry out Step (c):

```
song.append(lyrics);
```

Figure 5.8 shows the complete applet. The `for` loop that carries out the preceding repetition is highlighted in color. Also shown is the window produced by a sample run of the program.

FIGURE 5.8   OLD MACDONALD APPLET—MODIFIED

```java
/** OldMacDonald2.java displays the lyrics to "Old MacDonald."
 *  Input:   names of animals and the sounds they make
 *  Output:  the lyrics of the song
 *
 *  HTML note -- include the following in your web page:
 *     <APPLET CODE="OldMacDonald2.class" WIDTH=550 HEIGHT=350>
 *                                                        </APPLET>
 */

import javax.swing.*;              // JApplet, JTextArea, JLabel
public class OldMacDonald2 extends JApplet
{

/**  utility method to simplify verse-building
 *   Receive: creature, a String; sound, a String
 *   Return: a verse of "Old MacDonald" using creature and sound
 */

 private static String buildVerse(String creature, String sound)
 {
    return "\nOld MacDonald had a farm, E-I-E-I-O"
         + "\nAnd on this farm he had a " + creature + ", E-I-E-I-O"
         + "\nWith a " + sound + "-" + sound + " here and a " +
                  sound + "-" + sound + " there"
         + "\nHere a " + sound + " there a " + sound +
              " everywhere a " + sound + "-" + sound
         + "\nOld MacDonald had a farm, E-I-E-I-O\n";
 }

public void init()
 {
    final int NUMBER_OF_VERSES = 3;

    JTextArea song = new JTextArea();
    getContentPane().add(song, "West");

    JLabel farmerPicture = new JLabel(new ImageIcon("farmer.gif"));
    getContentPane().add(farmerPicture, "East");

    for (int count = 1; count <= NUMBER_OF_VERSES; count++)
    {
      String animalName
           = JOptionPane.showInputDialog("Animal #" + count + " name:");
      String animalSound
           = JOptionPane.showInputDialog("Animal #" + count + " sound:");
      String lyrics
           = buildVerse(animalName, animalSound);
      song.append(lyrics);
    }
 }
}
```

The output produced for the inputs "horse", "neigh", "cat", "Meow", "gorilla", and "G-R-R" is as follows:

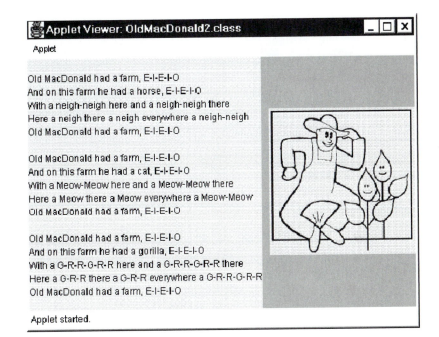

PART OF THE PICTURE: COMPUTABILITY THEORY

We have seen that if a needed operation is not predefined in Java, we can remedy the situation by designing and implementing a *method* to perform that operation. We have also seen how to build methods that use *sequential execution, selection* and *repetition.*

Selection and repetition enable us to build methods that are more powerful than those limited to sequential execution. There are methods that use sequence and selection for which there is no equivalent method that uses only sequential execution. Similarly, there are methods that use sequence, selection, and repetition for which there is no equivalent method that uses only sequence and selective execution.

Stated differently, *the set of all operations that can be performed using only sequential execution is a proper subset of the set of all operations that can be performed using sequence and selection. And the set of all operations that can be performed using only sequential and selective execution is a proper subset of the set of all operations that can be performed using sequence, selection, and repetition.*

The following **Venn Diagram** pictures the relationship between these three categories:

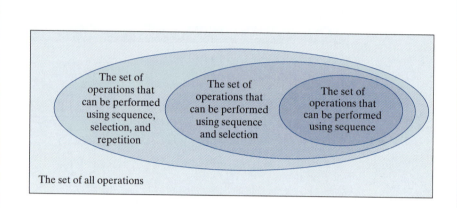

Selection statements allow us to design and implement operations that are more powerful than those we can build using only sequence; and repetition statements allow us to design and implement operations that are more powerful than those that can be built using only sequence and selection.

This is a result from **computability theory,** a branch of computer science that investigates (from a theoretical viewpoint) interesting questions such as the following:

❑ What kinds of operations can (or cannot) be computed?

❑ How can operations be classified, and what relationships exist among those classes?

❑ What is the most efficient algorithm for solving a particular problem?

Rather than ask questions about programs written in an existing language or that run on a particular hardware platform (both of which become obsolete all too soon), theoreticians represent programs *abstractly,* using mathematical models (e.g., *the set of all operations that use only sequence*). The advantage of this is that when a theoretician discovers something that is true about the model, then that result is true for all programs and methods represented by that model, regardless of the language in which they are written and regardless of the hardware on which they execute!

This **language and hardware independence** gives theoretical work a sense of *timelessness*—a theoretical result that is true today will still be true tomorrow. Although programming languages and hardware platforms come and go, theoretical results endure.

PART OF THE PICTURE: NUMERICAL METHODS

Mathematical models are used to solve problems in a wide variety of areas including science, engineering, business, and the social sciences. Many of these models consist of ordinary algebraic equations, differential equations, systems of equations, and so on, and the solution of the problem is obtained by finding solutions for these equations. Methods for solving such equations with a computer program are called **numerical methods,** and the development and analysis of such numerical methods is an important area of study.

Some of the major types of problems in which numerical methods are routinely used include the following:

1. *Curve fitting.* In many applications, the solution of a problem requires analyzing data consisting of pairs of values to determine whether the items in these pairs are related. For example, a sociologist might wish to determine whether there is a linear relationship between educational level and income level.

2. *Solving equations.* Such problems deal with finding the value of a variable that satisfies a given equation.

3. *Integration.* The solution of many problems such as finding the area under a curve, determining total revenue generated by sales of an item, calculating probabilities of certain events, and calculating work done by a force, require the evaluation of an integral. Often these integrals can only be evaluated using numerical techniques.

4. *Differential equations.* Differential equations are equations that involve one or more derivatives of unknown functions. They play an important role in many applications, and several effective and efficient numerical methods for solving these equations have been developed.

5. *Solving linear systems.* Linear systems consist of several equations, each of which has several unknowns. A solution of such a system is a collection of values for these unknowns that satisfies all of the equations simultaneously.

In this section, we present a simple but practical introduction to one of these areas: integration. Examples from some of the other areas are described in the exercises and in later chapters.

THE TRAPEZOID METHOD OF APPROXIMATING AREAS

One of the important problems in calculus is finding the area of a region having a curved boundary. Here we consider the simple case in which the region is bounded below by the x-axis, above by the graph of a function $y = f(x)$, on the left by the vertical line $x = a$, and on the right by the vertical line $x = b$:[6]

---

[6] More generally, the problem is to approximate the integral $\int_a^b f(x)dx$.

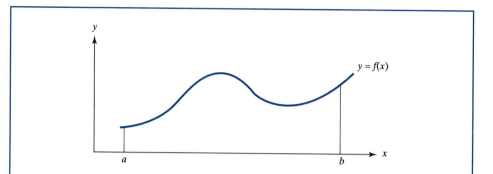

One commonly used mathematical method for approximating this area is to divide the region into strips and approximate the area of each strip by using a trapezoid. More precisely, we cut the interval $[a, b]$ into n parts, each of length $\Delta x = (b - a)/n$, using $n - 1$ equally spaced points $x_1, x_2, \ldots, x_{n-1}$. Locating the corresponding points on the curve and connecting consecutive points using line segments forms n trapezoids:

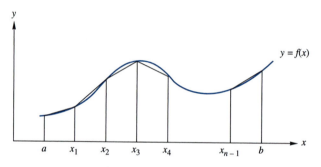

The sum of the areas of these trapezoids is approximately the area under the graph of f.

The bases of the first trapezoid are $y_0 = f(a)$ and $y_1 = f(x_1)$, and thus its area is[7]

$$\frac{1}{2}\Delta x(y_0 + y_1)$$

Similarly, the area of the second trapezoid is

$$\frac{1}{2}\Delta x(y_1 + y_2)$$

where $y_2 = f(x_2)$, and so on. The sum of the areas of the n trapezoids is

$$\frac{1}{2}\Delta x(y_0 + y_1) + \frac{1}{2}\Delta x(y_1 + y_2) + \frac{1}{2}\Delta x(y_2 + y_3) + \cdots + \frac{1}{2}\Delta x(y_{n-1} + y_n)$$

---

[7] The familiar formula from geometry for the area of a trapezoid with bases b_1 and b_2 and height h is $\frac{1}{2} h(b_1 + b_2)$. Note that in this problem, the bases are vertical and the "height" is horizontal.

where $y_0, y_1, \ldots, y_{n-1}, y_n$ are the values of the function f at $a, x_1, \ldots, x_{n-1}, b$, respectively. Combining terms, we can write this sum more simply as

$$\Delta x \left(\frac{y_0 + y_n}{2} + y_1 + y_2 + \cdots + y_{n-1} \right)$$

or, written more concisely using Σ (sigma) notation, as

$$\Delta x \left(\frac{y_0 + y_n}{2} + \sum_{i=1}^{n-1} y_i \right)$$

which is then an approximation of the area under the curve.

This formula can be treated as an algorithm for calculating the trapezoidal approximation to the area, which we can use to define a `TrapezoidalArea()` method, as shown in Figure 5.9. This particular definition reads the function values $y_0, y_1, \ldots, y_{n-1}, y_n$ from the keyboard.[8]

FIGURE 5.9   THE TRAPEZOIDAL METHOD

```
/** TrapezoidalArea.java computes the approximate area under a curve for
 *   which a collection of y values at equally spaced x values are
 *   entered from the keyboard.
 *   Receive:       n, number of subintervals along the x axis
 *                  intLength, the length of the interval on the x axis
 *   Precondition: the y values correspond to equally-spaced x values
 *                  in the interval on the x axis.
 *   Return:        the approximate area under the curve
 */

public static double TrapezoidalArea(int n, double intLength)
{
    Screem theScreen = new Screen();
    Keyboard theKeyboard  = new Keyroard();

    theScreen.print("First y value? ");
    double yValue = theKeyboard.readDouble(); // the first y value
    double sum = yValue / 2.0;                 // initialize sum to 1/2 of it

    for (int i = 1; i <= n - 1; i++)
    {
        theScreen.print("Next y value?   ");
        yValue = theKeyboard.readDouble();    // i-th y value
        sum += yValue;                         // add it to sum
    }

    theScreen.print("Last y value?   ");
    yValue = theKeyboard.readDouble();        // the last y value
    sum += yValue/ 2.0;                        // add 1/2 of it to sum

    double deltaX = intLength / (double) n;

    return deltaX * sum;                       // total area of trapezoids
}
```

---

[8] `TrapezoidalArea()` can be overloaded with other definitions that read the function values from a file, calculate them from an equation that defines the function, receive an array of function values from the caller (arrays are discussed in Chapter 9), and so on.

There are many other techniques for approximating areas such as the rectangle method, the midpoint method, Gaussian quadrature, and Simpson's rule (see Programming Problem 24 at the end of this chapter). One could develop an entire collection of Java methods that implement these various numerical methods.

There are many problems for which it is necessary to compute the area under a curve (or the more general problem of calculating an integral). We will now consider one such real-world problem and solve it using the trapezoidal method.

PROBLEM: ROAD CONSTRUCTION

A construction company has contracted to build a highway for the state highway commission. Several sections of this highway must pass through hills from which large amounts of dirt must be excavated to provide a flat and level roadbed. For example, one section that is 1000 feet in length must pass through a hill whose height (in feet) above the roadbed has been measured at equally spaced distances and tabulated as follows:

Distance	Height
0	0
100	6
200	10
300	13
400	17
500	22
600	25
700	20
800	13
900	5
1000	0

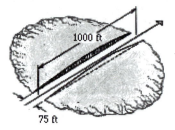

To estimate the construction costs, the company needs to know the volume of dirt that must be excavated from the hill.

OBJECT-CENTERED DESIGN

PRELIMINARY ANALYSIS. To estimate the volume of dirt to be removed, we will assume that the height of the hill does not vary from one side of the road to the other. The volume can then be calculated as

Volume = (cross-sectional area of the hill) × (width of the road)

1000 ft

The cross-sectional area of the hill can be computed using the trapezoidal method.

Freeway construction (F3 Freeway, Oahu Hawaii). Photo courtesy of Tony Stone Images.)

BEHAVIOR. The program should display on the screen a prompt for the length of the roadway passing through the hill and the number of points at which the height of the hill was measured and read these values. The program should then pass these values to `TrapezoidalArea()` to compute the cross-sectional area of the hill. It should then display a prompt for the width of the roadway, read this value from the keyboard, and then compute and display the volume of dirt to be removed.

PROBLEM'S OBJECTS. From our behavioral description, we can identify the following objects:

Description of problem's object	Type	Kind	Name
Length of roadway through the hill	double	varying	*roadLength*
Number of points where elevation was measured	int	varying	*numberOfPoints*
Cross-sectional area of the hill	double	varying	*hillCrossSectionalArea*
Width of the road	double	varying	*roadWidth*
Volume of dirt	double	varying	*dirtVolume*

We can then specify the task of the program as follows:

Input: The length of a section of road

A collection of heights at equally spaced points along this section

The width of the road

Output: The volume of dirt to be removed

OPERATIONS. From our behavioral description, making a list of the operations is straightforward:

i. Read a double from the keyboard (*roadLength* and *roadwidth*).
ii. Compute the cross-sectional area of the hill (`TrapezoidalArea()`).
iii. Store a real value in a real variable (*hillCrossSectionalArea, dirtVolume*).
iv. Multiply two real values.

ALGORITHM. These operations can be organized into an algorithm, as follows:

Algorithm for Highway Construction Problem

1. Prompt for and read the length of the roadway through the hill into *roadLength*.
2. Prompt for and read the number of points at which the hill elevation was measured into *numberOfPoints*.
3. Compute the approximate cross-sectional area of the hill and store it in *hillCrossSectionalArea*.
4. Prompt for and read the width of the road into *roadWidth*.
5. Compute the volume of dirt to be removed:

$$dirtVolume = hillCrossSectionalArea \times roadWidth$$

CODING AND TESTING. The program in Figure 5.10 implements this algorithm.

FIGURE 5.10   ROAD CONSTRUCTION

```
/** RoadConstruction.java uses the trapezoidal method to find the volume of
 *  dirt that must be removed to construct a road through a hill.
 *  Input:  the length of roadway through the hill,
 *          the number of points at which hill elevation was measured,
 *          the width of the roadway
 *  Output: the approximate volume of dirt removed
 */

import ann.easyio.*;               // Keyboard, Screen
```

```
class RoadConstruction extends Object
{
// Insert the method TrapezoidalArea here
 public static void main(String [] args)
  {
    Screen theScreen = new Screen();
    theScreen.print("Enter the length of roadway through the hill: ");
    Keyboard theKeyboard = new Keyboard();
    double roadLength = theKeyboard.readDouble();    // get the road length

    theScreen.print("Enter the number of points at which hill elevation "
                    + "was measured: ");

    int numberOfPoints = theKeyboard.readInt();      // get the number of points

    theScreen.println("Enter the hill elevations (y values) at the "
                    + numberOfPoints + " equally-spaced points.\n"
                    + "The amount of dirt to be removed"
                    + " from the hill will be computed.\n");

                                                // compute X-sectional area
    double hillCrossSectionalArea =
                        TrapezoidalArea(numberOfPoints - 1, roadLength);


   theScreen.print("Enter the width of the roadway: ");
   double roadWidth = theKeyboard.readDouble();     // get the road width
                                                    // compute volume
   double dirtVolume = roadWidth * hillCrossSectionalArea;
                                                    // display volume
   theScreen.println("\n--> The volume of dirt to be removed is "
                    + "\n   approximately " + dirtVolume + " cubic units.");
  }
}
```

Sample run:

```
Enter the length of roadway through the hill: 1000
Enter the number of points at which hill elevation was measured: 11
Enter the hill elevations (y values) at the 11 equally-spaced points.
The amount of dirt to be removed from the hill will be computed.

First y value? 0
Next y value?  6
Next y value?  10
Next y value?  13
Next y value?  17
Next y value?  22
Next y value?  25
Next y value?  20
Next y value?  13
Next y value?  5
Last y value?  0
Enter the width of the roadway: 75

--> The volume of dirt to be removed is
    approximately 982500.0 cubic units.
```

CHAPTER SUMMARY

KEY TERMS AND NOTES

block

box diagram

`break` statement

compound statement

flow diagram

`for` statement

forever loop

`if` statement

`if-break` combination

indefinite loop

loop

loop body

nested `if` statements

overload

posttest loop

pretest loop

repetition mechanism

selection

sentinel

sentinel-based input processing

sequential execution

signature

`System.err`

termination (or exit) condition

trace table

◎ Some problems require control mechanisms that are more powerful than sequential execution, namely, selection and repetition.

◎ *Sequential execution* refers to execution of a sequence of statements in the order in which they appear, so that each statement is executed exactly once.

◎ *Selective execution* refers to selecting and executing exactly one of a collection of alternative actions.

◎ The `if` statement is the most common selection structure for selecting between two alternatives.

◎ A *block* groups a sequence of statements into a single statement by enclosing them in curly braces ({ and }).

◎ `if` statements are useful for checking a method's preconditions.

◎ When one of the alternatives in an `if` statement contains another `if` statement, the second if statement is said to be *nested* in the first. In this case, an `else` clause is matched with the nearest preceding unmatched `if`.

◎ A method name can be overloaded, provided no two definitions of the method have the same signature.

◎ There are three parts to a *repetition* mechanism (also called a *loop*): (1) *initialization, repeated execution,* and *termination.*

◎ A `for` loop executes a statement repeatedly, as long as some boolean expression is true.

◎ Sentinel-based input processing can be used in many problems that involve processing lists of data. It uses an indefinite (forever) loop containing an `if-break` combination to exit the loop when a sentinel value is read.

Documentation

REFERENCE This chapter used no new classes from the Java API. The classes from Java's Swing packages that were used in the Graphical/Internet Java section were all described in similar sections in earlier chapters: `JApplet`, `JTextArea`, and `JLabel` in Chapter 4 and `JOptionPane` in Chapters 2 and 3. See the Documentation sections at the ends of these chapters along with the Java API documentation for information about these classes.

🖝 PROGRAMMING POINTERS

Several of the following programming pointers reiterate those in the preceding chapter and are included here for emphasis and for completeness. For additional explanation, details, and examples, see the Programming Pointers section in Chapter 4.

PROGRAM STYLE AND DESIGN

1. *Methods should be documented.* The documentation should include a statement of what it does and its *specification:* What it *receives, what is input to it, any preconditions, what it returns, what it outputs, and any postconditions.*

2. *Methods are separate components, and the white space in a program should reflect this.*

3. *Guidelines for programming style apply to methods.*

4. *Once a problem has been analyzed to identify its objects and the operations needed to solve it, an algorithm should be constructed that specifies the order in which the operations are applied to the data objects.*

5. *Operations that are not predefined (or are nontrivial) in Java should be encoded as methods.*

6. *A method that encodes an operation should be designed in the same manner as the main method.*

7. *A method that returns no values should have return type* `void`*.*

8. *A method that receives no values should have no parameters.*

9. *If a problem requires the selection of one or more operations, use a selection statement like the* `if` *statement.*

10. *If a problem requires the repetition of one or more operations, and the number of repetitions can be computed in advance, use a repetition statement like the* `for` *statement.*

11. *If a problem requires the repetition of one or more operations an indeterminate number of times, use a repetition statement like the forever loop.*

WATCH

OUT

POTENTIAL PITFALLS

1. *When a method is called, the list of arguments is matched against the list of parameters from left to right, with the leftmost argument associated with the leftmost parameter, the next argument associated with the next parameter, and so on. The number of arguments must be the same as the number of parameters in the method heading, and the type of each argument must be compatible with the type of the corresponding parameter.*

2. *Identifiers defined within a method (e.g., parameters, local variables, and local constants) are defined only during the execution of that method; they are undefined both before and after its execution.*

3. *Changing the value of a primitive-type parameter does not change the value of the corresponding argument; however, modifying the object referred to by a reference-type parameter (but not its address) does change the value of the object referred to by the corresponding argument, because both refer to the same object.*

4. *Each { must have a matching }.*

5. *A common programming error is using an assignment operator (=) when an equality operator (==) is intended. Each equality comparison in a boolean expression should be double-checked to make certain that the equality operator is being used and not the assignment operator.* It is easy to forget that, in Java, = is the assignment operator and to incorrectly encode an instruction of the form

> If *variable* is equal to *value*, then
> > *statement*

as

```
if (variable = value)
    statement
```

perhaps because = is used in many programming languages to check equality.

6. *In a nested if statement, each* `else` *clause is matched with the nearest preceding unmatched* `if`. For example, consider the following statements, which are given without indentation:

```
if (x > 0)
if (y > 0)
z = x + y;
else
z = x - y;
w = x * y * z;
```

With which `if` is the `else` associated? According to the rule just stated, these statements are executed as

```
if (x > 0)
    if (y > 0)
        z = x + y;
    else
        z = x - y;
w = x * y * z;
```

where the `else` clause matches the `if` statement containing the condition y > 0. Use indentation and alignment to show such associations.

7. *When using repetition, care must be taken to avoid infinite looping.*

❑ In a `for` statement, be sure that the boolean expression controlling repetition eventually becomes true. For example, executing the following code fragment,

```
for (double num = 0.0; num != 1.0; num += 0.3)
    theScreen.println(num);
```

results in an infinite loop

```
0.0
0.3
0.6
0.9
1.2
  .
  .
  .
```

because the boolean expression controlling the loop is always false. Rewriting the loop as

```
for (double num = 0.0; num <= 1.0; num += 0.3)
    theScreen.println(num);
```

corrects the problem.

❑ The body of a forever loop should always contain an if-break (or if-return) combination and statements that cause the exit condition of the loop to eventually become true.

8. *In a* for *loop, neither the control variable nor any variable involved in the loop condition should be modified within the body of the* for *loop, since it is intended to run through a specified range of values.* Strange or undesirable results may be produced otherwise. To illustrate, the statement

```
for (int i = 1; i <= 4; i++)
{
    theScreen.println(i);
    i++;
}
```

produces the output

```
1
3
```

The statement

```
for (int i = 1; i <= 4; i++)
{
    theScreen.println(i);
    i--;
}
```

results in an infinite loop, displaying the output

```
1
1
1
1
.
.
.
```

PROGRAMMING PROBLEMS

SECTIONS 5.1 & 5.2

1. Write a driver program to test the distance-calculation method of Exercise 11.

2. Write a driver program to test the quadratic-equation method of Exercise 12. Execute the program with the following values for a,b, and c: $1, -5, 6; 1, -2, 1; 1, 0, 4; 1, 1, 1; 2, 1, -3$.

3. Modify the quadratic-equation method of Exercise 12 so that it returns 0 if the quadratic equation has no real roots (discriminant is negative), 1 if it has a repeated real root (discriminant is 0), and 2 if it has two distinct real roots (discriminant is positive). Test the method with a driver program using the values in Problem 2 for $a, b,$ and c.

4. Construct a driver program to test the pollution-index method in Exercise 13 and execute it with the following data: $20, 45, 75, 35, 60$.

5. Construct a driver program to test the wind-chill method in Exercise 14 and execute it with the following data: $-80, 20, 0, -70, -10, -5, 10, -20, -40$.

6. Modify the wage-calculation program in Figure 5.1 as follows: If an employee's number is greater than or equal to 1000, the program should read an annual salary and calculate the employee's weekly pay as this salary divided by 52. If the employee's number is less than 1000, wages are calculated on an hourly basis, as described in Section 5.1. Execute the program with following data: $123, 38, 7.50; 175, 39.5, 7.85; 1217, 25500; 223, 40, 9.25; 375, 44.5, 8.35; 1343, 31775$.

SECTION 5.3

7. Write a driver program to test the summation method of Exercise 12.

8. Write a driver program to test the summation method of Exercise 13.

9. The sequence of *Fibonacci numbers* begins with the integers $1, 1, 2, 3, 5, 8, 13, 21, \ldots$ where each number after the first two is the sum of the two preceding numbers. Write a program that reads a positive integer n and uses a for loop to generate and display the first n Fibonacci numbers.

10. Ratios of consecutive Fibonacci numbers $1/1, 1/2, 2/3, 3/5, \ldots$ approach the *golden ratio* $(\sqrt{5} - 1)/2$. Modify the program in Problem 9 so that it also displays the decimal values of the ratios of consecutive Fibonacci numbers.

11. A certain product is to sell for `unitPrice` dollars. Write a program that reads values for `unitPrice` and `totalNumber` and then produces a table showing the total price of from 1 through `totalNumber` units. The table should have a format like the following:

```
Number of Units          Total Price
================          ============
            1             $ 1.50
            2             $ 3.00
            3             $ 4.50
            4             $ 6.00
            5             $ 7.50
```

12. Suppose that at a given time, genotypes AA, AB, and BB appear in the proportions x, y, and z, respectively, where $x = 0.25$, $y = 0.5$, and $z = 0.25$. If individuals of type AA cannot reproduce, the probability that one parent will donate gene A to an offspring is

$$p = \frac{1}{2}\left(\frac{y}{y + z}\right)$$

since $y / (y + z)$ is the probability that the parent is of type AB and 1/2 is the probability that such a parent will donate gene A. Then the proportions x', y', and z' of AA, AB, and BB, respectively, in each succeeding generation are given by

$$x' = p^2, y' = 2p(1 - p), z' = (1 - p)^2$$

and the new probability is given by

$$p' = \frac{1}{2}\left(\frac{y'}{y' + z'}\right)$$

Write a program to calculate and display the generation number and the proportions of AA, AB, and BB under appropriate headings for 30 generations. (Note that the proportions of AA and AB should approach 0, since gene A will gradually disappear.)

13. Write a program that uses a sentinel-based input loop to read data values as shown in the following table, calculates the miles per gallon in each case, and displays the values with appropriate labels:

Miles Traveled	Gallons of Gasoline Used
231	14.8
248	15.1
302	12.8
147	9.25
88	7
265	13.3

14. Write a program that uses a sentinel-based input loop to read several values representing miles, converts miles to kilometers (1 mile = 1.60935 kilometers), and displays all values with appropriate labels.

15. Write a program to read a set of numbers, count them, and calculate and display the mean, variance, and standard deviation of the set of numbers. The *mean* and *variance* of numbers $x_1, x_2, \ldots, x_n$ can be calculated using the formulas

$$\text{mean} = \frac{1}{n}\sum_{i=1}^{n} x_i \qquad \text{variance} = \frac{1}{n}\sum_{i=1}^{n} x_i^2 - \frac{1}{n^2}\left(\sum_{i=1}^{n} x_i\right)^2$$

The *standard deviation* is the square root of the variance.

SECTION 5.4

16. Modify the applet in Figure 5.8 so that the user enters the number of verses to generate.

17. Modify the applet in Figure 5.8 so that it allows the user to enter an animal's name, what sound it makes, and the name of a file containing a picture of the animal. Have it

display each verse of the song separately with the picture of Mr. MacDonald replaced by the picture of the animal described in that verse.

18. Proceed as in Problem 17, but you should locate the pictures of animals. Then have the program check with an `if` statement whether one of these pictures can be used for the animal entered by the user, and if so use it; if not, simply display the picture of Mr. Mac-Donald.

19. Proceed as in Problem 18, but in the last case, display below Mr. MacDonald's picture a message of the form "His *animal-name* goes *animal-sound.*"

For Problems 20–23, write and test a song-playing applet similar to that in Figure 5.8 for the specifed song. Lyrics can be found on the Internet using a search engine. You can also check the website for this book for links to where they can be found (see the preface).

20. "Happy Birthday to You" with the name of some person you know inserted at the appropriate place in the lyrics and using one or more appropriate pictures (e.g., a birthday cake or a photo of some person being honored).

21. "The Farmer in the Dell" with one or more appropriate pictures (e.g., the farmer, wife, child, nurse, cow, dog, cat, rat, cheese)

22. Some of the verses of "This Old Man" with one or more appropriate pictures.

23. Some of the verses of "The Hokey Pokey" with one or more appropriate pictures.

PART OF THE PICTURE: NUMERICAL METHODS

24. Another method of numerical integration that generally produces better approximations than the trapezoidal method is based on the use of parabolas and is known as *Simpson's rule*. In this method, the interval [a, b] is divided into an even number *n* of subintervals, each of length Δx, and the sum

$$\frac{\Delta x}{3}(y_0 + 4y_1 + 2y_2 + 4y_3 + 2y_4 + \cdots + 2y_{n-2} + 4y_{n-1} + y_n)$$

is used to find the area under the graph of *f* over the interval [a, b]. Write a method `SimpsonArea()` like `TrapezoidalArea()` in Figure 5.9 but use Simpson's rule. Then modify the program in Figure 5.10 to use this method to find the volume of dirt removed.

25. The work done (in joules) by a force (in newtons) that is applied at an angle θ (radians) as it moves an object from $x = a$ to $x = b$ on the *x* axis (with meters as units) is given by

$$w = \cos\theta \int_a^b F(x)dx$$

where $F(x)$ is the force applied at point *x* . That is, the work done is the area under the graph of $y = F(x)$ from $x = a$ to $x = b$ multiplied by cos θ. Write a program similar to that in Figure 5.10 to compute the work done for $\theta = 0.35$ radians, $a = 10.0$ m,

$b = 40.0$ m, and the following forces measured at equally-spaced points from a to b: 0.0, 4.5, 9.0, 13.0, 14.0, 10.5, 12.0, 7.8, 5.0 (all in newtons).

26. Repeat Problem 25 but use Simpson's rule (see Problem 24).

27. Overload the method `TrapezoidalArea()` in Figure 5.9 with a definition that has as parameters the endpoints a and b of the interval and the number n of points of subdivision, and which calls some method `F()` to calculate the function values rather than input them. Test your method with a driver program and method `F()` that calculates x^2. (Note: The area under the graph of $y = x^2$ from $x = a$ to $x = b$ is $(b^3 - a^3) / 3$.)

28. Another area of numerical methods is equation solving. One method for finding an approximate solution of an equation $f(x) = 0$ for some function f is the *bisection method*. In this method, we begin with two numbers a and b, where the function values $f(a)$ and $f(b)$ have opposite signs. If f is continuous between $x = a$ and $x = b$— that is, if there is no break in the graph of $y = f(x)$ between these two values—then the graph of f must cross the x-axis at least once between $x = a$ and $x = b$; thus, there must be at least one solution of the equation $f(x) = 0$ between a and b. To locate one of these solutions, we first bisect the interval $[a, b]$ and determine in which half f changes sign, thereby locating a smaller subinterval containing a solution of the equation. We bisect this subinterval and determine in which half f changes sign; this gives a still smaller subinterval containing a solution.

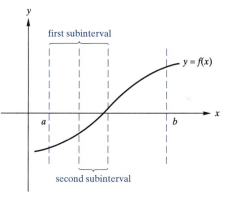

Repeating this process gives a sequence of subintervals, each of which contains a solution of the equation and whose length is one-half that of the preceding interval. Write a method to implement the bisection method and use it in a program to find a solution of the equation $x^3 + x - 5 = 0$.

MORE ABOUT CLASSES: INSTANCE METHODS

The old order changeth, yielding place to new. *Alfred Lord Tennyson*

. . . All manner of things—everything that begins with an M . . . such as mousetraps, and the moon, and memory, and muchness—you know you say things are "much of a muchness." *The Dormouse in Lewis Carroll's Alice's Adventures in Wonderland*

I'd never join a club that would accept someone like me as a member. *Groucho Marx*

■ Chapter Contents

Chapter Objectives

- Take a first look at how to build classes as types
- Study how to write instance methods and how they differ from static (class) methods
- See how to implement attributes as attribute variables (also called instance variables)
- Explain why encapsulation and information hiding are important and see how to realize them in class declarations
- Illustrate all of the preceding features by building a complete class to model temperatures

- Describe and give examples of the roles of:
  - → class constructors
  - → accessor methods
  - → mutator methods
  - → converter methods
  - → utility methods
- Take a closer look at graphics programming, showing especially how to paint in a frame created using Java's Swing components
- (Optional) Give an overview of artificial intelligence and some of the topics of study in this area of computer science

As we noted in Chapter 1, the word *class* is often used to describe a group or category of objects that have a set of attributes in common. For example, the high school football teams in one state are described as

- ❑ *class A,* if they have fewer than 100 students in 3 grades
- ❑ *class AA,* if they have between 101 and 500 students in 3 grades
- ❑ *class AAA,* if they have between 501 and 1000 students in 3 grades
- ❑ *class AAAA,* if they have 1000 or more students in 3 grades

The U.S. Navy describes ships as belonging to certain *classes;* for example, *Skipjack class, Thresher class,* and *Sturgeon class* have been used to characterize different kinds of submarines. Economists describe families as *lower class, middle class,* or *upper class,* based on their annual income. Used in this way, the word *class* is a synonym for the word *type,* since it provides a name for a group of related objects.

In the last chapter, we saw how a Java **class** can be used as a repository in which static methods can be stored for reuse by other classes. While this is a valid use of a class, a class whose methods are all static does not serve as a new *type,* in the sense that a state athletic association, the U.S. Navy, and economists have used the word. Put another way, *one cannot create useful* objects *from a class that contains only static methods.*

To create a class that serves as a *type* (i.e., from which objects can be created), the class must contain **instance methods**—messages that can be sent to an object as opposed to the class. In this chapter, we will learn to create such methods, and see how they differ from static methods.

6.1   INTRODUCTORY EXAMPLE: MODELING TEMPERATURES

PROBLEM: TEMPERATURE CONVERSION

Sally Science Major is taking a chemistry course at the local university. Many of her lab reports require reporting the temperature at which an experiment was conducted in one or more of the Fahrenheit, Celsius, or Kelvin scales. A program that converts a temperature in one of these scales to the other scales would be very helpful to her. Our problem is to design and develop this program.

Preliminary Analysis

If we follow the steps of object-centered design, we must model a *temperature* to solve this problem. A temperature has two attributes—its *number of degrees* and its *scale* (Fahrenheit, Celsius, or Kelvin). Of course, we could model this using two variables:

```
double itsDegrees = 100.0;
char   itsScale = 'C';
```

But this "separate variable approach" requires two variables (`itsDegrees` and `itsScale`) to model a single real-world object (a temperature). It would be more convenient if we had a `Temperature` *type* with which we could create a single software object to model this real-world object:

```
Temperature boilingPoint = new Temperature(100.0, 'C');
```

Similarly, to display a temperature, the separate-variable approach would require us to display the value of each variable separately

```
theScreen.print(itsDegrees + " " + itsScale);
```

instead of simply

```
theScreen.print(boilingPoint);
```

More generally, to apply some method `m()` to a temperature, the separate-variable approach requires that `m()` receive each variable used in our model as an argument,

```
m(itsDegrees, itsScale);
```

whereas a `Temperature` type could allow us instead to send a message to a `Temperature` object to invoke method `m()`:

```
boilingPoint.m();
```

The separate-variable approach is not unreasonable for objects that can be described with two attributes, but it quickly becomes unwieldy as the complexity of the object being modeled increases. Think how many variables would be needed to represent a tax form like that shown in Figure 6.1!

Recall that object-centered design as described in the preceding chapter consists of the following steps:

1. Identify the behavior required to solve the problem
2. Identify the objects

> For each object that cannot be *directly* represented with the existing types:
> Design and build a class to represent such objects

3. Identify the operations

> For each operation that is not predefined:

FIGURE 6.1—A W-2 Income Tax Form

Copy C For EMPLOYEE'S RECORDS (See Notice on back.)		2000	OMB No. 1545-0008
a Control number ABC-123	**1** Wages, tips, other comp. 1111.11	**2** Federal income tax withheld .00	
b Employer's ID number 123456789	**3** Social security wages	**4** Social security tax withheld 11.22	
	5 Medicare wages and tips	**6** Medicare tax withheld 22.11	

c Employer's name, address, and ZIP code

Dinoville Rock Quarry
1212 T-Rex Ave.
Bedrock, Prehistoria   00001

d Employee's social security number 987-675-4321

e Employee's name, and address, and ZIP code

Fred Flintstone
123 Cave A
Bedrock, Prehistoria   00002

7 Social security tips	**8** Allocated tips	**9** Advance EIC payment
10 Dependent care benefits	**11** Nonqualified plans	**12** Benefits included in box 1
13 See instrs. for box 13	**14** Other	

15	Statutory employee	Deceased	Pension plan	Legal rep.	Hshld. emp.	Subtotal	Deferred compensation

PR	123456789	1111.11	.00
16 State Employer's state I.D. #	**17** State wages, tips, etc.	**18** State income tax	
19 Locality name Bedrock	**20** Local wages, tips, etc. 1111.11	**21** Local income tax .00	

Form W-2 Wage and Tax Statement   Dept. of the Treasury -- IRS
This information is being furnished to the IRS. If you are required to file a tax return, a negligence penalty/other sanction may be imposed on you if this income is taxable and you fail to report it.

If the operation is an operation on a class object from step 2a,

    a. Design and build a method to perform that operation

    b. Store that method in the class responsible for providing the operation.

4. Organize the objects and operations into an algorithm

For our temperature problem, therefore, we should create a `Temperature` class containing both the scale and the degrees of an arbitrary temperature and methods to perform temperature conversions. Given such a class, solving the problem is straightforward.

 ## OBJECT-CENTERED DESIGN

BEHAVIOR. Our program should display on the screen a prompt for a temperature (degrees and scale), and should then read a temperature from the keyboard. It should then display the Fahrenheit, Celsius, and Kelvin equivalents of that temperature.

OBJECTS. We can identify the following objects in our problem:

Description of problem's object	Type	Kind	Name
Our program	??	—	none
The screen	`Screen`	varying	*theScreen*
A prompt	`String`	constant	none
A temperature	`Temperature`	varying	*temp*
The keyboard	`Keyboard`	varying	*theKeyboard*
The Fahrenheit equivalent	`Temperature`	varying	none
The Celsius equivalent	`Temperature`	varying	none
The Kelvin equivalent	`Temperature`	varying	none

Since our program will perform temperature conversions, we will name it `TemperatureConverter`.

OPERATIONS. The operations needed to solve this problem are as follows:

   i. Display a string on *theScreen*
  ii. Read a *Temperature* value from *theKeyboard*
 iii. Determine the Fahrenheit equivalent of a *Temperature*
 iv. Determine the Celsius equivalent of a *Temperature*
  v. Determine the Kelvin equivalent of a *Temperature*
 vi. Display a *Temperature* on *theScreen*

Here, only operation (i) is already available. It is provided by the `Screen` class from our `ann.easyio` package. We must build a `Temperature` class that provides methods to perform operations (ii–vi).

ALGORITHM. Assuming the availability of a `Temperature` class that provides operations ii–vi, we can organize the preceding operations into the following algorithm:

Algorithm for Temperature conversion

1. Declare *theScreen, theKeyboard, temp.*
2. Send *theScreen* a message asking it to display a prompt for a temperature.
3. Send *temp* a message asking it to read a *Temperature* value for itself from *theKeyboard.*
4. Send *theScreen* a message, asking it to display:
   a. the Fahrenheit equivalent of *temp.*
   b. the Celsius equivalent of *temp.*
   c. the Kelvin equivalent of *temp.*

CODING. Suppose that a `Temperature` class is available that provides the required operations on `Temperature` objects:

Method	Operation
`read(theKeyboard)`	Read a `Temperature` value from `theKeyboard`
`inFahrenheit()`	Return the Fahrenheit equivalent of `Temperature` object
`inCelsius()`	Return the Celsius equivalent of `Temperature` object
`inKelvin()`	Return the Kelvin equivalent of `Temperature` object

Then we can encode this algorithm in Java as shown in Figure 6.2. For convenience, we have wrapped this algorithm in an input loop, to process multiple temperatures without having to rerun the program.

FIGURE 6.2   A TEMPERATURE CONVERSION PROGRAM

```
/** TemperatureConverter.java
 *  Input:   a temperature value (e.g., 0 C).
 *  Output: that temperature in Celsius, Fahrenheit and Kelvin.
 */

import Temperature;
import ann.easyio.*;

class TemperatureConverter
{
 public static void main(String [] args)
  {
    Screen theScreen = new Screen();
    Temperature temp = new Temperature();
    Keyboard theKeyboard = new Keyboard();
    boolean inputOK;
    for (;;)
     {
       theScreen.print("\nTo perform a temperature conversion, enter\n"
                  + " a temperature (e.g., 0 C). Enter 0 A to stop: ");
       inputOK = temp.read(theKeyboard);

       if (!inputOK) break;

       theScreen.println("--> " + temp.inFahrenheit()
                    + " = " + temp.inCelsius()
                    + " = " + temp.inKelvin() );
     }
   }
 }
```

Sample run:

```
To perform a temperature conversion, enter
 a temperature (e.g., 0 C). Enter 0 A to stop: 100 C
--> 100.0 C = 373.15 K = 212.0 F

To perform a temperature conversion, enter
 a temperature (e.g., 0 C). Enter 0 A to stop: 32 f
--> 32.0 F = 0.0 C = 273.15 K

To perform a temperature conversion, enter
 a temperature (e.g., 0 C). Enter 0 A to stop: 0 k
--> 0.0 K = -273.15 C = -459.66999999999996 F

To perform a temperature conversion, enter
 a temperature (e.g., 0 C). Enter 0 A to stop: 0 A
```

We will design and build the `Temperature` class in the following sections, and use it to illustrate the principles of class design.

6.2   DESIGNING A CLASS

As with creating programs, building a class consists of two phases:

1. The design phase in which we plan the class
2. The implementation phase in which we encode our design in Java

This section explores the first phase. Sections 6.3 and 6.4 will examine the second phase.

Class Design

Designing a class consists first of identifying two things:

❑ its **behavior:** the *operations* that can be applied to a class object
❑ its **attributes:** the *data* that must be stored to characterize a class object

The next step, as we will show in subsequent sections, is to implement the *operations as methods* and the *attributes as variables or constants*. These are then "wrapped together" in a class declaration.

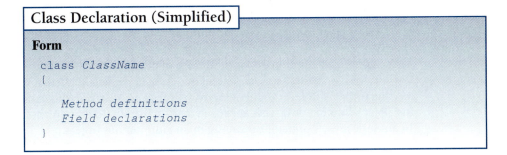

Class Declaration (Simplified)

Form
```
class ClassName
{

    Method definitions
    Field declarations

}
```

where:
   the method definitions are as described earlier; and
   the field declarations are declarations of variables (and constants).

Purpose

Defines a reference type named *ClassName*. The methods implement the operations that define the class' behavior. The variables (and constants) store values that represent the class' attributes. The values stored in them at any particular time determine the *state* of a class object at that time.

The behavior of a class is usually identified first, because often it is not obvious what the attributes of the class should be, and identifying the class behavior can sometimes clarify them. Also, if the behaviors are identified before any of the attribute details are established, they will remain independent of the details of how the attributes are implemented. This *independence from implementation details is an important principle of good class design.*

NOTE

The External and Internal Perspectives

Until now, our approach to programming has been that of an observer looking from outside the program into its details. Since we reside outside the program, this is a natural way to begin, and as long as we are only *using* predefined classes, this **external perspective** is adequate.

One of the most fundamental concepts of class design is **object autonomy,** embodied in the **I-can-do-it-myself principle,** which means that an object should carry within itself the ability to perform its operations. That is, rather than viewing a class operation as manipulation of an object by a program, object autonomy views a class operation as an object taking an action. To incorporate the I-can-do-it-myself principle into the design of a class, we must shift from the perspective of an external observer to the perspective of the object being designed. More precisely, we want to think through our design as though *we are the object.* The resulting approach describes an object in first person terminology, and it is thus called the **internal perspective.**

As a simple illustration of this difference of perspective, rather than describing the Temperature attributes as *its* degrees and *its* scale (which imply that we are outside, looking in), we will refer to them as *my* degrees and *my* scale (indicating that we are the object, looking out). This approach leads naturally to an implementation of the I-can-do-it-myself principle, resulting in an autonomous object.

In the sections that follow, we will use *both* perspectives. When *using* a class, we will use the *external* perspective. When *building* a class, we will use the *internal* perspective.

Class	Perspective
User	External
Builder	Internal

Temperature Behavior

From an internal perspective, a `Temperature` object must provide the following operations for the program in Figure 6.2 to work:

  i. Define myself *implicitly* by initializing my degrees and scale with default values

  ii. Read a temperature from a `Keyboard` object and store it within me

 iii. Compute the Fahrenheit temperature equivalent to me

  iv. Compute the Celsius temperature equivalent to me

  v. Compute the Kelvin temperature equivalent to me

  vi. Display my degrees and scale using a `Screen` object

Although these operations suffice to solve the problem at hand, designing a reusable class involves identifying other operations that a user of the class is likely to need. To that end, we might extend our list with the following operations:

 vii. Define myself *explicitly* by initializing my degrees and scale with specified values

 viii. Identify my number of degrees

  ix. Identify my scale

  x. Increase my temperature by a given number of degrees

xi. Decrease my temperature by a given number of degrees

xii. Compare myself to another `Temperature` object

xiii. Assign another `Temperature` value to me

This is not an exhaustive list, but it is a good start and will serve to introduce the details of class implementation. Other operations can be added later.

Temperature Attributes

To identify the attributes of a class, it is a good idea to go through the list of operations and identify what information each of them requires. If the same information is required by several different operations, then such information should probably be one of the object's attributes.

For example, if we examine the first twelve operations in our list, operations (i) and (vi)–(xi) indicate that, from an internal perspective, I, as a `Temperature` object, have two attributes:

1. my degrees

2. my scale

In fact, these are the only attributes needed for class `Temperature`. For other classes, a complete set of attributes may not be evident at the outset. In this case, others can be added later, when the implementation of an operation makes apparent the need for an attribute not in the list.

6.3   IMPLEMENTING CLASS ATTRIBUTES

Once we have a design for a class, we can use it as a blueprint for implementing the class. Since our class is a standalone class, we declare it in a separate file whose name should be the same as the name of the class (e.g., `Temperature.java`).

Given a class design that includes its attributes, our first task is to implement those attributes. In the case of attributes that change over time or that differ from one object to another, we must define variables to store their values. Attributes that are the same for all objects and do not change can be represented as constants (or as methods that return a literal). Attributes determine the **state** of a class object at a particular time.

For our `Temperature` class, the attributes—degrees and scale—will differ from one `Temperature` object to another and should therefore be stored in variables. We will use a `double` variable for the number of degrees with and a `char` variable for the scale:

```
/** Temperature.java
 *    . . .
 */

double myDegrees;
char    myScale;
```

These will become the **attribute variables**—also called **instance variables** or **data members** or **fields**—of our Temperature class. We will give the names of attribute variables the prefix my to indicate that these are attributes of the class and to reflect our internal perspective. And, as with all identifiers, the name of an attribute variable should be *self-documenting,* describing the attribute being stored.

Implementation Decisions. We could have used the String type to define myScale if we wanted to store the entire name of the scale, but we chose char instead because temperatures are usually written using a single character to indicate the scale (e.g., 98.6° F, 100° C, 273° K). In implementing attributes, the best choice may not always be clear, but a decision must be made before we can proceed. Such implementation decisions can be revised later if necessary.

Encapsulation

Once we have defined variables to represent the attributes of our class , we can actually create the class by wrapping them in a class declaration:

```
class Temperature
{
    double myDegrees;
    char    myScale;
}
```

This declaration creates a new type named Temperature. We can now use this type to declare objects. In the declarations

```
Temperature temp1 = new Temperature(),
            temp2 = new Temperature();
```

temp1 and temp2 each refer to a distinct Temperature object which contains two attribute variables: a double named myDegrees and a char named myScale. We might picture these objects as follows:

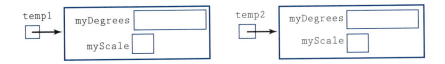

Wrapping the attribute variables in a class declaration and then using that class as a type to declare an object makes it possible for an object to store values of different types. In the vocabulary of programming languages, we say that class Temperature **encapsulates** the double attribute variable myDegrees and the char attribute variable myScale. Such encapsulation allows a *single* object to store values of different types (something not possible with primitive types) and thus have multiple attributes.

Information Hiding

As the attribute variables of a `Temperature` object are currently declared, they can be accessed directly[1]. For example, we can check the value of `temp1`'s scale:

```
if (temp1.myScale == 'F') // . . .
```

This is problematic, however, because there is nothing protecting an attribute from being accidentally modified. For example, a programmer might type X instead of C in an assignment statement,

```
temp1.myScale = 'X';
```

or set `myScale` to Kelvin when `myDegrees` is negative:

```
temp1.myScale = 'K';
```

In either case, the result would be an invalid temperature.

Such problems can be prevented by declaring the attribute variables to be **private:**

```
class Temperature
{
    private double myDegrees;
    private char   myScale;
}
```

This prevents direct access to the attribute variables from outside the class declaration. If an attempt is made to directly access a *private* attribute, the compiler will generate an error such as

```
Variable myScale in class Temperature not accessible. . .
```

Another reason for keeping attribute variables private is that it can help reduce program maintenance costs. To illustrate, we have defined `myScale` as a `char`, but we might decide in the future that a `String` representation would be better. If we omit the `private` specifier, a program can directly access the data member `myScale` as in

```
if (temp1.myScale == 'F') // . . .
```

However, if we were to later change the type of `myScale`, this revision would *break* that program, making it necessary to rewrite some of it as well. In some situations, the required revisions might be so extensive that software would not be ready on time and/or would be more expensive than was predicted, the obvious result of which would be a loss of sales.

The root of both of these problems is allowing a programmer to directly access the attribute variables of a class. By making them *private,* we prevent such direct access and prevent the problems from occurring.

---

[1] They can be accessed throughout the file (or package) that contains the class declaration, but not outside it.

This fundamental concept of class design is called **information hiding.** By preventing a program from directly accessing the data members of a class, we hide that information, thus removing the temptation to access the data members directly and preventing potential problems.

NOTE

> *It is good programming practice to hide all attribute variables of a class by making them **private**.*

Once we have the attribute variables encapsulated and hidden, we are almost ready to begin implementing the class operations.

Class Invariants

Before defining class operations, we should identify any restrictions on the values of the attributes of our class. For example, we might stipulate that the only valid values for the attribute variable myScale are the characters F, C, and K. If we identify and specify such restrictions at the outset, then we can implement the various class operations in a way that ensures that these restrictions are observed.

To document such limitations concisely, we usually define a condition (i.e., a boolean expression) that describes the restrictions. Such a condition should state the restrictions in terms of the attribute variables. For example, using both the preceding restriction on the temperature scale and the fact that the lower bound on a temperature is absolute zero, we might write the following condition to define what constitutes a valid Temperature:

```
   myScale == 'C' && myDegrees >= ABSOLUTE_ZERO_CELSIUS
|| myScale == 'F' && myDegrees >= ABSOLUTE_ZERO_FAHRENHEIT
|| myScale == 'K' && myDegrees >= ABSOLUTE_ZERO_KELVIN
```

Once we have such a condition, we want to make certain that none of the code we write for this class violates it—that is, we want the condition to be true, both before and after each call of a class operation. Because this condition must be true throughout the class, it is called a **class invariant.** When such an invariant is defined, it is good practice to record it in the documentation at the beginning of the class file.

```
/** Temperature.java
 *   Class Invariant: myScale == 'C' &&
 *                        myDegrees >= ABSOLUTE_ZERO_CELSIUS
 *                 || myScale == 'F' &&
 *                        myDegrees >= ABSOLUTE_ZERO_FAHRENHEIT
 *                 || myScale == 'K' &&
 *                        myDegrees >= ABSOLUTE_ZERO_KELVIN
 */

// . . .
```

```
class Temperature
{
   public final static double
                     ABSOLUTE_ZERO_FAHRENHEIT = -459.67,
                     ABSOLUTE_ZERO_CELSIUS    = -273.15,
                     ABSOLUTE_ZERO_KELVIN     = 0.0;

   private double myDegrees;   // >= ABSOLUTE_ZERO for myScale
   private char   myScale;     // 'F', 'C', or 'K'
}
```

Since our class invariant relies on the values of absolute zero in each of the different scales, we define constants for all three. Because these constants are likely to be generally useful to temperature-related programs, we define them as `public` **constants** so they are accessible both inside and outside the class declaration.

Note also that since the values of these constants will be the same for all `Temperature` objects, we use the `static` modifier to define them as **static constants** (or **class constants**) rather than **instance constants.** This means that *objects* share *these constants rather than carrying around their own copies of them, as would be the case if they were instance constants.* Static constants are accessed by sending messages to the class rather than to an instance of that class (i.e., an object); for example,

> NOTE

```
Temperature.ABSOLUTE_ZERO_CELSIUS
```

retrieves the value -273.15.

✔ Quick Quiz 6.3

1. For an object that cannot be directly represented with existing types, we design and build a(n) _____ to represent it.

2. The behavior of a class object is the collection of _____ that can be applied to the object.

3. The attributes of a class object consist of the _____ that must be stored to characterize the object.

4. (True or false) The attributes of a class are usually identified before the behavior.

5. Object autonomy is embodied in the _____ principle.

6. _____ allows a single object to store values of different types.

7. What is the purpose of hiding attribute variables in a class?

8. Data members are hidden by declaring them to be _____ .

9. A boolean expression that describes restrictions on the values of the attributes of a class is called a class _____ .

10. Declaring a constant in a class to be _____ makes it accessible outside the class.

11. The keyword _____ is used to declare a static (or class) constant.

12. What is the difference between a static (or class) constant and an instance constant?

6.4   IMPLEMENTING CLASS OPERATIONS

Once the attributes of a class have been *defined, encapsulated,* and *hidden,* we are ready to begin implementing the class *operations.* For most operations, this is done using **instance methods.** Recall the differences between static (or class) methods and instance (or object) methods described in Chapter 4:

Static (or class) methods	Instance (or object) methods
Declared with keyword `static`	No `static` modifier is used
Shared by all objects of the class	Each class object has its own copy
Invoked by sending a message to the class	Invoked by sending a message to a class object

Instance methods generally fall into one of the following categories:

1. **Constructors:** Methods that initialize attribute variables
2. **Accessors:** Methods that retrieve but do not change attribute variable values
3. **Mutators:** Methods that change attribute variable values
4. **Converters:** Methods that provide a representation of an object in a different type
5. **Utilities:** Methods used by other methods to simplify or avoid redundant coding

In this section, we will see examples of each of these categories of instance methods.

`Temperature` Output: A Convert-to-`String` Method

It is good practice to define methods for output early in the implementation process, because being able to view an object's value can help with checking the correctness of the other operations. For this reason we will begin by building an output method for our `Temperature` class.

In Java, the `print()` and `println()` methods can be used to display any value whose type is `Object` or any class that extends `Object`. These methods work by sending an object a message to convert itself to a `String` using its `toString()` method and then displaying the string returned by that method. Various other operations (e.g., the `String` concatenation operator +) also use `toString()` messages to convert objects to `Strings` so they can be processed. For these reasons, most classes should provide a `toString()` method. The existing `print()` and `println()` methods can then be used to display objects of that class without further work.

As its name suggests, the `toString()` method is a **converter** method. From an *external* perspective, an expression such as

```
temp1.toString()
```

should return a `String` containing the degrees and scale attributes of the `Temper-ature` object to which `temp1` refers.

From an *internal* perspective, when I (a `Temperature` object) receive the `toString()` message, it is as if someone called to me

"Hello there! Please give me a `String` representation of yourself!"

I should respond by returning a `String` containing the values stored in `myDegrees` and `myScale`, with a space separating them.

Thus, we can specify the behavior of `toString()` as follows:

Return: A `String` containing `myDegrees`, a space, and `myScale`

Since we can use the concatenation operator (+) to build this `String`, this method is easy to encode, as shown in Figure 6.3. (A complete definition of class `Tempera-ture` showing all of its methods, variables, and constants is given at the end of this section.)

FIGURE 6.3   DISPLAYING A `Temperature`

```
/** toString converter (used by +, print(), println(), ...).
 *  Return: a String representation of myself.
 */
public String toString()
{
  return myDegrees + " " + myScale;
}
```

Note that although a method from a different class is not permitted to access the private attribute variables of a class, a method defined within the same class can access them freely.

NOTE   As we have noted, *the `print()` and `println()` methods send the `toString()` message to any object they are asked to display.* A statement like

        theScreen.print(temp1);

therefore, will (behind the scenes) send `temp1` the `toString()` message to obtain a `String` representation of `temp1` and will then display the result. For the `toString()` method in Figure 6.3, the output produced by the above statement will be the value of `temp1.myDegrees` followed by a space and the value of `temp1.myScale`. Similarly,

        theScreen.print(temp2);

will display the value of `temp2.myDegrees`, a space, and the value of `temp2.myScale`.

Before this method is useful, however, the attribute variables `myDegrees` and `myScale` must have values. We therefore turn our attention to methods that enable attribute variables to be initialized.

Constructor Methods

A `Temperature` definition

```
Temperature temp1 = new Temperature(),
             temp2 = new Temperature();
```

defines `temp1` and `temp2` to be handles for `Temperature` objects that we can picture as follows:

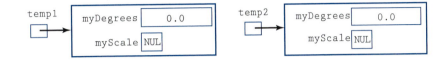

The values of the attribute variables in these objects are the default values specified in Java for their types. As we have seen (see Section 2.3) the default value for numeric types is zero. (The `char` value corresponding to Unicode representation 0 is the null character `'\u0000'`, commonly denoted by NUL.) We would prefer instead that such declarations define `temp1` and `temp2` with some default initial value that represents a valid `Temperature` value (e.g., 0 degrees Celsius):

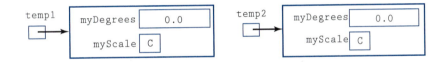

Java allows a class to define methods whose *purpose is to initialize the attribute variables* of the class. These special methods are called **constructors,** and *the name of a constructor is always the same as the name of the class.* A constructor that initializes the attribute variables to default values is called a **default-value constructor,** while a constructor that initializes the attribute variables to user-supplied values is called an **explicit-value constructor.**

The Default-Value Constructor. To be autonomous, a `Temperature` object should be able to initialize itself. Applying the I- can-do-it-myself principle, a constructor defines the sequence of actions that I (a `Temperature` object) take to initialize my attribute variables when I am created. Applying object-centered design from this internal perspective gives the following specification for the behavior of our default-value constructor:

Postcondition: `myDegrees == 0.0 && myScale == 'C'`

We specify the behavior of a constructor using a **postcondition,** a boolean expression that must be `true` when the method terminates.

Figure 6.4 shows the definition of a default-value constructor for our class Temperature.

FIGURE 6.4   THE Temperature DEFAULT-VALUE CONSTRUCTOR.

```
/** Temperature default-value constructor
 *   Postcondition: myDegrees == 0.0 && myScale == 'C'.
 */
public Temperature()
{
  myDegrees = 0.0;
  myScale = 'C';
}
```

Here we see some unusual features. The first is that there is no return type between public and the method's name because *constructor functions have no return type,* not even void. As an initialization method, a constructor never returns anything to its caller. Its sole purpose is to initialize an object's attribute variables. The other unusual feature is the method's name. The name of a constructor must always be the same as the name of the class.

Once these two methods are added to the class Temperature, a programmer can write a short driver program to test this much of the class:

```
import Temperature;
import ann.easyio.*;

class TemperatureTester
{
 public static void main(String [] args)
 {
    Screen aScreen = new Screen();
    Temperature temp1 = new Temperature();
    aScreen.println(temp1);
 }
}
```

When this program is executed, it will display

```
0 C
```

This output is produced because whenever the Java compiler processes the statement

```
Temperature temp1 = new Temperature();
```

it searches the class for a Temperature() method (i.e., a constructor) that it can use to initialize the newly-created object. Upon finding one, it invokes that method to initialize the object.[2] *A constructor is called by the compiler whenever a class object is defined using the* new *operator. For this reason, when building a class, always provide one or more constructors to initialize its attribute variables.*

NOTE

---

[2] If it does not find such a method and the class has no other constructors, the compiler will generate a default constructor and use it to initialize the attribute variables with the Java-specified default values.

Explicit-Value Constructors. The constructor method we just defined only allows us to initialize a `Temperature` object to the value 0 degrees Celsius. It would also be useful to allow initializations with other temperature values. This can be accomplished by defining a second `Temperature` constructor that receives the initial values via its parameters. From an internal perspective, object-centered design gives us the following specification for the operation's behavior:

> **Receive:** *degrees,* a `double`
> *scale,* a `char`
>
> **Precondition:** *scale* is one of {'F', 'f', 'C', 'c', 'K', 'k'} and *degrees* is valid for *scale.*
>
> **Postcondition:** `myDegrees ==` *degrees* `&& myScale ==` *scale* in uppercase.

Unlike the default-value constructor, this method receives its initialization values from the caller, and so our constructor must supply *parameters* to hold those values. For convenience, we will allow the user to give the scale in either upper or lower case, making six valid values for `myScale`: `'f'`, `'c'`, `'k'`, `'F'`, `'C'`, `'K'`. Since there is the possibility of the caller passing invalid values for *degrees* and/or *scale* and violating the precondition, our method must check that *degrees* and *scale* represent a valid temperature before proceeding with the initialization. Such checking is called **validation,** and any method that tries to change the value of an attribute variable should *validate* the new value before making the change. Since most classes contain several methods that can change the values of attribute variables, we will write a utility method `isValidTemperature()` that can be called to validate proposed temperature values.

If the values of *degrees* and *scale* represent a valid temperature, then we will use those values to initialize the attribute variables. If they do not, we will display a diagnostic message and terminate execution. Since this last action will be needed by other methods in the class that perform validation, we will build a second utility method `fatal()` to perform it.

Figure 6.5 gives a definition of the explicit-value constructor method. Note that the value of the parameter `scale` is converted to uppercase (if necessary) before it is assigned to the `myScale` attribute variable so that the *class invariant* is satisfied.

FIGURE 6.5 THE `Temperature` EXPLICIT-VALUE CONSTRUCTOR

```
/** Explicit-value constructor.
 *  Receive:       double degrees, char scale
 *  Precondition:  scale is one of 'f', 'F', 'c', 'C', 'k', or 'K'
 *                 and degrees is a valid number of degrees for scale.
 *  Postcondition: myDegrees == degrees && myScale == (uppercase) scale.
 */
public Temperature(double degrees, char scale)
{
 if (isValidTemperature(degrees, scale))
 {
   myDegrees = degrees;
   myScale = Character.toUpperCase(scale);
 }
 else
   fatal("Temperature(degrees, scale)", "invalid args: "
                                 + degrees + scale);
}
```

Given this constructor and definitions for `isValidTemperature()` and `fatal()` (see Figures 6.6 and 6.7), a programmer can now write

```
import Temperature;
import ann.easyio.*;

class TemperatureTester
{
  public static void main(String [] args)
  {
    Screen aScreen = new Screen();
    Temperature temp1 = new Temperature(98.6, 'F');

    Temperature temp2 = new Temperature();
    aScreen.println(temp1 + "\n" + temp2);
  }
}
```

When this program is compiled and run, the declarations

```
Temperature temp1 = new Temperature(98.6, 'F');
Temperature temp2 = new Temperature();
```

construct `temp1` using the explicit-value constructor and `temp2` using the default-value constructor. Represented graphically, these objects are thus initialized as follows:

The program will then display

```
98.6 F
0 C
```

for `temp1` and `temp2`.

Method Names and Overloading

Having two different methods with the same name is known as **overloading.** When the Java compiler processes the declaration

```
Temperature temp2 = new Temperature();
```

it searches the class for a method named `Temperature` (i.e., a constructor) that has no parameters. On finding one, it uses that constructor to perform the initialization.

By contrast, when the compiler sees the declaration

```
Temperature temp1 = new Temperature(98.6, 'F');
```

it searches the class for a method whose **signature** is consistent with the method call; that is, its name is `Temperature` (i.e., it is a constructor) and its list of parameter types) matches the argument types. On finding it, the compiler uses that constructor to perform the initialization.

More generally, a declaration statement of the form

```
ClassName variableName = new ClassName(argumentList);
```

causes the compiler to search the definition of class `ClassName` for a constructor whose parameter types match the types of the arguments in `argumentList`. If it finds such a constructor, it uses it to perform the initialization. If it does not find one, it generates a compilation error (except as noted in Footnote 2).

Utility Methods

A Utility Method: `isValidTemperature()`.

To validate the values of its parameters, our explicit-value constructor calls a method named `isValidTempera-ture()` that we must define. As we noted, other methods should be able to use this method to test whether or not a given pair of `double` and `char` values represents a valid temperature. We can thus specify the behavior of this method as follows:

Receive: *degrees,* a `double`; and *scale,* a `char`.

Return: true if and only if *(degrees, scale)* represents a valid temperature.

For our `Temperature` class, we allow any temperature greater than or equal to absolute zero. Since a temperature might be given in any of the three scales, we must compare the value of *degrees* to absolute zero separately for each scale. To do so, we can use an `if-else-if` statement, as shown in Figure 6.6.

FIGURE 6.6 `isValidTemperature()` UTILITY METHOD

```
/** Temperature validation utility.
 *  Receive: degrees, a double; scale, a char
 *  Return:  true if (degrees, scale) represent a valid temperature,
 *           false otherwise.
 */
public static boolean isValidTemperature(double degrees, char scale)
{
  if (scale == 'C' || scale == 'c')
    return degrees >= ABSOLUTE_ZERO_CELSIUS;
  else if (scale == 'F' || scale == 'f')
    return degrees >= ABSOLUTE_ZERO_FAHRENHEIT;
  else if (scale == 'K' || scale == 'k')
    return degrees >= ABSOLUTE_ZERO_KELVIN;
  else
    return false;
```

Note that this method does not access any attribute variables. Instead, it receives the values it is to test via its parameters, and accesses the absolute-zero class constants we defined earlier. Since it uses only class values and parameters, we define it as a static method rather than as an instance method (for the reasons stated later in this section).

A Utility Method: `fatal()`. If its parameters do not represent a valid `Temper-ature` value, our explicit-value constructor calls a method named `fatal()` to display a diagnostic message and then terminate execution. For diagnostic messages, it is our practice to have them display two pieces of information:

1. The method in which the problem was detected
2. A description of the problem

Accordingly, our `fatal()` method will behave according to the following specification:

Receive: *methodName,* a `String`; and *diagnostic,* a `String`

Output: *methodName* and *diagnostic,* formatted as an error message

Postcondition: The program has been terminated.

The Java `System` **class** (from package `java.lang`) contains an object named `err` that is normally used to display error/diagnostic messages. The implementation of `fatal()` in Figure 6.7 uses this object along with the `exit()` method from the `System` class. Since the package `java.lang` is automatically imported into every Java program, no additional steps are necessary to use `System.err`.

FIGURE 6.7   `fatal()` UTILITY METHOD.

```
/** Fatal error utility
 *  Receive:        methodName, the name of the method where the error
 *                  occurred, and diagnostic, a message explaining the problem
 *  Output:         an error message containing methodName and diagnostic
 *  Postcondition: Execution is terminated.
 */
private static void fatal(String methodName, String diagnostic)
{
  System.err.println("\n*** " + methodName + ": " + diagnostic);
  System.err.flush();
  System.exit(1);
}
```

This method begins by sending `System.err` the `println()` message with an error message argument that is built from parameters `methodName` and `diagnos-tic`, along with some formatting literals to give the appearance of an error message. It then sends `System.err` a message to use its `flush()` method, which ensures that the contents of `System.err` appear on the screen immediately. Finally, it terminates program execution by sending the `System` class the `exit()` message, with the argument 1 to indicate abnormal termination.

There is nothing about this utility method that restricts its use to the class `Tem-perature`. It can be used in any method where some error condition might occur. For this reason, we have also added it as a public static method to the `ann.util` package so that it can be used in later methods we develop.

Static vs. Instance Methods

We defined the `toString()` and constructor methods as *instance* methods, but we defined the `isValidTemperature()` and `fatal()` methods as *static* methods. This raises an important question: *When should a method be a static method and when should it be an instance method?*

The fundamental distinction between the two is that an instance method is invoked by a message that is sent to *an instance of a class,* that is, to an *object,* while a static method is invoked by a message that is sent to the *class* itself. Practically speaking, this has the following effects:

NOTE

- *A static method may access only static variables, static constants, and static methods,* that is, variables, constants, and methods that are also declared using the `static` modifier.

- *An instance method may access both instance and static variables, constants, and methods.*

- *Objects have their own distinct copies of attribute (or instance) variables, constants, and instance methods, but they share the same copy of static variables, constants, and methods.*

One consequence of these differences is that since constants represent values that do not change, *most constants should be declared as static constants* so that all objects share a single definition. For our `Temperature` class, we might picture this as follows:

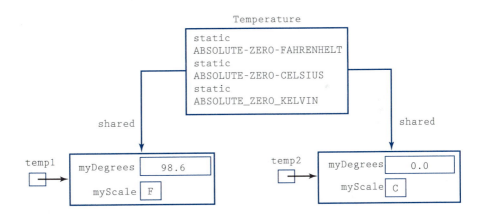

Using instance constants would waste memory because each object would have its own definition of each constant:

NOTE   In contrast, variables in a class generally represent values that can differ from object to object. As a result, *most variables should not be declared static,* because static variables cannot hold values that differ from one object to another since they are shared by all instances of the class. As we stated earlier, they determine the *state* of an object at a particular time.

For methods, here is a simple "rule-of-thumb" that we will follow:

NOTE

> *If a method needs to access attribute variables, then it must be defined as an instance method. Otherwise, it should be defined as a static method, and all information it requires should be passed to it via parameters or declared to be static.*

Following this rule, we defined `toString()` and our constructors as instance methods because they need to access the attribute variables of an object. By contrast, we made `isValidTemperature()` and `fatal()` static methods because they do not access an object's attribute variables. Instead, they receive all of the information they require via their parameters.

It is worth mentioning that it would not be appropriate to replace the `isValidTemperature()` class method with an instance method that returned `true` or `false` depending on the values of `myDegrees` and `myScale`. The class invariant stipulates that a `Temperature` object will *always* be valid, which means that this method would always have to return `true`, which is surely not very useful!

Accessor Methods

An **accessor** is a method that allows a programmer to retrieve, but not modify, some attribute of a class. From an external perspective, a programmer should be able to send a message

```
temp1.getDegrees()
```

to retrieve the number of degrees in a `Temperature` object `temp1` and a message

```
temp1.getScale()
```

to access the scale in `temp1`. As these names suggest, it is common practice for the name of an accessor method to begin with the prefix *get* followed by the attribute it is accessing.

An autonomous `Temperature` object will know how many degrees it has. From an internal perspective, when I (a `Temperature`) receive the `getDegrees()` message, I should return the number of degrees I have. We thus have this simple specification for the behavior of `getDegrees()`:

Return: `myDegrees`

The specification of the behavior of `getScale()` is similar:

Return: `myScale`

Figure 6.8 shows the definitions of these methods.

FIGURE 6.8   Temperature ACCESSOR METHODS

```
/** degrees accessor
 *   Return: myDegrees
 */
public double getDegrees()
{
  return myDegrees;
}

/** scale accessor
 *   Return: myScale
 */

public char getScale()
{
  return myScale;
}
```

From an external perspective, when the `getDegrees()` message is sent to a Temperature object, it will return the value stored in the attribute variable `myDegrees` in that object. To illustrate, given the declarations

```
Temperature temp1 = new Temperature(98.6, 'F'),
            temp2 = new Temperature();
```

the expression

```
temp1.getDegrees()
```

will return the value of `myDegrees` in `temp1` (i.e., 98.6), while the expression

```
temp2.getDegrees()
```

will return the value of `myDegrees` in `temp2` (i.e., 0.0). The `getScale()` method behaves in a similar manner using an object's attribute variable `myScale`.

Temperature Input: A Mutator Method

Java's use of the `toString()` method in defining the `print()` and `println()` methods provides an elegant solution to the problem of outputting an object's value. Unfortunately, there is no such analog for input. Our next task, therefore, is to define a method to read a `Temperature` value from a `Keyboard`. We want a statement such as

```
temp2.read(theKeyboard);
```

to read a number and a character from `theKeyboard` and store them in `temp2.myDegrees` and `temp2.myScale`, respectively. Methods that change the values of an object's attribute variables change the internal state of the object and are thus called **mutators.**

From an internal perspective, a `read()` method must contain the instructions that I (as an autonomous `Temperature` object) must follow to input a temperature. One decision that must be made is what to do if the user enters an invalid temperature.

One possibility is to generate a fatal error as we did with the explicit-value constructor. Another possibility is for our method to return a boolean value that indicates whether or not the input was valid. We will adopt this latter approach because it lets us use sentinels to control input loops.

From this perspective, object-centered design leads to the following specification:

Receive: *theKeyboard,* a `Keyboard` object

Input: *inDegrees,* a `double` value, and *inScale,* a `char` value

Precondition: *inScale* is one of {'f', 'c', 'k', 'F', 'C', 'K'} and *inDegrees* is valid for *inScale.*

Return: true if *(inScale, inDegrees)* represents a valid temperature and false otherwise

Postcondition: `myDegrees` == *inDegrees* && `myScale` == *inScale*

For user convenience, we will accept the scale in either upper or lowercase, converting lowercase entries to uppercase to satisfy the class invariant. To guard against an invalid scale, we must check that the scale that is input satisfies the precondition before modifying the data members. We can perform this validation using the `isValidTemperature()` utility. If the input is not valid, we will have the method return `false` and leave further action up to the caller. Figure 6.9 gives a definition of this method.

FIGURE 6.9   Temperature INPUT

```
/** read(Keyboard) using the ann Keyboard class.
 *   Receive:       theKeyboard, a Keyboard object
 *   Input:         degrees, a double, and scale, a char, from theKeyboard
 *   Return:        true if (degrees, scale) comprises a valid temperature,
 *                  false otherwise
 *   Postcondition: myDegrees == degrees && myScale == scale if a valid
 *                  temperature has been input; otherwise the data members
 *                  are unchanged.
 */
public boolean read(Keyboard theKeyboard)
{
  double inDegrees = theKeyboard.readDouble();
  char inScale    = theKeyboard.readChar();

  if (isValidTemperature(inDegrees, inScale))
  {
    myDegrees = inDegrees;
    myScale   = Character.toUpperCase(inScale);
    return true;
  }
  else
    return false;
}
```

Note that the structure of this method is quite similar to that of the explicit-value constructor. The primary differences are:

❑ A constructor gets its values from another method via parameters, but an input method gets its values from the user via the keyboard.

❑ Our explicit-value constructor generates a fatal error if its parameters represent an invalid temperature, but this method returns `false` if the user-entered values are invalid.

This different approach does not violate our class invariant, because we only change the values of the attribute variables if the input values comprise a valid temperature.

Given this method, a programmer can now use `read()` to input temperatures from a `Keyboard` object. To illustrate, we can build an input loop like the following to process multiple temperatures, using any invalid temperature as a sentinel:

```
// . . .
Temperature temp1 = new Temperature();
boolean validInput;

for (;;)
{
   theScreen.print("Enter a temperature, as in 98.6 F
   (0 A to quit): ");
   validInput = temp1.read(theKeyboard);

   if (!validInput) break;

   // . . . process the temperature in temp1 . . .
}
```

Conversion Methods

Next, we examine the methods that produce equivalent temperatures in different scales. We begin with a method to produce the Fahrenheit equivalent of a `Temperature`.

From an internal perspective, I (an autonomous `Temperature` object) should be able to compute the Fahrenheit `Temperature` equivalent of myself. Object-centered design produces the following specification for this behavior:

Return: The Fahrenheit temperature equivalent of myself

Because the particular formula used to compute the return value depends on the current value of `myScale`, we will use an `if-else-if` statement to select the appropriate formula. Since the method must return a `Temperature`, we use the explicit-value constructor to build the return-value. Figure 6.10 gives a definition of this method.

FIGURE 6.10   THE `inFahrenheit()` FUNCTION MEMBER

```
/** Fahrenheit converter
 *  Return: the Fahrenheit equivalent to myself
 */
public Temperature inFahrenheit()
{
  Temperature result = null;
```

```
   if (myScale == 'F')
     result = new Temperature(myDegrees, 'F');
   else if (myScale == 'C')
     result = new Temperature(myDegrees * 1.8 + 32.0, 'F');
   else if (myScale == 'K')
     result = new Temperature((myDegrees - 273.15) * 1.8 + 32.0, 'F');

   return result;
}
```

There are several things to note about this method. The first is that `result` is initialized to the special value `null`. We could have written

```
   Temperature result = new Temperature();
```

NOTE

but doing so is wasteful. The reason is that it would create a `Temperature` object that is then immediately thrown away when one of the branches of the if-else-if statement constructs and assigns a new `Temperature` value to `result`. For such situations, *Java provides the keyword* `null` *which can (and should) be used to give a reference-type variable an initial value that will be immediately overwritten.*

Another point to note is that this method constructs the `Temperature` value it returns by calling the explicit-value `Temperature` constructor. For example, in the first case, the expression

```
   new Temperature(myDegrees, 'F')
```

passes the arguments `myDegrees` and `'F'` to the explicit-value constructor, which constructs a `Temperature` object from these values in the memory location allocated by `new`. The `return` statement then makes this object the method's return-value. The other cases use this same constructor, but with different expressions for the first argument.

A final point to note is that our class invariant ensures that `myScale` is one of 'F', 'C', or 'K'. This means that `inFahrenheit()` and other non-mutator methods do not need to check for other values of `myScale`.

Given this method, a programmer can now write

```
   Temperature temp1 = new Temperature();   // default value: 0 C
   Temperature temp2 = temp1.inFahrenheit();

   theScreen.println(temp2);
```

and the Fahrenheit equivalent of 0 degrees Celsius will be displayed:

```
   32.0 F
```

The methods `inCelsius()` and `inKelvin()` are similar, and are left as exercises.

Raising (and Lowering) a `Temperature`

If `Temperature` objects `temp1` and `temp2` are constructed by

```
   Temperature temp1 = new Temperature(95.0, 'F'),
               temp2 = null;
```

it would be convenient if we had an operation to raise a temperature as in the statement

```
   temp2 = temp1.raise(3.6);
```

Such an operation would effectively build a new `Temperature` that represents raising the temperature `temp1` by a specified amount. Similarly, it would be convenient to have an operation to lower a `Temperature` by a given amount.

Using object-centered design, we can specify the behavior of `raise()` as follows:

Receive: *amount,* a `double` value

Precondition: (`myDegrees` + *amount,* `myScale`) is a valid temperature

Return: *resultTemp,* a `Temperature` such that
resultTemp.`myScale` == `myScale`, and
resultTemp.`myDegrees` == `myDegrees` + *amount*

As in previous methods, we will use `isValidTemperature()` to verify the precondition. If it is satisfied, we can use the explicit-value constructor to build the return value. If it is not, we will treat this as a fatal error and handle it with our `fatal()` utility. Figure 6.11 presents a definition of this method.

FIGURE 6.11   THE `raise()` METHOD

```
/** raise by a (double) amount in degrees of my scale.
 *  Receive:      double amount
 *  Precondition: myDegrees + amount produces a valid magnitude
 *                for a Temperature whose scale is myScale.
 *  Return:       a Temperature that is amount degrees higher than myself.
 */
public Temperature raise(double amount)
{
  double newDegrees = myDegrees + amount;

  if (!isValidTemperature(newDegrees, myScale))
    fatal("raise(double)", newDegrees + " " + myScale
                      + " is not a valid temperature");
  return new Temperature(newDegrees, myScale);
}
```

The definition of a `lower()` method for decreasing a `Temperature` by a given amount is similar and is left as an exercise.

Comparing `Temperature` Values

As we noted in Section 6.2, it would be useful if we could compare two `Temperature` objects using relational operators. Unfortunately, unlike C++, Java does not (at present) allow us to define operators for new types such as <, so we cannot build a method that lets us write

```
if (temp1 < temp2)   // WON'T work correctly
```

But we can write methods that provide the same functionality as the relational operators. For example, we can write a `lessThan()` method that could be used in statements like the following for programming a computer-controlled thermostat:

```
Temperature warm = new Temperature(20.0, 'C');
if (houseTemperature.lessThan(warm))
    furnace.run();
```

A similar `greaterThan()` method might be used in programming a computerized thermometer:

```
Temperature bodyTemperature = new Temperature(98.6, 'F');
if (yourTemperature.greaterThan(bodyTemperature))
    theScreen.println("You have a fever!");
```

To permit such operations, we must define a method for each of the relational operations for class `Temperature`. We will do this for two of them, the *less-than* operation and the *equality* operation. The others are similar and are left as exercises.

We begin with the `lessThan()` method. From an external perspective, we want to be able to write an expression like

```
temp1.lessThan(temp2)
```

and have it return `true` if and only if the `Temperature` referred to by `temp1` is less than that referred to by `temp2`. From an internal perspective, I (an autonomous `Temperature`) should return `true` if I am less than the `Temperature` parameter that accompanies the `lessThan()` message and should return false otherwise.

Using object-centered design, we can specify the behavior of `lessThan()` as follows:

Receive: *otherTemp,* a `Temperature` value

Return: `true` if and only if I am less than *otherTemp*

Note that if `temp1` refers to the `Temperature` 0° C and `temp2` refers to the `Temperature` 32° F, then the expression

```
temp1.lessThan(temp2)
```

should return `false`, since these two temperatures are in fact equal. Implementing `lessThan()` is thus complicated by the possibility that the scales for the two objects may not be the same. Figure 6.12 shows one way that this method can be defined.

FIGURE 6.12 A `lessThan()` RELATIONAL OPERATION

```
/** less-than comparison.
 *  Receive: otherTemp, a Temperature object
 *  Return:  true if and only if I am less than otherTemp
 */
public boolean lessThan(Temperature otherTemp)
{
    Temperature localTemp = null;           // the equivalent of otherTemp,
                                            //  but in my scale
    if (myScale == 'C')
      localTemp = otherTemp.Celsius();
    else if (myScale == 'F')
      localTemp = otherTemp.Fahrenheit();
    else
      localTemp = otherTemp.Kelvin();

    return myDegrees < localTemp.getDegrees();
}
```

This implementation of the method resolves the problem of different scales by using a local Temperature object `localTemp`, which it sets to the equivalent of `otherTemp` in the same scale as the `Temperature` object receiving the message. Once we have two temperatures in the same scale, we can simply compare their `myDegrees` values using the normal less-than operator.[3]

An `equals()` method that checks equality of two `Temperatures` can be defined using much the same approach, as shown in Figure 6.13.

FIGURE 6.13   AN `equals()` RELATIONAL OPERATOR

```
/** equality comparison.
 *    Receive: otherTemp, a Temperature object
 *    Return:  true if and only if I am equal to otherTemp.
 */
public boolean equals(Temperature otherTemp)
{
  Temperature localTemp = null;          // the equivalent of otherTemp,
                                         // but in my scale
  if (myScale == 'C')
    localTemp = otherTemp.Celsius();
  else if (myScale == 'F')
    localTemp = otherTemp.Fahrenheit();
  else
    localTemp = otherTemp.Kelvin();

  return myDegrees == localTemp.getDegrees();
}
```

Each of the other four relational operations can be implemented in a similar manner. However, a comparison of Figures 6.12 and 6.13 should make it clear that this approach involves a good deal of duplicate code.

What we can do instead is use an approach similar to that used in Java's `String`, `BigInteger`, and various other classes, and write a general `compareTo()` method that "factors out" the code that these relational operations have in common. More precisely, in keeping with these other classes, we can specify that our `compareTo()` method should behave as follows:

Receive: *otherTemp,* a `Temperature` object

Return: 0 if my temperature is equal to that of *otherTemp*
          A negative value if my temperature is less than that of *otherTemp*
          A positive value if my temperature is greater than that of *otherTemp*

We can generate this behavior by using the code common to Figure 6.12 and 6.13, but returning 0, −1, or +1 depending on whether `myDegrees` is equal to, less than, or greater than `otherTemp.myDegrees`. This is the approach used in Figure 6.14.

---

[3] A method can directly access the private attribute variables of a same-class object it receives via a parameter. For readability, we use an object's accessor method, rather than directly accessing its attribute variables.

FIGURE 6.14   A `compareTo()` **UTILITY METHOD**

```
/** compare utility method.
 *    Receive: otherTemp, the Temperature to which I'm being compared.
 *    Return:  a negative value, if I am <  otherTemp,
 *             0,                 if I am == otherTemp,
 *             a positive value, if I am > otherTemp.
 */
public int compareTo(Temperature otherTemp)
{
  Temperature localTemp = null;              // the equivalent of otherTemp,
                                             // but in my scale
  if (myScale == 'C')
    localTemp = otherTemp.inCelsius();
  else if (myScale == 'F')
    localTemp = otherTemp.inFahrenheit();
  else if (myScale == 'K')
    localTemp = otherTemp.inKelvin();

  if (myDegrees < localTemp.getDegrees())
    return -1.0;
  else if (myDegrees > localTemp.getDegrees())
    return 1.0;
  else
    return 0.0;
}
```

Given this method, the relational operators can now be implemented with almost no duplicate code. For example, Figure 6.15 shows how the `equals()` and `lessThan()` methods can be defined using `compareTo()`. The remaining relational operators can be defined in a similar fashion and are left as exercises.

FIGURE 6.15   THE `equals()` **AND** `lessThan()` **METHODS**

```
/** equality comparison.
 *  Receive: otherTemp, a Temperature object
 *  Return:  true if and only if I am equal to otherTemp
 */
public boolean equals(Temperature otherTemp)
{
  return compareTo(otherTemp)    == 0;
}

/** less-than comparison.
 *  Receive: otherTemp, a Temperature object
 *  Return:  true if and only if I am less than otherTemp
 */
public boolean lessThan(Temperature otherTemp)
{
  return compareTo(otherTemp)    < 0;
}
```

By "factoring out" the code common to each relational operation, this approach produces methods that are simpler and, therefore, easier to write and understand.

> *If you find yourself doing the same thing more than once, there is probably a better way to do what you are doing!*

Handles and Reference Type Copying

Several times since Chapter 2 we have indicated that Java's reference types are created from classes (or arrays or interfaces, as described later). In the world of computing, the word **reference** is a synonym for the word **address.** As we shall see, this is the origin of the phrase *reference type* in Java.

As we know, a primitive type declaration such as

```
int count = 0;
```

allocates memory space for an `int` variable, associates the name `count` with that space, and initializes that space to 0. We can visualize its effect as follows:

count

0

By contrast, the reference-type declaration

```
Temperature temp = new Temperature(0.0, 'C');
```

actually creates *two* distinct entities that we can visualize as follows:

temp   myDegrees   0.0
        myScale   C

The first entity is a reference-type variable named `temp`, whose value is the *memory address* of a `Temperature` object. The second entity is an unnamed `Temperature` object, whose attribute variables are initialized using the default-value constructor. When we say that `temp` *refers to* this `Temperature` object, what we mean is that `temp`'s value is the *memory address* of that object. Strictly speaking, `temp` and the `Temperature` object to which it refers are two distinct entities.

An analogy may help clarify this. A television remote control lets us perform operations on a television set (e.g., change its channel, adjust its volume, etc.). In a similar manner, the variable `temp` lets us perform operations on the `Temperature` object to which it refers. The expression

```
temp.getScale()
```

sends the getScale() message to the Temperature object to which temp refers, and the expression

```
temp.inFahrenheit()
```

sends an inFahrenheit() message to that same Temperature object via variable temp.

In fact, variable temp is the only way we can interact with that Temperature object because it has no name of its own. For this reason, a variable like temp is usually referred to as a **handle** for the object to which it refers. Just as in the real world, an object's handle is the way to grab that object, temp is how we "grab" or otherwise manipulate the Temperature object to which it refers.

The Reference Type Copying Problem.

Understanding the difference between a handle and the object to which it refers is important, since it can help you avoid a potential problem of dealing with reference types. Consider the statements:

```
Temperature temp = new Temperature(100, 'C');
Temperature saveTemp = temp;
```

How should we visualize temp and saveTemp? The key lies in the notion of handles. Because temp and saveTemp are handles for Temperature objects, the first statement creates a new Temperature object and initializes handle temp with its address:

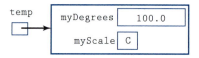

Since it does not use the new operator, the second statement does not create a new Temperature object. Instead, the second statement initializes handle saveTemp with the address from temp:

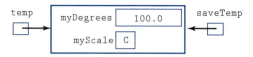

The result is that temp and saveTemp are both handles for the same Temperature object. This is probably not what the programmer intended, because if a mutator is applied to temp as in

```
temp.read(theKeyboard);
```

then any changes that are made to the `Temperature` object to which `temp` refers simultaneously change the `Temperature` object to which `saveTemp` refers. For example, if the user enters `98.6` and 'F', then our picture changes as follows:

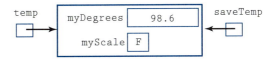

Again, since the attribute variables in the `Temperature` object to which `saveTemp` refers are being overwritten, this is most likely not what the programmer intended.

This copying problem for reference types is the same one we described in Chapter 4 when we studied the parameter-passing mechanism. As we noted there, it is known as the **alias problem** because it produces two names for the same thing.

To remedy it, a class can provide a `copy()` method—several Java API classes call this method `clone()`. From an external perspective, a `copy()` method should make and return a copy of the object that receives a message to invoke this method. From an internal perspective, if I (a `Temperature` object) receive a `copy()` message, I should build and return a copy of myself. This gives the following specification:

Return: A distinct `Temperature` equal to myself

The explicit-value constructor makes this an easy method to implement, as shown in Figure 6.16.

FIGURE 6.16   THE `copy()` METHOD

```
/** copy instance method, to support assignments, initializations.
 *  Return:  A distinct copy of myself
 */

public Temperature copy()
{
  return new Temperature(myDegrees, myScale);
}
```

Given such a method, a programmer can now write:

```
Temperature temp = new Temperature(100, 'C');
Temperature saveTemp = temp.copy();
```

and `saveTemp` will be initialized to a distinct copy of `temp`:

Application of a mutator to `temp`, as described previously,

```
temp.read(keyboard);
```

will then change the value of `temp`, but not the value of `saveTemp`:

Our `copy()` method is relatively simple because the types of all the attribute variables within class `Temperature` are primitive types. If the type of any of its attribute variables were a reference type, then such a copy would not make a distinct copy of that variable:

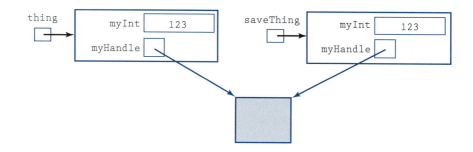

This is known as a **shallow copy.** To create a truly distinct copy, each reference type attribute variable would need to be copied separately, an operation known as a **deep copy:**

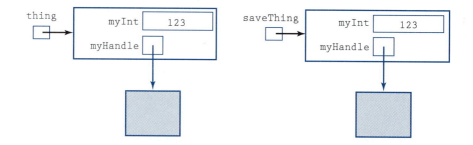

Summary: The `Temperature` Class

Figure 6.17 collects together all of the code fragments of class `Temperature` into one class declaration.

FIGURE 6.17 THE Temperature CLASS

```
/** Temperature.java
 *  Class Invariant: myScale == 'C' && myDegrees >= ABSOLUTE_ZERO_CELSIUS
 *                || myScale == 'F' && myDegrees >= ABSOLUTE_ZERO_FAHRENHEIT
 *                || myScale == 'K'  && myDegrees >= ABSOLUTE_ZERO_KELVIN
 */

import ann.easyio.Keyboard;

class Temperature
{
 public final static double ABSOLUTE_ZERO_FAHRENHEIT = -459.67,
                            ABSOLUTE_ZERO_CELSIUS     = -273.15,
                            ABSOLUTE_ZERO_KELVIN      =    0.0;

 //--- Constructors ---
 /** Default-value constructor.
  *  Postcondition: myDegrees == 0.0 && myScale == 'C'.
  */
 public Temperature()
 {
   myDegrees = 0.0;
   myScale = 'C';
 }

 /** Explicit-value constructor.
  *  Receive:       double degrees, char scale
  *  Precondition:  scale is one of 'f', 'F', 'c', 'C', 'k', or 'K'
  *                   and degrees is a valid number of degrees for scale.
  *  Postcondition: myDegrees == degrees && myScale == (uppercase) scale.
  */
 public Temperature(double degrees, char scale)
 {
   if (isValidTemperature(degrees, scale))
   {
     myDegrees = degrees;
     myScale = Character.toUpperCase(scale);
   }
   else
     fatal("Temperature(degrees, scale)", "invalid args: " + degrees + scale);
 }

 //--- Accessors ---
 /** degrees accessor.
  *  Return: myDegrees
  */
 public double getDegrees()
 {
   return myDegrees;
 }

 /** scale accessor.
  *  Return: myScale
  */
 public char getScale()
 {
   return myScale;
 }
```

FIGURE 6.17.   THE Temperature CLASS (cont'd)

```
//--- Input/Output ---
/** read(Keyboard) using the ann Keyboard class.
 *  Receive:       theKeyboard, a Keyboard object
 *  Input:         degrees, a double, and scale, a char, from theKeyboard
 *  Return:        true if (degrees, scale) comprises a valid temperature,
 *                 false otherwise
 *  Postcondition: myDegrees == degrees && myScale == scale if a valid
 *                 temperature has been input; otherwise the data members
 *                 are unchanged.
 */
public boolean read(Keyboard theKeyboard)
{
  double inDegrees = theKeyboard.readDouble();
  char inScale    = theKeyboard.readChar();

  if (isValidTemperature(inDegrees, inScale))
  {
    myDegrees = inDegrees;
    myScale   = Character.toUpperCase(inScale);
    return true;
  }
  else
    return false;
}

/** toString converter (used by +, print(), println(), ...).
 *  Return: a String representation of myself
 */
public String toString()
{
  return myDegrees + " " + myScale;
}

//--- Converters ---
/** Fahrenheit converter
 *  Return: the Fahrenheit equivalent to myself
 */
public Temperature inFahrenheit()
{
  Temperature result = null;

  if (myScale == 'F')
    result = new Temperature(myDegrees, 'F');
  else if (myScale == 'C')
    result = new Temperature(myDegrees * 1.8 + 32.0, 'F');
  else if (myScale == 'K')
    result = new Temperature((myDegrees - 273.15) * 1.8 + 32.0, 'F');

  return temp;
}


//--- Celsius and Kelvin
//--- converters go here


//--- Other Temperature Operations
/** raise by a (double) amount in degrees of my scale.
 *  Receive:      double amount
 *  Precondition: myDegrees + amount produces a valid magnitude
 *                for a Temperature whose scale is myScale.
 *  Return:       a Temperature that is amount degrees higher than myself.
 */
public Temperature raise(double amount)
{
  double newDegrees = myDegrees + amount;

  if (!isValidTemperature(newDegrees, myScale))
    Controller.fatal("raise(double)", newDegrees + " " + myScale
                              + " is not a valid temperature");

  return new Temperature(newDegrees, myScale);
}
```

NOTE

As this example demonstrates, it is our practice to organize a class as follows:

- ❑ We begin a class with any constants the class provides. This allows them to be quickly found when necessary.
- ❑ After the constants, we place the constructors, accessors, mutators, converters, and utilities. Since these represent the operations available to a user of the class, we want a reader of the class to see them as soon as possible.
- ❑ We place the attribute variable declarations (and private methods) last, because they represent the private internal implementation details of the class. Since a user of the class is not permitted to directly access them, a reader of the class should not have to wade through such details before getting to those parts of the class the reader can access. This is particularly important for more complex classes.

The Class Interface. The benefit of keeping attribute variables private is that it forces programs to interact with a class object through its public methods. The set of public operations can thus be thought of as an **interface** between the class and programs that use it. Since the interface provides the sole means of operating on an object, it is important that it be well-designed—a good interface must provide all of the functionality needed to operate on an object. *Designing a good interface thus requires much time and thought, and should not be hurried.*

NOTE

One reason for designing the interface carefully is that a class interface must be *stable*. If it changes frequently, then programs that use the class must be revised often to accommodate the changes. Programmers will eventually tire of revising their programs and will stop using the class. A stable interface is only possible if it is carefully designed from the outset.

If an interface is stable, then any program that uses the class solely through the interface will not break, even if the private portion of the class is modified extensively. Such extensive modifications are common in maintaining or upgrading many real-world systems. The attribute variables in a class may be replaced by others that more efficiently represent the object being modeled; private utility methods may be implemented more efficiently; and so on. If the interface is stable, the time required to upgrade such a system is only the time to modify the class—*programs that use the class will not require modification.* This means that such systems can be maintained more easily, saving time and money.

✔ Quick Quiz 6.4

1. Class operations are usually implemented using _____.
2. Methods that initialize attribute variables are called _____.
3. Methods that retrieve but do not change attribute variable values are called _____.
4. Methods that change attribute variable values are called _____.
5. Methods that provide a representation of an object in a different type are called _____.
6. Methods that other methods use to simplify or avoid redundant coding are called _____.
7. A constructor in a class `Student` will be named _____.
8. Name and describe two kinds of constructors.

9. A boolean expression that must be true when the method terminates is called a(n) _____ .

10. (True of false) Objects share instance variables, constants, and methods.

11. The word *reference* is a synonym for the word _____ .

12. A variable that stores the address of an object is called a(n) _____ for that object.

13. The set of public operations of a class acts as a(n) _____ between the class and programs that use it.

EXERCISES 6.4

1. Add a method to class `Temperature` that lowers a `Temperature` value by a numeric value.

2. Add a method to class `Temperature` that converts a `Temperature` value to its Celsius equivalent.

3. Add a method to class `Temperature` that converts a `Temperature` value to its Kelvin equivalent.

For Exercises 4–9, define the (private) attribute variables of a class to model the given item.

4. Date as a month, day, and year.

5. Time measured in hours, minutes, seconds, and AM or PM indicator.

6. A telephone number as area code, local exchange, and number

7. Cards in a deck of playing cards

8. A point (x, y) in a Cartesian coordinate system

9. A point (r, θ) in a polar coordinate system

For Exercises 10–15, complete the class declarations begun in Exercises 4–9 for the specified objects, supplying an appropriate set of operations for the class. You should write a driver program to test your class as Programming Problems 1–6 at the end of the chapter ask you to do.

10. Date as a month, day, and year

11. Time measured in hours, minutes, seconds, and AM or PM indicator

12. A telephone number as area code, local exchange, and number.

13. Cards in a deck of playing cards

14. A point (x, y) in a Cartesian coordinate system

15. A point (r, θ) in a polar coordinate system

For Exercises 16–18, develop a class for the given information, and then write operations appropriate for an object of that type. You should write a driver program to test your class as Programming Problems 7–9 at the end of the chapter ask you to do.

16. Information about a person: name, birthday, age, gender, social security number, height, weight, hair color, eye color, and marital status.

17. Statistics about a baseball player: name, age, birthdate, position (pitcher, catcher, infielder, outfielder).

18. Weather statistics: date; city and state, province, or country; time of day; temperature; barometric pressure; weather conditions (clear skies, partly cloudy, cloudy, stormy).

For Exercises 19–21, write appropriate class declarations to describe the information in the specified file. Descriptions of these files are given at the end of Chapter 10.

19.   `Student.txt`

20.   `Inventory.txt`

21.   `Users.txt`

6.5 GRAPHICAL/INTERNET JAVA: RAISE THE FLAG

The focus of this chapter has been on instance methods, and how they can be used to write reusable code. In this section, we take a closer look at how to generate simple computer graphics. Most of the methods provided in Java for graphics programming are instance methods that operate on graphics objects. As in our graphical/internet examples thus far, we will use the powerful and current tools provided by Java's Swing components.

A CloseableFrame Class

The applets we have build in earlier chapters have extended Java's JApplet class. The classes we have built thus far have extended Java's Object class. For simple graphics, we can build classes that extend CloseableFrame, a class provided in our ann.gui package that we have designed to make graphical programming easier. Here is a simple example:

```
class DrawingDemo extends CloseableFrame
{
 public static void main(String [] args)
 {
    DrawingDemo myGUI = new DrawingDemo();
    myGUI.setVisible(true);
 }
}
```

Note that the main method of this class is a bit different from others we have seen. It simply creates an instance of itself,

```
DrawingDemo myGUI = new DrawingDemo();
```

and then sends this object the setVisible() message to make it appear on the screen:

```
myGUI.setVisible(true);
```

The main methods of other object-oriented graphical user interface programs are usually similarly simple because the real work is done by methods in other classes—in this case, by setVisible() (from java.awt.Component).

Adding an import statement such as

```
import ann.gui.*;   // CloseableFrame
```

before this class declaration to import the class CloseableFrame yields a program that can be compiled and executed. When we do so, it creates a graphical user interface window like the following. In the absence of any other code, the window frame is blank. When its close box is clicked, the application that created the window is terminated and the window is destroyed.

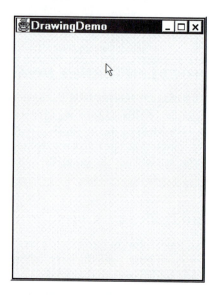

Recall that when a class *B extends* another class *A*, the Java compiler treats class *B* as a specialized version of *A*—an extension of class *A*. The benefit of this is that *B* *inherits* all of the attributes (variables and constants) and behaviors (methods) of *A* so that any message that can be sent to an *A* object can be sent to a *B* object as well.

This means that, in the current example, when we define the `DrawingDemo` class as an extension of `CloseableFrame`, any method in the class `CloseableFrame` (along with all those in its ancestor classes) can also be used with a `DrawingDemo` object. Table 6.1 lists a few of these methods. Others are given in the Documentation section of the chapter summary.

REFERENCE

TABLE 6.1   SOME `CloseableFrame` METHODS

Method	Description
`setTitle(str)`	Set the frame's title to `String str`
`setBackground(c)` `setForeground(c)`	Set the frame's background / foreground color to `Color c`
`setSize(width, height)`	Resize the frame to `height` rows by `width` columns, where `height` and `width` are integers
`getHeight()` `getWidth()`	Get the height / width of the frame
`setVisible(b)`	Make the frame visible or invisible based on boolean value `b`

Painting

In Section 4.5, we introduced the basic concepts involved in **painting** (i.e., drawing) in some region of the screen called a *window frame* (or simply *window* or *frame*) that has been designated for graphical output. As we noted there, Java's Swing classes provide a variety of **top-level containers** such as JApplet and JFrame that create these regions. In the preceding DrawingDemo example, the container Closeable-Frame created a window because it extends JFrame. But now we must figure out how to paint in this window frame.

These top-level containers contain other *intermediate* containers called **panes** or **panels.** The most important of these is the **content pane.** Usually there are several other containers between it and the top-level container, but in most cases, we need not be concerned with what they are. The content pane is used to group and position the components that do the painting. In our simple example we will use just one component, DrawingPane (rather than using a layout manager to position several components on the content pane):

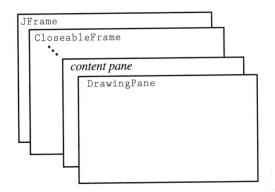

The definition of DrawingPane is given in Figure 6.18.

```
/** DrawingDemo.java
 *   Output: A closeable frame that displays its dimensions.
 */

import ann.gui.CloseableFrame;
import java.awt.*;
import javax.swing.*;

class DrawingDemo extends CloseableFrame
{
  public static void main(String [] args)
  {
```

FIGURE 6.18   `DrawingDemo.java`

```
   {
      DrawingDemo myGUI = new DrawingDemo();
      myGUI.setContentPane( new DrawingPane() );
      myGUI.setVisible(true);
   }
}

class DrawingPane extends JPanel
{
   final int MARGIN = 20;

   public DrawingPane()
   {
      setBackground(Color.white);
   }

   public void paintComponent(Graphics pen)
   {
      super.paintComponent(pen);

      int height = getHeight();
      int width = getWidth();
      pen.drawSing("This window-pane has height " + height +
                   " and width "  + width, MARGIN, height / 2);
   }
}
```

Here, the main method in `DrawingDemo` creates the frame `myGui` as before, and then constructs a `DrawingPane` and positions it on the content pane:

```
     myGUI.setContentPane( new DrawingPane() );
```

The last statement of the main method then makes it visible as before.

For the class `DrawingPane`, we have followed the widely recommended practice of using subclasses of `JPanel` for painting. One of the methods in this class is a constructor that sets the background of the panel to white (instead of the content pane's default color, gray), using the `setBackgound()` method inherited from `JPanel` (which it inherited from `JComponent`),

The other method defined in `DrawingPane` is `paintComponent()`. It is needed because the *painting of Swing components must always be performed by a method named* `paintComponent()`. This method's only parameter is a `Graphics` object, and it is here that the statements that do the actual painting reside:

```
     public void paintComponent(Graphics pen)
     {
        // statements to paint the component
     }
```

For the painting to be done correctly, `DrawingPane`'s `paintComponent()` method first invokes the `paintComponent()` method in its superclass `JPanel` (which inherits it from `JComponent`) to clear the background:

```
super.paintComponent(pen);
```

However, before `paintComponent()` can paint a message in this component displaying the dimensions of the panel, it must first get these dimensions. It accomplishes this by using the `getHeight()` and `getWidth()` methods which `DrawingPane` inherits from `JPanel` (which inherits them from `JComponent`):

```
int height = getHeight();
int width = getWidth();
```

The actual painting is done by `paintComponent()`'s parameter, the `Graphics` object—named pen in this case. `Graphics` is one of the classes in the `java.awt` package, Java's **Abstract Windowing Toolkit,** a collection of classes for building user interfaces in earlier versions of Java and upon which Swing is founded. (See Section 1.3 for more information about AWT.) The `Graphics` class provides a variety of messages that can be sent to `pen`. In our example, its `drawString()` method is invoked to display the pane's dimensions, 20 columns from the left edge of the frame, and roughly half-way between its top and bottom edges.

The `Graphics` class contains more than 40 different methods (see the Java API documentation for a complete list). A few of the simpler ones are given in Table 6.2. As we noted in Section 1.3, the location at which something is to be drawn is specified by giving its (x, y) coordinates, measured in **pixels (picture elements),** with location $(0, 0)$ referring to the upper-left corner of the window.

TABLE 6.2   SOME Graphics CLASS METHODS

Method	Description
	Draw a(n):
`drawArc(x, y, width, height, startAngle, arcAngle)`	arc that begins at `startAngle` and extends for `arcAngle` degrees and covers the specified rectangle (see `drawRect()`).
`drawLine(x1, y1, x2, y2)`	line from $(x1, y1)$ to $(x2, y2)$
`drawOval(x, y, width, height)`	oval covering the specified rectangle (see `drawRect()`)
`drawRect(x, y, width, height)`	rectangle of the given dimensions, whose upper left corner is at (x, y)
`drawString(str, x, y)`	String `str` at position (x, y)
	Draw a filled:
`fillArc(x, y, width, height, startAngle, arcAngle)`	arc (see `drawArc()`)
`fillOval(x, y, width, height)`	oval (see `drawOval()`)
`fillRect(x, y, width, height)`	rectangle (see `drawRect()`)
`translate(x, y)`	Shift the origin to position (x, y)

When the program in Figure 6.18 is executed, the following window is produced:

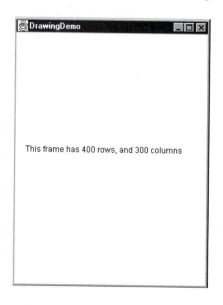

This frame has 400 rows, and 300 columns

A Dutch Flag GUI Application

Most countries have colorful flags, but while some of these flags have a fairly complex graphical structure, others are quite simple. One such flag is that of the Netherlands:

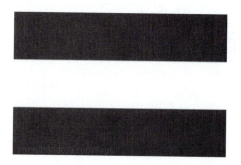

It consists of three equal-height horizontal stripes: a red stripe at the top, a white stripe in the middle, and a blue stripe at the bottom. (See the CD and the website for this text for a colored image of this flag and other colored screen snaps.) We will design a class to draw a picture of this flag.

Since our class is to be an application that draws a simple picture, we will define it by extending the `CloseableFrame` class as described previously. This will allow us to use `CloseableFrame`'s `setSize()` method to fix the flag's dimensions, the `setTitle()` method to set the name that appears on its title bar, and the `setBackground()` method with the argument `Color.white` to draw a white background, on top of which we will draw the red and blue stripes.

Figure 6.19 presents a class `DutchFlag1` that draws this flag.

FIGURE 6.19.   THE DUTCH FLAG

```java
/** DutchFlag1.java is a GUI application that draws a Dutch flag.
 *  Output: A graphic representing the flag of the Netherlands.
 */

import ann.gui.CloseableFrame;
import javax.swing.*'         // JPanel;
import java.awt.*;            // Graphics, Color, ...

public class DutchFlag1 extends CloseableFrame
{
 private static final int FLAG_WIDTH  = 350;
 private static final int FLAG_HEIGHT = 200;
 private static final int TITLE_ROWS = 30;

 public DutchFlag1()
 {
   JPanel flagPanel = new FlagOfHolland(FLAG_WIDTH, FLAG_HEIGHT);
   setContentPane(flagPanel);
 }

 public static void main(String [] args)
 {
   DutchFlag1 myPicture = new DutchFlag1();
   myPicture.setSize(FLAG_WIDTH, FLAG_HEIGHT + TITLE_ROWS);
   myPicture.setVisible(true);
 }
}

class FlagOfHolland extends JPanel
{
 public FlagOfHolland(int width, int height)
 {
   setSize(width, height);
   myHeight = height;
   myWidth = width;

   // draw white field as background
   setBackground(Color.white);

 }

 public void paintComponent(Graphics pen)
 {
   super.paintComponent(pen);

   myHeight = getHeight();
   myWidth = getWidth();

   int stripeHeight = myHeight / 3;

   // draw red stripe
   pen.setColor(Color.red);
   pen.fillRect(0, 0, myWidth, stripeHeight);

   // draw blue stripe
   pen.setColor(Color.blue);
   pen.fillRect(0, 2 * stripeHeight, myWidth, myHeight );
 }

 int myHeight, myWidth;
}
```

When this program is compiled and executed, it produces a frame containing a title bar and the Dutch flag below it:

The main method first invokes the class constructor,

```
DutchFlag1 myPicture = new DutchFlag1();
```

which creates a JPanel, whose size equals the size of the flag, and positions it on the content pane of the frame. It then sets the size of the resulting frame myPicture so that it is large enough to contain the title bar and this JPanel:

```
myPicture.setSize(FLAG_WIDTH, FLAG_HEIGHT + TITLE_ROWS);
```

Making this frame visible then produces the window shown above.

The paintComponent() method creates the red and blue stripes by simply drawing two rectangles. To control the drawing color, it sends a message to its parameter pen along with a Color argument to invoke pen's setColor() method and select this color. Each colored rectangle can then be drawn by sending pen a message to invoke its fillRect() method with arguments that determine the upper-left corner and the lower-right corner of the rectangle. The red rectangle has opposite corners at (0, 0) and (myWidth, stripeHeight), where myWidth is the flag's width and stripeHeight is one-third of myHeight, the flag's height. The upper-left corner of the blue stripe is at (0, 2 * stripeHeight), since we must move down by 2 stripes, and it's lower-right corner is at (0, myHeight).

A Dutch Flag Applet

Because many Swing components can be used in both applets and applications, writing an applet that draws the Dutch flag is an easy modification of the preceding GUI application. As Figure 6.20 shows, we need only have this class extend JApplet instead of CloseableFrame and change the main method to a non-static init() method.

FIGURE 6.20.   THE DUTCH FLAG APPLET

```java
/* DutchFlag2.java is an applet that draws a Dutch flag
 *  Output: A graphic representing the flag of the Netherlands.
 */

import javax.swing.*;        // JApplet, JPanel
import java.awt.*;           // Graphics, Color, ...
public class DutchFlag2 extends JApplet
{
 private static final int FLAG_WIDTH  = 350;
 private static final int FLAG_HEIGHT = 200;
 private static final int TITLE_ROWS = 30;

 public DutchFlag2()
 {
   JPanel flagPanel = new FlagOfHolland(FLAG_WIDTH, FLAG_HEIGHT);
   setContentPane(flagPanel);
 }

 public void init()
 {
   DutchFlag2 myPicture = new DutchFlag2();
   myPicture.setSize(FLAG_WIDTH, FLAG_HEIGHT + TITLE_ROWS);
   myPicture.setVisible(true);
 }
}

class FlagOfHolland extends JPanel
{
 public FlagOfHolland(int width, int height)
 {
   setSize(width, height);
   myHeight = height;
   myWidth = width;

   // draw white field as background
   setBackground(Color.white);

 }

 public void paintComponent(Graphics pen)
 {
   super.paintComponent(pen);

   myHeight = getHeight();
   myWidth = getWidth();

   int stripeHeight = myHeight / 3;

   // draw red stripe
   pen.setColor(Color.red);
   pen.fillRect(0, 0, myWidth, stripeHeight);

   // draw blue stripe
   pen.setColor(Color.blue);
   pen.fillRect(0, stripeHeight * 2, myWidth, myHeight );
 }

 int myHeight, myWidth;
}
```

The output produced by this applet is

PART OF THE PICTURE: ARTIFICIAL INTELLIGENCE

by Keith Vander Linden

Just over an hour into the 6th game of their chess match, Garry Kasparov, the reigning world champion, conceded defeat to Deep Blue, a chess-playing computer developed by IBM corporation. Kasparov lost the match, held in May of 1997, 3.5 games to 2.5 games. It marked the first time a computer program had defeated a world chess champion in anything approaching tournament conditions.

Although this result came as a surprise to many, it has been clear for some time that a computer would eventually beat a world champion player. Since their introduction to tournament play in the late 1960's, chess programs have made steady progress, defeating a chess master in 1983, a grandmaster in 1988, and now the world champion. This is by no means the end of the story, however. There are reservations concerning the validity of this most recent match: it was not really a tournament setting with multiple players, Kasparov was not allowed to study Deep Blue's previous matches, and he was under considerable pressure to hold off a perceived "attack on humanity" by computer programs. Nevertheless, another milestone has been passed.

The construction of game-playing programs such as Deep Blue is part of a subfield of Computer Science known as **Artificial Intelligence** or **AI.** Roughly speaking, AI is an attempt to program computers to perform intelligent tasks. Giving a precise definition of AI is difficult, however, and most AI textbooks spend a laborious opening chapter attempting to characterize the field. This difficulty comes about for two reasons: (1) because intelligent behavior is complex and hard to define; and (2) because the styles of programming used to implement this behavior are diverse.

INTELLIGENCE

We all have a general notion of what intelligence is. We presume to know who has it and who doesn't. Garry Kasparov, for example, is intelligent by any measure. He is the world champion of chess, a game long seen as a pinnacle of human intellectual achievement. But what about Deep Blue? Is it intelligent? It beat Garry Kasparov in a chess match, this must mean something.[4]

Clearly, Deep Blue has performed an intelligent feat. It has done so, however, in a very narrow domain. This is one thing that distinguishes its accomplishment from general human intelligence. Intelligent behavior, the "I" in AI, is diverse. Humans display profoundly complex behavior in many areas, all of which have been topics of study in AI, including:

- ❑ *Reasoning and problem solving*—Humans are able to reason about their world and to plan their own actions accordingly. This encompasses a variety of activities, including game playing, mathematical theorem proving, and the planning of actions. Examples of systems which perform these tasks include Deep Blue, the game-playing system just discussed; EQP, a system which, in 1996, proved a theorem that no human has successfully proven; and SPIKE, a system which plans observation schedules for the Hubble space telescope.

- ❑ *Memory*—Humans are able to remember things about their world. In AI, the study of this area is called **knowledge representation.** It serves as the foundation of all reasoning and problem solving. Deep Blue, for example, represents considerable knowledge about chess but, it must be said, little or nothing about anything else.

- ❑ *Motion and manipulation*—Humans are able to perform actions in their world. The area of AI which deals with this is called **robotics.** This area, much popularized in science fiction, includes the development of robotic arms for assembly lines, or of fully mobile agents such as Robosoft's Auto VacC, an autonomous vacuum cleaner.

- ❑ *Perception*—Humans are able to see and to hear. The areas of AI concerned with these behaviors are called **computer vision** and **speech recognition.** They have been successful in fielding systems, which convert written characters into ASCII characters, called optical character recognition systems and systems which convert spoken words into ASCII words, called speech-to-text dictation systems.

- ❑ *Language processing*—Humans are able to process natural, human languages. In AI, the behaviors studied include the ability to understand language **(natural language understanding),** the ability to produce language **(natural language generation),** and the ability to translate from one language to another **(machine translation).** Examples of this include Météo, a system which generates weather reports in English

---

[4] This is what makes the defeat such a shock for some. Kasparov is well-known as having been a child prodigy, the youngest world chess champion in history (gaining the title at age 22), highly articulate, multilingual, the author of several books, active in politics; in short, the clever sort of individual that should be able to defeat a computer if ever anyone could. He is the best player in the world, and by some accounts the best in history. It would thus be a pity if he were remembered only for being the first to be outsmarted by a computer.

and French, and Systran, a machine translation system used by the European Commission.

❑ *Learning*—Humans are also able to learn from past experiences. In AI, the study of this phenomenon is called **machine learning.** One practical application of this involves **data mining.** Data mining tools attempt to find consistent patterns in large amounts of data. One such tool, ISL's Clementine, has been trained to predict the audience-share for prospective new television shows on the BBC.

Deep Blue can play chess well, but doesn't exhibit any of the other behaviors just given. It can't even move its own chess pieces. At first glance, however, many of these other areas don't appear to be all that difficult, particularly when compared with chess. My four-year old son, for example, can't play chess very well yet, but he does exhibit all the other behaviors with relative ease. He remembers things, he perceives and manipulates things, he processes language, and he learns. These have all come naturally to him. Surely with a little extra work, Deep Blue could do them as well. This is a critical misconception. Just because a task is easy for people doesn't necessarily means that it is *simple.* In fact, some of the things humans find extremely easy to perform have turned out to be among the hardest to program. For example, in the area of natural language processing, we have not succeeded in producing a system capable of engaging in meaningful conversation except in narrowly defined contexts. Conversely, some of the greatest successes in AI have been in areas seen as requiring great skill such as chess playing, calculus, and medical diagnosis.

This paradox of sorts is part of the reason that early researchers in AI grossly underestimated the difficulties in AI programming. Indeed, the field of AI has been greatly damaged by overly-ambitious expectations. In the mid-to-late 50's, for example, many people felt that machine translation programs were just around the corner. In retrospect, this was an extraordinary claim given that at the time we barely knew how to translate FORTRAN into assembly language.

PROGRAMMING TECHNIQUES

Another point that distinguishes Deep Blue's accomplishment from general human intelligence is the mechanism by which it operates, the "A" in its AI. As there is a wide range of intelligent behavior, there is also a wide range of programming techniques used to implement them "artificially." These techniques include:

❑ *Heuristic search*—AI programs are frequently designed to consider a number of choices. This is called **search** because the program is said to search through a space of possible choices and their consequences. For example, before making a choice, Deep Blue considers many moves and what their consequences might be many steps into the future. It uses a 256-processor architecture to do this, considering on the order of 200 million board positions per second. Search alone is seldom sufficient, however. The nature of chess, for example, dictates that Deep Blue be selective in what moves it considers, and how far down the road it considers them. There are simply too many alternatives to consider them all. It, therefore, tends to ignore the less promising ones, and to focus on a few options. These options are chosen based on **heuristics,** or rules of thumb, such as "first, consider moves that gain control of the center of the board."

❑ *Logic programming*—This approach involves representing knowledge in a well-defined format and performing logical inferences on it. For example, EQP, the theorem-proving program mentioned earlier, uses such an approach to prove theorems. It takes a set of given knowledge, and attempts to derive the theorem logically from this knowledge. The programming language **Prolog** has been specifically designed to support logic programming.

❑ *Expert systems*—Expert systems encode knowledge elicited from an expert in some domain. Many of these systems have become commercial successes, including XCON (a system which configures computer components for DEC equipment), and SBDS (a system which diagnoses electrical problems in Ford automobile engines).

❑ *Neural networks*—The techniques given so far are programmed on computers that are built with digital circuitry. The human brain, on the other hand, is very different. It is constructed of very simple brain cells, called *neurons,* which are highly interconnected with one another. Computer models of this structure are called **neural networks** or **connectionist systems.** They display radically different characteristics from traditional techniques.

These techniques are not mutually exclusive, and may be used individually or in combinations to implement the intelligent behaviors discussed.

EXAMPLE: THE JACKDICE GAME

Early researchers in AI frequently used games such as chess as a vehicle for their research. Games tend to be limited in scope and to have well-defined rules. Chess, for example, has a 12×12 board with a finite set of pieces, where each piece has a well-defined set of possible moves. This allowed the researchers to avoid the problems involved in modeling the other areas of intelligent behavior. We, too, will take advantage of this and implement a program that plays **JackDice,** a simple dice game for two players.

JackDice is derived from Not-One, a dice game used in previous versions of this text, and from BlackJack, a common card game. In JackDice, each player takes a turn in which they roll two dice and remember the sum of the values. They may roll again as many times as they would like, summing up the values of each roll. The only stipulation is that the total sum of all their moves may not exceed 21. The player with the highest score after a set number of turns wins.[5]

We'll start by implementing a `play()` function for a `JackDice` game class (part of which is shown in Figure 6.21). This method runs a match with `gamesPerMatch` games, each with `turnsPerGame` rounds. It prints out the scores at the end of each turn, game, and match.[6]

---

[5] The strategy in this game, of course, comes in determining when to roll again, and when to "stay" with what you've got. Obviously, if you roll two sixes on the first try, you would stop immediately with a score of 12. If you roll a 7, however, the decision is less clear. There are, after all, six ways to roll a seven (i.e., a 6 and a 1, a 5 and a 2, a 4 and a 3, in either order) and the chance of re-rolling one of them is 1/6th (i.e., the 6 ways to roll a 7 out of the 36 possible rolls).

[6] This code was written by Wesley Morgan based on a C++ version of not-one, a similar game, built by Joel Adams, Christopher Hirt, Matthew Post, and Keith Vander Linden. A class-tournament version of this code with a Swing-based interface also exists.

FIGURE 6.21   A PORTION OF THE DRIVER FOR JackDice

```
//...
while ( ( player1GameScore < gamesPerMatch/2+1 ) &&
        ( player2GameScore < gamesPerMatch/2+1 ) )
{
    gameCounter++;
    player1Score = player2Score = 0;

    // Let the players initialize themselves for each game.
    player1.initialize();
    player2.initialize();

    for (int turn = 1; turn <= turnsPerGame; turn++)
    {
        theScreen.println( "\n------------------------\n"
                    + player1.name() + ", turn " + turn );
        player1RollTotal = player1.takeTurn( player2RollTotal, 1 );
        player1Score += player1RollTotal;

        theScreen.println( "\n------------------------\n"
                    + player2.Name() + ", turn " + turn );
        player2RollTotal = player2.takeTurn( player1RollTotal, 2 );
        player2Score += player2RollTotal;

        theScreen.println( "\n***********************\n"
                    + " Turn " + turn + " - "
                    + player1.name() + ": " + player1Score + "; "
                    + player2.name() + ": " + player2Score + '\n'
                    + "\n***********************\n" );
    }
}
```

The play() method makes use of two classes, Player1 and Player2, each
of which extends a parent Player class. The Player class implements the take-
Turn() method (shown in Figure 6.22), while the Player1 and Player2 classes implement the methods initialize() and name().[7]

---

[7] Method takeTurn() is declared final so that no class that extends Player can override it. The
method randomInt() is the following private method in Player that uses Java's Random class to generate random integers in the range min to max:

```
private int randomInt( int min, int max )
{
    Random randomNum = new Random();
    double randomDouble = randomNum.nextDouble();
    randomDouble *= max;
    randomDouble = min + ( randomDouble % ( max - min + 1 ) );
    return (int)randomDouble;
}
```

FIGURE 6.22   A TURN-TAKING METHOD FOR `JackDice`

```
public final int takeTurn( int opponentsLastRoll, int whichTurn )
{
   int myCurrentRoll = randomInt( 1, 6 ) + randomInt( 1, 6 );   // first roll

   int scoreSoFar = myCurrentRoll;
   theScreen.print( "rolls: " + myCurrentRoll + " " );
   updateData(opponentsLastRoll, myCurrentRoll);

   for (;;)    // keep rolling until the player tells us to stop
   {
      if ( stop() )
      {
         theScreen.println( "STOP" );
         break;
      }

      // if we made it here, the player must want to roll again
      myCurrentRoll = randomInt( 1, 6 ) + randomInt( 1, 6 );
      updateData( opponentsLastRoll, myCurrentRoll );
      theScreen.print( myCurrentRoll + " " );

      // if score goes above MAX_SCORE, all points are lost and the turn ends
      if ( ( scoreSoFar + myCurrentRoll ) > MAX_SCORE )
      {
         scoreSoFar = 0;
         theScreen.println( "FAIL" );
         break;
      }
      else scoreSoFar += myCurrentRoll;
   }

   theScreen.println( " score: " + scoreSoFar + '\n' );
   raiseScore(scoreSoFar);
   return scoreSoFar;
}
```

The `takeTurn()` method uses a random number generator to simulate rolling two dice and implements the player's turn with a loop that continues until either the player decides to stop, as determined by the `stop()` method, or the player goes over 21. The appropriate score is then returned.

There are many strategies that may be implemented for this game. Recall that Deep Blue used heuristic search in its strategy. That was appropriate in chess, but is not as useful here because `JackDice`'s decisions are, for the most part, made independently of what the other player is likely to do in the future. We will, therefore, use a scaled-down expert system approach in which we encode knowledge from expert players. The simplest strategy is to encode the somewhat dubious "knowledge" that a player should always accept his or her first roll. This strategy has the virtue of simplicity and also the advantage that it never gets a 0 for a turn because it never risks going over 21. It is implemented with the following `stop()` method:

```
boolean stop()
{
   return true;
}
```

Another simple strategy is to randomly determine whether to go on or not. This is implemented in the following `stop()` method:

```
boolean stop()
{
    int choice = randomInt(0, 1); // declare a random
coin
    if (choice == 1)
        return true;

    else
        return false;
}
```

A partial output for a game between these two strategies is shown in Figure 6.23. This output shows a 1 game match, with 3 turns per game, between Tux and Bill. Note that Bill's strategy got a bit greedy on the second turn and ended up going over 21 which lead to his ultimate defeat.

FIGURE 6.23   SAMPLE OUTPUT OF A JACKDICE GAME

```
Let's play some JackDice!
- - - - - - - - - - - - - - - - - - - - - -
Tux, turn 1
rolls: 4 12 STOP
  score: 16
- - - - - - - - - - - - - - - - - - - - - -
Bill, turn 1
rolls: 4 12 2 STOP
  score: 18
* * * * * * * * * * * * * * * * * * * * * * *
  Turn 1 - Tux: 16; Bill: 18
* * * * * * * * * * * * * * * * * * * * * * *

- - - - - - - - - - - - - - - - - - - - - -
Tux, turn 2
rolls: 4 2 8 STOP
  score: 14
- - - - - - - - - - - - - - - - - - - - - -
Bill, turn 2
rolls: 4 8 12 FAIL
  score: 0
* * * * * * * * * * * * * * * * * * * * * * *
  Turn 2 - Tux: 30; Bill: 18
* * * * * * * * * * * * * * * * * * * * * * *

- - - - - - - - - - - - - - - - - - - - - -
Tux, turn 3
rolls: 4 10 STOP
  score: 14
- - - - - - - - - - - - - - - - - - - - - -
Bill, turn 3
rolls: 4 9 5 STOP
  score: 18

* * * * * * * * * * * * * * * * * * * * * * *
  Turn 3 - Tux: 44; Bill: 36
* * * * * * * * * * * * * * * * * * * * * * *

Tux wins game 1!
Tux wins the match!
```

There are clearly more effective strategies for this game, that would most likely include additional expert knowledge about how to act in certain specific situations. An expert player, for example, might likely take more risks if they are far behind near the end of a game, or they might become more conservative if they have a "comfortable" lead. Other approaches might involve a statistical analysis of "optimal" choices. Implementing this additional knowledge is left as an exercise.

✍ EXERCISES

1. Using the `JackDice` skeleton given in this section, program the `JackDice` game with better heuristic functions for player 1 and player 2. Try pitting your strategy against those of your fellow colleagues.

2. Write a strategy that allows the user to play manually against other strategies.

3. Discuss the question of whether Deep Blue (or JackDice for that matter) is "intelligent" or not.

Further Reading

If you are interested in reading further on Artificial Intelligence, consider going to the following sources:

❑ Russell and Norvig's text *Artificial Intelligence, A Modern Approach,* Prentice Hall, 1995—This is a good, comprehensive introduction to the field, which discusses not only the computer science in AI, but also the influence of other disciplines such as philosophy, psychology, and linguistics. They also discuss many of the concepts and example systems mentioned in this section.

❑ Some of the early papers in AI are still as incisive today as they were when they first came out—Turing wrote a landmark paper on the nature of AI, "Computing Machinery and Intelligence," *Mind,* 59:433–460, 1950. Searle wrote an oft-cited critique of Turing's vision, "Minds, Brains and Programs," *Behavioral and Brain Sciences,* 3:417–424, 1980.

❑ There are also extensive materials available on the internet—Carnegie Mellon's AI repository at http://www.cs.cmu.edu/Groups/AI/html/repository.html has an extensive collection of documents and systems. The Kasparov vs. Deep Blue chess match is discussed at length at IBM's site, http://www.chess.ibm.com.

CHAPTER SUMMARY

KEY TERMS AND NOTES

Abstract Windowing Toolkit (AWT)	instance constant
accessor method	instance method
alias problem	instance variable
attribute	internal perspective
attribute variable	mutator method
behavior	`null`
class	object autonomy
class invariant	overloading
constructor	`paintComponent()`
convertor method	painting
data members	postcondition
deep copy	private
default-value constructor	public
encapsulation	reference
`err`	shallow copy
explicit-value constructor	signature
external perspective	state
field	static constant
`flush()`	static interface
`Graphics`	static variable
handle	`System` class
I-can-do-it-myself principle	utility method
information hiding	validation

◎ Designing a class consists of identifying its:
  ❑ *behavior:* the operations that can be applied to a class object
  ❑ *attributes:* the data that must be stored to characterize a class object

◎ Design a class's behavior (operations) independently of implementation details of its attributes.

◎ Objects should carry within themselves the ability to perform their operations.

◎ Use an *external* perspective when you are *using* a class; use an *internal* perspective when you are *building* a class.

◎ A class's behaviors should be identified before its attributes because:
  ❑ It is often not obvious what the attributes should be.
  ❑ Knowing the class behavior can help with identifying the attributes.
  ❑ Behaviors should be independent of any particular details of how the attributes are implemented.

◎ To identify a class's attributes, go through the list of operations and identify what information each requires. Information that is needed by several different operations is probably an attribute.

◎ For attributes that change over time or that differ from one object to another, define variables to store their values. Attributes that are the same for all objects and do not change can be represented as constants. Attributes determine the *state* of an object at a particular time.

◎ It is good programming practice to hide all attribute variables of a class by making them private.

◎ Objects share *static* (or *class*) constants and variables. Objects have their own copies of *non-static* constants and variables.

◎ Class operations are usually implemented using *instance* methods, of which five common categories are: constructors, accessors, mutators, convertors, and utilities.

◎ When implementing class operations with methods, it is a good practice to define methods that support output early.

◎ If a class has a `toString()` method, the existing `print()` and `println()` methods can then be used to display objects of that class, because they send the `toString()` message to any object they are asked to display.

◎ The compiler calls a constructor whenever a class object is defined using the `new` operator. For this reason, when building a class, always provide one or more constructors to initialize the attribute variables of the class. Otherwise, the compiler will generate a constructor to initialize them with default values.

◎ A *default constructor* is invoked when a declaration of an object provides no initial values for the attribute variables.

◎ An *explicit-value constructor* has parameters that are used to initialize some or all of an object's attribute variables.

◎ *Static* (or *class*) *methods* and *instance* (or *object*) *methods* have the following differences:

  ❑ Static methods are declared using the keyword `static`; instance methods are not.

  ❑ Instance methods may access both static and non-static variables, constants, and methods.

  ❑ Static methods may access only static variables, static constants, and static methods.

  ❑ Objects share the same copy of static variables, constants, and methods, but they have their own distinct copies of non-static variables, constants, and methods.

◎ A method that must access attribute variables must be defined as an instance method. Otherwise, it should be defined as a static method, and the information it needs should be passed to it via parameters or declared using static variables and constants.

◎ Since constants represent values that do not change, they should be declared as static constants.

◎ Explicit-value constructors are useful to construct objects that must be returned by a method.

◎ *Accessor* methods can be used to retrieve, but not modify, the value of an object's attribute variables.

◎ *Mutator* methods can change the values of an object's attribute variables. They should ensure that the modified object still satisfies the class invariant.

◎ The keyword `null` should be used to initialize reference-type variables that will immediately be assigned new values.

◎ Factoring out code that is common to several operations and encapsulating it in a separate method can result in methods that are simpler and, therefore, easier to write and understand.

◎ The *alias problem* arises when a copy operation does not produce a completely distinct copy because the address in a reference-type variable is copied rather than the object it refers to.

◎ A common arrangement of items in a class is as follows:

—Class constants first, so they can be quickly found
—The methods next, so it is easy to find the class' operations; they make up the class' interface
—Attribute variables last, so the user need not see them

◎ Painting a Swing component must always be done with a method named `paintCompo-nent()`.

Documentation

REFERENCE ■ `CloseableFrame` is a class we provide in the `ann.gui` package to make it a bit easier to do graphical programming. It extends Java's Swing class `JFrame`, which in turn extends `Frame` from `java.awt`, whose ancestor classes are `Window`, `Container`, `Component` (all from `java.awt`), and `Object`. Thus, in addition to the following methods, `CloseableFrame` also inherits methods from these classes.

SOME `CloseableFrame` METHODS (EXTENDS `javax.swing.JFrame`)

Method	Description
`void setTitle(String str)`	Set the frame's title to `str`
`Color getBackground()`	Return the frame's background `Color`
`Color getForeground()`	Return the frame's foreground `Color`
`int getWidth()`	Get the width of the frame
`int getHeight()`	Get the height of the frame
`Dimension getSize()`	Get the frame's size as a `Dimension` object
`boolean isVisible()`	Return `true` if the frame is visible and false otherwise
`void setBackground(Color c)`	Set the frame's background color to `c`
`void setForeground(Color c)`	Set the frame's foreground color to `c`
`void setSize(int width, int height)`	Resize the frame to the specified width and height
`void setSize(Dimension d)`	Set the frame's size as specified by `Dimension d`
`void setVisible(boolean b)`	Make the frame visible or invisible based on `b`

★ SOME Graphics CLASS METHODS (java.awt)

Method	Description

void drawArc(int *x*, int *y*,
          int *width*, int *height*,
          int *startAngle*, int *arcAngle*)
	Draw an arc that covers the specified rectangle

void drawLine(int *x1*, int *y1*, int *x2*, int *y2*)	Draw a line from ($x1,y1$) to ($x2,y2$)
void drawOval(int *x*, int *y*, int *width*, int *height*)	Draw an oval covering the specified rectangle
void drawRect(int *x*, int *y*, int *width*, int *height*)	Draw a rectangle of the given dimensions, whose upper left corner is at (x,y)
void drawString(String *str*, int *x*, int *y*)	Draw String *str* at position (x,y)

void fillArc(int *x*, int *y*,
          int *width*, int *height*,
          int *startAngle*, int *arcAngle*)
	Draw a filled arc that covers the specified rectangle

void fillOval(int *x*, int *y*, int *width*, int *height*)	Draw a filled oval covering the specified rectangle
void fillRect(int *x*, int *y*, int *width*, int *height*)	Draw a filled rectangle of the given dimensions, whose upper left corner is at (x,y)
void translate(int *x*, int *y*)	Shift the origin to position (x,y)

PROGRAMMING POINTERS

PROGRAM STYLE AND DESIGN

1. *When an object in a problem cannot be represented directly using predefined types, define a class to represent such objects.* The class is the central mechanism for defining new types in Java.

2. *Use classes to define new types whose values have attributes of various types.* One of the purposes of the class is to permit different data types to be encapsulated in a single object. For example, to model an address, we might declare:

```
class Address
{
  // . . . Public interface omitted . . .
 private int    myHouseNumber;
 private String myStreet,
                myCity,
                myState;
 private long   myZipCode;
}
```

3. *Use indentation to reflect the structure of your class, since this increases its readability.*

4. *Use descriptive identifiers for the attribute variable so they are self-documenting and describe the attributes being stored. Name choices should also reinforce the I-can-do-it-myself principle.* For example, begin each name of a data member with the prefix my.

5. *Place the methods before the attribute variables in a class declaration. They carry out operations, which make up the class's interface, and should be easy to find.* Users of your class should be able to find the class interface without wading through all of its private details.

6. *Designing a good interface requires much time and thought, and should not be hurried.* A class interface should be *stable* so that programs that use the class do not require modification when the class is changed.

7. *Keep all attribute variables of a class private and provide accessor functions to retrieve the values of those members.* One purpose of a class is to hide implementation details from programs that use an object. Providing a carefully designed interface and preventing programs from accessing the attribute variables except through this interface simplifies program maintenance.

8. *Most constants should be declared as static constants, so that all objects share a single definition.*

9. *Check the class invariant in every mutator method.*

10. *Use the keyword* null *to initialize a reference-type variable that will be immediately overwritten.*

11. *Factor out code that is common to several operations and encapsulate it in a separate method.* This can result in methods that are simpler and, therefore, easier to write and understand.

12. *Uses Java's Swing components where possible in graphics programming.* They have far greater capabilities than their AWT counterparts and greatly enhance a progammer's ability to build GUIs.

WATCH

!

OUT

POTENTIAL PITFALLS

1. *Members of a class that are declared following the keyword* private *are not accessible outside of the class.*

2. *The name of the constructor is the same as the name of the class, and the constructor has no return type.*

3. *Whereas an instance method may access both static and non-static variables, constants, and methods, a static method may access only static variables, constants, and methods.*

4. *Assigning the value of one reference-type variable to another variable of the sametype does not make a copy of the object referred to by the first variable.* For example, consider the declarations

```
Temperature temp1 = new Temperature(0, 'C');
Temperature temp2 = null;
```

The assignment statement

```
temp2 = temp1;
```

will simply copy the address of the `Temperature` object referred to by `temp1` into `temp2` with the result that both of the handles `temp1` and `temp2` refer to the same object.

Changing the value of the object via one of the reference-type variables also affects the other variable. To avoid this, one should write a method that can be used to produce a distinct copy of the object; for example,

```
t2 = t1.copy();
```

5. *Do not add components to or paint directly on Swing containers. Components are added to the container's content pane, and all painting is done with a* `paintComponent()` *method.*

PROGRAMMING PROBLEMS

SECTION 6.4

1. Write a driver program to test the date class of Exercise 10.
2. Write a driver program to test the time class of Exercise 11.
3. Write a driver program to test the phone-number class of Exercise 12.
4. Write a driver program to test the playing-cards class of Exercise 13.
5. Write a driver program to test the Cartesian-coordinate class of Exercise 14.
6. Write a driver program to test the polar-coordinate class of Exercise 15.
7. Write a driver program to test the personal-information class of Exercise 16.
8. Write a driver program to test the baseball-player class of Exercise 17.
9. Write a driver program to test the weather-statistics class of Exercise 18.
10. The *point-slope equation* of a line having slope m and passing through point P with co-ordinates (x_1, y_1) is

$$y - y_1 = m(x - x_1)$$

   (a) Write a `LineSegment` class, described by two `CartesianPoint` endpoints, where `CartesianPoint` is the class in Exercise 14. In addition to the usual operations, this class should provide operations to compute:

   (i) The midpoint of the line segment joining two points

   (ii) The equation of the perpendicular bisector of this line segment

   (b) Write a class for a `Line`, described by its slope and a point on the line, with operations that

   (i) Find the point-slope equation of the line

   (ii) Find the slope-intercept equation of the line

   (c) Write a program to read the point and slope information for two lines and to determine whether they intersect or are parallel. If they intersect, find the point of intersection and also determine whether they are perpendicular.

11. Write a program that accepts a time of day in military format and finds the corresponding standard representation in hours, minutes, and A.M./P.M., or accepts the time in the usual format and finds the corresponding military representation. For example, the input 0100 should produce 1:00 A.M. as output, and the input 3:45 P.M. should give 1545. Use a class to store the time, and provide extraction or conversion functions to display the time in either format. (See Programming Problem 2.)

12. A *complex number* has the form $a + bi$, where a and b are real numbers and $i^2 = -1$. The four basic arithmetic operations for complex numbers are defined as follows:

$$\text{addition:} \quad (a + bi) + (c + di) = (a + c) + (b + d)i$$

$$\text{subtraction:} \quad (a + bi) - (c + di) = (a - c) + (b - d)i$$

$$\text{multiplication:} \quad (a + bi)*(c + di) = (ac - bd) + (ad + bc)i$$

$$\text{division:} \quad \frac{a + bi}{c + di} = \frac{ac + bd}{c^2 + d^2} + \frac{bc - ad}{c^2 + d^2}i$$

$$\text{provided } c^2 + d^2 \neq 0.$$

(a) Write a class to store complex numbers and provide operations for the four basic arithmetic operations along with input and output operations.

(b) Write a program to read two complex numbers and a symbol for one of these operations and to perform the indicated operation.

13. A *rational number* has the form a/b, where a and b are integers with $b \neq 0$. Some of the basic operations on rational numbers are given in the following table:

Input	Output	Comments
3/8 + 1/6	13/24	$a/b + c/d = (ad + bc)/bd$ reduced to lowest terms
3/8 − 1/6	5/24	$a/b - c/d = (ad - bc)/bd$ reduced to lowest terms
3/8 * 1/6	1/16	$a/b * c/d = ac/bd$ reduced to lowest terms
3/8 / 1/6	9/4	$a/b / c/d = ad/bc$ reduced to lowest terms
3/8 I	8/3	Invert a/b
8/3 M	2 + 2/3	Write a/b as a mixed fraction
6/8 R	3/4	Reduce a/b to lowest terms
6/8 G	2	Greatest common divisor of numerator and denominator
1/6 L 3/8	24	Lowest common denominator of a/b and c/d

1/6 < 3/8	true	$a/b < c/d$?
1/6 <= 3/8	true	$a/b \leq c/d$?
1/6 > 3/8	false	$a/b > c/d$?
1/6 >= 3/8	false	$a/b \geq c/d$?
3/8 = 9/24	true	$a/b = c/d$?
2/3 X + 2 = 4/5	X = −9/5	Solution of linear equation $(a/b)X + c/d = e/f$

(a) Write a class to store rational numbers and provide operations for (some of) the basic arithmetic operations along with input and output operations that read and display all rational numbers in the format a/b, or simply a if the denominator is 1.

(b) Write a program to read two rational numbers and a symbol for one of these operations and to perform the indicated operation.

SECTION 6.6

For Problems 14–18, design a GUI application to display the flag for the specified nation. (See the CD or the websites given in the preface for colored images of these flags.)

14. Mauritius (from top to bottom: red, blue, yellow, light green stripes)

15. Italy (left stripe green, middle, stripe white, right stripe red)

16. Denmark (white stripe against red background)

17. Norway (red field, with a centered white cross running across that field, and a blue cross centered atop the white cross)

18. Japan (red circle against white background)

19–23.   Proceed as in Problems 14–18, but write applets instead of applications.

SELECTION

When you get to the fork in the road, take it. *Yogi Berra*

We are all special cases. *Albert Camus*

"Would you tell me, please, which way I ought to go from here?"
"That depends a great deal on where you want to get to," said the Cat. *Lewis Carroll*

If you believe you can, you probably can. If you believe you won't, you most assuredly won't. Belief is the ignition switch that gets you off the launching pad. *Denis Waitley*

■ Chapter Contents

Chapter Objectives

- Expand on the introduction to selection in Chapter 4
- Examine the `if` statement in more detail
- Study the `switch` statement and how it can be used to implement certain multialternative selections
- Introduce conditional expressions
- Introduce event-driven programming and use it in developing graphical user interfaces
- (Optional) See how `boolean` expressions can be used to model logical circuits

- (Optional) Take a detailed look at the architecture of typical computer systems

In Chapters 4, we saw that methods play an important role in programming in Java. We also saw that the logical flow of execution through a method is governed by three basic control mechanisms: **sequence, selection,** and **repetition**. In this chapter, we take a closer look at the selection mechanism. We will expand on our earlier look at the `if` statement; introduce the `switch` statement and conditional expressions; and take a first look at event-driven programming. The special Part of the Picture sections describe the role of boolean expressions in logical circuit design and offer a close look at computer architecture.

7.1 INTRODUCTORY EXAMPLE: THE MASCOT PROBLEM

PROBLEM

The Big 10 Conference of the NCAA consists of the following universities, whose common names and mascots are as shown:

University	Common Name	Mascot
University of Illinois	Illinois	Fighting Illini
University of Indiana	Indiana	Hoosiers
University of Iowa	Iowa	Hawkeyes
University of Michigan	Michigan	Wolverines
Michigan State University	Michigan State	Spartans
University of Minnesota	Minnesota	Golden Gophers
Northwestern University	Northwestern	Wildcats
Ohio State University	Ohio State	Buckeyes
Pennsylvania State University	Penn State	Nittany Lions
Purdue University	Purdue	Boilermakers
University of Wisconsin	Wisconsin	Badgers

Our problem is to develop a method `mascot()` that, given the name of a Big 10 university, returns its mascot.[1]

---

[1] We have restricted our universities to the Big 10 conference to keep the problem manageable in size. Extending the problem to include additional universities is not difficult, and is left as an exercise.

OBJECT-CENTERED DESIGN

BEHAVIOR. Our method should receive from its caller the common name of a Big 10 university. It should return the university's mascot.

PROBLEM'S OBJECTS. Examining this problem, we identify two objects:

Description of problem's objects	Type	Kind	Movement	Name
A Big 10 university's common name	String	varying	received	*university*
Its mascot	String	varying	returned	none

The problem can be specified in terms of these objects as follows:

Receive: *university,* a String

Precondition: *university* is the common name of a Big 10 university

Return: the mascot of *university,* a String

Given this specification, we can build the stub shown below for our method. Since Java methods must be in a class, we will create a Big10 class that contains our method:

```
class Big10
{
   public static String mascot(String university)
   {
   }
}
```

OPERATIONS. From the problem description, we can identify 11 operations:

  i. Compare *university* to "Illinois"; if equal, return "Fighting Illini"

 ii. Compare *university* to "Indiana"; if equal, return "Hoosiers"

iii. Compare *university* to "Iowa"; if equal, return "Hawkeyes"

.
.
.

xi. Compare *university* to "Wisconsin"; if equal, return "Badgers"

Because the String class defines methods to check if two String values are equal, an if-else-if statement can be used to perform these operations.

ALGORITHM. These operations can be organized into the following algorithm.

Algorithm for Big 10 University Mascot Computation
  1. If *university* is "Illinois"
        return "Fighting Illini".

2. Otherwise, if *university* is "Indiana"
        return "Hoosiers".

3. Otherwise, if *university* is "Iowa"
        return "Hawkeyes".

4. Otherwise, if *university* is "Michigan"
        return "Wolverines".

5. Otherwise, if *university* is "Michigan State"
        return "Spartans".

6. Otherwise, if *university* is "Minnesota"
        return "Golden Gophers".

7. Otherwise, if *university* is "Northwestern"
        return "Wildcats".

8. Otherwise, if *university* is "Ohio State"
        return "Buckeyes".

9. Otherwise, if *university* is "Penn State"
        return "Nittany Lions".

10. Otherwise, if *university* is "Purdue"
        return "Boilermakers".

11. Otherwise, if *university* is "Wisconsin"
        return "Badgers".

12. Otherwise
     a. Display an error message.
     b. Return "unknown" as a default value.

CODING. Given this algorithm, completing our method is straightforward, as shown in Figure 7.1. For the convenience of the user, we will use the `equalsIgnoreCase()` method of the `String` class, which performs the equality comparison, ignoring case differences.

FIGURE 7.1   THE `mascot()` METHOD

```
/** mascot () is a static method in class Big10 that finds the mascot
       of a Big 10 university.
 *  Receive        university, a String
 *  Precondition: university is a Big 10 university
 *  Return         the (String) mascot of university
 */

public static String mascot(String university)
{
  if ( university.equalsIgnoreCase("Illinois") )
    return "Fighting Illini";
  else if ( university.equalsIgnoreCase("Indiana") )
    return "Hoosiers";
  else if ( university.equalsIgnoreCase("Iowa") )
    return "Hawkeyes";
  else if ( university.equalsIgnoreCase("Michigan") )
    return "Wolverines";
  else if ( university.equalsIgnoreCase("Michigan State") )
    return "Spartans";
```

```
else if ( university.equalsIgnoreCase("Minnesota")  )
  return "Golden Gophers";
else if ( university.equalsIgnoreCase("Northwestern") )
  return "Wildcats";
else if ( university.equalsIgnoreCase("Ohio State") )
  return "Buckeyes";
else if ( university.equalsIgnoreCase("Penn State") )
  return "Nittany Lions";
else if ( university.equalsIgnoreCase("Purdue") )
  return "Boilermakers";
else if ( university.equalsIgnoreCase("Wisconsin")  )
  return "Badgers";
else
{
  System.err.println("\n*** mascot(university): " + university
                      + " is not a Big-10 university!");

  return "";
}
```

TESTING. To test our method, we write a simple driver program like that in Figure 7.2. Note that it uses the `Keyboard` method `readLine()` to read the name of a university, because some names consist of more than one word (e.g., Michigan State, Penn State). If we used the `readWord()` method, only the first word of such names would be read, but `readLine()` reads an entire line of input (including blanks).

FIGURE 7.2   DRIVER FOR THE `mascot()` **METHOD**

```
/** Big10Mascots.java is a simple driver program to test the (static) mascot()
 *    method in class Big10.
 *  Input:  name of Big 10 schools
 *  Output: prompts, mascots of schools
 */

import ann.easyio.*;        // Keyboard, Screen

class Big10Mascots
{
 public static void main(String [] args)
 {
   String school = "";
   Keyboard theKeyboard = new Keyboard();
   Screen theScreen = new Screen();
   theScreen.println("To identify a Big-10 university's mascot:");
   for (;;)
   {
     theScreen.print("\nEnter the name of a Big-10 university (Q to quit): ");
     school = theKeyboard.readLine();

     if ( school.equalsIgnoreCase("Q") ) break;

     theScreen.println( Big10.mascot(school) );
   }
 }
}
```

Sample run:

```
To identify a Big-10 university's mascot:

Enter the name of a Big 10 school (Q to quit): Michigan
Wolverines

Enter the name of a Big 10 school (Q to quit): Ohio State
Buckeyes

Enter the name of a Big 10 school (Q to quit): Missouri
Mascot: Missouri is not known by this program!

Enter the name of a Big 10 school (Q to quit): Minnesota
Golden Gophers

Enter the name of a Big 10 school (Q to quit): q
```

The sample run indicates that the method is working correctly.

7.2   SELECTION: THE `if` STATEMENT REVISITED

In Chapter 4, we saw three different forms of the `if` statement:
The **single-branch** or **simple** `if` form:

```
if (boolean_expression)
    statement
```

The **dual-branch** or `if-else` form:

```
if (boolean_expression)
    statement₁
else
    statement₂
```

The **multi-branch** or **if-else-if** form:

```
if (boolean_expression₁)
    statement₁
else if (boolean_expression₂)
    statement₂



else if (boolean_expressionₙ)
    statementₙ
else
    statementₙ₊₁
```

The boolean expressions in these `if` statements are sometimes called **conditions.**
    While these may look like three distinct statements, Java really has only one `if`
statement with two different forms:

The `if` Statement (General Form)

Forms:

```
if (booleanExpression) statement₁

if (booleanExpression) statement₁ else statement₂
```

where:
`if` and `else` are keywords; and
`statement₁` and `statement₂` are Java statements (individual or block).

Purpose:

If `booleanExpression` is true, then `statement₁` is executed and `statement₂` (if present) is bypassed. If the `booleanExpression` is false, then `statement₁` is bypassed and `statement₂` (if present) is executed. In either case, execution continues with the next statement in the program.

Understanding the Multibranch `if`

While it may look like a different statement, the multibranch or `if-else-if` form is really an `if` statement of the second form

```
if (booleanExpression) statement₁ else statement₂
```

where `statement₂` is another `if` statement.

It is important to understand that this multibranch form is simply a series of nested `if` statements written as one. That is, if we were to write a 5-branch `if-else-if` and we were to start each new `if` statement on a new line with each `else` aligned with its corresponding `if`, our code would appear as follows:

```
if (booleanExpression₁)
    statement₁
else
    if (booleanExpression₂)
        statement₂
    else
        if (booleanExpression₃)
            statement₃
        else
            if (booleanExpression₄)
                statement₄
            else
                statement₅
```

However, the free-form nature of Java allows us to write each nested `if` on the same line as the preceding `else` and align the `else-if` combinations:

```
if (booleanExpression₁)
    statement₁
else if (booleanExpression₂)
    statement₂
else if (booleanExpression₃)
    statement₃
else if (booleanExpression₄)
    statement₄
else
    statement₅
```

This latter style reflects more clearly the multibranch nature and is therefore more readable. It is, however, important to understand that each `else` is really a continuation of the preceding `if`:

```
if (boolean_expression₁)
    statement₁
else if (boolean_expression₂)
    statement₂
else if (boolean_expression₃)
    statement₃
else if (boolean_expression₄)
    statement₄
else
    statement₅
```

WATCH

OUT

PITFALL: THE DANGLING-ELSE PROBLEM

We have just seen that the multibranch form of the `if` statement is actually an `if-else` form

```
if (booleanExpression) statement₁ else statement₂
```

in which *statement₂* is another `if` statement. However, suppose that *statement₁* is another `if` statement; for example,

```
if (x > 0)
    if (y > 0)
        z = Math.sqrt(x) + Math.sqrt(y);
```

When such nested `if` statements are followed by an `else`, it is not evident with which `if` the `else` corresponds. Does the `else` match the outer `if`:

```
if (x > 0)
    if (y > 0)
        z = Math.sqrt(x) + Math.sqrt(y);
else
    System.err.println("\nUnable to compute z!");
```

Or does it match the inner `if`?

```
if (x > 0)
    if (y > 0)
        z = Math.sqrt(x) + Math.sqrt(y);
    else
        System.err.println("\nUnable to compute z!");
```

This ambiguity is known as the **dangling else problem,** and Java resolves it by stipulating that

> In a nested `if` statement, an `else` is matched with the nearest preceding unmatched `if`.

Thus, for the preceding `if` statement, the second matching is used; that is, the `else` is associated with the inner `if` (whose condition is `y > 0`). Consequently, the output statement is executed only in the case that x is positive and y is nonpositive. If we wish to associate this `else` with the outer `if`, we can force the association by surrounding the inner `if` with curly braces, as follows:

```
if (x > 0)
{
    if (y > 0)
        z = Math.sqrt(x) + Math.sqrt(y);
}
else
    System.err.println("\nUnable to compute z!");
```

Putting the inner `if` inside a block makes it a complete statement, so that the `else` must associate with the outer `if`. Thus, the output statement is executed whenever x is nonpositive.

WATCH

OUT

PITFALL: USING RELATIONAL OPERATORS WITH REFERENCE TYPES

Another common mistake is to compare reference types using a relational operator (i.e., ==, !=, <, >, <=, >=). To illustrate, consider the following definitions:

```
String s1 = new String("Hi!"),
       s2 = new String("Hi!"),
       s3 = s2;
```

If we compare s1 and s2 using the equality operator,

```
if (s1 == s2) aScreen.println("equal!");
else          aScreen.println("not equal!");
```

then "`not equal!`" is displayed. But if we compare s2 and s3,

```
if (s2 == s3) aScreen.println("equal!");
else          aScreen.println("not equal!");
```

"equal!" is displayed. How can this be, when s1, s2, and s3 all seem to be equal
to the same value?

The answer lies in the concept of handles, which we discussed in Section 6.4; s1,
s2, and s3 are *handles* (i.e., reference type variables), and the value of each is an address of a String object, which we can visualize as follows:[2]

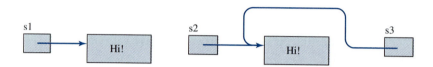

From this, it should be clear why s1 and s2 are not equal when compared with ==
but s2 and s3 are:

NOTE

   Relational operators compare the addresses in handles.

Because s1 and s2 refer to two distinct String objects and distinct String objects have distinct addresses, the expression

       s1 == s2

is false, regardless of the values of the String objects. By contrast, s2 and s3 refer
to the same String object, and since an object has only one address, the addresses
in s2 and s3 are the same, making the expression

       s2 == s3

true. Briefly, s2 and s3 are handles for the same String, so their addresses must be
the same.

To compare the *values* of objects instead of the *addresses* in their handles, reference types should usually be compared using one of the comparison methods provided
by their class. To illustrate, the statements

```
if (s1.equals(s2))
   aScreen.println("equal!");
else
   aScreen.println("not equal!");
```

will display "equal!", because the

   String *class methods* equals() *and* equalsIgnoreCase() *compare the*
   characters within String *objects, not the addresses in their handles.*

---

[2] The String literals "Hi!" are actually implemented in Java as references to the same String object.
Thus the two larger boxes really should contain arrows to a box containing "Hi!". We used this simpler
visualization, however, to keep from making the problem still more complex.

It follows that in designing a class for which it is necessary to compare objects, one should provide methods to perform the comparison operations (e.g., see the `equals()` method in the `Temperature` class in Section 6.4).

Using == to compare two handles is not a *syntax* error, and so the Java compiler will not produce an error message. However, comparing reference types with == is usually a *logic* error, and such errors can be fiendishly difficult to find, because == is the correct way to compare primitive types. *Any time an algorithm calls for a relational comparison, the types of the objects being compared should be carefully checked. A relational operator (e.g., ==) should be used to compare primitive types and a method provided by the class (e.g., `equals()`) should be used to compare reference types.*

NOTE

✍ EXERCISES 7.2

1. Describe the output produced by the following poorly-indented program segment:

    ```
    int number = 4;
    double alpha = -1.0;
    if (number > 0)
        if (alpha > 0)
            theScreen.println("first");
    else
        theScreen.println("second");
        theScreen.println("third");
    ```

    Exercises 2 and 3 refer to the following `if` statement, where `honors`, `awards`, and `good-Student` are of type `boolean`:

    ```
    if (honors)
        if (awards)
            goodStudent = true;
        else
            goodStudent = false;
    else if (!honors)
        goodStudent = false;
    ```

2. Write a simpler `if` statement that is equivalent to this one.

3. Write a single assignment statement that is equivalent to this `if` statement.

For Exercises 4–8, you are asked to write methods. To test these methods, you should write driver programs as instructed in Programming Problems 1–5 at the end of this chapter.

4. In a certain region, pesticide can be sprayed from an airplane only if the temperature is at least 70°, the relative humidity is between 15 and 35 percent, and the wind speed is at most 10 miles per hour. Write a method `okToSpray()` that receives three numbers representing temperature, relative humidity, and wind speed, and returns true if the conditions allow spraying and false otherwise.

5. A certain credit company will approve a loan application if the applicant's income is at least $25,000 or the applicant's assets are at least $100,000; in addition, the applicant's total liabilities must be less than $50,000. Write a method `creditApproved()` that receives three numbers representing income, assets, and liabilities, and returns true if the criteria for loan approval are satisfied and false otherwise.

6. Write a method that returns true if the value of an `int` parameter `year` is the number of a leap year and returns false otherwise. (A leap year is a multiple of 4; and if it is a multiple of 100, it must also be a multiple of 400.)

7. Write a method that returns the number of days in a given `int` parameter month (1, 2, . . . , 12) of a given parameter `year`. Use Exercise 6 to determine the number of days if the value of month is 2.

8. Proceed as in Exercise 7, but assume that `month` is a `String` parameter whose value is the name of `month`.

7.3   SELECTION: THE `switch` STATEMENT

An `if` statement can be used to implement a multialternative selection statement in which exactly one of several alternative actions is selected and performed. In the `if-else-if` form described in the preceding section, a selection is made by evaluating one or more boolean expressions. Because selection conditions can usually be formulated as boolean expressions, an `if-else-if` form can be used to implement virtually any multialternative selection.

In this section we describe another multialternative selection statement called the `switch` statement. Although it is not as widely applicable as the `if` statement, it is more efficient for implementing certain forms of selection. As usual, we begin with an example that illustrates the use of the statement.

PROBLEM: SELECTIVE TEMPERATURE CONVERSIONS

In Chapter 6, we built a `Temperature` class and used it to display a temperature's representation in the Fahrenheit, Celsius, and Kelvin scales. The key portion of this program was the output statement:

```
theScreen.println("-> " + temp.inFahrenheit()
            + " = " + temp.inCelsius()
            + " = " + temp.inKelvin() );
```

which sends `temp` three messages to get the different representations.

The only drawback to this approach is that it displays `temp`'s value in all three scales. The user already knows the value of `temp` in one of the scales—the value the user entered. Moreover, users may want to know only the equivalent temperature in one of the two remaining scales, not both.

Now that we know about selective execution, we can give users greater control by writing a program that allows them to choose which conversion they wish to have performed: convert to Fahrenheit, convert to Celsius, or convert to Kelvin.

 OBJECT-CENTERED DESIGN

PROBLEM. Write a program that allows users to select conversions to be applied to temperatures they enter.

BEHAVIOR. The program should display on the screen a menu of the possible conversion options and then read the desired conversion from the keyboard. Next, it should display on the screen a prompt for a temperature, which it should read from the keyboard. The program should then display the result of converting the input temperature, as determined by the specified conversion.

PROBLEM'S OBJECTS. From our behavioral description, we have the following objects:

Description of problem's objects	Type	Kind	Name
The program	??	—	—
The screen	Screen	varying	*theScreen*
A menu of options	String	constant	*MENU*
A prompt	String	constant	none
Conversion	char	varying	*menuChoice*
The keyboard	Keyboard	varying	*theKeyboard*
Temperature	Temperature	varying	*temp*
Result	Temperature	varying	none

We might visualize our menu as something like the following:

```
To convert a temperature between scales, enter:
A - to convert your temperature to Fahrenheit;
B - to convert your temperature to Celsius;
C - to convert your temperature to Kelvin; or
Q - to quit
->
```

We can thus specify the problem as follows:

Input: *temp,* a Temperature, and *menuChoice,* a char

Precondition: *menuChoice* is one of {A, a, B, b, C, c, Q, q}.

Output: *MENU,* prompts for input, and the result of converting the temperature

OPERATIONS. Our behavioral description leads to the following list of operations:

   i. Send *theScreen* messages to display *MENU* (String) and a prompt (String)
   ii. Send *temp* a message to read a Temperature value from *theKeyboard*
   iii. Send *theKeyboard* a message to read a char and store it in *menuChoice*
   iv. Send *temp* the conversion message corresponding to *menuChoice*

All of these are provided in our ann.easyio package and our Temperature class. For operation iv, we must compare *menuChoice* to each of the valid menu choices, and based upon that comparison, send *temp* the corresponding conversion message.

ALGORITHM. The following algorithm applies this strategy. For user convenience, we have added an input-loop to process several temperatures.

Algorithm to Convert Arbitrary Temperatures

Loop:

1. Tell *theScreen* to display *MENU*.
2. Tell *theKeyboard* to read a `char` into *menuChoice*.
3. If *menuChoice* is 'Q' or 'q', terminate repetition.
4. Tell *theScreen* to display a prompt for a temperature.
5. Tell *temp* to read a temperature value from *theKeyboard*.
6. If *menuChoice* is 'A' or 'a'

    a. Send *temp* a message to convert itself to Fahrenheit.

    b. Tell *theScreen* to display the resulting temperature.

    Otherwise, if *menuChoice* is 'B' or 'b'

    a. Send *temp* a message to convert itself to Celsius.

    b. Tell *theScreen* to display the resulting temperature.

    Otherwise, if *temp* is 'C' or 'c'

    a. Send *temp* a message to convert itself to Kelvin.

    b. Tell *theScreen* to display the resulting temperature.

    Otherwise

    Display an error message.

End loop

CODING AND TESTING. We could implement the algorithm using an `if-else-if` construct:

```
if (menuChoice == 'A' || menuChoice == 'a')
   theScreen.println( temp.inFahrenheit() );
else if (menuChoice == 'B' || menuChoice == 'b')
   theScreen.println( temp.inCelsius() );
else if (menuChoice == 'C' || menuChoice == 'c')
   theScreen.println( temp.inKelvin() );
else
   System.err.println("\nmain(): " + menuChoice + "
     is invalid\n");
```

The Java `switch` statement, however, provides a more convenient way to do this, as shown in the program in Figure 7.3.

FIGURE 7.3   ARBITRARY TEMPERATURE CONVERSIONS

```
/* TemperatureConverter.java converts temperatures between scales.
 * Input:    a character indicating a specific temperature conversion,
 *              and a temperature to be converted
 * Output: the converted temperature
 */

import Temperature;
import ann.easyio.*;                 // Keyboard, Screen
```

```
class TemperatureConverter
{
 public static void main(String [] args)
 {
   final String MENU = "\nTo convert a temperature between scales, enter:"
                   + "\n A - to convert your temperature to Fahrenheit;"
                   + "\n B - to convert your temperature to Celsius;"
                   + "\n C - to convert your temperature to Kelvin; and"
                   + "\n Q - to quit."
                   + "\n --> ";
   Screen theScreen = new Screen();
   Temperature temp = new Temperature();
   Keyboard theKeyboard = new Keyboard();
   char menuChoice;

   for (;;)
   {
     theScreen.print(MENU);
     menuChoice = theKeyboard.readChar();

     if (menuChoice == 'q' || menuChoice == 'Q') break;

     theScreen.print("Next, enter the temperature to be converted"
                   + "\n (e.g., 0 C): ");
     temp.read(theKeyboard);

     switch(menuChoice)
     {
       case 'A': case 'a':
         theScreen.println("\n" + temp + " in Fahrenheit is "
                           + temp.inFahrenheit());
         break;
       case 'B': case 'b':
         theScreen.println("\n" + temp + " in Celsius is "
                           + temp.inCelsius());
         break;
       case 'C': case 'c':
         theScreen.println("\n" + temp + " in Kelvin is "
                           + temp.inKelvin());
         break;
       default:
         System.err.println("\nmain(): " + menuChoice + " is invalid\n");
     }
   }
 }
}
```

Sample run:

```
To convert a temperature between scales, enter:
 A - to convert your temperature to Fahrenheit;
 B - to convert your temperature to Celsius;
 C - to convert your temperature to Kelvin; and
 Q - to quit.
 --> A
Next, enter the temperature to be converted
 (e.g., 0 C): 0 C

0.0 C in Fahrenheit is 32.0 F
```

```
To convert a temperature between scales, enter:
 A - to convert your temperature to Fahrenheit;
 B - to convert your temperature to Celsius;
 C - to convert your temperature to Kelvin; and
 Q - to quit.
 --> b
Next, enter the temperature to be converted
 (e.g., 0 C): 212 f

212.0 F in Celsius is 100.0 C

To convert a temperature between scales, enter:
 A - to convert your temperature to Fahrenheit;
 B - to convert your temperature to Celsius;
 C - to convert your temperature to Kelvin; and
 Q - to quit.
 --> Q
```

By allowing us to specify the cases for a given alternative, the `switch` gives us a convenient way to test the value of `menuChoice`, regardless of whether it is uppercase or lowercase:

```
switch(menuChoice)
{
    case 'A': case 'a':
       theScreen.println("\n" + temp + " in Fahrenheit is "
                         + temp.inFahrenheit());
       break;
    case 'B': case 'b':
       theScreen.println("\n" + temp + " in Celsius is "
                         + temp.inCelsius());
       break;
    case 'C': case 'c':
       theScreen.println("\n" + temp + " in Kelvin is "
                         + temp.inKelvin());
       break;
    default:
       System.err.println("\nmain(): " + menuChoice
                         + " is invalid\n");
}
```

Many people find the equivalent `if-else-if` version to be more work and less readable. In addition, using a `switch` statement to select from among several alternatives is typically *more time-efficient* than using an `if` statement, as discussed at the end of this section.

Form of the `switch` Statement

A (simplified) general form for the Java `switch` statement is as follows:

The `switch` Statement

Form:

```
switch (expression)
{
   caseList₁ : statementList₁;
   caseList₂ : statementList₂;
               .
               .
               .
   caseListₙ : statementListₙ
   default   : statementListₙ₊₁
}
```

where:
`switch` and `default` are keywords;
expression is a `char`, `byte`, `short`, or `int` expression;
each *caseListᵢ* is a sequence of cases of the form

`case constantValue :`

with the type of `constantValue` compatible with the type of *expression*;
the `default` clause is optional; and
each *statementListᵢ* is a sequence of statements.

Purpose:

When the `switch` statement is executed, *expression* is evaluated. If
the value of *expression* is in *caseListᵢ*, then execution begins in
statementListᵢ and continues until one of the following is reached:

> A `break` statement
> A `return` statement
> The end of the `switch` statement

If the value of *expression* is not in any *caseListᵢ*, then *statementListₙ₊₁* in the `default` clause is executed. If the `default` clause is
omitted and the value of *expression* is not in any *caseListᵢ*, then execution continues after the closing brace (}) of the `switch`.
  The type of *expression* is restricted to `char`, `byte`, `short`, or `int`. In
particular, it may not evaluate to a real or a `String` value.

The `break` Statement

As illustrated in the program in Figure 7.3, each of the statement lists in a `switch`
statement usually ends with a `break` statement of the form

```
break;
```

When it is executed, this statement transfers control to the first statement following
the `switch` statement. As we saw in Chapter 5, the `break` statement can also be
used to terminate the repetition of a loop. The behavior of the `break` is the same in

both statements: execution jumps to the first statement following the statement in which it appears.[3]

Drop-Through Behavior

An important feature to remember when using the `switch` statement is its *drop-through behavior*. To illustrate it, suppose we had written the `switch` statement in Figure 7.3 without the break statements

```
switch(menuChoice)
{
  case 'A': case 'a':
    screen.println("\n" + temp + " in Fahrenheit is "
                      + temp.inFahrenheit());
  case 'B': case 'b':
    screen.println("\n" + temp + " in Celsius is "
                      + temp.inCelsius());
  case 'C': case 'c':
    screen.println("\n" + temp + " in Kelvin is "
                      + temp.inKelvin());
  default:
    System.err.println("\nmain(): " + menuChoice
                          + " is invalid\n");
}
```

The output produced when this modified version is run may be rather unexpected. Here is one example:

```
To convert a temperature between scales, enter:
 A - to convert your temperature to Fahrenheit;
 B - to convert your temperature to Celsius;
 C - to convert your temperature to Kelvin; and
 Q - to quit.
 -> b
Next, enter the temperature to be converted
 (e.g., 0 C): 32 f

32.0 F in Celsius is 0.0 C
32.0 F in Kelvin is 273.15 K
main(): B is invalid!
```

As before, in the sample run in Figure 7.3, the value of `menuChoice` is `b`, so control is transferred to the statement:

```
theScreen.println("\n" + temp + " in Celsius is "
                      + temp.inCelsius());
```

---

[3] An alternative form of the break statement,

```
break label;
```

can be used to transfer control to a statement with the specified label. See Section 8.2 for more information.

However, there is no `break` following this statement to transfer control past the other statements, and so execution drops through to the statement in the next case,

```
theScreen.println("\n" + temp + " in Kelvin is "
                  + temp.inKelvin());
```

which displays the equivalent temperature in Kelvin. Again, there is no `break` statement, so execution drops through to the statement in the next (default) case

```
System.err.println("\nmain(): " + menuChoice
                   + " is invalid\n");
```

which displays an error message. All of this occurs because once a `case` is matched, the drop-through behavior continues until a `break`, a `return`, or the end of the `switch` statement is reached. Because there are no `break` or `return` statements here, execution proceeds through all of the statements in the `switch` that follow case `'b':`. To avoid this behavior, we must *remember to end each statement list in a* `switch` *statement with a* `break` *or* `return` *statement (except for the final statement list, where it is not necessary).*

WATCH

OUT

PROBLEM: CONVERTING NUMERIC CODES TO NAMES

The program in Figure 7.3 uses the `switch` statement in a `main` method, but it is perhaps more commonly used to control selection in methods other than `main`. In this case, the method is probably using the `switch` to select its return value, and so a `return` statement can be used instead of a `break` statement. The following example illustrates this.

Suppose that a university uses numeric codes to store certain information about a student: 1 for freshman, 2 for sophomore, 3 for junior, 4 for senior, and 5 for graduate. When information about a freshman named Jane Doe is displayed, output of the form

```
Doe, Jane D. (Freshman)
```

is more descriptive than

```
Doe, Jane D.    (1)
```

Write a method that, given the numeric code for a year, returns the name of the year corresponding to that code (e.g., 1 → Freshman, 2 → Sophomore, and so on).

PROBLEM'S OBJECTS. From our behavioral description, we have two objects:

Description of problem's object	Type	Kind	Movement	Name
A year code	`int`	varying	received	*yearCode*
The name of the year	`String`	varying	returned	none

We can thus specify our problem as:

Receive: *yearCode*, an integer

Precondition: *yearCode* is in the range 1–5

Return: The character string corresponding to that year code ("Freshman", "Sophomore", . . .)

From this specification, we can build the following stub for our method, which we might store in a class named `AcademicYear`:

```
class AcademicYear
{
   public static String yearNameFor(int yearCode)
   {
   }
}
```

OPERATIONS.   From the behavioral description, we have only one operation:

Return the name of the year corresponding to *yearCode*

Here, the key word is *corresponding*. Because we must return the name of the year corresponding to *yearCode,* we must compare *yearCode* to each of the possible year codes and then select an appropriate return statement.

ALGORITHM.   The following algorithm applies this strategy.

Algorithm to Convert a Year Code

If *yearCode* is 1
    Return "Freshman".

Otherwise, if *yearCode* is 2
    Return "Sophomore".

Otherwise, if *yearCode* is 3
    Return "Junior".

Otherwise, if *yearCode* is 4
    Return "Senior".

Otherwise, if *yearCode* is 5
    Return "Graduate".

Otherwise
    Display an error message.
    Return the empty string.

Although we clearly could implement this algorithm using an `if` statement, the method in Figure 7.4 solves this problem using a `switch` statement. Note that no `break` statements are required in the cases of this `switch` statement. The method uses the `switch` to select a `return` statement, and a `return` statement causes execution of the method to terminate.

FIGURE 7.4   YEAR-CODE CONVERSION

```
/** Static method yearNameFor() (in class AcademicYear) returns the name
 *      of an academic year, given its code.
 *   Receive:        yearCode, an int
 *   Precondition: 1 <= yearCode && yearCode <= 5.
 *   Return:         The appropriate (string) year name
 *                   (Freshman, Sophomore, Junior, Senior, Graduate)
 */

public static String yearNameFor()(intyearCode)
{
  switch (yearCode)
  {
    case 1:  return "Freshman";
    case 2:  return "Sophomore";
    case 3:  return "Junior";
    case 4:  return "Senior";
    case 5:  return "Graduate";
    default: System.err.println("\nyearNameFor() (int)invalid code "
                                 + yearCode);
             return "";
  }
}
```

TESTING. To test our method, we can write a simple driver program like that in Figure 7.5. Note the use of the `for` statement in testing our method. By varying `i` over the range 1–6 and passing each value of `i` to the method, we can easily check that the method is behaving correctly for each valid value and one invalid value.

FIGURE 7.5   DRIVER TO TEST yearNameFor()

```
/** AcademicYearDriver.java is a simple driver to test (static) method
 *     yearNameFor() in class AcademicYear.
 *   Input: none
 *   Output: names of years (Freshman, Sophomore, ...)
 */

import ann.easyio.Screen;

class AcademicYearDriver
{
 public static void main(String [] args)
 {
   Screen theScreen = new Screen();
   for (int number = 1; number <= 6; number++)
     theScreen.println( AcademicYear.yearNameFor (number) );
 }
}
```

Sample run:

```
Freshman
Sophomore
Junior
Senior
Graduate

yearNameFor(int): invalid code 6
```

Cases with No Action

Occasionally, no action is required for certain values of the expression in a `switch` statement. In such situations, the statement lists associated with these values should consist of a single `break` or `return` statement, so that no action is taken. For example, a program to count aces and face cards might use a `switch` statement like the following:

```
char card;
int aces = faceCards = 0;
        .
        .
        .

switch (card)
    {
        case 'A':                              aces++;
                                               break;
        case 'J': case 'Q': case 'K': faceCards++;
                                               break;
        case '2': case '3': case '4': // these 'cards' are
        case '5': case '6': case '7': // not being counted
        case '8': case '9': case '0':
                                               break;
        default:
            System.err.println("***Illegal card: " + card);
    }
```

NOTE   Note that white space is ignored in the case lists and statement lists. Where these items are positioned is largely a matter of personal style, but the goal should be to write readable `switch` statements in which there is a clear association between each case list and its corresponding statement list.

WATCH

!

OUT   It is important to remember that *the types of the expression of a* `switch` *and the constants in its case lists are restricted to* `char`, `byte`, `short`, *and* `int`. *In particular, they may not be real or* `String` *expressions.* For example, we cannot write the preceding `switch` as

```
String card;
int aces = faceCards = 0;
        .
        .
        .

switch (card)
    {
        case "ACE":                            aces++;        // STRINGS
                                               break;         // ARE
        case "JACK": case "QUEEN":                            // NOT
        case "KING":                           faceCards++;   // ALLOWED
                                               break;
                    .
                    .
                    .
    }
```

NOTE **Choosing the Proper Selection Statement**

Now that we have two different ways to perform multialternative selection, it is important to understand when an `if-else-if` statement should be used and when a `switch` statement is appropriate. If a selection step in an algorithm is written in the form

If *expression* is equal to *constant*$_1$
  statement_list$_1$

Otherwise, if *expression* is equal to *constant*$_2$
  statement_list$_2$

  .
  .
  .

Otherwise, if *expression* is equal to *constant*$_n$
  statement_list$_n$

Otherwise
  statement_list$_{n+1}$

and if *expression* is of type `char`, `byte`, `short`, or `int`, then this selection step is most effectively coded as a `switch` statement:

```
switch (expression)
{
    case constant₁: statementList₁
                    break;
    case constant₂: statementList₂
                    break;
        .
        .
        .
    case constantₙ: statementListₙ
                    break;

    default:        statementListₙ₊₁
}
```

The reason is that in the `if-else-if` form, execution of *statementList*$_1$ requires the evaluation of one boolean expression, execution of *statementList*$_2$ requires the evaluation of two boolean expressions, . . . , and execution of *statementList*$_n$ (or *statementList*$_{n+1}$) requires the evaluation of n boolean expressions. Because it takes time to evaluate each expression, there is a performance penalty associated with statements that occur later in an `if-else-if` construct.

For example, we already saw that it would be *correct* to code the temperature-conversion algorithm at the beginning of this section using an `if-else-if` as follows:

```
if (menuChoice == 'A' || menuChoice == 'a')
    theScreen.println(temp.inFahrenheight());
else if (menuChoice == 'B' || menuChoice == 'b')
    theScreen.println(temp.inCelsius());
```

```
else if (menuChoice == 'C' || menuChoice == 'c')
   theScreen.println(temp.inKelvin());
else
   System.err.println("main(): " + menuChoice
      + " is invalid");
```

But this requires that 5 or 6 boolean expressions be evaluated for a Kelvin conversion, compared to only 1 or 2 for a Fahrenheit conversion.

By contrast, a `switch` statement is usually implemented so that each statement list requires approximately one comparison,[4] regardless of whether it is first or last. A `switch` statement is thus to be preferred over the `if-else-if` when

1. The equality (==) comparison is being performed;
2. The same expression (e.g., `menuChoice`) is being compared in each condition; and
3. The type of the expression being compared is `char`, `byte`, `short`, or `int`.

EXAMPLE: AUTONOMOUS `AcademicYear` OBJECTS

To illustrate, suppose that instead of using the `AcademicYear` class only as a repository for class methods, we want to be able to construct autonomous `AcademicYear` objects.

OPERATIONS. To do this, we might begin with the following operations, expressed from the internal perspective:

- ❑ Construct (initialize) myself using a given academic year
- ❑ Construct (initialize) myself using a given year code
- ❑ Convert myself to a `String` representation (for output)

There are many other operations which could be provided (and should be provided in a real-world implementation)—input, advance to next academic year, and so on. We will leave these as exercises.

ATTRIBUTE VARIABLES. Our academic years have only one attribute: the name of the academic year (*Freshman, Sophomore, Junior, Senior,* or *Graduate*). We could represent this attribute using the integer year code described above. However, if we instead represent this attribute as a `String` named `myName`, then implementing the `toString()` method becomes a simple accessor method:

```
public String toString()
{
   return myName;
}
```

---

[4] The mechanism by which this is accomplished is beyond the scope of this text. The interested reader should see *Compilers: Principles, Techniques and Tools* by Aho, Sethi, and Ullman (Reading, Mass.: Addison-Wesley, 1986).

We thus add a declaration of `myName` to our `AcademicYear` class:

```
class AcademicYear
{
 // definition of yearNameFor() method
 private String myName;
}
```

CONSTRUCTOR FROM YEAR NAME. It would be convenient to be able to initialize an `AcademicYear` object using the name of the year; for example,

```
AcademicYear aYear = new AcademicYear("freshman");
```

For this, object-centered design leads to the following specification for the constructor:

Receive: *yearName,* a `String`

Precondition: *yearName* is one of "freshman", "sophomore", "junior", "senior", or "graduate" (ignoring case)

Postcondition: *myName* equals the year corresponding to *yearName*

To ensure its postcondition, this constructor can use selection to set attribute variable *myName* as follows:

If *yearName* is equal to "freshman" (ignoring case)
   Set *myName* to "Freshman"
Otherwise, if *yearName* is equal to "sophomore" (ignoring case)
   Set *myName* to "Sophomore"
Otherwise, if *yearName* is equal to "junior" (ignoring case)
   Set *myName* to "Junior"
Otherwise, if *yearName* is equal to "senior" (ignoring case)
   Set *myName* to "Senior"
Otherwise, if *yearName* is equal to "graduate" (ignoring case)
   Set *myName* to "Graduate"
Otherwise:
   Generate a fatal error message

In coding this algorithm, we must again decide whether to use an `if` or a `switch` statement. We use the three decision criteria to help us:

1. An equality (`==`) comparison is being performed;
2. The same expression (`yearCode`) is being compared in each condition; and
3. The type of the expression being compared is `char`, `byte`, `short`, or `int`.

Our algorithm meets conditions 1 and 2, but it fails condition 3. As a result, we must code this constructor using an `if` statement, as shown in the second explicit-value constructor in Figure 7.6.

CONSTRUCTOR FROM YEAR CODE. In addition to consructing an `AcademicYear` objects from year names, it would be convenient to be able to initialize them using the year codes described earlier; for example,

```
AcademicYear aYear = new AcademicYear(1);
```

For this, object-centered design leads to the following specification for the constructor:

Receive: *yearCode*, an `int`

Precondition: $1 <= yearCode$ && $yearCode <= 5$.

Postcondition: *myName* equals the academic year corresponding to *yearCode.*

To ensure its postcondition, this constructor can use selection to set attribute variable *myName* as follows:

> If *yearCode* is equal to 1
> > Set *myName* to "Freshman"
>
> Otherwise, if *yearCode* is equal to 2
> > Set *myName* to "Sophomore"
>
> Otherwise, if *yearCode* is equal to 3
> > Set *myName* to "Junior"
>
> Otherwise, if *yearCode* is equal to 4
> > Set *myName* to "Senior"
>
> Otherwise, if *yearCode* is equal to 5
> > Set *myName* to "Graduate"
>
> Otherwise:
> > Generate a fatal error message

To code this algorithm, do we use an `if` statement or a `switch` statement? To decide, we use the criteria given earlier:

1. An equality (==) comparison is being performed;
2. The same expression (`yearCode`) is being compared in each condition; and
3. The type of the expression being compared is `char`, `byte`, `short`, or `int`.

Because all three conditions hold, a `switch` is preferred over an `if`, and this is why we used it in the `yearNameFor()` method we developed earlier to convert a year code to its name. The first explicit-value constructor in Figure 7.6 simply invokes this method to set the value of `myName`. (Note that even though `yearNameFor()` is a static method, it can be invoked from inside the class without attaching the class name `AcademicYear`.)

Figure 7.6 gives the "complete" `AcademicYear` class. See the exercises for additional `AcademicYear` methods.

FIGURE 7.6   CLASS AcademicYear

```java
/* AcademicYear.java provides the AcademicYear class for modeling
 * academic years (freshman, sophomore, etc.).
 */

class AcademicYear
{
 /** Explicit-value constructor.
  *  Receive:        yearCode, an int
  *  Precondition:   1 <= yearCode && yearCode <= 5.
  *  Postcondition:  myName equals the academic year for yearCode.
  */
 public AcademicYear(int yearCode)
 {
   switch (yearCode)
   {
     case 1:  myName = "Freshman";
              break;
     case 2:  myName = "Sophomore";
              break;
     case 3:  myName = "Junior";
              break;
     case 4:  myName = "Senior";
              break;
     case 5:  myName = "Graduate";
              break;
     default: System.err.println("\nAcademicYear(int): invalid code "
                                   + yearCode);
              System.exit(1);
   }
 }

 /** Explicit-value constructor from year name.
  *  Receive:        yearName, a String
  *  Precondition: yearName is one of {freshman, sophomore, junior,
  *                   senior, graduate}, ignoring case.
  *  Postcondition:  myName equals the academic year for yearName.
  */
 public AcademicYear(String yearName)
 {
   if ( yearName.equalsIgnoreCase("freshman") )
     myName = "Freshman";
   else if ( yearName.equalsIgnoreCase("sophomore") )
     myName = "Sophomore";
   else if ( yearName.equalsIgnoreCase("junior") )
     myName = "Junior";
   else if ( yearName.equalsIgnoreCase("senior") )
     myName = "Senior";
   else if ( yearName.equalsIgnoreCase("graduate") )
     myName = "Graduate";
   else
   {
     System.err.println("\nAcademicYear(String): invalid name "
                          + yearName);
     System.exit(1);
   }
 }
```

```
/** yearNameFor() is a static method that returns the name of an
 *    academic year, given its code.
 *  Receive:      yearCode, an int
 *  Precondition: 1 <= yearCode && yearCode <= 5.
 *  Return:       the appropriate (string) year name
 *                  (Freshman, Sophomore, Junior, Senior, Graduate)
 */
  public static String yearNameFor(int yearCode)
  {
    switch (yearCode)
    {
      case 1:  return "Freshman";
      case 2:  return "Sophomore";
      case 3:  return "Junior";
      case 4:  return "Senior";
      case 5:  return "Graduate";
      default: System.err.println("\nyearNameFor(int):  invalid code"
                                    + yearCode);
               return "";
    }
  }

  /** AcademicYear-to-String converter
   *  Return: myName
   */
  public String toString()
  {
    return myName;
  }

  private String myName = "";
}
```

✔ Quick Quiz 7.3

For the following questions, assume that `number` is an `int` variable, `code` is a `char` variable, and `x` is a `double` variable.

1. If `number` has the value 99, tell what output is produced by the following `switch` statement, or indicate why an error occurs:

```
switch(number)
{
    case 99: theScreen.println(number + 99);
             break;
    case -1: theScreen.println(number - 1);
             break;
    default: theScreen.println("default)";
}
```

2. Proceed as in Question 1, but suppose the `break` statements are omitted.
3. Proceed as in Question 1, but suppose `number` has the value 50.
4. Proceed as in Question 2, but suppose `number` has the value 50.
5. Proceed as in Question 1, but suppose `number` has the value −1.
6. Proceed as in Question 2, but suppose `number` has the value −1.

7. If the value of `code` is the letter B, tell what output is produced by the following `switch` statement, or indicate why an error occurs:

```
switch (code)
{
   case 'A': case 'B':
      theScreen.println(123);
      break;
   case 'P': case 'R': case 'X':
      theScreen.println(456);
}
```

8. Proceed as in Question 7, but suppose the value of `code` is the letter X.

9. Proceed as in Question 7, but suppose the value of `code` is the letter M.

10. If the value of `x` is 2.0, tell what output is produced by the following `switch` statement, or indicate why an error occurs:

```
switch (x)
{
   case 1.0: theScreen.println(x + 1.0);
             break;
   case 2.0: theScreen.println(x + 2.0);
}
```

✍ EXERCISES 7.3

1. Write a `switch` statement that increases `balance` by adding `amount` to it if the value of the character variable `transCode is 'D'`; decreases `balance` by subtracting `amount` from it if `transCode is 'W'`; displays the value of `balance` if `transCode is 'P'`; and displays an illegal-transaction message otherwise.

2. Write a `switch` statement that, for two given integers a and b, and a given character `operator`, computes and displays a + b, a − b, a * b, or a / b according to whether `operator` is '+', '−', '*', or '/', and displays an illegal-operator message if it is not one of these.

For Exercises 3–6, write methods that use `switch` statements to compute what is required. To test these methods, you should write driver programs as instructed in Programming Problems 9–12 at the end of this chapter.

3. Given a number representing a TV channel, return the call letters of the station that corresponds to that number, or some message indicating that the channel is not used. Use the following channel numbers and call letters (or use those that are available in your locale):

   2: WCBS

   4: WNBC

   5: WNEW

   7: WABC

   9: WOR

      11: WPIX

      13: WNET

4. Given a distance less than 1000, return a shipping cost as determined by the following table:

Distance	Cost
0 through 100	5.00
More than 100 but not more than 300	8.00
More than 500 but less than 600	10.00
More than 600 but less than 1000	12.00

5. Given the number of a month, return the name of a month (or an error message indicating an illegal month number).

6. Proceed as in 5, but return the number of days in a month. (See Exercise 6 of Section 7.2 regarding the determination of leap years.)

For Exercises 7–9, write methods to add to the class `AcademicYear` to compute what is required. To test these methods, you should write driver programs as instructed in Programming Problems 13–15 at the end of this chapter.

7. An input method that reads a year code (1, 2, 3, 4, 5) and stores the corresponding year name in the attribute variable `myName`.

8. A case-insensitive input method that reads a year name (Freshman, Sophomore, Junior, Senior, Graduate) and stores it in the attribute variable `myName`.

9. A method that returns the minimum number of course credits needed for that academic-year classification. Suppose that these classifications are determined by the number of credit hours earned to date as given in the following table:

Year	Credit Hours Earned
Freshman	0–26
Sophomore	27–57
Junior	58–88
Senior	89–123
Graduate	124 and above

7.4   SELECTION: CONDITIONAL EXPRESSIONS

The selection statements (`if` and `switch`) we have considered thus far are similar to statements provided by other languages. However, Java has inherited a third selection mechanism from its ancestral language C, an expression that produces either of two values, based on the value of a boolean expression.

    To illustrate it, suppose we wish to determine whether a student is passing or failing, based on an average numeric score on homework and tests. If `average` contains this average and `PASS_FAIL_LINE` is a constant denoting the cutoff between passing and failing, then the statement

```
theScreen.println("You are " +
    ((average > PASS_FAIL_LINE) ? "passing." : "failing.") );
```

will display

```
You are passing.
```

if the condition `average > PASS_FAIL_LINE` is `true`, but it will display

```
You are failing.
```

if the condition `average > PASS_FAIL_LINE` is `false`.

Because the value produced by such expressions depends on the value of their conditions, they are called **conditional expressions,**[5] and have the following general form:

The Conditional Expression

Form:

```
condition ? expression₁ : expression₂
```

where:
`condition` is a boolean expression; and
`expression₁` and `expression₂` are type-compatible expressions.

Behavior:

`condition` is evaluated.
If `condition` is `true`,
    then the value of `expression₁` is produced as the result.
If `condition` is `false`,
    then the value of `expression₂` is produced as the result.

Note that in a conditional expression, only one of $expression_1$ and $expression_2$ is evaluated. Thus, an assignment such as

```
reciprocal = ( (x == 0) ? 0 : 1 / x );
```

is safe because if the value of `x` is zero, the expression `1 / x` will not be evaluated, and so no divide-by-zero error results. A conditional expression can thus sometimes be used in place of an `if` statement to guard a potentially unsafe operation. When it is used as a subexpression in another expression, the conditional expression should be enclosed in parentheses, because its precedence is lower than most of the other operators (see Appendix C).

This mechanism has many different uses, because it can be used anywhere that an expression can appear. In fact, conditional expressions can be used in place of most `if-else` statements. To illustrate, suppose that we wanted to write a method

---

[5] In a conditional expression of the form `C ? A : B, ?  :` is actually a **ternary** (three-operand) **operation** whose operands are `C`, `A`, and `B`.

`largerOf()` to find the maximum of two `int` values. Although we could do this with an `if` statement,

```
public static int largerOf(int value1, int value2)
{
    if (value1 > value2)
        return value1;
    else
        return value2;
}
```

a conditional expression provides a simpler alternative:

```
public static int largerOf(int value1, int value2)
{
    return ( (value1 > value2) ? value1 : value2 );
}
```

Using such a method, we can write

```
max = largerOf(x, y);
```

and `max` will be assigned the larger of the two values `x` and `y`.

As a final example, suppose that `numCourses` is an `int` variable containing the number of courses a student is taking in the current semester. Then the output statement

```
theScreen.println("\nYou are taking " + numCourses + " course"
        + ((numCourses == 1) ? "" : "s") + " this semester\n");
```

will display the *singular* message

```
You are taking 1 course this semester
```

if `numCourses` is equal to 1 and will display a *plural* message if `numCourses` has a value other than 1:

```
You are taking 3 courses this semester
```

✍ EXERCISES 7.4

1. Describe the operation that the following method performs:

```
public static int doSomething1(int value)
{
```

```
        return ( (value >= 0) ? value : -value );
    }
```

2. Describe the operation that the following method performs:

```
    public static char doSomething2(char ch)
    {
        return (char)( ( ('A' <= ch) && (ch <= 'Z') ) ?
                       ch + 32 : ch );
    }
```

3. Write conditional expressions that can replace the blanks in the output statement

```
    theScreen.println(_____ + month + "/"
                   + _____ + day + "/"
                   + _____ + year % 100);
```

so that the output produced will be as follows:

month	day	year	Output
12	25	1998	12/31/98
10	2	1999	10/02/99
2	14	2000	02/14/00
1	1	2001	01/01/01

4. Write a conditional expression that can replace the blank in the output statement

```
    theScreen.println(_____ + number);
```

so that the output produced will be as follows:

number	Output
123	123
23	023
3	003

5. Write a method `smallerOf()` that returns the smaller of two given integer values.
6. Using nested conditional expressions, write a method:
    (a) `largestOf()` that, given three `int` values, returns the largest of the three.
    (b) `smallestOf()` that, given three `int` values, returns the smallest of the three.
7. The mathematician Carl Friedrich Gauss discovered that the sum of the integers from 1 through n is given by the formula

$$\frac{n(n + 1)}{2}$$

Using a conditional expression, construct a method `sum()` that returns the value according to Gauss's formula if the value of its parameter is positive and zero otherwise.

7.5 GRAPHICAL/INTERNET JAVA: EVENT-DRIVEN PROGRAMMING

Programming has traditionally consisted of writing programs that consist of 3 steps:

1. Input values that need to be processed.
2. Process the values.
3. Output the results of the processing.

Many of our examples thus far have followed this model.

Graphical user interface (GUI) programs, however, do not simply input, process, and output. Instead, they must respond to mouse clicks, mouse movements, and keystrokes from the keyboard, and react differently to different occurrences. Such occurrences are called **events** and because GUI programs behave primarily in response to events, GUI programming is an example of **event-driven programming.**

Informally, an event can be defined as *any occurrence that is of interest to the executing program.* Some examples are:

- ❏ the user pressing a mouse button
- ❏ the user releasing a mouse button
- ❏ the user dragging the mouse
- ❏ the user pressing a keyboard key
- ❏ the user clicking the mouse on a graphical (on-screen) button
- ❏ the user entering text in a graphical (on-screen) text field

Each such occurrence is a *different event,* and so a program may have to respond to each in a different manner. Selection statements (e.g., if statements) are generally used to select the code that generates a program's response to a given event.

In this section, we will take a first look at event-driven programming. As usual, we will start with a problem.

PROBLEM 1: A GUI BIG-10-MASCOT PROGRAM

Write a GUI version of the Big-10-Mascot program in Section 7.1 that displays the mascot for any Big 10 university.

 OBJECT-CENTERED DESIGN

BEHAVIOR. The program should construct a window containing a prompt for a university name followed by a text field. When the user enters the common name of a Big 10 university, the program should display a "Mascot:" label, followed by a text field containing the name of the mascot for that university. If the user enters anything else, the program should just display the latter text field containing an error message.

As we have seen before, we can sketch the GUI's different appearances and link them together in a transition diagram. The following is one possible transition diagram for this problem:

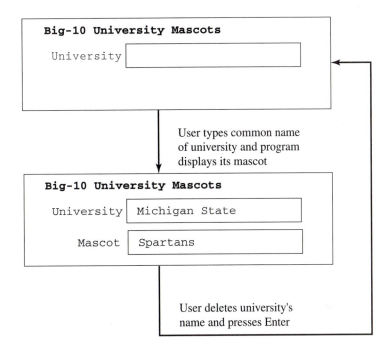

This design illustrates an important GUI design principle:

Only show users what they need to see.

For example, instead of making the "Mascot:" label and text field appear and disappear, we could keep things simpler and just display them at all times. However, doing so might lead users to believe that they can enter a *mascot* and the program will display the corresponding Big 10 university, which is not the case. By hiding everything except what the user needs to see, such confusion can be eliminated.

PROBLEM'S OBJECTS. From our behavioral description and transition diagram, we can identify these objects:

Description of problem's object	Type	Kind	Name
The program	??	—	??
A window	??	varying	*aGUI*
Prompt for university	JLabel	constant	*mySchoolLabel*
First text field	JTextField	varying	*mySchoolField*
A Big 10 common name	String	varying	*school*
Mascot label	JLabel	constant	*myMascotLabel*
Second text field	JTextField	varying	*myMascotField*
A mascot	String	varying	*mascot*

If we call our class `GUIBig10Mascots`, that will be the name of our program and its type. If we define `GUIBig10Mascots` to extend the class `CloseableFrame` from package `ann.gui`, then `GUIBig10Mascots` will also be the type for our window frame.

In earlier chapters, we have used several of Java's Swing components in building GUI applications and applets. In Section 6.5, we used our `CloseableFrame` class, which extends Swing's `JFrame` class, to create a frame and then used `JPanel` to create a pane (also called a panel) to place on its content pane. We also saw in Sections 4.5 and 5.4 how the `JLabel` class can be used to define text labels and prompts. We will use the `JTextField` class to define a box in which the user can enter a line of text. The methods provided in these classes for manipulating graphical objects are described in these sections and in the Documentation sections at the end of Chapters 4 and 6 and this chapter.

OPERATIONS. From our behavioral description, we can identify these operations:

i. Construct the graphical user interface by doing the following:
   a. Display a window frame
   b. Position a `JLabel` (university prompt, mascot label) in a window frame
   c. Position a `JTextField` (university text field, mascot text field) in a window frame
   d. Set the title of a window frame

ii. When the user enters something in a `JTextField` (university text field):
   a. Get the text from the `JTextField` (university text field)
   b. Set the text in a `JTextField` (mascot text field):
   c. Make a `JLabel` (mascot-label) disappear
   d. Make a `JTextField` disappear (university text field)
   e. Select between operations (ii-b), (ii-c) and (ii-d), based on the result of (ii-a)

Most (but not all) of these operations are straightforward: we simply send an appropriate message to the object in question. For example, as we saw in Section 6.5, a message of the form

```
guiComponent.setVisible(false);
```

can be used to hide a GUI component and

```
guiComponent.setVisible(true);
```

can be used to make it visible. GUI components are visible by default.

As another example, if `mySchoolField` and `myMascotField` are handles for `JTextField` objects, then the message

```
String school = mySchoolField.getText();
```

will retrieve the contents of the `JTextField` for which `mySchoolField` is the handle. Similarly, the message:

```
myMascotField.setText(mascot);
```

will set the contents of the `JTextField` referred to by `myMascotField` to the `String` referred to by `mascot`.

CODING. Since this is our first GUI application that does event-handling, we will go directly to the coding step and show how these operations are implemented. Then we will examine it step by step. Figure 7.7 gives the code for `GUIBig10Mascots.java`.

FIGURE 7.7   BIG10MASCOTS GUI APPLICATION

```
/** GUIBig10Mascots.java provides the class GUIBig10Mascots for building
 *    GUIs that can be used to find the mascots of Big-10 universities.
 */

import Big10;
import ann.gui.CloseableFrame;
import javax.swing.*;           // JLabel, JTextField, JPanel
import java.awt.*;              // Color
import java.awt.event.*;        // ActionEvent, ...

class GUIBig10Mascots extends CloseableFrame
                      implements ActionListener
{
 /** GUI constructor.
  *  Postcondition: the GUI has been constructed
  */
 public GUIBig10Mascots()
 {
    setTitle("Big-10 University Mascots");

    mySchoolLabel = new JLabel("University: ", SwingConstants.RIGHT);
    mySchoolField = new JTextField(14);
    mySchoolField.addActionListener(this);

    myMascotLabel = new JLabel("Mascot: ", SwingConstants.RIGHT);
    myMascotLabel.setVisible(false);

    myMascotField = new JTextField(14);
    myMascotField.setVisible(false);
    myMascotField.setEditable(false);

    myPanel = new JPanel();
    myPanel.setLayout( new GridLayout(2,2) ); // 2 rows, 2 columns
    myPanel.add(mySchoolLabel);                // row 1 column 1
    myPanel.add(mySchoolField);                // row 1 column 2
    myPanel.add(myMascotLabel);                // row 2 column 1
    myPanel.add(myMascotField);                // row 2 column 2
    setContentPane(myPanel);
 }


 /** ActionEvent handler
  *  Receive:       event, an ActionEvent
  *  Precondition:  event was generated by an 'Enter' in mySchoolField
  *  Postcondition: event has been processed
  */
 public void actionPerformed(ActionEvent event)
 {
    String school = mySchoolField.getText();
```

```
if (school.length() == 0)                          // no text entered
{
  myMascotLabel.setVisible(false);
  myMascotField.setText("");
  myMascotField.setVisible(false);
}
else
{
  String mascot = Big10.mascot(school);
  if (mascot.length() == 0)                         // non-Big-10 school
          myMascotLabel.setVisible(false);
          myMascotField.setText("Not in Big-10");
          myMascotField.setVisible(true);
      }
    else                                     // valid Big-10 school name
    {
      myMascotLabel.setVisible(true);
      myMascotField.setText(mascot);
      myMascotField.setVisible(true);
    }
  }
}

public static void main(String [] args)
{
  GUIBig10Mascots aGUI = new GUIBig10Mascots();
  aGUI.setBackground(Color.white);
  aGUI.pack();
  aGUI.setVisible(true);
}

private JLabel      mySchoolLabel, myMascotLabel;
private JTextField  mySchoolField, myMascotField;
private JPanel      myPanel;
}
```

TESTING. When executed, this application first generates the following window frame:

If the user enters the common name of a Big-10 university, the program displays its mascot:

If the user enters a string is entered that is not a Big-10 university, the program displays an error message:

If the user deletes the university name and presses *Enter,* the program returns to the original screen, providing the cyclic behavior shown in our transition diagram. Our application thus provides *continuous behavior*—the program will not terminate until the user clicks on the window-frame's close box. Such continuous behavior is fairly typical of GUI applications. In Java, such continuous behavior is provided by the underlying system, using an **event-processing loop** that behaves as follows:

Loop:

    a. Get *event,* the oldest event that has not yet been processed.

    b. If *event* is the terminate-event, terminate repetition.

    c. Process *event.*

End loop

> **NOTE** This makes our tasks as GUI programmers much easier: *a Java GUI application need not define an event-processing loop, because the repetitive behavior is provided by the underlying Java system.* An object whose class is an extension of `CloseableFrame` or `JApplet` automatically inherits this behavior from the class it extends.

Java's Event Model

To understand what is happening in Figure 7.7, we must first examine Java's system for dealing with events, which is called the **event delegation model.** In this system, some objects *generate* events (e.g., buttons, text fields, keyboard keys, and so on) and are called **event sources.** In Java jargon, an event source **fires** events. Other objects *respond* to events and are called **event-listeners,** or simply **listeners.**

Building a GUI program that uses Java's event delegation model involves three steps:

1. Define the event *source(s)*

2. Define the event *listener(s)*

3. *Register* a listener with each source, to handle the events generated by that source

We will look at these steps individually.

1. Event Sources. To define an event source we must define an event-generating component in our GUI, usually in its constructor. For example, one of the event sources in the class `GUIBig10Mascots` is the `JTextField` named `mySchoolField`. It is defined as an attribute variable,

```
private JTextField mySchoolField;
```

and is initialized in the usual manner, by using the `new` operator and a `JTextField` constructor,

```
mySchoolField = new JTextField(14);
```

which creates a text box with 14 columns (the length of the longest university name). This component is then placed on the window pane referred to by `myPanel` by using its `add()` method:

```
myPanel.add(mySchoolField);
```

Because a `JTextField` fires `ActionEvents`, our GUI now has an event source.

Java's Interface Mechanism. At the beginning of the declaration of the class `GUIBig10Mascots`,

```
class GUIBig10Mascots extends CloseableFrame
                          implements ActionListener
{
   // . . .
}
```

we see that this class *extends the class* `CloseableFrame` and thus inherits all of its instance fields and methods, but we also see a new feature, namely, that `GUIBig10Mascots` **implements** `ActionListener` (as indicated by the keyword `implements`).[6] `ActionListener` is not a class; it is an **interface** (not to be confused with user interfaces) defined in the `java.awt.event` package. Before discussing event-listeners, we must look first at Java's interface mechanism.

One difference between classes and interfaces is that classes contain *method definitions;*

❑ Interfaces contain only *method headings* (also called *prototypes*).

For example, here is the complete code for the interface `ActionListener`:

```
public interface ActionListener extends EventListener
{
   public void actionPerformed(ActionEvent e);
}
```

`ActionListener` contains only a heading for a method named `actionPerformed()`.

A class that implements an interface must provide a definition for each method whose heading appears in that interface. Said differently, an interface only *specifies* the behavior of a class by telling what methods it must have, but a class implementing that interface must *define* that behavior. Thus, when our `GUIBig10Mascot` class indicates that it is implementing the `ActionListener` interface, it is promising that it will provide a definition for the `actionPerformed()` method. If it does not, a compilation error will result.

---

[6] A class can extend only one superclass, but it can implement more than one interface. This makes it possible to accomplish in Java many of the same things that multiple inheritance makes possible in C++.

Another difference between classes and interfaces is:

❑ Interface objects cannot be created using `new`. Instead, they are created *indirectly* by creating an instance of a class that implements that interface.

Thus, when a `GUIBig10Mascots` object is created using the `new` operator,

```
GUIBig10Mascots aGUI = new GUIBig10Mascots();
```

the resulting object is simultaneously an instance of class `GUIBig10Mascots`, an extension of class `CloseableFrame`, and an implementation of interface `Action-Listener`. In other words, the resulting object is all three of these things simultaneously.

Although interface objects cannot be created directly, we can (i) create interface handles, and (ii) send an interface message to an object referred to by the handle. Java's notion of event listeners provides a good illustration of how this can be useful, so let's return to our discussion of Java's event-delegation model.

2. Event Listeners. To have a GUI *respond to* events from an event source such as a `JTextField`, we must

a. *Create a listener* for that event source; and

b. *Register the listener* with that event source.

The listener can be a separate object, but it is common practice in Java for a GUI application itself to serve as the listener. In our example, the definition

```
class GUIBig10Mascots extends CloseableFrame
                       implements ActionListener
{
    // . . .
}
```

specifies that in addition to being a specialized kind of `CloseableFrame`, `GUIBig10Mascots` is also an `ActionListener`. From what we said earlier, this means that when the main method creates a `GUIBig10Mascots` object,

```
GUIBig10Mascots aGUI = new GUIBig10Mascots();
```

it simultaneously creates:

1. A `CloseableFrame` object whose appearance is specified by the `GUIBig10Mascots` constructor

2. An `ActionListener` object that provides definitions of `ActionListener`'s methods

Since `ActionListener` has only one method, `actionPerformed()`, our `GUIBig10Mascots` class must provide a definition for it:

```
class GUIBig10Mascots extends CloseableFrame
                       implements ActionListener
{
    // . . . . constructor method

    public void actionPerformed(ActionEvent event)
```

```
    {
       // . . . what to do when an ActionEvent occurs
    }

    // . . . main method
  }
```

An `ActionListener` is required to handle `ActionEvents`, but other kinds of events require other kinds of listeners. See the Documentation in the chapter summary for more events and their listeners.

3. Registering Event Listeners with Event Sources. Once an event source and a listener for it have been created, the last step in Java's event-delegation model is to register the listener with the event-source(s). This is why `ActionEvent` sources provide an `addActionListener()` method. In our `GUIBig10Mascots` constructor, the statement

```
       mySchoolField.addActionListener(this);
```

sends a message to the `JTextField` object referred to by `mySchoolField`.

Because this statement is within the `GUIBig10Mascots` class constructor, the keyword `this` refers to the object being constructed, and so it is this object that is being passed as an argument to the `JTextField`, thereby registering itself as an `ActionListener`—as the listener for that `JTextField`. We say that this listener has been **bound** to that event source.

Once we have defined our event sources, defined listeners for their events, and registered the listeners with the sources, the underlying Java system then ensures that events are delivered to their associated listeners.

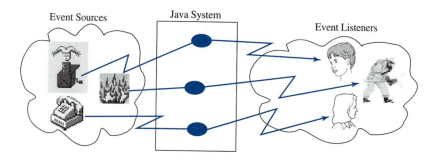

WATCH   If you find that a GUI component doesn't seem to be doing anything, check that you have created and registered a listener for its events. *If no listener is bound to an event source, events from that source will be ignored.*

OUT

The Usefulness of Interfaces. Earlier we noted that although interface objects cannot be created directly, interface handles can be created and messages can be sent to objects via those handles. We also said that event listeners provide a good illustration of why this is useful, and we can now show this.

A nested if statement is then used to determine whether or not mascot refers to an empty string:

```
if (mascot.length() == 0)        // not a Big 10 school
{
  myMascotLabel.setVisible(false);
  myMascotField.setText("Not in Big-10");
  myMascotField.setVisible(true);
}
else                             // a Big 10 school
{
  myMascotLabel.setVisible(true);
  myMascotField.setText(mascot);
  myMascotField.setVisible(true);
}
}
```

If mascot refers to an empty string, then school does not refer to the name of a Big 10 university, and so we hide the JLabel referred to by myMascotLabel, use the setText() method to display an error message in myMascotField's JTextField, and make that JTextField visible.

However, if mascot does not refer to an empty string, then it refers to the mascot of the Big 10 university to which school refers. In this case, we use setVisible() to ensure that both the JLabel and JTextField are visible, and setText() to display the mascot in the JTextField.

An Applet Version of the Big-10-Mascot Program

Converting the Big 10 Mascot GUI application into an applet is straightforward. We need only make the class extend JApplet instead of CloseableFrame,

```
public class GUIBig10Mascots2 extends JApplet
                              implements ActionListener
```

change the main() method to a non-static init() method,

```
public void init(String [] args)
{ . . .
}
```

and remove the call to setTitle(), since JApplet does not contain this method. Also, for the applet frame to have approximately the same dimensions as the windows for the GUI application, the HTML file should contain

```
<APPLET CODE="GUIBig10Mascots2.class"
   WIDTH=300 HEIGHT=60 <\APPLET>
```

The complete applet code can be found on the text's CD and website (see the preface).

PROBLEM 2: A GUI TEMPERATURE CONVERTER APPLICATION

To help with understanding what different GUI applications have in common and where they differ, we now look at a GUI version of our `TemperatureConverter` from Chapter 6.

Unlike `GUIBig10Mascots`, which has a single source of `ActionEvents`, our `GUITemperatureConverter` should let the user enter either a Fahrenheit, Celsius, or Kelvin temperature. To permit this, our `GUITemperatureConverter` will have three `JTextFields`—one for each of the Fahrenheit, Celsius, and Kelvin temperatures in degrees—and each of these can fire `ActionEvents`. Accordingly, our application must register itself as the listener for each of these `JTextFields`, and its `actionPerformed()` method must handle events from any of these event sources.

The complete code for this application is given in Figure 7.8.

FIGURE 7.8   `GUITemperatureConverter.java`

```java
// GUITemperatureConverter.java

import Temperature;
import ann.gui.CloseableFrame;
import javax.swing.*;              // JLabel, JTextField, ...
import java.awt.*;                 // Color, ...
import java.awt.event.*;           // ActionEvent, ...

class GUITemperatureConverter extends CloseableFrame
                              implements ActionListener
{
  final static int MAX_DIGITS = 12;  // size of JTextFields

 /** GUI constructor.
  *  Postcondition: The GUI has been constructed
  */
 public GUITemperatureConverter()
 {
  setTitle("Temperature Converter");

  myFahrField = new JTextField(MAX_DIGITS);
  myFahrField.setHorizontalAlignment(JTextField.RIGHT);
  myFahrField.addActionListener(this);
  myFahrLabel = new JLabel(" Fahrenheit", SwingConstants.LEFT);
```

```java
myCelsField = new JTextField(MAX_DIGITS);
myCelsField.setHorizontalAlignment(JTextField.RIGHT);
myCelsField.addActionListener(this);
myCelsLabel = new JLabel(" Celsius", SwingConstants.LEFT);

myKelvField = new JTextField(MAX_DIGITS);
myKelvField.setHorizontalAlignment(JTextField.RIGHT);
myKelvField.addActionListener(this);
myKelvLabel = new JLabel("  Kelvin", SwingConstants.LEFT);

myPanel = new JPanel( new GridLayout(3,2) ); // 3 rows, 2 cols
myPanel.setBackground(Color.white);
myPanel.add(myFahrField); myPanel.add(myFahrLabel); // row 1
myPanel.add(myCelsField); myPanel.add(myCelsLabel); // row 2
myPanel.add(myKelvField); myPanel.add(myKelvLabel); // row 3
setContentPane(myPanel);
}

/** Handler for ActionEvents.
 *  Receive:          event, an ActionEvent
 *  Precondition:     degrees was entered in myFahrField, myCelsField,
 *                       or myKelvField
 *  Postcondition:    the other two fields contain degrees in their
 *                       respective scales
 */
public void actionPerformed(ActionEvent event)
{
  Temperature fTemp = null, cTemp = null, kTemp = null;
  Object eventSource = event.getSource();

  if (eventSource instanceof JTextField)
  {
    JTextField eventSourceField = (JTextField)eventSource;
    String degreeString = eventSourceField.getText();

  if (degreeString.length() > 0)                     // text entered
  {
    double degrees = Double.parseDouble(degreeString);

    if ( eventSourceField.equals(myFahrField) )      // Fahrenheit
    {
      fTemp = new Temperature(degrees, 'F');
      cTemp = fTemp.inCelsius();
      myCelsField.setText( Double.toString( cTemp.getDegrees() ) );
      kTemp = fTemp.inKelvin();
      myKelvField.setText( Double.toString( kTemp.getDegrees() ) );
    }
    else if ( eventSourceField.equals(myCelsField) ) // Celsius
    {
      cTemp = new Temperature(degrees, 'C');
      fTemp = cTemp.inFahrenheit();
      myFahrField.setText( Double.toString( fTemp.getDegrees() ) );
      kTemp = cTemp.inKelvin();
      myKelvField.setText( Double.toString( kTemp.getDegrees() ) );
    }
    else if ( eventSourceField.equals(myKelvField) ) // Kelvin
    {
      kTemp = new Temperature(degrees, 'K');
      fTemp = kTemp.inFahrenheit();
      myFahrField.setText( Double.toString( fTemp.getDegrees() ) );
      cTemp = kTemp.inCelsius();
      myCelsField.setText( Double.toString( cTemp.getDegrees() ) );
    }
```

```
        else                                                // illegal scale
           System.err.println("actionPerformed(): event from JTextField: "
                              + eventSourceField + " not expected\n");
        }

      else                                            // no text entered
        {
          myFahrField.setText("");
          myCelsField.setText("");
          myKelvField.setText("");
        }
      }
    else
      System.err.println("actionPerformed(): unexpected event source: "
                        + eventSource + " from non-JTextField\n");
  }

  public static void main(String [] args)
  {
    GUITemperatureConverter myGUI = new GUITemperatureConverter();
    myGUI.pack();
    myGUI.setVisible(true);
  }

  private JLabel      myFahrLabel, myCelsLabel, myKelvLabel;
  private JTextField  myFahrField, myCelsField, myKelvField;
  private JPanel      myPanel;
}
```

As before, our constructor method is responsible for building the GUI. To do so, it follows steps similar to those we saw in Figure 7.7 and really does nothing new.

To determine the source of a given event, our `actionPerformed()` method sends its `ActionEvent` argument the `getSource()` message, which returns the event source that fired this particular event. Because `ActionEvents` are fired by GUI components other than `JTextFields` (see the Documentation section in the chapter summary), `getSource()` returns the event-source as type `Object`, rather than type `JTextField`.

Our `actionPerformed()` method then casts that `Object` into a `JTextField`, so that `JTextField` messages can be sent to it. Since *it is good practice to only perform such a cast when one is certain of the object's type,* we use an `if` statement and the `instanceof` **operator** to verify the type before performing the cast:

```
        if (eventSource instanceof JTextField)
        {
          JTextField eventSourceField = (JTextField)eventSource;
          // . . .
```

An expression of the form

```
        handle instanceof ClassName
```

produces the value `true` if `handle` refers to an object whose type is `ClassName`, and produces the value `false` otherwise.

The only other interesting feature of our `actionPerformed()` method is its use of an `if-else-if` statement and the `equals()` method to determine which `JTextField` is the source of the event:

```
if ( eventSourceField.equals(myFahrField) )
{
  // . . . update Celsius and Kelvin fields
}
else if ( eventSourceField.equals(myCelsField) )
{
  // . . . update Fahrenheit and Kelvin fields
}
else if ( eventSourceField.equals(myKelvField) )
{
  // . . . update Fahrenheit and Celsius fields
}
else
    // . . . error
```

Testing. When executed, this application displays the following window frame:

If the user enters a number in any of the text fields,

the program displays the equivalent temperature in the other two scales:

The application then provides for continuous execution, until the user clicks the window's close box.

An Applet Version of the Temperature Converter Program

The GUI application in Figure 7.8 can be converted to an applet in the same manner as the Big-10-Mascot application described earlier:

1. The class should extend `JApplet` instead of `CloseableFrame`:

```
public class GUITemperatureConverter2 extends JApplet
                             implements ActionListener
```

2. Replace `main()` with a non-static `init()` method:

```
public void init(String [] args)
{ . . .
}
```

3. Remove the call to `setTitle()`.
4. Set the dimensions of the applet frame in the HTML file:

```
<APPLET CODE="GUITemperatureConverter2.class"
   WIDTH=300 HEIGHT=60 </APPLET>
```

This will produce frames like the following:

The CD that accompanies this text and the book's website—see the preface for the URL—contain the complete applet code.

Conclusions

The `TemperatureConverter` application in Chapter 6 and the `GUITemperatureConverter` application in Figure 7.7 both accomplish basically the same thing: each reads a temperature and then displays the corresponding temperatures in different scales. These two programs in essence provide different user interfaces for our `Temperature` class. More precisely, the `TemperatureConverter` program provides a *textual user interface* for class `Temperature` while the `GUITemperatureConverter` program provides a *graphical user interface*.

In a similar fashion, the `Big10Mascots` application of Figure 7.2 and the `GUIBig10Mascots` of Figure 7.7 both do the same thing: These two programs thus represent different user interfaces to the functionality of the `Big10` class.

These examples illustrate an important design principle:

> *Objects and their user interfaces should be kept separate.*

Following this principle allows different user interfaces (e.g., `TemperatureConverter` and `GUITemperatureConverter`) to be defined for the same underlying object (e.g., a `Temperature`). A simple class design test is whether or not the class provides sufficient functionality for different user interfaces to interact with its objects.

✔ Quick Quiz 7.5

1. Mouse clicks, keystrokes, and other occurrence that are of interest to an executing program are examples of _____.

2. GUI programming is an example of _____-driven programming.

3. (True or false) The repetitive behavior is provided by the underlying Java system.

4. Java's system for dealing with events is called the _____ model.

5. An event source is said to _____ events.

6. What are the three steps used in building an event-driven GUI program?

7. A class contains method definitions, but an interface contains only method _____.

8. What must a class that implements an interface provide?

9. In Question 8, what happens if a class does not provide what is required?

10. Every Java graphical container has a(n) _____ that determines the appearance and layout of GUI components within that container.

11. A Swing window frame has a frame plus a number of _____. Graphical elements can be drawn on the _____.

12. When does a `JTextField` object generate an `ActionEvent`?

PART OF THE PICTURE: BOOLEAN LOGIC AND DIGITAL DESIGN

The *Part of the Picture: Introduction to Computer Organization* section in Chapter 0 and the *Part of the Picture: Computer Architecture* that follows this section describe one of a computer's components, the CPU (central processing unit). The arithmetic operations performed by the CPU must be carried out using special electrical circuits called **logic circuits** that are used to implement boolean (or digital) logic in hardware. In this section we investigate the design of such circuits, which is one small part of the broader area of computer architecture.

EARLY WORK

The foundations of circuit design were laid in the early 1900s by the English mathematician George Boole, after whom the Java `boolean` type is named. Boole formalized several axioms of logic, resulting in an algebra for writing logical expressions, which have since come to be known as boolean expressions.

In Java syntax, some of the basic axioms of boolean logic are as follows:[7]

The Relational Laws

1a. `!(X == Y) ≡ (X != Y)`   1b. `!(X != Y) ≡ (X == Y)`
2a. `!(X < Y) ≡ (X >= Y)`   2b. `!(X >= Y) ≡ (X < Y)`
3a. `!(X > Y) ≡ (X <= Y)`   3b. `!(X <= Y) ≡ (X > Y)`

The Boolean Laws

4a. `X || false ≡ X`   4b. `X && false ≡ false`
5a. `X || true ≡ true`   5b. `X && true ≡ X`

Idempotent Laws

6a. `X || X ≡ X`   6b. `X && X ≡ X`

Involution Law

7a. `!(!X) ≡ X`

Laws of Complementarity

8a. `X || (!X) ≡ true`   8b. `X && (!X) ≡ false`

Commutative Laws

9a. `X || Y ≡ Y || X`   9b. `X && Y ≡ Y && X`

Associative Laws

10a. `(X || Y) || Z ≡ X || (Y || Z)`   10b. `(X && Y) && Z ≡ X&& (Y && Z)`

Distributive Laws

11a. `X && (Y || Z) ≡ (X && Y)||(X && Z)`   11b. `X || (Y && Z) ≡ (X || Y) && (X || Z)`

Simplification Theorems

12a. `(X && Y) || (X && !Y) ≡ X`   12b. `(X || Y) && (X || !Y) ≡ X`
13a. `X || (X && Y) ≡ X`   13b. `X && (X || Y) ≡ X`
14a. `(X || !Y) && Y ≡ X && Y`   14b. `(X && !Y) || Y ≡ X || Y`

DeMorgan's Laws

15a. `!(X && Y) ≡ !X || !Y`   15b. `!(X || Y) ≡ !X && !Y`

[7] In the statements of these laws, the symbol ≡ denotes *is equivalent to.* A statement of the form $p \equiv q$ means that p and q always have the same truth values (true or false).

It is especially useful for programmers to know DeMorgan's Laws because they can simplify complicated boolean expressions. As a simple illustration, suppose that `done` and `error` are `boolean` variables, and consider the following `if` statement:

```
if (!done && !error)
    // . . . do something . . .
```

DeMorgan's law tells us that the boolean expression involving two negated values,

```
!done && !error
```

can be simplified to

```
!(done || error)
```

The original expression contained 2 NOT operations and 1 AND operation, but the simplified expression contains only 1 NOT operation and 1 OR operation—1 less operation. Applying DeMorgan's law repeatedly to a boolean expression of the form

$$!b_1 \text{ \&\& } !b_2 \text{ \&\& } \cdots \text{ \&\& } !b_n$$

containing n NOTs and $n - 1$ ANDs, gives the simpler expression

$$!(b_1 \text{ || } b_2 \text{ || } \cdots \text{ || } b_n)$$

containing only 1 NOT and $n - 1$ ORs. The complexity of the expression is thus reduced by $n - 1$ NOT operations, which can result in a significant increase in performance.

DIGITAL CIRCUITS

With the invention of the digital computer in the late 1930s, the work of Boole moved from obscurity to prominence. The axioms and theorems of his boolean algebra became extremely important as mathematicians, engineers, and physicists sought to build the arithmetic and logic circuitry of the early computers. These circuits utilize three basic electronic components: the **AND gate,** the **OR gate,** and the **NOT gate** or **inverter,** whose symbols are as follows:

ANDgate   ORgate   inverter

The inputs to these gates are electrical voltages, where a voltage that exceeds a certain threshold value is interpreted as 1 (i.e., true), and a voltage below that threshold is interpreted as 0 (i.e., false). In the case of an AND gate, a 1 is produced only when there are 1s on both input lines. An OR gate produces a 1 only when there is a 1 on at least one of the input lines. The output of a NOT gate is the opposite of its input. Because these three components behave in the same fashion as the AND, OR, and NOT operators from boolean algebra, a circuit can be constructed to represent any boolean expression, and boolean expressions can be used to design circuits.

CIRCUIT DESIGN: A BINARY HALF-ADDER

To illustrate, consider the problem of adding two binary digits `digit1` and `digit2`. The truth table below summarizes the behavior of the addition operation, which produces two results—a `sum` bit and a `carry` bit:

digit1	digit2	carry	sum
0	0	0	0
0	1	0	1
1	0	0	1
1	1	1	0

There are two important things to note:

1. The `carry` output is 1 (`true`) only when `digit1` and `digit2` are both 1 (`true`)
2. The `sum` output is 1 (`true`) only when `digit1` is 0 (`false`) and `digit2` is 1 (`true`), or when `digit1` is 1 (`true`) and `digit2` is 0 (`false`)

It is easy to see that we can represent these outputs by the following pair of boolean expressions:

```
boolean carry = digit1 && digit2,
        sum = (!digit1 && digit2) || (digit1 && !digit2);
```

The expression for `sum` has the form `(!A && B) || (A && !B)` and can be simplified by applying the axioms from boolean logic as follows:

<u>(!A && B)</u> || <u>(A && !B)</u>
　　　⇓　　　　　(Apply 9a to switch two operands of ||)
<u>(A && !B)</u> || <u>(!A && B)</u>
　　　⇓　　　　　(Apply 11b with X = (A && !B), Y = !A, Z = B)
((A && !B) || !A) && (<u>(A && !B) || B</u>))
　　　⇓　　　　　(Apply 14b to second expression with X = A and Y = B)
((A && !B) || !A) && (A || B)
　　　⇓　　　　　(Apply 9a to switch two operands of first &&)
(<u>(!B && A) || !A</u>) && (A || B)
　　　⇓　　　　　(Apply 14b to first expression with X = !B and Y = !A)

```
(!B || !A) && (A || B)
            ⇓              (Apply 15a to first || expression with X = B and Y
                            = A)
!(B && A) && (A || B)
            ⇓              (Apply 9a to switch two operands of first &&)
!(A && B) && (A || B)
            ⇓              (Apply 9a to switch two operands of second &&)
(A || B) && !(A && B)
```

This means that the boolean expression for sum can be rewritten as

```
sum = (digit1 || digit2) && !(digit1 && digit2);
```

which has one less NOT operation than the original expression.

This may seem like a lot of work for not much improvement. On the contrary, this simplification means that a circuit for this expression will require one less inverter than a circuit for the original expression and will therefore be less expensive to manufacture. If the adder on a CPU combines 32 of these circuits to add 32 bits simultaneously, then 32 fewer inverters are required per CPU. When those CPUs are mass-produced, this circuit may be manufactured millions of times for a total savings of millions of times the cost of an inverter!

Using the boolean expressions

```
boolean carry = digit1 && digit2,
        sum = (digit1 || digit2) && !(digit1 && digit2);
```

for sum and carry, we can design the following circuit, called a **binary half-adder,** that adds two binary digits:

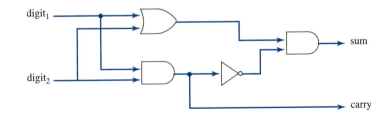

It accepts two inputs, digit1 and digit2, and produces two outputs, sum and carry.

Once a boolean expression is found to represent a circuit, it is easy to build a simple class to represent the circuit and check the correctness of the expression. To illustrate, Figure 7.9 provides a software representation of a binary half-adder.

In addition to the constructor and some utility methods, the class provides mutator methods to set a half-adder's two inputs, plus accessor methods to retrieve its sum and carry values. The highlighted code in the `sum()` and `carry()` methods encode the boolean expressions derived above.

FIGURE 7.9   A BINARY HALF-ADDER CLASS

```
/** HalfAdder.java represents a binary half-adder.  It calculates the
 *  output from boolean expressions that represent the logical circuit
 *  for a binary half-adder.
 */

class HalfAdder

/** Default constructor.

 *  Postcondition: attribute variables myInput1 and myInput2 are
 *                 set to false
 */
public HalfAdder()
{
  myInput1 = myInput2 = false;
}

/** setInput1() and setInput2() set the two binary inputs of the half-adder.
 *  Return:          digit, an integer
 *  Precondition:    digit is a binary digit (0 or 1)
 *  Postcondition: attribute variables myInput1 and myInput2 are
 *                 set to this bit.
 */

public void setInput1(int digit)
{
  if (isBinary(digit))

    myInput1 = toBoolean(digit);

  else
  {
    System.err.println("setInput1(int): non-binary input: " + digit);
    System.exit(1);
  }
}

public void setInput2(int digit)
{
  if (isBinary(digit))
    myInput2 = toBoolean(digit);
  else
  {
    System.err.println("setInput2(int): non-binary input: " + digit);
    System.exit(1);
  }
}

/** toString() converts outputs of binary half-adder to a String
 *      suitable for output to the screen.
 *  Return:  string containing sum and carry bits
 */

public String toString()
{
  return " sum: " + sum() + ", carry: " + carry();
}
```

```
/** sum() and carry() compute the outputs of binary half-adder.
 *  Return:  sum and carry bits
 */

public int sum()
{
  return toInt( (myInput1 || myInput2) && !(myInput1 && myInput2) );
}

public int carry()
{
  return toInt( myInput1 && myInput2 );
}

// -- Utility methods:
/** isBinary() checks if digit is a binary digit (0 or 1).
 *  Receive:  digit, an int
 *  Return:   true if digit is a bit, false otherwise
 */
 public static boolean isBinary(int digit)
 {
   return (digit == 0 || digit == 1);
 }

/** toBoolean() converts a bit to boolean value (0 -> false, 1 -> true)
 *  Receive:  bit, an int
 *  Return:   true if bit is 1, false if bit is 0
 */
public static boolean toBoolean(int digit)
{
  return !(digit == 0);
}
/** toInt() converts boolean value to a bit (false -> 0, true -> 1).
 *  Receive: input, a boolean
 *  Return:  1 if input it true, false if it is 0
 */
public static int toInt(boolean input)
{
  return ((input == true) ? 1 : 0);
}
private boolean myInput1,      // boolean representation, to ease
                myInput2;      //  the sum and carry computations
}
```

To simulate the use of a half-adder, we can write the program shown in Figure 7.10.

FIGURE 7.10   TESTING A BINARY HALF-ADDER

```
//HalfAdderTester.java

importHalfAdder;
import ann.easyio.*;                   // Keyboard, Screen
```

```
class HalfAdderTester extends Object
{
 public static void main(String [] args)
 { Screen theScreen = new Screen();
   Keyboard theKeyboard = new Keyboard();
   HalfAdder hAdder = new HalfAdder();
   intinput1,input2;
   theScreen.println("Binary Half-Adder Test Program\n");
   for(;;)
   {
      theScreen.print("\nEnter two binary digits (-1 to quit): ");
      input1=theKeyboard.readInt();
      input2 = theKeyboard.readInt();

      if (input1 < 0 || input2 < 0) break;

      hAdder.setInput1(input1); hAdder.setInput2(input2);
      theScreen.println("(carry,sum) = " + hAdder.carry()+  hAdder.sum()
   }
  }
 }
}
```

Sample runs:

```
BinaryHalf-AdderTestProgram

Enter two binary digits (-1 to quit): 0 0
(carry,sum)=00


Enter two binary digits (-1 to quit): 0 1
(carry,sum)=01


Enter two binary digits (-1 to quit): 1 0
(carry,sum)=01

Enter two binary digits (-1 to quit): 1 1
(carry,sum)=10

Enter two binary digits (-1 to quit): -1 0
```

A binary *full-adder* for adding two binary digits and a carry bit, and an *adder* for numbers having more than one binary digit, are described in the Programming Problems at the end of the chapter.

PART OF THE PICTURE: COMPUTER ARCHITECTURE

by William Stallings

At a top level, a computer consists of processor, memory, and I/O components, with one or more modules of each type. These components are interconnected in some fashion to achieve the main function of the computer, which is to execute programs. Thus, there are four main structural elements:

- **Processor:** Controls the operation of the computer and performs its data processing functions. When there is only one processor, it is often referred to as the central processing unit (CPU).
- **Main Memory:** Stores data and programs. This memory is typically volatile; it is also referred to as real memory or primary memory.
- **I/O Modules:** Move data between the computer and its external environment. The external environment consists of a variety of external devices, including secondary memory devices, communications equipment, and printers.
- **System Interconnection:** Some structure and mechanisms that provide for communication among processors, main memory, and I/O modules.

Figure 7.11 depicts these top-level components. The processor controls operations. One of its functions is to exchange data with memory. For this purpose, it typically makes use of two internal (to the processor) registers: a **memory address register (MAR),** which specifies the address in memory for the next read or write; and a **memory buffer register (MBR),** which contains the data to be written into memory or which receives the data read from memory. Similarly, an **I/O address register (I/OAR)** specifies a particular I/O device. An **I/O buffer register (I/OBR)** is used for the exchange of data between an I/O module and the processor.

A **memory module** consists of a set of locations, defined by sequentially numbered addresses. Each location contains a binary number that can be interpreted as either an instruction or data. An I/O module transfers data from external devices to processor and memory, and vice versa. It contains internal buffers for temporarily holding this data until it can be sent on.

Figure 7.11   Computer Components: Top-Level View

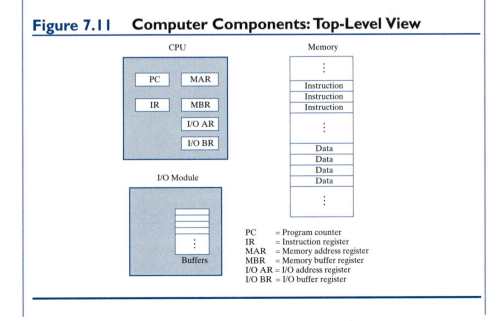

PC   = Program counter
IR   = Instruction register
MAR   = Memory address register
MBR   = Memory buffer register
I/O AR = I/O address register
I/O BR = I/O buffer register

PROCESSOR REGISTERS

Within the processor, there is a set of registers that provide a level of memory that is faster and smaller than main memory. The registers in the processor serve two functions:

- **User-visible registers:** These enable the assembly-language programmer to minimize main memory references by optimizing the use of registers. For high-level languages, an optimizing compiler will attempt to make intelligent choices of which variables to assign to registers and which to main memory locations. Some high-level languages, such as C and C++, allow the programmer to suggest to the compiler which variables should be held in registers.

- **Control and status registers:** These are used by the processor to control the operation of the processor and by privileged, operating-system routines to control the execution of programs.

There is not a clean separation of registers into these two categories. For example, on some machines the program counter is user visible, but on many it is not. For purposes of the following discussion, however, it is convenient to use these categories.

User-Visible Registers. A user-visible register is one that may be referenced by means of the machine language that the processor executes and that is generally available to all programs, including application programs as well as system programs. The following types of registers are typically available: data, address, and condition codes.

Data registers can be assigned to a variety of functions by the programmer. In some cases, they are general purpose in nature and can be used with any machine instruction that performs operations on data. Often, however, there are restrictions. For example, there may be dedicated registers for floating-point operations.

Address registers contain main memory addresses of data and instructions, or they contain a portion of the address that is used in the calculation of the complete address. These registers may themselves be somewhat general purpose, or they may be devoted to a particular addressing mode.

Examples include:

- **Index register:** Indexed addressing is a common mode of addressing that involves adding an index to a base value to get the effective address.

- **Segment pointer:** With segmented addressing, memory is divided into variable-length blocks of words called segments. A memory reference consists of a reference to a particular segment and an offset within the segment; this mode of addressing is important in memory management. In this mode of addressing, a register is used to hold the address of the base (starting location) of the segment. There may be multiple registers; for example, one for the operating system (i.e., when operating-system code is executing on the processor) and one for the currently executing application.

❑ **Stack pointer:** If there is user-visible stack addressing, then typically the stack is in main memory and there is a dedicated register that points to the top of the stack. This allows the use of instructions that contain no address field, such as push and pop.

A final category of registers, which is at least partially visible to the user, holds **condition codes** (also referred to as flags). Condition codes are bits set by the processor hardware as the result of operations. For example, an arithmetic operation may produce a positive, negative, zero, or overflow result. In addition to the result itself being stored in a register or memory, a condition code is also set. The code may subsequently be tested as part of a conditional branch operation. Condition code bits are collected into one or more registers. Usually, they form part of a control register. Generally, machine instructions allow these bits to be read by implicit reference, but they cannot be altered by the programmer.

Control and Status Registers. There are a variety of processor registers that are employed to control the operation of the processor. Most of these, on most machines, are not visible to the user. Some of them may be accessible by machine instructions executed in a control or operating-system mode.

Of course, different machines will have different register organizations and use different terminology. We will list common register types, with a brief description.

In addition to the MAR, MBR, IOAR, and IOBR registers mentioned earlier, the following are essential to instruction execution:

❑ Program counter (PC): Contains the address of an instruction to be fetched.
❑ Instruction register (IR): Contains the instruction most recently fetched.

All processor designs also include a register or set of registers, often known as the **program status word (PSW),** which contains status information. The PSW typically contains condition codes plus other status information. Common fields and flags include the following:

❑ **Sign:** Contains the sign bit of the last arithmetic operation.
❑ **Zero:** Set when the result of an arithmetic operation is zero.
❑ **Carry:** Set if an operation resulted in a carry (addition) into or borrow (subtraction) out of a high-order bit. Used for multi-word arithmetic operations.
❑ **Equal:** Set if a logical compare result is equality.
❑ **Overflow:** Used to indicate arithmetic overflow.
❑ **Interrupt Enable/Disable:** Used to disable or enable interrupts. When interrupts are disabled, the processor ignores them. This is often desirable when the operating system is in the midst of dealing with another interrupt.

❑ **Supervisor:** Indicates whether the processor is executing in supervisor or user mode. Certain privileged instructions can be executed only in supervisor mode, and certain areas of memory can be accessed only in supervisor mode.

There are a number of other registers related to status and control that might be found in a particular processor design. In addition to the PSW, there may be a pointer to a block of memory containing additional status information. In machines using multiple types of interrupts, a set of registers may be provided, with one pointer to each interrupt-handling routine. If a stack is used to implement certain functions (e.g., procedure call), then a system stack pointer is needed. Memory management hardware requires dedicated registers. Finally, registers may be used in the control of I/O operations.

A number of factors go into the design of the control and status register organization. One key issue is operating system support. Certain types of control information are of specific utility to the operating system. If the processor designer has a functional understanding of the operating system to be used, then the register organization can to some extent be tailored to the operating system.

Another key design decision is the allocation of control information between registers and memory. It is common to dedicate the first (lowest) few hundred or thousand words of memory for control purposes. The designer must decide how much control information should be in more expensive, faster registers and how much in less expensive, slower main memory.

INSTRUCTION EXECUTION

The basic function performed by a computer is program execution. The program to be executed consists of a set of instructions stored in memory. The processor does the actual work by executing instructions specified in the program.

The simplest point of view is to consider instruction processing as consisting of two steps: The processor reads (fetches) instructions from memory one at a time, and executes each instruction. Program execution consists of repeating the process of instruction fetch and instruction execution. The instruction execution may involve several operations and depends on the nature of the instruction.

The processing required for a single instruction is called an instruction cycle. In simple terms, the instruction cycle consists of a fetch cycle, in which the processor reads an instruction from memory, and the execute cycle, in which the processor executes the instruction. This instruction cycle is performed repeatedly.

INSTRUCTION FETCH AND EXECUTE

At the beginning of each instruction cycle, the processor fetches an instruction from memory. In a typical processor, a register called the **program counter (PC)** is used to keep track of which instruction is to be fetched next. Unless told otherwise, the processor always increments the PC after each instruction fetch so that it will fetch the next instruction in sequence (i.e., the instruction located at the next higher memory address). So, for example, consider a computer in which each instruction occupies one 16-bit word of memory. Assume that the program counter is set to word location 300. The processor will next fetch the instruction at location 300. On succeeding instruction cycles, it will fetch instructions from locations 301, 302, 303, and so on. This sequence may be altered, as explained presently.

The fetched instruction is loaded into a register in the processor known as the **instruction register (IR).** The instruction is in the form of a binary code that specifies what action the processor is to take. The processor interprets the instruction and performs the required action. In general, these actions fall into four categories:

- ❑ **Processor-memory:** Data may be transferred from processor to memory or from memory to processor.

- ❑ **Processor-I/O:** Data may be transferred to or from a peripheral device by transferring between the processor and an I/O module.

- ❑ **Data processing:** The processor may perform some arithmetic or logic operation on data.

- ❑ **Control:** An instruction may specify that the sequence of execution be altered. For example, the processor may fetch an instruction from location 149, which specifies that the next instruction be from location 182. The processor will remember this fact by setting the program counter to 182. Thus, on the next fetch cycle, the instruction will be fetched from location 182 rather than 150.

Of course, an instruction's execution may involve a combination of these actions.

Let us consider a simple example using a hypothetical machine that includes the characteristics listed in Figure 7.12. The processor contains a single data register, called an **accumulator (AC).** Both instructions and data are 16 bits long. Thus it is convenient to organize memory using 16-bit locations, or words. The instruc-

Figure 7.12   Characteristics of a Hypothetical Machine

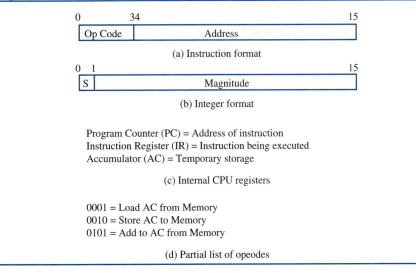

0   34   15

Op Code	Address

(a) Instruction format

0   1   15

S	Magnitude

(b) Integer format

Program Counter (PC) = Address of instruction
Instruction Register (IR) = Instruction being executed
Accumulator (AC) = Temporary storage

(c) Internal CPU registers

0001 = Load AC from Memory
0010 = Store AC to Memory
0101 = Add to AC from Memory

(d) Partial list of opeodes

tion format provides four bits for the opcode; thus there can be as many as $2^4 =$ 16 different opcodes, and up to $2^{12} = 4{,}096$ (4K) words of memory can be directly addressed.

Figure 7.13 illustrates a partial program execution, showing the relevant portions of memory and processor registers. The program fragment shown adds the contents of the memory word at address 940 to the contents of the memory word at address 941 and stores the result in the latter location. Three instructions, which can be described as three fetch and three execute cycles, are required:

1. The program counter (PC) contains 300, the address of the first instruction. This address is loaded into the instruction register (IR). Note that this process would involve the use of a memory address register (MAR) and a memory buffer register (MBR). For simplicity, these intermediate registers are ignored.

2. The first 4 bits in the IR indicate that the accumulator (AC) is to be loaded. The remaining 12 bits specify the address, which is 940.

3. After the load is complete, the PC is incremented and the next instruction is fetched.

4. The old contents of the AC and the contents of location 941 are added and the result is stored in the AC.

5. The PC is incremented and the next instruction is fetched.

6. The contents of the AC are stored in location 941.

Figure 7.13   Example of Program Execution

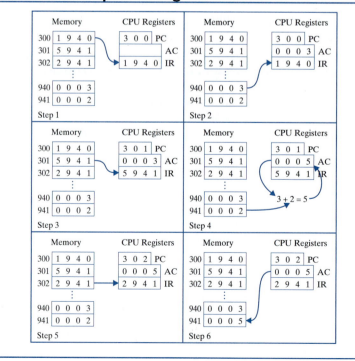

In this example, three instruction cycles, each consisting of a fetch cycle and an execute cycle, are needed to add the contents of location 940 to the contents of 941. With a more complex set of instructions, fewer cycles would be needed. Most modern processors include instructions that contain more than one address. Thus the execution cycle for a particular instruction may involve more than one reference to memory. Also, instead of memory references, an instruction may specify an I/O operation.

FUNCTION

An I/O module (e.g., a disk controller) can exchange data directly with the processor. Just as the processor can initiate a read or write with memory, designating the address of a specific location, the processor can also read data from or write data to an I/O module. In this latter case, the processor identifies a specific device that is controlled by a particular I/O module. Thus, an instruction sequence similar in form to that of Figure 7.13 could occur, with I/O instructions rather than memory-referencing instructions.

In some cases, it is desirable to allow I/O exchanges to occur directly with memory. In such a case, the processor grants to an I/O module the authority to read from or write to memory, so that the I/O-memory transfer can occur without tying up the processor. During such a transfer, the I/O module issues read or write commands to memory, relieving the processor of responsibility for the exchange. This operation is known as **direct memory access (DMA).**

THE MEMORY HIERARCHY

The design constraints on a computer's memory can be summed up by three questions: How much? How fast? How expensive?

The question of how much is somewhat open-ended. If the capacity is there, applications will likely be developed to use it. The question of how fast is, in a sense, easier to answer. To achieve greatest performance, the memory must be able to keep up with the processor. That is, as the processor is executing instructions, we would not want it to have to pause waiting for instructions or operands. The final question must also be considered. For a practical system, the cost of memory must be reasonable in relationship to other components.

As might be expected, there is a tradeoff among the three key characteristics of memory: namely cost, capacity, and access time. At any given time, a variety of technologies are used to implement memory systems. Across this spectrum of technologies, the following relationships hold:

- ❏ Smaller access time, greater cost per bit
- ❏ Greater capacity, smaller cost per bit
- ❏ Greater capacity, greater access time

The dilemma facing the designer is clear. The designer would like to use memory technologies that provide for large-capacity memory, both because the capacity is needed and because the cost per bit is low. However, to meet performance requirements, the designer needs to use expensive, relatively lower-capacity memories with fast access times.

The way out of this dilemma is not to rely on a single memory component or technology, but to employ a **memory hierarchy.** A traditional hierarchy is illustrated in Figure 7.14. As one goes down the hierarchy, the following occur:

Figure 7.14   The Memory Hierarchy

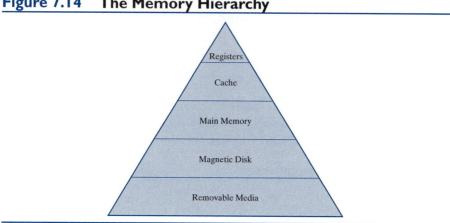

(a) Decreasing cost/bit

(b) Increasing capacity

(c) Increasing access time

(d) Decreasing frequency of access of the memory by the processor

Thus, smaller, more expensive, faster memories are supplemented by larger, cheaper, slower memories. By employing a variety of technologies, a spectrum of memory systems exist that satisfy conditions (a) through (c). Fortunately, condition (d) is also generally valid.

The basis for the validity of condition (d) is a principle known as locality of reference. During the course of execution of a program, memory references by the processor, for both instructions and data, tend to cluster. Programs typically contain a number of iterative loops and subroutines. Once a loop or subroutine is entered, there are repeated references to a small set of instructions. Similarly, operations on tables and arrays involve access to a clustered set of data words. Over a long period of time, the clusters in use change, but over a short period of time, the processor is primarily working with fixed clusters of memory references.

Accordingly, it is possible to organize data across the hierarchy such that the percentage of accesses to each successively lower level is substantially less than that of the level above. Consider a simple two-level memory. Let Level 2 memory contain all program instructions and data. The current clusters can be temporarily placed in Level 1. From time to time, one of the clusters in Level 1 will have to be swapped back to Level 2 to make room for a new cluster coming in to Level 1. On average, however, most references will be to instructions and data contained in Level 1.

This principle can be applied across more than two levels of memory. Consider the hierarchy shown in Figure 7.14. The fastest, smallest, and most expensive type of memory consists of the registers internal to the processor. Typically, a processor will contain a few dozen such registers, although some machines contain hundreds of registers. Skipping down two levels, main memory, also referred to as real memory, is the principal internal memory system of the computer. Each location in main memory has a unique address, and most machine instructions refer to one or more main memory addresses. Main memory is usually extended with a higher-speed, smaller cache. The cache is not usually visible to the programmer or, indeed, to the processor. It is a device for staging the movement of data between main memory and processor registers to improve performance.

The three forms of memory just described are, typically, volatile and employ semiconductor technology. The use of three levels exploits the fact that semiconductor memory comes in a variety of types, which differ in speed and cost. Data are stored more permanently on external mass storage devices, of which the most common are hard disk and removable media, such as removable disk, tape, and optical storage. External, nonvolatile memory is also referred to as secondary or auxiliary memory. These are used to store program and data files and are usually visible to the programmer only in terms of files and records, as opposed to individual bytes or words. Disk is also used to provide an extension to main memory known as virtual storage or virtual memory.

INPUT/OUTPUT ORGANIZATION

In addition to one or more processors and a set of memory modules, the third key element of a computer system is a set of I/O modules. Each module interfaces to the system bus or other interconnection structure and controls one or more external devices. An I/O module is not simply mechanical connectors that wire a device into the system bus. Rather, the I/O module contains some "intelligence," that is, it contains logic for controlling the flow of data between the external device and the bus.

An I/O module has two major functions:

- ❑ Interface to the processor and memory via the system bus or other interconnection structure.
- ❑ Interface to one or more external devices by tailored data links.

I/O MODULE FUNCTION

The major functions or requirements for an I/O module fall into the following categories:

- ❑ Control and timing
- ❑ Communication with processor
- ❑ Communication with external device
- ❑ Data buffering
- ❑ Error detection

During any period of time, the processor may communicate with one or more external devices in unpredictable patterns, depending on the program's need for

I/O. The internal resources, such as main memory and the system bus, must be shared among a number of activities, including I/O. Thus, the I/O function includes a **control and timing** requirement, to coordinate the flow of traffic between internal resources and external devices. For example, the control of the transfer of data from an external device to the processor might involve the following sequence of steps:

1. The processor interrogates the I/O module to check the status of the attached device.
2. The I/O module returns the device status.
3. If the device is operational and ready to transmit, the processor requests the transfer of data, by means of a command to the I/O module.
4. The I/O module obtains a unit of data (e.g., 8 or 16 bits) from the external device.
5. The data are transferred from the I/O module to the processor.

If the system employs a bus, then each of the interactions between the processor and the I/O module involves one or more bus events.

The preceding simplified scenario also illustrates that the I/O module must have the capability to engage in **communication with the processor** and with the external device. Communication with the processor involves:

❑ **Command decoding:** The I/O module accepts commands from the processor. These commands are generally sent as signals on the control bus. For example, an I/O module for a disk drive might accept the following commands: READ SECTOR, WRITE SECTOR, SEEK track number, and SCAN record ID. The latter two commands each include a parameter that is sent on the data bus.

❑ **Data:** Data are exchanged between the processor and the I/O module over the data bus.

❑ **Status reporting:** Because peripherals are so slow, it is important to know the status of the I/O module. For example, if an I/O module is asked to send data to the processor (read), it may not be ready to do so because it is still working on the previous command. This fact can be reported with a status signal. Common status signals are BUSY and READY. There may also be signals to report various error conditions.

❑ **Address recognition:** Just as each word of memory has an address, so does each I/O device. Thus, an I/O module must recognize one unique address for each peripheral it controls.

On the other side, the I/O module must be able to communicate with external devices. This communication also involves commands, status information, and data.

An essential task of an I/O module is data buffering. Whereas the transfer rate into and out of main memory or the processor is quite high, the rate is orders of magnitude lower for most peripheral devices. Data coming from main memory are sent to an I/O module in a rapid burst. The data are buffered in the I/O module and then sent to the external device at its data rate. In the opposite direction, data are buffered so as not to tie up the memory in a slow transfer operation. Thus, the I/O module must be able to operate at both device and memory speeds.

Finally, an I/O module is often responsible for error detection and for subsequently reporting errors to the processor. One class of errors includes mechanical and electrical malfunctions reported by the device (e.g., paper jam, bad disk track). Another class consists of unintentional changes to the bit pattern as it is transmitted from device to I/O module. Some form of error-detecting code is often used to detect transmission errors. A common example is the use of a parity bit on each character of data. For example, the ASCII character occupies 7 bits of a byte. The eighth bit is set so that the total number of 1s in the byte is even (even parity) or odd (odd parity). When a byte is received, the I/O module checks the parity to determine whether an error has occurred.

TO PROBE FURTHER

The topics in this section are covered in detail in *Computer Organization and Architecture: Designing for Performance, Fourth Edition,* by William Stallings (Prentice Hall, 1996). Links to web sites with further information can be found at `http://www.WilliamStallings.com/`.

CHAPTER SUMMARY

KEY TERMS AND NOTES

bound to an event source	fire
`break` statement	handle
condition	`implements`
conditional expression	`instanceof` operator
continuous behavior	interface
dangling else problem	layout manager
drop-through behavior	listener
dual-branch or `if-else` form	multi-branch `if` or `if-else-if` form
event	prototype
event delegation model	reference type
event-driven programming	single-branch or simple `if` form
event listener	`switch` statement
event-processing loop	ternary operation
event source	

◎ The multibranch if is a series of nested if statements written as one.

◎ In a nested if, each else is matched with the nearest preceding unmatched if.

◎ Relational operators compare the addresses in handles, not the objects to which they refer.

◎ To compare the *values* of objects instead of the *addresses* in their handles, use one of the comparison methods provided by their class—for example, equals() *and* equalsIgnoreCase() for the String class.

◎ To prevent drop-through behavior in a switch statement, remember to end the statement list in each case with a break or return statement (except for the final statement list, where it is not needed).

◎ Remember that the types of the expression of a switch and the constants in its case lists must be char, byte, short, or int. Note that they may not be real or String expressions.

◎ In deciding which statement to use to implement a selection, use a switch if all of the following hold and an if otherwise:

1. An equality (==) comparison is being performed.
2. The same expression is being compared in each condition.
3. The type of the expression being compared is char, byte, short, or int.

◎ Conditional expressions can be used in place of most if-else statements and sometimes provide a simpler alternative.

◎ GUI programs not only perform input, process, and output, but they must also respond to mouse clicks, mouse movements, and keystrokes from the keyboard, and react differently to different events.

◎ In Java, GUI applications need not define an event-processing loop because the underlying Java system provides repetitive behavior.

◎ To define an event source in a GUI, one must define an event-generating component, usually in the GUI's constructor.

◎ An interface only *specifies* the behavior of a class by telling what methods it must have; but a class implementing that interface must *define* that behavior by providing a definition of each method whose heading appears in that interface.

◎ Interface objects cannot be created using new. However, interface messages can be sent to instances (objects) of a class that implements that interface.

◎ A JTextField allows input of one line of text, but also fires ActionEvents.

◎ It is common practice in Java to have a GUI application itself serve as a listener for an event source.

◎ If you find that a GUI component isn't working, check that you have created and registered a listener for its events. If you haven't, events from that event source will be ignored.

◎ The following procedure can be used to build simple GUIs:

1. Create the GUI components (JLabels, JTextFields, etc.), their listener(s), and register the listener(s) with those that fire events.
2. Create a JPanel on which to mount the GUI components.
3. Tell the JPanel which layout manager you want it to use.
4. Mount the GUI components on the JPanel, usually using its add() method.
5. Make the JPanel the content pane of your window frame.

Documentation

REFERENCE ■ JTextField Summary

- ❏ A JTextField object generates an ActionEvent when the Enter key is pressed within the field.
- ❏ An ActionListener is the listener for ActionEvent objects.
- ❏ To be an ActionListener, an object's class must implement the ActionListener interface.
- ❏ A GUI can bind a listener to a JTextField object using the addActionListener() method.
- ❏ A JTextField object sends its listener the actionPerformed() message when *Enter* is pressed within the field.
- ❏ An ActionListener must provide a definition of actionPerformed() to handle an ActionEvent when it occurs.

■ SOME METHODS

Method	Description
JTextField()	Constructs a new empty text field
JTextArea(int columns)	Like the preceding, but with specified number of columns
JTextField(String text)	Constructs a new text area containing the specified text
JTextArea(String text, int columns)	Like the preceding, but with specified number of columns
void addActionListener (ActionListener l)	Adds the action listener l to the list of listeners that are to receive action events
int getColumns()	Returns the number of columns in the text field
protected String paramString()	Returns a string representation of this text field
void removeActionListener (ActionListener l)	Removes listener l from the list of listeners
void setColumns(n)	Sets the number of columns in the text area to n
Methods inherited from JTextComponent	
String getText()	Returns the text contained in this text field
void setText(String t)	Sets the text of this text field to t

■ High-Level Events and Listeners

The following table lists some of the Swing GUI components, the events they fire, the listeners for such events, and the methods that must be overloaded by a listener. See the Java API documentation for more information. Each listener method has a single parameter whose type is the particular event associated with that listener. For example, `actionPerformed()` has a parameter of type `ActionEvent`, `itemStateChanged()` has a parameter of type `ItemEvent`, and so on.

SOME JAVA HIGH LEVEL EVENTS, SOURCES, AND LISTENERS

Source(s)	Fires event	Requires listener	Listener methods
`JTextField` `JButton` `JRadioButton` `JComboBox` `JMenuItem`[8]	`ActionEvent`	`ActionListener`	`actionPerformed()`
`JCheckBox`	`ItemEvent`	`ItemListener`	`itemStateChanged()`
`JList`	`ListSelection-Event`	`ListSelection-Listener`	`valueChanged()`
`JSlider`	`ChangeEvent`	`ChangeEvent-Listener`	`stateChanged()`

■ Low-Level Events and Listeners

In addition to these sources of "high-level" events, Java also treats the user's mouse and keyboard as sources of "low-level" events. The following table presents some of Java's low-level events, the listener for each kind of event, and the methods that must be defined to implement the listener's interface. As before, each listener method has a single parameter whose type is the particular event associated with that listener.

SOME JAVA LOW-LEVEL EVENTS, SOURCES, AND LISTENERS

Source(s)	Event	Requires listener	Listener methods
Within a GUI Component: A keystroke	`KeyEvent`	`KeyListener`	`keyPressed()` `keyReleased()` `keyTyped()`
A mouse-button clicked	`MouseEvent`	`MouseListener`	`mousePressed()` `mouseReleased()`

---

[8] A `JMenuItem` fires `ActionEvents` and requires an `ActionListener`; a `JCheckBoxMenuItem` fires `ItemEvents` and requires an `ItemListener`; and a `JRadioButtonMenuItem` fires both kinds of events, and either kind of listener can be used to handle its events.

			mouseEntered()
			mouseExited()
			mouseClicked()
The mouse is moved	MouseEvent	MouseMotion-Listener	mouseDragged() mouseMoved()
	FocusEvent	FocusListener	focusGained() focusLost()
A window is manipulated	WindowEvent	WindowListener	windowClosing() windowOpened() windowIconified() windowDeiconified() windowClosed() windowActivated() windowDeactivated()

☞ PROGRAMMING POINTERS

PROGRAM STYLE AND DESIGN

In this text, we use the following conventions for formatting the selection statements considered in this chapter.

1. *For an* if *statement,* if (boolean_expression) *is on one line, with its statement indented on the next line. If there is an* else *clause,* else *is on a separate line, aligned with* if, *and its statement is indented on the next line. If the statements are compound, the curly braces are aligned with the* if *and* else *and the statements inside the block are indented.*

```
if (boolean_expression)
    statement₁
else
    statement₂

if (boolean_expression)
{
    statement₁
       .  .  .
    statementₖ
}
else
{
    statementₖ₊₁
       .  .  .
    statementₙ
}
```

An exception is made when the if-else-if *form is used to implement a multialternative selection structure. In this case the format used is*

```
if (boolean_expression₁)
    statement₁
```

```
else if (boolean_expression₂)
    statement₂
        .
        .
        .
else if (boolean_expressionₙ)
    statementₙ
else
    statementₙ₊₁
```

2. *For a* switch *statement,* switch (expression) *is on one line, with its curly braces aligned and on separate lines; each case list is indented within the curly braces; and each statement list and* break *or* return *statement is indented past its particular case list.*

```
switch (expression)
{
    case_list₁:  statement_list₁
                 break;                  // or return
    case_list₂:  statement_list₂
                 break;                  // or return
                     .
                     .
                     .
    case_listₙ:  statement_listₙ
                 break;                  // or return
    default:     statement_listₙ₊₁
}
```

Alternatively, each statement_listᵢ may be positioned on the line following case_listᵢ.

3. *Program defensively by using the* if *statement to test for illegal values.* For an example, see the first if statement in the method displayGrade() in the next programming pointer.

4. *Multialternative selection constructs can be implemented more efficiently with an* if-else-if *construct than with a sequence of separate* if *statements.* For example, consider the method

```
static public void displayGrade(int score)
{
    if (score < 0 || score > 100)
        theScreen.println(score + " is not a valid score.");
    if (score >= 90) && (score <= 100))
        theScreen.println('A');
    if ((score >= 80) && (score < 90))
        theScreen.println('B');
    if ((score >= 70) && (score < 80))
        theScreen.println('C');
    if ((score >= 60) && (score < 70))
        theScreen.println('D');
    if (score < 60)
        theScreen.println('F');
}
```

Here, all the `if` statements are executed for each score processed and 5 of the boolean expressions are compound expressions, so that a total of 16 operations are performed, regardless of the score being processed. By contrast, for the method

```
static public void displayGrade(int score)
{
    if (score < 0 || score > 100)
        theScreen.println(score + " is not a valid score.");
    else if (score >= 90)
        theScreen.println('A');
    else if (score >= 80)
        theScreen.println('B');
    else if (score >= 70)
        theScreen.println('C');
    else if (score >= 60)
        theScreen.println('C');
    else
        theScreen.println('F');
}
```

most of the boolean expressions are simple, and not all of them are evaluated for each score, so that only 3 to 7 operations are performed, depending on the score being processed.

5. *Multialternative selection statements of the form*

```
if (expression == constant₁)
    statement₁
else if (expression == constant₂)
    statement₂

    .
    .
    .

else if (expression == constantₙ)
    statementₙ
else
    statementₙ₊₁
```

where the type of `expression` *and each* `constantᵢ` *is* `char, byte, short,` *or* `int, are usually implemented more efficiently using a* `switch` *statement. For example, we might implement* `displayGrade()` *even more efficiently as follows:*

```
static public void displayGrade(int score)
{
    switch (score / 10)
    {
        case 10: case 9: theScreen.println('A');
                         break;

        case 8:          theScreen.println('B');
                         break;

        case 7:          theScreen.println('C');
                         break;
```

```
      case 6:                 theScreen.println('D');
                              break;

      case 5: case 4:
      case 3: case 2:
      case 1: case 0:  theScreen.println('F');
                              break;

      default:                theScreen.println(score +
                              " is not a valid score.");

  }

}
```

This version of `displayGrade()` will perform the same number of operations regardless of the value of `score`.

A second advantage of the `switch` statement is that a problem solution implemented with a `switch` is often more readable than an equivalent solution implemented using an `if` statement. For example, consider the problem of classifying the value of a `char` variable ch as an arithmetic operator (+, −, *, /, %), a relational operator (<, >), an assignment operator (=), or a punctuation symbol (semicolon, or comma). Using a `switch` statement, we might write

```
switch (ch)
{
    case '+': case '-':
    case '*': case '/':
    case '%':               theScreen.println("Arithmetic operator)";
                            break;

    case '<': case '>': theScreen.println("Relational operator)";
                            break;

    case '=':               theScreen.println("Assignment operator)";
                            break;

    case ';': case ',': theScreen.println("Punctuation)";
                            break;

    default:                theScreen.println("identification of "
                            + ch + " is not supported.)";
}
```

which is more readable than an equivalent implementation using an `if` statement:

```
if ((ch == '+') || (ch == '-') || (ch == '*')
  || (ch == '/') || (ch == '%'))
    theScreen.println("Arithmetic operator)";
else if ((ch == '<') || (ch == '>'))
    theScreen.println("Relational operator)";
else if (ch == '=')
    theScreen.println("Assignment operator)";
else if ((ch == ';') || (ch == ','))
    theScreen.println("Punctuation)";
else
    theScreen.println("identification of "
                        + ch + " is not supported.)";
```

6. *In designing a GUI, show users only what they need to see.*

7. *A Java GUI application need not define an event-processing loop, because the repetitive behavior is provided by the underlying Java system.*

8. *Objects and their user interfaces should be kept separate.* This allows different user interfaces (UI)—e.g., a textual UI and a graphical UI—for the same underlying object.

WATCH

!

OUT

POTENTIAL PITFALLS

1. *A common programming error in an* `if` *statement is using an assignment operator (=) when an equality operator (==) is intended.*

2. *When real quantities that are algebraically equal are compared with* ==, *the result may be a false boolean expression, because most real numbers are not stored exactly.* For example, even though the two real expressions x * (1/x) and 1.0 are algebraically equal, the boolean expression x * (1/x) == 1.0 may be false for some real numbers x.

3. *Comparing reference-type expressions with relational operators (==, !=, . . .) compares addresses of objects and not the objects themselves.* Use a comparison method provided in the class to compare the objects.

4. *In a nested* `if` *statement, each* `else` *clause is matched with the nearest preceding unmatched* `if`. For example, consider the following statements, which are given without indentation:

```
if (x > 0)
if y > 0)
z = x + y;
else
z = x - y;
w = x * y * z;
```

With which `if` is the `else` associated? According to the rule just stated, these statements are executed as

```
if (x > 0)
    if (y > 0)
        z = x + y;
    else
        z = x - y;
w = x * y * z;
```

where the `else` clause matches the `if` statement containing the condition y > 0. Use indentation and alignment to show such associations.

5. *Each* `switch` *statement and block must contain matching curly braces.* A missing } can be very difficult to locate. In certain situations, the compiler may not find that a { is unmatched until it reaches the end of the file. In such cases, an error message such as

```
Error. . . : Compound statement missing } in method . . .
```

will be generated.

6. *The selector in a* `switch` *statement must be of type* `char`, `byte`, `short`, *or* `int`. In particular, the values of the selector in label lists

❑ May *not* be real constants, such as 1.5, -2.3, 3.414159 or 2.998E8; and

❑ May *not* be string constants such as "JACK", "QUEEN", or "KING".

7. *A class that implements an interface must provide a definition for each method whose heading appears in that interface or a compiler error will result.*

PROGRAMMING PROBLEMS

SECTION 7.2

1. Write a driver program to test the `oKToSpray()` method of Exercise 4.

2. Write a driver program to test the `creditApproved()` method of Exercise 5.

3. Write a driver program to test the leap-year method of Exercise 6.

4. Write a driver program to test the days-in-a-month method of Exercise 7.

5. Write a driver program to test the days-in-a-month method of Exercise 8.

6. Suppose that charges by a gas company are based on consumption according to the following table:

Gas Used	Rate
First 70 cubic meters	$5.00 minimum cost
Next 100 cubic meters	5.0¢ per cubic meter
Next 230 cubic meters	2.5¢ per cubic meter
Above 400 cubic meters	1.5¢ per cubic meter

Write a method that computes the charges for a given amount of gas usage. Use this method in a program in which the meter reading for the previous month and the current meter reading are entered, each a four-digit number and each representing cubic meters, and that then calculates and displays the amount of the bill. *Note:* The current reading may be less than the previous one because the meter "rolled over" from 9999 to 0000. For example, the previous reading may be 9897, and the current one may be 0103. Execute the program with the following pairs of meter readings: 3450, 3495; 8810, 8900; 9950, 0190; 1275, 1982; 9872, 0444.

7. Write a program that reads values for the coefficients A, B, C, D, E, and F of the equations

$$Ax + By = C$$

$$Dx + Ey = F$$

of two straight lines, and then determine whether the lines are parallel (their slopes are equal) or the lines intersect. If they intersect, determine whether the lines are perpendicular (the product of their slopes is equal to -1).

8. Write a program that reads the coordinates of three points and then determines whether they are collinear.

SECTIONS 7.3 & 7.4

9. Write a driver program to test the TV-channel method of Exercise 3.

10. Write a driver program to test the distance-cost method of Exercise 4.

11. Write a driver program to test the month-name method of Exercise 5.

12. Write a driver program to test the days-in-month method of Exercise 6.

13. Write a driver program to test the year-name method of Exercise 7.

14. Write a driver program to test the input method of Exercise 8.

15. Write a driver program to test the course-credits method of Exercise 9.

16. Locating avenues' addresses in mid-Manhattan is not easy; for example, the nearest cross street to 866 Third Avenue is 53rd Street, whereas the nearest cross street to 866 Second Avenue is 46th Street. To locate approximately the nearest numbered cross street for a given avenue address, the following algorithm can be used:

Cancel the last digit of the address, divide by 2, and add or subtract the number given in the following abbreviated table:

1st Ave.	Add 3
2nd Ave.	Add 3
3rd Ave.	Add 10
4th Ave.	Add 8
5th Ave. up to 200	Add 13
5th Ave. up to 400	Add 16
6th Ave. (Ave. of the Americas)	Subtract 12
7th Ave.	Add 12
8th Ave.	Add 10
10th Ave.	Add 14

Write a method that uses a switch statement to determine the number of the nearest cross street for a given address and avenue number according to the preceding algorithm. Then write a program to test your method.

17. A wholesale office supply company discounts the price of each of its products depending on the number of units bought and the price per unit. The discount increases as the number of units bought and/or the unit price increases. These discounts are given in the following table:

Number Bought	Unit Price (dollars)		
	0–10.00	10.01–100.00	100.01–
1–9	0%	2%	5%
10–19	5%	7%	9%
20–49	9%	15%	21%
50–99	14%	23%	32%
100–	21%	32%	43%

Write a method that calculates the percentage discount for a specified number of units and unit price. Use this method in a program that reads the number of units bought and the unit price and then calculates and displays the total full cost, the total amount of the discount, and the total discounted cost.

18. An airline vice president in charge of operations needs to determine whether the current estimates of flight times are accurate. Because there is a larger possibility of variations due to weather and air traffic in the longer flights, he allows a larger error in the time estimates for them. He compares an actual flight time with the estimated flight time and considers the estimate to be too large, acceptable, or too small, depending on the following table of acceptable error margins:

Estimated Flight Time in Minutes	Acceptable Error Margin in Minutes
0–29	1
30–59	2
60–89	3
90–119	4
120–179	6
180–239	8
240–359	13
360 or more	17

For example, if an estimated flight time is 106 minutes, the acceptable error margin is 4 minutes. Thus, the estimated flight time is too large if the actual flight time is less than 102 minutes, or the estimated flight time is too small if the actual flight time is greater than 110 minutes; otherwise, the estimate is acceptable. Write a method that uses a switch statement to determine the acceptable error for a given estimated flight time, according to this table. Use your method in a program that reads an estimated flight time and an actual flight time and then determines whether the estimated time is too large, acceptable, or too small. If the estimated flight time is too large or too small, the program should also print the amount of the overestimate or underestimate.

19. Build a class MetricConverter that contains a method convertLength() that receives a real value and two strings inUnits and outUnits, then converts a value given in inUnits to the equivalent metric value in outUnits and returns this value. The method should carry out the following conversions:

inUnits		outUnits
I	c	(inches to centimeters; 1 in = 2.54001 cm)
F	c	(feet to centimeters; 1 ft = 30.4801 cm)
F	m	(feet to meters; 1 ft = 0.304801 m)
Y	m	(yards to meters; 1 yd = 0.914402 m)
M	k	(miles to kilometers; 1 mi = 1.60935 km)

Also, write a driver program to test your method. What happens if you enter units other than those listed?

20. For the MetricConverter class in Problem 19, add a method convertWeight() that carries out the following conversions:

inUnits	outUnits	
O	g	(ounces to grams; 1 oz = 28.349527 g)
P	k	(pounds to kilograms; 1 lb = 0.453592 kg)

Also, modify the driver program from Problem 19 to test your method.

21. For the MetricConverter class in Problem 19, add a method convertVolume() that carries out the following conversions:

inUnits	outUnits	
P	1	(pints to liters; 1 pt = 0.473167 L)
Q	1	(quarts to liters; 1 qt = 0.94633 L)
G	1	(gallons to liters; 1 gal = 3.78541 L)

Also, modify the driver program from Problem 19 to test your method.

22. Write a menu-driven program to test the three methods of Problems 19–21. It should allow the user to select one of three options according to whether lengths, weights, or volumes are to be converted, read the value to be converted and the units, and then call the appropriate method to carry out the conversion.

SECTION 7.5

23. (a) Add a `university()` method to the class `Big10` from Section 7.1 that receives a university's mascot and returns the university's common name.

    (b) Now modify `GUIBig10Mascots` to display the university's common name if its mascot is entered in the "mascot" text field.

24. (a) Add a boolean method `isMember()` to the class `Big10` from Section 7.1 that receives a string and returns true if this string is the common name of a Big 10 university and returns false otherwise.

    (b) Now modify `GUIBig10Mascots` so that it only uses the `mascot()` method if `school` is a Big 10 university.

Part of the Picture: Boolean Logic and Digital Design

25. Add a method to the class `HalfAdder` in Figure 7.9 that sets both inputs at once. Also modify the driver program in Figure 7.10 to test your method.

26. A *binary full-adder* has three inputs: the two bits a and b being added, and a "carry-in" bit.

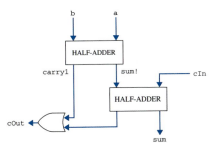

cIn (representing the carry bit that results from adding the bits to the right of a and b in two binary numbers). It can be constructed from two binary half-adders and an OR gate:

(a) Write boolean expressions for

    (i) `sum1` and `carry1` in terms of a and b

    (ii) `sum` and `carry` in terms of `cIn`, `sum1`, and `carry1`

(b) Build a class for this binary full-adder, and use it in a program to verify the results shown in the following table:

a	b	cIn	sum	carry
0	0	0	0	0
0	0	1	1	0
0	1	0	1	0
0	1	1	0	1
1	0	0	1	0
1	0	1	0	1
1	1	0	0	1
1	1	1	1	1

27. An *adder* to calculate binary sums of two-bit numbers

```
        a2 a1
    +   b2 b1
    ─────────
   cOut s2 s1
```

where `s1` and `s2` are the sum bits and `cOut` is the carry-out bit, can be constructed from a binary half-adder and a binary full-adder:

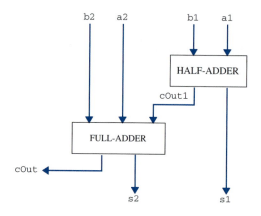

(a) Write logical expressions for

    (i) `s1` and `cOut1` in terms of `a1` and `b1`

    (ii) `s2` and `cOut` in terms of `a2`, `b2`, and `cOut1`

(b) Build a class for this adder and use it in a program to demonstrate that $00 + 00 = 000, 01 + 00 = 001, 01 + 01 = 010, 10 + 01 = 011, 10 + 10 = 100, 11 + 10 = 101$, and $11 + 11 = 110$.

REPETITION STRUCTURES

But what has been said once can always be repeated. *Zeno of Elea*

It's *deja vu* all over again. *Yogi Berra*

So, naturalists observe, a flea
Hath smaller fleas that on him prey;
And these have smaller fleas to bite 'em
and so proceed *ad infinitum*. *Jonathan Swift*

A rose is a rose is a rose. *Gertrude Stein*

Before one can understand recursion, one must understand recursion. *V. Orehck III (fictitious)*

■ Chapter Contents

Chapter Objectives

- Expand on the introduction to repetition in Chapter 4
- Examine for loops and Java's `for` statement in more detail
- Study while and do loops and the corresponding Java `while` and `do-while` statements
- Introduce recursion by describing it and illustrating it with several examples
- Take another look at event-driven programming and at how state diagrams are useful in designing such programs

- (Optional) Take a first look at the important area of computer science known as algorithm analysis

As we saw in Chapter 5, the three control mechanisms used in writing methods are **sequence, selection,** and **repetition.** In Chapter 7, we examined selection in detail, and in this chapter we take a closer look at the third control structure, repetition. We also introduce *recursion,* another control mechanism that is a form of repetition.

8.1 INTRODUCTORY EXAMPLE: THE PUNISHMENT OF GAUSS

Although sequence and selection are powerful control mechanisms, they are by themselves not powerful enough to solve all computing problems. In this section, we examine a problem that can be solved using repetition and review the most familiar Java repetition statement: the `for` statement.

THE SUMMATION PROBLEM

Our problem begins with an incident in the life of Carl Friedrich Gauss, one of the greatest mathematicians of all time. When Gauss was young, he attended a school in Brunswick, Germany. One day when the students were being particularly mischievous, their teacher asked them to sum the numbers from 1 to 100, expecting that this would keep them busy for quite awhile. However, Gauss produced the correct answer (5050) to the problem almost immediately, using a particularly clever approach described at the end of this chapter.

Although calculating the sum of the integers from 1 to 100 is not a particularly important computation, a generalization of this problem has many applications. The problem is to construct a method that, given a positive integer n, calculates the sum of the integers from 1 to n:

$$1 + 2 + \cdots + n$$

Thus, Gauss and his classmates were asked to compute a particular *instance* of the summation problem with $n = 100$.

 OBJECT-CENTERED DESIGN

BEHAVIOR. The method should receive the value n from its caller. It should compute the sum $1 + 2 + \cdots + n$ and return this value to its caller.

PROBLEM'S OBJECTS. Obviously, the value n is required if we are to compute the sum of the integers from 1 to n. We can thus list the following objects for this problem:

Description of problem's object	Type	Kind	Movement	Name
The limit value, n	integer	varying	received	n
$1 + 2 + \cdots + n$	integer	varying	returned	none

This allows us to specify the problem as follows: Write a method `summation()` that will

Receive: an integer value n

Return: $1 + 2 + \cdots + n$

This specification lets us build a stub for this method, which we will store in a `Formula` class:

```
public class Formula
{
   public static int summation(int n)
   {
   }
}
```

OPERATIONS. Because most of us do not have Gauss' ability, we will solve this problem using the approach probably used by his classmates (and intended by his teacher). We simply begin adding consecutive integers, keeping a running total as we proceed:

$$
\begin{array}{rl}
0 & \leftarrow \textit{running total} \\
+\ 1 & \leftarrow \textit{count} \\ \hline
1 & \leftarrow \textit{running total} \\
+\ 2 & \leftarrow \textit{count} \\ \hline
3 & \leftarrow \textit{running total} \\
+\ 3 & \leftarrow \textit{count} \\ \hline
6 & \leftarrow \textit{running total} \\
+\ 4 & \leftarrow \textit{count} \\ \hline
10 & \leftarrow \textit{running total} \\
+\ 5 & \leftarrow \textit{count} \\ \hline
15 & \leftarrow \textit{running total} \\
\vdots &
\end{array}
$$

This procedure consists of the following steps:

1. Initialize a *running total* to 0.
2. Initialize *count* to 1.
3. Loop through the following steps:
   a. Add *count* to the *running total.*
   b. Add 1 to count.

The steps in the loop must be repeated as long as the value of *count* is less than or equal to *n*. Thus, if *n* has the value 100, the loop must be repeated as long as *count* is less than or equal to 100:

$$\vdots$$

$$
\begin{array}{ll}
4950 & \leftarrow running\ total \\
+\ \ 100 & \leftarrow count \\
\hline
5050 & \leftarrow running\ total
\end{array}
$$

It is apparent that this procedure uses two previously unmentioned quantities— the *running total* and the *count*—and that when the procedure is finished, the value of the *running total* is the sum of the integers from 1 to *n* and is therefore the value to be returned by the method. We can thus amend our list of problem objects as follows:

Description of problem's object	Type	Kind	Movement	Name
The limit value, *n*	integer	varying	received	*n*
$1 + 2 + \cdots + n$	integer	varying	returned	*runningTotal*
A counter	integer	varying	none	*count*

The preceding description of how the problem can be solved suggests that the following operations are needed:

   i. Receive an integer (*n*)
   ii. Initialize an integer (*runningTotal* to zero, *count* to 1)
   iii. Add two integers (*count* and *runningTotal*) and store the result
   iv. Repeat the preceding step for each value of *count* in the range 1 through *n*
   v. Return an integer (*runningTotal*)

All of these can be implemented using operations and statements provided in Java. In particular, the repetition in (iv) can be implemented using a for loop as described in Chapter 5.

ALGORITHM. We organize these operations in the following algorithm:

Algorithm for the Summation Problem

1. Initialize *runningTotal* to 0.
2. For each value of *count* in the range 1 through *n*:

   Add *count* to *runningTotal.*
3. Return *runningTotal.*

CODING AND TESTING. Note that although the algorithm makes use of *running-Total* and *count*, these values are not received by the method from its caller, but they are required to solve the problem. It is important to remember that such objects should be declared as *local variables within the definition of the method* `summa-tion()`. By contrast, the specification tells us that *n* must be *received* from whatever method calls `summation()`, and so it is declared as a *parameter* of the method. Figure 8.1 presents an implementation of method `summation()`. In the next section we will review the `for` statement used to implement the loop in `summation()`.

FIGURE 8.1   METHOD `summation()`—FOR LOOP VERSION

```
/** summation(n) computes 1 +2 + ... + n, using a for loop.
 *   Receive:     n, an integer
 *   Precondition: n > 0.
 *   Return:      the value 1 + 2 + ... + n.
 */

public static int summation (int n)
{
   int runningTotal = 0;

   for (int count = 1; count <= n; count++)
      runningTotal += count;

   return runningTotal;
}
```

The driver program in Figure 8.2 illustrates how this method can be used to solve any instance of the summation problem.

FIGURE 8.2   DRIVER PROGRAM FOR `summation()`

```
// SummationTest.java is a simple driver program to test method sum().

//--- Insert definition of summation() here ---

class SummationTest extends Object
{
 public static void main(String [] args)
 {
    Screen theScreen = new Screen();
    Keyboard theKeyboard = new Keyboard();
    theScreen.print("To compute the sum of the integers from "
                + "1 through n,\n please enter a value for n: ");
    int n = theKeyboard.readInt();
    theScreen.println("--> 1 + ... + " + n + " = " + summation(n) );
 }
}
```

Sample runs:

```
To compute the sum of the integers from 1 through n,
  please enter a value for n: 5
--> 1 + ... + 5 = 15


To compute the sum of the integers from 1 through n,
  please enter a value for n: 100
--> 1 + ... + 100 = 5050
```

8.2   REPETITION: THE FOR LOOP REVISITED

Counting loops, or **counter-controlled loops,** are loops in which a set of statements is executed once for each value in a specified range:

> for each value of a *counter-variable* in a specified range:
>   *statement*

For example, our solution to the summation problem uses a counting loop, since it executes the statement

```
runningTotal += count;
```

once for each value of `count` in the range 1 through n.

Counting loops are used so frequently that almost all programming languages provide a special statement called a `for` **statement** to implement them, and this loop is therefore commonly called a **for loop.** We have seen the four components of the `for` statement before:

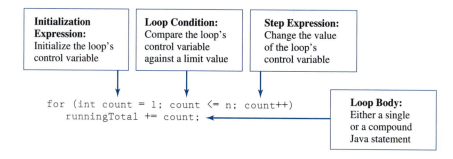

We have also seen that a trace table is a useful tool to trace the action of a loop (especially in debugging). For example, in the first sample run of Figure 8.2 where the value 5 is entered for n, the loop counts through the values 1 through 5, so that the body of the for loop is executed five times. The following table shows the values of the variables `count`, `n`, and `runningTotal` and the boolean expression that controls repetition as the method `summation()` executes:

count	n	count <= n	Action	runningTotal
1	5	true	Execute loop body	1
2	5	true	Execute loop body	3
3	5	true	Execute loop body	6
4	5	true	Execute loop body	10
5	5	true	Execute loop body	15
6	5	false	Terminate repetition	15

A similar trace table for the second sample run where n has the value 100 would show that the loop counts through the values 1 through 100, so that the loop body is executed 100 times.

In general, there are two common forms of `for` statements that implement counting loops: an ascending form, in which the loop control variable is incremented,

```
for (int control_variable = initial_value;
         control_variable <= limit_value;
         increment_expression)
    statement
```

and a descending form, in which the loop control variable is decremented:

```
for (int control_variable = initial_value;
         control_variable >= limit_value;
         decrement_expression)
    statement
```

The first form counts through an *ascending range,* and the second counts through a *descending range.*

To illustrate the first form, consider the `for` statement

```
for (int number = 1; number <= 10; number++)
    theScreen.println( "\t" + number + "\t"
                       + Math.pow(number, 2) );
```

Here, `number` is the control variable, the initial value is `1`, the limit value is `10`, and the step expression is `number++`. This for loop will execute the statement

```
theScreen.println( "\t" + number + "\t"
                   + Math.pow(number, 2) );
```

once for each value of `number` in the ascending range 1 through 10. On the first pass through the loop, `number` will have the value 1; on the second pass it will have the value 2, and so on until the final pass when `number` will have the value 10. Thus, the output produced will be:

```
1       1
2       4
3       9
4       16
5       25
6       36
7       49
8       64
9       81
10      100
```

By using an appropriate increment expression, a `for` statement can be used to step through a range of values in increments other than 1. For example, the `for` statement

```
for (int number = 1; number <= 100; number += 20)
    theScreen.println( "\t" + number + "\t"
                            + Math.pow(number, 2) );
```

uses the increment expression

```
number += 20
```

to count upwards by increments of 20, producing the output:

```
0       0
20      400
40      1600
60      3600
80      6400
100     10000
```

The second form of a for loop performs a decrement operation following each execution of the loop body. For example,

```
for (int number = 10; number > 5; number--)
    theScreen.println( "\t" + number + "\t"
                            + Math.pow(number, 2) );
```

will count downward from 10 to 6, producing the output:

```
10      100
9       81
8       64
7       49
6       36
```

Note that whereas the ascending form continues the repetition as long as the control variable is less than or equal to the limit value, the descending form is counting downwards, and so must continue the repetition as long as the control variable is *greater than* or equal to the limit value.

Nested Loops: Displaying a Multiplication Table

The statement that appears within a `for` statement may itself be a `for` statement; that is, one for loop may be *nested within* another for loop. As an example, Figure 8.3 presents a program that displays a multiplication table by calculating and displaying products of the form x `*` y for each x in the range 1 through `lastX` and each y in the range 1 through `lastY` (where `lastX` and `lastY` are arbitrary integers). The multiplication table is generated by using nested `for` statements:

```
for (int x = 1; x <= lastX; x++)
    for (int y = 1; y <= lastY; y++)
    {
        product = x * y;
        theScreen.println( x + " * " + y + " = " + product );
    }
```

The loop that has `x` as its control variable is referred to as the **outer loop,** and the loop that has `y` as its control variable is referred to as the **inner loop.**

FIGURE 8.3   PRINTING A MULTIPLICATION TABLE

```
/** MultiplicationTable.java displays a multiplication table.
 *  Input:    lastX and lastY, the largest numbers to be multiplied
 *  Output:   A list of products: 1*1, 1*2, ..., lastX * lastY
 */

import ann.easyio.*;

class MultiplicationTable
{
 public static void main(String [] args)
 {
   Screen theScreen = new Screen();
   Keyboard theKeyboard = new Keyboard();
   theScreen.print("To generate a multiplication table "
                   + "for the values 1*1 through x*y,\n"
                   + "please enter two integer limit values "
                   + "(one for x, one for y): ");

   int lastX = theKeyboard.readInt(), // the largest numbers being multipli
       lastY = theKeyboard.readInt(),
       product;                        // the product of the two numbers
   for (int x = 1; x <= lastX; x++)
     for (int y = 1; y <= lastY; y++)
     {
       product = x * y;
       theScreen.println( x + " * " + y + " = " + product );
     }
 }
}
```

Sample run:

```
To generate a multiplication table for the values 1*1 through x*y,
please enter two integer limit values (one for x, one for y): 3 4
1 * 1 = 1
1 * 2 = 2
1 * 3 = 3
1 * 4 = 4
2 * 1 = 2
2 * 2 = 4
2 * 3 = 6
2 * 4 = 8
3 * 1 = 3
3 * 2 = 6
3 * 3 = 9
3 * 4 = 12
```

In the sample run, `lastX` is given the value 3 and `lastY` is given the value 4. When control reaches the outer loop,

```
for (int x = 1; x <= lastX; x++)
```

its control variable `x` is assigned its initial value 1. The statement it controls (the inner loop),

```
for (int y = 1; y <= lastY; y++)
{
    product = x * y;
    theScreen.println( x + " * " + y + " = " + product );
}
```

is then executed. This inner loop counts through the values 1 through 4 and calculates and displays the first four products: 1 * 1, 1 * 2, 1 * 3, and 1 * 4. Control then passes from the inner loop to the increment expression of the outer loop, where the value of `x` is incremented to 2. The statement it controls (the inner loop) is then executed again. It again counts through the values 1 through 4 for `y`, but since the value of `x` is now 2, this pass calculates and displays the next four products: 2 * 1, 2 * 2, 2 * 3, and 2 * 4. The control variable `x` is then incremented to 3, so that when the inner loop is executed again, the last four products, 3 * 1, 3 * 2, 3 * 3, and 3 * 4, are produced. `x` is then incremented again (to 4), making the loop condition `x <= lastX` false, so that repetition stops. The compound statement

```
{
    product = x * y;
    theScreen.println( x + " * " + y + " = " + product );
}
```

is executed a total of 12 times, because the inner loop is executed 4 times for each of the 3 executions of the outer loop.

WATCH OUT   *WORDS OF WARNING*

A `for` loop must be constructed carefully to ensure that its initialization expression, loop condition, and step (increment or decrement) expression will eventually cause the loop condition to become false. In particular:

> *If the body of a counting loop alters the values of any variables involved in the loop condition, then the number of repetitions may be changed.*

It is generally considered poor programming practice to alter the value of any variables in the loop condition within the body of a counting loop, because this can produce unexpected results. For example, execution of

```
int limit = 1;

for (int i = 0; i <= limit; i++)
{
   theScreen.println(i);
   limit++;
}
```

produces an infinite sequence of integers

```
0
1
2
3
.
.
.
```

because on each pass through the loop, the expression `limit++` increments `limit` by 1 before `i++` increments `i`. As a result, the loop condition `i <= limit` is always true.

Similarly, the loop

```
for (int i = 0; i <= limit; i++)
{
   theScreen.println(i);
   i--;
}
```

will output infinitely many zeros,

```
0
0
0
.
.
.
```

because the expression `i--` in the body of the loop decrements `i` by 1 before the increment expression `i++` increments it by 1. As a result, `i` is always 0 when the loop condition is tested.

Forever Loops

The primary use of for loops is to implement counting loops where the number of repetitions is known (or can be computed) in advance. For example, in computing the sum of the integers from 1 to n, we know that the loop's body must be executed exactly n times. However, there are many problems in which the number of repetitions cannot be determined in advance. For these situations, many modern programming languages provide a general loop statement that provides for *indefinite repetition.* This loop is often implemented by a language statement that is different from the statements for other loops.[1]

Java, however, does not provide a syntactically distinct statement, but instead allows the programmer to construct such a loop from other loops. As we saw in Chapter 5, one way this can be done is by removing the initialization expression, the loop condition, and the step expression from a `for` statement:[2]

```
for ( ; ; )                    // forever loop
    statement
```

Because such a loop contains no loop condition specifying the condition under which repetition terminates, it is an **indefinite loop** that executes the statements in its body without stopping. We will call such a loop a **forever loop.**

To illustrate, consider the following forever loop:

```
for ( ; ; )                    // forever loop
    theScreen.println( "Help! I'm caught in a loop!" );
```

This statement will produce the output

```
Help! I'm caught in a loop!
Help! I'm caught in a loop!
Help! I'm caught in a loop!
Help! I'm caught in a loop!
            .
            .
            .
```

an unlimited number of times, unless the user *interrupts* execution (usually by pressing the `Control` and `C` keys).

To avoid this infinite looping behavior, the body of a forever loop is usually a compound statement, containing

1. Those statements that must be executed repeatedly in order to solve the problem; and
2. A statement that will terminate execution of the loop when some condition is satisfied.

As we saw in Chapter 5, loop termination is usually accomplished with a `break` statement or a `return` statement.

---

[1] For example, *Ada* and *Turing* have the `loop` statement; *Modula-2* and *Modula-3* have the `LOOP` statement.

[2] Alternatively, we can achieve the same effect with either of these forms: `while (true) statement` or `do { statementlist } while (true);`

The `break` and `continue` Statements;
Labeled Statements

A `break` **statement** can be used to terminate execution of an enclosing loop or `switch` statement. It has two forms:

The `break` Statement

Forms:
```
break;
break identifier;
```
where:
  `break` is a Java keyword;
  this statement is contained in a loop or `switch` statement; and
  `identifier` is a Java identifier that labels an enclosing statement.

Behavior:

In the first form, control transfers to the innermost enclosing loop or `switch` statement and its execution is terminated.

In the second form, `identifier` is the label of a **labeled statement** of the form

```
identifier : Statement
```

where `Statement` encloses the `break` statement. Control transfers to this enclosing labeled statement and its execution is terminated.[3]

If there is no enclosing loop or `switch` statement for the first form or an enclosing labeled statement for the second form, a compile-time error results.

Most of the forever loops we have considered up to now have had the following form:

```
for (;;)                          // loop:
{
    statement_list₁
    if (termination_condition) break;
    statement_list₂
}                                 // end loop
```

where either $statement\_list_1$ or $statement\_list_2$ can be empty. Note that unlike other loops (counting loops and the loops considered in the next sections), repetition continues as long as the condition in the `if`-`break` combination is *false*— it terminates when the condition becomes true. To distinguish this condition from the loop conditions of the other loops we will call it a **termination condition** instead of a *loop condition*.

---

[3] Labeled breaks are an alternative to the `goto` statement that is present in many other languages (e.g., C++), which is not provided in Java.

To illustrate forever loops, here is a useful utility method called `getMenu-Choice()` that receives a menu and the characters that denote the first and last choices from the menu. (A precondition of this method is that the menu choices are a closed range such as A-D.) It repeatedly displays the menu and reads the user's choice until that choice is in the range of valid choices:

```
public static char getMenuChoice(string MENU, char firstChoice,
                                               char lastChoice)
{
    char choice;                            // what the user enters

    for (;;)                                // loop:
    {
        theScreen.print(MENU);              // statement_list₁
        choice = theKeyboard.readChar();
                                            // if-break combination
        if ((choice >= firstChoice) && (choice <= lastChoice))
            break;
                                            // statement_list₂
        theScreen.println("\nI'm sorry, but " + choice
                          + " is not a valid menu choice." );
    }                                       // end loop

    return choice;
}
```

The effect is to "trap" the user inside the forever loop until a valid menu choice is entered. That is, when the user enters an invalid menu choice, the termination condition is false. As a result, the `break` statement is bypassed and the output statement displays an error message. Control then returns to the beginning of the loop for the next repetition and gives the user another chance. When a valid choice is entered, the termination condition becomes true, so the `break` statement is executed and transfers control to the `return` statement following the loop.

A labeled `break` is useful when we have nested loops (or nested `switch` statements). An unlabeled `break` inside an inner loop can only cause control to transfer out of that loop:

```
for (...)
{
    ...
    for (...)
    {  ...
        if (condition) break;
        ...
    }
    //-- break will transfer control here
    ...
}
```

If we want execution to transfer out of both loops, we can use a labeled `break` as in the following:

```
outer: for (...)
{
   ...
   for (...)
   {  ...
      if (condition) break outer;
      ...
   }
   ...
}
//- break will transfer control here
```

When the *condition* becomes true, break outer will transfer control to the statement labeled outer, which is the outer loop, and cause execution of it to terminate.

A related statement that is sometimes useful for modifying (but not terminating) execution of a loop is the continue **statement.** It has the following form:

The continue Statement

Forms:

```
continue;
continue label;
```
where:
continue is a Java keyword;
this statement is contained in a loop; and
label is a Java identifier that labels an enclosing loop.

Behavior:

In the first form, control transfers to the innermost enclosing loop, the current iteration is terminated, and a new one begins.

In the second form, control transfers to the enclosing labeled loop, the current iteration is terminated, and a new one begins

If there is no enclosing loop, a compile-time error results.

The continue statement is useful when one wants to skip to the bottom part of a loop if a certain condition is true:

```
for (...)
{
   ...
   if (condition) continue;
   //- Skip from here to end of loop body if
   //- condition is true and begin a new iteration
}
```

Like labeled break statements, labeled continue statements are useful in the case of nested loops.

Returning from a Loop. In methods like `getMenuChoice()` where the statement following a forever loop is a `return` statement, it is slightly more efficient to replace the `break` statement with a `return` statement:

```
public static char getMenuChoice(string MENU, char firstChoice,
                                                 char lastChoice)
{
   char choice;                             // what the user enters

   for (;;)                                 // loop:
   {
      theScreen.print(MENU);                // statement_list₁
      choice = theKeyboard.readChar();
                                            // if-return combination
      if ((choice >= firstChoice) && (choice <= lastChoice))
         return choice;
                                            // statement_list₂
      theScreen.println("\nI'm sorry, but " + choice
                        + " is not a valid menu choice." );
   }                                        // end loop
}
```

As before, if the user enters an invalid choice, an error message is displayed and the body of the loop is repeated. However, when the user enters a valid choice, the termination condition is true, and so the `return` statement is selected. Since execution of a `return` statement causes the method to terminate, it also terminates the loop within that method.

8.3   REPETITION: THE WHILE LOOP

A loop of the form

> loop
>> if (*termination_condition*) exit the loop.
>> other statements
> end loop

in which the termination test occurs before the loop's statements are executed is called a **pretest** or **test-at-the-top** loop. Such loops can be implemented in Java using a forever loop:

```
for (;;)                                   // loop:
{
   if (termination_condition) break;
   statement_list
}                                          // end loop
```

However, most programming languages, including Java, provide another statement with a simpler syntax for these pretest loops—a `while` **statement**—and this loop is thus also called a **while loop.** We will use a while loop to solve the following problem.

PROBLEM: FOLLOW THE BOUNCING BALL

Suppose that when a ball is dropped, it bounces from the pavement to a height one-half of its previous height. We want to write a program that will simulate the behavior of the ball when it is dropped from a given height. It should display the number of each bounce and the height of that bounce, repeating this until the height of the ball is very small (e.g., less than 1 millimeter).

 OBJECT-CENTERED DESIGN

BEHAVIOR. The program should first display on the screen a prompt for the initial height, and then read this quantity from the keyboard. It should then display 1 and the height of the first rebound, display 2 and the height of the second rebound, and so on, until the height of the rebound is less than some very small number.

PROBLEM'S OBJECTS. Given the preceding description of the behavior, we can identify the following objects in this problem:

Description of problem's object	Type	Kind	Name
The current height	real	variable	*height*
The bounce number	integer	variable	*bounce*
A very small number	real	constant	*SMALL_NUMBER*

This list allows us to specify our problem as follows:

Input: The initial *height* of a ball

Output: For each rebound of the ball:
       the number of the rebound and
       the height of that rebound, assuming that the height of each
          rebound is one-half the previous height

OPERATIONS. The operations that must be performed are:

  i. Display a prompt

  ii. Input a real value (the original *height*)

  iii. Initialize *bounce* to zero

  iv. Divide the *height* by 2 (to compute the rebound height)

  v. Increment *bounce*

  vi. Display the current *bounce* number and *height*

  vii. Repeat operations iv–vi as long as *height* ≥ *SMALL_NUMBER*

ALGORITHM. Each of these operations is available through the operators and statements of Java. However, for the loop in vii we must ask where the termination condition should be placed. It should be clear that if *height* is initially less than

SMALL_NUMBER, then none of the operations in (iv)–(vi) should be performed. This suggests that we use a pretest loop as in the following algorithm:

Algorithm for Bouncing Ball Problem

1. Initialize *bounce* to 0.
2. Prompt for and read a value for *height*.
3. Display original *height* value with appropriate label.
4. Loop:
   - a. If *height* < *SMALL_NUMBER*, terminate the repetition.
   - b. Replace *height* with *height* divided by 2.
   - c. Add 1 to *bounce*.
   - d. Display *bounce* and *height*.

   End Loop

CODING. We could code this algorithm using a pretest form of a forever loop, but as we noted earlier, the Java while loop has a simpler syntax. The program in Figure 8.4 implements this algorithm, using a while loop to implement the loop in Step 4.

FIGURE 8.4   COMPUTING REBOUND HEIGHT

```
/** BallBounce.java calculates and displays the rebound heights
 *    of a dropped ball.
 *
 *  Input:  A real height from which a ball is dropped.
 *  Output: For each rebound of the ball from the pavement below:
 *              the number of the rebound and
 *              the height of that rebound, assuming that the height
 *               of each rebound is one-half the previous height
 */

import ann.easyio.*;          // Keyboard, Screen

class BallBounce
{
 public static void main(String [] args)
 {
    final double SMALL_NUMBER = 1.0e-3,      // 1 millimeter.
              REBOUND_FACTOR = 0.5;
    Screen theScreen = new Screen();
    Keyboard theKeyboard = new Keyboard();

    theScreen.print(
          "\nTo compute the rebound number and height for a dropped ball,"
       + "\n enter the starting height (in meters): ");

    double height = theKeyboard.readDouble();

    theScreen.println("\nStarting height: " + height + " meters.");
```

```
    int bounce = 0;
    while (height >= SMALL_NUMBER)
    {
      height *= REBOUND_FACTOR;
      bounce++;
      theScreen.println("Rebound #" + bounce + ": "
                        + height + " meters.");
    }
  }
}
```

Sample Run:

```
To compute the rebound number and height for a dropped ball,
 enter the starting height (in meters): 15

Starting height: 15.0 meters.
Rebound #1: 7.5 meters.
Rebound #2: 3.75 meters.
Rebound #3: 1.875 meters.
Rebound #4: 0.9375 meters.
Rebound #5: 0.46875 meters.
Rebound #6: 0.234375 meters.
Rebound #7: 0.1171875 meters.
Rebound #8: 0.05859375 meters.
Rebound #9: 0.029296875 meters.
Rebound #10: 0.0146484375 meters.
Rebound #11: 0.00732421875 meters.
Rebound #12: 0.003662109375 meters.
Rebound #13: 0.0018310546875 meters.
Rebound #14: 9.1552734375E-4 meters..
```

The while Statement

While loops are implemented in Java using a while **statement** of the following form:

The while Statement

Form:
```
while (loop_condition)
    statement
```
where:
   while is a Java keyword;
   loop_condition is a boolean expression; and
   statement is a simple or compound statement.

Behavior:

When execution reaches a while statement:

1. loop_condition is evaluated.

2. If loop_condition is true:

   a. The specified statement, called the **body** of the loop, is executed.

   b. Control returns to Step 1.

   Otherwise
      Control is transferred to the statement following the while statement.

Like a for loop, a while loop has a loop condition that controls repetition. The placement of this loop condition before the body of the loop is significant because it means that a while loop is a pretest loop so that when it is executed, this condition is evaluated *before* the body of the loop is executed. This can be pictured as follows:

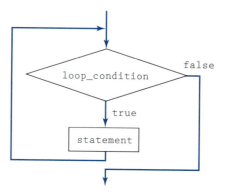

As this diagram indicates, execution of the specified statement is repeated as long as the loop condition remains true and terminates when it becomes false. For example, the following table provides a partial trace of the repetitions of the while loop in Figure 8.4, showing the values of the relevant variables and expressions:

height	bounce	height >= SMALL_NUMBER	Action
15.0	0	true	Execute loop body
7.5	1	true	Execute loop body
3.75	2	true	Execute loop body
1.875	3	true	Execute loop body
.	.	.	.
.	.	.	.
.	.	.	.
0.0018310546875	13	true	Execute loop body
9.1552734375E−4	14	false	Terminate repetition

The preceding diagram indicates that the loop condition is evaluated before the loop body is executed, and thus if this condition is initially false, the body of the loop will not be executed. Stated differently, the body of a pretest loop will be executed *zero or more times,* and so these loops are said to exhibit **zero-trip behavior.** Thus, in the program in Figure 8.4, if the value entered for height is less than SMALL_NUMBER, the statements in the while loop will not be executed, because the condition height >= SMALL_NUMBER that controls the repetition will be false the first time it is evaluated. As we shall see, it is this zero-trip behavior that distinguishes the while loop from other noncounting loops. It is important to keep this characteristic in mind when designing a solution to a problem, because it influences the decision of which loop to use.

Loop Conditions vs. Termination Conditions

A forever loop continues the repetition when its condition is `false` and terminates the repetition when that condition is `true`. A while loop behaves in precisely the opposite manner: a while loop *continues* the repetition as long as its condition is `true`, and *terminates* the repetition when its condition is `false`. Put differently, the condition controlling a while loop must always be the *negation* of the condition controlling an equivalent forever loop.

```
for (;;)                         while (!condition)
{                                {
   if (condition) break;            statements
   statements                    }
}
```

To illustrate, the while loop in the bouncing-ball program in Figure 8.4 continues the repetition so long as `height` is greater than or equal to SMALL_NUMBER:

```
while (height >= SMALL_NUMBER)
{
   height *= REBOUND_FACTOR;
   bounce++;
   theScreen.println("Rebound #" + bounce + ": "
                     + height + " meters.");
}
```

The equivalent forever loop version would control the repetition by terminating when `height` is less than SMALL_NUMBER:

```
for (;;)
{
   if (height < SMALL_NUMBER) break;
   height *= REBOUND_FACTOR;
   bounce++;
   theScreen.println("Rebound #" + bounce + ": "
                     + height + " meters.");
}
```

WATCH

OUT

WORDS OF WARNING

As with other loops, it is important to ensure that the body of a while loop will eventually cause its loop condition to become `false`, since otherwise an *infinite loop* will result. To illustrate, consider the while loop

```
counter = 1;
while (counter < 100)
{
   theScreen.println(counter);
   counter--;
}
```

Here, `counter` is initially less than 100, and since `counter--` decrements `counter` by 1, the value of `counter` will always be less than 100. Thus, the condition `counter < 100` will always be `true`, resulting in an infinite loop that produces the output:

```
1
0
-1
-2
-3
.
.
.
```

Another common mistake is illustrated by the following code segment:

```
counter = 1;
while (counter < 100)
   theScreen.println( counter );
   counter++;
```

This code segment will display the value 1 infinitely many times:

```
1
1
1
1
1
.
.
.
```

Errors of this kind can be fiendishly difficult to find, because the indentation of the statements makes them appear correct. The problem here is that the loop body is a single statement. Thus, in the absence of curly braces, only the statement

```
theScreen.println( counter );
```

is in the body of the loop. To include the statement

```
counter++;
```

both statements must be surrounded with curly braces:

```
counter = 1;
while (counter < 100)
{
    theScreen.println( counter );
    counter++;
}
```

8.4   REPETITION: THE DO LOOP

In the last section, we saw that the `while` statement provides a loop that evaluates its loop condition prior to executing the statement it controls. We also saw that such pretest loops are useful in solving problems where zero-trip behavior is required.

There are some repetition problems, however, for which zero-trip behavior is not appropriate. For such problems, many languages provide a *posttest loop* called the *do loop*, which is described in this section.

PROBLEM: MAKING A PROGRAM PAUSE

It is sometimes useful to make a program pause for a specified length of time. For example, a program that displays information too quickly may need to pause to give a user time to read the information. Here we consider how to write a method that, given a length of time, will make a program pause for that length of time.

OBJECT-CENTERED DESIGN

PRELIMINARY ANALYSIS. If we search the Java API for time-related methods, we find that the `System` class from package `java.lang` provides a `current-TimeMillis()` method that returns the number of milliseconds since January 1, 1970 as a `long` value. We can use this method to help solve our problem by recording the starting time of the pause and then repeatedly reading the current time until the difference between the current and starting times exceeds the given length of time. This technique is called **busy-waiting,** because it makes a program *wait* by keeping the computer's CPU *busy.*

BEHAVIOR. Our method should receive a value from its caller representing the number of seconds the program should pause. The method should note the time, and then repeatedly recheck the time until the specified number of seconds have passed.

PROBLEM'S OBJECTS. From the behavioral description, we can identify the following data objects in this problem:

Description of problem's object	Type	Kind	Movement	Name
The number of seconds	double	varying	received	*seconds*
The number of milliseconds	long	varying	none	*milliseconds*
The starting time	long	constant	none	*START_TIME*
The current time	long	varying	none	*currentTime*

In order to allow the caller to pass fractional values for the number of seconds (e.g., 1.5), we will use a `double` parameter to store these values.

Another detail is that we are allowing the user to specify a given number of seconds as a `double`, but the `currentTimeMillis()` method returns the time in milliseconds as a `long` value. Since we must compare these times, we will have to convert

the (double) number of seconds into the (long) equivalent number of milliseconds.

All of this suggests the following specification for our method:

Receive: *seconds,* a double value

Precondition: *seconds* > 0

Postcondition: *seconds* is time that has elapsed since the method began execution

This specification allows us to build a stub for our method, which we call pause().
Since it controls program execution, we will store it (along with other control-related
methods) in a class named Controller in the ann.util package:

```
public class Controller
{
  public static void pause(double seconds)
  {
  }
}
```

OPERATIONS. From the preceding observations we can identify the following operations:

  i. Receive a double value from the caller (*seconds*)
  ii. Check the precondition
  iii. Convert a double (*seconds*) to a long (*milliseconds*)
    a. Multiply a double by 1000 (*seconds*)
    b. Round that product to a long (*milliseconds*)
  iv. Get the current time (*currentTime*)
  v. Subtract two long values (*currentTime, START_TIME*)
  vi. Repeat iv–v while one long value (*currentTime − START_TIME*) is less than another
  (*milliseconds*)

Each of these operations is provided in Java, either as an operator or as a statement.

ALGORITHM. There are two things to note about the repetition in operation vi:

  1. Operations iv and v are to be repeated so long as *currentTime − START_TIME <
  milliseconds* is true.
  2. In order to evaluate this loop condition, we must get the current time *at least once.*

These observations suggest that the loop condition should be evaluated at the "bottom" of the loop, as in the following algorithm:

Algorithm to Pause Execution (Busy-Waiting)

1. Receive *seconds.*
2. Initialize *START_TIME.*
3. If *seconds* > 0:
       a. Compute *milliseconds* from *seconds.*
       b. Loop:
           i. Get *currentTime.*
           ii. If *currentTime* – *START_TIME* > *milliseconds*
               Terminate the repetition.
       End loop
   Else
       Display error message.

CODING. As we have seen before, the loop in such an algorithm can be implemented using a forever loop:

```
for (;;)
{
    currentTime = currentTimeMillis();
    if (currentTime - START_TIME > milliseconds) break;
}
```

However, Java has an alternative repetition statement that provides a more convenient syntax for posttest or test-at-the-bottom loops. This statement is the do statement and is illustrated in Figure 8.5.

FIGURE 8.5   METHOD pause()

```
/** pause(n) pauses program execution for n seconds.
 * Receive:       seconds, a double value
 * Precondition:  seconds > 0.
 * Postcondition: seconds time has elapsed since invocation.
 */

public static void pause(double seconds)
{
  final long START_TIME = System.currentTimeMillis();
  if (seconds > 0)
  {
    long currentTime = 0,
         milliSeconds = (long)(1000 * seconds + 0.5);

    do
      currentTime = System.currentTimeMillis();
    while((currentTime - START_TIME) <= milliSeconds);
  }
  else
    fatal("pause(n):", "negative n received");
}
```

Since the `fatal()` method presented in Figure 6.7 is also a program-control method, we will store it along with `pause( )` and other program-control methods in our

Controller class in the `ann.util` package provided with this text, so that they can be conveniently reused by any program needing them.

TESTING. A simple driver program to test method `pause()` is given in Figure 8.6. When executed, there is a noticeably longer delay as each line is output, and the length of each delay can be verified (roughly) using a watch or clock.

FIGURE 8.6   DRIVER FOR METHOD `pause()`

```
// PauseTester.java is a simple driver program to test the method pause().

import ann.util.Controller;
class PauseTester
{
  public static void main(String [] args)
  {
    for (double count = 1.0; count <= 5.0; count += 0.5)
    {
      System.err.println("Pausing for " + count + " seconds.");
      Controller.pause(count);
    }
    System.err.println("Test complete.");
  }
}
```

Sample runs:

```
Pausing for 1.0 seconds.
Pausing for 1.5 seconds.
Pausing for 2.0 seconds.
Pausing for 2.5 seconds.
Pausing for 3.0 seconds.
Pausing for 3.5 seconds.
Pausing for 4.0 seconds.
Pausing for 4.5 seconds.
Pausing for 5.0 seconds.
Test complete.
```

A Posttest Loop

The method in Figure 8.6 uses a new Java repetition statement—the do **statement,** which has the following form:

The do Statement

Form:

```
do
    statement
while (loop_condition);
```

where:

> do and while are Java keywords;
> loop_condition is a boolean expression;
> statement is a simple or compound statement; and
> a semicolon must follow the expression at the end of the statement.

Behavior:

When execution reaches a do loop:

(1) statement is executed.

(2) loop_condition is evaluated.

(3) If loop_condition is true, then
>   Control returns to step (1).
> Otherwise
>   Control passes to the first statement following the do loop.

Note that the loop condition in a do statement appears *after* the body of the loop, indicating that it is evaluated at the end, or "bottom," of the loop. The do loop is thus a **posttest** or **test-at-the-bottom** loop, in which execution flows as pictured in the following diagram:

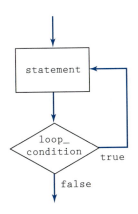

The fact that the loop condition is evaluated after the body of the loop has been executed guarantees that the body of the loop will be executed at least once. Thus, in contrast to the zero-trip behavior of pretest loops, posttest loops are said to exhibit **one-trip behavior.**

Loop Conditions vs. Termination Conditions

A do loop uses a loop condition that continues the repetition so long as the condition is true, and terminates the repetition when the condition becomes false. As with the while loop, the loop condition is the negation of the termination condition used in an equivalent forever loop.

To illustrate, the do loop in the pause-execution problem uses a *less-than-or-equal-to* comparison as a loop condition:

```
do
   currentTime = System.currentTimeMillis();
while((currentTime - START_TIME) <= milliSeconds);
```

An equivalent forever loop would use a *greater-than* comparison:

```
for (;;)
{
   currentTime = currentTimeMillis();
   if (currentTime - START_TIME > milliseconds) break;
}
```

WATCH **WORDS OF WARNING**

!

OUT

Do Not Forget the Semicolon. The syntax of the do statement is different from that of the while statement and is designed to indicate clearly that it is a posttest loop. However, there is another, less obvious, difference between while and do statements that is a common source of programming errors:

> *The do statement must be terminated with a semicolon, but a semicolon after the block in a while statement is an error.*

The reason is that the final component in each of the other loops is a statement, but the final component of a do loop is a boolean expression, which must be terminated with a semicolon.

Avoid Infinite Loops. As with while loops, it is important to ensure that the statements within a do loop will eventually cause repetition to terminate, because an infinite loop will result otherwise. For example, in the do loop

```
counter = 1;
do
{
   theScreen.println(counter);
   counter--;
}
while (counter < 100);
```

the termination condition is always true because counter is initially less than 100 and counter-- decrements counter by 1, causing the value of counter to always be less than 100. Thus, this is an infinite loop, producing an unlimited amount of output:

```
  1
  0
 -1
 -2
 -3
  .
  .
  .
```

Input Do Loops: The Query Approach

In Chapter 5, we described two different approaches to input loops: the **counting approach** and the **sentinel approach.**

The counting approach begins by asking the user how many values they have to process, and then uses a for loop to iterate that many times. The general pattern is as follows:

Pattern for Counting Input Loop

Display a prompt (for the number of values to be processed).
Read *numberOfValues* to be processed.
`for (int var = 1; var <= numberOfValues; var++)`
`{`

    Display a prompt for a data value.
    Read *theValue* to be processed.
    Process *theValue.*

`}`

The sentinel approach uses a special value called an **end-of-data flag** or **sentinel** to mark the end of the data values to be processed. A forever loop can be used to read an input value and `if-break` (or `if-return`) combination to terminate the repetition if that value is the sentinel value:

Pattern for Sentinel Input Loop (forever Loop Version)

`for(;;)`
`{`

    Display a prompt (for a data value).
    Read *theValue* to be processed.
    If (*theValue* is the sentinel) terminate the repetition.
    Process *theValue.*

`}`

Each of these approaches has its disadvantages. The counting loop approach requires its user to know in advance the number of values to be entered, which may be difficult to determine for large data sets. The program is much more flexible and user-friendly if the computer, rather than the user, does the counting. Sentinels can only be used in problems where some value can serve as the sentinel, and for some problems, there may be no suitable value. For example, for a program that encrypts characters, it may not be possible to designate one character as a sentinel without limit-ing the usefulness of the program.

In this subsection, we examine a final approach that, although not without flaws, is the most broadly applicable. In a nutshell, this approach is simply to **query the user** at the end of each repetition whether there is more data to process. Figure 8.7 illus-trates this approach. It is a modification of the programs in Section 5.3 for calculat-ing factorials that uses querying to control the number of factorials to be calculated. It uses the method `factorial()`—see Figure 5.7—from the class `ann.math.For-mula` provided with this text.

FIGURE 8.7   THE QUERY APPROACH

```
/**  factorials.java computes factorials, using a query-controlled loop
 *      to input a series of integers.
 *   Input:        A series of integer values.
 *   Precondition: Each value >= 0.
 *   Output:       The factorial of each value.
 */

import ann.easyio.*;                  // Keyboard, Screen
import ann.math.Formula;             // factorial()
import java.math.BigInteger;

class factorials
{
 public static void main(String [] args)
  {
    Screen theScreen = new Screen();
    Keyboard theKeyboard = new Keyboard();
    String numberString;
    char response;
    do
     {
        theScreen.print("To compute n!, enter n: ");
        numberString = theKeyboard.readWord();

        theScreen.println( numberString + "! = "
                      + Formula.factorial( new BigInteger(numberString) )

        theScreen.print("\nDo you have more values to enter (y or n)? ");
        response = theKeyboard.readChar();
     }
    while (response == 'y' || response == 'Y');
  }
}
```

Sample Run:

```
To compute n!, enter n: 0
0! = 1

Do you have more values to enter (y or n)? y

To compute n!, enter n: 1
1! = 1

Do you have more values to enter (y or n)? y

To compute n!, enter n: 2
2! = 2

Do you have more values to enter (y or n)? y
```

```
To compute n!, enter n: 5
5! = 120

Do you have more values to enter (y or n)? y

To compute n!, enter n: 100
100! =
93326215443944152681699238856266700490715968264381621468592963895217599
932299156089414639761565182862536979208272237582511852109168640000000000
00000000000000

Do you have more values to enter (y or n)? n
```

This program uses the query

```
Do you have more values to enter (y or n)?
```

and then reads the user's response (presumably y or n) from the keyboard. The boolean expression

```
response == 'y' || response == 'Y'
```

is used as the loop condition. Execution of such a loop will continue until the user enters a response indicating no further input.

In problems where it is reasonable to assume that the user has at least one value to be entered and processed, the query and the corresponding loop condition are placed at the bottom of the loop, making it a posttest loop.[4] This suggests the following *pattern* for a query-controlled input loop:

Pattern for Query-Controlled Input Loop

```
char response;

do
{
```
    Display a prompt for a data value.
    Input *theValue* to be processed.
    Process *theValue*.

    Display a query that asks if there is more data.
    Input the user's response (y or n).
```
}
while ((response == 'y') || (response == 'Y'));
```

---

[4] In problems where there might be no values to enter and process, the forever loop can be used:

```
char response;
double value;
for (;;)
{
    theScreen.print( "\nDo you wish to continue (y or n)? ");
    response = keyboard.readChar();
    if (response == 'n' || response == 'N') break;
    theScreen.print("\nEnter a value: ");
    value = theKeyboard.readDouble();
    // process value
}
```

Query Methods. The code to perform a query tends to clutter a loop, and this may obscure the program's structure. One way to avoid this is by constructing a **query method** like the following to perform the query and to return true or false based on the user's response:

```
public class Query
{
   public static boolean moreValues()
   {
      theScreen.print("Do you have more values to enter (y or n)? ");
      char answer = theKeyboard.readChar();
      return (answer == 'y') || (answer == 'Y');
   }

   // . . . other query methods
}
```

Since it returns a boolean value, a call to such a **query method** can be used as the loop condition. To illustrate, we could modify the factorial program in Figure 8.7 to use the preceding query method `moreValues()` as shown in the program in Figure 8.8. The `Query` class is stored in the package `ann.util` provided with this text.

FIGURE 8.8   THE QUERY METHOD APPROACH

```
/** factorials2.java computes factorials using a query-controlled loop
 *    to input a series of integers.
 *    Input:        A series of integer values.
 *    Precondition: Each value >= 0.
 *    Output:       The factorial of each value.
 */

import ann.easyio.*;        // Keyboard, Screen
import ann.math.Formula;    // factorial()
import ann.util.Query;      // moreValues()
import java.math.BigInteger;

class factorials2 extends Object
{
 public static void main(String [] args)
 {
   Screen theScreen = new Screen();
   Keyboard theKeyboard = new Keyboard();
   String numberString;

   do
   {
      theScreen.print("To compute n!, enter n: ");
      numberString = theKeyboard.readWord();

      theScreen.println( numberString + "! = "
                   + Formula.factorial( new BigInteger(numberString) )
   }
   while ( Query.moreValues() );
 }
}
```

When execution reaches the loop condition of the do loop in this program, the method moreValues() is called. It queries the user, reads the response, and returns true if the response was either y or Y and returns false otherwise. If moreValues() returns true, the body of the do loop is repeated, but if it returns false, repetition is terminated.

This version of a query-controlled loop is easier to read than the earlier version in Figure 8.7, because the statements that perform the querying (including the declaration of a character variable to hold the response) are now hidden in the method moreValues().

Another advantage of this approach is that a query method can be stored in a class (e.g., Query), from which it can be accessed by any program requiring a query-controlled loop. Since this particular query,

```
Do you have more values to enter (y or n)?
```

may be less appropriate for a different program, such a class might contain a variety of query methods:

```
moreValues():    Asks if there are more values
continue():      Asks if the user wants to continue
done():          Asks if the user is finished
```

A program that uses the Query class can use whichever query method is most appropriate.

A pattern for a loop controlled by a query method is as follows:

Pattern for Input Loop Controlled by a Query Method

```
import ann.util.Query;
     .
     .
     .
do
{
    Display a prompt for a data value.
    Input theValue to be processed.
    Process theValue.
}
while ( Query.queryMethod() );
```

The Disadvantage of the Query Approach. The sentinel and counting approaches require one interaction by the user to enter each data value, but the query approach requires two—one for the data value, and one for the response to the query. This doubling of user effort may make the query approach too cumbersome for large data sets.

8.5   CHOOSING THE RIGHT LOOP

With so many different kinds of loops, it can be difficult for a programmer to decide which is best for a particular problem. One simple guideline is the following:

> *The choice of a loop should be determined by the nature of the problem.*

This means that choosing a loop is part of the design phase of program development. It should be done only after the algorithm has been developed in some detail, because the algorithm will provide clues as to which loop to use.

Decision #1: Use a Counting Loop or a General Loop?

The first question to ask is

> *Does the algorithm require counting through some fixed range of values?*

If the answer is yes, then a counting loop is needed, and a for loop is the appropriate choice. However, if solving the problem does not involve repeating the execution of statements a fixed number of times, then one of the more general loops—while, do, or forever—is a better choice.

Decision #2: Which General Loop?

If one of the general loops should be used, then the next question is: Which one? One way to proceed is to begin with a *generic loop* of the form

```
Loop
    body-of-the-loop
End Loop
```

in the algorithm. Then continue to develop the algorithm, adding any necessary initialization statements before the loop together with the statements that make up the body of the loop:

```
initialization statements
Loop
    statement₁
        .
        .
        .
    statementₙ
End Loop
```

Finally, formulate an appropriate termination condition and determine where it should be placed in the loop. This will determine which kind of loop to use:

> If the termination condition appears
>
> ❏ At the beginning of the loop, the loop is a pretest loop; choose a while loop;
> ❏ At the bottom of the loop, the loop is a posttest loop; choose a do loop;
> ❏ Within the list of statements, the loop is a test-in-the-middle loop; choose a forever loop with an `if-break` (or `if-return`) combination.

To illustrate, consider again the problem of designing an algorithm for the bouncing-ball problem of Section 8.3. Using a generic loop, we write a first version of the algorithm as follows:

1. Initialize *bounce* to 0.
2. Enter a value for *height*.
3. Display original *height* value with appropriate label.
4. Loop

       Replace *height* with *height* divided by 2.

       Add 1 to *bounce.*

       Display *bounce* and *height.*

    End Loop

Because repetition is to stop when *height* is less than some *SMALL_NUMBER,* the condition

$$height < SMALL\_NUMBER$$

can be used as a termination condition for the loop. However, the user could have entered zero or a negative value for *height,* in which case the body of the loop should not be executed. Thus, we should evaluate this condition immediately upon entering the loop:

1. Initialize *bounce* to 0.
2. Enter a value for *height.*
3. Display original *height* value with appropriate label.
4. Loop

    a. If *height* < *SMALL_NUMBER,* terminate the repetition.

    b. Replace *height* with *height* divided by 2.

    c. Add 1 to *bounce.*

    d. Display bounce and height.

    End Loop

This is a pretest loop; and we should therefore use a `while` loop to implement it.

By contrast, if we reconsider the sentinel approach to reading a collection of values, we begin by constructing the generic loop

Loop
    Display a prompt for input.
    Input *theValue.*
    Process *theValue.*
End loop

Since we are using the sentinel approach, an appropriate termination condition is

theValue is the sentinel

Before this termination condition can be evaluated, *theValue* must have a value, which means that the termination condition must appear after the input statement. Also, a sentinel value must not be processed, which means that the termination condition should be placed before the processing statements:

Loop

   a. Display a prompt for input.

   b. Input *theValue.*

   c. If *theValue* is the sentinel, then terminate repetition.

   d. Process *theValue.*

End Loop

This is a test-in-the-middle loop; we should therefore implement it using a forever loop.

✔ Quick Quiz 8.5

1. Name the three kinds of input loops.
2. _____ loops execute a set of statements once for each value in a specified range and they are implemented in Java by a(n) _____ statement.
3. What are the four components of a counting for loop?
4. (True or false) The counting method of input is one of the most flexible methods.
5. A special value used to signal the end of data is called a(n) _____ or _____.
6. (True or false) A disadvantage of using a while loop instead of a forever loop for sentinel-based input is that duplicate input steps are often required.
7. A _____ is a question asked of the user to determine whether there are more data values.
8. The terminating statement in a forever loop is usually a(n) _____ combination.

Answer Questions 9–12 using "pretest" or "posttest".

9. A while loop is a _____ loop.
10. A do loop is a _____ loop.
11. The body of a _____ loop is always executed at least once.
12. A _____ loop has zero-trip behavior.

For Questions 13–20, describe the output produced.

13.
```
for (int i = 0; i < 10; i++)
    theScreen.println("2i = " + 2*i);
```

14.
```
for (int i = 0; i <= 5; i++)
    theScreen.print( (2*i + 1) + " ");
theScreen.println( );
```

15.
```
for (int i = 1; i < 4; i++)
{
    theScreen.print(i);
    for (int j = i; j >= 1; j--)
        theScreen.println(j);
}
```

16.
```
int i = 0, j = 0, k;
for (;;)
{
    k = 2 * i * j;
    if (k > 10) break;
    theScreen.println(i + " " + j + " " + k);
    i++;
    j++;
}
theScreen.println(k);
```

17.
```
int k = 5;
int i = -2;
while (i <= k)
{
    i += 2;
    k--;
    theScreen.println(i + k);
}
```

18.
```
int i = 4;
while (i >= 0)
{
    i--;
    theScreen.println(i);
}
theScreen.println("\n*****");
```

19.
```
int i = 0, k;
do
{
    k = i * i + 1;
    theScreen.println(i + " " + k);
    i++;
}
while (k <= 10);
```

```
20.  int i = 4, k;
     do
     {
         k = i * i - 4;
         theScreen.println(i + " " + k);
         i--;
     }
     while (k >= 0);
```

✍ EXERCISES 8.5

For Exercises 1–14, describe the output produced.

1. ```
   for (int i = 10; i > 0; i--)
       theScreen.println(i + " cubed = " + i*i*i);
   ```

2. ```
   for (int i = 10; i > 0; i -= 2)
       theScreen.println(i + " squared = " + i*i);
   ```

3. ```
   for (int i = 1; i <= 5; i++)
   {
       theScreen.println(i);
       for (int j = i; j >= 1; j -= 2)
           theScreen.println(j);
   }
   ```

4. ```
   int k = 5;
   for (int i = -2; i < 5; i += 2)
   {
       theScreen.println(i + k);
       k = 1;
   }
   ```

5. ```
   for (int i = 3; i > 0; i--)
       for (int j = 1; j <= i; j++)
           for (int k = i; k >= j; k--)
               theScreen.println(i + " " + j + " " + k);
   ```

6. ```
   for (int i = 1; i <= 3; i++)
       for (int j = 1; j <= 3; j++)
       {
           for (int k = i; k <= j; k++)
               theScreen.println(i + " " + j + " " + k);
           theScreen.println( );
       }
   ```

7. ```
   for (int i = 1; i <= 2; i++)
       for (int j = 1; j <= 3; j++)
           for (int k = 1; k <= 4; k++)
           {
               if (i + j < k) break;
               theScreen.println(i + " " + j + " " + k);
           }
   ```
   ```

8.
```
for (int i = 1; i <= 2; i++)
    for (int j = 1; j <= 3; j++)
        for (int k = 1; k <= 4; k++)
        {
            if (i - j > k) continue;
            theScreen.println(i + " " + j + " " + k);
        }
```

9.
```
for (int i = 1; i <= 2; i++)
    for (int j = 1; j <= 3; j++)
    {
        if (i > j) continue;

        for (int k = 1; k <= 4; k++)
            theScreen.println(i + " " + j + " " + k);
    }
```

10.
```
here: for (int i = 1; i <= 2; i++)
    for (int j = 1; j <= 3; j++)
        for (int k = 1; k <= 4; k++)
        {
            if (i + j < k) break here;
            theScreen.println(i + " " + j + " " + k);
        }
```

11.
```
here: for (int i = 1; i <= 2; i++)
    for (int j = 1; j <= 3; j++)
        for (int k = 1; k <= 4; k++)
        {
            if (i - j > k) continue here;
            theScreen.println(i + " " + j + " " + k);
        }
```

12.
```
int i = 5, j = 1, k;
for (;;)
{
    k = 2 * i - j;
    if (k < 0) break;
    theScreen.println(i + " " + j + " " + k);
    j++;
    i--;
}
theScreen.println(i + " " + j + " " + k);
```

13.
```
int i = 0, j = 10, k;
for (;;)
{
    k = 2 * i + j;
    if (k > 15) break;
    theScreen.println(i + " " + j + " " + k);
    if (i + j < 10) break;
    i++;
    j--;
}
theScreen.println(i + " " + j + " " + k);
```

14.
```
int i = 0, j = 10, k;
for (;;)
{
    k = 2 * i + j;
    if (k > 20) break;
    theScreen.println(i + " " + j + " " + k);
    if (i + j < 10) break;
    i++;
    j--;
}
theScreen.println(i + " " + j + " " + k);
```

15.
```
int i = 5, j;
for (;;)
{
    theScreen.println(i);
    i -= 2;
    if (i < 1) break;
    j = 0;
    for (;;)
    {
        j++;
        theScreen.println(j);
        if (j >= i) break;
    }
    theScreen.println("###");
}
theScreen.println("***");
```

16.
```
int k = 5, i = 32;
while (i > 0)
{
    theScreen.println("base-2 log of " + i + " = " + k);
    i /= 2;
    k--;
}
```

17.
```
int i = 1, j;
while (i*i < 10)
{
    j = i;
    while (j*j < 100)
    {
        theScreen.println(i + j);
        j *= 2;
    }
    i++;
}
theScreen.println("\n*****");
```

18.
```
int i = 0, k;
do
{
    k = i * i * i - 3 * i + 1;
    theScreen.println(i + " " + k);
    i++;
}
while (k <= 2);
```

19.
```
int i = 0, j, k;
do
{
    j = i * i * i;
    theScreen.print(i);
    do
    {
        k = i + 2 * j;
        theScreen.print(j);
        theScreen.print(k);
        j += 2;
    }
    while ( k <= 10);
    theScreen.println("*****");
    i++;
}
while (j <= 5);
```

Each of the loops in the following program segment is intended to find the smallest value of number for which the product $1 \times 2 \times \cdots \times$ number is greater than limit. For each of Exercises 20–22, make three trace tables, one for each loop, that display the values of number and product for the given value of limit.

```
/* A. Using a while loop */
number = 0;
product = 1;
while (product <= limit)
{
    number++;
    product *= number;
}

/* B. Using a do loop */
number = 0;
product = 1;
do
{
    number++;
    product *= number;
}
while (product <= limit);
```

```
/* C. Using a test-in-the middle loop */
number = 0;
product = 1;
for (;;)
{
    number++;
    if (product > limit) break;
    product *= number;
}
```

20. limit = 20

21. limit = 1

22. limit = 0

For Exercises 23–27, write a loop to do what is required.

23. Display the value of x and decrease x by 0.5 as long as x is positive.

24. Display the squares of the first 50 positive even integers in increasing order.

25. Display the square roots of the real numbers 1.0, 1.25, 1.5, 1.75, 2.0, . . . , 5.0.

26. The sequence of *Fibonacci numbers* begins with the integers 1, 1, 2, 3, 5, 8, 13, 21, . . . where each number after the first two is the sum of the two preceding numbers. Display the Fibonacci numbers less than 500.

27. Repeatedly prompt for and read a real number until the user enters a positive number.

For Exercises 28–35, write methods that will do what is required. To test these methods, you should write driver programs as instructed in Programming Problems 1–8 at the end of this chapter.

28. Modify the version of the method `summation()` in Section 8.1 so that it calculates the sum of the integers from `first` through `last`, where `first` and `last` are integers.

29. Write a `BigInteger` version of the method `summation()` in Section 8.1.

30. Proceed as in Exercise 28, but write a `BigInteger` version.

31. Given a real number x and a nonnegative integer n, use a loop to calculate x^n, and return this value.

32. Proceed as in Exercise 31, but allow n to be negative. (x^{-n} is defined to be $1 / x^n$, provided $x \neq 0$.)

33. Given a positive integer n, return the sum of the proper divisors of n, that is, the sum of the divisors that are less than n. For example, for $n = 10$, the method should return $1 + 2 + 5 = 8$.

34. Given an integer n, return true if n is prime and false otherwise. (A *prime number* is an integer $n > 1$ whose only divisors are 1 and n.)

35. Given a positive integer n, return the least nonnegative integer k for which $2^k \geq n$.

8.6   INTRODUCTION TO RECURSION

All the examples of method calls considered thus far have involved one method m1 () calling a different method m2 () (with the calling method m1 () often being the main method). However, a method may also *call itself,* a phenomenon known as **recursion,** and in this section, we show how recursion is implemented in Java.

PROBLEM 1: THE FACTORIAL PROBLEM REVISITED

To illustrate the basic idea of recursion, we reconsider the problem of calculating factorials.

 PROBLEM'S OBJECTS. The objects and specification of this problem were given in Section 5.3. The specification,

Receive: *n,* an integer.

Return: $n! = 1 \times 2 \times \cdots \times n$

gives rise to the following stub for the method:

```
public static int factorial(int n)
{
}
```

OPERATIONS. Although the first definition of the factorial *n*! of an integer *n* that one usually learns is

$$n! = \begin{cases} 1 & \text{if } n \text{ is } 0 \\ 1 \times 2 \times \cdots n & \text{if } n > 0 \end{cases}$$

it would be foolish to use it to calculate a sequence of consecutive factorials; that is, to multiply together the numbers from 1 through *n* each time:

$$0! = 1$$

$$1! = 1$$

$$2! = 1 \times 2 = 2$$

$$3! = 1 \times 2 \times 3 = 6$$

$$4! = 1 \times 2 \times 3 \times 4 = 24$$

$$5! = 1 \times 2 \times 3 \times 4 \times 5 = 120$$

A great deal of the effort would be redundant, because it is clear that once a factorial has been calculated, it can be used to calculate the next factorial. For example, given the value 4! = 24, the value 5! can be computed simply by multiplying the value of 4! by 5:

$$5! = 5 \times 4! = 5 \times 24 = 120$$

This value of 5! can in turn be used to calculate 6!,

$$6! = 6 \times 5! = 6 \times 120 = 720$$

and so on. Indeed, to calculate $n!$ for any positive integer n, we need only know the value of 0!,

$$0! = 1$$

and the fundamental relation between one factorial and the next:

$$n! = n \times (n - 1)!$$

In general, an operation is said to be **defined recursively** if its definition consists of two parts:

1. An **anchor** or **base case,** in which the value produced by the operation is specified for one or more values of the operands
2. An **inductive** or **recursive step,** in which the value produced for the current value of the operands is defined in terms of previously defined results and/or operand values.

For the factorial operation ! we have:

$0! = 1$ (the anchor or base case)
For $n > 0, n! = n \times (n - 1)!$ (the inductive or recursive step)

The first statement specifies a particular value produced by !, and the second statement defines the value produced for n in terms of the value produced for $n - 1$.

Algorithm. This approach to calculating factorials leads to the following recursive definition of $n!$,

$$n! = \begin{cases} 1 & \text{if } n \text{ is } 0 \\ n \times (n - 1)! & \text{if } n > 0 \end{cases}$$

which can be used as an algorithm[5] for completing the stub of `factorial()`. To see how it works, consider using it to calculate 5!. We must first calculate 4! because 5! is

---

[5] Note that a recursive definition with a slightly different anchor case can be given by observing that 0! and 1! are both 1. Although this alternative definition leads to a slightly more efficient implementation of `factorial()`, we will use the simpler definition in this introduction to recursion.

defined as the product of 5 and 4!. But to calculate 4! we must calculate 3! because 4! is defined as $4 \times 3!$. And to calculate 3!, we must apply the inductive step of the definition again, $3! = 3 \times 2!$, then again to find 2!, which is defined as $2! = 2 \times 1!$, and once again to find $1! = 1 \times 0!$. Now we have finally reached the anchor case:

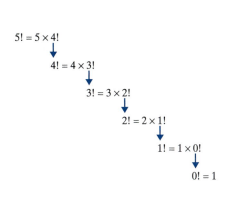

Since the value of 0! is given, we can now backtrack to find the value of 1!,

then backtrack again to find the value of 2!,

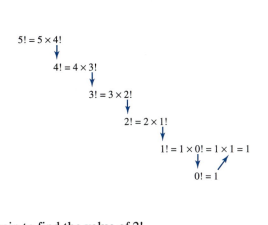

and so on, until we eventually obtain the value 120 for 5!:

$$5! = 5 \times 4! = 5 \times 24 = 120$$
$$4! = 4 \times 3! = 4 \times 6 = 24$$
$$3! = 3 \times 2! = 3 \times 2 = 6$$
$$2! = 2 \times 1! = 2 \times 1 = 2$$
$$1! = 1 \times 0! = 1 \times 1 = 1$$
$$0! = 1$$

As this example demonstrates, a recursive definition may require considerable bookkeeping to record information at the various levels of the recursion, because this information is used *after* the anchor case is reached to backtrack from one level to the preceding one. Fortunately, most modern high-level languages (including Java) support recursion by automatically performing all of the necessary bookkeeping and backtracking.

CODING. Figure 8.9 shows a definition of factorial() that implements this algorithm.

FIGURE 8.9   COMPUTING N! RECURSIVELY

```
/** factorial() computes n! recursively.
 *
 *   Receive:       n, an integer
 *   Precondition:  n >= 0.
 *   Return:        n! (or -1 if n is negative)
 */

public static int factorial(int n)
{
   if (n == 0)
      return 1;                         // anchor case
   else if (n > 0)
      return n * factorial(n-1);   // inductive step

   else                                 // invalid parameter
   {
      System.err.println( "n! is not defined for negative n");
      return -1;
   }
}
```

When this method is called with an argument greater than zero, the inductive step

```
        else if (n > 0)
           return n * factorial(n−1);
```

causes the method to call itself repeatedly, each time with a smaller parameter, until the anchor case

```
if (n == 0)
    return 1;
```

is reached.

To illustrate, consider the statement

```
int fact = factorial(4);
```

that calls the method `factorial()` to calculate 4!. Since the value of n (4) is not 0, the inductive step executes

```
return n * factorial(n-1);
```

which calls `factorial(3)`. Before control is transferred to `factorial(3)`, the current value (4) of the parameter n is saved so that the value of n can be restored when control returns. This might be pictured as follows

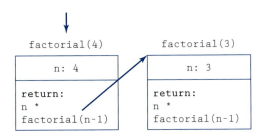

Since the value of n (3) in this method call is not 0, the inductive step in this second call to `factorial()` generates another call `factorial(n-1)` passing it the argument 2. Once again, the value of n (3) is saved so that it can be restored later:

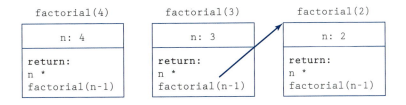

Since the value of n (2) in this method call is not 0, the inductive step in this third call to `factorial()` generates another call `factorial(n-1)` passing it the argument

1. Once again, the value of n (2) is saved so that it can be restored later. The call `factorial(1)` in turn generates another call, `factorial(0)`:

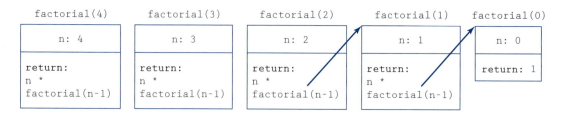

Because the anchor condition

```
if (n == 0)
    return 1;
```

is now satisfied in this last method call, no additional recursive calls are generated. Instead, the value 1 is returned as the value for `factorial(0)`:

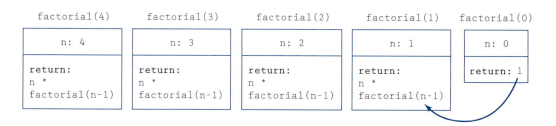

Now that `factorial(0)` has completed its computation, execution resumes in `factorial(1)`, where this returned value can now be used to complete the evaluation of

```
n * factorial(n − 1) = 1 * factorial(0) = 1 * 1 = 1
```

giving 1 as the return value for `factorial(1)`:

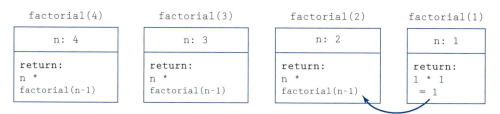

Once `factorial(1)` has completed its computation, execution resumes in `factorial(2)` where the return value of `factorial(1)` can now be used to complete the evaluation of

```
n * factorial(n − 1) = 2 * factorial(1) = 2 * 1 = 2
```

giving 2 as the return value for `factorial(2)`:

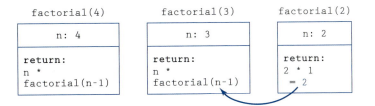

Since `factorial(2)` has completed its computation, execution resumes in `factorial(3)` where the return value of `factorial(2)` is used to complete the evaluation of

$$n \ * \ factorial(n \ - \ 1) \ = \ 3 \ * \ factorial(2) \ = \ 3 \ * \ 2 \ = \ 6$$

giving 6 as the return value for `factorial(3)`:

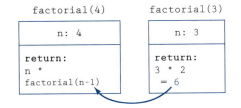

This completes the method call to `factorial(3)`, and so execution resumes in the call to `factorial(4)`, which computes and returns the value

$$n \ * \ factorial(n \ - \ 1) \ = \ 4 \ * \ factorial(3) \ = \ 4 \ * \ 6 \ = \ 24$$

giving 24 as the return value for `factorial(4)`:

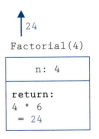

Note that in the definition `factorial()` we test both of the conditions in our algorithm,

```
if (n == 0)
    return 1;                           // trivial case
else if (n > 0)
    return n * factorial(n-1);   // inductive step
else                                    // invalid parameter
{
    System.err.println("n! is not defined for negative n");
    return -1;
}
```

and use the final `else` to handle cases where the parameter `n` is a negative integer. To see the reason for this, consider what would happen if we had written the method without this `else` clause,

```
if (n == 0)
    return 1;
else
    return n * factorial(n - 1);
```

and the method were called with a negative integer, as in

```
int fact = factorial(-1);
```

Since −1 is not equal to 0, the inductive step

```
else
    return n * factorial(n-1);
```

would be performed, recursively calling `factorial(-2)`. Execution of this call would begin, and since −2 is not equal to 0, the inductive step

```
else
    return n * factorial(n-1);
```

would be performed, recursively calling `factorial(-3)`. This behavior would continue until memory was exhausted, at which point the program would terminate abnormally, possibly producing an error message like

```
Stack overruns Heap.
```

Such behavior is described as **infinite recursion** and is obviously undesirable. To avoid it we programmed defensively by including the parameter-validity check.

PROBLEM 2: RECURSIVE EXPONENTIATION

Another classic example of an operation that can be calculated recursively is exponentiation: calculating x^n, where x is a real value and n is a nonnegative integer. The first definition of x^n that one learns is usually an iterative (nonrecursive) one:

$$x^n = \underbrace{x \times x \times \cdots \times x}_{n \; x's}$$

and later one learns that x^0 is defined to be 1. (For convenience, we assume here that x^0 is 1 also when x is 0, although in this case, it is usually left undefined.)

PROBLEM'S OBJECTS. For this problem, we can identify three objects:

Description of problem's object	Type	Kind	Movement	Name
The base value	double	varying	received	x
The exponent	int	varying	received	n
x raised to the power n	double	varying	returned	none

This gives the specification

Receive: x, a real value, and n, an integer;

Precondition: $n \geq 0$

Return: x^n, a real value

which suggests the following method stub:

```
public static double power(double x, int n)
{
}
```

OPERATIONS. To solve a problem recursively, we must identify the anchor and inductive cases. The anchor step is clear: $x^0 = 1$. For the inductive case, we look at an example:

$$5.0^4 = 5.0 \times 5.0 \times 5.0 \times 5.0 = (5.0 \times 5.0 \times 5.0) \times 5.0 = 5.0^3 \times 5.0$$

In general,

$$x^n = x^{n-1} \times x$$

ALGORITHM. Combining our anchor and inductive steps provides the following recursive definition of x^n:

$$x^n = \begin{cases} 1 & \text{if } n \text{ is zero} \quad \text{(the anchor case)} \\ x^{n-1} \times x & \text{if } n \text{ is greater than } 0 \text{ (the inductive case)} \end{cases}$$

As with the factorial method, this definition is an algorithm from which a recursive method can be written, as shown in Figure 8.10.

FIGURE 8.10   PERFORMING EXPONENTIATION RECURSIVELY

```
/** power recursively computes x raised to the power n.
 *
 *  Receive:       x, a double, and n, an integer
 *  Precondition:  n >= 0
 *  Return:        x raised to the power n (or -1 if n is negative)
 */

public static double power(double x, int n)
{
   if (n == 0)
      return 1.0;                      // anchor case
   else if (n > 0)
      return power(x, n - 1) * x;      // inductive step (n > 0)
   else                                // invalid parameter n
   {
      cerr << "*** power has received a negative exponent.\n";
      return -1.0;
   }
}
```

The following diagram pictures the five levels of method calls generated when this method is called with Power(3.0, 4):

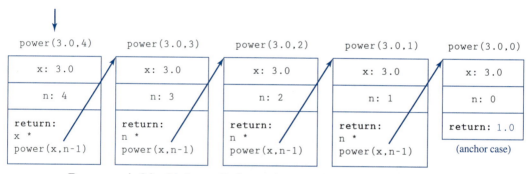

Because n is 0 in this last call, the anchor case has been reached, stopping the recursion. This sequence of recursive calls from an initial call to the anchor case is sometimes referred to as the *winding phase* of the recursion, because like a wind-up clock that is powered by winding a spring, the computation of a recursive method is powered by this sequence of calls that culminates in the anchor case.

Once the anchor case has been reached, the backtracking behavior begins that actually performs the computation, as shown in the following diagram:

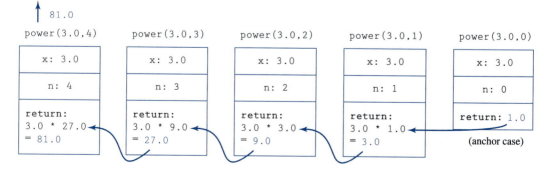

This phase in which values are returned from the anchor case back through each of the previous calls is sometimes referred to as the *unwinding phase* of the recursion, because like a wind-up clock performing its task as its spring unwinds, a recursive method performs its task by "unwinding" the recursive calls stacked up in its winding phase.

PROBLEM 3: DRY BONES!

The Old Testament book of Ezekiel is a book of vivid images that chronicle the siege of Jerusalem by the Babylonians and the subsequent forced relocation (known as the *exile*) of the Israelites following Jerusalem's fall. Chapter 37 describes a powerful vision of Ezekiel in which a valley of dry bones becomes reconnected as he prophesied. Tendons, muscle, and skin regrow on the reconnected bones and the dead skeletons return to life forming a vast army that fills the valley. This vision of new life arising from dry bones provided the homesick Israelites with hope that the "dry bones" of defeated Israel would "come back to life" and they could one day be free of their oppressors, the Babylonians.

Before the American Civil War, many black men and women in the United States found themselves in a situation similar to that of the Israelites, having been forcibly relocated from their homelands and brought to the United States to serve as slaves. One way that they were able to keep their hopes alive was through singing songs that spoke of freedom. However, songs that expressed such hopes directly could result in a beating for the singer, and so these sentiments had to be cleverly encoded in lyrics that would not catch the attention of the slaves' overseers.

One way this was done was by singing **spirituals**—songs whose lyrics referred to stories from the Bible that carried themes of hope and freedom. Songs like *Go Down Moses, Swing Low, Sweet Chariot,* and *Bright Canaan* are examples of spirituals that, in addition to their overt spiritual message, carried a second level of meaning that provided these men and women with the hope that they could one day be free of oppression.

One of the most subtle spirituals is *Dry Bones*. It makes no direct references to freedom, but uses the imagery of scattered bones being reconnected to encode the same message of hope conveyed in Ezekiel 37. With its message of freedom carefully hidden, such a song could be sung in the presence of even the harshest overseer:

```
Ezekiel cried, "Dem dry bones!"
Ezekiel cried, "Dem dry bones!"
Ezekiel cried, "Dem dry bones!"
Oh, hear the word of the Lord.

The foot bone connected to the leg bone,
The leg bone connected to the knee bone,
The knee bone connected to the thigh bone,
The thigh bone connected to the back bone,
The back bone connected to the neck bone,
The neck bone connected to the head bone,
Oh, hear the word of the Lord!
```

```
Dem bones, dem bones gonna walk aroun'
Dem bones, dem bones gonna walk aroun'
Dem bones, dem bones gonna walk aroun'
Oh, hear the word of the Lord.

The head bone connected to the neck bone,
The neck bone connected to the back bone,
The back bone connected to the thigh bone,
The thigh bone connected to the knee bone,
The knee bone connected to the leg bone,
The leg bone connected to the foot bone,
Oh, hear the word of the Lord!

Dem bones, dem bones gonna walk aroun'
Dem bones, dem bones gonna walk aroun'
Dem bones, dem bones gonna walk aroun'
Oh, hear the word of the Lord.
```

The structure of the song is interesting, because it can be partitioned into the following steps, which together comprise an algorithm for printing the song:

   a. Print the "`Ezekiel cried`" variation of the chorus.

   b. Print the *bone lyrics* from foot to head.

   c. Print the "`Dem bones`" variation of the chorus.

   d. Print the *bone lyrics* from toe to head.

   e. Print the "`Dem bones`" variation of the chorus.

What makes the structure interesting is that while Steps b and d are similar, they proceed in reverse order; that is, with the bones reversed. So in Step b, the lines have the form

```
The X bone connected to the Y bone,
```

while in Step d, the corresponding lines are in reverse order, with the bones reversed:

```
The Y bone connected to the X bone,
```

Because of this reversal, the actions performed in Steps b–d can be described using recursion. More precisely, Step c occurs in the middle, and so provides us with an anchor case:

   X == "head" → Print the "Dem bones" variation of the chorus

and every other case can be performed recursively, using this strategy :

   1. Identify the next bone Y.

   2. Print "`The X bone connected to the Y bone,`".

   3. Recursively print the lyrics for bone Y.

   4. Print "`The Y bone connected to the X bone,`".

The method `printBoneLyrics()` in Figure 8.11 encodes this recursive logic.

FIGURE 8.11   DRY BONES!

```
/* DryBones.java displays the lyrics of the song "Dry Bones."
 *
 * Output: lyrics of "Dry Bones"
 */

import ann.easyio.*;                 // Screen

class DryBones extends Object
{
 /** chorus() returns the lyrics of the chorus of the song,
  *  of which there are two variations.
  *  Receive:  variation, a String
  *  Return:   the chorus with the specified variation
  */
  private static String chorus(String variation)
  {
     return variation + variation + variation + lastLine();
  }

 /** lastLine() returns the last line of each verse & chorus.
  *  Receive:  variation, a String
  *  Return:  the last line of each verse and of the chorus
  */
  private static String lastLine()
  {
     return "Oh, hear the word of the Lord!\n\n";
  }

 /** getNext gets the next bone.
  *  Receive:        aBone, a String
  *  Precondition: aBone is a valid bone (in the song).
  *  Return:         the bone above aBone.
  */

  private static String getNext(String aBone)
  {
     if ( aBone.equals("foot") )
        return "leg";
     else if ( aBone.equals("leg") )
        return "knee";
     else if ( aBone.equals("knee") )
        return "thigh";
     else if ( aBone.equals("thigh") )
        return "back";
     else if ( aBone.equals("back") )
        return "neck";
     else if ( aBone.equals("neck") )
          return "head";
       else
       (
          System.err.println("\n*** getNext(): "
                             + aBone + " is unknown!");
          return "";
       }
    }
```

```
/** boneLyrics returns the lyrics for a given bone.
 *   Receive: bone, a String
 *   Return:  the lyrics for that bone and (recursively) the lyrics
 *            for the bones "beneath" it (during winding) and then
 *            for the bones "above" it (during unwinding)
 */
private static String boneLyrics (String bone)
{
    if ( bone.equals("head") )                 // Anchor: bPart == head
       return                                  //   return last line and
          lastLine()                           //   chorus variation
        + chorus("Dem bones, dem bones gonna walk aroun'\n");

    else
    {                                          // Ind-Step: bPart < head
       String
          nextBone = getNext(bone),            //   find next body part
          upLyric =  "The " + bone             //   do 'upward' lyric
             + " bone connected to the "       //   before recursion
             + nextBone + " bone,\n",          //   (winding)

          rest = boneLyrics(nextBone),         //   do rest recursively

          downLyric = "The " + nextBone        //   do 'downward' lyric
             + " bone connected to the "       //   after recursion
             + bone + " bone,\n";              //   (unwinding)

       return upLyric + rest + downLyric;
    }
}

public static void main(String [] args)
{
    Screen theScreen = new Screen();
    theScreen.println(
              chorus("Ezekiel cried, \"Dem dry bones!\"\n")
            + boneLyrics("foot")
            + lastLine()
            + chorus("Dem bones, dem bones gonna walk aroun'\n") );
}

}
```

As this example illustrates, recursion is not limited to methods such as `factorial()` and `power()` that return values. Neither is it limited to numeric problems, but rather can be applied to solve any of the wide variety of problems whose solutions are inherently recursive. The Towers of Hanoi problem that we consider next is another example of such a problem.

PROBLEM 4: TOWERS OF HANOI

The **Towers of Hanoi** problem is to solve the puzzle shown in the following figure, in which one must move the disks from the left peg to the right peg according to the following rules:

1. When a disk is moved, it must be placed on one of the three pegs.

2. Only one disk may be moved at a time, and it must be the top disk on one of the pegs.

3. A larger disk may never be placed on top of a smaller one.

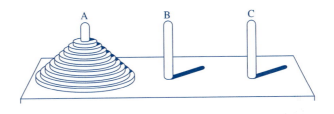

The following *game tree* shows the various configurations that are possible in the problem with two disks; the highlighted path in the tree shows a solution to the two-disk problem:

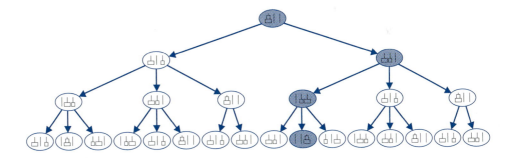

Legend has it that the priests in the Temple of Bramah were given a puzzle consisting of a golden platform with three diamond needles on which were placed sixty-four golden disks. The priests were to move one disk per day, following the preceding rules, and when they had successfully finished moving the disks to another needle, time would end. (*Question:* If the priests moved one disk per day and began their work in year 0, when would time end?)

Novices usually find the puzzle easy to solve for a small number of disks, but they have more difficulty as the number of disks grows to seven, eight, and beyond. To a computer scientist, however, the Towers of Hanoi puzzle is easy. We begin by identifying a base case, for which the problem is trivial to solve:

If there is one disk, then move it from Peg A to Peg C.

The puzzle is thus easily solved for $n = 1$ disk. We then seek an inductive solution for $n > 1$ disks, in which we assume that a solution exists for $n - 1$ disks:

1. *Move the topmost $n - 1$ disks from Peg A to Peg B, using Peg C for temporary storage.*
2. *Move the final disk remaining on Peg A to Peg C.*
3. *Move the $n - 1$ disks from Peg B to Peg C, using Peg A for temporary storage.*

This scheme is implemented by the recursive method `move()` in Figure 8.12, which solves the Towers of Hanoi puzzle for n disks.

FIGURE 8.12   SOLVING THE TOWERS OF HANOI PROBLEM RECURSIVELY

```
/** move() is a recursive method to solve the Hanoi Towers puzzle.
 *   Receive: integer n, the number of disks to be moved,
 *            char source, the needle the disks are to be moved from,
 *            char destination, the needle the disks are to be moved to, and
 *            char spare, the needle that can be used to store disks
 *              temporarily
 *   Return:  sequence of moves that solves the puzzle
 */

public static String move(int n, char source, char destination, char spare)
{
   if (n <= 1)                                    // anchor
      return "Move the top disk from " + source
             + " to " + destination + "\n";
   else                                           // inductive case
      return
         move(n-1, source, spare, destination)
       + move(1, source, destination, spare)
       + move(n-1, spare, destination, source);
}
```

Figure 8.13 presents a driver program that uses `move()` to solve the Hanoi Towers problem, and an execution in which the problem is solved for 4 disks.

FIGURE 8.13   TOWERS OF HANOI DRIVER PROGRAM

```
/* Hanoi.java solves the Towers of Hanoi puzzle recursively.
 *
 * Input:  numDisks, the number of disks to be moved
 * Output: a sequence of moves that solve the puzzle
 */
```

```
import ann.easyio.*;                    // Keyboard, Screen

class Hanoi extends Object
{

  // Insert definition of move() from Figure 8.12 here

  public static void main(String [] args)
  {
     final char PEG1 = 'A',                    // the three pegs
               PEG2 = 'B',
               PEG3 = 'C';

     Screen theScreen = new Screen();
     theScreen.println("This program solves the Hanoi Towers puzzle.\n");

     theScreen.print("Enter the number of disks: ");
     Keyboard theKeyboard = new Keyboard();

     int numDisks = theKeyboard.readInt(); // the number of disks to be moved

                                           // output the solution
     theScreen.println("\n"
                 + move(numDisks, PEG1, PEG2, PEG3) );
  }
}
```

Sample run:

```
This program solves the Hanoi Towers puzzle.

Enter the number of disks: 4

Move the top disk from A to C
Move the top disk from A to B
Move the top disk from C to B
Move the top disk from A to C
Move the top disk from B to A
Move the top disk from B to C
Move the top disk from A to C
Move the top disk from A to B
Move the top disk from C to B
Move the top disk from C to A
Move the top disk from B to A
Move the top disk from C to B
Move the top disk from A to C
Move the top disk from A to B
Move the top disk from C to B
```

Many problems can be solved with equal ease using either a recursive or an iterative algorithm. For example, we implemented the factorial, power, and "dem-bones" methods in this section as recursive methods, but they can be written nonrecursively just as easily. For some problems, however, such as the Towers of Hanoi problem, recursion is the most natural and straightforward technique. For these problems, nonrecursive algorithms may not be obvious, may be more difficult to develop, and may be less readable than recursive ones.

✔ Quick Quiz 8.6

1. _____ is the phenomenon of a method calling itself.
2. Name and describe the two parts of a recursive definition of a method.
3. For the following recursive method, find `f(5)`.

```
public static int f(int n)
{
    if (n == 0)
        return 0;
    else
        return n + f(n - 1);
}
```

4. For the method in Question 3, find `f(0)`.
5. For the method in Question 3, suppose + is changed to * in the inductive step. Find `f(5)`.
6. For the method in Question 4, what happens with the method call `f(-1)`?

✍ EXERCISES 8.6

Exercises 1–11 assume the following method `f`:

```
public static void f(int num)
{
    if ((1 <= num) && (num <= 8))
    {
        f(num - 1);
        theScreen.print(num);
    }
    else
        theScreen.println( );
}
```

For Exercises 1–3, tell what output is produced by the method call.

1. `f(3);`   2. `f(7);`   3. `f(10);`

4–6. Tell what output is produced by the method calls in Exercises 1–3 if `num - 1` is replaced by `num + 1` in the method definition.

7–9. Tell what output is produced by the method calls in Exercises 1–3 if the statement `theScreen.print(num);` and the recursive call to `f()` are interchanged.

10–12. Tell what output is produced by the method calls in Exercises 1–3 if a copy of the statement `theScreen.print(num);` is inserted before the recursive call to `f()`.

13. Given the following method `f()`, use the method illustrated in this section to trace the sequence of method calls and returns in evaluating `f(1, 5)`.

```
public static int f(int num1, int num2)
{
    if (num1 > num2)
        return 0;
```

```
    else if (num2 == num1 + 1)
        return 1;
    else
        return f(num1 + 1, num2 - 1) + 2;
}
```

14. Proceed as in Exercise 13, but for f(8, 3).

Exercises 15–17 assume the following method g():

```
public static void g(int num1, int num2)
{
    if (num2 <= 0)
        theScreen.println();
    else
    {
        g(num1 - 1, num2 - 1);
        theScreen.print(num1);
        g(num1 + 1, num2 - 1);
    }
}
```

15. What output is produced by the method call g(14, 4)? (*Hint:* First try g(14, 2), then g(14, 3)).

16. How many letters are output by the call g(14, 10)?

17. If the statement theScreen.print(num1); is moved before the first recursive call to g(), what output will be produced by g(14, 4)?

For Exercises 18–22, determine what is calculated by the given recursive method.

18.
```
public static int f(int n)
{
    if (n == 0)
        return 0;
    else
        return n * f(n - 1);
}
```

19.
```
public static double f(double x, int n)
{
    if (n == 0)
        return 0;
    else
        return x + f(x, n - 1);
}
```

20.
```
public static int f(int n)
{
    if (n < 2)
        return 0;
    else
        return 1 + f(n / 2);
}
```

```
21.  public static int f(int n)
     {
        if (n == 0)
           return 0;
        else
           return f(n / 10) + n % 10;
     }


22.  public static int f(int n)
     {
        if (n < 0)
           return f(-n);
        else if (n < 10)
           return n;
        else
           return f(n / 10);
     }
```

For Exercises 23–27, write a nonrecursive version of the method.

23. The method in Exercise 18.

24. The method in Exercise 19.

25. The method in Exercise 20.

26. The method in Exercise 21.

27. The method in Exercise 22.

Exercises 28–33 ask you to write methods to compute various quantities. To test these methods, you should write driver programs as instructed in Programming Problems 22–25 at the end of this chapter.

28. Write a recursive method that returns the number of digits in a nonnegative integer.

29. Write a nonrecursive version of the method in Exercise 28.

30. Write a recursive method `printReverse()` that displays an integer's digits in reverse order.

31. Write a nonrecursive version of the method `printReverse()` in Exercise 30.

32. Modify the recursive exponentiation method in the text so that it also works for negative exponents. One approach is to modify the recursive definition of x^n so that for negative values of n, division is used instead of multiplication and n is incremented rather than decremented:

$$x^n = \begin{cases} 1 & \text{if } n \text{ is zero} \\ x^{n+1} \times x & \text{if } n \text{ is greater than } 0 \\ x^{n+1}/x & \text{otherwise} \end{cases}$$

33. The **greatest common divisor** of two integers a and b, GCD(a, b), not both of which are zero, is the largest positive integer that divides both a and b. The **Euclidean algorithm** for finding this greatest common divisor of a and b is as follows: Divide a by b to

obtain the integer quotient q and remainder r, so that $a = bq + r$. (If $b = 0$, GCD(a, b) = a.) Then GCD(a, b) = GCD(b, r). Replace a with b and b with r, and repeat this procedure. Since the remainders are decreasing, eventually a remainder of 0 will result. The last nonzero remainder is GCD(a, b). For example,

$$1260 = 198 \times 6 + 72 \quad GCD(1260, 198) = GCD(198, 72)$$

$$198 = 72 \times 2 + 54 \qquad\qquad = GCD(72, 54)$$

$$72 = 54 \times 1 + 18 \qquad\qquad = GCD(54, 18)$$

$$54 = 18 \times 3 + 0 \qquad\qquad = 18$$

(*Note:* If either a or b is negative, replace it with its absolute value.) Write a recursive method that calculates the greatest common divisor of two integers using the Euclidean algorithm.

34.   Write a nonrecursive version of the GCD method in Exercise 33.

35.   For the method `move()` in Figure 8.12, trace the execution of the method call `move(4, 'A', 'B', 'C');` far enough to produce the first five moves. Does your answer agree with the program output in Figure 8.13?

36.   Proceed as in Exercise 35 but for the call `move(5, 'A', 'B, 'C');`

8.7   GRAPHICAL/INTERNET JAVA: A GUESSING GAME

In the two-player game "Twenty Questions," one player thinks of something and the other player may ask up to twenty Yes–No questions in which to identify it. "Twenty Guesses" is a numerical version of this game, in which one player thinks of an integer and the other player is allowed up to twenty guesses. For each incorrect guess, the first player tells the second player whether the guess is too high, too low, or is the number. The second player then uses this information in the next guess. In this section, we will build a program to play this game, with the user in the role of the first player and the computer in the role of the second player.

PROBLEM: TWENTY GUESSES

Write a program with a graphical user interface to play the role of the guesser in the Twenty Guesses game. A common guessing strategy, and the one that we will use, is a binary-search strategy. The guesser keeps track of a low value and a high value that bound the search range and on each turn, guesses the number halfway between them. If the guess is too high, then the guesser replaces the upper bound by one less than the guess; if the guess is too low, then the lower bound is replaced by one more than the guess.

OBJECT-CENTERED DESIGN

BEHAVIOR. Our program should begin by asking the user to pick an integer and display a "Begin" button and a "Quit" button. If the user clicks the "Quit" button, the program should terminate. If the user clicks the "Begin" button, the program should play the game using the binary-search strategy, display a "Lower", an "Equal", and a "Higher" button by which the user can respond to the program's guess, and replace the "Begin" button with a "Reset" button. This behavior should continue until (i) the program guesses the integer, (ii) the program has guessed 20 times without guessing the integer; (iii) the user clicks the "Quit" button in which case the program should terminate; or (iv) the user clicks the "Reset" button in which case the program should reset for a new game.

TRANSITION DIAGRAM. To clarify the behavior, we might draw a transition diagram like the following that shows sketches of the different views we want our GUI to exhibit:

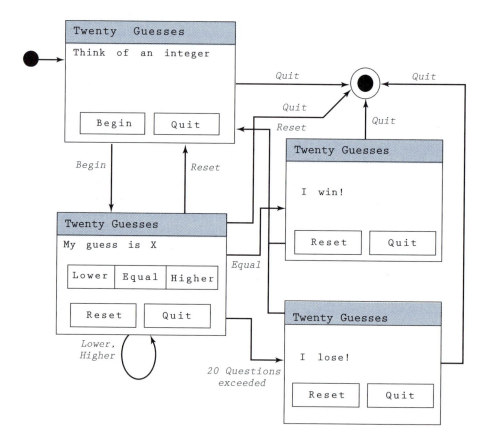

PROBLEM'S OBJECTS. From the preceding discussion, we can identify these objects in this problem:

Description of problem's object	Type	Kind	Name
The program	??	varying	??
A prompt	JLabel	varying	*myPromptLabel*
Prompt message	String	varying	none
A "Begin" button	JButton	varying	*myBeginButton*
A "Quit" button	JButton	varying	*myQuitButton*
A "Lower" button	JButton	varying	*myLowerButton*
An "Equal" button	JButton	varying	*myEqualButton*
A "Higher" button	JButton	varying	*myHigherButton*
A "Reset" button	JButton	varying	*myResetButton*
A guess	int	varying	*myGuess*
Count of guesses	int	varying	*myGuessCount*
A lowest possible value	int	varying	*myLoBound*
A highest possible value	int	varying	*myHiBound*

We will call our class `GUIGuessingGame`, which will provide both a type and a name for the program.

Our GUI uses `JButton` objects, which fire `ActionEvent` objects when clicked by the user. (See the Documentation sections of the summaries of Chapter 7 and this chapter for more information.) As we described in Section 7.5, to listen for `ActionEvent` objects, our `GUIGuessingGame` will need to implement the `ActionListener` interface, and register itself as the listener for each button.

The only tricky part of this program is getting both a "Begin" and a "Reset" button to appear at the same position in the window frame. To accomplish this, we will define a `JButton` named `myBeginButton`, a `JButton` named `myResetButton`, and a `JButton` *handle* named `myBeginResetButton`. Our code will then make `myBeginResetButton` the handle for either `myBeginButton` or `myResetButton`, as appropriate.

In addition to these objects, we will need a counter to keep track of how many questions have been asked and a few `JPanel` objects to group our components in an aesthetic way.

OPERATIONS.   From our GUI examples in Chapter 7, we can identify the following operations:

   i. A constructor method to build the GUI.

   ii. An `actionPerformed()` method to implement the `ActionListener` interface. To register itself as the listener for each button, our class will need to send the `addActionListener()` message to each button.

   iii. A main method to create an instance of the class and make it visible.

Technically, these three methods are all that are needed. However, another way to organize the code that is often more useful in event-driven programs is to convert the transition diagram into a **state diagram**—a transition diagram with most of the details removed. To illustrate, here is a state diagram for the transition diagram given earlier:

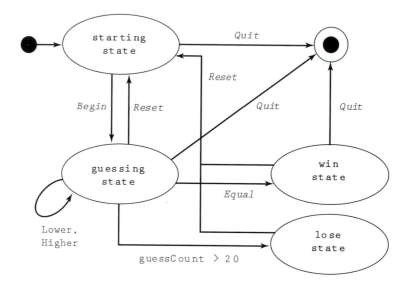

CODING. We can be certain that our GUI always has the correct appearance by writing a method for each state to define its appearance in that state. To illustrate, here is a method to initialize the program in its starting state:

```
private void enterStartingState()
{
   myGuessCount = 0;
   myLoBound = Integer.MIN_VALUE;
   myHiBound = Integer.MAX_VALUE;

   myPromptLabel.setText("Choose an integer for me to guess...");

   myBeginResetButton.setText("Begin");

   myBeginResetButton.setVisible(true);

   myQuitButton.setVisible(true);

   myLowerButton.setVisible(false);
   myEqualButton.setVisible(false);
   myHigherButton.setVisible(false);
}
```

Since this method is responsible for the appearance of the GUI at the outset and when the "Reset" button is clicked, it sets each of the variables used by the program to its initial state, and then sets the attributes of each of the buttons as shown in our transition diagram.

Every `JButton` has a label attribute that can be set using the `setText()` message. This lets us give the button referred to by `myBeginResetButton` a "Begin" label in the starting state and a "Reset" label in every other state. To illustrate, here is the method to enter the guessing state:

```
private void enterGuessingState()
{
    myGuess = (myHiBound + myLoBound) / 2;
    myGuessCount++;

    myPromptLabel.setText("Guess #" + myGuessCount
                       + ": Is your number " + myGuess + "?");

    myLowerButton.setVisible(true);
    myEqualButton.setVisible(true);
    myHigherButton.setVisible(true);

    myBeginResetButton.setText("Reset");
    myBeginResetButton.setVisible(true);
    myQuitButton.setVisible(true);
}
```

Upon entering the guessing state, this method generates a new guess based on the high and low values, increments the guess counter, updates the prompt label with the guess, and then sets the attributes of each of the buttons as specified in our transition diagram.

The `actionPerformed()` method uses the `getText()` message to retrieve the label of the button whose handle is `myBeginResetButton`, in order to distinguish a click on "Begin" from a click on "Reset":

```
if ( eventButton.equals(myBeginResetButton) )
{
    String itsLabel = eventButton.getText();
    if ( itsLabel.equals("Begin") )
        enterGuessingState();
    else if ( itsLabel.equals("Reset") )
        enterStartingState();
    else
        Controller.fatal("actionPerformed()", "unknown button");
}
```

Figure 8.14 gives the complete code for our Twenty Guesses Game.

FIGURE 8.14 THE TWENTY GUESSES GAME

```java
// GUIGuessingGame.java plays the 20-guesses game.

import ann.gui.CloseableFrame;
import ann.util.Controller;
import javax.swing.*;           // JButton, JFrame, ...
import java.awt.*;              // FlowLayout, GridLayout, ...
import java.awt.event.*;        // ActionEvent, ...

class GUIGuessingGame extends CloseableFrame
                      implements ActionListener
{
 final static int MAX_GUESSES = 20;

 public GUIGuessingGame()
 {
  setTitle(MAX_GUESSES + " Guesses");
  myPromptLabel = new JLabel();

  myLowerButton = new JButton("Lower");                 // create the buttons
  myLowerButton.addActionListener(this);
  myEqualButton = new JButton("Equal");
  myEqualButton.addActionListener(this);
  myHigherButton = new JButton("Higher");
  myHigherButton.addActionListener(this);
  myBeginResetButton = new JButton();
  myBeginResetButton.addActionListener(this);
  myQuitButton = new JButton("Quit");
  myQuitButton.addActionListener(this);

  enterStartingState();                                 // set their states

  myTopPane  = new JPanel( new FlowLayout() );          // build rows
  myTopPane.add(myPromptLabel);
  myMiddlePane = new JPanel( new GridLayout(1,3) );
  myMiddlePane.add(myLowerButton);
  myMiddlePane.add(myEqualButton);
  myMiddlePane.add(myHigherButton);
  myBottomPane = new JPanel( new FlowLayout() );
  myBottomPane.add(myBeginResetButton);
  myBottomPane.add(myQuitButton);

  myContentPane = new JPanel( new GridLayout(3,1) ); // build content pane
  myContentPane.setBackground(Color.white);
  myContentPane.add(myTopPane);
  myContentPane.add(myMiddlePane);
  myContentPane.add(myBottomPane);

  setContentPane(myContentPane);
 }

 private void enterStartingState()
 {
  myGuessCount = 0;
  myLoBound = Integer.MIN_VALUE;
  myHiBound = Integer.MAX_VALUE;
```

```java
    myPromptLabel.setText("Choose an integer for me to guess...");
    myBeginResetButton.setText("Begin");
    myBeginResetButton.setVisible(true);
    myQuitButton.setVisible(true);
    myLowerButton.setVisible(false);
    myEqualButton.setVisible(false);
    myHigherButton.setVisible(false);
}

public void actionPerformed(ActionEvent event)
{
  Object eventSource = event.getSource();
  if (eventSource instanceof JButton)
  {
    JButton eventButton = (JButton) eventSource;
    if ( eventButton.equals(myBeginResetButton) )
    {
      String itsLabel = eventButton.getText();
      if ( itsLabel.equals("Begin") )
        enterGuessingState();
      else if ( itsLabel.equals("Reset") )
        enterStartingState();
      else
        Controller.fatal("actionPerformed()", "unknown button");
    }
    else if ( eventButton.equals(myQuitButton) )
      System.exit(0);
    else if ( eventButton.equals(myEqualButton) )
      enterWinState();
    else if (myGuessCount < MAX_GUESSES)
      if ( eventButton.equals(myLowerButton) )
      {
        myHiBound = myGuess-1;
        enterGuessingState();
      }
      else if ( eventButton.equals(myHigherButton) )
      {
        myLoBound = myGuess+1;
        enterGuessingState();
      }
      else
        Controller.fatal("actionPerformed()", "unknown button " + event);
    else
      enterLoseState();
  }
  else
    Controller.fatal("actionPerformed()", "unknown event " + event);
}

private void enterGuessingState()
{
  myGuessCount++;
  myGuess = (myHiBound + myLoBound) / 2;
  myPromptLabel.setText("Guess #" + myGuessCount
                        + ": Is your number " + myGuess + "?");
  myLowerButton.setVisible(true);
  myEqualButton.setVisible(true);
  myHigherButton.setVisible(true);
```

```
    myBeginResetButton.setText("Reset");
    myBeginResetButton.setVisible(true);
    myQuitButton.setVisible(true);
  }

  private void enterWinState()
  {
    myPromptLabel.setText("I win!  Care to try again?");
    enterFinalState();
  }

  private void enterLoseState()
  {
    myPromptLabel.setText("Boo-hoo...  Want to play again? ");
    enterFinalState();
  }

  private void enterFinalState()
  {
    myLowerButton.setVisible(false);
    myEqualButton.setVisible(false);
    myHigherButton.setVisible(false);
    myBeginResetButton.setText("Reset");
    myBeginResetButton.setVisible(true);
    myQuitButton.setVisible(true);
  }

  public static void main(String [] args)
  {
    GUIGuessingGame game = new GUIGuessingGame();
    game.setSize(400,150);
    game.setVisible(true);
  }

  long    myGuessCount, myLoBound, myHiBound, myGuess;
  JLabel  myPromptLabel;
  JButton myQuitButton, myBeginResetButton,
          myLowerButton, myEqualButton, myHigherButton;
  JPanel  myContentPane, myTopPane, myMiddlePane, myBottomPane;
}
```

TESTING. When executed, our program begins by displaying the window frame shown below:

If the user clicks the "Quit" button, then the program terminates in this and all subsequent states. If the user clicks the "Begin" button, then the window frame changes as the program enters the guessing state:

If during the course of the game the program guesses the user's integer and the user presses the "Equal" button, then the window frame changes as the program enters the win state:

If, however, the program exhausts its guesses without guessing the user's integer, then the window frame changes as the program enters the lose state:

Pressing the "Reset" button in any of these states returns the program to the starting state. As discussed in Section 7.5, no repetition statement is needed within our program to elicit this continuous execution, because the event-handling loop is supplied by Java's underlying graphics system. Our program participates in this system by extending the `CloseableFrame` class.

An Applet Version of the GUI Guessing Program

Converson of the GUI guessing application to an applet follows a procedure like that used in the preceding chapter:

1. Make the class extend `JApplet` instead of `CloseableFrame`:

```
public class GUIGuessingGame2 extends JApplet
                            implements ActionListener
```

2. Replace `main()` with a non-static `init()` method:

```
public void init(String [] args)
{ . . .
}
```

3. Remove the call to `setTitle()`.

4. Adjust the dimensions of the applet frame in the HTML file so that it resembles the frame for the application in Figure 8.20:

```
<APPLET CODE="GUIGuessingGame2.class"
WIDTH=400 HEIGHT=100 </APPLET>
```

This will produce frames like the following:

The complete applet code can be found on the text's CD and website (see the preface). It has been renamed `GUIGuessingGame2` so all references to the class also need to be changed.

PART OF THE PICTURE: INTRODUCTION TO ALGORITHM ANALYSIS

In the incident described in Section 8.1, the student Gauss responded almost immediately when he was given the problem of summing the integers from 1 through 100. The simplicity and efficiency of his algorithm compared to the repetitive algorithm we used is an indication of his genius. We will describe his algorithm here and use it to introduce the area of computer science known as algorithm analysis.

To compute the sum of the integers from 1 through 100, Gauss perhaps observed that writing the sum forward,

$$sum = 1 + 2 + 3 + \cdots + 98 + 99 + 100$$

and then backwards,

$$sum = 100 + 99 + 98 + \cdots + 3 + 2 + 1$$

and then adding corresponding terms in these two equations gives

$$2 \times sum = 101 + 101 + 101 + \cdots + 101 + 101 + 101$$

$$= 100 \times 101$$

Thus the sum is equal to

$$sum = \frac{100 \times 101}{2} = 5050$$

Applying his algorithm to the more general summation problem, we begin with the sum

$$sum = 1 + 2 + 3 + \cdots + (n{-}2) + (n{-}1) + n$$

reverse it,

$$sum = n + (n{-}1) + (n{-}2) + \cdots + 3 + 2 + 1$$

and then add these two equations to get

$$2 \times sum = (n + 1) + (n + 1) + (n + 1) + \cdots + (n + 1) + (n + 1) + (n + 1)$$

$$= n \times (n + 1)$$

Dividing by 2 gives

$$sum = \frac{n \times (n + 1)}{2}$$

This formula implies that method `summation()` can be written without using a loop at all, as shown in Figure 8.15.

FIGURE 8.15 METHOD `summation()`—GAUSSIAN VERSION

```
class Formula
{
  /** summation(long n) computes the sum of the integers from 1 to n
   *  using Gauss' formula.
   *  Receive:      n, a long
   *  Precondition: n > 0
   *  Return:       the long value = 1 + 2 + ... + n
   */
```

```
public static long summation(long n)
{
  if (n > 0)
    return n * (n+1) / 2;
  else
  {
    Controller.fatal("summation(n)", "non-positive n received");
    return 0;
  }
}

// ... other Formula methods
}
```

This solution is better than one that uses a loop, because it solves the same problem *in less time*. To see why, suppose we want to compute the sum of the integers from 1 through 1000. A version of `summation()` that uses a loop (such as that in Figure 8.1) must repeat the body of the loop 1,000 times. That means it must perform:

> 1,000 additions of `count` to `runningTotal`,
> 1,000 assignments of that result to `runningTotal`,
> 1,000 increments of `count`, and
> 1,000 comparisons of `count` to n,

for a total of 4,000 operations. For an arbitrary value of n, each of these operations would be performed n times for a total of 4n operations. We say that the number of operations performed by the loop version of `summation()` **grows linearly** with the value of its parameter n.

By contrast, the final version of `summation()` always does

> 1 addition,
> 1 multiplication, and
> 1 division,

for a total of 3 operations, *regardless of the value of* n. Thus the time taken by the latter version of `summation()` is **constant,** regardless of the value of its parameter n.

This is our first look at an important area of computer science called **analysis of algorithms.** We have seen two algorithms that solve the summation problem. To determine which of them is "better", we analyze the number of operations each requires to solve the problem. The algorithm using Gauss' formula solves the problem in constant time, while the algorithm using a loop solves the problem in time proportional to n, and consequently, Gauss' algorithm is to be preferred.

CHAPTER SUMMARY

KEY TERMS AND NOTES

anchor or base case	one-trip behavior
counting (or counter-controlled) loops	outer loop
counting input loop	posttest loop
do loop	pretest loop
end-of-data flag	query-controlled input loop
for loop	recursion
forever loop	recursive definition of an operation
indefinite loop	sentinel
inductive or recursive step	state diagram
infinite recursion	termination condition
inner loop	Towers of Hanoi
labeled statement	while loop
nested loops	zero-trip behavior

◉ A trace table is a good tool to trace the action of a loop (especially in debugging).

◉ By using an appropriate increment expression, a `for` statement can be used to step through a range of values with any increment.

◉ It is (usually) unwise to change the value of any variables in the loop condition within the body of a counting loop, because this can produce unexpected results; in particular, the number of repetitions may change.

◉ An indefinite loop is usually implemented in Java with a `for` statement with no loop condition: `for(;;){ . . . }`.

◉ A forever loop continues repetition when its termination condition is false and terminates repetition when that condition is true.

◉ A `break` statement can be used to terminate execution of an enclosing loop or `switch` statement. An unlabeled `break` terminates the innermost enclosing loop or `switch`; a labeled `break` terminates execution of the enclosing statement that has that label. A labeled `break` is useful for breaking out of nested loops.

◉ In some cases, a `return` statement is a useful alternative to `break` for terminating execution of a method and returning to the calling method.

◉ A `continue` statement is useful for skipping the rest of the current iteration and beginning a new one.

◉ A *while* loop is a *pretest* (or test-at-the-top) loop. It continues repetition so long as its condition is true, and terminates repetition when that condition is false. A while loop has *zero-trip behavior.*

◉ A *do* loop is a *posttest* (or test-at-the-bottom) loop. Because its loop body will always be executed at least one before the loop condition is tested, it is said to have *one-trip behavior.*

◉ Three common kinds of input loops are:

❏ *Counting* loops in which the number of input items is known in advance

❏ *Sentinel-controlled* loops in which an end-of-data flag (or sentinel) signals the end of data

❏ *Query-controlled* loops in which the user is asked whether there is more data

◉ The following guidelines may help with deciding which kind of loop to use:

1. If the algorithm requires counting through some fixed range of values, use a counting loop.

2. If a general loop is required, use a generic indefinite loop to formulate the algorithm. Then determine where the termination condition should go. If at the beginning, use a while loop; it at the end, use a do loop; if somewhere else, use a forever loop with an `if-break` or `if-return`.

◉ A recursive method must have an anchor that will eventually be executed and cause a return from the method. It must also have an inductive step that specifies the current action of the method in terms of previously defined actions.

Documentation

REFERENCE The GUI example in Section 8.7 used several of the same Swing classes—`JTextField`, `JPanel`, and `JFrame` (and our extension `CloseableFrame`)—and event-handling classes—`ActionEvent` from `java.awt.event`—as the GUI examples in Section 7.5. See the presentation there and the Documentation section of the summary for Chapter 7 for information about them. The following table descrbes a few of the many methods provided for `JButton`, the only Swing component not described in earlier chapters. See Java's API documentation for more information.

■ SOME `JButton` METHODS (`javax.swing`)

Method	Description
Constructors:	Creates button with:
`JButton()`	no text or icon
`JButton(String text)`	specified text but no icon
`JButton(Icon icon)`	no text but with specified icon
`JButton(String text,` `      Icon icon)`	with specified text and icon
`String paramString()`	Returns a string representation of this `JButton`.
Methods inherited from `AbstractButton`:	
`void addActionListener(` `          ActionListener l)`	Adds `ActionListener` `l` to the button's listener list
`String getText()`	Returns the button's text
`boolean isSelected()`	Returns the state of the button
`void removeActionListener(` `          ActionListener l)`	Removes `ActionListener` `l` from the button's listener list
`void setText(String text)`	Sets the button's text to `text`

PROGRAMMING POINTERS

PROGRAM STYLE AND DESIGN

In this text, we use the following conventions for formatting the control statements considered in this chapter:

1. *The statement in a* `for`, `while`, `do`, *and forever loop is indented. If the statement is compound, the opening curly brace* `{` *is aligned with its closing curly brace* `}`; *the lines within the loop body are indented. In a do loop,* `do` *is aligned with its corresponding* `while`.

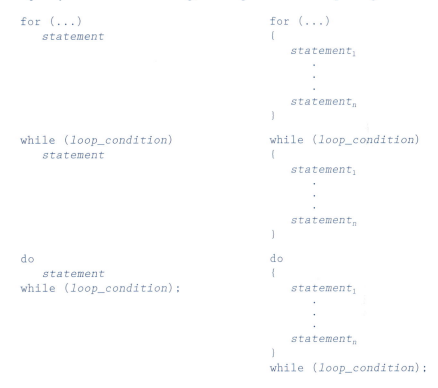

```
for (...)
    statement
```

```
for (...)
{
    statement₁
        .
        .
        .
    statementₙ
}
```

```
while (loop_condition)
    statement
```

```
while (loop_condition)
{
    statement₁
        .
        .
        .
    statementₙ
}
```

```
do
    statement
while (loop_condition);
```

```
do
{
    statement₁
        .
        .
        .
    statementₙ
}
while (loop_condition);
```

2. *Anything that can be computed can be computed using (only) the three control structures:* sequence, selection, *and* repetition.

3. *Repetition structures can be implemented in Java using the* `for`, `while`, *and* `do` *statements, and it is important to select the one that best implements the repetition structure required in a given problem.* Some guidelines for choosing the appropriate loop are:

❑ *The for loop is most appropriate for performing repetition when the number of repetitions can be determined before the loop is entered.*

❑ *The while loop is most appropriate for performing repetition when zero-trip behavior is desired.* Since the loop condition appears at the top of the loop, the body of the loop will not be entered inadvertently if the loop condition is false initially.

❑ *The do loop is most appropriate for performing repetition when one-trip behavior is desired.* Since the loop condition appears at the bottom of the loop, the body of the loop will be executed at least once before repetition is terminated.

❑ *The forever loop can be used to perform repetition when neither zero-trip nor one-trip behavior is desired.* An `if-break` or an `if-return` combination is usually used to terminate repetition.

4. *Recursive methods should be clearly marked as such.* For clarity and readability, the anchor case and inductive steps of a recursive method should be marked with comments.

WATCH

OUT

POTENTIAL PITFALLS

1. *Care must be taken to avoid infinite looping.*

❑ The loop condition of a for loop must eventually become *false;* the body of a while loop or a do loop must contain statements that eventually cause its loop condition to become *false.* For example, the code fragment

```
double x = 0.0;
do
{
    aScreen.println(x);
    x += 0.3;
}
while (x != 1.0);
```

produces an infinite loop:

```
0.0
0.3
0.6
0.9
1.2
1.5
1.8
 .
 .
 .
```

Since the value of x is never equal to 1.0, repetition is not terminated.

❑ The body of a forever loop should always contain an `if-break` or `if-return` combination and statements that ensure that the termination condition of the loop will eventually become *true.*

2. *In a while loop, the loop condition that controls repetition is evaluated before execution of the body of the loop. In a do loop, the loop condition that controls repetition is evaluated after execution of the body of the loop.* Thus, the body of a while loop will not be executed if the loop condition is false, but the statements within a do loop are always executed at least once.

3. *The* `for`, `while`, do *and forever loops control a single statement.* **For example, the following poorly-indented segment**

```
for (int i = 1; i <= 10; i++)
    j = i*i;
    aScreen.println(j);
```

will display only a single value,

```
100
```

since the output statement is outside the body of the loop. Likewise, the segment:

```
int count = 1;
while (count <= 10)
    aScreen.println(count + '\t' + count*count);
    count++;
```

will produce an infinite loop,

```
1       1
1       1
1       1
        .
        .
        .
```

because the statement that increments `count` is outside the body of the loop.

4. *In a do loop, the closing* `while (loop_condition)` *must be followed by a semicolon, or a syntax error will result.*

5. *In a for loop, neither the control variable nor any variable involved in the loop condition should be modified within the body of the loop, since it is intended to run through a specified range of consecutive values.* **Strange and undesirable results may be produced otherwise. To illustrate, the statement**

```
for (int i = 1; i <= 4; i++)
{
    aScreen.println(i);
    i++;
}
```

produces the output

```
1
3
```

The statement

```
for (int i = 1; i <= 4; i++)
{
    aScreen.println(i);
    i--;
}
```

results in an infinite loop, displaying the output

```
1
1
1
1
.
.
.
```

6. *Care must be taken to ensure that the anchor in a recursive method will eventually be reached.* Each recursive call should make progress towards the anchor case, or infinite recursion can result.

PROGRAMMING PROBLEMS

SECTIONS 8.1–8.5

1. Write a driver program to test the modified method `summation()` of Exercise 28 of Section 8.5.

2. Write a driver program to test the `BigInteger` version of the method `summation()` of Exercise 29 of Section 8.5.

3. Write a driver program to test the modified `BigInteger` version of the method `summation()` of Exercise 30 of Section 8.5.

4. Write a driver program to test the power method of Exercise 31 of Section 8.5.

5. Write a driver program to test the modified power method of Exercise 32 of Section 8.5.

6. Write a driver program to test the sum-of-divisors method of Exercise 33 of Section 8.5.

7. Write a driver program to test the prime-checker method of Exercise 34 of Section 8.5.

8. Write a driver program to test the power-of-two method of Exercise 35 of Section 8.5.

9. Write a program that displays the following multiplication table:

```
      1    2    3    4    5    6    7    8    9
 1    1
 2    2    4
 3    3    6    9
 4    4    8   12   16
 5    5   10   15   20   25
 6    6   12   18   24   30   36
 7    7   14   21   28   35   42   49
 8    8   16   24   32   40   48   56   64
 9    9   18   27   36   45   54   63   72   81
```

10. A positive integer is said to be a *deficient, perfect,* or *abundant* number if the sum of its proper divisors is less than, equal to, or greater than the number, respectively. For example, 8 is deficient because its proper divisors are 1, 2, and 4, and $1 + 2 + 4 < 8$; 6 is perfect, because $1 + 2 + 3 = 6$; 12 is abundant, because $1 + 2 + 3 + 4 + 6 > 12$. Write a

program that classifies n as being deficient, perfect, or abundant for $n = 20$ to 30, then for $n = 490$ to 500, and finally for $n = 8120$ to 8130. It should use the method from Exercise 33 of Section 8.5 to find the sum of the proper divisors.

Extra: Find the smallest odd abundant number. *Warning:* An attempt to find an odd perfect number will probably fail, because none has yet been found, although it has not been proven that such numbers do not exist.

11. The Rinky Dooflingy Company currently sells 200 dooflingies per month at a profit of $300 per dooflingy. The company now spends $2000 per month on advertising and has fixed operating costs of $1000 per month that do not depend on the volume of sales. If the company doubles the amount spent on advertising, sales will increase by 20 percent. Write a program that prints under appropriate headings the amount spent on advertising, the number of sales made, and the net profit. Begin with the company's current status and successively double the amount spent on advertising until the net profit "goes over the hump;" that is, begins to decline. The output should include the amounts up through the first time that the net profit begins to decline.

12. The *divide-and-average* algorithm for approximating the square root of any positive number a is as follows: take any initial approximation x that is positive, and then find a new approximation by calculating the average of x and a / x, that is, $(x + a / x) / 2$. Repeat this procedure with x replaced by this new approximation, stopping when x and a / x differ in absolute value by some specified error allowance, such as 0.00001. Write a program that reads values for x, a, and the small error allowance, and then uses this divide-and-average algorithm to find the approximate square root of x. Have the program display each of the successive approximations. Execute the program with $a = 3$ and error allowance $= 0.00001$, and use the following initial approximations: 1, 10, 0.01, and 100. Also execute the program with $a = 4$, error allowance $= 0.00001$, and initial approximations 1 and 2.

13. Write a program that accepts a positive integer and gives its prime factorization; that is, expresses the integer as a product of primes or indicates that it is a prime. (See Exercise 34 of Section 8.5 for the definition of a prime number.)

14. Write a program to read a set of numbers, count them, and find and print the largest and smallest numbers in the list and their positions in the list.

15. Write a program that reads an exchange rate for converting English currency to U.S. currency and then reads several several values in English currency and converts each amount to the equivalent U.S. currency. Display all amounts with appropriate labels. Use sentinel-controlled loops for the input.

16. Proceed as in the preceding exercise, but convert several values from U.S. currency to English currency.

17. One method for finding the *base-b representation* of a positive integer given in base-10 notation is to divide the integer repeatedly by b until a quotient of zero results. The successive remainders are the digits from right to left of the base-b representation. For example, the binary representation of 26 is 11010_2, as the following computation shows:

$$
\begin{array}{r}
0 \text{ R1} \\
2\overline{)1} \text{ R1} \\
2\overline{)3} \text{ R0} \\
2\overline{)6} \text{ R1} \\
2\overline{)13} \text{ R0} \\
2\overline{)26}
\end{array}
$$

Write a program to accept various integers and bases and display the digits of the base-*b* representation for each integer. You may assume that each base is in the range 2 through 10.

18. Proceed as in Problem 17, but convert integers from base 10 to hexadecimal (base 16). Use a `switch` statement to display the symbols A, B, C, D, E, and F for 10, 11, 12, 13, 14, and 15, respectively.

19. Write a program that reads the amount of a loan, the annual interest rate, and a monthly payment and then displays the payment number, the interest for that month, the balance remaining after that payment, and the total interest paid to date in a table with appropriate headings. (The monthly interest is $r / 12$ percent of the unpaid balance after the payment is subtracted, where *r* is the annual interest rate.) Use a method to display these tables. Design the program so it can process several different loan amounts, interest rates, and monthly payments, including at least the following triples of values: $100, 18 percent, $10 , and $500, 12 percent, $25. (*Note:* In general, the last payment will not be the same as the monthly payment; the program should show the exact amount of the last payment due.)

20. Proceed as in Problem 19 but with the following modifications: During program execution, have the user enter a payment amount and a day of the month on which this payment was made. The monthly interest is to be calculated on the *average daily balance* for that month. (Assume, for simplicity, that the billing date is the first of the month.) For example, if the balance on June 1 is $500 and a payment of $20 is received on June 12, the interest will be computed on (500 * 11 + 480 * 19)/30 dollars, which represents the average daily balance for that month.

21. Suppose that on January 1, April 1, July 1, and October 1 of each year, some fixed *amount* is invested and earns interest at some annual interest rate *r* compounded quarterly (that is, $r / 4$ percent is added at the end of each quarter). Write a program that reads a number of years and that calculates and displays a table showing the year, the yearly dividend (total interest earned for that year), and the total savings accumulated through that year. Design the program to process several different inputs and to call a method to display the table for each input.

A possible modification/addition to your program: Instead of investing *amount* dollars each quarter, invest *amount* / 3 dollars on the first of each month. Then in each quarter, the first payment earns interest for three months ($r / 4$ percent), the second for two months ($r / 6$ percent), and the third for one month ($r / 12$ percent).

SECTION 8.6

22. Write a driver program to test the digit-counting methods of Exercises 28 and 29.

23. Write a driver program to test the reverse-printing methods of Exercises 30 and 31.

24. Write a driver program to test the modified exponentiation method of Exercise 32.

25. Write a driver program to test the GCD methods of Exercises 33 and 34.

26. Write a test driver for one of the methods in Exercises 18–23. Add output statements to the method to trace its actions as it executes. For example, the trace displayed for `f(21)` for the methods in Exercise 20 should have a form like the following:

```
f(21) = 1 + f(10)
   f(10) = 1 + f(5)
      f(5) = 1 + f(2)
         f(2) = 1 + f(1)
            f(1) returns 0
         f(2) returns 1
      f(5) returns 2
   f(10) returns 3
f(21) returns 4
```

where the indentation level reflects the depth of the recursion.

27. Proceed as in Problem 26 but for the method `printReverse()` of Exercise 30. The trace for the method call `printReverse(9254)` should have a form like the following:

```
printReverse(9254): Output 4, then call printReverse(925).
   printReverse(925): Output 5, then call printReverse(92).
      printReverse(92): Output 2, then call printReverse(9).
         printReverse(9): Output 9 and \n.
         printReverse(9) returns.
      printReverse(92) returns.
   printReverse(925) returns.
printReverse(9254) returns.
```

28. Write a recursive method that prints the lyrics of the song *Bingo*:

Verse 1:   There was a farmer had a dog,
         And Bingo was his name-o.
            B-I-N-G-O!
            B-I-N-G-O!
            B-I-N-G-O!
         And Bingo was his name-o!

Verse 2:   Same as verse 1, but lines 3, 4, and 5 are:
         (Clap)-I-N-G-O!

Verse 3:   Same as verse 1, but lines 3, 4, and 5 are:
         (Clap, clap)-N-G-O!

Verse 4:   Same as verse 1, but lines 3, 4, and 5 are:
         (Clap, clap, clap)-G-O!

Verse 5:   Same as verse 1, but lines 3, 4, and 5 are:
         (Clap, clap, clap, clap)-O!

Verse 6:   Same as verse 1, but lines 3, 4, and 5 are:
         (Clap, clap, clap, clap, clap)

Also write a driver program to test your method.

29. Write a recursive method that prints a nonnegative integer with commas in the correct locations. For example, it should print 20131 as 20,131. Write a driver program to test your method.

30. The sequence of *Fibonacci numbers*, 1, 1, 2, 3, 5, 8, 13, 21, . . . , (see Programming Problem 9 in Chapter 5) can be defined recursively by:

$$f_1 = f_2 = 0 \qquad \text{(anchor)}$$
$$\text{For } n \geq 3, f_n = f_{n-1} + f_{n-2} \text{ (inductive step)}$$

A recursive method seems like a natural way to calculate these numbers. Write such a method and then write a driver program to test your method. (*Note:* You will probably find that this method is very inefficient. See if you can figure out why by tracing some method calls as was done in the text.)

31. Write a recursive method to find the prime factorization of a positive integer, that is, to express the integer as a product of primes or indicate that it is a prime. Display the prime factors in descending order. Write a driver program to test the method. See Exercise 34 of Section 8.5 for the definition of a prime number.

32. Consider a network of streets laid out in a rectangular grid; for example,

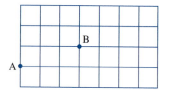

In a *northeast path* from one point in the grid to another, one may walk only to the north (up) and to the east (right). For example, there are four northeast paths from A to B in the preceding grid:

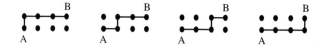

Write a recursive method to count the number of northeast paths from one point to another in a rectangular grid. Write a driver program to test your method.

33. Develop a recursive method to generate all of the $n!$ permutations of the set $\{1, 2, \ldots, n\}$. (*Hint:* The permutations of $\{1, 2, \ldots, k\}$ can be obtained by considering each permutation of $\{1, 2, \ldots, k-1\}$ as an ordered list and inserting k into each of the k possible positions in this list, including at the front and at the rear. For example, the permutations of $\{1, 2\}$ are $(1, 2)$ and $(2, 1)$. Inserting 3 into each of the three possible positions of the first permutation yields the permutations $(3, 1, 2)$, $(1, 3, 2)$, and $(1, 2, 3)$ of $\{1, 2, 3\}$, and using the second permutation gives $(3, 2, 1)$, $(2, 3, 1)$, and $(2, 1, 3)$. Write a driver program to test your method.

SECTION 8.7

34. The number-guessing program in Figure 8.14 always begins with `Integer.MAX_VALUE` as the lower bound on the range of numbers and `Integer.MIN_VALUE` as the upper bound (which always produces 0 as the initial guess). The binary-search strategy then makes it impossible to guess small integers in 20 guesses. Modify the program so that the initial lower and upper bounds are given by programmer-defined constants and the initial display informs the user in what range the integer to be guessed must be selected.

35. Proceed as in Problem 34, but let the user specify the initial lower and upper bounds.

36. The number-guessing program in Figure 8.14 always starts with the same first guess. Modify it so that it starts with a random guess.

ARRAYS

With silver bells, and cockle shells,
And pretty maids all in a row. *Mother Goose*

I've got a little list, I've got a little list. *Gilbert and Sullivan, The Mikado*

Would someone please wake the person who's sleeping in row 2 seat 3? *V. Orehck III*
(fictitious—during a lecture on matrices)

Chapter Contents

Chapter Objectives

- Investigate one-dimensional arrays as implemented in Java
- Study the important problems of sorting and searching lists
- See how command-line arguments can be implemented in Java
- Introduce two-dimensional arrays
- Build a class for matrices that provides several of the common matrix operations
- Show how arrays can be used in graphical programming by building a pie chart

- (Optional) Describe how matrix methods can be used to solve linear systems

We have seen that a single `String` object can store a collection of `char` values. It is also an *indexed* object, because if `aString` is of type `String`, `aString.charAt(i)` can be used to access the `char` in `aString` whose index is `i`. In this chapter, we examine a new structure of Java called the **array** that, like a `String`, can store multiple values, each of which can be accessed via an index. However, whereas a `String` is limited to storing `char` values, arrays can store values of *any* type.

9.1 INTRODUCTORY EXAMPLE: MS. WHITE'S TEST SCORE ANALYZER

We begin with a problem that can be conveniently solved using arrays.

PROBLEM: ANALYZING TEST SCORES

Ms. White has been recruited to teach in a remote mining community. To help her analyze the students' performance on tests, she would like a program that displays each student's name and lets her enter the test score for that student, computes and displays the average test score, and then displays each student's name, score, and the difference of that score from the average. Currently, there are seven students at the school.

 OBJECT-CENTERED DESIGN

BEHAVIOR. Using a sequence of student names, the program should display on the screen a student's name in a prompt for that student's test score and read the corresponding score from the keyboard. It should then compute the average of the sequence of scores. Finally, it should display each student's name, test score, and the difference of that score from the average.

PROBLEM'S OBJECTS. The objects in this problem are as follows:

Description of problem's object	Type	Kind	Name
A sequence of names	String[]	constant	*STUDENTS*
Each student's name	String	constant	*STUDENTS[i]*
The sequence of scores	double[]	varying	*scores*
Each student's score	double	varying	*scores[i]*
The screen	Screen	varying	*theScreen*
The keyboard	Keyboard	varying	*theKeyboard*
A prompt for each score	String	varying	none
The average of the scores	double	varying	*average*

The brackets ([and]) in the second and fourth object names will be explained in the next section.

OPERATIONS. The operations needed to solve the problem are

   i. Display a `String` on the screen
   ii. Read a `double` from the keyboard
   iii. Repeat operations (i) and (ii) for each value in a sequence of `Strings`
   iv. Compute the average of a sequence of `double` values
   v. Compute the difference of two `double` values
   vi. Access the ith value in a sequence of values
   vii. Display a `String` and two `double` values on the screen
   viii. Repeat operations (v–vii) for each value in a sequence

With the exception of operation (iv), each of these operations is either predefined in Java or is easily implemented using just a few Java statements.

To perform operation (iv), we provide a class `DoubleArrays` in the package `ann.math` that contains a class method named `average()` for computing the average of a sequence of `double` values. This and related array-processing methods will be discussed in the next section.

ALGORITHM. Assuming that the above-mentioned `average()` method is available, we can use the following algorithm to solve our problem:

Algorithm for Test Score Analysis

   1. Define an array *STUDENTS* containing the names of the students and an array *scores* to hold the students' test scores.

   2. For each student name in the array *STUDENTS*:

      a. Display on *theScreen* a string containing that name and a prompt for the test score for that student.

      b. Read a double from *theKeyboard*, storing it in the position in *scores* that corresponds to this student.

   3. Compute the *average* of the values in *scores*.

   4. Display *average* on *theScreen*.

   5. For each student in the array *STUDENTS*:

      Display on the screen that student's name, test score, and difference between that score and *average*.

CODING. The program in Figure 9.1 implements this algorithm. To avoid having to recompute the number of students for other sequences, we have added a constant `NUMBER_OF_STUDENTS` to store this value.

FIGURE 9.1   MS. WHITE'S `TestScoreAnalyzer` CLASS

```
/** TestScoreAnalyzer.java is a simple program to compare test scores.
 *
 *  Input:   a sequence of student test scores
 *  Output:  prompts, average test score, and a list of student names,
 *           test scores, and differences of scores from the average.
 */

import ann.easyio.*;              // Keyboard, Screen
import ann.math.DoubleArrays;

class TestScoreAnalyzer
{
  public static void main(String [] args)
  {
    final String [] STUDENTS = {"Bashful", "Doc", "Dopey", "Grumpy",
                                "Happy", "Sleepy", "Sneezy"};
    final int NUMBER_OF_STUDENTS = STUDENTS.length;
    double [] scores = new double [NUMBER_OF_STUDENTS];
    Screen theScreen = new Screen();
    Keyboard theKeyboard = new Keyboard();

    theScreen.println("To compare the scores of your students.");

    for (int i = 0; i < NUMBER_OF_STUDENTS; i++)
    {
      theScreen.print(" enter " + STUDENTS[i] + "'s score: ");
      scores[i] = theKeyboard.readDouble();
    }

    double average = DoubleArrays.average(scores);

    theScreen.println("\nThe average of the scores is " + average + "\n");

    for (int i = 0; i < NUMBER_OF_STUDENTS; i++)
    {
      theScreen.print(STUDENTS[i] + "\t" + scores[i] + "\t(");
      theScreen.printFormatted(scores[i] - average);
      theScreen.println(")");
    }
  }
}
```

Sample run:

```
To compare the scores of your students,
 enter Bashful's score: 80
 enter Doc's score: 90
 enter Dopey's score: 30
 enter Grumpy's score: 50
 enter Happy's score: 70
 enter Sleepy's score: 40
 enter Sneezy's score: 60

The average of the scores is 60.0

Bashful 80.0      (20)
Doc      90.0     (30)
Dopey    30.0     (-30)
Grumpy   50.0     (-10)
Happy    70.0     (10)
Sleepy   40.0     (-20)
Sneezy   60.0     (0)
```

9.2 ARRAYS

In this section, we will use the program in Figure 9.1 to study the details of Java arrays.

Array Definitions

Java arrays are objects, which means that they must be accessed via handles. To define an array handle, the following pattern can be used:

```
Type [] name
```

where `Type` specifies the kind of values the array can store, the brackets (`[]`) indicate that an array is being defined, and `name` is the handle by which the array can be accessed. Thus, the notation

```
double [] price;
```

defines `price` as a handle for an array that can store `double` values, whereas

```
String [] item;
```

defines `item` as a handle for an array capable of storing `String` values. Similarly, to define a handle named `count` for an array of `int` values, we would write:

```
int [] count;
```

Handles can thus be defined for arrays capable of storing arbitrary types.

Because no initial values were provided in the preceding declarations, `price`, `item`, and `count` will be initialized to `null`. When arrays are created for them, they will store the addresses of these arrays. We will now describe the two ways that array objects can be created: with array literals or by using the `new` operation.

Definitions Using Array Literals. When the exact size and initial values of an array are known in advance, we can define an **array literal** to initialize an array handle. For example, suppose we need four counter variables to solve some problem. Instead of defining four different variables, we could instead define `count` as the handle for an array of four `int` values, each initialized to zero, by writing:

```
int [] count = {0, 0, 0, 0};
```

We might visualize the resulting array as follows:

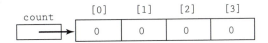

As this example illustrates, an array literal consists of a sequence of literals surrounded by braces (`{` and `}`), where the types of the literals match the type used to define the array's handle. An `int` array literal has `int` literals surrounded by braces; a `String`

array literal consists of `String` literals surrounded by braces; a `char` array literal has `char` literals surrounded by braces; and so on.

In our problem from Section 9.1, the number of students and their names are known in advance. As a result, the program in Figure 9.1 uses an array literal to define STUDENTS:

```
final String []
        STUDENTS = { "Bashful", "Doc", "Dopey", "Grumpy",
                     "Happy", "Sleepy", "Sneezy" };
```

This statement defines STUDENTS as the handle for an array of seven `String` values, which we might visualize as follows:

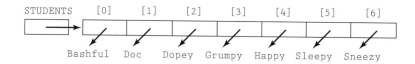

The "slots" in an array where values are stored are called **components** of the array, and the values stored in these components are called the **elements** of the array. Thus, each element of the `count` array has the value zero, whereas the elements of the STUDENTS array are handles for `Strings`. More generally, the elements of an array of primitive type values are *values* of that type, but the elements of an array of reference type values are *handles* for that reference type.

Array length. The number of components in an array is known as its **size** or **length.** This is very useful information when processing the values in an array. For this reason, every array has a public `length` **attribute** that can be accessed using dot notation. The program in Figure 9.1 uses this attribute to define NUMBER_OF_STUDENTS in the statement

```
final int NUMBER_OF_STUDENTS = STUDENTS.length;
```

Since there are seven elements in the array referred to by STUDENTS, this statement initializes NUMBER_OF_STUDENTS to the value 7. By contrast, for the `int` array `count` we defined earlier, the value of the expression

```
count.length
```

is 4.

Unlike arrays in some languages, Java *arrays are **zero-based**: that is, the index of the first component of a Java array is zero.* This means that because the `length` attribute gives the number of elements in the array, the value of the expression

```
arrayName.length − 1
```

is the index of the last element of the array referred to by *arrayName*. To illustrate, for the `count` array, the value of the expression `count.length − 1` is 3, which is the index of its last element; and for the STUDENTS array, the value of the expression STUDENTS.length − 1 is 6, which is the index of its last element.

Definitions Using `new`. The second way to define an array is with the customary approach for reference types: use the `new` **operation.** The program in Figure 9.1 uses this approach to define its second array with the statement

```
double [] scores = new double [NUMBER_OF_STUDENTS];
```

Since the value of `NUMBER_OF_STUDENTS` is seven, the expression

```
new double [NUMBER_OF_STUDENTS]
```

allocates a block of memory large enough to hold seven `double` values and returns the address of this block. With seven elements, the value of `scores.length` is 7, and the elements of `scores` are indexed 0 through 6:

```
scores      [0]    [1]    [2]    [3]    [4]    [5]    [6]
┌─────────┐    ┌──────┬──────┬──────┬──────┬──────┬──────┬──────┐
│      ───┼───▶│  0   │  0   │  0   │  0   │  0   │  0   │  0   │
└─────────┘    └──────┴──────┴──────┴──────┴──────┴──────┴──────┘
```

Java will automatically initialize the elements in such arrays to their default values—zero for primitive numeric types, `false` for `boolean` type, and `null` for reference types.

In this example, `scores` is an array of `double` values, but arrays of other element types may be created in the same way. For example, the declarations

```
final int NUM_ELEMENTS = 4;

// 4 char elements
char    [] charArray = new char[NUM_ELEMENTS];

// 4 int elements
int     [] intArray = new int[NUM_ELEMENTS];

// 4 String elements
String [] stringArray = new String[NUM_ELEMENTS];
```

construct three arrays, each having four components, (i.e., having length 4). The array associated with `charArray` has space for 4 `char` values (a total of 4 × 2 bytes = 8 bytes):

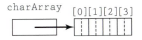

The array associated with `intArray` has space for 4 `int` values (a total of 4 × 4 bytes = 16 bytes):

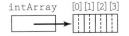

The array associated with `stringArray` has space for the handles of 4 `String` objects, similar to the diagram of STUDENTS we saw earlier.

Array Declarations. The declarations of arrays in our examples have all had the following general form:

Array Declaration (simplified)

Forms

```
ElementType [] arrayName;
ElementType [] arrayName = new ElementType [size];
ElementType [] arrayName = array-literal;
```

where:
ElementType is any type (including an array type);
arrayName is the handle for the array object being defined;
size is an expression specifying the number of components in the array; and
array-literal is a list of literals of type *ElementType*, enclosed between curly braces ({ and }).

Purpose

The first form declares that *arrayName* is a handle for an array to be created later whose elements are of type *ElementType*. The other forms request the Java system to:

1. Allocate memory for an array with the specified number of objects of type *Element-Type*—*size* for the second form and the number of values listed in the array literal for the third.

2. Initialize this block of memory with default *ElementType* values for the second form and with the values given in the array literal for the third.

3. Store the address of this memory block in *arrayName*.

Note that in the second declaration, an array's size is specified by an *expression*. This means that the size of the array need not be known when the program is compiled—it can be a value entered during execution; for example,

```
int arraySize  = keyboard.readInt();
double anArray = new double [arraySize];
```

This makes it possible to tailor the size of an array to the number of values it must store.

Don't Specify an Array's Size with a Literal. When specifying the size of an array, it is good programming practice to use a named constant or variable rather than a literal in the array declaration. For example, the array declaration in

```
final int SIZE = 5;
int [] count = new int[SIZE];
      .
      .
      .
```

NOTE

```
for (int i = 0; i < SIZE; i++)
    aScreen.println( count[i] );
```

is preferable to a definition using a literal:

```
int [] count = new int[5];
    .
    .
    .
for (int i = 0; i < 5; i++)
    aScreen.println( count[i] );
```

The reason is that it may be necessary to modify the array's size after the program has been in use for some time. If literals are used, making these modifications requires finding and changing each one throughout the entire program:

```
double count[100];
    .
    .
    .
for (int i = 0; i < 100; i++)
    aScreen.println( count[i] );
```

But if a named constant (such as SIZE) is used instead, then modifying the size of the array requires only a single modification—changing the declaration of the constant:

```
final int SIZE = 100;
double count[SIZE];
    .
    .
    .
for (int i = 0; i < SIZE; i++)
    aScreen.println( count[i] );
```

When the program is recompiled, the compiler will update all uses of SIZE with the new value, saving time and ensuring consistent sizes in all accesses to the array.

Processing Array Elements

We have seen that the individual characters in a String object can be accessed using the charAt() method and an index. More precisely, the character at index i within String object aString can be accessed by using aString.charAt(i).

By contrast, the value at index *i* in an array named *anArray* can be accessed using

> *anArray*[*i*]

i is called the **index** (or **subscript**) in this expression. For example, for the array STU-DENTS in Figure 9.1, STUDENTS[0] refers to the string "Bashful", STUDENTS[1] refers to the string "Doc", and so on. The values of scores[0] is 90, the value of scores[1] is 80, and so on. Each of scores[0], scores[1],... is thus a variable, called an **indexed variable** (or **subscripted variable**) of type `double`. Similarly, `STUDENTS[0]`, `STUDENTS[1]`,... are indexed constants of type `String`.

A for loop is useful for implementing many array operations, because its loop-control variable can be used to vary the index in an indexed variable (or constant). For an array declared by

```
aType [] anArray = new aType [ size ];
```

the indices range from 0 through $size - 1$. Each element of the array can be accessed in turn by using an indexed variable (or constant) `anArray[i]` in the body of a for loop in which the loop-control variable i counts from 0 to `anArray.length` $- 1$:

```
for (int i = 0; i < anArray.length; i++)
    // ... do something with anArray[i]
```

The program in Figure 9.1 uses this approach both to fill `scores` with values and to display `STUDENTS`, `scores`, and the difference of each score and the average. In the for loop

```
for (int i = 0; i < NUMBER_OF_STUDENTS; i++)
{
    theScreen.print(" enter " + STUDENTS[i] + "'s score: ");
    scores[i] = theKeyboard.readDouble();
}
```

the statement

```
theScreen.print(" enter " + STUDENTS[i] + "'s score: ");
```

is used to access and display the name of the student stored at index i in `STUDENTS`; and then the statement

```
scores[i] = theKeyboard.readDouble();
```

stores the value entered at the keyboard in the component of `scores` with index i. Because i is the loop control variable, its value is 0 on the first pass through the loop so the `double` value entered from the keyboard is stored in `score[0]`; i's value is 1 on the second pass, so the next score is stored in `score[1]`; and so on until the seventh pass, after which the loop terminates. In the sample run in Figure 9.1, the user enters the values 80, 90, 30, 50, 70, 40, and 60, so when the loop terminates, the elements of scores are as follows:

scores	[0]	[1]	[2]	[3]	[4]	[5]	[6]
	80.0	90.0	30.0	50.0	70.0	40.0	60.0

After computing the average of the scores, the following for loop that varies the index i from 0 to the number of students is used to generate the program's output:

```
for (int i = 0; i < NUMBER_OF_STUDENTS; i++)
{
    theScreen.print(STUDENTS[i] + "\t" + scores[i] + "\t(");
```

```
                theScreen.printFormatted(scores[i] - average);
                theScreen.println(")");
        }
```

In the first iteration of the loop, i is 0, so STUDENTS[i] accesses the value "Bash-ful" and scores[i] accesses the value 80.0, producing the output

```
        Bashful 80.0 (20)
```

On the second iteration, i is 1, so STUDENTS[i] accesses the value "Doc" and scores[i] accesses the value 90.0, producing the output

```
        Doc 90.0 (30)
```

The remaining lines of output are generated in a similar way.

It is worth noting that any operation that is defined for a given type can be applied to an array element of that type. For example, any operation that can be applied to the type double can be applied to an element of a double array, as in

```
    for (int i = 0; i < realArray.length; i++)
        theScreen.println( Math.sqrt(realArray[i]) ); // sqrt(double)
```

Similarly, any message that can be sent to a String can be sent to any of the elements of a String array. For example, here is a loop that finds "Happy" and displays his score:

```
    for (int i = 0; i < STUDENTS.length; i++)
        if ( name[i].equals("Happy") )            // String.equals(String)
            theScreen.println("Happy's score is " + scores[i]);
```

In mathematical formulas, subscripted notation like v_i has historically been used to denote the ith element in a sequence v. Because array components are subscripted variables, single-letter identifiers like i, j, and k are commonly used as names for array indices. This is one of the few cases where single letters are acceptable as identifier names.

Arrays and Methods

Array Parameters. Methods can be written that accept arrays via parameters and then operate on the arrays by operating on individual array elements. For example, we could use a method like the following to sum the elements of a double array:

```
        public static double sum(double [] array)
        {
            double result = 0.0;

            for (int i = 0; i < array.length; i++)
                result += array[i];

            return result;
        }
```

NOTE As this example illustrates, declaring a parameter with a type that includes a pair of brackets ([]) indicates that the parameter is an array. *An array of any size may be passed to the method via such a parameter.* Also, we see once again the usefulness of an array's length attribute to determine an array parameter's size within a method.

This sum() method is, in fact, defined (along with average()) in the DoubleArrays class that we have included in the ann.math package. Its availability makes the average() method quite simple:

```
public static double average(double [] array)
{
    if (array.length <= 0)   // check precondition
       Controller.fatal("DoubleArrays.average()", "array is empty!");

    return sum(array) / array.length;
}
```

Array Return Values. A method may also return an array as its result. To illustrate, the following method readArray() from the DoubleArrays class begins by reading the number of values in a sequence, uses that value to allocate an array of the necessary size, reads the sequence and stores it in the array, and finally, returns the array containing the input values:

```
public static double [] readArray()
{
   Screen theScreen = new Screen();
   theScreen.print("Enter the number of values you wish to store: ");
   Keyboard theKeyboard = new Keyboard();
   int n = theKeyboard.readInt();    // read n, the number of values

   double [] result = new double[n];// allocate array of size n

   for (int i = 0; i < n; i++)       // read n values into result
   {
      theScreen.print("Enter value " + i + ": ");
      result[i] = theKeyboard.readDouble();
   }

   return result;
}
```

We can then use this method to input an array of doubles as follows:

```
        double [] anArray = DoubleArrays.readArray();
```

Writing a corresponding method to output the values in an array is left as an exercise.

Predefined Array Operations

Java does provide a few operations that can be used with arrays, including the assignment operator (=), the clone() method, and the equals() method. We will now take a closer look at each of these operations.

The Assignment Operation. Java permits assignment expressions using array operands. For example, suppose that a program contains the following statements:

```
int [] original = {11, 22, 33, 44, 55};
int [] copy;
copy = original;
```

Although one might expect the third statement to define `copy` as a distinct copy of `original`, this is not what happens. The reason is that `original` and `copy` are both *handles* for array objects and are not arrays themselves. To see the difficulty, suppose we visualize the effect of the first statement as follows:

Once `copy` has been declared, the third (assignment) statement simply copies the *address* from the handle `original` into the handle `copy`, which we might picture as

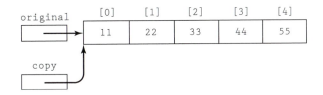

Thus, `original` and `copy` both refer to the same array object, instead of to distinct array objects. If the programmer was relying on the two handles referring to distinct arrays, then this represents a logic error—any change to the array referred to by one of the handles—`original` or `copy`—will simultaneously change the array referred to by the other handle.

WATCH

OUT

Indiscriminate use of the assignment operator with array objects can thus produce another example of the *aliasing problem* for reference types, which we first discussed in Section 4.2. For this reason, the assignment operator should never be used to make a copy of an array, since it does not do so.

Array Cloning

As described in Section 6.4, the aliasing problem can occur any time an attempt is made to copy an object by assigning one handle to another. Because the values of handles are addresses, such an assignment merely copies an address from one handle to another, instead of copying the object to which those handles refer.

To circumvent this problem, most predefined Java objects—arrays, in particular— have a `clone()` method that tells an object to make a copy of itself and return the address of the copy. To illustrate, if `copy` and `original` are handles for integer arrays as before,

```
int [] original = {11, 22, 33, 44, 55};
int [] copy;
```

and we want `copy` to be a distinct copy of `original`, we can write:

```
copy = original.clone();
```

The `clone()` method makes a distinct copy of the array `original`. We can picture the result as follows:

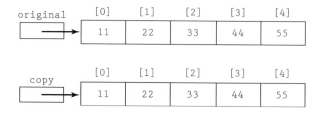

The `clone()` method can thus be used to make a distinct copy of an array. It is important to note, however, that (for the sake of efficiency) `clone()` just makes a *simple copy* of the object's memory. For arrays of primitive types such as `original`, this produces a completely distinct copy but *not* for arrays of reference types.

To illustrate, consider the following:

```
StringBuffer [] names = { new StringBuffer("Abby"),
                          new StringBuffer("Bob"),
                          new StringBuffer("Chris") };
StringBuffer [] copy =   (StringBuffer []) names.clone();
```

We can picture the objects produced by these statements as follows:

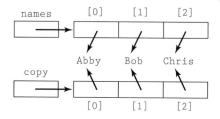

Here, the `clone()` method does makes a copy of the array `names`, but it is not a completely distinct copy. The reason is that `names` is an array of `StringBuffer` values, which means that its elements are `StringBuffer` handles. When `names` is sent the `clone()` message, it makes a copy of itself by a simple copy of its memory. This creates a second array whose elements are copies of its elements, and since those elements are `StringBuffer` handles containing addresses, the `StringBuffer` handles in this copy contain *the same addresses*. Put differently, the elements of `names` and the elements of `copy` are *different handles for the same sequence* of values. Because it copies handles without copying the objects to which they refer, the `clone()` method's operation is sometimes referred to as a **shallow copy operation.**

In some situations, shallow copying can lead to an aliasing problem. The most common problem occurs if we change the objects to which the handles in a shallow copy refer. For example, if we use `names` to change the 'o' in "Bob" to 'u',

```
names[1].setCharAt(1, 'u');
```

This change simultaneously affects the `StringBuffer` to which both `names[1]` and `copy[1]` refer:

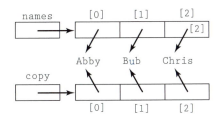

To avoid such problems, we can write our own **deep copying** method. To illustrate, here is such a method for an array of `StringBuffer` objects:

```
public static StringBuffer [] deepCopy(StringBuffer [] original)
{
    StringBuffer [] result = new StringBuffer[original.length];

    for (int i = 0; i < original.length; i++)
        result[i] = original[i].clone();

    return result;
}
```

There are many situations in which the `clone()` method's shallow copy is perfectly adequate, however. For example, if we assign `names[1]` the value "Bill", `copy[1]` will still refer to "Bob":

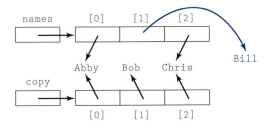

Array Equality

Java's `Object` class defines an `equals()` message that can be sent to an array object:

```
if (a1.equals(a2) ) // ...
```

Unfortunately, this method simply compares the addresses in the *handles* `a1` and `a2`. If they refer to the same object, then it returns true; otherwise it returns false. To actually compare the *elements* of two arrays, we must write our own method. To illustrate, the following class method `equals()` from the `DoubleArrays` class in our `ann.math` package can be used to compare the elements of two arrays of `doubles`, `array1` and `array2`:

```
public static boolean equals(double [] array1, double [] array2)
{
  if (array1.length == array2.length)
  {
    for (int i = 0; i < array1.length; i++)
      if (!(array1[i] == array2[i]))
        return false;

    return true;
  }

  else
    return false;
}
```

Because this is a static method, we invoke it by sending a message to the class `DoubleArrays` as in

```
if ( DoubleArrays.equals(a1, a2) ) // . . .
```

The method first checks whether the lengths of the two arrays are the same; if not, it returns false. Otherwise, it iterates through the index values, comparing the two arrays an element at a time. The method returns false if a mismatch is found, but returns true if it makes it through all index values without finding a mismatch.

A method to determine if two arrays of `String` values are equal uses the `equals()` method in place of `==` to compare the array elements. This is because the elements of the array are handles for `String` values, and the `String` class supplies its own definition of `equals()` to properly compare `String` values.

```
public static boolean equals(String [] array1, String [] array2)
{
  if (array1.length == array2.length)
  {
    for (int i = 0; i < array1.length; i++)
      if (!(array1[i].equals(array2[i])))
        return false;

    return true;
  }
```

```
      else
         return false;
   }
```

A similar method can be used to compare arrays whose elements are of other reference types that define `equals()` properly.

The `Vector` Class

One problem with arrays is that they have a fixed capacity. They can neither grow nor shrink. However, Java does provide an array-based container whose size can change, namely, the `Vector` class in the `java.util.` package. More precisely, the capacity of a `Vector` can increase to accommodate adding a new item.

Some of the methods used to process `Vector`s are the following. See the Documentation section of the chapter summary and the Java API documentation for others.

TABLE 9.1   SOME VECTOR METHODS

Vector method	Description
`Vector()`	Constructor: e.g., `Vector v = new Vector();` creates v as an empty `Vector`
`v.addElement(obj)`	Adds object *obj* at the end of v. If v is full (i.e., `v.size() == v.capacity()`), its capacity will be increased.
`v.add(obj, i)`	Adds object *obj* at index *i* of v. Elements at position *i* and following will be shifted right to make room.
`v.removeElement(obj)`	Removes object *obj* from v. If *obj* is found, elements following that position will be shifted left to close the gap.
`v.elementAt(i)`	Returns element of v with index *i*
`v.contains(obj)`	Returns true if object *obj* is in v and false otherwise.
`v.firstElement()`	Returns the first element of v
`v.lastElement()`	Returns the last element of v
`v.size()`	Returns the size of v

One of the difficulties of working with `Vector`s is that their *components must be objects.* This means that using primitive types for components is not permitted; instead, the corresponding wrapper classes must be used. Also, the methods of `Vector` that accept or return elements have `Object` as their parameter types and return types. This means that to retrieve a particular element from a `Vector`, a typecast must be used to convert it to its original reference type.

An alternative container that can grow when necessary and that does not have these deficiencies is the `ArrayList`. This container is described in Chapter 12.

✔ Quick Quiz 9.2

Questions 1–8 assume the following definitions:

```
double [] a = new double [5],
          b = {0,0,0,0,0},
          c = {1,2,3,4,5},
          d = {0};
```

1. (True or false) a is an array indexed 0, 1, 2, 3, 4, 5.
2. (True or false) b is an array indexed 0, 1, 2, 3, 4.
3. (True or false) All elements of a are initialized to 0.
4. (True or false) All elements of b are initialized to 0.
5. (True or false) c[3] == 3.
6. The value of a.length is _____.
7. The value of d.length is _____.
8. (True or false) b.equals(d).

Questions 9–16 assume the declarations:

```
int [] number = {1,3,5,7,9};
int [] value = new int [5];
double [] xValue = new double [5];
```

Tell what values will be stored in all the arrays involved or indicate why an error occurs.

9.
```
for (int i = 0; i <= 4; i++)
    xValue[i] = (double) i / 2.0
```

10.
```
for (int i = 0; i < number.length; i++)
    if (i % 2 == 0)
        number[i] = 2 * i;
    else
        number[i] = 2 * i + 1;
```

11.
```
for (int i = 1; i < 5; i++)
    number[i] = 2 * number[i - 1];
```

12.
```
for (int i = 3; i >= 0; i--)
    number[i] = 2 * number[i + 1];
```

13.
```
value = number;
number[1] = 0;
```

14.
```
value = number.clone();
number[1] = 0;
```

15. (True or false) The copying carried out by the first statement in Question 13 is a deep copy.

16. The copying carried out by the first statement in Question 14 is known as a(n) _____ copy.

✍ EXERCISES 9.2

For Exercises 1–7, assume that the following declarations have been made:

```
final int LITTLE = 5,
          MEDIUM = 9,
          BIG = 20;
int i, j, temp;
int [] number = {99, 33, 44, 88, 22, 11, 55, 66, 77};
double [] value = new double [LITTLE],
         large = new double [BIG];
```

Tell what values (if any) will be stored in all the arrays involved or explain why an error occurs.

1.  ```
    for (i = 0; i < LITTLE; i++)
        number[i] = i / 2;
    ```

2.  ```
    for (i = 0; i < number.length; i += 2)
        number[i] = i * i;

    for (i = LITTLE; i < number.length; i++)
        number[i] = number[i - 5];
    ```

3.  ```
    for (i = 0; i < 3; i++)
        value[i] = 0;

    for (i = 3; i < LITTLE; i++)
        value[i] = 1;
    ```

4.  ```
    for (i = 1; i < LITTLE; i += 2)
    {
        value[i - 1] = (double) i / 2.0;
        value[i] = 10.0 * value[i - 1];
    }
    ```

5.  ```
    i = 0;
    while (i != BIG)
    {
        if (i % 3 == 0)
            large[i] = 0;
        else
            large[i] = (double) i;
        i++;
    }
    ```

6.  ```
    number[0] = 1;
    i = 2;
    do
    {
        number[i] = 2 * number[i - 1];
        i++;
    }
    while (i < MEDIUM);
    ```

```
7.  for (i = 0; i < > ; i++)
    {
        for (j = i; j < > ; j++)
            if (number[j] > number[j + 1])
            {
                temp = number[j];
                number[j] = number[j + 1];
                number[j + 1] = temp;
            }
    }
```

For Exercises 8–14 write definitions of the given arrays.

8. An array of size 10 in which each element is an integer.

9. An array whose indices are integers from 0 through 10 and in which each element is a real value.

10. An array of size 10 in which each element is an integer, all of which are initially 0.

11. An array that can store 5 strings.

12. An array that can store 5 characters and is initialized with the vowels a, e, i, o, and u.

13. An array that can store 100 values, each of which is either `true` or `false`.

For Exercises 14–16, write definitions and statements to construct the given array.

14. An array whose indices are the integers from 0 through 99 and in which the value stored in each element is the same as the index.

15. An array whose indices are the integers from 0 through 99 and in which the values stored in the elements are the indices in reverse order.

16. An array of size 50 in which the value stored in an element is true if the corresponding index is even and false otherwise.

Exercises 17–23 ask you to write methods to do various things. To test these methods, you should write driver programs as instructed in Programming Problems 1–6 at the end of this chapter.

17. Output an array of doubles.

18. Return the smallest value stored in an array of integers.

19. Return the largest value stored in an array of integers.

20. Return the range of values stored in an array of integers; that is, the difference between the largest value and the smallest value.

21. Return `true` if the values stored in an array are in ascending order and `false` otherwise.

22. Insert a value into an array of integers at a specified position in the array.

23. Remove a value from an array of integers at a specified position in the array.

9.3   SORTING

A common programming problem is **sorting,** that is, arranging the items in a list so that they are in either ascending or descending order. There are many sorting methods, most of which assume that the items to be sorted are stored in an array. In this section we describe two of the simplest methods, *simple selection sort* and *linear insertion sort,* and one of the most efficient methods, *quicksort.* (Other sorting schemes will be described in the sequel to this text.)

Simple Selection Sort

The basic idea of a selection sort of a list is to make a number of passes through the list or a part of the list, and on each pass select one item to be correctly positioned. For example, on each pass through a sublist, the smallest item in the sublist might be found and moved to its proper position.

As an illustration, suppose that the following list is to be sorted into ascending order:

$$67, 33, 21, 84, 49, 50, 75$$

We locate the smallest item and find it in position 3:

$$67, 33, 21, 84, 49, 50, 75$$

We interchange this item with the first item and thus properly position the smallest item at the beginning of the list:

21 , 33 , 67 , 84 , 49 , 50 , 75

We now consider the sublist consisting of the items from position 2 on,

21 , 33 , 67 , 84 , 49 , 50 , 75

to find the smallest item and exchange it with the second item (itself in this case) and thus properly position the next-to-smallest item in position 2:

We continue in this manner, locating the smallest item in the sublist of items from position 3 on and interchanging it with the third item, then properly positioning the smallest item in the sublist of items from position 4 on, and so on until we eventually do this for the sublist consisting of the last two items:

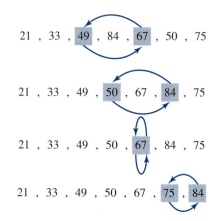

Positioning the smallest item in this last sublist obviously also positions the last item correctly, and thus completes the sort.

Writing statements to implement simple selection sort is straightforward. The following statements sort a list of n doubles stored in an array x into ascending order:

```
for (int i = 0; i < n - 1; i++)
{
   // First find smallest element in sublist x[i],....,x[n-1]
   double smallest = x[i];
   int smallPos = i;

   for (int j = i + 1; i <= n - 1; i++)
      if (x[j] < smallest)  // smaller item found
      {
         smallest = x[j];
         smallPos = j;
      }

   // Swap smallest item with item at front of sublist
   x[smallPos] = x[i];
   x[i] = smallest;
}
```

The primary virtue of simple selection sort is its simplicity. It is too inefficient, however, for use as a general sorting scheme, especially for large lists.

Linear Insertion Sort

One of the fastest sorting methods for small lists is linear insertion sort. It is based on the idea of repeatedly inserting a new element into a list of already sorted elements so that the resulting list is still sorted. The following sequence of diagrams demonstrates this method for the list 67, 33, 21, 84, 49, 50, 75. The sorted sublist produced at each stage is highlighted.

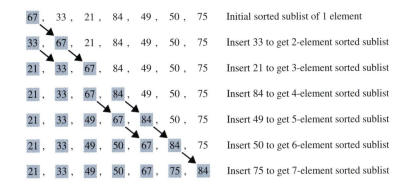

67,	33,	21,	84,	49,	50,	75	Initial sorted sublist of 1 element
33,	67,	21,	84,	49,	50,	75	Insert 33 to get 2-element sorted sublist
21,	33,	67,	84,	49,	50,	75	Insert 21 to get 3-element sorted sublist
21,	33,	67,	84,	49,	50,	75	Insert 84 to get 4-element sorted sublist
21,	33,	49,	67,	84,	50,	75	Insert 49 to get 5-element sorted sublist
21,	33,	49,	50,	67,	84,	75	Insert 50 to get 6-element sorted sublist
21,	33,	49,	50,	67,	75,	84	Insert 75 to get 7-element sorted sublist

The following algorithm describes this procedure for lists stored in arrays. At the ith stage, $x[i]$ is inserted into its proper place among the already sorted $x[0], \ldots, x[i-1]$. We do this by comparing x_i with each of these elements, starting from the right end, and shifting them to the right as necessary.

Linear Insertion Sort Algorithm

For $i = 1$ to $n - 1$ do the following:

// Insert $x[i]$ into its proper position among $x[0], \ldots, x[i-1]$.

a. Set *nextElement* equal to $x[i]$.

b. Set j equal to i.

c. While j > 0 and *nextElement* < $x[j-1]$ do the following:

// Shift element to the right to open a spot

i. Set $x[j]$ equal to $x[j-1]$.

ii. Decrement j by 1.

// Now drop *nextElement* into the open spot.

d. Set $x[j]$ equal to *nextElement*.

Quicksort

The **quicksort** method of sorting is more efficient than simple selection sort and linear insertion sort. It is in fact one of the fastest methods of sorting and is most often implemented by a recursive algorithm. The basic idea of quicksort is to choose some element called a **pivot** and then to perform a sequence of exchanges so that all elements that are less than this pivot are to its left and all elements that are greater than the pivot are to its right. This correctly positions the pivot and divides the (sub)list into two smaller sublists, each of which may then be sorted independently in the *same* way. This **divide-and-conquer** strategy leads naturally to a recursive sorting algorithm.

To illustrate this splitting of a list into two sublists, consider the following list of integers:

$$75, 70, 65, 84, 98, 78, 100, 93, 55, 61, 81, 68$$

If we select the first number as the pivot, we must rearrange the list so that $70, 65, 55, 61$, and 68 are placed before 75, and $84, 98, 78, 100, 93$, and 81 are placed after it. To carry out this rearrangement, we search from the right end of the list for an element less than 75 and from the left end for an item greater than 75.

$$75, \; 70, \; 65, \; \boxed{84}, \; 98, \; 78, \; 100, \; 93, \; 55, \; 61, \; 81, \; \boxed{68}$$

This locates the two numbers 68 and 84, which we now interchange to obtain

$$75, \; 70, \; 65, \; \boxed{68}, \; 98, \; 78, \; 100, \; 93, \; 55, \; 61, \; 81, \; \boxed{84}$$

We then resume the search from the right for a number less than 75 and from the left for a number greater than 75:

$$75, \; 70, \; 65, \; 68, \; \boxed{98}, \; 78, \; 100, \; 93, \; 55, \; \boxed{61}, \; 81, \; 84$$

This locates the numbers 61 and 98, which are then interchanged:

$$75, \; 70, \; 65, \; 68, \; \boxed{61}, \; 78, \; 100, \; 93, \; 55, \; \boxed{98}, \; 81, \; 84$$

A continuation of the searches locates 78 and 55:

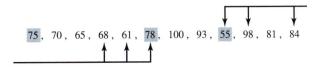

75 , 70 , 65 , 68 , 61 , 78 , 100 , 93 , 55 , 98 , 81 , 84

Interchanging these gives

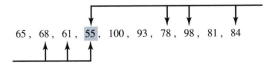

55 , 100 , 93 , 78 , 98 , 81 , 84

Now, when we resume our search from the right, we locate the element 55 that was found on the previous search from the left:

65 , 68 , 61 , 55 , 100 , 93 , 78 , 98 , 81 , 84

The "pointers" for the left and right searches have thus met, and this signals the end of the two searches. We now interchange 55 and the pivot 75:

55 , 70 , 65 , 68 , 61 , 75 , 100 , 93 , 78 , 98 , 81 , 84

Note that all elements to the left of 75 are less than 75 and that all those to its right are greater than 75, and thus the pivot 75 has been properly positioned.

The left sublist

55, 70, 65, 68, 61

and the right sublist

100, 93, 78, 98, 81, 84

can now be sorted *independently, using any sorting scheme desired.* Quicksort uses the same scheme we have just illustrated for the entire list; that is, these sublists must themselves be split by choosing and correctly positioning one pivot element (the first) in each of them.

A recursive method to sort a list is then easy to write and we leave it as an exercise. The anchor case occurs when the list being examined is empty or contains a single element; in this case the list is in order, and nothing needs to be done. The inductive case occurs when the list contains two or more elements, in which case the list can be sorted by:

1. Splitting the list into two sublists;
2. Recursively sorting the left sublist; and
3. Recursively sorting the right sublist.

✔ Quick Quiz 9.3

1. Describe how simple selection sort works.
2. Describe how linear insertion sort works.
3. (True or false) Linear insertion sort performs well for small lists.
4. Describe how quicksort uses a divide-and-conquer sorting strategy.
5. The item properly positioned at each call to quicksort is called a(n) _____.

✍ EXERCISES 9.3

For each of the arrays x in Exercises 1–4, show x after each of the first four passes of simple selection sort.

1.

i	0	1	2	3	4	5	6	7
$x[i]$	30	50	80	10	60	20	70	40

2.

i	0	1	2	3	4	5	6	7
$x[i]$	20	40	70	60	80	50	30	10

3.

i	0	1	2	3	4	5	6	7
$x[i]$	80	70	60	50	40	30	20	10

4.

i	0	1	2	3	4	5	6	7
$x[i]$	10	20	30	40	50	60	70	80

5–8. For the arrays x in Exercises 1–4, trace the action of linear insertion sort with diagrams like that in the text.

9. One variation of simple selection sort for a list stored in an array $x[0], \ldots, x[n-1]$ is to locate both the smallest and the largest elements while scanning the list and to position them at the beginning and the end of the list, respectively. On the next scan,

this process is repeated for the sublist $x[1], \ldots, x[n-2]$, and so on. Write an algorithm to implement this double-ended selection sort.

10–13. For the arrays x in Exercises 1–4 show x after each pass of the double-ended selection sort described in Exercise 9.

14. For the following array x, give a sequence of diagrams like those in the text that trace the action of quicksort as it splits the list by properly positioning the pivot 45:

i	0	1	2	3	4	5	6	7	8	9
$x[i]$	45	20	50	30	80	10	60	70	40	90

9.4   SEARCHING

Another important problem is **searching** a collection of data for a specified item and retrieving some information associated with that item. For example, one searches a telephone directory for a specific name in order to retrieve the phone number listed with that name. We consider two kinds of searches, linear search and binary search.

Linear Search

A **linear search** begins with the first item in a list and searches sequentially until either the desired item is found or the end of the list is reached. The following algorithm uses this method for searching a list of n elements stored in an array, $x[0], x[1], \ldots,$ $x[n-1]$, for *itemSought*. It returns the location of *itemSought* if the search is successful, or the value n otherwise.

Linear Search Algorithm
1. Initialize *location* to 0 and *found* to false.
2. While *location* $< n$ and not *found,* do the following:

   If *itemSought* is equal to $x[location]$, then

   Set *found* to true.

   Otherwise

   Increment *location* by 1.

Binary Search

If a list has been sorted, binary search can be used to search for an item more efficiently than linear search. Linear search may require n comparisons to locate a particular item, but binary search will require at most $\log_2 n$ comparisons. For example, for a list of 1024 $(= 2^{10})$ items, binary search will locate an item using at most 10 comparisons, whereas linear search may require 1024 comparisons.

In the binary search method, we first examine the middle element in the list, and if this is the desired element, the search is successful. Otherwise we determine whether the item being sought is in the first half or in the second half of the list and then repeat this process, using the middle element of that list.

To illustrate, suppose the list to be searched is

1279
1331
1373
1555
1824
1898
1995
2002
2335
2665
3103

and we are looking for 1995. We first examine the middle number 1898 in the sixth position. Because 1995 is greater than 1898, we can disregard the first half of the list and concentrate on the second half.

1955
2002
2335
2665
3103

The middle number in this sublist is 2335, and the desired item 1995 is less than 2335, so we discard the second half of this sublist and concentrate on the first half.

1995
2002

Because there is no middle number in this sublist, we examine the number immediately preceding the middle position—the number 1995—and locate our number.

The following algorithm uses binary search to search a list of n elements stored in an array, $x[0], x[1], \ldots , x[n - 1]$, that has been ordered so the elements are in ascending order. If *itemSought* is found, its location in the array is returned; otherwise, the value n is returned.

Binary Search Algorithm

1. Initialize *first* to 0 and *last* to $n - 1$. These values represent the positions of the first and last items of the list or sublist being searched.

2. Initialize the logical variable *found* to false.

3. While *first* $\leq$ *last* and not *found,* do the following:

   a. Find the middle position in the sublist by setting *middle* equal to the integer quotient $(first + last) / 2$.

   b. Compare *itemSought* being searched for with $x[middle]$. There are three possibilities:

      i. *itemSought* $< x[middle]$: *itemSought* is in the first half of the sublist; set *last* equal to *middle* $- 1$.

      ii. *itemSought* $> x[middle]$: *itemSought* is in the second half of the sublist; set *first* equal to *middle* $+ 1$.

iii. *itemSought* = *x*[*middle*]: *itemSought* has been found; set *location* equal to *middle* and *found* to true.

5. If *found*, return *middle*; otherwise return *n*.

9.5 PROCESSING COMMAND-LINE ARGUMENTS

Since our very first Java program in Chapter 1, we have seen that every Java application has a method whose name is `main`. The main method differs from other methods in a number of ways. One difference is that the main method can be passed arguments via its `args` parameter:

```
public static void main(String [] args)
{
    statementList
}
```

From what we have studied in this chapter, we see that `args` is a handle for an array of `String` values. Learning how to use this parameter is the topic of this section.

Command-Line Environments and Arguments

In **command-line environments** such as the Unix and MS-DOS operating systems, the user interacts with the system by typing *commands*. For example, the command

```
mkdir projects
```

is used in Unix to create a new subdirectory named `projects`. Similarly, the command

```
cd projects
```

will change the user's location in the directory structure to the subdirectory `projects`. In each case a program is being executed (one named `mkdir`, and the other named `cd`), and the name `projects` is passed to that program as an *argument*. Because such arguments are typed on the command-line, they are known as **command-line arguments** to the program being executed.

In Java, the `args` parameter of a `main` method provides a mechanism for a program to retrieve command-line arguments. In this section, we examine how this can be done.

Running Java From The Command Line

As you may already know, a Java program can be executed in a command-line environment by typing

```
java ClassName
```

Here, `java` is the name of the Java interpreter, and `ClassName` is the name of the class that defines the application being executed. This command initiates execution of the Java interpreter, which sends class `ClassName` the `main` message, initiating execution of the `main` method.

Command-line arguments may also be used. That is, we could type

$$\text{java } \textit{ClassName } \textit{Argument}_0 \textit{ Argument}_1 \ldots \textit{Argument}_{N-1}$$

When this occurs[1], the Java interpreter will automatically build a `String` array of N elements, such that

- ☐ `args[0]` is a handle for $\textit{Argument}_0$
- ☐ `args[1]` is a handle for $\textit{Argument}_1$

.

.

.

- ☐ `args[N−1]` is a handle for $\textit{Argument}_{N-1}$

The simple Java program in Figure 9.2 illustrates how the `main` method can then access the individual argument values via its `args` parameter.

FIGURE 9.2   USING COMMAND-LINE ARGUMENTS

```
/** ArgumentClinic.java shows how to process command-line arguments.
 *   ...
 *  Output:   The number of command line arguments and the strings in argc
 */

class ArgumentClinic
{
  public static void main(String [] args)
  {
    System.out.println("There are " + args.length +
                   + " arguments on the command-line");
    for (int i = 0; i < args.length; i++)
      System.out.println("args[" + i + "]: " + args[i]);
  }
}
```

If this program is executed by entering the command

```
java ArgumentClinic
```

the output produced will be

```
There are 0 arguments on the command line
```

---

[1] Some IDEs handle command-line arguments more gracefully, without forcing the user to use a command-line environment. For example, in WinEdit, holding down the *Shift* key while selecting the *Macro* → *Run Java* menu choice displays a dialog box in which such arguments can be entered.

Note that the for loop is skipped because the absence of command-line arguments makes `args.length` have the value 0, and so the for loop's condition (being a pretest loop) is initially false. If we execute the program by entering the command

```
java ArgumentClinic Argument
```

then the output produced is

```
There are 1 arguments on the command line:
args[0]: Argument
```

We see in this execution that `args.length` has the value 1, and `args[0]` is a handle for the character string `Argument`. If we execute the program by entering

```
java ArgumentClinic I want an argument
```

then the output is:

```
There are 4 arguments on the command line:
args[0]: I
args[1]: want
args[2]: an
args[3]: argument
```

From these examples it should be evident that the values in `args` depend on what is entered on the command line when the program is invoked. If the user enters the name of the program followed by n arguments, then the value of `args.length` will be n, the number of argument strings entered on the command line; `args[0]` through `args[n-1]` will refer to the n arguments that were entered.

EXAMPLE: A SQUARE ROOT CALCULATOR

As a simple illustration of the use of command-line arguments, consider the problem of designing a square root calculator that allows the user to enter the value(s) to be processed on the command line.

PROBLEM. Construct a program `Sqrt` that, given a real value, displays the square root of that value; the input value is to be entered on the command line. For example, if the command

```
java Sqrt 4
```

is entered, the value 2 should be displayed; and if

```
java Sqrt 4 9 16 25
```

is entered, the values 2, 3, 4, and 5 should be displayed.

PROBLEM'S OBJECTS. From the problem description, we can identify the following objects:

Description of problem's object	Type	Kind	Name
A sequence of command-line arguments	`String []`	variable	`args`
The number of command-line arguments	`int`	variable	`args.length`
A particular command-line argument	`double`	variable	*value*
The square root of an argument	`double`	variable	—

Since the program must process command-line arguments, it *receives* the arguments through the parameter of the main method (i.e., `args`). We can thus specify the problem as follows:

Receive: One or more command-line arguments

Precondition: The command-line arguments are positive numeric values.

Output: The square roots of those values

On the basis of this specification, we can write the following stub for the program:

```
class Sqrt
{
 public static void main(String [] args)
 {
 }
}
```

OPERATIONS. In designing the solution, we identify the following operations:

i. Retrieve command-line arguments
ii. Take the square root of each argument
iii. Output the resulting value(s)

Taking the square root of each argument and outputting the resulting value is straightforward, but retrieving the arguments requires the use of `args`. Consider what the user might enter:

<u>java Sqrt</u>   // error — no data to process (args.length is 0)

<u>java Sqrt 9</u>   // one value (args.length is 1, args[0] is "9")

<u>java Sqrt 4 9</u>   // two values (args.length is 2,
                 // args[0] is "4", args[1] is "9")

Generalizing, we see that if the user supplies n values to be processed, then `args.length` will equal n, `args[0]` will refer to the first value, `args[1]` will refer to the second value, and so on. We can thus use `args[i]` to retrieve the arguments, with i varying from 0 through `args.length` − 1.

However, each `args[i]` refers to a `String`, and we must take the square root of a value of type `double`. This means that the string referred to by `args[i]` must be converted to the corresponding `double` value, which we have done many times before.

Once we have converted the character string to the corresponding `double` value, all that remains is to find its square root, which is easy, using the `sqrt()` method from the `Math` class. We then simply display the value and its square root.

Algorithm.   We can thus construct the following algorithm, which checks that at least one command-line argument has been given and if so, uses a loop to process each argument.

Algorithm for `Sqrt`

1. If `args.length` is less than 1, display an "incorrect usage" error message and quit.
2. For each integer *i* in the range 0 through `args.length` − 1:
   a. Get *value,* the double equivalent to argument *i.*
   b. Display *value* and its square root.

CODING.   Given this algorithm, we can encode it in Java as shown in Figure 9.3.

FIGURE 9.3   ENCODING SQRT

```
/** Sqrt.java gives a command-line square root calculator.
 *
 *  Input:  a sequence of numeric (double) values
 *  Output: the square root of each input value
 */

class Sqrt
{
  public static void main(String [] args)
  {
    double value;
    if (args.length > 0)
      for (int i = 0; i < args.length; i++)
      {
        value = Double.parseDouble(args[i]);
        System.out.println("The square root of " + value
                           + " is " + Math.sqrt(value) );
      }
    else
      System.err.println("\n*** Usage: java Sqrt <valueList>\n");
  }
}
```

Sample runs:

```
java Sqrt

*** Usage: java Sqrt <valueList>
```

```
java Sqrt 4

The square root of 4.0 is 2.0

java Sqrt 1 7 9

The square root of 1.0 is 1.0
The square root of 7.0 is 2.6457513110645907
The square root of 9.0 is 3.0
```

9.6   MULTIDIMENSIONAL ARRAYS

The arrays we have considered thus far store sequences of values. Each of these arrays thus has one dimension: its *length*, which is the number of values in the sequence. In addition to these *one-dimensional arrays*, Java allows a programmer to define arrays with more than one dimension. As we shall see, a *two-dimensional array* can be used to store a data set whose values are arranged in *rows* and *columns*. Similarly, a *three-dimensional array* is an appropriate storage structure when the data can be arranged in *rows, columns,* and *ranks*. When there are several characteristics associated with the data, still higher dimensions may be useful, with each dimension corresponding to one of these characteristics. In this section we consider the use of *multidimensional arrays* in Java programs.

PROBLEM

The German transportation tycoon Otto Bonn is expanding his trucking business into Florida, with shipping centers in Daytona Beach, Gainesville, Jacksonville, Miami, Tallahassee, and Tampa. He has hired us as software consultants to create a computerized mileage chart for his truck drivers. Given any two of these cities, our program must display the approximate mileage between them.

Preliminary Analysis

From a road atlas, we find the following mileages between Florida cities:

	Daytona Beach	Gainesville	Jacksonville	Miami	Tallahassee	Tampa
Daytona Beach	0	97	90	268	262	130
Gainesville	97	0	74	337	144	128
Jacksonville	90	74	0	354	174	201
Miami	268	337	354	0	475	269
Tallahassee	262	144	174	475	0	238
Tampa	130	128	201	269	238	0

The basic idea is to create a software representation of such a chart, and then use it to look up the distance between any two of the cities.

 ## OBJECT-CENTERED DESIGN

BEHAVIOR. For simplicity, our program will begin by displaying on the screen a numbered menu of the cities. It should then read the numbers of two cities from the keyboard. Next, it should look up the mileage between those cities in a software mileage chart. Finally, it should display that mileage.

PROBLEM'S OBJECTS. To save space, we omit the now-familiar screen and keyboard objects:

Description of problem's object	Type	Kind	Name
A menu of cities	`String`	constant	*MENU*
The number of a city	`int`	varying	*city1*
The number of another city	`int`	varying	*city2*
A mileage chart	`int[][]`	constant	*MILEAGE_CHART*
The mileage	`int`	varying	*mileage*

As we shall see, the type `int[][]` refers to a two-dimensional array of integers, which provides a convenient way to represent our mileage chart.

OPERATIONS. Our behavioral description gives the following set of operations:

i. Define a two-dimensional array with initial values
ii. Display a string on the screen
iii. Read two integers from the keyboard
iv. Look up an entry in a two-dimensional array
v. Output an integer

ALGORITHM. These operations are easily organized into the following algorithm:

Algorithm for City Mileages

0. Define *MILEAGE_CHART*, a two-dimensional array of city mileages, and *MENU*, a menu of the supported cities.
1. Via the screen, display *MENU*.
2. From the keyboard, read two integers into *city1* and *city2*.
3. Compute *mileage*, by looking up *MILEAGE_CHART*[*city1*][*city2*].
4. Via `theScreen`, display *mileage*.

CODING. The preceding algorithm is easily encoded in Java, as shown in Figure 9.4.

FIGURE 9.4   A MILEAGE CALCULATOR FOR MAJOR FLORIDA CITIES

```
/** MileageCalculator.java calculates mileage between major Florida cities.
 *
 *  Input:        city1 and city2, two integers representing cities
 *  Precondition: For n cities, city1 and city2 are in the range 0 to n-1.
 *  Output:       The mileage between city1 and city2
 */

import ann.easyio.*;              // Keyboard, Screen

class MileageCalculator
{
 public static void main(String [] args)
 {
    final int [][] MILEAGE_CHART
              = { {   0,  97,  90, 268, 262, 130 },   // Daytona Beach
                  {  97,   0,  74, 337, 144, 128 },   // Gainesville
                  {  90,  74,   0, 354, 174, 201 },   // Jacksonville
                  { 268, 337, 354,   0, 475, 269 },   // Miami
                  { 262, 144, 174, 475,   0, 238 },   // Tallahassee
                  { 130, 128, 201, 269, 238,   0 } };// Tampa

    final String MENU = "To determine the mileage between two cities,\n"
          + " please enter the numbers for two cities from this menu:\n\n"
          + "      0 for Daytona Beach,    1 for Gainesville\n"
          + "      2 for Jacksonville,     3 for Miami\n"
          + "      4 for Tallahassee,      5 for Tampa\n\n"
          + "--> ";

    Screen theScreen = new Screen();
    theScreen.print(MENU);
    Keyboard theKeyboard = new Keyboard();

    int city1 = theKeyboard.readInt(),
        city2 = theKeyboard.readInt(),
        mileage = MILEAGE_CHART[city1][city2];

    theScreen.println("The mileage between those 2 cities is "
                      + mileage + " miles.");
 }
}
```

Sample run:

```
To determine the mileage between two cities,
please enter the numbers of 2 cities from this menu:

    0 for Daytona Beach,    1 for Gainesville
    2 for Jacksonville,     3 for Miami
    4 for Tallahassee,      5 for Tampa

--> 2 5

The mileage between those 2 cities is 201 miles.
```

There are many problems in which the data being processed can be naturally organized as a *table*. The preceding mileage problem is such a problem since mileage charts are commonly given in tabular form. For such problems, two-dimensional arrays provide a way to build a software model of a table.

Defining a Two-Dimensional Array

The program in Figure 9.4 illustrates how a two-dimensional array can be defined and initialized. The statement

```
final int [][] MILEAGE_CHART
            = { {   0,  97,  90, 268, 262, 130 },   // Daytona Beach
                {  97,   0,  74, 337, 144, 128 },   // Gainesville
                {  90,  74,   0, 354, 174, 201 },   // Jacksonville
                { 268, 337, 354,   0, 475, 269 },   // Miami
                { 262, 144, 174, 475,   0, 238 },   // Tallahassee
                { 130, 128, 201, 269, 238,   0 } };// Tampa
```

defines the object MILEAGE_CHART as a constant two-dimensional array of integers, consisting of six rows and six columns, which we might visualize as follows:

	[0]	[1]	[2]	[3]	[4]	[5]
[0]	0	97	90	268	262	130
[1]	97	0	74	337	144	128
[2]	90	74	0	354	174	201
[3]	268	337	354	0	475	269
[4]	262	144	174	475	0	238
[5]	130	128	201	269	238	0

As with one-dimensional arrays, each dimension of a two-dimensional array is indexed starting with zero, so the six rows are indexed from zero to five as are the six columns. As we shall see, these row and column indices are used to uniquely identify each element in the array.

This example shows how a two-dimensional array object can be initialized using a two-dimensional array literal, by listing the initial values in curly braces. Although not required, the values for each row are enclosed in their own pair of curly braces. A two-dimensional array literal is, therefore, a list of one-dimensional array literals, all of which have the same number of elements.

Two-dimensional arrays like MILEAGE_CHART that have the same number of rows as columns are called *square* arrays. But non-square arrays are needed for some problems. For example, consider the screen on a standard computer monitor. A typical screen can display 24 lines, with 80 characters on each line. The standard way to describe the screen is in terms of horizontal rows and vertical columns, with the rows being numbered from 0 through 23 and the columns numbered from 0 through 79. The position at row 0 and column 0 is usually in the upper left corner of the screen, giving the screen the following layout:

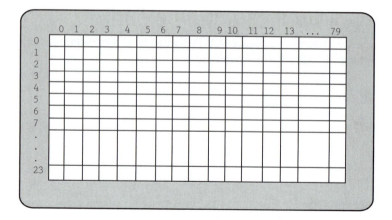

Such a screen can be modeled in software using a two-dimensional array of characters, declared as follows:

```
final int ROWS = 24,
          COLUMNS = 80;

char [][] screen = new char[ROWS][COLUMNS];
```

Note that this definition creates `screen` as a two-dimensional *variable* array object, whereas `MILEAGE_CHART` in Figure 9.4 is a two-dimensional *constant* array object.

As the preceeding examples illustrate, two-dimensional arrays are natural extensions of those for one-dimensional arrays described in Section 9.2. In general, they can have the following forms:

Two-Dimensional Array Declaration

Form

```
ElementType [][] arrayName;
ElementType [][] arrayName = new ElementType [DIM₁][DIM₂];
ElementType [][] arrayName = array-literal;
```

where:
`ElementType` is any type;
`arrayName` is the handle for the array object being defined;
DIM_1 and DIM_2 are expressions that evaluate to nonnegative integers; and
`array-literal` is a list of the form
    {one-dim-lit₁, one-dim-lit₂, . . . , one-dim-litₘ}
    where each `one-dim-litᵢ` is a one-dimensional array literal containing the same number of `ElementType` values (optionally enclosed in curly braces).

Purpose

The first form declares that `arrayName` is a handle for a two-dimensional array to be created later whose elements are of type `ElementType`. The other forms request the Java system to:

> **1.** Allocate memory for a two-dimensional array with elements of type *ElementType*: for the second form, the array will have DIM_1 rows and DIM_2 columns; for the third form. the array will have *m* rows and the number of columns will be the number of values in the one-dimensional array literals..
>
> **2.** Initialize this block of memory with default *ElementType* values for the second form and with the values given in the *array-literal* for the third.
>
> **3.** Store the address of this memory block in *arrayName*.

Predefined Two-Dimensional Array Operations

As with one-dimensional arrays, the central predefined operation for two-dimensional arrays is accessing its elements. A one-dimensional array uses a single index to accomplish this, as in

```
double aOneDimensionalArray = new double[10];
     .
     .
     .
aOneDimensionalArray[0] = 2.5;
```

Objects like MILEAGE_CHART and screen are two-dimensional objects and require two indices, one for each dimension. The element in row 0, column 0, of MILEAGE_CHART can be accessed using

```
MILEAGE_CHART[0][0]
```

The element of MILEAGE_CHART in the second column of the first row can be accessed using

```
MILEAGE_CHART[0][1]
```

the element at row 4, column 3 using

```
MILEAGE_CHART[4][3]
```

and so on. In general, the notation

```
MILEAGE_CHART[r][c]
```

can be used to access the value at row r and column c. The program in Figure 9.4 looked up the mileage between city1 and city2, by accessing the element at row city1 and column city2:

```
int mileage = MILEAGE_CHART[city1][city2];
```

Because MILEAGE_CHART is a constant object, we are only permitted to read (i.e., look up) its values. If we try to change one of the elements of MILEAGE_CHART,

```
MILEAGE_CHART[r][c] = theKeyboard.readInt();
```

the compiler will generate an error because we may not alter the value of a constant object.

By contrast, the `screen` object described above is a *variable* object, so values can be assigned to it. For example, the statement

```
screen[0][0] = 'X';
```

assigns the character 'X' to the element in row 0 and column 0.

Defining Two-Dimensional Array Operations

Just as one-dimensional array variables and constants are handles of array objects, two-dimensional array variables and constants are also handles. As we saw with one-dimensional arrays, care must be used with the assignment operator, because it may not produce the desired behavior. Instead, the `clone()` method can be used to make a shallow copy of a two-dimensional array.

Similarly, the `equals()` method only compares the *handles* of two-dimensional arrays. If we want to compare the *elements* of 2 two-dimensional arrays, we must define our own `equals()` method. For example, to compare 2 two-dimensional `int` arrays, we might use the following method:

```
public static boolean equals(int [][] array1, int [][] array2)
{
   if (array1.length != array2.length)            // check # of rows
      return false;
   else
   {
      for (int r = 0; r < array1.length; r++)      // for each row:
         if (array1[r].length != array2[r].length) // check # of columns
            return false;
         else                                       // compare elements
            for (int c = 0; c < array1[r].length; c++)
               if (array1[r][c] != array2[r][c])
                  return false;

      return true;              // all rows, columns, elements are equal
   }
}
```

Note that whereas operations on one-dimensional arrays typically use a single for loop to count through the index values;

```
for (int i = 0; i < numberOfValues; i++)
   // ... do something with oneDimensionalArray[i]
```

operations that access the values stored in a two-dimensional array use *two* nested for loops: an outer loop that counts through the rows, and an inner loop that counts through the columns:

```
for (int r = 0; r < numberOfRows; r++)
   for (int c = 0; c < numberOfColumns; c++)
      // ... do something with twoDimensionalArray[r][c]
```

In the next subsection, we will see several examples of methods that use this approach.

A Matrix Class

A two-dimensional numeric array having m rows and n columns is called an **$m \times n$ matrix.** In this section, we briefly examine how to build part of a `Matrix` class that contains several useful operations. There are many different matrix operations; to illustrate their implementation, we will build a method to perform **matrix multiplication.** Other operations such as matrix addition are described in the exercises. The Part of the Picture section that follows describes one of the many important applications of matrices.

Matrix Multiplication. Suppose that *mat1* is an $m \times n$ matrix and *mat2* is an $n \times p$ matrix. The product *mat3* of *mat1* and *mat2* is an $m \times p$ matrix in which the entry *mat3*[i][j], which appears in the ith row and the jth column, is given by

$$mat3[i][j] = \text{The sum of the products of the entries in row } i \text{ of}$$
$$mat1 \text{ with the entries of column } j \text{ of } mat2$$

$$= mat1[i][1] * mat2[1][j] + mat1[i][2] * mat2[2][j]$$
$$+ \cdots + mat1[i][n] * mat2[n][j]$$

Note that the number of columns (n) in *mat1* must equal the number of rows in *mat2* for the product of *mat1* with *mat2* to be defined.

To illustrate the operation, suppose that *mat1* is the 2×3 matrix

$$\begin{bmatrix} 1 & 0 & 2 \\ 3 & 0 & 4 \end{bmatrix}$$

and that *mat2* is the 3×4 matrix

$$\begin{bmatrix} 4 & 2 & 5 & 3 \\ 6 & 4 & 1 & 8 \\ 9 & 0 & 0 & 2 \end{bmatrix}$$

Because the number of columns (3) in *mat1* equals the number of rows in *mat2*, the product matrix *mat3* is defined. The entry in the first row and first column is obtained by multiplying the first row of mat1 with the first column of mat2, element by element, and adding these products:

$$\begin{bmatrix} 1 & 0 & 2 \\ 3 & 0 & 4 \end{bmatrix} \begin{bmatrix} 4 & 2 & 5 & 3 \\ 6 & 4 & 1 & 8 \\ 9 & 0 & 0 & 2 \end{bmatrix}$$

$$1 * 4 + 0 * 6 + 2 * 9 = 22$$

Similarly, the entry in the first row and second column is

$$\begin{bmatrix} 1 & 0 & 2 \\ 3 & 0 & 4 \end{bmatrix} \begin{bmatrix} 4 & 2 & 5 & 3 \\ 6 & 4 & 1 & 8 \\ 9 & 0 & 0 & 2 \end{bmatrix}$$

$$1 * 2 + 0 * 4 + 2 * 0 = 2$$

The complete product matrix *mat3* is the 2 × 4 matrix given by

$$\begin{bmatrix} 22 & 2 & 5 & 7 \\ 48 & 6 & 15 & 17 \end{bmatrix}$$

In general, the algorithm for multiplying matrices is as follows:

Matrix Multiplication Algorithm

1. If the number of columns in *mat1* ≠ the number of rows in *mat2*, then the product *mat3* = *mat1* * *mat2* is not defined; terminate the algorithm.
2. For each row *i* in *mat1*, do the following:

   For each column *j* in *mat2* do the following:

   a. Set *sum* equal to 0.

   b. For each column *k* in *mat1* (= the number of rows in *mat2*):

   Add *mat1*[*i*][*k*] * *mat2*[*k*][*j*] to *sum*.

   c. Set *mat3*[*i*][*j*] equal to *sum*.

Before we can encode this algorithm, we need a `Matrix` class in which to store the method.

Building a `Matrix` Class

To build a `Matrix` class, we begin by identifying the operations our class will need to provide. Some of these operations are:

❑ A default-value constructor: Initialize myself to an empty matrix
❑ An explicit-value constructor: Initialize myself to have a specified size
❑ Input: Fill myself with values from the keyboard
❑ Output: Convert myself to a `String` representation
❑ Retrieve my element at row r column c
❑ Change my element at row r column c
❑ Return the product of myself with another matrix

Other common operations such as addition, subtraction, and multiplication by a constant would also be added. We leave these as exercises.

If we begin with a class skeleton, we can supply stubs for each of these methods:

```
public class Matrix
{
 public Matrix() {}
 public Matrix(int rows, int columns) {}
 public void read() {}
 public String toString() {}
 public double getElement(int row, int column) {}
 public void setElement(int row, int column, double value) {}
 public Matrix times(Matrix mat2) {}
}
```

Note that the structure of each stub follows naturally from a careful description of what the operation is to perform.

Once we have the class skeleton and stubs, we are ready to add attribute variables. For convenience, we will store a matrix as a two-dimensional array of double values and also store the number of rows and the number of columns in the array.

```
public class Matrix
{
 public Matrix() {}
 public Matrix(int rows, int columns) {}
 public void read() {}
 public String toString() {}
 public double getElement(int row, int column) {}
 public void setElement(int row, int column, double value) {}
 public Matrix times(Matrix mat2) {}

 private int myRows;
 private int myColumns;
 private double [] [] myArray;
}
```

The Default Constructor. Because the default constructor just initializes fields with values appropriate for an empty matrix, it is quite simple, as shown in Figure 9.5:

FIGURE 9.5   MATRIX DEFAULT CONSTRUCTOR

```
public Matrix()
{
   myArray = null;
   myRows = 0;
   myColumns = 0;
}
```

Given this method, a programmer can write

```
Matrix aMatrix = new Matrix();
```

and aMatrix will be the handle for an empty Matrix object.

The Explicit-Value Constructor. Because the explicit-value constructor initializes attribute variables with values supplied by the user (who might pass erroneous values), these values must be validated before they are used. This validation makes the explicit value constructor a bit more complex, as shown in Figure 9.6:

FIGURE 9.6   MATRIX EXPLICIT-VALUE CONSTRUCTOR

```
public Matrix(int rows, int columns)
{
  if (rows < 0)
    Controller.fatal("Matrix.Matrix()", "invalid row parameter");
  else if (columns < 0)
    Controller.fatal("Matrix.Matrix()", "invalid column parameter");
  else
  {
    myArray = new double[rows][columns];
    myRows = rows;
    myColumns = columns;
  }
}
```

A declaration of the form

```
Matrix aMatrix = new Matrix(m, n);
```

will make aMatrix a handle for a Matrix object with m rows and n columns.

Output. We will build a method to perform output next, since it is useful in debugging other methods. As we have seen before, all that is needed is to implement the toString() method for our class. Figure 9.7 provides a possible implementation. Note that to process each value in the two-dimensional array, we use nested for loops, as described previously.

FIGURE 9.7   MATRIX OUTPUT (STRING CONVERSION)

```
public String toString()
{
  String result = "";

  for (int r = 0; r < myRows; r++)
  {
    for (int c = 0; c < myColumns; c++)
      result += "\t" + myArray[r][c];

    result += "\n";
  }

  return result;
}
```

To produce a reasonable table output (at least for small matrices), this method prints a tab character to separate the columns in a row. And at the end of each row, a newline character is used to start the next row on a new line. Given this method, we can display the values in a matrix in the same way as we display any other kind of object's value; for example,

```
theScreen.println(aMatrix);
```

Input. For input, we will assume that the user enters the number of rows, then the number of columns, and finally the values to go into the matrix. This leads to the `read()` method shown in Figure 9.8. Note that because the matrix being input may have a size already specified, we must validate the dimensions entered by the user.

FIGURE 9.8   MATRIX INPUT

```
public void read()
{
  Keyboard myKeyboard = new Keyboard();
  int rows = myKeyboard.readInt();
  int columns = myKeyboard.readInt();

  if ( (rows <= 0) || (myRows > 0 && rows != myRows) )
    Controller.fatal("Matrix.read()", "input row value is invalid");
  else if ( (columns <= 0) || (myColumns > 0 && columns != myColumns ) )
    Controller.fatal("Matrix.read()", "input column value is invalid");
  else
  {
    myArray = new double[rows][columns];

    for (int r = 0; r < rows; r++)
      for (int c = 0; c < columns; c++)
        myArray[r][c] = myKeyboard.readDouble();

    myRows = rows;
    myColumns = columns;
  }
}
```

Note that `myKeyboard` is not really an attribute of our `Matrix` class, because it is only needed in this (input) method. Because of this, we declare it locally within this method, rather than as an attribute variable.

Given this method, a programmer can now write

```
Matrix aMatrix = new Matrix();
aMatrix.read();
```

and `aMatrix` will fill itself with values entered at the keyboard, unless the user enters invalid dimensions for the matrix.

Matrix Attribute Accessors. Our class has two attributes to which we might want to grant a user access: the number of rows and the number of columns. For this reason we provide accessor methods for these two attributes as shown in Figure 9.9:

FIGURE 9.9   MATRIX ATTRIBUTE ACCESSOR

```
public int rows()
{
  return myRows;
}

public int columns()
{
  return myColumns;
}
```

A programmer can use the expressions `aMatrix.rows()` and `aMatrix.columns()` to determine the number of rows and columns, respectively, in the `Matrix` referred to by `aMatrix`.

Element Accessor and Mutator Methods. Our operations list includes two methods to manipulate individual elements of a matrix. The first method lets a user of the `Matrix` class retrieve the value at a given row and column, and the second lets a user change the value at a given row and column. We call these methods `getElement()` and `setElement()`, respectively.

In each method, the caller must supply the indices of the row and column being accessed. To guard against errors, these values should be validated. Since this validation is useful in other methods we would normally add to the class, we use a utility method `isValid()` to check the validity of a given row and column pair. Figure 9.10 shows this method along with the `setElement()` and `getElement()` methods.

FIGURE 9.10   MATRIX ELEMENT ACCESSOR AND MUTATOR

```
private boolean isValid(int row, int column)
{
  return 0 <= row && row < myRows
         && 0 <= column && column < myColumns;
}
public void setElement(int row, int column, double value)
{
  if (! isValid(row, column))
    Controller.fatal("Matrix.setElement()",
                     "invalid [row][column] parameters");

  myArray[row][column] = value;
}

public double getElement(int row, int column)
{
  if (! isValid(row, column))
    Controller.fatal("Matrix.getElement()",
                     "invalid [row][column] parameters: ["
                     + row + "][" + column + "]");

  return myArray[row][column];
}
```

Given these methods, expressions of the form

```
aMatrix.getElement(r, c)
```

can be used to retrieve the value of the element at row r, column c, and

```
aMatrix.setElement(r, c, v);
```

to set the element at row r, column c to value v.

Matrix Multiplication. The final operation we add to our class is matrix multiplication. Figure 9.11 presents a `times()` method that implements the algorithm given earlier.

FIGURE 9.11   MATRIX MULTIPLICATION METHOD

```
public Matrix times(Matrix mat2)
{
  if (columns() != mat2.rows())
    Controller.fatal("Matrix.times()", "myColumns: " + myColumns
                     + " != mat2.rows(): " + mat2.rows());

  Matrix mat3 = new Matrix(myRows, mat2.columns());

  for (int i = 0; i < myRows; i++)
    for (int j = 0; j < mat2.columns(); j++)
    {
       double sum = 0.0;
       for (int k = 0; k < myColumns; k++)
         sum += myArray[i][k] * mat2.getElement(k, j);
       mat3.setElement(i, j, sum);
    }

  return mat3;
}
```

The matrix multiplication algorithm given earlier described how to multiply two matrices *mat1* and *mat2* to produce a third matrix *mat3*. Note that instead of this external perspective, our implementation is from an internal perspective. There is no reference to *mat1* anywhere in the method, because it is the object itself. The code reflects this perspective: for example, the statement:

```
sum += myArray[i][k] * mat2.getElement(k, j);
```

accesses the element at row i, column k within `myArray`, and accesses the element at row k, column j in `mat2`. Since `mat2` is a different `Matrix` object, we use its `getElement()` method to perform the access.

Given this method and `Matrix` objects referred to by m1 and m2, a programmer can now compute the product of those objects by writing:

```
Matrix m3 = m1.times(m2);
```

Program To Do Matrix Multiplication. We have now defined a minimal `Matrix` class. (See the exercises for additional `Matrix` operations that can be added.) A program can use its methods in the same manner as those of any other class, as illustrated in Figure 9.12. Note that we have included this `Matrix` class in the package `ann.math` provided with this text.

FIGURE 9.12   PROGRAM TO MULTIPLY MATRICES

```
/** MatrixMultiplier.java illustrates use of the matrix multiplication meth
 *
 *  Input:   two matrices
 *  Output: the matrices together with their product (provided it is define
 */

import ann.easyio.*;      // Screen
import ann.math.Matrix;

class MatrixMultiplier
{
  public static void main(String [] args)
  {
    Screen theScreen = new Screen();
    theScreen.println("This program multiplies two matrices.\n"
       + "Enter the number of rows, columns, and elements of matrix 1: ");
    Matrix mat1 = new Matrix();
    mat1.read();
    theScreen.println(
       "\nEnter the number of rows, columns, and elements of matrix 2: ");
    Matrix mat2 = new Matrix();
    mat2.read();

    Matrix mat3 = mat1.times(mat2);

    theScreen.println("\nmatrix 1 * matrix 2 = \n" + mat3);
  }
}
```

Sample run:

```
To multiply two matrices,
enter the number of rows, columns, and elements of matrix 1:
2 3
1 0 2
3 0 4

Enter the number of rows, columns, and elements of matrix 2:
3 4
4 2 5 3
6 4 1 8
9 0 0 2

matrix 1 * matrix 2 =
       22.0     2.0      5.0      7.0
       48.0     6.0     15.0     17.0
```

Note the various places that this program uses the `Matrix` class operations. The statements:

```
Matrix mat1 = new Matrix();
...
Matrix mat2 = new Matrix()
```

construct `mat1` and `mat2` as empty matrices. The statements

```
mat1.read();
...
mat2.read();
```

use the `read()` method to fill these matrices with values entered at the keyboard. The statement

```
Matrix mat3 = mat1.times(mat2);
```

sends `mat1` the `times()` message, which computes and returns the product of itself and `mat2`. Finally, the statement

```
the Screen.println("\nmatrix 1 * matrix 2 = \n" + mat3);
```

implicitly calls the `Matrix toString()` method to display the contents of `mat3`.

Higher-Dimensional Arrays

We have now seen how to define arrays having two dimensions. The techniques can also be extended to arrays of higher dimensions. For example, suppose that a retailer maintains an inventory of jeans. She carries several different brands of jeans and for each brand she stocks a variety of styles, waist sizes, and inseam lengths. A four-dimensional array can be used to record the inventory, with each element of the array being the number of jeans of a particular brand, style, waist size, and inseam length currently in stock. The first index represents the brand, which we might represent by

```
final int LEVI              = 0,  // define brand information
          WRANGLER          = 1,
          CALVIN_KLEIN      = 2,
          LEE               = 3,
          NUMBER_OF_BRANDS  = 4;
```

The second index represents the style, for which we might write something like

```
final int WIDE_BOTTOM       = 0,  // style information
          RELAXED_FIT       = 1,
          STRAIGHT_LEG      = 2,
          REGULAR_FIT       = 3,
          NUMBER_OF_STYLES  = 4;
```

The third and fourth indices represent waist size and inseam length, respectively. To represent waist sizes ranging from 28 through 48 and inseam lengths ranging from 26 through 36, we might use

```
final int W28 = 0, W29 = 1, W30 = 2, W31 = 3,  // waist sizes
          W32 = 4, W33 = 5, W34 = 6, W35 = 7,
          W36 = 8, W37 = 9, W38 = 10, W39 = 11, W40 = 12,
          W41 = 13, W42 = 14, W43 = 15, W44 = 16, W45 = 17,
          W46 = 18, W47 = 19, W48 = 20,
          NUMBER_OF_WAIST_SIZES = 21;
```

```
final int I26 = 0,  I27 = 1,  I28 = 2,  I29 = 3,   // inseam sizes
          I30 = 4,  I31 = 5,  I32 = 6,  I33 = 7,
          I34 = 8,  I35 = 9,  I36 = 10,
          NUMBER_OF_INSEAM_SIZES = 11;
```

Since each of these constant-ranges corresponds to a range of index values, we can use the constants in each range as array indices.

To maintain the inventory, we can declare a four-dimensional array object:

```
int [][][][] jeansInventory =
    new int [NUMBER_OF_BRANDS] [NUMBER_OF_STYLES]
            [NUMBER_OF_WAIST_SIZES] [NUMBER_OF_INSEAM_SIZES];
```

The value of the expression

```
jeansInventory[LEVI] [RELAXED_FIT] [W32] [I31]
```

is the number of Levi's relaxed fit 32 × 31 jeans that are in stock. The statement

```
jeansInventory[brand] [style] [waist] [inseam] --;
```

can be used to record the sale (i.e., decrement the inventory) of one pair of jeans of a specified *brand*, *style*, *waist* size, and *inseam* length.

Java places no limit on the number of dimensions of an array. This means that for arbitrary values of *n*, *n*-dimensional arrays can be defined, the array's elements can be accessed using *n* indices, and the values in the array can be processed using *n* nested for loops. The forms of array declarations for two dimensions extend naturally to higher dimensions.

✔ Quick Quiz 9.4

1. A(n) _____ array is useful for storing data arranged in rows and columns.
2. A(n) _____ array is useful for storing data arranged in rows, columns, and ranks.
3. Arrays with the same number of rows as columns are said to be _____ arrays.

Questions 4–14 refer to the following two-dimensional array:

		[0]	[1]	[2]	[3]
	[0]	11	22	0	43
	[1]	1	-1	0	999
mat:	[2]	-5	39	15	82
	[3]	1	2	3	4
	[4]	44	33	22	11

Find the value of each expression in Questions 4–9.

4. `mat[2][4]`   5. `mat[4][1]`   6. `mat[1][1]`

7. `mat[0][0]+ mat[0][1]`   8. `mat[0][0] + mat[1][0]`   9. `mat[3]`

Find the value of x in each of Questions 10–14:

10.
```
int x = 0;
   for (int i = 0; i <= 4; i++)
      x += mat[i][1];
```

11.
```
int x = 0;
   for (int j = 0; j < 4; j++)
      x += mat[1][j];
```

12.
```
int x = 0;
   for (int k = 0; k <= 3; k++)
      x += mat[k][k];
```

13.
```
int x = 0;
   for (int i = 0; i < 5; i++)
      for (int j = 0; j < 4; j++)
         x += mat[i][j];
```

14.
```
int x = 0;
   for (int j = 0; j < 4; j++)
      for (int i = 0; i < 5; i++)
         x += mat[i][j];
```

15. A two-dimensional numeric array having m rows and n columns is called a(n) _____.

Questions 16–18 assume the following matrices:

$$A = \begin{bmatrix} 1 & 0 & 2 \\ 3 & 0 & 4 \end{bmatrix}, B = \begin{bmatrix} 1 & 0 \\ 2 & -1 \\ 1 & 3 \end{bmatrix}$$

16. $A * B$ will be a(n) _____ × _____ matrix.

17. Calculate $A * B$.

18. Calculate $B * A$ or explain why it is not defined.

✎ EXERCISES 9.4

For Exercises 1–6, tell how many elements `array` will have.

1. `int [][] array = new int [50][100]`

2. `char [][] array = new char [26][26]`

3. `boolean [][] array = new boolean [2][2]`

4. `double [][][] array = new double [1][2][3]`

5. `double [][][] array = new double [6][10][20]`

6. `boolean [][][][] array = new boolean [2][2][2][2]`

Exercises 7–10 assume that the following declaration has been made:

```
int [][] mat = new int [3][3];
```

Tell what value (if any) is stored in each array element, or explain why an error occurs.

7.  ```
    for (int i = 0; i < 3; i++)
        for (int j = 0; j < 3; j++)
            mat[i][j] = i + j;
    ```

8.  ```
    for (int i = 0; i < 3; i++)
        for (int j = 2; j >= 0; j--)
            if (i == j)
                mat[i][j] = 0;
            else
                mat[i][j] = 1;
    ```

9.  ```
    for (int i = 0; i < 3; i++)
        for (int j = 0; j < 3; j++)
            if (i < j)
                mat[i][j] = -1
            else if (i == j)
                mat[i][j] = 0;
            else
                mat[i][j] = 1;
    ```

10. ```
    for (int i = 0; i < 3; i++)
    {
        for (int j = 0; j < i; j++)
            mat[i][j] = 0;
        for (j = i; j < 3; j++)
            mat[i][j] = 2
    }
    ```

Exercises 11–14 assume that the following declaration has been made:

```
int [][] num = { {0,2,4,6,8}, {1,3,5,7,9} };
```

Tell what output will be produced or explain why an error occurs.

11. ```
    for (int i = 0; i < 2; i++)
    {
        for (int j = 0; j < 5; j++)
            theScreen.print( num[i][j] + " " );
        theScreen.println();
    }
    ```

12. ```
    for (int j = 0; j < 5; j++)
    {
        for (int i = 0; i < 2; i++)
            theScreen.print( num[i][j] + " " );
        theScreen.println();
    }
    ```

13.
```
for (int i = 0; i < 2; i++)
{
    for (int j = 0; j < 7; j++)
        theScreen.print( num[j][i] + " " );
    theScreen.println();
}
```

14.
```
for (int i = 0; i < 2; i++)
{
    for (int j = 4; j >= 0; j--)
        theScreen.print( num[i][j] + " " );
    theScreen.println();
}
```

15. Write a method that, given a two-dimensional array with m rows and n columns, will calculate and return the average of each row.

16. Proceed as in Exercise 15, but find the average of each column.

17. Following the example of the four-dimensional array `jeansInventory` in the text, write declarations for recording sales of ten different automobile models by eight different employees at an auto dealership. Using these types, build a class whose basic operations are the input and output of sales tables. The output operator should display the sales table with the rows labeled with the automobile models and the columns labeled with the employees' names.

18. Add a constructor to class `Matrix` that, upon receiving a one-dimensional array of `double` values, builds a `Matrix` having only one row that contains the elements of that array.

19. Add a constructor to class `Matrix` that, upon receiving a one-dimensional array of `double` values, builds a `Matrix` having only one column that contains the elements of that array.

20. Add an addition operation to class `Matrix`. The sum of two matrices is defined as follows: If A_{ij} and B_{ij} are the entries in the ith row and jth column of $m \times n$ matrices A and B, respectively, then $A_{ij} + B_{ij}$ is the entry in the ith row and jth column of the sum, which will also be an $m \times n$ matrix. For example,

$$\begin{bmatrix} 1 & 0 & 2 \\ -1 & 3 & 5 \end{bmatrix} + \begin{bmatrix} 4 & 2 & 1 \\ 7 & 0 & 3 \end{bmatrix} = \begin{bmatrix} 5 & 2 & 3 \\ -6 & 3 & 8 \end{bmatrix}$$

21. Add a subtraction operation to class `Matrix`. The definition of the difference of two matrices is the same as that for the sum in Exercise 20 except that the entries of the second matrix B are subtracted from the first matrix A.

22. Add a method to class `Matrix` to find the transpose of a matrix, which is defined as follows: Suppose that A is an $m \times n$ matrix, and that A_{ij} is the entry in the ith row and jth column of A. The transpose of A is an $n \times m$ matrix T in which $T_{ji} = A_{ij}$, for all indices i and j. For example, if A is the 2×3 matrix

$$\begin{bmatrix} 1 & 0 & 2 \\ -1 & 3 & 5 \end{bmatrix}$$

the transpose of A is the 3×2 matrix

$$\begin{bmatrix} 1 & -1 \\ 0 & 3 \\ 2 & 5 \end{bmatrix}$$

9.7 GRAPHICAL/INTERNET JAVA: A PIE-CHART CLASS

In this section, we examine a graphics-related problem for which the array provides a convenient solution.

PROBLEM: PROFIT ANALYSIS FOR THE MIDDLE EARTH TOURING COMPANY[2]

After the War of the Rings, some hobbits decide to form a company to organize tours of the various sites of interest during the war. After much deliberation, they name their company the Middle Earth Touring Company. To test the waters, they decide to start with a tour of the Shire, a tour of the cities of Gondor, and a tour of what is left of Mordor. After 6 months of running their tours, they decide that they need a program to help them see how popular each tour is. They have hired us to write a program that prompts for the proceeds earned on each tour, and then displays a pie chart showing the relative percentage of profit for each tour. The program should be easy to upgrade, because the hobbits are thinking of adding more tours in the near future.

 OBJECT-CENTERED DESIGN

BEHAVIOR. For each tour being offered, the program should display a prompt for the proceeds of that tour and read those profits. The program should then build a well-labeled pie chart showing the percentage of the total proceeds earned by each tour.

PRELIMINARY SKETCH. We can use input dialogs from Java's `JOptionPane` class to perform the input steps. However, Java provides no predefined class for building a pie chart, so we will need to build one ourselves. We might sketch a preliminary design for such a *PieChart* object, laying out some of the relevant measurements as follows:

---

[2] With apologies to J.R.R. Tolkien.

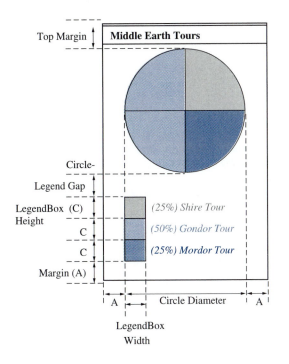

These are not all of the relevant measurements, but they provide a start. More will be identified as we build our pie-chart class.

Since the program must represent multiple tours and each tour can be represented by a `String`, we can represent multiple tours with a `String` array. Similarly, we can represent the proceeds from the tours with a `double` array.

PROBLEM'S OBJECTS   From our behavioral description, we can identify these objects:

Description of problem's objects	Type	Kind	Name
The tours being offered	`String[]`	constant	*TOURS*
A prompt	`String`	constant	none
The tour proceeds	`double[]`	varying	*proceeds*
A particular tour	`String`	varying	*TOURS[i]*
A particular tour's proceeds	`double`	varying	*proceeds[i]*
A pie chart	`PieChart`	varying	*proceedsChart*

Our behavioral description actually describes additional objects. However, these objects are items to be displayed by our `PieChart` class. Because of this, these objects will be the responsibility of this class rather than our application.

OPERATIONS. The behavioral description requires the following operations:

i. Display a `String`

ii. Read a `double`

iii. Repeat (i) and (ii) for each `String` in an array

iv. Build a `PieChart` from a `String` array and a `double` array

v. Display a `PieChart`

ALGORITHM. Assuming that we can build a `PieChart` class to provide the final two operations, we can use the following algorithm to solve the problem.

Algorithm for Middle Earth Tours Problem

1. Define *TOURS*, a `String` array of tour names, and *proceeds*, a `double` array having the same length as *TOURS*.
2. For each index *i* from 0 though (length of *TOURS*) − 1:
   a. Display a prompt for the proceeds from *TOURS*[*i*].
   b. Read the input into *proceeds*[*i*].
3. Build *proceedsChart*, showing *TOURS* and *proceeds*.
4. Display *proceedsChart*.

CODING. Figure 9.13 shows an implementation of this algorithm for the three tours described in the problem.

FIGURE 9.13   PROCCEDS FROM MIDDLE EARTH TOURS—VERSION 1

```
/** TourAnalyzer1.java
 *
 *   Input: The proceeds from 3 tours
 *   Output: A pie chart for those proceeds
 */

import javax.swing.*;        // JOptionPane
import PieChart;
class TourAnalyzer1 extends Object
{
 public static void main(String [] args)
 {
    final String [] TOURS = {"Shire Tour", "Gondor Tour", "Mordor Tour"};

    double [] proceeds = new double[TOURS.length];

    for (int i = 0; i < TOURS.length; i++)
    {
      String proceedsString = JOptionPane.showInputDialog(
                        "Enter proceeds from " + TOURS[i] + ":");
      proceeds[i] = Double.parseDouble(proceedsString);
    }

    PieChart profitChart = new PieChart(TOURS, proceeds);
    profitChart.setTitle("Middle Earth Tours");
    profitChart.setVisible(true);
 }
}
```

TESTING Given the `PieChart` class, this program will prompt us for the first tour's proceeds,

followed by a prompt for the second tour's proceeds,

and finally, a prompt for the third tour's proceeds:

Following this last dialog, the program builds and displays a pie chart representing the relative percentages of the input values:

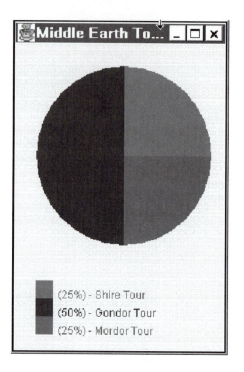

Of course this last occurrence will not happen without a `PieChart` class. We build this class next.

Pie-Chart Classes

OPERATIONS. We begin the construction of our `PieChart` class by identifying the operations we want it to provide. Since a pie chart consists of slices, we start with these operations:

- **i.** Construct a pie chart, given a `String` array containing slice labels and a `double` array containing raw values for slices.
- **ii.** Draw (paint) the pie chart.
- **iii.** Change the color of a given slice.
- **iv.** Change the raw value of a given slice.

From these descriptions, we might begin with the following class skeleton:

```
public class PieChartPanel extends JPanel
{
 public PieChartPanel(final String [] SLICE_LABELS,
                double [] sliceValues) {}
 public void paintComponent(Graphics pen) {}
 public void setSliceColor(int sliceNumber, Color newColor) {}
 public void setSliceValue(int sliceNumber, double newValue) {}
}
```

Our `PieChart` class will then extend `CloseableFrame`,

```
class PieChart extends CloseableFrame
```

and will simply place the `PieChartPanel` that contains the actual pie chart on the content pane of this frame.

Attributes. Before we begin implementing these methods, we need to identify the attributes of the `PieChartPanel` class. Some of these attributes can be gleaned from our sketch. For example, it identifies values such as the top margin and the margin between the pie chart's elements and the edge of the frame, so we define constants for these values to make it easy to adjust them. In addition, we add a constant for the degrees in a circle, a constant defining the maximum number of slices a pie chart can have, and a constant for the offset from the top of the window to where we begin drawing the chart's legend:

```
public class PieChartPanel extends JPanel
{
 private final static int
    MARGIN            = 25,
    TOP_MARGIN        = 25,
    CIRCLE_DIAMETER   = 200,
    CIRCLE_LEGEND_GAP = 40,
    LEGEND_OFFSET     = TOP_MARGIN + CIRCLE_DIAMETER
                        + CIRCLE_LEGEND_GAP,
    LEGEND_BOX_SIZE   = 20,
    LEGEND_LABEL_GAP  = 5,
    DEGREES_IN_CIRCLE = 360,
    MAX_SLICES        = 6;

 // methods will go here ...
}
```

Other attributes follow from thinking carefully about the kinds of information the operations require the class to store. For example, if the `paintComponent()` method is to draw a label for each slice, those labels must be stored somewhere. If it is to draw slices as angles proportional to a slice-value's relative percentage, then those slice percentages must be stored by the class. If we wish to allow a user to change the raw value of a slice percentage, then we must store the raw values for each slice. Similarly, if we wish to allow a user to change the color of a slice, then our class must store the color for each slice and use this stored color when it paints the slice. Finally, if we want to display the raw values (or percentages) of each slice in its label, we should format this `double` value to only a few decimal places. These plus a few other attribute variables to simplify some of our computations give us the following attribute variables:

```
class PieChartPanel extends JPanel
{
  // Constants and method stubs omitted ...

 private String [] mySliceLabel;   // label for a slice
 private double [] mySliceValue;   // raw value for a slice
 private double [] mySlicePct;     // percentage for a slice
 private Color  [] mySliceColor    // default slice colors
              = {Color.green, Color.blue, Color.red,
                 Color.orange, Color.gray, Color.cyan};
 private int       mySlices,       // number of slices
                   myWidth,        // window-frame dimensions
                   myHeight;
 private NumberFormat myFormatter; // display numbers
                                   // as percentages
}
```

Once we have identified the attributes, we can begin implementing the methods. (Also, we can always add more if we have forgotten any.)

The `PieChartPanel` Constructor. The role of the constructor is to initialize the attribute variables of the class. We can thus specify the task our `PieChartPanel` constructor must perform as follows:

Receive: SLICE_LABELS, a constant `String` array
                    `sliceValues`, a `double` array

Precondition: SLICE_LABLES.length == sliceValues.length
   &&   sliceLabels.length is in the range 2..MAX_SLICES
   &&   sliceValues.length is in the range 2..MAX_SLICES

Postcondition: mySliceLabels is a copy of SLICE_LABELS
   &&   mySliceValues is a copy of sliceValues
   &&   mySlices = sliceValues.length
   &&   myWidth, myHeight are set to my dimensions

To satisfy these conditions, we can write a method that tests the preconditions and then uses assignments to initialize the attribute variables as follows. The complete method is given in Figure 9.14.

```
public PieChartPanel(final String [] sliceLabels,
                     double [] sliceValues)
{
  //... check precondition

  mySlices = sliceValues.length;
  mySliceLabel = new String[mySlices];
  mySliceValue = new double[mySlices];
```

```
for (int i = 0; i < mySlices; i++)
{
  mySliceLabel[i] = sliceLabels[i];
  mySliceValue[i] = sliceValues[i];
}

myFormatter = NumberFormat.getPercentInstance();
mySlicePct = new double[MAX_SLICES];
computePercentages();

myWidth = MARGIN + CIRCLE_DIAMETER + MARGIN;
myHeight = LEGEND_OFFSET + mySlices * LEGEND_BOX_SIZE + MARGIN;
setSize(myWidth, myHeight);
setBackground(Color.white);
}
```

This definition uses a utility method `computePercentages()` to initialize the attribute variable `mySlicePercent`. The reason is that if we think ahead a bit, the user may use the `setSliceValue()` method to change the raw value of a slice. This will require recomputing the values in the attribute variable `mySlicePercent` each time we repaint the screen. Since this is a nontrivial operation, we encode it as a method so that both this constructor and the `paintComponent()` method can use the same code. The method, which is given in Figure 9.14, simply sums the values in `mySliceValue` and then computes each value in `mySlicePercent` by dividing the corresponding value in `mySliceValue` by the sum of the values.

The `paintComponent()` Method. Since the Swing components use `paint-Component()` to paint in a frame, we must define this method to actually draw the pie chart. If we study the drawing methods in Java's `Graphics` class, we see that we can use the `fillArc()` method to draw a particular slice, the `fillRect()` method to draw a legend box, and the `drawString()` method to label a legend box. Each of these methods is described in the Java API documentation.

To simplify the `paintComponent()` method, we first define the following `drawSlice()` method to draw a particular slice (`sliceNumber`) of the pie chart, starting at a particular angle (`startAngle`), through a given angle (`arcAngle`), using our method's `Graphics` context (`pen`). Each of these values must be supplied via a parameter.

```
private void drawSlice(int sliceNumber, int startAngle,
                       int arcAngle, Graphics pen)
{
  if (sliceNumber < 0 || sliceNumber >= mySlices)
    Controller.fatal("drawSlice()", "invalid sliceNumber");
  else if (startAngle < 0)
    Controller.fatal("drawSlice()", "negative startAngle");
  else if (arcAngle < 0)
    Controller.fatal("drawSlice()", "negative arcAngle");
  pen.setColor(mySliceColor[sliceNumber]);
  pen.fillArc(MARGIN, TOP_MARGIN, CIRCLE_DIAMETER, CIRCLE_DIAMETER,
              startAngle, arcAngle);
```

```
    pen.fillRect(MARGIN,
                 LEGEND_OFFSET + sliceNumber*LEGEND_BOX_SIZE,
                 LEGEND_BOX_SIZE, LEGEND_BOX_SIZE);
    pen.drawString("(" + myFormatter.format(mySlicePct[sliceNumber])
                   + ") - " + mySliceLabel[sliceNumber],
                 MARGIN + LEGEND_BOX_SIZE + LEGEND_LABEL_GAP,
                 LEGEND_OFFSET + (sliceNumber+1)*LEGEND_BOX_SIZE);
  }
```

Getting the correct arguments to `fillArc()`, `fillRect()`, and `drawString()` takes some experimentation, but the constant attributes we defined earlier simplify the process greatly.

The `paintComponent()` method then draws each slice in turn by computing its starting angle and how big its angle should be, and then passing these values to the `drawSlice()` method:

```
        public void paintComponent(Graphics pen)
        {
          super.paintComponent(pen);
          setSize(myWidth, myHeight);
          int startAngle = 0;
          int arcAngle = 0;
          for (int i = 0; i < mySlices; i++)
          {
            startAngle += arcAngle;
            arcAngle = round(mySlicePct[i] * DEGREES_IN_CIRCLE);
            drawSlice(i, startAngle, arcAngle, pen);
          }
        }
```

The `setSliceColor()` Mutator. We can specify the problem of letting the user change a slice color as follows:

Receive: `sliceNumber`, the number of the slice whose color is being changed; `newColor`, the new color

Precondition: `sliceNumber` is in the range 0..`mySlices`

Postcondition: `mySliceColor[sliceNumber] == newColor`

Implementing a method to satisfy these conditions is straightforward:

```
public void setSliceColor(int sliceNumber, Color newColor)
{
  if (sliceNumber < 0 || sliceNumber >= mySlices)
    Controller.fatal("setSliceColor(int,Color)", " invalid slice "
                     + sliceNumber);
  mySliceColor[sliceNumber] = newColor;
  repaint();
}
```

Note that we must call `repaint()` at the end of the method if we want our `PieChart` to be updated with the new slice color when this method terminates.

Given this method, a programmer can now write

```
myChart.setSliceColor(i, differentColor);
```

to set the color of the slice whose index is *i* to *differentColor*.

The `setSliceValue()` **Mutator.** We can specify the problem of letting the user change a slice value as follows:

Receive: sliceNumber, the number of the slice whose color is being changed; newValue, the new value for the slice

Precondition: sliceNumber is in the range 0..mySlices

Postcondition: mySliceValue[sliceNumber] == newValue

A method to satisfy these conditions is given in Figure 9.14. It is straightforward and similar to `setSliceColor()`. The only significant difference is that we must be sure to recompute `mySlicePercentages` before repainting, so that the size of a given slice is properly updated.

The Pie-Chart Classes. Figure 9.14 gives the complete `PieChart` and `PieChart-Panel` classes.

FIGURE 9.14   PIE-CHART CLASSES

```
/** PieChartPanel.java provides a pie chart.
 *  Attributes: arrays of slice labes, slice colors, slice sizes, and
 *              slice colors; number of lices; dimensions of window frame;
 *              formatter to display numbers and percentages
 *  Methods:    constructor of a pie chart with a set of slice labels and
 *              values; paintComponent(); draw slize with a given number,
 *              start and arc angles; set slice color or value
 *              private method to compute percentages amd a rounding method
 */

import java.awt.*;                        // Graphics, Color, ...
import javax.swing.JPanel;
import java.text.NumberFormat;
import ann.utility.Controller;

class PieChartPanel extends JPanel
{
  private final static int
    MARGIN             = 25,
    TOP_MARGIN         = 25,
    CIRCLE_DIAMETER    = 200,
    CIRCLE_LEGEND_GAP  = 40,
    LEGEND_OFFSET      = TOP_MARGIN + CIRCLE_DIAMETER + CIRCLE_LEGEND_GAP,
    LEGEND_BOX_SIZE    = 20,
    LEGEND_LABEL_GAP   = 5,
    DEGREES_IN_CIRCLE  = 360,
    MAX_SLICES         = 6;
```

```
/** Constructor
 *   Receive:           sliceLabels, an array of String;
 *                      sliceValues, an array of double;
 *   Precondition:      sliceLabels.length = sliceValues.length
 *                      && sliceLabels.length >= 2
 *                      && sliceLabels.length <= MAX_SLICES
 *                      && sliceValues.length >= 2
 *                      && sliceValues.length <= MAX_SLICES.
 *   Postcondition: for each index i in 0..MAX_SLICES-1:
 *                      mySliceLabel[i].equals(sliceLabels[i])
 *                      && mySliceValue[i] == sliceValues[i]
 *                      && mySlices == sliceValues.length
 *                      && myWidth and myHeight are set appropriately.
 */
public PieChartPanel(final String [] sliceLabels, double [] sliceValues)
{
  if (sliceLabels.length != sliceValues.length)
    Controller.fatal("PieChart(String[], double[])",
                     "arrays different lengths");
  else if (sliceLabels.length < 2)
    Controller.fatal("PieChart(String[], double[])",
                     "2 values minimum");
  else if (sliceLabels.length > MAX_SLICES)
    Controller.fatal("PieChart(String[], double[])",
                     MAX_SLICES + " values maximum");
  mySlices = sliceValues.length;
  mySliceLabel = new String[mySlices];
  mySliceValue = new double[mySlices];

  for (int i = 0; i < mySlices; i++)
  {
    mySliceLabel[i] = sliceLabels[i];
    mySliceValue[i] = sliceValues[i];
  }

  myFormatter = NumberFormat.getPercentInstance();
  mySlicePct = new double[mySlices];
  computePercentages();

  myWidth  = MARGIN + CIRCLE_DIAMETER + MARGIN;
  myHeight = LEGEND_OFFSET + mySlices * LEGEND_BOX_SIZE + MARGIN;
  setSize(myWidth, myHeight);
  setBackground(Color.white);
}

/** Utility method to comute percentages for slices.
 *   Postcondition: Attribute variable mySlicePct has been initialized.
 */
private void computePercentages()
{
  double valuesSum = 0.0;

  for (int i = 0; i < mySlices; i++)
    valuesSum += mySliceValue[i];

  for (int i = 0; i < mySlices; i++)
    mySlicePct[i] = mySliceValue[i] / valuesSum;
}

/** Utility to draw 1 slice, its legend-box, and label.
 *   Receive:           sliceNumber, the index of the slice we are drawing;
 *                      startAngle and arcAngle of the slice, two ints;
 *
```

```java
public void paintComponent(Graphics pen)
{
  super.paintComponent(pen);
  setSize(myWidth, myHeight);

  int startAngle = 0;
  int arcAngle = 0;

  for (int i = 0; i < mySlices; i++)
  {
    startAngle += arcAngle;
    arcAngle = round(mySlicePct[i] * DEGREES_IN_CIRCLE);
    drawSlice(i, startAngle, arcAngle, pen);
  }
}

/** Utility to draw 1 slice, its legend-box, and label.
 *  Receive:       sliceNumber, the index of the slice we are drawing;
 *                 startAngle and arcAngle of the slice, two ints;
 *                 pen, a Graphics object
 *    Precondition:  0 <= sliceNumber && sliceNumber < mySlices
 *                 &&  startAngle and arcAngle are valid angles.
 *    Postcondition: slice sliceNumber has been drawn correctly.
 */
private void drawSlice(int sliceNumber, int startAngle, int arcAngle,
                       Graphics pen)
{
  if (sliceNumber < 0 || sliceNumber >= mySlices)
    Controller.fatal("drawSlice()", "invalid sliceNumber");
  else if (startAngle < 0)
    Controller.fatal("drawSlice()", "negative startAngle");
  else if (arcAngle < 0)
    Controller.fatal("drawSlice()", "negative arcAngle");

  pen.setColor(mySliceColor[sliceNumber]);
  pen.fillArc(MARGIN, TOP_MARGIN, CIRCLE_DIAMETER, CIRCLE_DIAMETER,
              startAngle, arcAngle);
  pen.fillRect(MARGIN,
              LEGEND_OFFSET + sliceNumber*LEGEND_BOX_SIZE,
              LEGEND_BOX_SIZE, LEGEND_BOX_SIZE);
   pen.drawString("(" + myFormatter.format(mySlicePct[sliceNumber]) + ")"
              + mySliceLabel[sliceNumber],
              MARGIN + LEGEND_BOX_SIZE + LEGEND_LABEL_GAP,
              LEGEND_OFFSET + (sliceNumber+1)*LEGEND_BOX_SIZE);
}

/** Mutator so that programmers can customize slice colors.
 *  Receive:       int sliceNumber, Color newColor
 *  Precondition:  0 <= sliceNumber && sliceNumber < mySlices
 *                 && newColor is a valid Color.
 *  Postcondition: mySliceColor[sliceNumber] == newColor.
 */
public void setSliceColor(int sliceNumber, Color newColor)
{
  if (sliceNumber < 0 || sliceNumber >= mySlices)
    Controller.fatal("setSliceColor(int,Color)", " invalid slice "
                     + sliceNumber);

  mySliceColor[sliceNumber] = newColor;
  repaint();
}
```

```
/** Mutator so that programmers can modify slice percentages.
 *  Receive          int sliceNumber, double newValue
 *  Precondition:    0 <= sliceNumber && sliceNumber < mySlices
 *                   && newValue is a valid percentage.
 *  Postcondition: mySliceValue[sliceNumber] == newValue.
 */
public void setSliceValue(int sliceNumber, double newValue)
{
  if (sliceNumber < 0 || sliceNumber >= mySlices)
    Controller.fatal("setSlicePercent(int,double)", " invalid slice "
                   + sliceNumber);

  mySliceValue[sliceNumber] = newValue;
  computePercentages();
  repaint();


  /** double-to-int rounding utility
   *  Receive: value, a double
   *  Return:  an int == value rounded off
   */
  private int round(double value)
  {
    return (int) (value + 0.5);
  }

//--- Attribute variables ---
 private String [] mySliceLabel;    // label for a given slice
 private double [] mySliceValue;    // raw value for a given slice
 private double [] mySlicePct;      // percentage for a given slice
 private Color [] mySliceColor      // color for a given slice
                    = {Color.green, Color.blue, Color.red,
                       Color.orange, Color.gray, Color.cyan};
 private int       mySlices,        // number of slices
                   myWidth,         // window-frame dimensions
                   myHeight;
 private NumberFormat myFormatter; // display numbers as percentages
}


/** PieChart.java wraps a PieChartPanel in a CloseableFrame.
 */

import java.awt.*;                      // Graphics, Color, ...
import ann.gui.CloseableFrame;
import PieChartPanel;

//--- Constructor ---
class PieChart extends CloseableFrame
{
  final int TITLE_BAR_SIZE = 25;

  public PieChart(final String [] sliceLabels, final double [] sliceValues)
  {
    myPanel = new PieChartPanel(sliceLabels, sliceValues);
    setContentPane(myPanel);
    setSize(myPanel.getWidth(), myPanel.getHeight() + TITLE_BAR_SIZE);
  }

  private PieChartPanel myPanel;
}
```

The advantage of this approach is its reusability and simplicity of maintenance. When the hobbits call us back in a year and tell us they would like to add two new tours to the program, it is easy to make this change, as shown in Figure 9.15. The changes are shown in color. No other changes are required! However, to make updates this easy, we had to keep reusability in mind from the outset in designing the pie-chart classes!

FIGURE 9.15   PROCEEDS FROM MIDDLE EARTH TOURS—VERSION 2

```java
/** TourAnalyzer1.java
 *
 *   Input: The proceeds from 3 tours
 *   Output: A pie chart for those proceeds
 */

import javax.swing.*;      // JOptionPane
import PieChart;

class TourAnalyzer1 extends Object
{
  public static void main(String [] args)
  {
    final String [] TOURS = {"Shire Tour", "Gondor Tour", "Mordor Tour"};

    double [] proceeds = new double[TOURS.length];

    for (int i = 0; i < TOURS.length; i++)
    {
      String proceedsString = JOptionPane.showInputDialog(
                        "Enter proceeds from " + TOURS[i] + ":");
      proceeds[i] = Double.parseDouble(proceedsString);
    }

    PieChart profitChart = new PieChart(TOURS, proceeds);
    profitChart.setTitle("Middle Earth Tours");
    profitChart.setVisible(true);
  }
}
```

Here is the output from a sample run of the updated program:

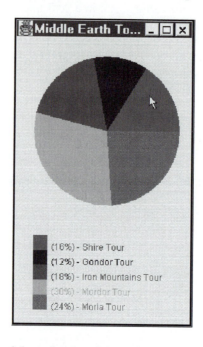

The array is thus a useful mechanism for storing many values of the same type in a single container. An array parameter allows many values to be passed to a method via a single parameter.

As an Applet

As in the preceding chapters, transforming the GUI applications in this section into applets is straightforward. No changes are needed in the `PieChart` and `PieChart-Panel` classes. For the `TourAnalyzer` classes, we need only have them extend `JApplet` rather than `Object`,

```
public class TourAnalyzer3 extends JApplet
```

and change the `main()` method to an `init()` method:

```
public void init (String [] args)
```

PART OF THE PICTURE: NUMERICAL METHODS

As noted in the second Part of the Picture section of Chapter 5, one of the important types of problems in which numerical methods are used is in solving systems of linear equations, each of which has several unknowns. This section illustrates how matrices are commonly used for solving such linear systems.

APPLICATION OF MATRICES: SOLVING LINEAR SYSTEMS

A linear system is a set of linear equations, each of which involves several unknowns; for example,

$$5x_1 - x_2 - 2x_3 = 11$$

$$-x_1 + 5x_2 - 2x_3 = 0$$

$$-2x_1 - 2x_2 + 7x_3 = 0$$

is a linear system of three equations involving the three unknowns $x_1, x_2,$ and x_3. A solution of such a system is a collection of values for these unknowns that satisfies all of the equations simultaneously.

One method for solving a linear system is called **Gaussian elimination.** In this method, we first eliminate x_1 from the second equation by adding 1/5 times the first equation to the second equation and, from the third equation, by adding 2/5 times the first equation to the third equation. This yields the linear system

$$5x_1 - x_2 - 2x_3 = 11$$

$$4.8x_2 - 2.4x_3 = 2.2$$

$$-2.4x_2 + 6.2x_3 = 4.4$$

which is equivalent to the first system because it has the same solution as the original system. We next eliminate x_2 from the third equation by adding 2.4/4.8 = 1/2 times the second equation to the third, giving the new equivalent linear system:

$$5x_1 - x_2 - 2x_3 = 11$$

$$4.8x_2 - 2.4x_3 = 2.2$$

$$5x_3 = 5.5$$

Once the original system has been reduced to such a *triangular* form, it is easy to find the solution. It is clear from the last equation that the value of x_3 is

$$x_3 = \frac{5.5}{5} = 1.100$$

Substituting this value for x_3 in the second equation and solving for x_2 gives

$$x_2 = \frac{2.2 + 2.4(1.1)}{4.8} = 1.008$$

and substituting these values for x_2 and x_3 in the first equation gives

$$x_1 = \frac{11 + 1.008 + 2(1.100)}{5} = 2.842$$

The original linear system can also be written as a single matrix equation

$$Ax = b$$

where A is the 3×3 **coefficient matrix,** b is the 3×1 **constant vector,** and x is the 3×1 **vector of unknowns:**

$$A = \begin{bmatrix} 5 & -1 & -2 \\ -1 & 5 & -2 \\ -2 & -2 & 7 \end{bmatrix}, \quad x = \begin{bmatrix} x_1 \\ x_2 \\ x_3 \end{bmatrix}, \quad b = \begin{bmatrix} 11 \\ 0 \\ 0 \end{bmatrix}$$

The operations used to reduce the original linear system to triangular form use only the coefficient matrix A and the constant vector b. Thus, if we combine these into a single matrix by adjoining b to A as a last column,

$$Aug = \begin{bmatrix} 5 & -1 & -2 & 11 \\ -1 & 5 & -2 & 0 \\ -2 & -2 & 7 & 0 \end{bmatrix}$$

we can carry out the required operations on this new matrix, called the **augmented matrix,** without writing down the unknowns at each step. Thus we add $-Aug[1][0]/\ Aug[0][0] = 1/5$ times the first row of Aug to the second row, and $-Aug[2][0]/Aug[0][0] = 2/5$ times the first row of Aug to the third row, to obtain the new matrix:

$$Aug = \begin{bmatrix} 5 & -1 & -2 & 11 \\ 0 & 4.8 & -2.4 & 2.2 \\ 0 & -2.4 & 6.2 & 4.4 \end{bmatrix}$$

Then, adding $-Aug[2][1]/Aug[1][1] = 1/2$ times the second row to the third row gives the following *triangular* matrix, which corresponds to the final triangular system of equations:

$$Aug = \begin{bmatrix} 5 & -1 & -2 & 11 \\ 0 & 4.8 & -2.4 & 2.2 \\ 0 & 0 & 5 & 5.5 \end{bmatrix}$$

From this example, we see that the basic row operation performed at the ith step of the reduction process is:

> for $k = i + 1, i + 2, \ldots, n$
>
> $$\text{Replace row}_k \text{ by row}_k - \frac{Aug[k][i]}{Aug[i][i]} \times \text{row}_i$$

Clearly, for this to be possible, the element $Aug[i][i]$, called a **pivot** element, must be nonzero. If it is not, we must interchange the ith row with a later row to produce a nonzero pivot.

An algorithm and a program for solving linear systems using Gaussian elimination can be found on the websites for this text (see the preface.)

CHAPTER SUMMARY

KEY TERMS AND NOTES

aliasing problem	linear insertion sort
`args` parameter	linear search
array	$m \times n$ matrix
array components	matrix multiplication
array declaration	multidimensional array
array elements	`new` operation
array literal	pivot
array size or length	quicksort
binary search	searching
`clone()` method	shallow copy
command-line argument	simple selection sort
command-line environment	sorting
deep copy	subscript
index	subscripted variable
indexed variable	`Vector`
`length` attribute	zero-based

- ◎ Java arrays are *objects*, which means that they must be accessed via handles.
- ◎ A simple form of an array declaration is `Type [] name;`, where `Type` is the type of elements in the array and `name` is a handle by which these elements can be accessed.
- ◎ The array `name` can be initialized with an *array literal:* `Type [] name = {list};`, where `list` is a list of values of type `Type` that will be stored in `name[0]`, `name[1]`,....
- ◎ The `new` operator can be used to create an array with a specified number N of elements: `Type [] name = new Type[N]`. The elements `name[0]`, `name[1]`,.... `name[N−1]` will be initialized to default values of type `Type`.
- ◎ Java arrays are *zero-based*; that is, the index of the first element is zero.
- ◎ If `Type` is a primitive type, the elements of `name` will be *values* of that type. If `Type` is a reference type, the elements of `name` will be *handles* for that reference type.
- ◎ Every array has a public `length` *attribute* that can be accessed: `name.length`.
- ◎ A for loop whose loop-control variable is an array index is useful for implementing array operations, because it can vary this index in an indexed variable.
- ◎ Arrays may be passed to methods via parameters and may also be returned by methods.
- ◎ Java provides the following operations for arrays: assignment (=), the `clone()` method to copy an array, and the `equals()` method to check if two arrays are the same.
- ◎ Array assignment assigns the value of one array handle to another, with the result that both handles refer to the same array. This is another instance of the *aliasing problem*.

◎ The clone() method makes a copy of an object's memory. This produces a completely distinct copy for arrays of primitive types, but *not* for arrays of reference types. This is called a *shallow copy*. For a *deep copy*, we must write our own clone() method.

◎ The expression array.equals(array2) simply compares array handles. To compare the actual arrays to which they refer, we must write our own equals() method.

◎ The Vector class in java.util is an array-based container whose size can change to accommodate new elements.

◎ Linear insertion sort is one of the fastest sorts for small lists. Quicksort sorts a list recursively and is one of the fastest sorting methods for large lists.

◎ Linear search can be used with any list. Binary search is faster than linear search, but can only be used with ordered lists.

◎ Two-dimensional arrays can be used to store data values arranged in rows and columns, and three-dimensional arrays to store data values arranged in rows, columns, and ranks.

◎ Nested for loops are often used to access the elements of a two-dimensional array: an outer loop that counts through the rows, and an inner loop that counts through the columns.

REFERENCE

Documentation

■ **SOME** Vector **METHODS** (java.util)

Method	Description
Vector()	Constructs an empty vector
Vector(Collection c)	Constructs vector containing the elements of c
Vector(int cap)	Constructs empty vector with initial capacity cap
Vector(int cap, int capInc)	Constructs empty vector with the initial capacity cap and capacity increment capInc
void add(int i, Object obj)	Inserts obj at position i of vector; appends obj if i is omitted
boolean addAll(int i, Collection c)	Inserts all of c's elements at position i of vector; appends them if i is omitted
void addElement(Object obj)	Adds obj at the end of the vector, increasing its size by 1
int capacity()	Returns capacity of vector
void clear()	Clears all the elements of vector, making it empty
Object clone()	Returns a clone of the vector
bool contains(Object obj)	Returns true if obj is in vector and false otherwise

`boolean containsAll` `        (Collection c)`	Returns true if all elements of c are in vector and false otherwise.
`void copyInto(` `        Object[] arr)`	Copies elements of vector into the array arr
`Object elementAt(int i)`	Returns element of vector at location i
`boolean equals(Object obj)`	Compares vector with obj for equality
`Object firstElement()`	Returns the first element of vector
`Object get(int i)`	Gets element of vector at location i
`int indexOf(Object obj,` `          int i)`	Searches vector for obj, starting at index i, using `equals()` for comparison. Returns index of first occurrence of obj found, -1 if obj not found. Starts search at position 0 if i is omitted.
`void insertElementAt` `    (Object obj, int i)`	Inserts obj in vector at location i
`boolean isEmpty()`	Returns true if vector is empty, false if not
`Object lastElement()`	Returns the last element of vector
`int lastIndexOf(Object obj,` `              int i)`	Searches vector for obj, backwards from index i, using `equals()` for comparison. Returns index of first occurrence of obj found, -1 if obj not found. Starts search at end of vector if i is omitted.
`Object remove(int i)`	Removes the element at position i
`boolean remove(Object obj)`	Removes first occurrence of obj in vector; if found, returns true, and false otherwise
`boolean removeAll` `        (Collection c)`	Removes all elements of c from vector; if some elements are found, returns true, and false otherwise
`void removeAllElements()`	Removes all elements of vector
`boolean removeElement` `        (Object obj)`	See `remove()`
`void removeElement (int i)`	Removes element at position i
`boolean retainAll` `        (Collection c)`	Removes from vector all elements not in c; if some elements are found, returns true, and false otherwise
`Object set(int i,` `          Object obj)`	Replaces element at position i in vector with obj. Returns element that was replaced
`void setElementAt` `    (Object obj, int i)`	Replaces element at position i in vector with obj; previous element is discarded
`void setSize(int n)`	Sets size of vector to n

`v.size()`	Returns the size of `v`
`Object[] toArray()`	Returns array containing all of the elements in a vector
`String toString()`	Returns a string representation of a vector, containing the `String` representation of each element
`void trimToSize()`	Trims vector's capacity to be its current size

☞ PROGRAMMING POINTERS

PROGRAM STYLE AND DESIGN

1. *Arrays can be used to store sequences of values* since the elements of an array all have the same type.

2. *When using an array, always define its capacity using a named constant or variable, not a literal.* Such an identifier can be used to control for loops, passed to methods, and so on, which simplifies program maintenance if the array must be resized.

3. *Use of a multidimensional array is appropriate when a table of data values, a list of tables, and so on must be stored in main memory for processing.* Using a multidimensional array when it is not necessary, however, can tie up a large block of memory locations. The amount of memory required to store a multidimensional array may be quite large, even though each index is restricted to a small range of values. For example, the three-dimensional array `threeD` declared by

   ```
   int [][][] threeD = new int [20][20][20];
   ```

   requires $20 \times 20 \times 20 = 8000$ memory locations.

WATCH OUT

POTENTIAL PITFALLS

1. *In Java, array indices are enclosed between a pair of square brackets, not between parentheses.* An attempt to access element i of an array a by using `a(i)` will be interpreted by the Java compiler as a call to a method named a, passing it the argument i. A compile-time error will result unless such a method exists, in which case a logic error will result.

2. *The first element of a Java array has the index value 0—not 1, as in many programming languages.* Forgetting this can produce some puzzling results.

3. *Attempting to copy one array into another by using the assignment operator (=) only copies the address of the second array to the first so that both handles refer to the same array.* Changing an element in either array will change both arrays. This is an example of the *aliasing problem*.

4. *The `clone()` method can be used to produce a distinct copy of an array.* For an array a whose elements are of some primitive type, `a.clone()` will produce a completely separate copy of a. For arrays whose elements are handles, however, *shallow copying* results so that an element in `a.clone()` will refer to the same object as the corresponding element in a.

5. *In Java, multiple indices are each enclosed in brackets ([and]) and attached to the array name.* In some languages, a single pair of brackets (or parentheses) is used to enclose a list of indices. However, attempting to access the value in row i and column j of a two-dimensional array a in Java by using

        a[i,j]

will cause a compile-time error.

6. *When processing the elements of a multidimensional array using nested loops, the loops must be arranged so that the indices vary in the appropriate order.* To illustrate, suppose that the two-dimensional array table is declared by

        int [][] table = new int[3][4];

and the following data values are to be read into the array:

        11 22 27 35 39 40 48 51 57 66 67 92

If these values are to be read and assigned in a row-wise manner so that the value is the table

$$
\begin{array}{cccc}
11 & 22 & 27 & 35 \\
39 & 40 & 48 & 51 \\
57 & 66 & 67 & 92
\end{array}
$$

then the following nested for loops are appropriate:

        for (int row = 0; row < 3; row++)
           for (int col = 0; col < 4; col++)
              table[row][col] = theKeyboard.readInt();

If the order of these loops is reversed,

        for (int col = 0; col < 4; col++)
           for (int row = 0; row < 3; row++)
              table[row][col] = theKeyboard.readInt();

then table will be loaded column-by-column, instead of row-by-row,

$$
\begin{array}{cccc}
11 & 35 & 48 & 66 \\
22 & 39 & 51 & 67 \\
27 & 40 & 57 & 92
\end{array}
$$

and operations applied to table will produce incorrect results.

PROGRAMMING PROBLEMS

SECTION 9.2

1. Write a driver program to test the output method of Exercise 17.
2. Write a driver program to test the min and max methods of Exercises 18 and 19.
3. Write a driver program to test the range method of Exercise 20.
4. Write a driver program to test the ascending-order method of Exercise 21.
5. Write a driver program to test the insert method of Exercise 22.

6. Write a driver program to test the remove method of Exercise 23.

7. The Rinky Dooflingy Company records the number of cases of dooflingies produced each day over a four-week period. Write a program that reads these production numbers and stores them in an array. The program should then accept from the user a week number and a day number, and should display the production level for that day. Assume that each week consists of five workdays.

8. The Rinky Dooflingy Company maintains two warehouses, one in Chicago and one in Detroit, each of which stocks at most 25 different items. Write a program that first reads the product numbers of items stored in the Chicago warehouse and stores them in an array Chicago, and then repeats this for the items stored in the Detroit warehouse, storing these product numbers in an array Detroit. The program should then find and display the *intersection* of these two lists of numbers, that is, the collection of product numbers common to both sequences. The lists should not be assumed to have the same number of elements.

9. Repeat Problem 8 but find and display the *union* of the two lists, that is, the collection of product numbers that are elements of at least one of the sequences of numbers.

10. Suppose that mailboxes in a row are numbered 1 through 150 and that, beginning with mailbox 2, we open the doors of all the even-numbered mailboxes. Next, beginning with mailbox 3, we go to every third mail box, opening its door if it is closed and closing it if it is open. We repeat this procedure with every fourth mailbox, then every fifth mailbox, and so on. Using an array to model the mailboxes, write a program to determine which mailboxes will be closed when this procedure is completed.

11. If $\bar{x}$ denotes the mean of a sequence of numbers $x_1, x_2, \ldots, x_n$, the *variance* is the average of the squares of the deviations of the numbers from the mean,

$$\text{variance} = \frac{1}{n} \sum_{i=1}^{n} (x_i - \bar{x})^2$$

and the *standard deviation* is the square root of the variance. Write methods to calculate the mean, variance, and standard deviation of the values stored in an array, and a driver program to test your methods.

12. Letter grades are sometimes assigned to numeric scores by using the grading scheme commonly called *grading on the curve*. In this scheme, a letter grade is assigned to a numeric score according to the following table, where m is the mean score and σ (sigma) is the standard deviation.

x = Numeric Score	Letter Grade
$x < m - \dfrac{3}{2}\sigma$	F
$m - \dfrac{3}{2}\sigma \leq x < m - \dfrac{1}{2}\sigma$	D
$m - \dfrac{1}{2}\sigma \leq x < m + \dfrac{1}{2}\sigma$	C
$m + \dfrac{1}{2}\sigma \leq x < m + \dfrac{3}{2}\sigma$	B
$m + \dfrac{3}{2}\sigma \leq x$	A

Write a program that reads a list of real numbers representing numeric scores, stores them in an array, calls the methods from Problem 11 to calculate their mean and standard deviation, and then calls another method to display the letter grade corresponding to each numeric score.

13. A prime number is an integer greater than 1 whose only positive divisors are 1 and the integer itself. The Greek mathematician Eratosthenes developed an algorithm, known as the *Sieve of Eratosthenes,* for finding all prime numbers less than or equal to a given number n; that is, all primes in the range 2 through n. Consider the list of numbers from 2 through n. Two is the first prime number, but the multiples of 2 (4, 6, 8, . . .) are not, and so they are crossed out in the list. The first number after 2 that was not crossed out is 3, the next prime. We then cross out from the list all higher multiples of 3 (6, 9, 12, . . .). The next number not crossed out is 5, the next prime, and so we cross out all higher multiples of 5 (10, 15, 20, . . .). We repeat this procedure until we reach the first number in the list that has not been crossed out and whose square is greater than n. All the numbers that remain in the list are the primes from 2 through n. Write a program that uses this sieve method and an array to find all the prime numbers from 2 through n. Run it for $n = 50$ and for $n = 500$.

SECTION 9.3

14. Write and test a method for simple selection sort.

15. Write and test a method for linear insertion sort.

16. Write and test a method for quicksort.

17. Write and test a method for double-ended selection sort described in Exercise 9.

18. The investment company of Pickum & Loozem has been recording the trading price of a particular stock over a 15-day period. Write a program that reads these prices and sorts them into increasing order, using one of the sort methods in Problems 14–17. The program should display the trading range; that is, the lowest and the highest prices recorded, and also the median price (see Problem 24).

SECTION 9.4

19. Write and test a method for linear search.

20. Write and test a method for binary search.

21. The Rinky Dooflingy Company manufactures different kinds of dooflingies, each identified by a product number. Write a program that reads product numbers and prices, and stores these values in two arrays, `number` and `price`; `number[0]` and `price[0]` are the product number and unit price for the first item, `number[1]` and `price[1]` are the product number and unit price for the second item, and so on. The program should then allow the user to select one of the following options:

   (a) Retrieve and display the price of a product whose number is entered by the user (Use the linear search procedure developed in Problem 19 to determine the index of the specified item in the array `number`.)

   (b) Print a table displaying the product number and the price of each item.

SECTION 9.5

22. Write a program `binary` so that the command

```
java binary decimalValue
```

will calculate and display the binary representation of `decimalValue`.

23. Write a program to find the average of a list of numbers, so that a command of the form

```
java average list_of_numbers
```

will calculate and display the average of the values in the list.

24. The *median* of a list of n numbers is a value such that $n / 2$ of the values are greater than that value, and $n / 2$ of the values are less than that value. The usual procedure to find the median is to sort the list and then pick the middle number as the median if the list has an odd number of elements, or the average of the two middle numbers if the number of elements is even. Write a program to find the median of a list of numbers so that a command of the form

```
java median list_of_numbers
```

will calculate and display the median of the values in the list.

SECTION 9.6

25. Write a program to calculate and display the first ten rows of Pascal's triangle. The first part of the triangle has the form

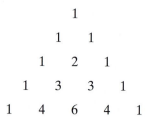

in which each row begins and ends with 1, and each of the other entries in a row is the sum of the two entries just above it. If this form for the output seems too challenging, you might display the triangle as

```
1
1  1
1  2  1
1  3  3  1
1  4  6  4  1
```

26. A demographic study of the metropolitan area around Dogpatch divided it into three regions: urban, suburban, and exurban, and published the following table showing the annual migration from one region to another (the numbers represent percentages):

↱	Urban	Suburban	Exurban
Urban	1.1	0.3	0.7
Suburban	0.1	1.2	0.3
Exurban	0.2	0.6	1.3

For example, 0.3 percent of the urbanites (0.003 times the current population) move to the suburbs each year. The diagonal entries represent internal growth rates. Using a two-dimensional array to store this table, write a program to determine the population of each region after 10, 20, 30, 40, and 50 years. Assume that the current populations of the urban, suburban, and exurban regions are 2.1, 1.4, and 0.9 million, respectively.

27. The famous mathematician G. H. Hardy once mentioned to the brilliant young Indian mathematician Ramanujan that he had just ridden in a taxi whose number he considered to be very dull. Ramanujan promptly replied that, on the contrary, the number was very interesting because it was the smallest positive integer that could be written as the sum of two cubes (that is, written in the form $x^3 + y^3$, with x and y integers) in two different ways. Write a program to find the number of Hardy's taxi.

28. The group CAN (Citizens Against Noise) has collected some data on the noise level (measured in decibels) produced at seven different speeds by six different models of cars. This data is summarized in the following table:

	Speed(MPH)						
Car	20	30	40	50	60	70	80
1	88	90	94	102	111	122	134
2	75	77	80	86	94	103	113
3	80	83	85	94	100	111	121
4	68	71	76	85	96	110	125
5	77	84	91	98	105	112	119
6	81	85	90	96	102	109	120

Write a program that will display this table in easy-to-read format, and that will calculate and display the average noise level for each car model, the average noise level at each speed, and the overall average noise level.

29. Suppose that a certain automobile dealership sells ten different models of automobiles and employs eight salespersons. A record of sales for each month can be represented by a table in which each row contains the number of sales of a given model by all salespersons, and each column contains the number of sales of all models by a given salesperson. For example, suppose that the sales table for a certain month is as follows:

```
0  0  2  0  5  6  3  0
5  1  9  0  0  2  3  2
0  0  0  1  0  0  0  0
1  1  1  0  2  2  2  1
5  3  2  0  0  2  5  5
2  2  1  0  1  1  0  0
3  2  5  0  1  2  0  4
3  0  7  1  3  5  2  4
0  2  6  1  0  5  2  1
4  0  2  0  3  2  1  0
```

Write a program to produce a monthly sales report, displaying the monthly sales table in the form:

```
                                    Salesperson
Model       :    1    2    3    4    5    6    7    8   :  Totals
-----------------------------------------------------------------------
  1         :    0    0    2    0    5    6    3    0   :    16
  2         :    5    1    9    0    0    2    3    2   :    22
  3         :    0    0    0    1    0    0    0    0   :     1
  4         :    1    1    1    0    2    2    2    1   :    10
  5         :    5    3    2    0    0    2    5    5   :    22
  6         :    2    2    1    0    1    1    0    0   :     7
  7         :    3    2    5    0    1    2    0    4   :    17
  8         :    3    0    7    1    3    5    2    4   :    25
  9         :    0    2    6    1    0    5    2    1   :    17
 10         :    4    0    2    0    3    2    1    0   :    12
-----------------------------------------------------------------------
Totals      :   23   11   35    3   15   27   18   17
```

As indicated, the report should also display the total number of automobiles sold by each salesperson and the total number of each model sold by all salespersons.

30. Suppose that the prices for the ten automobile models in Problem 29 are as follows:

Model #	Model Price
1	$ 7,450
2	$ 9,995
3	$26,500
4	$ 5,999
5	$10,400
6	$ 8,885

7	$11,700
8	$14,440
9	$17,900
10	$ 9,550

Write a program to read this list of prices and the sales table given in Problem 29, and calculate the total dollar sales for each salesperson and the total dollar sales for all salespersons.

31. A certain company has a product line that includes five items that sell for $100, $75, $120, $150, and $35. There are four salespersons working for this company, and the following table gives the sales report for a typical week:

Salesperson number	Item number 1	2	3	4	5
1	10	4	5	6	7
2	7	0	12	1	3
3	4	9	5	0	8
4	3	2	1	5	6

Write a program to

(a) Compute the total dollar sales for each salesperson

(b) Compute the total commission for each salesperson if the commission rate is 10 percent

(c) Find the total income for each salesperson for the week if each salesperson receives a fixed salary of $200 per week in addition to commission payments

32. A number of students from several different engineering sections performed the same experiment to determine the tensile strength of sheets made from two different alloys. Each of these strength measurements is a real number in the range 0 through 10. Write a program to read several lines of data, each consisting of a section number and the tensile strength of the two types of sheets recorded by a student in that section, and store these values in a two-dimensional array. Then calculate:

(a) For each section, the average of the tensile strengths for each type of alloy

(b) The number of persons in a given section who recorded strength measures of 5 or higher

(c) The average of the tensile strengths recorded for alloy 2 by students who recorded a tensile strength lower than 3 for alloy 1.

33. A *magic square* is an $n \times n$ table in which each of the integers $1, 2, 3, \ldots, n^2$ appears exactly once and all column sums, row sums, and diagonal sums are equal. For example, the following is a 5×5 magic square in which all the rows, columns, and diagonals add up to 65:

17	24	1	8	15
23	5	7	14	16
4	6	13	20	22
10	12	19	21	3
11	18	25	2	9

The following is a procedure for constructing an $n \times n$ magic square for any odd integer n. Place 1 in the middle of the top row. Then after integer k has been placed, move up one row and one column to the right to place the next integer $k + 1$, unless one of the following occurs:

   (i) If a move takes you above the top row in the jth column, move to the bottom of the jth column and place the integer $k + 1$ there.

  (ii) If a move takes you outside to the right of the square in the ith row, place $k + 1$ in the ith row at the left side.

 (iii) If a move takes you to an already filled square or if you move out of the square at the upper right-hand corner, place $k + 1$ immediately below k.

Write a program to construct an $n \times n$ magic square for any odd value of n.

34. Consider a square grid, with some cells empty and others containing an asterisk. Define two asterisks to be *contiguous* if they are adjacent to each other in the same row or in the same column. Now suppose we define a *blob* as follows:

  (a) A blob contains at least one asterisk

  (b) If an asterisk is in a blob, then so is any asterisk that is contiguous to it

  (c) If a blob has more than two asterisks, then each asterisk in it is contiguous to at least one other asterisk in the blob. For example, there are four blobs in the partial grid

*			*	*			*		*	*
							*		*	*

seven blobs in

*		*		*			*		*	*
				*					*	
*				*						

and only one in

		*	*	*		*	*	*		
			*			*		*		
			*	*	*					

Write a program to count the number of blobs in a square grid. Input to the program should consist of the locations of the asterisks in the grid, and the program should display the grid and the blob count.

35. The game of *Life,* invented by the mathematician John H. Conway, is intended to model life in a society of organisms. Consider a rectangular array of cells, each of which may contain an organism. If the array is assumed to extend indefinitely in both directions, each cell will have eight neighbors, the eight cells surrounding it. Births and deaths occur according to the following rules:

(a) An organism is born in an empty cell that has exactly three neighbors

(b) An organism will die from isolation if it has fewer than two neighbors

(c) An organism will die from overcrowding if it has more than three neighbors

The following display shows the first five generations of a particular configuration of organisms:

Write a program to play the game of *Life* and investigate the patterns produced by various initial configurations. Some configurations die off rather quickly; others repeat after a certain number of generations; others change shape and size and may move across the array; and still others may produce "gliders" that detach themselves from the society and sail off into space.

36. The game of *Nim* is played by two players. There are usually three piles of objects, and on his or her turn, each player is allowed to take any number (at least one) of objects from one pile. The player taking the last object loses. Write a program that allows the user to play Nim against the computer. You might have the computer play a perfect game, or you might design the program to "teach" the computer. One way for the computer to "learn" is to assign a value to every possible move, based on experience gained from playing games. The value of each possible move is stored in some array; initially, each value is 0. The value of each move in a winning sequence of moves is increased by 1, and those in a losing sequence are decreased by 1. At each stage, the computer selects the best possible move (that having the highest value).

37. Write a program that allows the user to play tic-tac-toe against the computer.

Matrix Problems

38. Write a driver program to test the `Matrix` constructor in Exercise 18.

39. Write a driver program to test the `Matrix` constructor in Exercise 19.

40. Write a driver program to test the `Matrix` addition operator in Exercise 20.

41. Write a driver program to test the `Matrix` subtraction operator in Exercise 21.

42. Write a driver program to test the `Matrix` transpose method in Exercise 22.

43. A certain company manufactures four electronic devices using five different components that cost $10.95, $6.30, $14.75, $11.25, and $5.00, respectively. The number of components used in each device is given in the following table:

Device	Component number				
number	1	2	3	4	5
1	10	4	5	6	7
2	7	0	12	1	3
3	4	9	5	0	8
4	3	2	1	5	6

Write a program that uses matrix multiplication to

(a) Calculate the total cost of each device

(b) Calculate the total cost of producing each device if the estimated labor cost for each device is 10 percent of the cost in part (a).

44. The *vector-matrix equation*

$$\begin{bmatrix} N \\ E \\ D \end{bmatrix} = \begin{bmatrix} \cos\alpha & -\sin\alpha & 0 \\ \sin\alpha & \cos\alpha & 0 \\ 0 & 0 & 1 \end{bmatrix} \begin{bmatrix} \cos\beta & 0 & \sin\beta \\ 0 & 0 & 0 \\ -\sin\beta & 0 & \cos\beta \end{bmatrix} \begin{bmatrix} 1 & 0 & 0 \\ 0 & \cos\gamma & -\sin\gamma \\ 0 & \sin\gamma & \cos\gamma \end{bmatrix} \begin{bmatrix} I \\ J \\ K \end{bmatrix}$$

is used to transform local coordinates (I, J, K) for a space vehicle to inertial coordinates (N, E, D). Write a program that reads values for α, β, and γ and a set of local coordinates (I, J, K) and then uses matrix multiplication to determine the corresponding inertial coordinates.

45. A *Markov chain* is a system that moves through a discrete set of states in such a way that when the system is in state i there is probability P_{ij} that it will next move to state j. These probabilities are given by a transition matrix P, whose (i, j) entry is P_{ij}. It is easy to show that the (i, j) entry of P^n then gives the probability of starting in state i and ending in state j after n steps.

To illustrate, suppose there are two urns A and B containing a given number of balls. At each instant, a ball is chosen at random and is transferred to the other urn. This is a Markov chain if we take as a state the number of balls in urn A and let P_{ij} be the probability that a ball is transferred from A to B if there are i balls in urn A. For example, for four balls, the transition matrix P is given by

$$\begin{bmatrix} 0 & 1 & 0 & 0 & 0 \\ 1/4 & 0 & 3/4 & 0 & 0 \\ 0 & 1/2 & 0 & 1/2 & 0 \\ 0 & 0 & 3/4 & 0 & 1/4 \\ 0 & 0 & 0 & 1 & 0 \end{bmatrix}$$

Write a program that reads a transition matrix P for such a Markov chain and calculates and displays the value of n and P^n for several values of n.

46. A *directed graph,* or *digraph,* consists of a set of vertices and a set of directed arcs joining certain of these vertices. For example, the following diagram pictures a directed graph having five vertices numbered $1, 2, 3, 4$, and 5, and seven directed arcs joining vertices 1 to 2, 1 to 4, 1 to 5, 3 to 1, 3 to itself, 4 to 3, and 5 to 1:

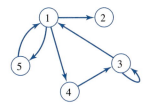

A directed graph having n vertices can be represented by its *adjacency matrix,* which is an $n \times n$ matrix, with the entry in the ith row and jth column 1 if vertex i is joined to vertex j, and 0 otherwise. The adjacency matrix for this graph is

$$
\begin{bmatrix}
0 & 1 & 0 & 1 & 1 \\
0 & 0 & 0 & 0 & 0 \\
1 & 0 & 1 & 0 & 0 \\
0 & 0 & 1 & 0 & 0 \\
1 & 0 & 0 & 0 & 0
\end{bmatrix}
$$

If A is the adjacency matrix for a directed graph, the entry in the ith row and jth column of A^k gives the number of ways that vertex j can be reached from the vertex i by following k edges. Write a program to read the number of vertices in a directed graph and a collection of ordered pairs of vertices representing directed arcs, construct the adjacency matrix, and then find the number of ways that each vertex can be reached from every other vertex by following k edges for some value of k.

47. A company produces three different products. They are processed through four different departments, A, B, C, and D, and the following table gives the number of hours that each department spends on each product:

Product	A	B	C	D
1	20	10	15	13
2	18	11	11	10
3	28	0	16	17

The cost per hour of operation in each of the departments is as follows:

Department	A	B	C	D
Cost per hour	$140	$295	$225	$95

Write a program that uses matrix multiplication to find the total cost of each of the products.

FILE I/O

I can only assume that a "Do Not File" document is filed in a "Do Not File" file. *Senator Frank Church*

. . . it became increasingly apparent to me that, over the years, Federal agencies have amassed vast amounts of information about virtually every American citizen. This fact, coupled with technological advances in data collection and dissemination, raised the possibility that information about individuals conceivably could be used for other than legitimate purposes and without the prior knowledge or consent of the individuals involved. *President Gerald R. Ford*

The rights of the people to be secure in their persons, houses, papers, and effects against unreasonable searches and seizures, shall not be violated. . . . *Fourth Amendment of the U. S. Constitution*

Human beings, for all their pretensions, have a remarkable propensity for lending themselves to classification somewhere within neatly labeled categories. Even the outrageous exceptions may be classified as outrageous exceptions! *W. J. Reichmann*

Chapter Contents

Chapter Objectives

- Study Java's support for input and output with text and binary files
- Examine the important role that exceptions plan in Java, especially in input and output
- [a] See how files can be used in GUI programs by studying an information-retrieval problem

• (Optional) Learn about the role files play in database management systems

Many computer users have had the unfortunate experience of having their word processor (or text editor) unexpectedly fail while they were editing a document. This is especially annoying because all of the information entered since the last save operation is lost. This happens because a word processor is an executable program, and the information being edited (documents, programs, input data, etc.) is stored in the section of main memory allocated to the word processor. When the word processing program terminates, this memory is deallocated and its contents are lost.

To alleviate this problem, many word processors and text editors provide an *autosave* feature that periodically saves the information to secondary memory to minimize the amount of information lost should a power outage occur. Examples of secondary memory include hard disks, floppy disks, zip disks, CDs, and tape cartridges.

Information that is saved in secondary memory must be stored in such a way that:

1. It can be retrieved in the future.
2. It is kept separate from all other documents, programs, and so on, that are saved.

To achieve these goals, secondary memory is organized into distinct containers called **files,** in which information—e.g., documents and programs—can be stored. When a document must be edited, the word processor *loads* it from secondary memory to main memory by *reading* from the file containing the document. The operation of *saving* information to secondary memory involves *writing* the document to a file.

In addition to providing a stable place to store *documents* and *programs,* files can also be used to store *data.* If a large set of data values is to be processed, then those values can be stored in a file, and a program can be written to read these values from the file and process them. This capability is especially useful in testing and debugging a program because the data does not have to be reentered each time the program is executed.

Files are usually classified by the kind of data stored in them. Those that contain textual characters (such as the source code for a program and numbers entered with a text editor) are called **text files.** By contrast, files that contain non-textual characters (such as the binary code for a compiled program or control codes for a word processor) are called **binary files.** In this chapter, we will discuss Java's support for input and output using both kinds of files. We will also consider the role of exceptions in Java.

10.1   INTRODUCTORY EXAMPLE: WEATHER DATA ANALYSIS

Until now our programs have been *interactive,* meaning that the user entered data directly from the keyboard in response to prompts and/or queries displayed on the screen. There are many problems, however, in which the sheer volume of data to be processed makes it impractical to enter it from the keyboard. For such problems, the data can be stored in a text file and the program designed to read data values from that file. The data file only needs to be prepared one time, but the data can be read and processed by programs over and over. In this section we look at one such problem.

PROBLEM: PROCESSING METEOROLOGICAL DATA

A meteorologist, Willie Weatherman, records and processes large amounts of weather-related data. One part of this data consists of thousands of atmospheric pressure readings that were recorded every 15 minutes for the past year. This data has been stored in a text file named `pressure.dat`, one `double` value per line. The minimum, maximum, and average of these readings must be computed. Willie needs a program to read this data, calculate these statistics, and write the results to a text output file.

Solution

Because input and output via files in Java is rather complicated, especially when dealing with text files, we will forego the usual design steps in this example and instead present the Java code for the solution in Figure 10.1, and then explain how it solves the problem. Subsequent sections will explain and illustrate the Java I/O system in more detail.

FIGURE 10.1   ANALYZING A FILE OF NUMERIC DATA

```
/** DataAnalyzer.java computes the minimum, maximum, and average
 *    of an arbitrary sequence of numbers stored in a text file.
 *    Input:   double values from an input file
 *    Receive: name of input file (via main's args)
 *    Output:  count, average, maximum, and minimum of these values
 *             to an output file
 */

import ann.util.*;            // Controller
import java.io.*;             // BufferedReader, FileReader, ...

class DataAnalyzer extends Object
{
 public static void main(String [] args)
 {
    if (args.length < 1)
      Controller.fatal("DataAnalyser.main()",
        "\nUsage: java DataAnalyzer <inputfile> [ <outputfile> ]");

    try                                                    // try block
    {
       BufferedReader in = new BufferedReader(             // connect to
                        new FileReader( args[0]) ); // input file
       int    count = 0;
       String valueString = "";
       double value,
              minimum = Integer.MAX_VALUE,                 // start big,
              maximum = Integer.MIN_VALUE,                 //  and small
              sum = 0.0;
```

```
        for (;;)                                        // input loop
        {
            valueString = in.readLine();                // read string

            if ( valueString == null ) break;           // end-of-file
            if ( valueString.equals("") ) continue;     // empty line

            value = Double.parseDouble(valueString);    // string->double

            count++;                                     // update count,
            sum += value;                                //    sum,
            if (value < minimum) minimum = value;        //    minimum,
            if (value > maximum) maximum = value;        //    maximum
        }

        in.close();                                      // disconnect

        PrintWriter out = new PrintWriter(               // connect to
                        new BufferedWriter(              //    output file
                          new FileWriter( args[1] )));

        out.println("\nOf " + count   + "values,");      // output count,

        if (count > 0)
        {
            out.println("minimum = " + minimum);         //    minimum,
            out.println("maximum = " + maximum);         //    maximum,
            out.println("average = " + sum/count);       //    average
        }

        out.close();                                     // disconnect

        System.out.println("\nProcessing complete.\n");  // user feedback
    }

    catch (Exception anException)
    {
        Controller.fatal("DataAnalyzer.main()", anException.toString() );
    }
  }
}
```

Solution Overview

Getting the File Names. Our solution obtains the names of the input and output files via the main method's `args` parameter, which was described in Section 9.5. The input and output file names will be accessible via `args[0]` and `args[1]`, respectively.

Opening a Text Input File. The program begins by opening a connection to the input file. This is accomplished using two classes: the `FileReader` class whose constructor establishes a connection to the input file whose name it receives via its parameter; and the `BufferedReader` class that provides the `readLine()` method to read a `String` from a file. In Java 2, text input is generally accomplished using *Reader* classes.

Reading Text From an Input File. To process the values in the input file, the program uses an input loop that reads the values from the file a line at a time, using the

`BufferedReader` method `readline()`, which reads a line of text and returns it as a `String`. This `String` is then converted to a numeric value using the `Double` class method `parseDouble()`. Java does not provide a class that lets us read a `double` value directly from a text file, and so this rather convoluted approach is necessary for now.

The input loop also counts and sums these numeric values because these quantities are needed to compute the average. It also computes the minimum and maximum by comparing each numeric value against the smallest and largest values seen thus far and updating these values as necessary.

Closing an Input File. When all the values in the input file have been processed, the program breaks its connection to the input file. This is accomplished by sending the `BufferedReader` a `close()` message. A file should always be closed when it is no longer needed.

Opening a Text Output File. The program's next task is to open a connection to an output file. This is accomplished with a combination of three classes:

- ☐ a `FileWriter` to establish the connection
- ☐ a `BufferedWriter` to improve the output efficiency
- ☐ a `PrintWriter` to provide convenient `print()` and `println()` methods for performing the output.

Writing to a disk is hundreds of times *slower* than writing to main memory. If every output statement wrote directly to the disk, programs would run very slowly. A `BufferedWriter` improves performance by temporarily storing the output values in a section of main memory called a **buffer,** and then writing the contents of the buffer to disk all at once.

Writing Text Values to a File. To actually write the count, minimum, maximum, and average values to the output file, our program uses the `println()` method provided by class `PrintWriter`.

Closing an Output File. The connection to an output file is broken the same way as the connection to an input file: by sending the `PrintWriter` a `close()` message. This is especially important when the `PrintWriter` is constructed from a `BufferedWriter`, because the `close()` message **flushes** the `BufferedWriter`'s buffer, causing all of the values to actually be written to the disk.

Handling Exceptions. There are many things that can go wrong when dealing with files. For example, the input file might not exist when we try to access it or it might contain invalid data. The output file might be unavailable (e.g., it might be in use by another program). If such a problem occurs, the method in which the problem occurred creates and *throws* an **exception**—the abstraction Java uses to represent an abnormal occurrence. For an exception to be caught and handled, the method must be invoked in a **try block,** so most of our program statements are wrapped in a try block.

A try block is followed by one or more **catch blocks** that contain statements to be executed if a given exception occurs. The code in a catch block is described as *ex-*

ception-handling code. The final piece of our program is a catch block that displays the exception and then terminates the program.

Testing

To test the correctness of our program, we construct several **test files,** each of which contains a small set of data values that will be used to check whether or not the program is performing correctly. For example, we might place an odd number of values in ascending order in a file `data1.txt`,

```
11
12
13
14
15
```

an even number of values in descending order in a file `data2.txt`,

```
90
80
70
60
50
40
```

and so on. We thus create test files that *exercise* the program, looking for conditions under which it might fail. Figure 10.2 shows sample runs of the program using these two files.

FIGURE 10.2   TESTING THE PROGRAM IN FIGURE 10.1

Sample run #1 (Unix):

```
$ java DataAnalyzer data1.txt analysis1.txt

Processing complete.

$ more analysis1.txt

Of 5 values,
minimum = 11.0
maximum = 15.0
average = 13.0
```

Sample run #2 (MS-DOS):

```
C:\ java DataAnalyzer data2.txt analysis2.txt

Processing complete.

C:\ type analysis2.txt

Of 6 values,
minimum = 40.0
maximum = 90.0
average = 65.0
```

Note that in these sample runs of the program, the only output that appears on the screen is the termination message `Processing complete`. The rest of the output is written to the output file specified by the user. The program retrieves the two file-names from the command-line, and all other input data is read from the input file.

When our program has been thoroughly tested, we can execute it with the original data file (`pressure.dat`) and have confidence in the results it produces.

10.2   JAVA'S I/O SYSTEM: READERS, WRITERS, AND STREAMS

If you study the Java API, you will find a bewildering assortment of classes provided in Java for performing input and output. This plethora of I/O classes makes it possible to combine them in ways that meet the requirements of a wide variety of specialized situations, ranging from classes for reading files, keeping track of line numbers (`LineNumberReader`) to classes for writing files using ZIP compression (`ZipOutputStream`). In this section, we will focus on what one needs to know in order to use Java's I/O system to perform text I/O and binary I/O, and ignore most of these more specialized capabilities.

Java I/O

All input and output in Java is accomplished using classes that are collectively known as **streams.** As the name implies, a Java stream is an abstraction for a means of *moving information* between a program and a device—a disk, a keyboard, a screen or window, and so on.

There are several ways that streams can be categorized. Perhaps the most basic division is between **input streams** and **output streams.** An input stream provides support for moving information from an input device to a program, and an output stream provides support for transferring information from a program to an output device.

Predefined Streams. The `System` class in the `java.lang` package provides three public class variables that are streams:

❑ `System.in` is an `InputStream` object associated with "standard input" (usually the computer's keyboard)

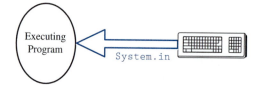

❑ `System.out` is a buffered `PrintStream` object associated with "standard output" (usually the computer's screen or active window)

❑ `System.err` is an unbuffered `PrintStream` object associated with "standard error" (usually the computer's screen or console window)

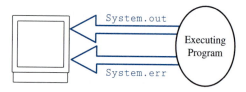

While the `PrintStream` class provides reasonably convenient methods for outputting primitive type values, the `InputStream` class only provides methods for reading byte values. If we wish to read at a "higher level" than the byte level, we must "wrap" `System.in` with another class that provides the higher-level methods.

To illustrate this idea of wrapping one class in another, consider the `BufferedReader` class. It provides a `read()` method that returns a (16-bit) `char` value (returning it as an `int`), and a `readLine()` method that reads an entire line and returns it as a `String`. Although there is no `BufferedReader` constructor that lets us wrap a `BufferedReader` around an `InputStream`, there is one that allows us to wrap a `BufferedReader` around an `InputStreamReader`, and an `Input-StreamReader` constructor that lets us wrap an `InputStreamReader` around an `InputStream`. This means that we can wrap an `InputStreamReader` around `System.in`, and then wrap a `BufferedReader` around the resulting `Input-StreamReader`:

```
BufferedReader myReader =
    new BufferedReader( new InputStreamReader(System.in) );
```

Now we can send `myReader` the `read()` message to read a single `char` value,

```
char ch = (char) myReader.read();
```

or send it the `readLine()` message to read an entire line of text:

```
String str = myReader.readLine();
```

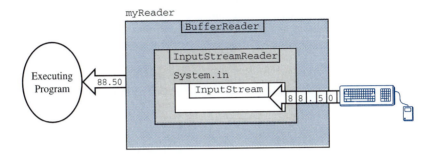

These are the only input methods available in class `BufferedReader`, however, so if we need more powerful input methods—e.g., `readInt()` to read `int`s, `read-Double()` to read `double`s, and so on—we must build them ourselves using the `read()` and `readLine()` methods. This is in fact the approach we took in writing the `Keyboard` class in the `ann.easyio` package we have been using for interactive input and output thus far. We encourage you to study this class to see examples of how to build more powerful methods from more primitive methods.

In contrast to `InputStream`, Java's `PrintStream` class provides convenient `print()` and `println()` methods to output primitive type values. As a result, the `print()` and `println()` methods provided by the `Screen` class in our `ann.easyio` package simply send the corresponding messages to `System.out`.

I/O Using Readers and Writers

Another way to categorize Java's I/O classes is as follows:

- ❑ The *Reader* and *Writer* collection of classes provide support for `char` (16-bit Unicode) input and output, respectively.
- ❑ The *InputStream* and *OutputStream* collection of classes provide support for byte (8-bit) input and output, respectively.

Java's I/O system is a bit unstable at the time of this writing: the *Reader* and *Writer* classes and extensions of them are new in Java 2, and the use of several (but not all) of the `Stream` classes from Java 1.1 has been deprecated. Our "rule of thumb" is to

NOTE *use a Reader or Writer class whenever possible, and use a Stream class only when there is no Reader or Writer that does what you need.*

Using a Reader. To illustrate, the program in Figure 10.1 must read text values from a file. If we search through the API, we find a `FileReader` class that provides a way to build a stream from a file to our program by sending the name of the file to its constructor:

```
FileReader(input_filename)
```

But we cannot use a `FileReader` to read numbers or even `String` values from the file, because its `read()` method only reads a single `char` value.

The `BufferedReader` class, however, has a `readLine()` method that can read `String` values, and it has a constructor that lets us wrap a `BufferedReader` around any `Reader`, in particular, around a `FileReader`. So we can write

```
BufferedReader in = new BufferedReader(
                        new FileReader(input_filename) );
```

to create an input stream connecting the file to our program.

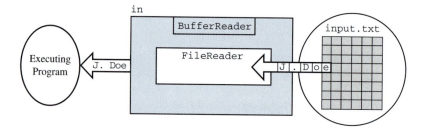

For example, we can "hardwire" the name of an input file into a program as in

```
BufferedReader in = new BufferedReader(
                        new FileReader("input.txt") );
```

or we can have the user enter the file name as we did in Figure 10.1, having the program obtain it from the command line via its `args` parameter:

```
BufferedReader in = new BufferedReader(
                        new FileReader( args[0]) );
```

Once this connection to the file has been established, lines of text can be read from the file by sending the `BufferedReader` a `readLine()` message of the form

```
string_variable = buffered_reader_object.readLine();
```

For example in the program in Figure 10.1, we used

```
valueString = in.readLine();
```

in an input loop to read lines (not including end-of-line characters) from the input file.

A `BufferedReader` is so named because it *buffers* the input from the file to improve program performance. Without buffering, each invocation of `read()` or `read-Line()` could cause values to be read directly from the disk and then returned to the program. However, disk accesses can take thousands (or millions) of times as long as a typical CPU operation. With buffering, values are obtained from the disk in advance and stored in a section of main memory called a *buffer,* so that calls to `read()` and `readLine()` can obtain these values from main memory, which takes much less time than for disk accesses:

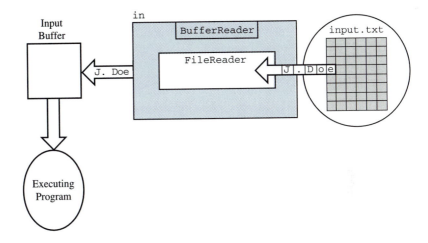

When no values remain to be read, the `readLine()` method returns `null`. We can use this to formulate a termination condition for the input loop:

```
for (;;)
{
    valueString = in.readLine();

    if (valueString == null) break; // end-of-file

    ...
}
```

If `readLine()` encounters an empty line in the file, it returns the empty string (`""`). The program in Figure 10.1 uses this property to test for empty lines so they can be skipped since they cannot be converted to numbers:

```
for (;;)
{
    valueString = in.readLine();

    if (valueString == null) break;          // end-of-file
    if (valueString.equals("")) continue; // empty line

    ...
}
```

Recall that a `break` statement terminates repetition by transferring control to the first statement following the loop and that a `continue` statement continues repetition by transferring control back to the "top" of the loop, thus skipping the rest of the loop body.

Note that the first `if` in this loop tests the value of handle `valueString` against the `null` value, and so uses the equality operator (==). By contrast, the second `if` tests the `String` object to which `valueString` refers against the empty string, and so must use the `equals()` method. Note also that the order of these `if`s is significant, because sending an `equals()` message to a `String` handle whose value is `null` will generate a run-time error.

If neither `if`'s condition is true, then control continues within the loop to the statements that follow the second `if`:

```
for (;;)
{
    valueString = in.readLine();

    if (valueString == null) break;

    if (valueString.equals("") continue;

    value = Double.parseDouble(valueString);

    count++;
    sum += value;
    if (value < minimum) minimum = value;
    if (value > maximum) maximum = value;
}
```

These statements convert the (non-null, non-empty) `String` returned by `readLine()` into the corresponding number, and then update the count, sum, minimum, and maximum values.

When control leaves this loop because all of the values in the input file have been processed, we send the `close()` message to the `BufferedReader`,

```
in.close();
```

to terminate the connection to the file.

What we have illustrated is a fairly standard procedure for reading values from a text file. We can summarize the steps as follows:

Text Input Pattern

1. Build a `BufferedReader` by wrapping one around a `FileReader`.

2. Use an input loop to read lines of text from the `BufferedReader` (converting those lines to numeric values if necessary).

3. Close the `BufferedReader`.

Using a Writer. If a problem requires us to write values to a text file, then our rule of thumb suggests using one of the `Writer` classes. To illustrate, the program in Figure 10.1 must write `double` values and their labels (i.e., `String` values) to a text file. The Java API tells us that the `FileWriter` class provides a way to build a stream from a program to a file, but its various `write()` methods will only write `char` and `String` values. However, the `PrintWriter` class provides `print()` and `println()` methods to write each of the primitive type values as well as `String` values.

We could simply wrap a `PrintWriter` around a `FileWriter`,

```
PrintWriter pw = new PrintWriter(                    // valid, but
                    new FileWriter( args[1] ));   // inefficient
```

but this would result in poor program performance for basically the same reason as we described for file input. Each call to `print()` or `println()` would generate a disk access, which requires much more time than typical CPU operations. To avoid this sluggish behavior, we can instead wrap the `FileWriter` in a `BufferedWriter`, and then wrap the `BufferedWriter` in our `PrintWriter`:

```
PrintWriter out = new PrintWriter(
                    new BufferedWriter(
                        new FileWriter( args[1] ) ) );
```

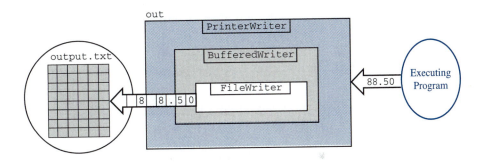

A `BufferedWriter` improves program performance by buffering output values. Values to be written to a disk are temporarily stored in a buffer (in main memory), and are actually written to the disk at some later time.

To illustrate the difference, if we had used (unbuffered) `pw` to perform our program's output,

```
pw.println("minimum = " + minimum);
pw.println("maximum = " + maximum);
pw.println("average = " + sum/count);
```

then each `println()` message would cause a separate disk access. By contrast, using a `PrintWriter` that wraps a `BufferedWriter`,

```
out.println("minimum = " + minimum);
out.println("maximum = " + maximum);
out.println("average = " + sum/count);
```

will not cause disk accesses, because the `BufferedWriter` only writes its buffer to the disk when it receives the `close()` message

```
out.close();
```

or the buffer becomes full.[1]

10.3   EXCEPTIONS

As you have undoubtedly experienced several times, it is very easy for things to go wrong with a program—the program logic may be faulty, the user might enter invalid input values, or any number of other things. In Java, such situations are viewed as *exceptional occurrences,* and Java accordingly provides an `Exception` **class** to represent such things. Put differently, an `Exception` is the type of object Java uses to indicate that *something abnormal occurred.*

Try-Catch Blocks

To signal an abnormal occurrence, a method can **throw an exception.** Such methods can be called from inside a **try block,** which may be followed by one or more **catch blocks** containing code that specifies what to do if the exception occurs. The (simplified) structure is as follows:

Try-Catch Blocks

Form:

```
try
{
    statement-list₀, including an invocation of
    a method that can throw an exception
}
catch (Exception_Type₁ variable_name₁)
{
    statement-list₁
}
catch (Exception_Type₂ variable_name₂)
{
    statement-list₂
}
...
finally
{
    statement-listₙ
}

statement-listₙ₊₁
```

---

[1] The `Writer` then writes the contents of the buffer to disk to make room for more values. Also, the `flush()` message can be used to tell a `Writer` to write its buffer to disk immediately.

where:
  each *statement-list_i* is a sequence of Java statements;
  each *variable_name_i* is a valid Java identifier;
  there may be zero or more catch blocks; and
  the `finally` block is optional.

Purpose

If an exception is thrown during execution of the method call in *statement-list$_0$*, execution leaves the try block and the attached catch blocks are searched for one that corresponds to the type of the exception thrown. If some *Exeception_Type$_i$* is found, *statement-list$_i$* is executed. Execution then continues with *statement-list$_n$* in the `finally` block, or with *statement-list$_{n+1}$* if there is no `finally` block. If no exception is found, execution terminates. If the method does not throw an exception, all of the catch blocks are skipped and execution continues with *statement-list$_n$* or *statement-list$_{n+1}$* as just described.

The program in Figure 10.1 uses a try-catch block because many of Java's file-handling methods throw exceptions. For example, the `FileReader(`*fileName*`)` constructor, where *fileName* is of type `String`, throws a `FileNotFoundException` if no file with the name *fileName* can be found. In this case, the catch block will be executed; it causes execution to terminate with an appropriate error message. By contrast, the `FileWriter(`*fileName*`)` constructor creates *fileName* if it can't be found. However, another program could be using the file, or something else could go wrong, in which case this method throws an `IOException`. Similarly, the `readLine()` method throws an `IOException` if something unexpected occurs.

The benefit of an exception-catching mechanism is that it leaves the decision of how to respond to an exception in the hands of the programmer who invoked the method instead of the person who wrote the method. While the most common response in a catch block is to display the string associated with the exception and terminate the program, for example, with statements like

```
System.err.println(anException.toString());
System.exit(1);
```

the programmer is not limited to this and may implement some other appropriate response instead.

The downside of this flexibility is the added complexity and clutter to one's code: the need for try blocks to invoke exception-throwing methods and catch blocks to catch and handle exceptions.

The Exception Hierarchy

Java provides several different predefined exceptions and organizes them into an Exception class hierarchy, a small part of which is shown in the following diagram:

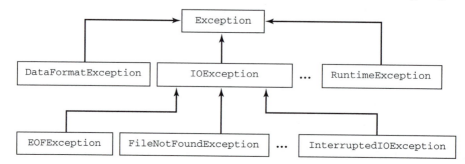

The Exception class is the most general of these classes; as one descends through the hierarchy, the exceptions become increasingly specialized.

NOTE

When many different things can go wrong in a program, a programmer has several options:

1. *The simplest approach is to wrap all of the calls to methods that throw exceptions in a single try block followed by a single catch block that catches an* Exception:

```
try
{
    invoke methods that throw various exceptions
}
catch (Exception anException)
{
    response when anException occurs
}
```

A catch block that catches an Exception will catch anything that is an extension of Exception. As indicated by the preceding Exception hierarchy, IOException, FileNotFoundException, and so on are all extensions of Exception. So long as it is acceptable to respond to all exceptions in a uniform way, this one catch block can be used to deal with all exceptions. This is the approach that was used in Figure 10.1.

2. *A more common approach is to wrap all of the calls to methods that can throw exceptions in a single try block, followed by a sequence of catch blocks, one for each of the exceptions those methods can throw:*

```
try
{
    invoke methods that throw various exceptions
}
catch (FileNotFoundException e1)
{
    response when a file is not found
}
```

```
catch (IOException e2)
{
   response for more general I/O problems
}
catch (Exception anException)
{
   response when any other exception occurs
}
 .
 .
 .
```

As indicated, a try block can be followed by an arbitrary number of catch blocks, each of which can be parameterized with a different exception class. This allows the programmer to stipulate different responses to different exceptions.

3. *The most highly-structured approach is to wrap each call to a method that throws an exception in its own try block with a catch block for the particular exception it throws:*

```
try
{
   invoke a method that throws FileNotFoundException
}
catch (FileNotFoundException e)
{
   response when a file is not found
}

try
{
   invoke a method that throws EOFException
}
catch (EOFException e)
{
   response for more end-of-file exceptions
}
 .
 .
 .

try
{
   invoke a method that throws RuntimeException
}
catch (RuntimeException e)
{
   response for run-time exceptions
}
```

This approach provides for a tailored response to each different kind of exception.

Most of Java's standard I/O methods (and those of many other classes) throw exceptions, and so mastering the use of try-catch blocks is a necessity for programming in Java.

Throwing Exceptions

When we design methods in which errors might occur—e.g., input / output methods for classes we are building—we may want to design these methods to throw exceptions. An example of this is the `read()` method for the class `Student` in Section 10.6, where we need to decide what should happen when there are no more values left in the input file. In keeping with Java's philosophy, we throw an exception and leave it up to the caller to decide what to do. As we show there, if `read()` is invoked when the input file is empty, the statements

```
aLine = aReader.readLine();
     .
     .
     .
if (aLine == null)                    // if nothing
    throw new EOFException();         // indicate EOF
```

will detect this and create and throw an instance of the predefined `EOFException` class.

A method that throws an exception must explicitly state this in its heading; for example:

```
public void read(BufferedReader aReader) throws EOFException
```

It is then the responsibility of the calling method to invoke this method within a `try-catch` block that handles the exception.

10.4 MORE ABOUT I/O STREAMS

In general, text-based input or output can be carried out using a *Reader* or a *Writer*. However, it is sometimes useful to be able to store values (numeric or otherwise) in their internal *binary format* rather than as text. To illustrate, suppose that an `int` variable has the value 1024 and we need to store this value in a file. If we use a *Writer* and `println()` as described earlier, then the Unicode characters '1', '0', '2', and '4' will be written to the file:

$$\underbrace{00000000\ 00110001}_{1}\ \underbrace{00000000\ 00110000}_{0}\ \underbrace{00000000\ 00110010}_{2}\ \underbrace{00000000\ 00110100}_{4}$$

Note that this requires a total of $4 \times 2 = 8$ bytes of storage. But if we instead write 1024 in base-two format, then its binary representation is written to the file and stored as one 4-byte `int`:

> 00000000   00000000   00000100   00000000

Since most files contain thousands of values, storing them in binary format can potentially save a large amount of space.

In Java, the *Stream* classes provide (8-bit) byte-level operations. Thus, any time a problem calls for byte-level input or output, look to the Java *Stream* classes to do the job. One distinction to keep in mind is that the *Writer* output methods use the word *print*, but the *Stream* output methods generally use the word *write*. However, both the *Reader* and *Stream* input methods use the word *read*.

To open a file for byte output, Java provides the `FileOutputStream` class, and to open a file for byte input, Java provides the `FileInputStream` class. Beyond their constructors, each of these files provides only primitive I/O operations on bytes and byte-arrays.

For the sake of efficiency, Java also provides `BufferedOutputStream` and `BufferedInputStream` classes. These classes should normally be used to wrap a `FileInputStream` or `FileOutputStream`, respectively, to avoid the poor performance caused by frequent disk accesses as described earlier.

To allow primitive types to be written or read conveniently, Java provides the `DataOutputStream` and `DataInputStream` classes. These classes provide type-specific methods as given in Table 10.1.

TABLE 10.1   BYTE-LEVEL I/O METHODS FOR PRIMITIVE TYPES

Type	DataOutputStream Method	Bytes Used	DataInputStream Method
boolean	writeBoolean(*boolean_val*)	1	readBoolean()
byte	writeByte(*byte_val*)	1	readByte()
char	writeChar(*int_val*)	2	readChar()
short	writeShort(*short_val*)	2	readShort()
int	writeInt(*int_val*)	4	readInt()
long	writeLong(*long_val*)	8	readLong()
float	writeFloat(*float_val*)	4	readFloat()
double	writeDouble(*double_val*)	8	readDouble()
String	writeChars(*String_val*) writeBytes(*String_val*) writeUTF(*String_val*)	—	readUTF()

To illustrate these methods, Figure 10.3 presents a program that writes a sequence of `double` values to a binary data file, and then reads them back and displays them.

FIGURE 10.3   DATA STREAM DEMONSTRATION

```java
/** DataStreamDemo.java
 * ...
 */

import ann.util.*;        // Controller
import java.io.*;         // DataOutputStream, DataInputStream...

class DataStreamDemo extends Object
{
 public static void main(String [] args)
 {
    DataOutputStream dataOut = null;
    DataInputStream dataIn = null;

    try
    {
      dataOut = new DataOutputStream(
                 new BufferedOutputStream(
                  new FileOutputStream("numbers.dat")));

      for (double val = 1; val <= 10000; val *= 10)
        dataOut.writeDouble(val);

      dataOut.close();

      try
      {
        dataIn = new DataInputStream(
                  new BufferedInputStream(
                   new FileInputStream("numbers.dat") ));
        double value;
        for (;;)
        {
          value = dataIn.readDouble(); // EOFException breaks if no more data
          System.out.println(value);
        }
      }
      catch (EOFException e)
      {
        dataIn.close();
        System.out.println("Processing complete.\n");
      }
    }
  catch (Exception e)
  {
    Controller.fatal("main()", e.toString());
  }
 }
}
```

Sample Run (MS-DOS):

```
C:\ java DataStreamDemo
1.0
10.0
100.0
1000.0
10000.0
Processing complete.

C:\ type numbers.dat
?_      @$      @Y      @Å@      @+ê
```

Note that as with *Readers* and *Writers,* when a program is done using a `Data-InputStream` or `DataOutputStream`, the stream should be sent the `close()` message.

According to the Java API, the various `DataInputStream` read methods throw an `EOFException` if there are no values remaining in the file to be read. The `Data-StreamDemo` program uses this in the termination test of the input loop. That is, instead of an input loop with the usual structure,

```
for (;;)
{
    read a value
    if there were no more values, terminate repetition
    process the value
}
close the stream
```

this program uses an input loop with a very different structure:

```
try
{
    for (;;)
    {
    read a value from the DataInputStream, which throws
        an EOFException if there are no more values
    process the value
    }
}
catch (EOFException e)
{
    close the DataInputStream
}
```

This is the standard way to build an input loop when using Java `DataInputStream` methods. However, the `close()` method can throw an `IOException`. Because of this, the program in Figure 10.3 nests this try-catch block within another try block to catch this exception.

Note also that the data file `numbers.dat` produced by the program is formatted for readability by a data stream, not by a human. The 64-bit binary representations of `double` values are written to this file.[2] If an attempt is made to display these values as text—e.g., with the `type` command as in Figure 10.3—each consecutive pair of bytes in these representations is interpreted as a character, which usually produces "garbage" output like that shown.

Note that different types of values can be written to the same file (e.g., `char`, `int` and `double` values). However, as we saw already in Chapter 2, the number of bits used to represent a value varies from one type to another—e.g., 16 bits for `char`, 32 bits for `int`, and 64 bits for `double`. This means that when such a file is subsequently read, the file's values must be read back in exactly the same order they were written.

---

[2] See the section "Part of the Picture: Data Representation" in Chapter 2.

For example, suppose that an output loop writes a sequence of records to a file, where each record consists of a char, an int, and a double:

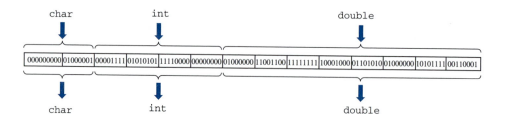

Then each repetition of an input loop to read back those records should read the values in the same order: a char, an int, and a double. Reading them in some other order such as int, double, char will produce incorrect (garbage) values since different bit sequences are being read:

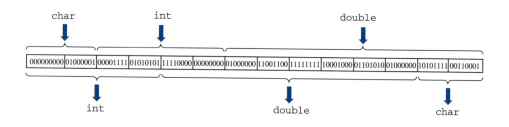

A clean way to ensure that values are read in the same order as they were written is to represent such a record with a class, and have the class provide its own write() method to write its values to a DataOutputStream, and its own read() method to fill itself with values from a DataInputStream.

To illustrate, if a problem involved reading and writing student records to/from a binary file, then we might build a class like the following:

```java
// StudentRecord.java

class StudentRecord extends Object
{
    // ... constructors, accessors, ...

public void write(DataOutputStream out)
{
    out.writeChar(myGender);
    out.writeInt(myYear);
    out.writeDouble(myGPA);
}
```

```
public void read(DataInputStream in)
{
   try
   {
      myChar = in.readChar();
      if (myGender != 'M' && myGender != 'F')
        Controller.fatal(...);

      myYear = in.readInt();
      if (myYear < 0 || myYear > 5)
        Controller.fatal(...);

      myGPA = in.readDouble();
      if (myGPA < 0.0 || myGPA > 4.0)
        Controller.fatal(...);
   }
   catch (IOException err)
   {
      Controller.fatal(...);
   }
}

private char   myGender;
private int    myYear;
private double myGPA;
}
```

The `write()` method is fairly simple; the `read()` method is bit more complicated because the `DataInputStream` methods may throw an `IOException`.

Summary of File I/O in Java

The following points summarize some of the important points regarding file I/O in Java that have been described in this chapter:

❑ A text file is simply a container for Unicode character values stored on a secondary memory device.

❑ A binary file is a container for byte values stored on a secondary memory device.

❑ A file cannot be accessed directly from a program, but must be accessed indirectly through a stream—an abstract conduit between the program and the file through which the program can perform input from and/or output to the file.

❑ Text input files can be read using a `FileReader` wrapped in a `BufferedReader`. The `read()` method reads a single character, and the `readLine()` method reads a `String`.

❑ Text output files can be written using a `FileWriter` wrapped in a `BufferedWriter` wrapped in a `PrintWriter`. The `print()` and `println()` methods are each defined for the various primitive data types, as well as `String` values.

❑ Binary input files can be read using a `FileInputStream` wrapped in a `Buffered-InputStream` wrapped in a `DataInputStream`. A primitive type value can be read using the `readT()` method, where `T` is a primitive type (e.g., `readInt()`, `read-Char()`, and so on).

❑ Binary output files can be written using a `FileOutputStream` wrapped in a `BufferedOutputStream` wrapped in a `DataOutputStream`. A value of some primitive type *T* can be written using the `writeT()` method (e.g., `writeInt()` and `writeChar()`).

❑ Most of the standard Java I/O methods throw exceptions. To catch and handle such exceptions, the method must be invoked in a try block, followed by one or more catch blocks containing code to handle that exception. Java's exceptions are organized into an exception hierarchy, with a very general `Exception` class at the top of the hierarchy, and increasingly specific subclasses in the lower levels of the hierarchy.

✔ Quick Quiz 10.4

1. All input and output in Java is accomplished using classes known as _____.
2. The public class variable provided in Java's `System` class for standard input is _____.
3. The public class variable provided in Java's `System` class for standard output is _____.
4. The public class variable provided in Java's `System` class for standard error is _____.
5. What is the basic difference between the *Reader / Writer* and *InputStream / OutputStream* collections of classes?
6. (True or false) Retrieving values from a file on disk is considerably faster than most CPU operations.
7. A section of main memory that is loaded with values from a disk in advance so they can be used for input in a program is known as a(n) _____.
8. The performance of a program that does output to a file can be improved by writing the values to a(n) _____ from which they can be transferred to disk later.
9. In Java, an object of type _____ is used to signal that something abnormal has occurred.
10. A method can _____ an exception to signal that something out of the ordinary has occurred.
11. A program must invoke a method that throws an exception in a(n) _____ block if it is to detect the occurrence of that exception and handle it.
12 Exceptions are handled in a calling program by _____ blocks.
13. Contrast text files and binary files.

✎ EXERCISES 10.4

1. Write statements to construct a `BufferedReader` object named `input` as a connection to an input file named `InData.txt`.

2. Proceed as in Exercise 1 but open a `PrintWriter` object named `outputStream` as a connection to an output file named `OutData.txt`.

3. Proceed as in Exercise 1 but have the user enter the name of the file on the command line.

4. Proceed as in Exercise 2 but have the user enter the name of the file on the command line.

For Exercises 5–8, assume that `input` is the `BufferedReader` from Exercise 1 or 3 that is connected to a file containing daily sales for a company:

```
555.90
777.34
1211.08
957.55
  .
  .
  .
```

Write statements to do what is asked for.

5. Read a line from this file into a `double` variable named `dailySales`.

6. Read through the entire file and count how many lines are in the file.

7. Read through the file and calculate the total sales for the company and the average daily sales.

8. Read through the file and determine on which days the maximum and minimum sales occurred.

10.5   EXAMPLE: SCANNING FOR A VIRUS

A computer **virus** is a piece of software that, when executed, attempts to hide itself within other executable programs. When it succeeds, the executable program becomes a **host** for the virus, so that when it is executed, the virus tries to "infect" other programs. That is, if the programs on one computer are infected with a virus and a user copies one of those programs onto a floppy disk and then takes the floppy disk to another computer to execute that program, the virus will try to replicate itself by infecting the programs on that computer. A computer virus can thus spread quickly among a community of computer users if they share infected software applications.

There are a number of organizations that write software products to combat viruses. These products utilize two basic approaches:

❑ Virus *detection & recovery* to identify viruses in a system and remove them (hopefully without damaging their hosts).

❑ Virus *prevention* to keep new viruses from infecting a computer's programs, by watching for behavior characteristic of viruses.

A virus can be very malicious. An example is the infamous Michelangelo virus, which is programmed to do nothing (but replicate itself) until March 6 (the birthday of Michelangelo) when it erases the hard disk of the computer whose software it infects. By contrast, the CODE 252 virus activates whenever an infected system or application is executed, and displays the annoying message:

```
You have a virus
Ha Ha Ha Ha Ha Ha Ha
Now erasing all disks...
Ha Ha Ha Ha Ha Ha Ha
P.S. Have a nice day
```

```
Ha Ha Ha Ha Ha Ha Ha
(Click to continue...)
```

Fortunately, this message is a "practical joke" as the virus does not actually delete any files or directories.

For viruses that display such messages, the character string displayed is typically stored within the virus as a constant. That means that to identify whether or not a program is a host for a virus, a virus-detection program can simply scan the suspected host for the appropriate string. This is the approach used to detect the ANTI virus; virus-detection programs simply scan executable programs suspected of being hosts for the string "ANTI".

The program in Figure 10.4 simulates this detection technique. It uses the capabilities provided by the `String` class and an end-of-file controlled loop to implement the following algorithm:

Virus-Detection Algorithm

1. Repeat the following:
   a. Read a line from a file.
   b. If no line is read because the end of the file was reached, terminate repetition.
   c. Otherwise scan that line for a given string of text.
   d. If the string of text is found, stop reading from the file.
2. Display a message indicating whether the string was found.

The sample run in Figure 10.4 uses a file named `binary.exe`, a text file (simulating a binary file) in which we have embedded the Unicode string "ANTI" to simulate infection with the ANTI virus.

FIGURE 10.4   SIMULATED VIRUS SCANNING

```
/** VirusScanner.java simulates the scan for a virus signature.
 *     Input:    lines of text from an input file
 *     Receive:  name of input file (via main's args)
 *               string to be checked (via main's args)
 *     Output:   a message indicating whether the input string occurs
 *               in the input file
 */

import java.io.*;              // BufferedReader, FileReader, ...
import ann.util.*;            // Controller

class VirusScanner extends Object
{
 public static void main(String [] args)
 {
   if (args.length != 2)
     Controller.fatal("VirusScanner.main()",
                  "Usage: java VirusScanner <file> <VirusSignature>");
   try
   {
     BufferedReader myReader  = new BufferedReader(
                               new FileReader( args[0] ));
     String inString = null;
     boolean signatureFound = false;
```

```
        do
        {
          inString = myReader.readLine();

          if (inString == null) break;

          if (inString.indexOf( args[1] ) >= 0)
            signatureFound = true;
        }
        while (!signatureFound);

        myReader.close();

        System.out.print("*** Virus signature '" + args[1]);
        if (signatureFound)
          System.out.println"' found in " + args[0]);
        else
          System.out.println("' not found in " + args[0]);
      }
    catch (Exception e)
      {
        Controller.fatal("main()", e.toString());
      }
  }
}
```

Listing of simulated virus-infected file

```
&1/4&L&Æ&ø&_&_&_&_&_&_&+&+&_&_&+&+&+&+&+
&+&-&-&+&-&+&_&_&+&+&-&-&_&_&-&+&-&-&-&-&+
&+&+&+&+&+&+&+&_&_&_&_&_&_&·&_&_&_&_&Ê&_
&_&_&_&_&_&_&_&_&Ò&_&_&_&_&^&_&¯&_&·&_
&n&_&_&_'' ' ' ' ' ' '''
'''''_' &+&+&_&_&+ANTI' '_&+&+&_&_&+
''' ' ' ' ' ' '&_&_&_&n&_&·&_&¯&_
&^&_&_&_&_&Ò&_&_&_&_&_&_&_&_&_&Ê&_&_&_
&_&·&_&_&_&_&_&_&+&+&+&+&+&+&+&+&+&-&-&-&·&-
&+&-&_&_-&-&+&+&_&_&+&-&+&+&-&-&+&+&+&+&+&+
&_&_&+&+&_&_&_&_&_&_&_&Ø&Æ&•&1/4
```

Sample run (MS-DOS):

```
C:\ java VirusScanner binary.exe ANTI

*** Virus signature 'ANTI' found in binary.exe
```

10.6   EXAMPLE: RETRIEVING STUDENT INFORMATION

Classes allow us to represent complex objects in software. In this section, we build an information retrieval system that a university registrar might use to maintain student records.

PROBLEM: INFORMATION RETRIEVAL

The registrar at IO University has a text file named `students.txt` that contains student records:

```
111223333 Bill Board Freshman 16.0 3.15
666554444 Jose Canusee Sophomore 16.0 3.25
777889999 Ben Dover Junior 16.0 2.5
333221111 Stan Dupp Senior 8.0 3.75
444556666 Ellie Kat Senior 16.0 3.125
999887777 Isabelle Ringing Junior 16.0 3.8
              .
              .
              .
```

Each line in this file has the form

> *studentNumber firstName lastName studentYear credits gradePointAverage*

where

> *studentNumber* is a 9-digit (integer) student ID number,
> *firstName, lastName,* and *studentYear* are character strings,
> *credits* is the (real) number of credits this student carried this semester, and
> *gradePointAverage* is the (real) grade point average of the student this semester.

The registrar at IOU needs a program that will let her enter student numbers, and that will retrieve and display the information for those students. For simplicity, we will assume that the first line of the file `students.txt` is an integer indicating the number of students listed in the file.[3]

 ## OBJECT-CENTERED DESIGN

BEHAVIOR. The program should read a sequence of students from the input file `students.txt`. It should then repeatedly prompt for and read a student ID number from the keyboard, search the sequence of students for the position of the student with that student ID number, and if found, display the information for that student.

---

[3] Chapter 12 shows how to avoid this limitation using the `ArrayList` or `LinkedList` classes.

PROBLEM'S OBJECTS. An abbreviated list of the objects in this problem is as follows:

Description of problem's object	Type	Kind	Name
Individual students	`Student`	varying	—
Number of students	`int`	varying	*numberOfStudents*
A sequence of students	`StudentSequence`	varying	*students*
Name of the input file	`String`	constant	`args[0]`
A student ID number	`int`	varying	*studentID*
The position of the student	`int`	varying	*position*

Since the primary objects we need to represent are students, and there is no predefined type that we can use for this, we will build a `Student` class.

Although we could simply use an array to store our sequence of students, we will instead define a separate `StudentSequence` class. Building a separate class allows us to implement reusable operations on the sequence and, in addition, lets us change the underlying (array) implementation if we should discover a better approach in the future.

OPERATIONS. The operations needed to solve this problem are as follows:

i. Construct a `StudentSequence` from an input file
  a. Access the input file
  b. Read the number of students from the input file
  c. Build a `Student` array with a given number of entries
  d. Read a sequence of `Students` from the input file
ii. Display a prompt for a student ID number
iii. Read an integer from the keyboard
  a. Build a `BufferedReader` for `System.in`
  b. Read a `String` of digits from a `BufferedReader`
  c. Convert the `String` of digits into an `int`
iv. Find the index of a `Student` with a given ID number within a `StudentSequence`
v. Retrieve the `Student` at a given index within a `StudentSequence`
vi. Display a `Student`
vii. Repeat operations ii–vi an arbitrary number of times

The "I can do it myself" principle suggests that operations i, iv, and v are the responsibility of the `StudentSequence` class. Operation vi should be the responsibility of the `Student` class, along with the usual assortment of constructors, accessors, and so on. Also, operation i-d suggests that our `Student` class should supply a method to fill itself with values (from a `BufferedReader`, since these are text values).

ALGORITHM. Assuming that we have `Student` and `StudentSequence` classes that provide the appropriate operations, we can organize the preceding operations into the following algorithm:

Algorithm for Student Information Retrieval

1. Build *students* as a `StudentSequence`, initialized from an input file (whose name is received via `main()`'s `args` parameter).
2. Repeatedly do the following:
   a. Prompt for and read *studentID*.
   b. Search *students* for the student whose ID is *studentID*, returning its *position*.
   c. If the search was successful
      Display the student at *position*.
      Otherwise
      Display an error message.

The `Student` class. Before we can code this algorithm, we must build the `Student` class. The operations required of a `Student` include:

i. Initialize itself with default values
ii. Initialize itself with explicitly supplied values
iii. Read its attributes from a `BufferedReader` and store them in itself
iv. Convert itself to a `String`
v. Access its GPA

These are the minimal operations needed to solve the problem. To make the class truly reusable, we should add (at least) the following operations:

vi. Access each of its attributes
vii. Change any of its attributes

The `Student` attributes required to solve this problem minimally include the attributes stored in the input file:

id number, first name, last name, year, credits, and *GPA*

Figure 10.5 presents our `Student` class.

FIGURE 10.5   CLASS Student

```
/** Student.java models a university student.
 *   Attributes:  ID number, first name, last name, year, credits, GPA
 *   Class Invariant: ID number> 0 && ID number< 999999999
 *                    && year (ignoring case) is one of "freshman",
 *                       "sophomore", "junior", "senior", "graduate"
 *                    && credits >= 0.0 && credits < 500
 *                    && GPA >= 0.0 && GPA <= 4.0
 *   Methods:  Constructors, attribute accessors, read(), toString(), print()
 */
```

```
import java.io.*;             // BufferedReader, Writer, IOException, ...
import java.util.*;           // StringTokenizer, NoSuchElementException, ...
import ann.util.*;            // Controller

class Student extends Object
{
 //--- Constructors ---
 /** Student default-value constructor
  *  Postcondition: myID == 0 && myFirstName == myLastName == myYear == ""
  *                 && myCredits == myGPA == 0
  */
 public Student()
 {
    myID = 0;
    myFirstName = myLastName = myYear = "";
    myCredits = myGPA = 0.0;
 }

 /** Student explicit-value constructor
  *  Receive:       int idNumber; Strings firstName, lastName, and year;
  *                 doubles credits and gpa
  *  Precondition:  idNumber> 0 && idNumber< 999999999 && year (ignoring
  *                 case) is one of "freshman", "sophomore", "junior",
  *                 "senior", "graduate" && credits >= 0.0 && credits < 500
  *                 && gpa >= 0.0 && gpa <= 4.0.
  *  Postcondition: myID == idNumber && myFirstName == firstName &&
  *                 myLastName == lastName && myYear == year &&
  *                 myCredits  == credits  && myGPA  == gpa.
  */
 public Student(int idNumber, String firstName, String lastName,
                String year, double credits, double gpa)
 {
    if (idNumber > 0 && idNumber < 999999999) // validate idNumber
      myID = idNumber;
    else
      Controller.fatal("Student()",
                       "invalid student id number");

    myFirstName = firstName;
    myLastName = lastName;

    if (year.equalsIgnoreCase("freshman")    // validate year
       || year.equalsIgnoreCase("sophomore")
       || year.equalsIgnoreCase("junior")
       || year.equalsIgnoreCase("senior")
       || year.equalsIgnoreCase("graduate") )
      myYear = year;

    if (credits >= 0.0 && credits < 500)     // validate credits
      myCredits = credits;

    if (gpa >= 0.0 && gpa <= 4.0)            // validate gpa
      myGPA = gpa;

 }
 //--- Accessors ---
 /** id Number accessor
  *  Return: myID */
 public int getIdNumber()  { return myID; }

 /** first and last name accessors
  *  Return: myFirstName and myLastName */
 public String getFirstName() { return myFirstName; }
 public String getLastName()  { return myLastName; }
```

```
  /** year accessor
   *  Return: myYear */
   public String getYear(){ return myYear; }

  /** credits and GPA accessors
   *  Return: myCredits and myGPA */
   public double getCredits() { return myCredits; }
   public double getGPA()     { return myGPA; }


  //--- Input method---
  /** Inputs a Student
   *  Receive:        BufferedReader aReader
   *  Precondition:   aReader has been connected with a text file
   *  Input (file):   aLine, a line of text
   *  Postcondition: EOFException thrown if end of file is reached; otherwise,
   *                  values are read for myIdNumber, myFirstName, myLastName,
   *                  myYear, myCredits, and myGPA and attributes are set to
   *                  these values or a fatal error occurs if class invariant
   *                  fails to hold or an input error occurs.
   */
   public void read(BufferedReader aReader) throws EOFException
   {
     String aLine = null,
            idString = null,
            creditsString = null,
            gpaString = null;
     StringTokenizer tokenizer = null;
     try
     {
       String aLine = aReader.readLine();        // read record

       if (aLine == null)                        // if nothing
         throw new EOFException();                //   indicate EOF
       else if (aLine.equals(""))                // if blank
         ;                                        //   do nothing
       else                                      // otherwise
       {                                          //   tokenize record
         tokenizer = new StringTokenizer(aLine);

         idString = tokenizer.nextToken();       //  get and validate id
         myID = Integer.parseInt(idString);
         if (myID < 0 || myID > 999999999)
           Controller.fatal("Student.read()",
                            "invalid id number");

         myFirstName = tokenizer.nextToken();   // get names
         myLastName = tokenizer.nextToken();

         myYear = tokenizer.nextToken();         // get and validate year
         if (!myYear.equalsIgnoreCase("freshman")
             && !myYear.equalsIgnoreCase("sophomore")
             && !myYear.equalsIgnoreCase("junior")
             && !myYear.equalsIgnoreCase("senior")
             && myYear.equalsIgnoreCase("graduate") )
           Controller.fatal("Student.read()",
                           "invalid year entry " + myYear);

                                                 // get and validate credits
         creditsString = tokenizer.nextToken();
         myCredits = Double.parseDouble(creditsString);
         if (myCredits < 0.0 || myCredits > 500)
           Controller.fatal("Student.read()",
                            "invalid credits entry");
```

```
                                                // get and validate gpa
        gpaString = tokenizer.nextToken();
        myGPA = Double.parseDouble(gpaString);
        if (myGPA < 0.0 || myGPA > 4.0)
          Controller.fatal("Student.read()",
                           "invalid credits entry");
      }
    }                                   // deal with exceptions:
    catch (NoSuchElementException e)    //  tokenizer.nextToken()
    {
      Controller.fatal("Student.read()", "missing values on line");
    }
    catch (IOException e)                     // aReader.readLine()
    {
      Controller.fatal("Student.read()", e.toString() );
    }
  }

  //--- Output methods ---
  /** toString converter -- used by System's print, println(), etc.
   *  Return: a String representation of Student
   */
  public String toString()
  {
    return "" + myID + " "

          + myFirstName + " " + myLastName + " "
          + myYear + " " + myCredits + " " + myGPA;
  }

  /** output to a file
   *  Receive:      PrintWriter aWriter
   *  Precondition: aWriter has been connected with a text file
   *  Output:       a Student record to aWriter
   */
  public void print(PrintWriter aWriter)
  {
    aWriter.println(myID);
    aWriter.println(myLastName + ", " + myFirstName);
    aWriter.println(myYear + "\t" + myCredits + "\t" + myGPA);
  }

  //--- Attribute variables ---
  private int    myID;
  private String myFirstName, myLastName, myYear;
  private double myCredits, myGPA;
}
```

Note that the layout of the input file determines the arrangement of the attribute variables in the input statement in the `read()` method: a student's ID number comes first, followed by the student's name (first, then last), followed by the remainder of the student's data (year, credit hours, and GPA). The to-string conversion method produces output having the same format.

One new issue that had to be resolved in writing the `read()` method is this: *what should a* Student *do in the* `read()` *method when there are no values remaining in the file?* In keeping with Java's philosophy, we throw an exception as described in

Section 10.3 and leave it up to the caller to decide what to do. More precisely, if read() is invoked when nothing remains to be read in the input file, the statements

```
aLine = aReader.readLine();
      .
      .
      .
if (aLine == null)                      // if nothing
    throw new EOFException();           // indicate EOF
```

will detect this circumstance and create and throw an instance of the predefined EOFException class. A method that throws an exception must explicitly state this in its heading, and so our read() method's heading is as follows:

```
public void read(BufferedReader aReader) throws EOFException
```

The method that sends the read() message is then responsible for invoking this method within a try-catch block that handles the exception.

The other issue that had to be resolved was this: *The* readLine() *method reads and returns an entire line as a* String. *How do we extract our* Student *attributes from that* String? The answer is to use the remarkable **StringTokenizer class** from package java.util:

```
tokenizer = new StringTokenizer(aLine);
```

The StringTokenizer constructor breaks a String into "words" or substrings called **tokens,** which can then be retrieved using the nextToken() **method:**

```
String idString = tokenizer.nextToken();
      .
      .
      .
myFirstName = tokenizer.nextToken();
myLastName = tokenizer.nextToken();
      .
      .
      .
```

In this problem, we know that a line should have six tokens on it. When such information is not known, the hasMoreTokens() **method** can be used to control a loop that retrieves the tokens:

```
while ( tokenizer.hasMoreTokens() )
{
    String nextValue = tokenizer.nextToken();
    // process nextValue
}
```

The StudentSequence Class. Our StudentSequence class must provide the operations described previously:

   i. Initialize itself with values from a given input file

  ii. Search itself for the index of a Student with a given ID number

 iii. Access the Student at a given index

We also provide a `length()` method that can be used to determine the number of students in the sequence. These are the only methods needed to solve the student-information-retrieval problem. Other useful methods (e.g., modify the `Student` at a given index) are left as exercises.

These operations only require a single attribute variable: an array of `Student` values. Figure 10.6 shows the resulting `StudentSequence` class.

FIGURE 10.6   CLASS StudentSequence

```
/** StudentSequence.java models a sequence of Students.
 *  Attributes:  An array of Students
 *  Methods:     Constructor (to construct sequence from a file),
 *                 search sequence for a given student ID, retrieve
 *                 student info, length of sequence (number of students)
 */

import Student;
import ann.util.*;            // Controller
import java.io.*;             // BufferedReader, FileReader, ...

class StudentSequence extends Object
{
 /** StudentSequence constructor
  *  Receive:       String fileName
  *  Precondition:  First line of fileName contains number of students in the
  *                   sequence; each line thereafter contains a Student record.
  *  Postcondition: Array myStudents is created and filled with Student
  *                   records from file; or a fatal I/O error occurs.
  */
 public StudentSequence(String fileName)
 {
   BufferedReader aReader = null;
   String numberString = null;

   try
   {
     aReader = new BufferedReader(
               new FileReader(fileName) );
     numberString = aReader.readLine();            // number of students
     int numberOfStudents = Integer.parseInt(numberString);

     myStudents = new Student[numberOfStudents];  // array of Students --
     for (int i = 0; i < myStudents.length; i++)  //  fill it with Student
     {                                            //  records from file
       myStudents[i] = new Student();
       myStudents[i].read(aReader);
     }

     aReader.close();
   }
   catch (IOException e)
   {
     Controller.fatal("StudentRetriever.main()",
                      e.toString());
   }
 }
```

```
/** Linear Search
 * Receive:        int id
 * Precondition:   0 <= id <= 999999999
 * Return:         index in myStudents of Student record containing id
 *                 or -1 if no such record is found
 * PostCondition:  Search terminated or a fatal error occurred caused by
 *                 illegal value of id.
 */

public int find(int id)
{
   if (id < 0 || id > 999999999)
     Controller.fatal("StudentArray.find(id)",
                   "invalid id received: " + id);
   int i;
   for (i = myStudents.length - 1; i >= 0; i--)
     if (myStudents[i].getIdNumber() == id)
       break;

   return i;
}

/** Retrieve Student record
 * Receive:        int i
 * Precondition:   0 <= i <= myStudents.length.
 * Return:         Student record at index i in myRecords
 * PostCondition:  Student record at index i is retireved and returned
 *                 or a fatal error occurs because of illegal value for i.
 */
public Student getStudent(int i)
{
   if (i < 0 || i >= myStudents.length)
     Controller.fatal("StudentArray.getStudent(i)",
                   "invalid index i received: " + i);

   return myStudents[i];
}

/** Length of sequence
 * Return:    length of myStudents
 */
public int length() { return myStudents.length; }

//--- Attribute variable ---
private Student [] myStudents = null;
}
```

Note that the StudentSequence constructor uses a for loop rather than an input loop to read the values from a file. It can do so because of our precondition that the first line of the input file indicates the number of Student records in the file. An alternative approach that does not require knowing the number of records is given in Chapter 12.

Note also that the body of this for loop is relatively simple, because a Student "knows" how to fill itself with values from a BufferedReader:

```
   for (int i = 0; i < myStudents.length; i++)
   {
      myStudents[i] = new Student();
      myStudents[i].read(aReader);
   }
```

That is, once `myStudents[i]` refers to a `Student`, we simply send that `Student` the `read()` message and it fills itself with values! The "I can do it myself" principle produces a simple and easy-to-read solution because it properly divides the responsibility for an operation among a program's objects.

The `StudentRetriever` Class. Given the `Student` and `StudentSequence` classes, our algorithm for the student-information-retrieval problem is relatively easy to implement. The basic idea is to define a `StudentSequence` object named `students` to store the sequence of `Student` values from the input file:

```
   StudentSequence students = new StudentSequence( args[0] );
```

The effect of this is to create an array of student objects that we can visualize as follows:

We can then apply the methods provided by `StudentSequence` to solve the problem. Figure 10.7 gives the implementation of the algorithm using this approach.

FIGURE 10.7   STUDENT INFORMATION RETRIEVAL

```
/** StudentRetriever.java retrieves student data from a "database".
 *  Input (from file):  a sequence of Students
 *  Input (keyboard):   one or more student ID-numbers
 *  Output:             data for students
 */

import Student;
import StudentSequence;
import ann.util.*;          // Controller
import java.io.*;           // BufferedReader, FileReader, ...

class StudentRetriever extends Object
{
 public static void main(String [] args)
 {
   if (args.length < 1)
     Controller.fatal("StudentRetriever.main()",
                   "Usage: java StudentRetriever <studentFile>");

   // Construct StudentSequence students from file
   StudentSequence students = new StudentSequence(args[0]);
```

```
      String numberString = null;
      try
      {
        BufferedReader aReader = new BufferedReader(
                              new InputStreamReader( System.in ) );
        int id;
        System.out.println("\nTo retrieve a student's information...");

        // Repeatedly read ids from the keyboard, search students for Student
        // with that id, and retrieve information about that student
        for (;;)
        {
          System.out.print("\nEnter a student's id # (-1 to quit): ");
          numberString = aReader.readLine();
          id = Integer.parseInt(numberString);

          if (id < 0) break;

          int position = students.find(id);

          if (position >= 0)
            System.out.println("\n\t" + students.getStudent(position) );
          else
            System.out.println("\n\tNo student found with id # " + id);
        }
      }
      catch (IOException e)
      {
        Controller.fatal("StudentRetriever.main()", e.toString());
      }
    }
  }
```

Listing of input file `students.txt`:

```
6
111223333 Bill Board        Freshman  16.0 3.15
666554444 Jose Canusee      Sophomore 16.0 3.25
777889999 Ben Dover         Junior    16.0 2.5
333221111 Stan Dupp         Senior     8.0 3.75
444556666 Ellie Kat         Senior    16.0 3.125
999887777 Isabelle Ringing Junior    16.0 3.8
```

Sample run:

```
C:\> java StudentRetriever students.txt

To retrieve a student's information...

Enter a student's id # (-1 to quit): 111223333

        111223333 Bill Board Freshman 16.0 3.15

Enter a student's id # (-1 to quit): 999887777
        999887777 Isabelle Ringing Junior 16.0 3.8

Enter a student's id # (-1 to quit): -1
```

Note that because this chapter is about Java's I/O system and exceptions, we chose not to use our `ann.easyio` package. If we had, our main method would be simpler:

```
public static void main(String [] args)
{
  if (args.length < 1)
    Controller.fatal("StudentRetriever.main()",
                     "Usage: java StudentRetriever <studentFile>");

  StudentSequence students = new StudentSequence(args[0]);
  Keyboard theKeyboard = new Keyboard();
  Screen theScreen = new Screen();

  theScreen.println("\nTo retrieve a student's information...");
  for (;;)
  {
    theScreen.print("\nEnter a student's id # (-1 to quit): ");
    int id = theKeyboard.readInt();

    if (id < 0) break;

    int position = students.find(id);

    if (position >= 0)
      theScreen.println("\n\t" + students.getStudent(position) );
    else
      theScreen.println("\n\tNo student found with id # " + id);
  }
}
```

Summary. Taking the time to implement an object as a class is an *investment for the future*—if the registrar subsequently asks us to write a program to create a list of all students who will be graduating with honors, our `Student` and `StudentSequence` class makes this easy:

```
StudentSequence students = new StudentSequence( args[0] );

System.out.println("Seniors whose GPA is 3.5 or greater:\n");
for (int i = 0; i < students.length(); i++;)
{
    Student stu = students.getStudent(i);
    if (stu.getYear().equals("Senior") && stu.getGPA() >= 3.5)
      System.out.println( stu );
}
```

By planning for the future and designing a class to be reusable, we can save ourselves (and others) time and effort, as demonstrated in the next section.

10.7 GRAPHICAL/INTERNET JAVA: STUDENT DATA RETRIEVAL GUI

In this section, we conclude our study of file I/O by building a graphical user interface for the student data retrieval problem presented in the preceding section. Although the program presented there solves the problem, such text-based user interfaces seem increasingly anachronous in today's world of Apple's MacOS, Microsoft's Windows, and the Unix X-window system. A graphical user interface is almost essential for any new application to be successful today.

Our problem remains the same and much of the work we did to solve it—creating the `Student` and `StudentSequence` classes—can be reused now. The only component we must replace is the `StudentRetriever` class, since it provided the text-based user interface that we intend to replace with a graphical user interface. Our task then is to build a GUI version of the `StudentRetriever` class.

Behavior

As was the case with `StudentRetriever`, the first thing our application must do is get the name of the student information file. While `GUIStudentRetriever` could do this in the same way as `StudentRetriever` (using the main method's `args` parameter), we will instead introduce a new Java GUI component called a `FileDialog`. As its name suggests, a `FileDialog` is a GUI dialog box that allows the user to select the name of a file from a list of files, which may be either input files or output files.

Once it has the name of the input file, our application can then pass it on to the `StudentSequence` constructor, build the GUI's initial view, and begin a cycle of reading a student's ID number and retrieving and displaying the information for that student. To begin, our application must read a student ID number from the user, and so our initial view will simply present a prompt-label and a text-box where the user can enter a student ID; all other components will be kept hidden until they are needed:

GUIStudentRetriever	
Enter a Student ID:	
Space for other (hidden) components	

Once a student ID has been entered, there are two possibilities. The first is that the user entered a valid ID, in which case our GUI should display the information for that student:

```
┌─────────────────────────────────────────────────┐
│ GUIStudentRetriever                               │
├─────────────────────────────────────────────────┤
│                   ┌─────────────────────────────┐ │
│  Enter a Student ID: │ 111223333                 │ │
│                   └─────────────────────────────┘ │
│  ┌──────────────┐  ┌─────────────────────────────┐ │
│  │ Bill         │  │ Board                       │ │
│  └──────────────┘  └─────────────────────────────┘ │
│  ┌──────────┐         ┌──────────┐  ┌───────────┐ │
│  │ Freshman │ Credits: │ 16.0     │ GPA: │ 3.15  │ │
│  └──────────┘         └──────────┘  └───────────┘ │
│                                                   │
└─────────────────────────────────────────────────┘
```

The second possibility is that the user entered an invalid ID, in which case our GUI should "blank out" the information fields and display a diagnostic message in the box we have reserved for this purpose at the bottom:

```
┌─────────────────────────────────────────────────┐
│ GUIStudentRetriever                               │
├─────────────────────────────────────────────────┤
│                   ┌─────────────────────────────┐ │
│  Enter a Student ID: │ 11111111                  │ │
│                   └─────────────────────────────┘ │
│  ┌──────────────┐  ┌─────────────────────────────┐ │
│  │              │  │                             │ │
│  └──────────────┘  └─────────────────────────────┘ │
│  ┌──────────┐         ┌──────────┐  ┌───────────┐ │
│  │          │ Credits: │          │ GPA: │       │ │
│  └──────────┘         └──────────┘  └───────────┘ │
│  No student found with that ID                    │
└─────────────────────────────────────────────────┘
```

To make this happen, our GUI will require `JLabel` attribute variables for the various labels, as well as `JTextField` variables for the various input/output boxes. In addition, we will need to group the components for a given row within three `JPanel` attribute variables:

```
┌─────────────────────────────────────────────────┐
│ GUIStudentRetriever                               │
├─────────────────────────────────────────────────┤
│                   ┌─────────────────────────────┐ │
│  Enter a Student ID: │ 11111111                  │ │
│                   └─────────────────────────────┘ │
│  ┌──────────────┐  ┌─────────────────────────────┐ │
│  │              │  │                             │ │
│  └──────────────┘  └─────────────────────────────┘ │
│  ┌──────────┐         ┌──────────┐  ┌───────────┐ │
│  │          │ Credits: │          │ GPA: │       │ │
│  └──────────┘         └──────────┘  └───────────┘ │
│  No student found with that ID                    │
└─────────────────────────────────────────────────┘
```

Lastly, we need to be able to keep the bottom three rows hidden in our first view. If we group these rows within their own `JPanel`, then we can hide them simply by hiding the `JPanel`:

```
GUIStudentRetriever

Enter a Student ID:    11111111



                      Credits:        GPA:

No student found with that ID
```

GUI Behavior. As we have seen before, it is useful to connect our preliminary sketch/views into a state diagram that indicates the events that cause a transition from one view to another. This state diagram then becomes a "blueprint" for our application.

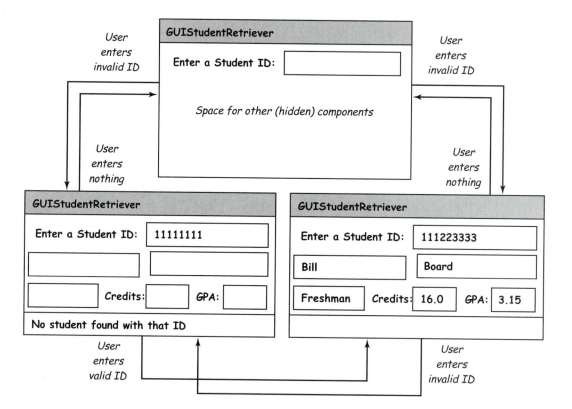

This helps us to identify the operations for our GUI. In addition to a constructor and an `actionPerformed()` event-handling method, we will need three "change-state" methods that we will call `enterInitialState()`, `enterGoodIDState()`, and `enterErrorState()`, respectively.

Implementation

We can begin our implementation of GUIStudentRetriever with a "skeleton" class that contains stubs for each of its methods:

```
/** GUIStudentRetriever.java
 *  ...
 */

class GUIStudentRetriever extends CloseableFrame
                                 implements ActionListener
{
  public GUIStudentRetriever() {}
  public void actionPerformed(ActionEvent event) {}
  public void enterInitialState() {}
  public void enterGoodIDState() {}
  public void enterErrorState() {}
}
```

To this, we add the attribute variables we will need:

```
class GUIStudentRetriever extends CloseableFrame
                                 implements ActionListener
{
 public GUIStudentRetriever() {}
 public void actionPerformed(ActionEvent event) {}
 public void enterInitialState() {}
 public void enterGoodIDState() {}
 public void enterErrorState() {}

 private StudentSequence myStudents;
 private JLabel     myIdLabel, myCreditsLabel, myGPALabel;
 private JTextField myIdField, myFirstNameField, myLastNameField,
                    myYearField, myCreditsField, myGPAField,
                    myStatusField;
 private JPanel     myInputPane, myOutputPane, myNamePane, myDataPane;
}
```

Constructor. Our constructor method must initialize these attributes in such a way as to build the graphical user interface. Here is its definition:

```
public GUIStudentRetriever()
{
  FileDialog fDialog = new FileDialog(this, "Select Student Input File");
  fDialog.show();
  String fileName = fDialog().getDirectory() + "/" + fDialog.getFile();
  if (fileName == null)                    // user pressed "Cancel"
     System.exit(0);                       // so quit
  else
     myStudents = new StudentSequence(fileName);
  myIdLabel = new JLabel("Enter ID Number: ", SwingConstants.RIGHT);
  myIdField = new JTextField("");
  myIdField.addActionListener(this);
```

```
        myInputPane = new JPanel( new GridLayout(1, 2) );
        myInputPane.add(myIdLabel);
        myInputPane.add(myIdField);
        myInputPane.setBackground(Color.white);

        myFirstNameField = new JTextField(15);
        myFirstNameField.setEditable(false);
        myFirstNameField.setBackground(Color.yellow);
        myLastNameField = new JTextField(15);
        myLastNameField.setEditable(false);
        myLastNameField.setBackground(Color.yellow);
        myNamePane = new JPanel( new FlowLayout() );
        myNamePane.add(myFirstNameField);
        myNamePane.add(myLastNameField);
        myNamePane.setBackground(Color.white);

        myYearField = new JTextField(10);
        myYearField.setEditable(false);
        myYearField.setBackground(Color.yellow);
        myCreditsLabel = new JLabel("Credits:");
        myCreditsField = new JTextField(6);
        myCreditsField.setEditable(false);
        myCreditsField.setBackground(Color.yellow);
        myGPALabel = newJLabel("GPA:");
        myGPAField = new JTextField(6);
        myGPAField.setEditable(false);
        myGPAField.setBackground(Color.yellow);
        myDataPane = new JPanel( new FlowLayout() );
        myDataPane.add(myYearField);
        myDataPane.add(myCreditsLabel);
        myDataPane.add(myCreditsField);
        myDataPane.add(myGPALabel);
        myDataPane.add(myGPAField);
        myDataPane.setBackground(Color.white);

        myStatusField = new JTextField("");
        myStatusField.setEditable(false);
        myStatusField.setBackground(Color.white);
        myOutputPane = new JPanel( new GridLayout(3,1) );
        myOutputPane.add(myNamePane);
        myOutputPane.add(myDataPane);
        myOutputPane.add(myStatusField);

        getContentPane().setLayout( new BorderLayout() );
        getContentPane().add(myInputPane, BorderLayout.NORTH);
        getContentPane().add(myOutputPane, borderLayout.SOUTH);
        getContentPane().setBackground(Color.white);
        pack();
        enterInitialState();
    }
```

There are only two new features in this method. The first it its use of the `FileDialog` mentioned earlier:

```
FileDialog fDialog
    = new FileDialog(this, "Select Student Input File");
```

initializes the `FileDialog`. Parameter `this` tells it that *we* are its owner-window, and the second parameter gives it a suitable title.[4] The second statement:

```
fDialog.show();
```

makes the `FileDialog` appear, and remain until the user selects a file. The third statement:

```
String fileName
    = fDialog.getDirectory()+ "/" + FDialog.getFile();
```

retrieves the name of the file selected by the user (or null if the user pressed "Cancel"). The `if` statement either terminates the program (if the user pressed "Cancel") or initializes `myStudents`:

```
if (fileName == null)     // user pressed "Cancel"
    System.exit(0);       // so quit
else
    myStudents = new StudentSequence(fileName);
```

The second new feature in this method is its nesting of `JPanel` components within `JPanel` components. The statements

```
myNamePane.add(myFirstNameField);
myNamePane.add(myLastNameField);
```

build the second row of our GUI by storing `myFirstNameField` and `myLastNameField` in the `JPanel` named `myNamePane`. Since the layout manager of `myNamePane` is a 1-by-2 `GridLayout`, these fields will be equally sized and spaced. The statements

```
myDataPane.add(myYearField);
myDataPane.add(myCreditsLabel);
myDataPane.add(myCreditsField);
myDataPane.add(myGPALabel);
myDataPane.add(myGPAField);
```

---

[4] This form is for getting the name of an *input* file. To get the name of an output file, use something like:
```
FileDialog fDialog
    = new FileDialog(this, "Output File?", FileDialog.SAVE);
```

build the third row of our GUI by storing the various fields and labels in the `JPanel` named `myDataPane`. Since `myDataPane` has a `FlowLayout` for its layout manager, these components "flow" from left-to-right across the `JPanel`. The statements

```
myOutputPane.add(myNamePane);
myOutputPane.add(myDataPane);
myOutputPane.add(myStatusField);
```

then add those two `JPanel` components and a `JTextField` to a `JPanel` named `myOutputPane`. Since the layout manager of `myOutputPane` is a 3-by-1 `GridLayout`, this will create three equally-sized rows. We can visualize the structure as follows:

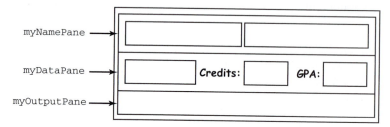

Beyond producing an aesthetically acceptable GUI, the primary benefit of this approach is that a single statement like:

```
myOutputPane.setVisible(false);
```

can be used to hide all of the components stored in `myOutputPane`, and

```
myOutputPane.setVisible(true);
```

can be used to make them all appear.

The Event-Handler Method. Since we only have a single component from which the user can generate events (`myIDField`), our `actionPerformed()` method is fairly simple:

```
public void actionPerformed(ActionEvent event)
{
  String idString = myIdField.getText();
  if ( idString.equals("") )
    enterInitialState();
  else
  {
    int id = Integer.parseInt(idString);
    int position = myStudents.find(id);
    if (position >= 0)
      enterGoodIDState( myStudents.getStudent(position) );
    else
      enterErrorState("No student found with that ID");
  }
}
```

This method generates the change-state behavior we designed. After retrieving the `String` entered by the user, we check it to see if the transition to the initial state is required. If not, we then convert that `String` to the corresponding `int` ID number, and then use the `StudentSequence find()` method to search `myStudents` for a `Student` with that ID number. If such a `Student` exists, we pass him or her to our `enterGoodIDState()` method; otherwise, we pass an error message to our `enterErrorState()` method.

The Initial View. Our method to generate the initial view is quite simple:

```
public void enterInitialState()
{
  myOutputPane.setVisible(false);
}
```

Since our interface has already been constructed, all that is needed to generate this view is to hide the various components in which we display output values. Since we have stored all of those components in a single `JPanel`, one statement is sufficient to hide all of them; otherwise, this method would be much longer. Since we are hiding these components, we need not bother changing their values (e.g., to empty strings).

The Valid ID View. If the user enters a valid student ID, then we must fill in `myFirstNameField`, `myLastNameField`, `myYearField`, `myCreditsField`, `myGPAField`, and `myStatusField` with the corresponding attributes of the `Student` we receive via the parameter, and then make these values appear. Achieving this is straightforward: we simply set each `JTextField` in `myOutputPane` to the `String` value appropriate for the valid ID state and then make them visible:

```
public void enterGoodIDState(Student stu)
{
  myFirstNameField.setText( stu.getFirstName() );
  myLastNameField.setText( stu.getLastName() );
  myYearField.setText( stu.getYear() );
  myCreditsField.setText( Double.toString(stu.getCredits() ) );
  myGPAField.setText( Double.toString( stu.getGPA() ) );
  myStatusField.setText("");
  myOutputPane.setVisible(true);
}
```

The Invalid ID View. If a user enters an invalid student ID, then we must make the transition to an error state. Our error-state method must display in `myStatusField` the diagnostic message it receives via its parameter, and blank out the other output fields:

```
public void enterErrorState(String statusMsg)
{
  myFirstNameField.setText("");
  myLastNameField.setText("");
  myYearField.setText("");
  myCreditsField.setText("");
  myGPAField.setText("");
  myStatusField.setText(statusMsg);
  myOutputPane.setVisible(true);
}
```

Put differently, we must again set each `JTextField` in `myOutputPane`, but this time to a value appropriate for an error state.

The main Method. Thanks to all of the work by the other methods, our main method has nothing to do beyond creating an instance of the class and making it visible.

```java
public static void main(String [] args)
{
    GUIStudentRetriever myGUI = new GUIStudentRetriever();
    myGUI.setVisible(true);
}
```

That completes our class. Figure 10.8 presents the complete class.

FIGURE 10.8   GUI STUDENT INFORMATION RETRIEVAL

```java
/** GUIStudentRetriever.java provides a simple 3-state GUI
 *   to retrieve student information from a student "database".
 */

import java.awt.*;
import java.awt.event.*;
import javax.swing.*;
import ann.gui.CloseableFrame;
import StudentSequence;
import Student;

class GUIStudentRetriever extends CloseableFrame
                          implements ActionListener
{
/** GUI Constructor
 *   Input:          the name of the student input file.
 *   Postcondition: My attribute variables are initialized.
 */
 public GUIStudentRetriever()
 {
  FileDialog fDialog = new FileDialog(this, "Select Student Input File");
  fDialog.show();
  String fileName = fDialog.getDirectory() + "/" + fDialog.getFile();
  if (fileName == null)                      // user pressed "Cancel"
    System.exit(0);                          //  so quit
  else
    myStudents = new StudentSequence(fileName);

  myIdLabel = new JLabel("Enter ID Number: ", SwingConstants.RIGHT);
  myIdField = new JTextField("");
  myIdField.addActionListener(this);
  myInputPane = new JPanel( new GridLayout(1, 2) );
  myInputPane.add(myIdLabel);
  myInputPane.add(myIdField);
  myInputPane.setBackground(Color.white);

  myFirstNameField = new JTextField(15);
  myFirstNameField.setEditable(false);
  myFirstNameField.setBackground(Color.yellow);
  myLastNameField = new JTextField(15);
  myLastNameField.setEditable(false);
  myLastNameField.setBackground(Color.yellow);
```

```
    myNamePane = new JPanel( new FlowLayout() );
    myNamePane.add(myFirstNameField);
    myNamePane.add(myLastNameField);
    myNamePane.setBackground(Color.white);
    myYearField = new JTextField(10);
    myYearField.setEditable(false);
    myYearField.setBackground(Color.yellow);
    myCreditsLabel = new JLabel("Credits:");
    myCreditsField = new JTextField(6);
    myCreditsField.setEditable(false);
    myCreditsField.setBackground(Color.yellow);
    myGPALabel = new JLabel("GPA:");
    myGPAField = new JTextField(6);
    myGPAField.setEditable(false);
    myGPAField.setBackground(Color.yellow);
    myDataPane = new JPanel( new FlowLayout() );
    myDataPane.add(myYearField);

    myDataPane.add(myCreditsLabel);
    myDataPane.add(myCreditsField);
    myDataPane.add(myGPALabel);
    myDataPane.add(myGPAField);
    myDataPane.setBackground(Color.white);

    myStatusField = new JTextField("");
    myStatusField.setEditable(false);
    myStatusField.setBackground(Color.white);

    myOutputPane = new JPanel( new GridLayout(3,1) );
    myOutputPane.add(myNamePane);
    myOutputPane.add(myDataPane);
    myOutputPane.add(myStatusField);

    getContentPane().setLayout( new BorderLayout() );
    getContentPane().add(myInputPane, BorderLayout.NORTH);
    getContentPane().add(myOutputPane, BorderLayout.SOUTH);
    getContentPane().setBackground(Color.white);
    pack();
    enterInitialState();
  }

/** action-event handler
 *  Precondition:  The user has pressed 'Enter' in myIdField
 *  Postcondition: I have changed state according to the user's input:
 *                    valid id -> good-id-state
 *                 invalid id -> error-state
 *                  no input -> initial-state
 */
public void actionPerformed(ActionEvent event)
  {
    String idString = myIdField.getText();
    if ( idString.equals("") )
      enterInitialState();
    else
    {
      int id = Integer.parseInt(idString);
      int position = myStudents.find(id);
      if (position >= 0)
        enterGoodIDState( myStudents.getStudent(position) );
      else
        enterErrorState("No student found with that ID");
    }
  }
```

```java
/** initial and no-input state
 * Precondition:  myIdField is empty
 * Postcondition: myOutputPane is hidden
 */
public void enterInitialState()
{
   myOutputPane.setVisible(false);
}

/** valid input state
 *   Receive:       stu, a Student
 *   Precondition:  stu is an initialized Student
 *   Postcondition: For each Student attribute A:
 *                       myAField == stu.getA()
 *                    && myStatusField == ""
 *                    && myOutputPane is visible
 */
public void enterGoodIDState(Student stu)
{
   myFirstNameField.setText( stu.getFirstName() );
   myLastNameField.setText( stu.getLastName() );
   myYearField.setText( stu.getYear() );
   myCreditsField.setText( Double.toString(stu.getCredits() ) );
   myGPAField.setText( Double.toString( stu.getGPA() ) );
   myStatusField.setText("");
   myOutputPane.setVisible(true);
}


/** invalid input state
 *   Receive:       statusMsg, a String
 *   Precondition:  statusMsg contains a diagnostic message
 *   Postcondition: For each Student attribute A:
 *                       myAField == ""
 *                    && myStatusField.equals(statusMsg)
 *                    && myOutputPane is visible
 */
public void enterErrorState(String statusMsg)
{
   myFirstNameField.setText("");
   myLastNameField.setText("");
   myYearField.setText("");
   myCreditsField.setText("");
   myGPAField.setText("");
   myStatusField.setText(statusMsg);
   myOutputPane.setVisible(true);
}


// main method
public static void main(String [] args)
{
   GUIStudentRetriever myGUI = new GUIStudentRetriever();
   myGUI.setVisible(true);
}


// Attribute variables
private StudentSequence myStudents;
private JLabel          myIdLabel, myCreditsLabel, myGPALabel;
private JTextField      myIdField, myFirstNameField, myLastNameField,
                        myYearField, myCreditsField, myGPAField,
                        myStatusField;
private JPanel          myInputPane, myOutputPane, myNamePane, myDataPane;
}
```

Testing

To test our program, we run it in the usual fashion (without any command-line arguments). The program begins by building a `GUIStudentRetriever` object, whose constructor pops up the `FileDialog` described earlier:

Once the user has selected an input file, our constructor builds the graphical user interface and then enters the initial state:

From this point on, the GUI's appearance changes as specified by our state diagram. If the string the user enters is a valid ID, `actionPerformed()` invokes the `enterGoodIDState()` which generates the correct display:

If the string the user enters is not the ID of any student, `actionPerformed()` invokes the `enterErrorState()` method which generates the appropriate display:

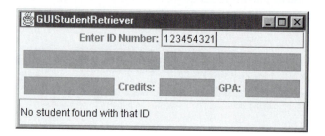

Since all state-transitions are controlled by `actionPerformed()`, we can change from any state to any other state. For example, if the user should delete all input and press the 'Enter' key, then we return to the initial state:

Building graphical user interfaces requires practice, planning, and patience. We encourage you to experiment with this class and perhaps add new features to it. We also encourage you to design graphical user interfaces for your own applications, because it is only through hands-on experimentation that you truly begin to master Java's exciting GUI-building facilities.

PART OF THE PICTURE: DATABASE SYSTEMS

by Keith Vander Linden, Calvin College

One of our local supermarket chains keeps detailed records of its products, sales, customers, and suppliers. They can tell you the current price of any item in any of their stores, who supplied it, and how long it's been on the shelf. They can tell you how many people bought tortilla chips at the rock-bottom sale price last weekend and whether they also bought salsa and bean-dip to go with them. Not surprisingly, this level of record keeping produces a staggering volume of information, commonly called data. Why do they go to all this trouble? The answer—they have to make business decisions and these decisions are based on data. The more accurate and detailed the data, the better the decisions can be. Was the rock-bottom sale price for the chips too high, or too low? Did they make an overall profit? How many units of chips should they stock next time? The data can help answer these questions, and thus is critical to business in a competitive market.

This use of data is not unique to the grocery business. Banks keep records of our accounts and our transactions, universities and colleges keep records of our tuition costs and our performance, airlines keep records on which planes are flying where and who has paid to ride on them. As in the case of the supermarket, these data sets can become very large, and must be maintained for long periods of time. Furthermore, they must be conveniently accessible to many people. It is useful, therefore, to store and maintain them on computers. The data sets themselves, when stored on a computer, are commonly called **databases,** and the programs designed to maintain them are called **database management systems (DBMS).**

The current chapter has discussed files, and it is not hard to see that their ability to store large amounts of data in a persistent manner is important for database systems. Section 10.1 gives an example of how files can be used to maintain a small meteorological database. As we work with that database, however, a problem arises—the database will change, as all realistic databases do. We may, for example, want to add temperature readings to the pressure readings already contained there. Adding this information to the file is easy enough, but we must also modify the code by adding an additional variable to store the temperature, an extra input command to read the value, and we must know the order in which the pressure and temperature readings are stored in the file. Another complication would arise if we wanted to add information on the particular instruments used to collect the readings. This would probably require a separate file of information for each of the instruments, new code to read and process this file, and some additional code allowing us to record which readings were taken with which instruments.

What started as a fairly simple problem, with a small driver program and a single data file, has become much more complex. In addition, this complexity is likely to increase as the database grows, and as more and more people want to access it. Database systems are designed to address these problems. Although varied, they tend to provide a number of common facilities:

- ❑ *High-level views of the data*—Database systems allow programmers to view the data at a higher level, ignoring some of the details of the location and format of the files.

- ❑ *Access routines*—A high-level view of the data wouldn't be of much use if the programmer couldn't retrieve and manipulate the data. Database systems, therefore, provide what is called a **query language,** which provides a set of operations that a programmer can use when accessing and manipulating a database.

- ❑ *Support for large databases*—Databases tend to be large, frequently too large to fit into a computer's main memory. For example, the supermarket database mentioned above maintains approximately one terabyte of data, that's 10^{12} bytes, or

1,000 gigabytes. Database systems are designed to manipulate large databases such as this without reading them into main memory all at once.

❑ *Security*—It is frequently important to restrict access to sensitive or proprietary data in a database. Most database systems provide this capability.

❑ *Data sharing*—The data stored in a database is often of interest to many different people. Several people may, therefore, want to retrieve or modify the data at the same time. Database systems typically provide a check-in/check-out protocol for the data, much like the protocol for checking out books at a public library. This ensures that only one person can manipulate a particular data element at any one time.

❑ *Data integrity*—The access routines that manipulate the database must maintain the data's internal consistency. For example, a simple money transfer from one bank account to another generally involves two operations, reducing the funds in one account and increasing them in another. These two operations, which taken together form a single unit called a *transaction,* should be done together or not at all, otherwise the data becomes inconsistent. Database systems tend to provide this capability, even in the context of disk crashes and power outages.

THE RELATIONAL MODEL

Database systems can be based on different models, each of which attempts to provide the features just mentioned. One particular model, called the **relational model,** has become an industry standard. In this model, the database is viewed as a set of **tables,** called **relations,** with one row for each entry. For instance, the data from a simple employee database would be viewed as follows:

Name	ID number	Pay rate	Department
Jon	45678	7.50	Accounting
Mark	56789	8.75	Accounting
Paul	67891	9.35	Marketing
Matthew	78912	10.50	Accounting
Gabriel	89123	6.35	Marketing
Joe	91234	10.50	Development
Naomi	98765	7.15	Development
Jamie	12345	9.15	Development
April	23456	8.75	Accounting
Jodi	34567	10.50	Service

In this relation, the top row specifies the contents of each column of data. In this case we have the employee's name, ID number, pay rate, and department. The relation has one row, called a **record,** for each employee, and each record has one entry for each column, called a **field.** We will call this table the `Employee` relation. Note that there is no mention here of the files that contain the data, or in what format the data is represented. The database system takes care of these details so the programmer doesn't have to.

One popular query language for the relational model is called **SQL** (for "Structured Query Language"). SQL provides commands to add data to relations, retrieve data from relations, and modify data in relations. For example, consider the following command:

```
SELECT * FROM Employee WHERE Rate = 10.5 ;
```

This command will retrieve, or *select,* all the records (specified by the "*") from the Employee relation that have a pay rate of $10.50. The resulting records are as follows:

Name	ID number	Pay rate	Department
Jon	45678	7.50	Accounting
Mark	56789	8.75	Accounting
Paul	67891	9.35	Marketing
Matthew	78912	10.50	Accounting
Joe	91234	10.50	Development
Jodi	34567	10.50	Service

Note that the result is itself a relation. This elegant feature allows the output of one SQL command to be used as the input to another.

AN EXAMPLE: THE SELECT COMMAND

To gain a better understanding of the relationship between file manipulation and database management, we will build a simple relational database system with a scaled-down implementation of the select command. We will construct the classes very much as was done in the student information example shown in section 10.6, except that we will implement a relational view of the data.

Recall that the student information example implemented a StudentSequence class that contained an array of Student classes, each of which hardcoded the fields it contained. The relational data model is more flexible. It views a database as a relation or a set of relations where the structure of each relation is specified by indicating the fields it will contain, and the type of data stored in each field. This structure is called a **schema.** A very simple schema for the Employee relation is as follows:

```
Name        string
ID          int
Rate        double
Department  string
```

This schema says that `Employee` will contain a record for each employee and that each record will contain the employee's name (a string), the employee's ID number (an int), his or her pay rate (a double), and a department name (a string). We will store this schema in a schema file named `Employee.schema`. The actual data for `Employee` will be stored in a separate data file named `Employee.data`. The contents of this file for the `Employee` relation are as follows:

```
Jon       45678    7.50    Accounting
Mark      56789    8.75    Accounting
Paul      67891    9.35    Marketing
Matthew   78912   10.50    Accounting
Gabriel   89123    6.35    Marketing
Joe       91234   10.50    Development
Naomi     98765    7.15    Development
Jamie     12345    9.15    Development
April     23456    8.75    Accounting
Jodi      34567   10.50    Service
```

Notice how the columns in `Employee.data` match the rows in `Employee.schema`. The first column is the name (a `String`), second column is the ID number (an `int`), and so forth.

The representation of the `Employee` relation, therefore, consists of two files: `Employee.schema` and `Employee.data`. We can now implement a `Relation` class that makes use of these files and implements a `select()` method. The constructor function for the `Relation` class will load the data and schema files, and the `select()` method will return all the records in the given relation whose specified field is equal to the specified value. For example, we might call the `select()` method as follows:

```
Relation relation = new Relation("Employee");
relation.select("Rate", "=", "10.50");
```

Here, the first command creates a new relation by calling the `Relation()` constructor method, which takes the name of the relation and loads the two implementation files (`Employee.schema` and `Employee.data`). The second command calls the `select()` method for the relation and prints all the records in the `Employee` relation for which the `Rate` is 10.50. As this code illustrates, database programming is done at a high level. There are no file manipulation commands here, no for loops, no I/O streams, and the programmer doesn't know anything about the `.schema` and `.data` files or their format. All of these things are maintained within the `Relation` class, and thus do not concern the database programmer.

Given this class, it is not difficult to write a simple SQL parser that can behave as follows:

```
Welcome to SelectBase
a (very) simple relational database system
```

```
SQL> SELECT * FROM Employee WHERE Rate = 10.50 ;
Matthew   78912   10.50   Accounting
Joe       91234   10.50   Development
Jodi      34567   10.50   Service
```

To see the implementation of the `select()` method, consider the class definition for the `Relation` class, shown here:[5]

```
class Relation extends Object
{

  // To save space, we'll leave out the constructor.

  public void select(String fieldName, String operator,
                     String fieldValue)
  {
    for (int i = 0; i < records.size(); i++)
      if (((Record)(records.elementAt(i))).satisfies(
                          fieldName, operator, fieldValue))
      System.out.println(records.elementAt(i).toString());
  }

  public Vector records;
}
```

Here, the `Relation` class maintains a `Vector` of the records in the specified relation. The `select()` method can loop through this `Vector` in search of records that match the `WHERE` condition. Matches are determined by the `satisfies()` method, implemented as part of the `Record` class (analogous to the `Student` class in the student information system). The beauty of this database system approach is that we can create new relations simply by building new `.schema` and `.data` files; we don't need to modify the database system code at all.

FURTHER READING
The field of database systems is active, both in research and in applications. If you are interested in reading additional material, consider going to the following sources:

❑ Ullman and Widom's text *A First Course in Database Systems,* Prentice Hall, 1997— This is a good, current overview of the field of database systems. It covers the Relational model, and also deals with newer object-oriented approaches to database modeling.

---

[5] Note that the if condition in this code must cast the type of the elements of the records `Vector` to `Record`. For more information about the `Vector` class, see Section 9.2.

❏ E. F. Codd's original paper, "A Relational Model of Data for Large Shared Data Banks," *Communications of the ACM,* 1970, 13(6), pages 377–387—This is a seminal paper on the relational database model.

❏ For information on some current database systems, visit the Oracle or Sybase corporation web sites: `www.oracle.com`; `www.sybase.com`.

✍ EXERCISES

1. Because the SQL interpreter discussed in the chapter reads relational tables based on a schema, you can perform many useful database operations without modifying the code. Try some of the following:

   (a) Add a field to the database for the employee's last name. Remember that you'll have to modify both the schema and the data file in a consistent manner.

   (b) Create a new relation for a college bookstore that maintains information on books (e.g., the title, author, ISBN number, and price).

   (c) Create a new relation for your class, including fields for student names, ID numbers, and grades for the various projects you've done.

2. Modify the program in this section to add column headers to the relation output. The headers should be based on the names of the fields given in the schema file.

3. The implementation of `select()` for this chapter only supports a single `WHERE` condition that uses either the `==` or the `!=` operator. Modify it to support multiple conditions using any relational operator (i.e., $<$, $>$, $<=$, and $>=$).

4. Modify the program from Exercise 3 to write the results of the select command to a file rather than writing them to the screen. The program should prompt the user for a output file name. It should then write the results to this file, or to the screen if no filename is given. Now, use this program to select the following records:

   (a) Find the employees in `Employee` with a pay rate equal to $10.50 and a Department of Accounting.

   (b) Find the employees in `Employee` with a pay rate greater than $8.00 and less than $10.00.

5. The relational model also supports a command that returns a specified column (or columns) from a relation rather than returning the full record. This command, called **project,** is implemented in SQL by allowing the programmer to replace the "*" in the `SELECT` clause of the select command with a list of field names. Modify the program in this section to support this. You should allow the user to enter either a "*" in the `SELECT` clause, or a specific field name. For example, if the user enters "*" in the `SELECT` clause, full records will be returned:

```
Welcome to SelectBase
a (very) simple relational database system

SQL> SELECT * FROM Employee WHERE Department = Development ;
```

```
Joe        91234   10.50   Development
Naomi      98765   7.15    Development
Jamie      12345   9.15    Development
```

If, on the other hand, the user enters a field name in the SELECT clause, only the value of that field will be returned:

```
Welcome to SelectBase
a (very) simple relational database system

SQL> SELECT Name FROM Employee WHERE Department = Development ;

Joe
Naomi
Jamie
```

CHAPTER SUMMARY

KEY TERMS AND NOTES

binary file	hasMoreTokens() method
buffer	input stream
BufferedReader	nextToken() method
BufferedWriter	output stream
catch block	PrintWriter
close()	stream
exception	StringTokenizer class
Exception hierarchy	System.err
exception-handling code	System.in
file	System.out
FileDialog	text file
FileReader	throw an exception
FileWriter	token
flush a buffer	try block

◎ All input and output in Java is accomplished using classes that are collectively known as *streams*. The System class in the java.lang package provides three public class variables that are streams:

❑ System.in: an InputStream object associated with "standard input" (usually the keyboard)

❑ System.out: a buffered PrintStream object associated with "standard output" (usually the computer's screen or active window)

❑ System.err: an unbuffered PrintStream object associated with "standard error" (usually the computer's screen or console window)

◎ The `InputStream` class only provides methods for reading byte values. To read at a higher level, `System.in` must be wrapped in another class: for example, in an `Input-StreamReader` and then wrap a `BufferedReader` around the resulting `Input-StreamReader`.

◎ A *text file* is simply a container for Unicode character values stored on a secondary memory device. A *binary file* is a container for byte values stored on a secondary memory device.

◎ A file cannot be accessed directly from a program, but must be accessed indirectly through a stream—an abstract conduit between the program and the file through which the program can perform input from and/or output to the file.

◎ A file should always be closed when it is no longer needed.

◎ Writing to a disk and reading from a disk are much slower than writing to and reading from main memory. `BufferedWriter`s improve performance by temporarily storing output values in a section of main memory called an *output buffer,* and then writing the contents of the buffer to the disk all at once. Similarly, `BufferedReader`s store input values in an *input buffer* and values are then read from this buffer rather than directly from the disk.

◎ Text output files can be written using a `FileWriter` wrapped in a `BufferedWriter` wrapped in a `PrintWriter`. The `print()` and `println()` methods are each defined for the various primitive data types, as well as `String` values.

◎ Text input files can be read using a `FileReader` wrapped in a `BufferedReader`. The `read()` method reads a single character, and the `readLine()` method reads a `String`.

◎ Most standard Java I/O methods throw exceptions. Catching and handling such exceptions is accomplished by calling the methods in a try block, followed by catch blocks containing code to handle the exceptions.

◎ Java's exceptions are organized into an exception hierarchy, with a very general `Exception` class at the top of the hierarchy, and increasingly specific subclasses in the lower levels of the hierarchy.

◎ A method that throws an exception must explicitly state this in its heading:

```
ReturnType name(param-list) throws ExceptionName
```

The exception is actually thrown with a `throw` statement; for example,

```
if (...)     // no more data
   throw new EOFException();
```

◎ Binary output files can be written using a `FileOutputStream` wrapped in a `BufferedOutputStream` wrapped in a `DataOutputStream`. A primitive type value can be written using the `writeT()` method, where `T` is a primitive type (e.g., `writeInt()`, `writeChar()`, and so on).

◎ Binary input files can be read using a `FileInputStream` wrapped in a `BufferedInputStream` wrapped in a `DataInputStream`. A primitive type value can be read using the `readT()` method, where `T` is a primitive type (e.g., `readInt()`, `readChar()`, and so on).

◎ `Reader` and `Writer` classes support `char` (16-bit Unicode) input and output. `InputStream` and `OutputStream` classes support byte (8-bit) input and output.

◎ The `StringTokenizer` class from package `java.util` breaks a `String` into "words" or substrings called *tokens.*

◎ A `FileDialog` is a GUI dialog box that allows the user to select the name of a file from a list of files, which may be either input files or output files.

Documentation

This chapter focused on file I/O. The following tables describe several of the methods used for the various streams, readers, and writers used in this chapter for dealing with files as well as some methods used with exceptions. See the Java API documentation for more details.

■ SOME `PrintStream` METHODS

Method	Description

`PrintStream(OutputStream out)`
 	
`PrintStream(OutputStream out, boolean autoflush)`
	Constructs a print stream; values will be printed to output stream `out`. The output buffer will not be flushed automatically in the first form; in the second, if `autoflush` is true, it will be flushed whenever a byte array is written, one of the `println()` methods is invoked, or a newline character or byte ('\n') is written

`void flush()`	Flush the stream
`void close()`	Flush the stream and then close it
`void print(T value)`	Display a value of type `T`, which may be `boolean`, `char`, `char[]`, `double`, `float`, `int`, `long`, `Object`, or `String`
`void println(T value)` `void println()`	Display a value as with `print()` and then advance to a new line; in the second form, simply advance to a new line

■ SOME `BufferedReader` METHODS

Method	Description
`BufferedReader(Reader in)`	Constructs an input stream for characters using a buffer of some default size
`BufferedReader(Reader in, int size)`	Constructs an input stream for characters using a buffer with the specified `size`
`void close()`	Close the input stream
`int read()`	Read a character
`String readLine()`	Returns a line of text, not including end-of-line characters, or `null` if the end of the stream has been reached
`long skip(long n)`	Skip n characters

■ SOME `PrintWriter` METHODS

Method	Description

`PrintWriter(OutputStream out)`
 	
`PrintWriter`
`(OutputStream out, boolean autoflush)`
	Constructs a `PrintWriter` object from an existing output stream `out`, without automatic line flushing in the first form; in the second, if `autoflush` is true, `println()` methods will flush the output buffer.

`void flush()`	Flush the stream
`void close()`	Flush the stream and then close it
`void print(T value)`	Display a value of type T, which may be `boolean`, `char`, `char[]`, `double`, `floats`, `int`, `long`, `Object`, or `String`
`void println(T value)` `void println()`	Display a value as with `print()` and then advance to a new line; in the second form, simply advance to a new line

■ SOME `DataOutputStream` METHODS

Method	Description
`DataOutputStream(OutputStream out)`	Creates a new data output stream to write data to the underlying output stream `out`
`void flush()`	Flush the data output stream
`int size()`	Returns the current number of bytes written to this data output stream so far

`void writeBoolean(boolean val)`
`void writeByte(byte val)`
`void writeChar(int val)`
`void writeShort(short val)`
`void writeInt(int val)`
`void writeLong(long val)`
`void writeFloat(float val)`
`void writeDouble(double val)`
`void writeChars(String val)`
`void writeBytes(String val)`
`void writeUTF(String val)`
	Write a value of the various primitive types or `String` to the data stream. `writeBytes()` writes `val` as a sequence of one-byte characters; `writeChars()` writes `val` as a sequence of two-byte (Unicode) characters; `writeUTF()` writes `val` using UTF-8 encoding. (UTF-8 is a transmission format for Unicode that is safe for Unix file systems.)

`void write(byte[] b, int off,` `            int len) )`	Write `len` bytes from the specified byte array starting at offset `off` to the data output stream

■ **SOME** `DataInputStream` **METHODS**

Method	Description
`DataInputStream(InputStream in)`	Creates a new data input stream to read data from the underlying input stream `in`

`boolean readBoolean()`
`byte readByte()`
`char readChar()`
`short readShort()`
`int readInt()`
`long readLong()`
`float readFloat()`
`double readDouble()`
`String readUTF()`
	Read and return a value of the various primitive types or `String` from the data stream.

■ **SOME** `Exception` **METHODS**

Method	Description
`Exception()`	Constructs an exception with no specified detail message
`Exception(String str)`	Constructs an exception with detail message `str`
`String getMessage()`	Returns the error message string of this exception; `null` if there is none (inherited from class `Throwable`)
`String toString()`	Returns a short description of this exception. If it was created with an error message string, this string will be the concatenation of: ❑ The name of the actual class of this object ❑ `": "` (a colon and a space) ❑ The string returned by `getMessage()` If this exception was created with no error message string, then the name of the actual class of this object is returned. (Inherited from class `Throwable`)

The GUI example in Section 10.7 used several of the same Swing classes—`JTextField`, `JPanel`, and `JFrame` (and our extension `CloseableFrame`)—and event-handling classes—`ActionEvent` from `java.awt.event`—as the GUI examples in Section 7.5. See the presentation there and the Documentation section of the summary for Chapter 7 for information about them. The following table describes a few of the many methods provided for `FileDialog`. See Java's API documentation for more information.

■ SOME `FileDialog` METHODS

Method	Description

`FileDialog(Frame parent)`
 	
`FileDialog(Frame parent,`
`        String title)`
 	
`FileDialog(Frame parent,`
` String title, int mode)`
	Creates a file dialog with owner-window specified by `parent`. In the first form, the title will be empty, and for the other forms will have the specified title. In the last form, the value of `mode` is oneof the constants LOAD or SAVE (defined in this class), which specify whether the file dialog window will be used to locate an input file or an output file. In the first form, the default value is LOAD.

`int getMode()`	Returns the mode of this file dialog (see above)
`void setMode(int mode)`	Sets the mode of this file dialog (see above)
`String getFile()`	Returns the selected file of this file dialog or null if none is selected.
`void setFile(String file)`	Sets the selected file for this file dialog window to `file`. This will be the default file if it is set before the file dialog window is first shown.
`String getDirectory()`	Returns the directory of this file dialog window
`void setDirectory(String dir)`	Sets the directory of this file dialog window to `dir`

 ## PROGRAMMING POINTERS

 ### PROGRAM STYLE AND DESIGN

1. *If a program is to read data from a file, an input stream must be constructed to connect the program and the file. If it is to write data to a file, an output stream must be constructed as a connection between the program and the file.*

2. *Use one of the Reader or Writer subclasses whenever possible rather than one of the Stream subclasses.* The classes in the *Reader* and *Writer* hierarchies are new to Java 2, and many of the *Stream* classes (from Java 1) are deprecated in Java 2, which means they will be phased out in later versions of the language.

3. *A suggested pattern for input of text from a file:*

a. Build a `BufferedReader` by wrapping one around a `FileReader`:

```
BufferedReader in = new BufferedReader(
                        new FileReader(input_filename) );
```

b. Use an input loop to read lines of text from the `BufferedReader` (converting those lines to numeric values if necessary):

```
for (;;)
{
  valueString = in.readLine();
  if (valueString == null) break; // end-of-file
  ...
}
```

c. Close the `BufferedReader`:

```
in.close();
```

4. *A suggested pattern for output of text to a file:*

a. Build a `PrintWriter` by wrapping a `FileWriter` in a `BufferedWriter` and wrapping it in a `PrintWriter`:

```
PrintWriter out = new PrintWriter (
                    new BufferedReader(input_filename);
                    new FileReader(output_filename) ) ) ;
```

b. Use the `print()` and `println()` methods provided in `PrintWriter` to write values to the file::

```
out.print(value);
out.println(value);
```

c. Close the `PrintWriter`:

```
out.close();
```

5. *Use* `DataInputStream`*s and* `DataOutputStream`*s for binary input/output with files.*

6. *A catch block of the form*

```
catch (Exception variable)
{
    // exception-handling statements
)
```

can be used to handle any exception.

POTENTIAL PITFALLS

1. *Most Java I/O methods throw exceptions.*

2. *To detect and handle an exception that a method throws, the method must be invoked in a try block followed by one of more catch blocks that specify what to do if an exception occurs:*

```
try
{
  // method call
}
catch (ExceptionType variable)
{
  // exception-handling statements
)
  // ... more catch blocks may go here
finally                //optional finally block
(
  // statements for things to be done for all
  // exceptions or if there were none
}
```

WATCH

OUT

PROGRAMMING PROBLEMS

SECTIONS 10.1–10.4

1. Write a program to test the line-counting code in Exercise 6 of Section 10.4.

2. Write a program to test the average daily sales code in Exercise 7 of Section 10.4.

3. Write a program to test the code in Exercise 8 of Section 10.4 for finding the days when the maximum and minimum sales occurred.

4. Write a program to concatenate two text files; that is, to produce a file that contains the first file followed by the second file.

5. Write a program to copy one text file into another text file in which the lines are numbered 1, 2, 3, . . . with a number at the left of each line.

6. Write a program that reads a text file and counts how many lines in the file contain a specified string entered during execution of the program.

7. Proceed as in Problem 6 but find the total number of occurrences of the string.

8. Write a program that reads a text file and counts the vowels in the file.

9. Write a program that reads a text file and counts the characters in each line. The program should display the line number and the length of the shortest and longest lines in the file, as well as the average number of characters per line.

10. Write a program that reads a text file and writes it to another text file, but with leading blanks and blank lines removed. Run this program using as input files the last two Java programs you have written, and comment on whether you think indenting Java programs makes them more readable.

11. Write a file pagination program that reads a text file and prints it in blocks of 20 lines. If after printing a block of lines, there still are lines in the file, the program should allow

the user to indicate whether more output is desired; if so, the next block should be printed; otherwise, execution of the program should terminate.

12. Proceed as in Problem 5, but use Java's `LineNumberReader` class.

13. Proceed as in Problem 9, but use Java's `LineNumberReader` class.

14. Write a program that uses Java's `ZipOutputStream` class to create a compressed file.

15. Write a program that uses Java's `ZipInputStream` class to extract information from the compressed file generated in Problem 14.

SECTION 10.5–10.6

16. People from three different income levels, A, B, and C, rated each of two different products with a number from 0 through 10. Construct a file in which each line contains the income level and product rankings for one respondent. Then write a program that reads this information and calculates

   (a) For each income bracket, the average rating for Product 1

   (b) The number of persons in income bracket B who rated both products with a score of 5 or higher

   (c) The average rating for Product 2 by persons who rated Product 1 lower than 3

   Label all output and design the program so that it automatically counts the number of respondents.

17. Suppose that each line of a file contains a student's last name and exam score. Write a program that reads and counts the students, then calculates the mean score, the variance and the standard deviation. Display how many scores there are and their mean, variance, and standard deviation with appropriate labels. (See Programming Problem 11 in Chapter 9 for definitions of mean, variance, and standard deviation.)

18. Extend the program of Problem 17 to read the student information in the file, calculate the mean and standard deviation of the scores, and produce another file containing each student's name, exam score, and the letter grade corresponding to that score. (See Programming Problem 12 in Chapter 9 for a description of grading on the curve.)

19. Suppose that a device monitoring a process records time, temperature, pressure, and volume and stores this data in a file. Each line in this file contains the following readings in the order given: time, temperature, pressure, and volume; for example,

```
1200 34.2 32.2 101.5
1300 38.8 32.2 112.1
1400 44.8 32.4 142.5
1500 51.3 32.0 152.0
  .     .    .     .
  .     .    .     .
  .     .    .     .
```

The value for time is an integer representing the time at which the measurements were taken. The values for temperature, pressure, and volume are real numbers. Design, implement, and test a program to read the values for the temperature and volume, display these values in tabular form like the following;

```
Temperature        Volume
===========        ======
      34.2         101.5
      38.8         112.1
      44.8         142.5
      51.3         152.0
```

20. Write a program that reads the time, temperature, pressure, and volume measurements from a data file like that described in Problem 19; converts the time from military to ordinary time (e.g., 0900 is 9:00 A.M., 1500 is 3:00 P.M.); calculates the average temperature, average pressure, and average volume; and displays a table like the following:

```
TIME            TEMPERATURE      PRESSURE         VOLUME
========================================================
12:00 PM           34.2            32.2           101.5
                    .               .               .
                    .               .               .
                    .               .               .
10:00 PM           88.9            33.0           318.6
========================================================
AVERAGES            ?               ?               ?
```

(with the ?s replaced by the appropriate averages).

21. Write a program to search the file Users (see description following this problem set) to find and display the resources used to date for specified users whose identification numbers are entered during execution of the program.

22. Write a program to search the file Inventory (see description following this problem set) to find an item with a specified item number. If a match is found, display the item number and the number currently in stock; otherwise, display a message indicating that it was not found.

23. At the end of each month, a report is produced that shows the status of each user's account in Users (see description following this problem set). Write a program to accept the current date and produce a report of the following form:

```
              USER ACCOUNTS—mm/dd/yy
                      RESOURCE            RESOURCES
   USER-ID             LIMIT                USED
====================================================
   10101              $750                 $381
   10102              $650                 $599***
     .                  .                    .
     .                  .                    .
     .                  .                    .
```

where mm/dd/yy is the current data and the three asterisks (***) indicate that the user has already used 90 percent or more of the resources available to him or her.

24. Write a program that reads a text file, counting the nonblank characters, the nonblank lines, the words, and the sentences, and then calculates the average number of characters per word and the average number of words per sentence. You may assume the following: The file contains only letters, blanks, commas, periods, semicolons, and colons; a word is any sequence of letters that begins a line or is preceded by one or more blanks and that is terminated by a blank, comma, semicolon, colon, period, or the end of a line; and a sentence is terminated by a period.

25. (Project) Write a menu-driven program that uses the files `Student` and `StudentUp-date` (see descriptions following this problem set) and allows (some of) the following options. For each option, write a separate function so that options and corresponding functions can be easily added or removed.

(1) Locate a student's permanent record when given his or her student number, and print it in a nicer format than that in which it is stored.

(2) Same as option 1, but locate the record when given the student's name.

(3) Print a list of all student names and numbers in a given class $(1, 2, 3, 4, 5)$.

(4) Same as option 3 but for a given major.

(5) Same as option 3 but for a given range of cumulative GPAs.

(6) Find the average cumulative GPAs for (a) all females, (b) all males, (c) all students with a specified major, and (d) all students.

(7) Produce updated grade reports with the following format (where xx is the current year):

```
        GRADE REPORT—SEMESTER 2   5/29/xx
              DISPATCH UNIVERSITY
    10103       James L. Johnson
                            GRADE       CREDITS
                            =====       =======
    ENGL 176                  C            4
    EDUC 268                  B            4
    EDUC 330                  B+           3
    P E 281                   C            3
    ENGR 317                  D            4

    Cumulative Credits:        28
    Current GPA:             1.61
    Cumulative GPA:          2.64
```

Here, letter grades are assigned according to the following scheme: A = 4.0, A− = 3.7, B+ = 3.3, B = 3.0, B− = 2.7, C+ = 2.3, C = 2.0, C− = 1.7, D+ = 1.3, D = 1.0, D− = 0.7, and F = 0.0. (See Programming Problem 5 in Chapter 3 for details on the calculation of GPAs.)

(8) Same as option 7, but instead of producing grade reports, produce a new file containing the updated total credits and new cumulative GPAs.

(9) Produce an updated file when a student (a) drops or (b) adds a course.

(10) Produce an updated file when a student (a) transfers into or (b) withdraws from the university.

SECTION 10.7

26. Design, implement, and test a GUI application calculating student letter grades using the grading-on-the-curve method described in Problem 18.

27. Design, implement, and test a GUI application for the computer-user problem in Problem 21.

28. Design, implement, and test a GUI application for the inventory problem in Problem 22.

DESCRIPTIONS OF DATA FILES

The following describe the contents of data files used in exercises in the text. Listings of them are available on the CD and at the websites for this text.

`Inventory.txt`
Item number: an integer
Number currently in stock: an integer (in the range 0 through 999)
Unit price: a real value
Minimum inventory level: an integer (in the range 0 through 999)
Item name: a character string

File is sorted so that item numbers are in increasing order.

`Student.txt`
This is a file of student records, each of which is organized as follows. They are arranged so that student numbers are in increasing order.

Student number: an integer
Student's name: two strings (last, first) and a character (middle-initial)
Hometown: two strings of the form city, state
Phone number: a string
Gender: a character (M or F)
Year: a 1-digit integer (1, 2, 3, 4, or 5 for special)
Major: a string
Total credits earned to date: an integer
Cumulative GPA: a real value

`StudentUpdate.txt`
This is a file of student grade records organized as follows. They are sorted so that student numbers are in increasing order. There is one update record for each student in the file `Student`.

Student number: an integer (same as those used in the file `Student`)
For each of five courses:
    Course name: a seven-character string (e.g., CPSC131)
    Letter grade: a two-character string (e.g., A−, B+, C♭)
    Course credit: an integer

`Users.txt`
This is a file of computer system user records, each of which is organized as follows: They are arranged so that identification numbers are in increasing order.

Indentification number: an integer
User's name: Two strings of the form last-name, first-name
Password: a string
Resource limit (in dollars): an integer with up to four digits
Resources used to date: a real value

`LeastSquares.txt`
This is a text file in which each line contains a pair of real numbers representing the x coordinate and the y coordinate of a point.

INHERITANCE AND OOP

A wise old owl sat upon an oak
The more he saw the less he spoke
The less he spoke the more he heard
Why aren't we like that wise old bird? *Edward Hersey Richards*

It could probably be shown by facts and figures that there is no distinctly American criminal class except Congress. *Mark Twain*

Blessed are the young for they shall inherit the national debt. *Herbert Hoover*

A rock pile ceases to be a rock pile the moment a single man contemplates it, bearing within him the image of a cathedral. *Antoine de Saint-Exupery*

Chapter Contents

Chapter Objectives

- Learn how classes are designed and built
- Learn about inheritance and polymorphsm, the two basic concepts of OOP
- Illustrate the power of inheritance and polymorphism with case studies: aviary simulation, geological classification, and payroll processing
- Use OOD to develop a function-plotting GUI application

Objects are often categorized into groups that share similar characteristics. To illustrate:

❑ The terms *vanilla, chocolate, strawberry, cookies-and-cream, mint-chocolate-chip, moose-tracks,* and others refer to *flavors of ice cream.*

657

❑ The elements *helium, neon, argon, krypton, xenon,* and *radon* are known as the *inert* (or *noble*) *gasses* because each has the full complement of eight electrons in its outermost atomic shell, and thus does not react readily with other elements.

❑ People who work as *internists, pediatricians, surgeons, gynecologists, neurologists, general practitioners,* and other specialists have something in common: they are all *doctors.*

❑ Similarly, *doctors, nurses, medical technicians, receptionists,* and *administrative staff* who work at a given hospital are all *employees* of that hospital.

These are just a few of the many situations in which we organize objects into groups because of their common characteristics. When two or more objects have some characteristic in common, those objects are said to be *related* by virtue of sharing that characteristic.

Much of the history of science has involved the classification of objects by identifying their common characteristics. For example, when biologists discover a new species, they study all of its characteristics to determine where it fits into their elaborate classification scheme.

One of the aims of object-oriented programming is to simplify the process of building software models of real-world objects. Since real-world objects may be related to one another, an object-oriented language must provide some mechanism for modeling such relationships. In Java, the keyword `extends` serves this purpose. In this chapter, we study Java's `extends` mechanism, and see how it can be used to save coding effort in a carefully designed system.

11.1 INTRODUCTORY EXAMPLE: A TRIP TO THE AVIARY

PROBLEM

The city of Drib has a brand new aviary that houses a few of each of the following birds:

❑ Gray geese that eat bugs and walk about calling "Honk!"
❑ Brown ostriches that eat grass and walk about calling "Neek-neek!"
❑ Brown screech owls that eat mice and fly about calling "Screeeeeeeeeeech!"
❑ White snow owls that eat mice and fly about calling "Hoo!" from 1 to 4 times.
❑ Parrots that eat fruit and fly about calling "Squawk!" Most of these are green.
❑ Parrots that eat fruit and fly about calling "Polly wanna cracker!", "Pieces of eight!", "You're a pretty boy!", and "I wonder if this thing can talk." Most of these are red.

We will create a program to simulate this aviary.

Because we are introducing a new topic, we will briefly describe our design strategy, present our coded solution to the problem, and then explain the thought process behind the design in the next section.

Design Sketch

The key to solving this problem in a way that minimizes coding effort and is easy to maintain is to design a `Bird` **class hierarchy.** More precisely, we begin by designing classes for the objects in our problem. We then identify what characteristics different classes have in common, and design **superclasses** to store those common characteristics. To illustrate, we can build a `SnowOwl` class to represent a snow owl, and a `ScreechOwl` class to represent a screech owl. However, both of these eat mice, so rather than store that information redundantly in both classes, we can define an `Owl` superclass to represent this common information. We can then use Java's `extends` mechanism to derive `SnowOwl` and `ScreechOwl` from `Owl`, so that these two classes inherit the characteristic of eating mice.

We continue this design process until each of the objects holds an appropriate place within a single unified hierarchy that has in its top level a `Bird` class containing the characteristics common to all of the birds. The resulting class hierarchy is as follows:

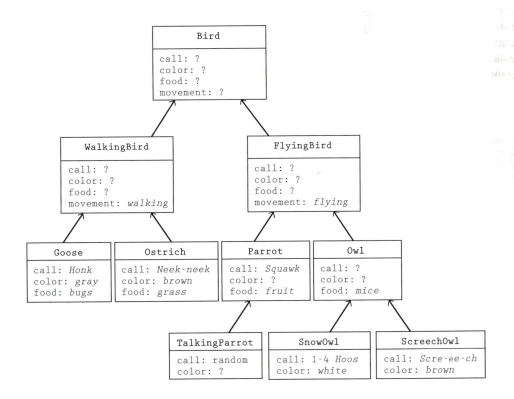

This class hierarchy serves as a blueprint for the coding, which we present next. We begin coding at the **root** (i.e., the top) of the hierarchy (`Bird`), and then work our way down towards the object classes. (Note: To save space, we will keep the documentation rather brief in these classes.)

Coding

Figure 11.1 presents the `Bird` class. It represents the attributes *color, food,* and *movement* that are common to all of the birds as pictured in our hierarchy.

FIGURE 11.1   CLASS `Bird`

```
/** Bird.java provides a class (abstract) to store attributes common to
 *   all birds -- color, food, and movement -- with methods to access
 *   these attributes and to convert them to a string for output purposes.
 *   A static randomInt() method is also provided to generate random
 *   integers for birds that exhibit randomness in their calls.
 */

import java.util.Random;

abstract class Bird extends Object
{
  /** Bird constructor
   *   Receive:       Strings color, food, and movement
   *   Postcondition: A Bird object is constructed with myColor == color
   *                    && myFood == food && myMovement == movement.
   */
  public Bird(String color, String food, String movement)
  {
    myColor = color;
    myFood = food;
    myMovement = movement;
  }

  //--- Accessors ---
  /** color accessor
   *   Return: myColor */
  public String getColor()     { return myColor; }

  /** food accessor
   *   Return: myFood */
  public String getFood()      { return myFood;  }

  /** movement accessor
   *   Return: myMovement */
  public String getMovement() { return myMovement; }

  /** (abstract) call accessor
   *   Return: myMovement
   *   Definition supplied by subclasses */
  abstract String getCall();

  //--- Output method ---
  /** toString converter
   *   Return a String representation of a Bird's attributes
   */
  public String toString()                    // output my
  {                                           // attributes:
    return "a " + getColor()                  //   color
         + " " + getClass().getName()         //   name
         + " " + getMovement()                //   movement
         + " by hunting " + getFood()         //   food
         + ",\n calling " + getCall();        //   call
  }
```

```
//--- Random number generator ---
/** Static random integer generator
 *   Receive: int upperBound
 *   Return:  a random int from the range 0..upperBound-1
 */
protected static int randomInt(int upperBound)
{
  return myRandom.nextInt(upperBound);
}

//--- Attribute variables ---
private String myColor, myFood, myMovement;
private static Random myRandom = new Random();
}
```

This class introduces a few new features that need explanation. First, note that there is no `myCall` attribute variable in class `Bird` to store a bird's call. This is because the calls of some birds (e.g., `TalkingParrot`, `SnowOwl`) vary in a "random" fashion. However, to make it possible to send a `Bird` object the `getCall()` message, we have included a `getCall()` method, but we have made it an **abstract method.** This means that although there is no definition for `getCall()` in class `Bird`, classes that extend this class will provide a definition. A class such as `Bird` that contains one or more abstract methods is called an **abstract class.** To indicate this, we preface both the declaration of `getCall()` and the declaration of class `Bird` with the keyword `abstract`. We will see the advantages of making `Bird` an abstract class in the next section.

A second new feature occurs in the `toString()` method, which invokes the accessor methods to build a description of a `Bird` object for output purposes. Note that one of the methods it invokes is the abstract `getCall()` method. This is legal, because any non-abstract class that extends our `Bird` class *must* either inherit or supply a definition for this method.

To access a bird's name, the `toString()` method uses the `getClass()` **method** from class `Object`. It returns a representation (of type `Class`) of the current object for which we invoke its `getName()` message to retrieve the name of the class as a `String`. This technique may seem somewhat awkward, but it can be used to retrieve the name of *any* class.

Finally, to simulate the "random" behavior of some birds, we define a `randomInt()` class method that returns a randomly generated integer in a specified range. To do this, we add to our class a static variable `myRandom` of type `Random`, which is a class in the package `java.util`. We make `randomInt()` a static method and `myRandom` a static variable so that all of our subsequent classes can share this method and variable.

Figure 11.2 presents the `WalkingBird` class. It extends our `Bird` class, which is called the **parent class** or **superclass** of `WalkingBird`. `WalkingBird` provides no additional functionality beyond a constructor. Because the *movement* attribute of a `WalkingBird` is "walking," this constructor has parameters for only the *color* and *food* attributes. The statement

```
super(color, food, "walking");
```

passes these values, along with the `String` literal `"walking"` to the `Bird` class constructor, which uses them to initialize the attribute variables defined in class `Bird`. The declaration of the `FlyingBird` class in Figure 11.3 is similar.

FIGURE 11.2   CLASS `WalkingBird`

```
/** WalkingBird.java provides a subclass (abstract) of Bird to model
 *   walking birds. Its only method is a constructor.
 */

abstract class WalkingBird extends Bird
{
  public WalkingBird(String color, String food)
  {
    super(color, food, "walking");
  }
}
```

FIGURE 11.3   CLASS `FlyingBird`

```
/** FlyingBird.java provides a subclass (abstract) of Bird to model
 *   flying birds. Its only method is a constructor.
 */

abstract class FlyingBird extends Bird
{
  public FlyingBird(String color, String food)
  {
    super(color, food, "flying");
  }
}
```

Figures 11.4 and 11.5 present the `Goose` and `Ostrich` classes, both of which extend the `WalkingBird` class.[1] Each provides a constructor that simply passes the appropriate *color* and *food* attributes to the `WalkingBird` constructor. They also define the `getCall()` method with behavior appropriate for a goose or ostrich, respectively.

FIGURE 11.4   CLASS `Goose`

```
/** Goose.java provides a subclass of WalkingBird that models a goose.
 *   It provides a constructor and a definition of getCall().
 */

class Goose extends WalkingBird
{
  public Goose()               { super("gray", "bugs"); }
  public String getCall() { return "Honk!"; }
}
```

---

[1] Apparently the geese have had their wings clipped so they don't fly away.

FIGURE 11.5   CLASS Ostrich

```
/** Ostrich.java provides a subclass of WalkingBird that models an ostrich.
 *  It provides a constructor and a definition of getCall().
 */

class Ostrich extends WalkingBird
{
  public Ostrich()         { super("brown", "grass"); }
  public String getCall() { return "Neek-neek!"; }
}
```

Figure 11.6 defines the `Parrot` class. Because a parrot *is* a flying bird, this class extends `FlyingBird`; and since different parrots have different colors, but all of them eat fruit, the constructor only needs a single parameter for the *color* attribute. It passes this value on to the `FlyingBird` constructor, along with the `String` literal "`fruit`" for its *food* attribute. Unless a parrot is taught to speak, it says "Squawk!", and so we define the `getCall()` method to return that `String` literal.

FIGURE 11.6   CLASS Parrot

```
/** Parrot.java provides a subclass of FlyingBird that models the parrots.
 *  It provides a constructor and a definition of getCall().
 */

class Parrot extends FlyingBird
{
  public Parrot(String color) { super(color, "fruit"); }
  public String getCall()      { return "Squawk!"; }
}
```

By contrast, a `TalkingParrot` speaks one of several phrases selected at random. As a result, its `getCall()` method is a bit more complex, as shown in Figure 11.7.

FIGURE 11.7   CLASS TalkingParrot

```
/** TalkingParrot.java provides a subclass of Parrot that models a talking
 *  parrot. Its attribute variable is an array that stores the phrases it
 *  can speak. It provides a constructor and a definition of getCall().
 */

class TalkingParrot extends Parrot
{
  public TalkingParrot(String color, String [] phrases)
  {
    super(color);
    myPhrases = phrases;
  }

  public String getCall()
  {
    int randomIndex = randomInt(myPhrases.length);
    return myPhrases[randomIndex];
  }

  private String [] myPhrases;
}
```

Because a talking parrot can speak several different phrases, this class uses a `String` array attribute variable named `myPhrases` to store these values. Its constructor receives via parameters not only its *color* attribute, but also the specific phrases a given parrot can speak (because different talking parrots "know" different phrases). The `getCall()` method uses the `randomInt()` method it inherits from class `Bird` to generate a random integer in the range 0 through `myPhrases.length − 1`, and then returns the element of `myPhrase` with that index. This causes `getCall()` to return a random phrase each time it is invoked.

Figure 11.8 presents the `Owl` class, which also extends the `FlyingBird` class. It supplies no functionality aside from a constructor. Since all of the owls eat mice but can have different colors, this constructor has a parameter for its *color* attribute, but none for a *food* attribute. When invoked, it simply passes the *color* it receives from its caller along with the `String` literal "mice" to its superclass (i.e., `FlyingBird`) constructor.

FIGURE 11.8   CLASS `Owl`

```
/** Owl.java provides a subclass (abstract) of Bird to model
 *   owls. Its only method is a constructor.
 */

abstract class Owl extends FlyingBird
{
  public Owl(String color) { super(color, "mice"); }
}
```

The `ScreechOwl` and `SnowOwl` classes then extend class `Owl`. Figure 11.9 presents the `ScreechOwl` class. Its contructor invokes the `Owl` constructor with the appropriate `String` literal for its *color* attribute. Since its *call* is always the same, the `getCall()` method simply returns the appropriate `String` for its *call*.

FIGURE 11.9   CLASS `ScreechOwl`

```
/** ScreechOwl.java provides a subclass of Own that models a screech owl.
 *   It provides a constructor and a definition of getCall().
 */

class ScreechOwl extends Owl
{
  public ScreechOwl()      { super("brown"); }
  public String getCall() { return "Screeeeeeeech!"; }
}
```

By contrast, a snow owl's *call* consists of 1 to 4 Hoo values. Figure 11.10 presents the `SnowOwl` class, whose `getCall()` method achieves this behavior by initializing its local `call` variable to the empty string, and then using the `randomInt()` method inherited from class `Bird` to generate a random number in the range 1 through 4. It then uses that random number to specify the number of repetitions of a for loop that concatenates that many "Hoo" literals to the `call` variable, and returns this string.

FIGURE 11.10   CLASS SnowOwl

```
/** SnowOwl.java provides a subclass of Own that models a snow owl.
 *  It provides a constructor and a definition of getCall().
 */

class SnowOwl extends Owl
{
  public SnowOwl() { super("white"); }

  public String getCall()
  {
    String call = "";
    int randomNumber = randomInt(4) + 1;              // 1..4

    for (int count = 1; count <= randomNumber; count++)
      call += "Hoo";

    return call + "!";
  }
}
```

This completes our `Bird` class hierarchy, and so we are ready to implement the `Aviary` class, which is shown in Figure 11.11.

FIGURE 11.11 CLASS Aviary

```
/** Aviary.java simulates a bird park.
 *  Output: A welcome message followed by the birds seen and heard
 *          on a simulated walk through the aviary.
 */

import ann.util.Controller;
import java.util.Random;

class Aviary extends Object
{
  public static void main(String [] args)
  {
    String [] parrotPhrases = {"Polly wanna cracker!",
                               "Pieces of eight!  Pieces of eight!",
                               "You're a pretty boy!",
                               "I wonder if this thing can talk?"};
    Bird [] birdArray = { new Ostrich(),
                          new Goose(),
                          new Parrot("green"),
                          new TalkingParrot("red", parrotPhrases),
```

```
                         new ScreechOwl(),
                         new SnowOwl()
                      };
      Random aRandom = new Random();
      int randomIndex, randomTime;
      Bird aBird = null;
      System.out.println("Welcome to the Aviary!\n (type Ctrl-c to quit));
      for (;;)
      {
         randomTime = aRandom.nextInt(10) + 1;           // pause from
         Controller.pause(randomTime);                   //   1..10 secs

         randomIndex = aRandom.nextInt(birdArray.length); // select a
         aBird = birdArray[randomIndex];                  //   random bird

         System.out.println("\nThere's " + aBird);        // display it
      }
   }
}
```

This program is deceptively simple, because most of the work is hidden in our `Bird` hierarchy. The program begins by building the array of phrases for the talking parrots. It then builds an array of `Bird` handles, each referring to a different kind of bird. This is legitimate, because an `Ostrich` *is a* (i.e., extends) `WalkingBird`, which *is a* `Bird`; a `TalkingParrot` *is a* `Parrot`, which *is a* `FlyingBird`, which *is a* `Bird`, and so on. (Note that although we pass only a *color* when we construct a `Parrot`, we must pass a *color* and an array of *phrases* when we construct a `TalkingParrot` object.) We then declare some local variables, display a greeting message, and enter a loop that drives the simulation.

The loop begins by pausing for 1 to 10 seconds, to simulate the time intervals between our observations of different birds. It then generates a random index into the array of `Bird` handles and outputs the bird at that index. This implicitly calls the `toString()` method defined in the `Bird` class, which calls each of the accessor methods. Execution then returns to the top of the loop where the cycle begins again.

Here is a sample run of the program:

Sample Run:

```
Welcome to the Aviary!
 (type Ctrl-c to quit)

There's a red TalkingParrot flying by hunting fruit,
 calling Polly wanna cracker!

There's a red TalkingParrot flying by hunting fruit,
 calling I wonder if this thing can talk?

There's a white SnowOwl flying by hunting mice,
 calling Hoo!

There's a green Parrot flying by hunting fruit,
 calling Squawk!
```

```
There's a gray Goose walking by hunting bugs,
  calling Honk!

There's a gray Goose walking by hunting bugs,
  calling Honk!

There's a brown Ostrich walking by hunting grass,
  calling Neek-neek!

There's a gray Goose walking by hunting bugs,
  calling Honk!

There's a white SnowOwl flying by hunting mice,
  calling Hoo!

There's a brown ScreechOwl flying by hunting mice,
  calling Screeeeeeeech!

There's a white SnowOwl flying by hunting mice,
  calling HooHoo!

There's a brown Ostrich walking by hunting grass,
  calling Neek-neek!

There's a red TalkingParrot flying by hunting fruit,
  calling Polly wanna cracker!

There's a green Parrot flying by hunting fruit,
  calling Squawk!

There's a brown Ostrich walking by hunting grass,
  calling Neek-neek!

There's a white SnowOwl flying by hunting mice,
  calling HooHooHooHoo!

There's a red TalkingParrot flying by hunting fruit,
  calling Pieces of eight! Pieces of eight!

There's a green Parrot flying by hunting fruit,
  calling Squawk!

There's a gray Goose walking by hunting bugs,
  calling Honk!

There's a red TalkingParrot flying by hunting fruit,
  calling You're a pretty boy!
        .
        .
        .
```

In the next section, we examine in detail some key aspects of the behavior of this program.

✔ Quick Quiz 11.1

1. A method in a class *C* is said to be _____ if it has no definition in *C* but subclasses of *C* will provide definitions.

2. An abstract class contains one or more _____ methods.

3. How is a class specified to be an abstract class?

For Questions 4–7, assume class declarations of the form

```
class Y extends Z {...}
class X extends Y {...}
```

4. X is called a(n) _____ of Y.

5. Y is called a(n) _____ of X.

6. (True or false) X extends Z.

7. Write a statement that the constructor in X can use to invoke a constructor in Y and pass it the values a and b.

11.2   INHERITANCE AND POLYMORPHISM

When we declare a class B to `extend` another class A,

```
class B extends A
{ ... }
```

this declaration means that class B **is a specialization of** class A; or more simply, that every B object *is an* A object. Graphically, this relationship is commonly drawn with an arrow from B to A to denote this extends or ***is-a* relationship:**

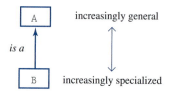

In this relationship, class A is called the **superclass** or **parent class,** and class B is called the **subclass** or **child class.** (The terms *superclass* and *subclass* correspond to *superset* and *subset* in mathematics: a superset has more general characteristics and a subset has more specialized characteristics.)

If we subsequently declare a class C that extends B,

```
class C extends B
{ ... }
```

then C *is a* B; and since B *is an* A, we can also say that C *is an* A:

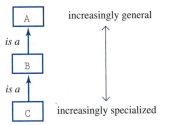

In mathematics, this is known as the **transitive** property of the *is-a* (or *extends*) relation.

Inheritance

Many people find the terms *parent class* and *child class* more intuitive than *super-class* and *subclass,* because they indicate the *inherits-from* relationship: when we write

```
class B extends A
{ ... }
```

the child class B **inherits** the characteristics (attribute variables and methods) of its parent class A. In Section 11.1, the class declarations

```
class Bird extends Object { ... }
class WalkingBird extends Bird { ... }
class FlyingBird extends Bird { ... }
class Goose extends WalkingBird { ... }
class Ostrich extends WalkingBird { ... }
class Parrot extends FlyingBird { ... }
class TalkingParrot extends Parrot { ... }
class Owl extends FlyingBird { ... }
class ScreechOwl extends Owl { ... }
class SnowOwl extends Owl { ... }
```

inform the Java compiler that these classes are related as follows:

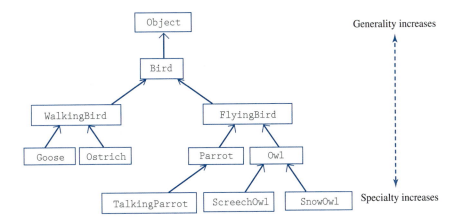

In a class hierarchy such as this, all of the classes from the parent of any class *B* up to and including the `Object` class are called **ancestor classes** of *B*. Similarly, for any class *A,* we will describe the set of all classes that have *A* as their ancestor as **descendant classes** of *A*. For example, the ancestor classes of `Goose` are `Walking-Bird`, `Bird`, and `Object`; the descendant classes of `FlyingBird` are `Parrot`, `Owl`, `TalkingParrot`, `ScreechOwl`, and `SnowOwl`.

In a class hierarchy such as this, each class *inherits the attributes and methods* of its ancestor classes. Thus, class `Bird` inherits the attributes and methods of its parent class `Object`. Classes `WalkingBird` and `FlyingBird` inherit the attributes and methods of their ancestor classes `Bird` and `Object`. Classes `Goose` and `Ostrich` inherit the attributes and methods of their ancestor classes `WalkingBird`, `Bird`, and `Object`; and so on.

This means that any of the methods defined in `Object`, `Bird`, or `WalkingBird` are also methods for a `Goose` or `Ostrich` object. For example, we can write

```
Goose aGoose = new Goose();
System.out.println( aGoose.getFood() );
```

because although there is no `getFood()` method defined in class `Goose` (see Figure 11.4), it inherits a `getFood()` method from class `Bird`, so this message invokes that `getFood()` method.

By contrast, if we write

```
Parrot aParrot = new Parrot("green");
System.out.println( aParrot.getCall() );
```

then we send `aParrot` the `getCall()` message. As we saw in Figure 11.7, the `Parrot` class does contain a `getCall()` method, and so this method is invoked.

Inheritance is a very powerful technique that can be used to eliminate redundant coding effort. To illustrate, we can send the `toString()` message to a `Goose`, `Ostrich`, `Parrot`, `TalkingParrot`, `ScreechOwl` or `SnowOwl`, even though none of those classes implements the method. By defining `toString()` once, in class `Bird`, we saved ourselves considerable coding effort because we did not have to redefine it in any of these subclasses, .

Handles and `extends`

In contrast to the preceding examples, suppose that we write

```
Bird aBird = new Goose();
```

NOTE

Because `aBird` is a `Bird` handle, and a `Goose` object *is a* `Bird`, this is a legal statement. *A handle for a class C can store a reference to any object whose class is a descendant of C.* Thus the preceding statement is valid because `Goose` is a descendant of `Bird`.

However, the opposite statement

```
Goose aGoose = new Bird("gray", "walking", "bugs");    // ERROR!
```

is *not* valid, primarily because although a `Goose` is a `Bird`, a `Bird` is not necessarily a `Goose`.[2] That is, extends is a unidirectional relation: *B* extends *A* does not imply that *A* extends *B*. This makes sense: *all geese are birds, but not all birds are geese.*

Polymorphism

Combining some of the preceding observations, we can write a statement like

```
Bird bird1 = new Parrot("green"),
     bird2 = new TalkingParrot("red", phrases);
```

and then send messages to the resulting objects to use their `getFood()` methods:

```
System.out.println( bird1.getFood() );
System.out.println( bird2.getFood() );
```

The `getFood()` method that `Parrot` and `TalkingParrot` inherit from class `Bird` will be invoked.

Things get more interesting if we write

```
System.out.println( bird1.getCall() );
System.out.println( bird2.getCall() );
```

In the first statement, we send a `Parrot` object the `getCall()` message. Even though we are sending it via a `Bird` handle, the `getCall()` method within class `Parrot` is invoked. Similarly, the second statement sends a `TalkingParrot` object the `getCall()` message. Even though we are sending the message via a `Bird` handle, this invokes the `getCall()` method defined within class `TalkingParrot`. We can think of how this works as follows:

NOTE

Message-Handling Mechanism

When a message is sent to an object of class *C* to use method *m*():

> If there is a definition of *m*() in *C*, then that definition is invoked;
> Otherwise, the parent of class *C* is searched for a definition of *m*(), continuing on through the ancestors of *C*.

Now consider the following fragment from the program in Figure 11.11, especially the statement highlighted in color:

```
randomIndex = aRandom.nextInt(birdArray.length); // select a
aBird = birdArray[randomIndex];                   // random bird

System.out.println("\nThere's" + aBird);          // display it
```

---

[2] A secondary reason is that `Bird` is an *abstract* class, and Java does not permit instances of an abstract class to be created.

We can picture the situation as follows, where the light arrows indicate possible references to Bird objects and the colored arrow represents the one randomly selected:

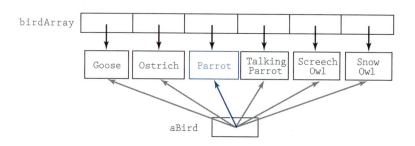

The first two statements make aBird refer to a randomly selected bird object. The third statement invokes the String concatenation operator (+) with aBird as an operand, which implicitly sends aBird the toString() message. This in turn invokes the toString() method the object inherits from class Bird. Its statement

```
return "a " + getColor()                    // color
      + " " + getClass().getName()          // name
      + " " + getMovement()                 // movement
      + " by hunting " + getFood()          // food
      + ",\n calling " + getCall();         // call
```

invokes the various accessor methods for a bird's attributes.

Here are the important points in this example:

NOTE

1. *A method defined in a class is inherited by all descendants of that class.* Because toString() is defined in class Bird, it is inherited by every descendant class of Bird.[3] Thus, if toString() is sent to a TalkingParrot, that TalkingParrot object executes the toString() method it inherits from Bird.

2. *When a message is sent to an object to use method m( ), any messages that m( ) sends will also be sent to that same object.* In our example, this means that when a TalkingParrot object is sent a message to use toString(), the toString() method it inherits from Bird sends getColor(), getClass(), getName(), getMovement(), getFood(), and getCall() messages. These messages are sent to this same TalkingParrot object.

3. *If the object receiving a message does not have a definition of the method requested, an inherited definition is invoked.* Since TalkingParrot has no definitions for the getColor(), getClass(), getName(), getMovement(), or getFood(), these messages invoke the methods that TalkingParrot inherits from class Bird.

---

[3] As noted later, a descendent class may choose to **override** an inherited definition by redefining it, as we did with getCall().

4. *If the object receiving a message has a definition of the requested method, that definition is invoked.* Since `TalkingParrot` has a definition for `getCall()`, the `getCall()` message invokes the definition of `getCall()` that is in `TalkingParrot`.

In connection with this last point, note that if `TalkingParrot` did not have a definition for `getCall()`, then the `getCall()` method it inherits from class `Parrot` would be invoked. However, because `TalkingParrot` requires a different behavior for `getCall()` than that provided by the method defined in `Parrot`, `TalkingParrot` supplies its own definition for `getCall()`. This is known as **overriding** an inherited method. *Any time that an inherited method does not supply the desired behavior, a class should override that method with a definition that does.*

NOTE

The preceding rules imply that a single message such as:

```
aBird.getCall()
```

can actually invoke different `getCall()` methods at different times, depending on the particular object to which `aBird` refers. Because one message can invoke many different methods, this kind of message behavior is called **polymorphic** behavior, or **polymorphism.**[4] Polymorphism directly supports the "I can do it myself" principle of object-oriented programming, because when a message is sent to an object, polymorphism ensures that the right method—the one defined in that object's class—is invoked.

Java methods are polymorphic by default. We need to do nothing special to "turn on" polymorphic behavior for a method.[5]

To summarize:

> *When a message is sent to an object to use method m( ), the Java system first looks at the class of the object to which it is sent. If that class contains a definition of m( ), then it is invoked. Otherwise, the Java system looks for a definition of m( ) one level up in the hierarchy—in the parent class—where the process begins again. If the Java compiler processes a statement that sends a message for which there is no method definition, the compiler will generate a compilation error. However, there are conditions (albeit unusual) under which a compiled program can send a message and the Java system is unable to find a definition of the corresponding method.[6] In such cases, the Java system throws a* `NoSuchMethod-Exception`.

---

[4] In Greek *poly* means "many" and *morph* means "form," so *polymorphism* describes what happens when a single statement can take on many different forms or definitions.

[5] Polymorphism is the default behavior for a Java method, and searching for the method definition slows down a method's execution. To improve a method's performance when polymorphism is not needed, polymorphic behavior can be "turned off" by preceding the method's definition with the keyword `final`.

[6] For example, *B* extends *C*, which contains *m*( ). *B* is compiled. Method *m*( ) is removed from *C* before *C* is compiled. During run time, the *B* object *b* invokes *m*( ), and a run-time error occurs.

The Java Hierarchy

If you have been using the Java API, you should know by now that Java's classes are organized into an extensive **class hierarchy.** There are far too many classes—more than 1600—to show, but the root of this hierarchy is the `Object` class, making it the **common ancestor** of all Java classes:

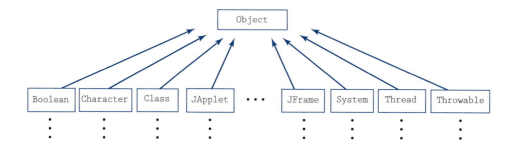

This means that *every class* inherits the characterists of the class `Object`, such as the methods `clone()`, `equals()`, `getClass()`, and `toString()`.

NOTE

In Java, every class except `object` *must be an extension of some other class.* If a programmer does not specify an `extends` relationship for a class, then that class extends the `Object` class *by default.* Java's `Object` class thus serves as a default super class.

Another way of saying the same thing is that *every class must fit somewhere within the Java class hierarchy.* While most of the programs we have written for this text have extended the `Object` class, most applets extend the `JApplet` class, and our GUI programs often extend our `CloseableFrame` class (which in turn extends the `JFrame` class).

The point of requiring every class to extend an existing class is to *avoid redundant coding effort.* For example, a class that extends our `CloseableFrame` class inherits the code that causes the close box to terminate the program, which saves us the effort of having to re-implement that same functionality in each new GUI class we write. Similarly, a program that extends `JApplet` inherits the various capabilities of the `JApplet` class, saving us the effort of re-implementing those same capabilities in our applets. Choosing which class to extend is an important part of the **object-oriented design** process, which we examine next.

Object-Oriented Design (OOD)

Thus far, we have designed most of the programs in the book using *object-centered design (OCD),* which is an object-based design methodology for beginning programmers. Now that we know about inheritance and polymorphism, we can expand OCD as follows:

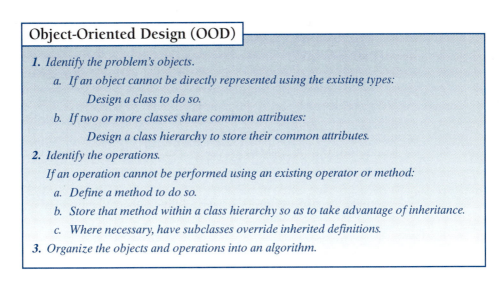

Object-Oriented Design (OOD)

1. Identify the problem's objects.

   a. If an object cannot be directly represented using the existing types:

      Design a class to do so.

   b. If two or more classes share common attributes:

      Design a class hierarchy to store their common attributes.

2. Identify the operations.

   If an operation cannot be performed using an existing operator or method:

   a. Define a method to do so.

   b. Store that method within a class hierarchy so as to take advantage of inheritance.

   c. Where necessary, have subclasses override inherited definitions.

3. Organize the objects and operations into an algorithm.

The resulting design methodology is a simple version of **object-oriented design (OOD),** which is the best-known technique for reducing the cost of maintaining a software system. By consolidating common characteristics (including functionality) within a class hierarchy, a given method is defined just once, avoiding redundant coding effort. This reduces maintenance costs, because if a class or method needs to be upgraded, all changes are localized to that class or method, and all subclasses of that class automatically inherit the changes.

We used OOD to design the class hierarchy in Section 11.1. We began by designing classes for the objects in our problem (Step 1a):

```
Goose, Ostrich, Parrot, ScreechOwl, SnowOwl, TalkingParrot
```

We then identified common attributes, and built a class hierarchy to consolidate those attributes. This is a "bottom-up" process, in which we begin with our objects at the bottom of the hierarchy and work our way upwards:

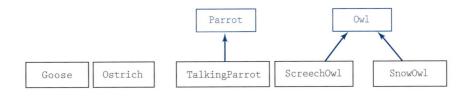

We then repeat the process, seeking suitable superclasses to categorize each class that has no parent class:

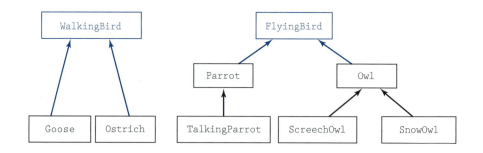

We continue this process until we have a fully-connected hierarchy:

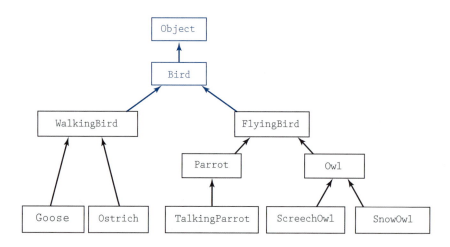

We then identify the operations and decide which class should be responsible for which operation—so as to take advantage of inheritance—using polymorphism where necessary in order for a method to behave as needed in a particular class (e.g., `get-Call()` in `TalkingParrot`).

Hierarchy design is thus a *bottom-up process;* implementing the design proceeds top-down.

O-O Design Issues

We have just seen an example of object-oriented design. There are, however, several issues that must be addressed in using it.

Using `extends` Correctly. Our first design issue is the decision of where to place a class in the hierarchy: *which class should a new class extend?* If we wish to take advantage of inheritance to avoid redundant coding effort, we may wish to choose a class other than `Object` as the superclass of the class we are designing. Our rule of thumb on this issue is as follows:

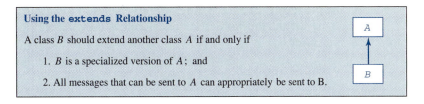

Using the `extends` Relationship

A class *B* should extend another class *A* if and only if

1. *B* is a specialized version of *A*; and
2. All messages that can be sent to *A* can appropriately be sent to B.

A child class *B* inherits the methods of its parent class *A*, so any message that can be sent to *A* can also be sent to *B*. This means that if there are any methods in *A* that would be inappropriate to send to a *B* object, then *B* should *not* extend *A*.

There are some situations where it may be unclear whether one class should extend another class. In this case the following "need a . . . use a . . ." test may help:

If all you need is an A, can you use a B?

For example, if all you need is a bird to be admitted to a bird-training seminar, could you use your pet toucan? Yes, so it would be appropriate for a `Toucan` class to extend the `Bird` class. Could you use a stuffed toy toucan to gain admittance? Probably not, so making a class `ToucanToy` a subclass of `Bird` is not appropriate; a stuffed toucan toy *is not* a bird. Even though the class `ToucanToy` might have many of the same characteristics as `Bird`, this is not good design.

NOTE

Using inheritance merely to avoid some code writing is not acceptable.

Abstract Methods and Classes. Our second design issue occurs when it should be possible to send some message to a class, but there is no clear way to define the corresponding method *in that class.* For example, every bird has a call, and so it would seem that a `Bird` should respond to the `getCall()` message. However, bird calls are highly specialized from one bird to another, which makes it difficult to think of an appropriate way to define a `getCall()` method in the `Bird` class. There are two different ways to resolve this difficulty:

1. Define a "generic method" within the class that provides some default behavior and let subclasses override it when necessary; or
2. Declare the method within the class as `abstract`, and leave it up to the subclasses to supply the specific behavior.

Using the first approach, we could define within `Bird` a generic `getCall()` method, such as

```
public String getCall() { return "Tweet-Tweet!"; }
```

Subclasses of `Bird` can then either choose to use this inherited default `getCall()` behavior, or to override it by supplying their own definition for `getCall()`. It is worth mentioning that although we did not use this approach for the `Bird` class in Figure 11.1, we did use it in Figure 11.6 for the `Parrot` class, whose `getCall()` method returns a default "`Squawk!`", while allowing subclasses like `TalkingParrot` (Figure 11.7) to override this behavior by redefining `getCall()`.

Using the second approach, we declared `getCall()` within `Bird` as an **abstract method,** by writing the word `abstract` followed by the method heading, followed by a semicolon:

```
abstract String getCall();
```

Such a declaration has three effects:

1. It makes it possible to send the `getCall()` message to a `Bird` subclass via a `Bird` handle.
2. It makes the `Bird` class into an **abstract class,** meaning that instances of `Bird` can not be created. The keyword `abstract` should precede the `Bird` class declaration.
3. It imposes the following requirement on subclasses: a definition of this method must reach any non-abstract subclass of `Bird`, either through inheritance or through a local definition of the method.

In Figure 11.1, we chose the second approach for our `Bird` class. Accordingly, the keyword `abstract` precedes both the class declaration and the declaration of `getCall()`. Note that because no definition of `getCall()` reaches `WalkingBird` (Figure 11.2) or `FlyingBird` (Figure 11.3), these classes must also be declared as `abstract` classes, or a compilation error will result.

Attribute Variables vs. Methods. Our final design issue concerns whether to represent a particular attribute using both an attribute variable and an accessor method, or only a method. For example, in Figure 11.1, we represented the *movement* attribute with an attribute variable and an accessor method:

```
public String getMovement() { return myMovement; }
        .
        .
        .
private String myMovement;
```

But we represented the *call* attribute with an abstract method, whose definition is supplied by the subclasses:

```
abstract public String getCall();
```

Why this difference?

We could have instead defined `getMovement()` as an abstract method of class `Bird`,

```
abstract public String getMovement();
```

and then had the `WalkingBird` class and the `FlyingBird` class supply definitions for this method:

```
// WalkingBird.java
        .
        .
        .
public String getMovement() { return "walking"; }
```

```
// FlyingBird.java
   .
   .
   .

public String getMovement() { return "flying"; }
```

This approach would eliminate the need for the attribute variable `myMovement`, which in turn would eliminate one parameter from the `Bird` constructor, simplifying it a bit. So why did we not use this approach?

Our rule of thumb for making this decision is as follows:

> **Choosing a Method or an Attribute variable and an Accessor**
>
> *If an attribute can be stored in an attribute variable and retrieved using an accessor method, then do so in such a way as to exploit inheritance and avoid redundant coding effort; otherwise declare an abstract method and leave it to subclasses to supply its definition.*

In following this rule, there is nothing about a bird's *movement* attribute that prevents it from being stored in an attribute variable. Since all birds move, we declare this variable and its accessor method in class `Bird`, so that every subclass will automatically inherit the attribute.

By contrast, consider a bird's *call* attribute. Some birds always give similar calls while other birds emit completely different calls at different times. This **behavioral variance** makes it difficult to store a bird's call in an attribute variable. As a result, we declare `getCall()` as an abstract method, and leave it to the individual subclasses to define its behavior.

When the degree of behavioral variance in an attribute makes it difficult to store that attribute in an attribute variable, we use this latter approach of declaring an abstract method, leaving it to each subclass to supply its definition in whatever way is appropriate for that subclass.

O-O Coding Issues

We complete this section with a discussion of some coding-specific issues that arise in implementing an object-oriented design. All of these result from the organization of classes into hierarchies. Our first two issues stem from attribute variables being kept private.

Initializing Inherited Attributes. Our first issue centers around the constructor method, whose task is to initialize attribute variables. As we have seen, attribute variables are declared as private to prevent programs from accessing them directly and becoming dependent on particular variable names or other details. Since private attribute variables cannot be accessed outside of their class, they cannot be accessed by methods in a child class. This creates the following problem: *How can a child class constructor initialize the attribute variables it inherits from its parent class, when it is not permitted to access directly those (private) attribute variables?*

The solution lies in the word *directly*. Although a child class method cannot directly access private inherited attribute variables, it can access them *indirectly* through methods provided by the parent class. More precisely, if a parent class provides a constructor to initialize its attribute variables (as every good class should), then a child class can invoke this parent class constructor to initialize its inherited attribute variables.

In Java, a child class constructor can invoke a constructor from its parent class using the **keyword** `super`. Our `Bird` hierarchy illustrates this. For example, the `Bird` constructor from Figure 11.1 is as follows:

```
public Bird(String color, String food, String movement)
{
  myColor = color;
  myFood = food;
  myMovement = movement;
}
```

The `WalkingBird` constructor from Figure 11.2 invokes this constructor:

```
public WalkingBird(String color, String food)
{
  super(color, food, "walking");
}
```

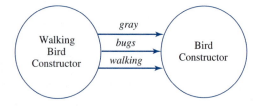

The `Goose` constructor from Figure 11.4 invokes the `WalkingBird` constructor:

```
public Goose() { super("gray", "bugs"); }
```

A statement

```
Bird aBird = new Goose();
```

thus invokes the `Goose` constructor, which invokes the `WalkingBird` constructor passing it the strings "gray" and "bugs", which invokes the `Bird` constructor passing it the strings "gray", "bugs", and "walking", which the `Bird` constructor then assigns to the attribute variables `myColor`, `myFood`, and `myMovement`:

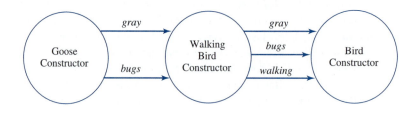

This statement thus constructs `aBird` as a gray bird that eats bugs and walks.

The following rules must be remembered when invoking the constructor in a parent class. A compilation error will result if either of them is violated.

Invoking a Constructor in a Parent Class

1. *Because it invokes a constructor, the* `super()` *method can only be invoked in another constructor method.*

2. *It must be the first statement in that method, so that the inherited attribute variables are initialized before any normal (non-inherited) attribute variables.*

Accessing Private Information from an Ancestor Class. A second coding issue arises when a descendant class needs to access or modify an attribute in an ancestor class. If the ancestor class declares the attribute as public, then the descendant can modify the variable, but so can any other user of the class. If the ancestor declares the attribute as private, then users of the class are prevented from accessing the attribute, but so are descendant classes.

For such circumstances, Java provides the `protected` modifier. If an attribute is declared as `protected`, then users of the class cannot access the attribute, but descendants of the class can. The `protected` **modifier** thus provides an intermediate level of protection between `private` and `public`.

It is our practice to always declare attribute variables as `private`, and if we wish to allow descendant classes to change the value of an attribute variable, to declare a *protected mutator method* for that attribute variable. This keeps both users and descendants of a class from directly accessing the attribute variable, but allows descendants to modify the attribute variable through the mutator.

It may seem simpler to make the attribute variable `protected` instead of `private`. Why force descendant classes to access an attribute variable through a `protected` mutator method? The answer is validation. If we make an attribute variable protected, then descendant classes can change that variable without the new value being validated. *By requiring a descendant class to access the private data through a mutator, we can ensure the validity of any new value by having the mutator check it.*

NOTE

To illustrate, suppose that we decided to permit descendants of class `Bird` to modify the `myMovement` attribute variable. If we simply make `myMovement` protected, then a descendant class could (erroneously) change `myMovement` to an invalid value,

```
myMovement = "space-walking";
```

and our simulation would continue with this "corrupted" information. We prefer instead to keep `myMovement` private and define a protected `setMovement()` mutator method in `Bird`:

```
protected void setMovement(String newMovement) throws Exception
{
    if ( !newMovement.equals("walking")
        && !newMovement.equals("flying")
        && !newMovement.equals("running")
        // ... check for each valid movement ...
```

```
              && !newMovement.equals("swimming") )
         throw new Exception("Invalid Bird movement: " + newMovement);

      myMovement = newMovement;
   }
```

Then any attempt to change the value of `myMovement` to an invalid value as in

```
         aBird.setMovement("space-walking");
```

will cause `setMovement()` to throw an exception.

Note that the `Bird` class in Figure 11.1 has a `randomInt()` method that is declared as `protected`. The motivation for this is a bit different. Because `randomInt()` is a utility method, we want to allow descendant classes to use this method; but it isn't really the sort of message one should send to a `Bird`. By declaring `randomInt()` as `protected`, descendant classes can use it as a utility, while casual users of class `Bird` are prevented from using it. This allows us to keep the `Bird` class `myRandom` variable `private`, as it should be.

Invoking An Inherited Method of the Same Name. Although it does not happen in our class hierarchy from Section 11.1, sometimes a method that overrides an inherited method needs to invoke that inherited method. To illustrate, suppose that the `getCall()` method class `TalkingParrot` needs to return a `String` consisting of a `Parrot`'s call (i.e., "Squawk!") followed by one of the `TalkingParrot`'s phrases selected at random. We cannot write

```
         public String getCall()
         {
            randomIndex = randomInt(myPhrases.length);
            return getCall() + myPhrases[randomIndex];   // LOGIC ERROR!
         }
```

in `TalkingParrot`, because this would invoke the `getCall()` message in `TalkingParrot`, producing an infinite recursion! What is needed is a way to invoke the `getCall()` method in the parent class `Parrot`. In Java, this can be done by **qualifying** a method name with the prefix `super`. Thus, in place of the preceding definition of `getCall()`, we could write

```
         public String getCall()
         {
            randomIndex = randomInt(myPhrases.length);
            return super.getCall() + myPhrases[randomIndex];   // Correct!
         }
```

NOTE

Generally speaking, *if a child class overrides a method* `m()` *inherited from its parent class and wishes to invoke the inherited method, the notation*

```
         super.m()
```

can be used.

This completes our discussion of inheritance, polymorphism and object-oriented design, all of which are of fundamental importance in Java. The remaining sections in this chapter will provide examples that apply these principles.

✔ Quick Quiz 11.2

For Questions 1–10, assume class declarations of the form

```
class Z
{ void m1() {...} // A
  void m2() {...} // B
}
class Y extends Z
{ void m1() {...} // C
}
class X extends Y
{ void m1() {...} // D
}

Z obj = new X();
```

1.   X is called a(n) _____ or _____ of Y.
2.   Y is called a(n) _____ or _____ of X.
3.   X is called a(n) _____ of Z.
4.   Z is called a(n) _____ of X.
5.   X _____ the characteristics (attribute variables and methods) of Y.
6.   For the statement obj.m1();, which of the methods labeled A, B, C, D is invoked?
7.   The definition of m1() in X is said to _____ the definition of m1() in Y.
8.   Describe what happens when the statement obj.m2(); is encountered.
9.   Tell how the method m1() labeled A could be invoked from inside class Y.
10.   _____ is the common ancestor of all Java classes
11.   The word _____ means "many forms."
12.   (True or false) Every class must be a subclass of some other class.

✍ EXERCISES 11.2

For Exercises 1–11, determine whether it would be appropriate for one of the two classes to be a subclass of the other. If it is, tell which would be the subclass. If is it not, explain why not.

1.   Lines and rectangles
2.   Squares and rectangles
3.   Triangles and rectangles
4.   Students at Universal University and GPAs
5.   Students and the library at Universal University
6.   Professors and employees at Universal University

7. Employees and persons at Universal University

8. Computers and electronic equipment

9. Computers and operating systems

10. Computers and highway systems

11. Computers and CPUs

For Exercises 12–15, draw a diagram that pictures an appropriate class hierarchy to model the given objects.

12. Circle, triangle, square, rectangle, polygon, geometric figure, hexagon.

13. Bulldog, Chihuahua, Collie, Miniature Collie, horse, cat, reptile, dog, snake, lizard, canine, mammal, animal.

14. Driver's license, chauffeur's license, hunting license, pet license, duck-hunting license, fishing license, deer-hunting license, dog license, marriage license, license.

15. Bank account, savings account, loan, checking account, student loan, free checking account, money-market savings account, home equity loan, graduate-school student loan.

For Exercises 16–19, add at least 4 more classes to the hierarchies of Exercises 12–15.

16. The hierarchy in Exercise 12

17. The hierarchy in Exercise 13

18. The hierarchy in Exercise 14

19. The hierarchy in Exercise 15

For Exercises 20–22, proceed as in Exercises 12–15, but make a class hierarchy with at least 12 descendant classes of the given class and that contains at least 3 levels.

20. Motorized vehicles

21. Computer equipment

22. Shoes

23. Write declarations for:

    (a) A class *License* with a person's name, age, and id number as attributes; a constructor method that initializes the attribute variables; and an output method.

    (b) A subclass *HuntingLicense* with the name of the prey as a new attribute; a constructor method that initializes the attribute variables; an accessor for this new attribute; and an output method that overrides that in the *License* class.

24. Write a declaration for a subclass *DeerHuntingLicense* of the *HuntingLicense* class in Exercise 23 with a new attribute that indicates whether hunting does is permitted, a constructor method that initializes the attribute variables, an accessor and a mutator for this new attribute, and an output method that overrides that in the *HuntingLicense* class.

25. Write declarations for:

    (a) A class *BankAccount* with a customer's name, account number, and account balance as attributes; a constructor method that initializes the attribute variables; and a method that displays the account number and the current balance.

    (b) A subclass *CheckingAccount* with service charge as a new attribute; a constructor method that initializes the attribute variables; a deposit method; and a withdrawal method.

(c) A subclass *Loan* with interest rate as a new attribute; a constructor method; a make-payment method; and an add-interest method.

26. Write a declaration for a subclass *StudentLoan* that is a subclass of the *Loan* class in Exercise 25 with the loan term (number of years to pay it off) and monthly payment as new attributes; a constructor method that initializes the attribute variables; and a method that returns the number of payments remaining.

11.3   EXAMPLE: GEOLOGICAL CLASSIFICATION

In this section we develop a simple rock classification program.

PROBLEM

In geology, rocks are classified according to the nature of their origin. More precisely, a given rock is described as:

- ❏ *Sedimentary,* if the rock was formed by the laying down of deposits of sediment
- ❏ *Igneous,* if it is volcanic in origin (i.e., formed by cooling magma)
- ❏ *Metamorphic,* if the rock was formed from some other rock by temperature or pressure changes and/or some fluid

Chalk, limestone, sandstone, and shale are *sedimentary* rocks. Basalt, granite, and obsidian are *igneous* rocks. Marble, quartzite, and slate are *metamorphic* rocks.

Knowing the different categories of rocks can make outdoor activities such as backpacking or canoeing more interesting. For example, if one is hiking through a valley whose walls contain layers of sandstone, then the walls of the valley may have once been under water and may contain fossils of water creatures. By contrast, a valley with granite walls means that there was once a volcano in the vicinity, and finding it can make for an interesting diversion in the trip.

In this section, we will develop a program that, given the name of a rock, displays a (very simplified) geological classification of that rock. The rocks our program will support will be those described above: chalk, limestone, sandstone, shale, basalt, granite, obsidian, marble, quartzite, and slate. However, thanks to object-oriented design, extending our program to handle additional rocks will be easy.

 ## OBJECT-ORIENTED DESIGN

BEHAVIOR. Our program should display on the screen a prompt for a rock, and read its name from the keyboard. For any of the rocks—chalk, limestone, sandstone, shale, basalt, granite, obsidian, marble, quartzite, or slate—our program should display a *description* of that rock.

PROBLEM'S OBJECTS. Ignoring the keyboard and screen, we can identify the following objects in this problem:

Description of problem's object	Type	Kind	Name
A rock	`Rock`	varying	*aRock*
chalk	`Chalk`	constant	—
limestone	`Limestone`	constant	—
sandstone	`Sandstone`	constant	—
shale	`Shale`	constant	—
basalt	`Basalt`	constant	—
granite	`Granite`	constant	—
obsidian	`Obsidian`	constant	—
marble	`Marble`	constant	—
quartzite	`Quartzite`	constant	—
slate	`Slate`	constant	—
description	`String`	varying	*aRock.getDescription()*

Because chalk, limestone, . . . , quartzite, and slate are all different kinds of rocks, we will create `Chalk`, `Limestone`,..., `Quartzite`, and `Slate` classes—a different class for each kind of rock. Finally, because *classification* is a characteristic of all rocks, we will represent this using an attribute variable (of type `String`) in our `Rock` class and supply a `getClassification()` accessor method by which this attribute can be retrieved.

We have seen that in the real world, these rocks are related as follows:

❑ chalk, limestone, sandstone, and shale are *sedimentary* rocks;
❑ basalt, granite, and obsidian are *igneous* rocks; and
❑ marble, quartzite, and slate are *metamorphic* rocks.

Chalk, limestone, sandstone, and shale thus share certain attributes. To store these common attributes, we will build a `SedimentaryRock` class. By having the `Chalk`, `Limestone`, `Sandstone`, and `Shale` classes extend this class, they will inherit the common attributes.

As igneous rocks, basalt, granite, and obsidian all have common attributes, so we will build an `IgneousRock` class to store these attributes. If our `Basalt`, `Granite`, and `Obsidian` classes then extend this `IgneousRock` class, each will inherit the common attributes.

As metamorphic rocks, marble, quartzite, and slate also have common attributes, so we will build a `MetamorphicRock` class to store them. If the `Marble`, `Quartzite`, and `Slate` classes then extend the `MetamorphicRock` class, they will inherit these common attributes.

Finally, sedimentary, igneous, and metamorphic rocks are all *rocks,* meaning they have characteristics in common with one other. To consolidate those common characteristics in one place, we will build a `Rock` class to house such attributes, and then define `SedimentaryRock`, `IgneousRock`, and `MetamorphicRock` classes as extensions of class `Rock`.

We can summarize these relationships in a class hierarchy diagram:

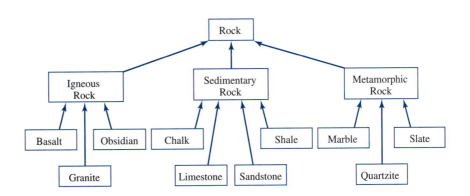

Each arrow in this diagram denotes the `extends` *or is-a relation* described in Section 11.2.

OPERATIONS. Once we have our classes organized into a hierarchy, we then want to identify the required operations and assign responsibility for them to particular classes. At the very least, each class should have

- ❑ A constructor
- ❑ Accessor methods for class attributes
- ❑ A `toString()` method to facilitate output

In addition to these operations, our program will display a *description* of a given rock. Since this seems likely to provide more details than a `String` representation of a rock, we will define a separate `getDescription()` method in each class.

Every rock has a classification—igneous, sedimentary, metamorphic. In the rock class, therefore, we will define an attribute variable for this classification and an accessor method for it.

A bit of research tells us that igneous rocks are categorized by (among other things) their *texture,* so we will define an attribute variable and accessor method within class `IgneousRock` to represent this information. Sedimentary rocks are categorized by (among other things) the *kinds of particles* from which they are formed, and so we will use an attribute variable and accessor method for it within class `Sedimentary-Rock`. Building a class for metamorphic rocks is left as an exercise.

We now have a class hierarchy, and the operations and attributes for each class in it. Together, these serve as a blueprint for building our system.

CODING. Figure 11.12 shows our Rock class. As before, our documentation of the classes is kept rather brief to save space in this text.

FIGURE 11.12   CLASS Rock

```
/** Rock.java provides a general Rock class to store a classification
 *   attribute common to all rocks .
 *   Methods are:  a constructor to create a Rock object from a String;
 *   an accessor method for the classification attribute;  a method that
 *   returns a description of the rock; and a to-String converter for
 *   output purposes.
 */

import ann.util.Controller;

class Rock extends Object
{
/** Rock constructor
 *   Receive:       String kind
 *   Postcondition:  myKind = kind or fatal error occurs if kind is invalid.
 */
 public Rock(String kind)
 {
   String theKind = kind.toLowerCase();
   if (theKind.equals("sedimentary")
      || theKind.equals("igneous")
      || theKind.equals("metamorphic") )
     myClassification = kind;
   else
     Controller.fatal("Rock(kind)", "invalid kind: " + kind);
 }

/** Classification accessor
 *   Return: classification */
 public String getClassification()
 {
   return myClassification;
 }

/** Description of rock
 *   Return: description of rock
 */
 public String getDescription()
 {
   return "a " + getClassification() + " rock";
 }

/** String converter
 *   Return: string representation of rock -- for output purposes */
 public String toString()
 {
   return getClass().getName()
         + " (a(n) " + getClassification() + " rock)";
 }

//--- Attribute variable ---
 private String myClassification;
}
```

Using our research to identify the valid textures for igneous rocks, we might define the `IgneousRock` class as shown in Figure 11.13.

FIGURE 11.13   CLASS `IgneousRock`

```
/** IgneousRock.java models igneous rocks, whose common attribute is texture.
 *  Methods are:  a constructor from a String; an accessor method for the
 *  texture attribute;  a method () that returns a description of the rock
 *  -- overloads inherited method.
 */

import Rock;
import ann.util.Controller;

class IgneousRock extends Rock
{
/** IgneousRock constructor
 * Receive:       String texture
 * Postcondition: myClassification == "Igneous" && myTexture == texture
 *                or fatal error occurs if texture is invalid.
 */
 public IgneousRock(String texture)
 {
   super("Igneous");
   if (texture.equals("glassy")
        || texture.equals("fine")
        || texture.equals("medium")
        || texture.equals("coarse") )
     myTexture = texture;
   else
     Controller.fatal("IgneousRock(texture)",
       "texture must be 'glassy', 'fine', 'medium', or 'coarse'");
 }

/** Texture accessor
 *  Return: texture */
 public String getTexture()
 {
   return myTexture;
 }

/** Description of rock
 *  Return: description of rock -- overrides inherited method */
 public String getDescription()
 {
   return "Igneous rocks are formed when magma or lava cools slowly,\n"
        + " and can be classified by granularity or texture.\n"
        + "Igneous rocks that cool underground are called 'intrusive'\n"
        + " and tend to have larger crystals or more coarse granularity.\n"
        + "Igneous rocks that cool at the surface are called 'extrusive'\n"
        + " and tend to have smaller crystals or finer granularity.";
 }

//--- Attribute variable ---
 private String myTexture;
}
```

Note that our `getDescription()` method provides generic information relevant to all igneous rocks. The subclasses of `IgneousRock` can then make use of this common information, and avoid redundant coding effort.

Using our research on the kinds of particles used to categorize sedimentary rocks, we might define class `SedimentaryRock` as shown in Figure 11.14.

FIGURE 11.14   CLASS `SedimentaryRock`

```
/** SedimentaryRock.java models sedimentary rocks, whose common attribute is
 *  the kind of particles in the rock.
 *  Methods are:  a constructor from a String; an accessor method for the
 *  particle attribute;  a method () that returns a description of the rock
 *  -- overloads inherited method.
 */

import Rock;
import ann.util.Controller;

class SedimentaryRock extends Rock
{
/** SedimentaryRock constructor
 * Receive:       String particleKind
 * Postcondition: myClassification == "Sedimentary"  &&
 *                myParticleKind == particleKind
 *                   or fatal error occurs if particleKind is invalid
 */
 public SedimentaryRock(String particleKind)
 { super("Sedimentary");
   if (particleKind.equals("clastic")
       || particleKind.equals("chemical")
       || particleKind.equals("organic") )
     myParticleKind = particleKind;
   else
     Controller.fatal("SedimentaryRock(particleKind)",
            " particleKind must be 'clastic', 'chemical', or 'organic'");
 }

/** Particle-kind accessor
 * Return: kind of particle */
 public String getParticleKind()
 {
   return myParticleKind;
 }

/** Description of rock
 * Return: description of rock -- overrides inherited method */
 public String getDescription()
 {
   return "Sedimentary rocks consist of layers of compacted particles,\n"
 + " which may be:\n"
 + "   'clastic' (wind, water or ice-born particles),\n"
 + "   'chemical' (particles precipitated from a water solution), or\n"
 + "   'organic' (particles precipitated or accumulated because of\n"
 + "             the activity of biological agents).";
 }
//---Attribute variable ---
 private String myParticleKind;
}
```

As before, we include a `getDescription()` method that provides a "generic" description suitable for all sedimentary rocks. The subclasses of `SedimentaryRock` can then each make use of this common description.

Dropping down in our hierarchy, we can define the `Basalt` class as shown in Figure 11.15.

FIGURE 11.15 CLASS Basalt

```
/** Basalt.java models basalt rocks.
 *  Methods are:  a default constructor;  a method () that returns a
 *  description of the rock -- overloads inherited method.
 */

class Basalt extends IgneousRock
{
/** Basalt constructor
 * Postcondition: myClassification (inherited) == "Igneous" &&
 *                myTexture (inherited) == "medium" */
 public Basalt()
 { super("medium"); }

/** Description of Basalt
 *  Return: description of basalt -- overrides inherited method */
 public String getDescription()
 {
   return "Basalt is an extrusive igneous rock with medium granularity.\n"
        + super.getDescription();

 }
}
```

This class definition is relatively simple, because it only includes the information unique to basalt—that it has *medium* granularity/texture. The properies that it has in common with other igneous rocks are inherited from class `IgneousRock`. Note that its `getDescription()` uses the call

```
        super.getDescription()
```

to invoke the `getDescription()` method from class `IgneousRock`. Thanks to this, the `Basalt` `getDescription()` method will return a description unique to `Basalt`, followed by the "generic" description that is common to all igneous rocks:

```
        Basalt is an extrusive igneous rock with medium granularity.
        Igneous rocks are formed when magma or lava cools slowly,
         and can be classified by granularity or texture.
        Igneous rocks that cool underground are called 'intrusive'
         and tend to have larger crystals or more coarse granularity.
        Igneous rocks that cool at the surface are called 'extrusive'
         and tend to have smaller crystals or finer granularity.
```

Thus, although it overrides the definition of `getDescription()`, it makes use of that definition to avoid redundant coding effort.

A `Chalk` class is similarly simple, but extends class `SedimentaryRock`, as shown in Figure 11.16.

Figure 11.16   Class Chalk

```
/** Chalk.java models chalk.
 *  Methods are:  a default constructor;  a method () that returns a
 *  description of the rock -- overloads inherited method.
 */

import SedimentaryRock;

class Chalk extends SedimentaryRock
{
/** Chalk constructor
 * Postcondition:  myClassification (inherited) == "Sedimentary" &&
 *                 myTexture (inherited) == "organic" */
 public Chalk()
 { super("organic"); }

/** Description of Chalk
 *  Return: description of chalk -- overrides inherited method */
 public String getDescription()
 {
    return "Chalk is an organic sedimentary rock\n"
           + " made from microscopic coccolith shells.\n"
           + super.getDescription();
 }
}
```

Here we use the same basic technique to avoid redundant coding: our `getDe-scription()` method returns a description unique to `Chalk`, followed by the "generic" description that is common to all sedimentary rocks. As a result, this method returns:

```
Chalk is an organic sedimentary rock
 made from microscopic coccolith shells.
Sedimentary rocks consist of layers of compacted particles,
 which may be:
     'clastic' (wind, water or ice-born particles),
     'chemical' (particles precipitated from a water solution), or
     'organic' (particles precipitated or accumulated because of
                the activity of biological agents).
```

We continue this process until each class in our hierarchy has been implemented in a similar fashion. Given such a hierarchy, we can then solve the rock classification problem with a fairly simple program, which is given in Figure 11.17.

Figure 11.17   Class RockClassifier

```
/** RockClassifier.java classifies rocks of various kinds.
 *  Input:  names of rocks
 *  Output: attributes of rocks
 */

import ann.easyio.*;                        // Screen, Keyboard
```

```
class RockClassifier extends Object
{
  public static void main(String [] args)
  {
    Screen theScreen = new Screen();
    Keyboard theKeyboard = new Keyboard();
    String rockString = "";
    Rock aRock = null;

    for (;;)
    {
      theScreen.print("\nTo see the attributes of a rock, enter its name\n'
                      + " (enter a non-rock to quit): ");
      rockString = theKeyboard.readWord();

      try
      {
        aRock = (Rock) Class.forName(rockString).newInstance();
      }
      catch (Exception anException)
      {
        System.exit(0);
      }

      theScreen.println("\n" + aRock.getDescription() );
    }
  }
}
```

Sample run:

```
To see the attributes of a rock, enter its name
 (enter a non-rock to quit): Chalk

Chalk is an organic sedimentary rock
  made from microscopic coccolith shells.
Sedimentary rocks consist of layers of compacted particles,
 which may be:
     'clastic' (wind, water or ice-born particles),
     'chemical' (particles precipitated from a water solution), or
     'organic' (particles precipitated or accumulated because of
               the activity of biological agents).

To see the attributes of a rock, enter its name
 (enter a non-rock to quit): Basalt

Basalt is an extrusive igneous rock with medium granularity.
Igneous rocks are formed when magma or lava cools slowly,
 and can be classified by granularity / texture.
Igneous rocks that cool underground are called 'intrusive'
 and tend to have larger crystals or more coarse granularity.
Igneous rocks that cool at the surface are called 'extrusive'
 and tend to have smaller crystals or finer granularity.

To see the attributes of a rock, enter its name
 (enter a non-rock to quit): Sandstone
```

```
    Sandstone is a clastic sedimentary rock made from quartz fragments.
    Sedimentary rocks consist of layers of compacted particles,
      which may be:
        'clastic' (wind, water or ice-born particles),
        'chemical' (particles precipitated from a water solution), or
        'organic' (particles precipitated or accumulated because of
                        the activity of biological agents).

    To see the attributes of a rock, enter its name
      (enter a non-rock to quit): quit
```

The structure of this program is quite simple, as the following algorithm shows:

ROCK CLASSIFICATION ALGORITHM

1. Prompt the user for the name of a rock.
2. Read the name of the rock into *rockString*.
3. Build an instance of the class whose name is stored in *rockString*.
4. Display the result of sending that object the *getDescription( )* message.

The only complicated part of this algorithm is in Step 3. To build an instance of a class from a `String` naming that class, we could have used a multi-branch `if` statement:

```
if (rockString.equals("Basalt"))
    aRock = new Basalt();

else if (rockString.equals("Granite"))
    aRock = new Granite();

...

else if (rockString.equals("Slate"))
    aRock = new Slate();

else
    System.exit(0);
```

While more familiar than the code in Figure 11.17, this approach has the disadvantage of "hard-wiring" the names of the rocks into our program. If we wish to add a new kind of rock at a later date, we must not only create a class for it, but also add a branch to this program's `if` statement to test for and create an instance of this new class.

The code in Figure 11.17 avoids this by using Java's `Class` class:

```
aRock = (Rock) Class.forName(rockString).newInstance();
```

Java's `Class` **class** provides various operations for manipulating classes. To illustrate, suppose that `rockString` is "Chalk". We pass `rockString` to the `forName()` class method, which, given a `String` naming a class, returns a `Class` object representing that class:

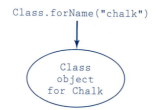

```
Class.forName("chalk")
```

Class
object
for Chalk

We then send that `Class` object the `newInstance()` message, which creates an actual instance of that class, and returns a reference to it:

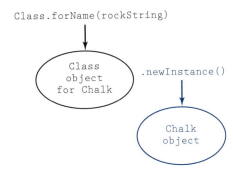

However, this reference is to an `Object`, and so it must be cast into our handle's type—`Rock` in this case. In general, one wants to cast to the type that is the nearest common ancestor of any of the classes being created—in this case `Rock`.

We can summarize this capability as follows:

Constructing An Object From A String

Form

 `Class.forName( StringVariable ).newInstance()`

where:
 `StringVariable` refers to a `String` containing the name of a class.

Purpose

Returns an instance of the class whose name is stored in *StringVariable*, created using the default constructor of that class. The `newInstance()` method returns that instance as an `Object` (and so it must be cast to an appropriate type, usually the nearest ancestor).

This technique allows us to enter the name of any of the rocks for which we have defined classes, and will then create an instance of that class. We will demonstrate this technique again in the next section, using file input.

11.4   EXAMPLE: AN O-O PAYROLL PROGRAM

Our earlier payroll programs in Chapters 2 and 5 were quite simple in that they calculated wages only for hourly employees. In this section we develop a somewhat more sophisticated payroll program for a company with different kinds of employees whose wages are determined in different ways. The program will be developed using the OOD principles we have considered thus far in this chapter.

PROBLEM

Ms. White and her students have decided to start a company named ComDot.com and have hired us to write a program to generate the monthly paychecks for their managers, secretaries, programmers, and consultants. Managers and programmers are paid a monthly salary, while secretaries and consultants are paid on an hourly basis. The relevant information about each employee is stored in a data file.

 ## OBJECT-ORIENTED DESIGN

BEHAVIOR. Our program should read a sequence of employees from an input file, (managers, secretaries, programmers, and consultants). It should compute their pay and print a paycheck for each employee, showing the employee's name, ID, and pay.

PROBLEM'S OBJECTS. From this description, we can identify the following objects in this problem:

Description of problem's object	Type	Kind	Name
Our program	`PayrollGenerator`	—	—
Employee sequence	`Employee []`	varying	*employee*
Input file (stream)	`BufferedReader( FileReader( fileName))`	varying	*empFile*
Input file name	`String`	varying	*args*[0]
Employee	`Employee`	varying	*employee*[*i*]
Managers	`Manager`	varying	—
Secretaries	`Secretary`	varying	—
Programmers	`Programmer`	varying	—
Consultants	`Consultant`	varying	—
Pay	`double`	varying	*employee*[*i*].*pay*()
Paycheck	`Paycheck`	varying	*paycheck*
Employee's name	`String`	varying	*employee*[*i*].*name*()

ANALYSIS. As salaried employees, managers and programmers have a common attribute: their *salary*. We will thus design a `SalariedEmployee` class to house this attribute, and define `Manager` and `Programmer` classes as extensions of this class.

As hourly employees, secretaries and consultants have common attributes: their *hourly wage,* and the number of *hours* they worked in a given pay period. We will thus design an `HourlyEmployee` class to house these attributes, and define `Secretary` and `Consultant` classes as extensions of this class.

In addition, salaried employees and hourly employees share common attributes: a name, ID number, pay, and so on. We will thus design an `Employee` class to house the information common to all employees, and define the `SalariedEmployee` and `HourlyEmployee` classes as extensions of this class.

While our `PayrollGenerator` will generate `Paycheck` objects, these classes have no common attributes, and so we will define them as extensions of the `Object` class. This gives the following class hierarchy:

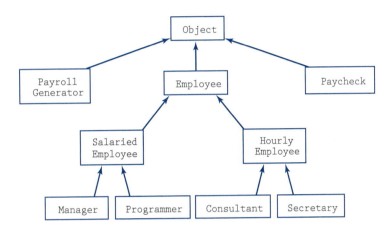

OPERATIONS. We can identify the following operations for our objects:

Operation	Responsibility of
i. Read a sequence of employees from a file (open a stream to a file,	`PayrollGenerator`
read an `Employee` from a stream, close a stream to a file)	`Employee`, subclasses
ii. Compute an employee's pay	`Employee`
iii. Construct a paycheck	`Paycheck`
iv. Access an employee's name	`Employee`
v. Access an employee's ID number	`Employee`
vi. Access an employee's pay	`Employee`, subclasses

`PayrollGenerator` will thus have two methods: `main()` and `readFile()`. The remaining methods will be distributed among the class hierarchy as shown below, along with suitable constructors and `toString()` methods:

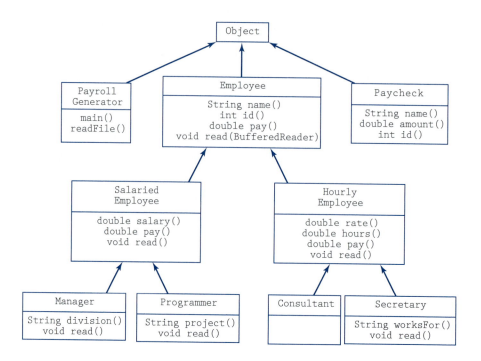

FILE FORMAT. The first line contains the number of employees. Subsequent lines contain information in employee records. Each record contains all of the attributes for a given employee, and different records contain different attributes; for example:

Number of employees	7
Employee #1 kind	Manager
Employee #1 name	Grumpy
Employee #1 id	4
Employee #1 salary	950.00
Employee #1 division	Javadoc
Employee #2 kind	Secretary
Employee #2 name	Bashful
Employee #2 id	1
Employee #2 wage	8.75
Employee #2 hours	40
Employee #2 works for	Grumpy
...	...

ALGORITHM. Given the class hierarchy, an algorithm for the payroll generator is quite simple:

Payroll Algorithm

1. Read the sequence of employee records from the input file into *employee* array.
2. For each index *i* of *employee*:
   a. Build a *paycheck* for *employee*[*i*].
   b. Output that *paycheck*.

CODING. We begin by encoding the Employee class, since it represents the common ancestor of most of our classes. Figure 11.18 presents its definition. (Note that to save space in this text, we are keeping documentation to a minimum in this example.)

FIGURE 11.18   CLASS Employee

```
/** Employee.java provides a class (abstract) to model employees.
 *   Attribute variables store an employee's name and ID number.
 *   Methods:  Constructors: default and one to construct an Employee
 *             from a name and ID number; accessors; to-string converter
 *             for output purposes; reader to read a name and ID number
 */

import java.io.*;    // BufferedReader, ...

abstract class Employee extends Object
{
 //--- Employee default constructor ---
 public Employee()
 {
   myName = "";
   myID = -1;
 }

 //--- Employee explicit-value constructor ---
 public Employee(String name, int id)
 {
   myName = name;
   myID = id;          // validation omitted
 }

 //--- Accessor methods ---
 public String name() { return myName; }
 public int id()      { return myID;   }

 //--- String converter (for output) ---
 public String toString() { return myName + "\n" + myID; }

//--- File input ---
 void read(BufferedReader reader)
 {
   try
   {
     myName = reader.readLine();
     myID   = new Integer(reader.readLine()).intValue();
   }
```

```
    catch (Exception error)
    {
      System.err.println("Employee:read(): " + error);
      System.exit(1);
    }
  }

  //--- Abstract pay method ---
  abstract public double pay();

  //--- Attribute variables ---
  private String myName;
  private int    myID;
}
```

Note that because an employee's pay is computed differently for salaried and hourly employees, we declare an abstract pay() method in class Employee so that pay() messages can be sent to an Employee handle. But only subclasses SalariedEmployee and HourlyEmployee will know how to compute their pay, and so we leave it to them to supply a definition for this method.

Figure 11.19 presents class SalariedEmployee.

FIGURE 11.19   CLASS SalariedEmployee

```
/** SalariedEmployee.java provides a subclass of Employee to model salaried
 *   employees. New attribute variable stores employee's salary.
 *   Methods: Constructors: default and one to construct a SalariedEmployee
 *            from a name, ID number, and salary;   accessors;
 *            pay calculator;  to-string converter for output purposes;
 *            reader to read a name, ID number, and salary.
 */

import Employee;
import java.io.*;                          // BufferedReader, ...

class SalariedEmployee extends Employee
{
  //--- SalariedEmployee default constructor ---
  public SalariedEmployee()
  {
    super();
    mySalary = 0.0;
  }

  //--- SalariedEmployee explicit-value constructor ---
  public SalariedEmployee(String name, int id, double salary)
  {
    super(name, id);
    mySalary = salary;
  }

  //--- Accessor methods ---
  public double salary() { return mySalary; }
  public double pay()    { return salary(); }

  //--- String converter (for output) ---
  public String toString()
  {
    return super.toString() + "\n" + mySalary;
  }
```

```
//--- File input ---
void read(BufferedReader reader)
{
  super.read(reader);
  try
  {
    mySalary = new Double( reader.readLine() ).doubleValue();
  }
  catch (Exception error)
  {
    System.err.println("SalariedEmployee:read(): " + error);
    System.exit(1);
  }
}

//--- Attribute variables ---
private double mySalary;
}
```

Note that the constructors use `super()` to initialize the inherited attribute variables. Similarly, the `toString()` and `read()` methods use `super.`*`methodName`*`()` to invoke the same method in the parent class to output and input the inherited attributes.

The `HourlyEmployee` class is similar, as shown in Figure 11.20.

FIGURE 11.20   CLASS `HourlyEmployee`

```
/** HourlyEmployee.java provides a subclass of Employee to model hourly
 *   employees. New attribute variable stores employee's salary.
 *   Constants: OVERTIME_THRESHOLD  = 40;  OVERTIME_FACTOR = 1.5
 *   Methods: Constructors: default and one to construct an HourlyEmployee
 *     from a name, ID number, hourly rate, and hours worked;
 *     accessors;  pay calculator;
 *     to-string converter for output purposes;
 *     reader to read a name,ID number, hourly rate, and hours worked
 */

import Employee;
import java.io.*;                         // BufferedReader, ...

class HourlyEmployee extends Employee
{
 public final static double OVERTIME_THRESHOLD  = 40;
 public final static double OVERTIME_FACTOR     = 1.5;

 //--- HourlyEmployee default constructor ---
 public HourlyEmployee()
 {
   super();
   myHourlyRate = myHours = 0.0;
 }

 //--- HourlyEmployee explicit-value constructor ---
 public HourlyEmployee(String name, int id, double rate, double hours)
 {
   super(name, id);
   myHourlyRate = rate;
   myHours = hours;
 }
```

```
//--- Accessor methods ---
public double hourlyRate() { return myHourlyRate; }
public double hours()      { return myHours; }

//--- Pay for hourly employee ---
public double pay()
{
  if (myHours <= OVERTIME_THRESHOLD)
    return myHours * myHourlyRate;
  else
    return OVERTIME_THRESHOLD * myHourlyRate +
           (myHours - OVERTIME_THRESHOLD) *
             myHourlyRate * OVERTIME_FACTOR;
}

//--- String converter (for output) ---
public String toString()
{
  return super.toString() + " " + myHourlyRate + " " + myHours;
}

//--- File input ---
void read(BufferedReader reader)
{
  super.read(reader);
  try
  {
    myHourlyRate = new Double(reader.readLine()).doubleValue();
    myHours = new Integer(reader.readLine()).intValue();
  }
  catch (Exception e)
  {
    System.err.println("HourlyEmployee:read() " + e);
    System.exit(1);
  }
}

//--- Attribute variables ---
private double myHourlyRate;
private double myHours;
}
```

Note the difference in the `pay()` definitions for `SalariedEmployee` and `HourlyEmployee`. We define each method as appropriate for its respective class, and rely on polymorphism for proper handling of `pay()` messages.

Descending a level in our hierarchy, we build the `Manager` class as shown in Figure 11.21.

FIGURE 11.21   CLASS Manager

```
/** Manager.java provides a subclass of SalariedEmployee to model
 *  managers.  New attribute variable stores manager's division.
 *  Methods: Constructors: default and one to construct a SalariedEmployee
 *           from a name, ID number, salary, and division;  accessors;
 *           to-string converter for output purposes;
 *           reader to read a name, ID number, salary, and division
 */

import SalariedEmployee;
import java.io.*;                          // BufferedReader, ...

class Manager extends SalariedEmployee
{
 //--- Manager default constructor ---
 public Manager()
 {
   super();
   myDivision = "";
 }

 //--- Manager explicit-value constructor ---
 public Manager(String name, int id, double salary, String division)
 {
   super(name, id, salary);
   myDivision = division;
 }

 //--- Accessor method ---
 public String division() { return myDivision; }

 //--- String converter (for output) ---
 public String toString()
 {
   return super.toString() + " " + division();
 }

 //--- File input ---
 void read(BufferedReader reader)
 {
   super.read(reader);
   try
   {
     myDivision = reader.readLine();
   }
   catch (Exception e)
   {
     System.err.println("Manager:read(): " + e);
     System.exit(1);
   }
 }

 //--- Attribute variable ---
 private String myDivision;
}
```

As before, our child class is responsible for providing the functionality related to its own attributes, and relies on the inherited methods to provide the functionality related to inherited attributes.

Figure 11.22 presents our `Programmer` class.

FIGURE 11.22   CLASS Programmer

```
/** Programmer.java provides a subclass of SalariedEmployee to model
 *   programmers. New attribute variable stores programmer's project.
 *   Methods: Constructors: default and one to construct a SalariedEmployee
 *            from a name, ID number, salary, and project;  accessors;
 *            to-string converter for output purposes;
 *            reader to read a name, ID number, salary, and project
 */

import SalariedEmployee;
import java.io.*;                          // BufferedReader, ...
class Programmer extends SalariedEmployee
{
 //--- Programmer default constructor ---
 public Programmer()
 {
   super();
   myProject = "";
 }

 //--- Programmer explicit-value constructor ---
 public Programmer(String name, int id, double salary, String project)
 {
   super(name, id, salary);
   myProject = project;
 }

 //--- Accessor method ---
 public String project() { return myProject; }

 //--- String converter (for output) ---
 public String toString()
 {
   return super.toString() + "\n" + myProject;
 }

 //--- File input ---
 public void read(BufferedReader reader)
 {
   super.read(reader);
   try
   {
     myProject = reader.readLine();
   }
   catch (Exception e)
   {
     System.err.println("Programmer.read(): " + e);
     System.exit(1);
   }
 }

 //--- Attribute variable ---
 private String myProject;
}
```

The other child classes Secretary and Consultant are similar to these, and their implementations are left as exercises.

The next class we will build is the Paycheck class, which is presented in Figure 11.23.

FIGURE 11.23   CLASS Paycheck

```
/** Paycheck.java provides a class to model paychecks.
 *  New attribute variables store a name, check amount, and ID number.
 *  Methods: Constructors: to construct a Paycheck from an Employee
 *     accessors; to-string converter for output purposes;
 */

import Employee;
import java.text.*;          // NumberFormat

class Paycheck extends Object
{
 //--- Paycheck constructor ---
 public Paycheck(Employee employee)
 {
   myName   = employee.name();
   myAmount = employee.pay();
   myID     = employee.id();
 }

 //--- Accessor methods ---
 public String name()    { return myName; }
 public double amount()  { return myAmount; }
 public int id()         { return myID; }

 //--- String converter (for output) ---
 public String toString()
 {
   NumberFormat cf = NumberFormat.getCurrencyInstance();
   String formattedAmount = cf.format(myAmount);
   return myName + "\t\t" + formattedAmount + "\n" + myID;
 }

 //--- Attribute variables ---
 private String myName;
 private double myAmount;
 private int    myID;
}
```

Since the paycheck's amount is a monetary value, we use the NumberFormat class method getCurrencyInstance(), which creates a number formatter set up to format monetary values. We then send that object the format() message accompanied by the amount we want formatted, which returns a String with the appropriate format. We then display this String, accompanied by the other relevant information for a pay check.

Given these classes, writing our PayrollGenerator is straightforward, as shown in Figure 11.24.

FIGURE 11.24   CLASS PayrollGenerator

```
/** PayrollGenerator.java calculates wages and prepares paychecks
 *  for employees:
 *  Input:  employee records (from a file)
 *  Output: paycheck information
 */

import Employee;
import Paycheck;
import java.io.*;            //BufferedReader, FileReader, ...
```

```
class PayrollGenerator
{
public static void main(String [] args)
{
   Employee [] employee = readFile(args[0]);

   for (int i = 0; i < employee.length; i++)
   {
      Paycheck check = new Paycheck(employee[i]);
      System.out.println(check + "\n");
   }
 }

public static Employee [] readFile(String fileName)
{
  BufferedReader empFile = null;
  int numberOfEmployees = 0;
  Employee [] result = null;

  try
  {
    empFile = new BufferedReader(
             new FileReader(fileName));

    numberOfEmployees = new Integer(empFile.readLine()).intValue();
    result = new Employee[numberOfEmployees];

    int i = 0;

    String className = "";
    for (;;)
    {
      String blankLine = empFile.readLine(); // eat blank line
      className = empFile.readLine();

      if (className == null || className == ""    // end of stream
          || i == result.length)                  // end of array
        break;

      result[i] = (Employee) Class.forName(className).newInstance();

      result[i].read(empFile);
      i++;
    }

    empFile.close();
  }
  catch (Exception e)
  {
      System.err.println(e); System.exit(1);
  }
  return result;
 }
}
```

Sample Input File: employees.txt

```
7

Manager
Grumpy
4
950.00
Java
```

```
Secretary
Bashful
1
8.00
45
Happy

Programmer
Happy
5
850.00
Java IDE

Consultant
Doc
2
15.90
20

Programmer
Sneezy
7
850.00
Java Debug

Consultant
Dopey
3
0.50
40

Programmer
Sleepy
6
900.00
Java Threads
```

Sample Run:

<u>java PayrollGenerator employees.txt</u>

```
Grumpy          $950.00
4

Bashful         $380.00
1

Happy           $850.00
5

Doc             $318.00
2

Sneezy          $850.00
7

Dopey           $20.00
3

Sleepy          $900.00
6
```

While not trivial, this payroll program is relatively simple. In fact, reading the employees from the input file is the most complex part, because of the complexity of Java's file-I/O mechanism. Even so, the `readFile()` method is much simpler than it might be, thanks to the following statements:

```
className = reader.readLine();

if (className == null || className == ""    // end of stream
        || i == result.length)              // end of array
   break;

result[i] = (Employee) Class.forName(className).newInstance();

result[i].read(reader);
```

The first line reads the name of the class from the input file (e.g., `Manager`, `Secretary`, etc.). After checking for end-of-file, the next line creates an instance of that class, using the `Class.forName().newInstance()` mechanism discussed in the preceding section. Once we have created an instance of the particular class, we send it the `read()` message, which (thanks to polymorphism) invokes the `read()` method in the newly created object.

Note that if the company decides to hire a janitor, all we have to do is

1. Build a `Janitor` class that extends `SalariedEmployee` or `HourlyEmployee`
2. Hire a janitor and add his/her data to the data file

That's it! Nothing else needs to be modified in order to add new kinds of *Employees* to the system. The cost of maintaining this system can't get much lower!

> *OOD lets you build sophisticated systems in which*
>
> ❑ *existing objects can have their implementations modified, or*
> ❑ *new objects can be added to the system,*
>
> *without having to modify existing parts of the system.*

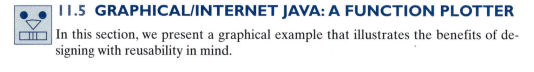

11.5 GRAPHICAL/INTERNET JAVA: A FUNCTION PLOTTER

In this section, we present a graphical example that illustrates the benefits of designing with reusability in mind.

PROBLEM

We want to develop a function-plotting program that high school (and other) mathematics students might use to visualize the behavior of functions. It should allow the user to select a function to be plotted as well as a range of values. It should also be relatively easy to modify the program to include new functions.

OBJECT-ORIENTED DESIGN

BEHAVIOR. The program should provide a graphical user interface that allows the user to select any of several different functions to display on a Cartesian grid. The program should also allow the user to adjust the axes, specify the color used to plot a function, and clear the grid.

PRELIMINARY SKETCHES. Here is a preliminary sketch of our graphical user interface:

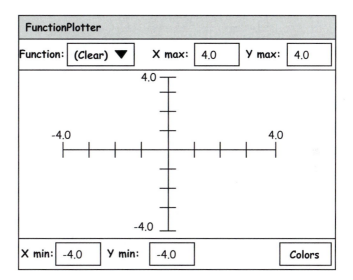

The component next to the label "Function:" is called a `JComboBox`. Although it looks like a button, clicking on it displays a scrollable drop-down menu, from which the user can select any of a number of choices. We will use this component to list the functions supported by our program:

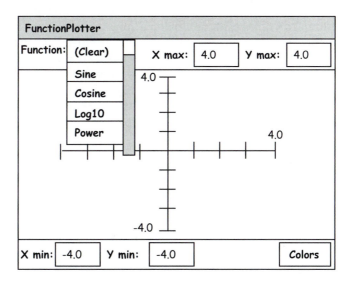

Whatever function the user selects from this list will then be drawn on the grid:

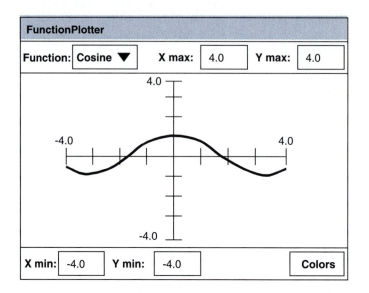

The four text boxes specifying the minimum and maximum *x* and *y* coordinates will allow the user to dynamically adjust the endpoints of the axes, providing a primitive "zoom" capability. The button on the lower-right corner will bring up a JColor-Chooser, which is a Java Swing dialog component that allows the user to select a particular drawing color.

In implementing this GUI, we will make use of a reusable custom component CartesianPanel class to provide the axes and point-plotting capabilities needed for the central panel of our GUI. We have defined this class in our ann.gui package as an extension of a JPanel.

NOTE   As we have seen before, when Java's Swing components are used to draw custom graphics, each component that must draw something on-screen should do so within (and only within) a method named paintComponent(). Because the CartesianPanel class already has a paintComponent() method defined, we should not modify it to draw our functions, because doing so could cause problems for other classes that use CartesianPanel. Instead, we can create a class that *extends* CartesianPanel, and override the paintComponent() method in this subclass to draw the functions. We will call this new class FunctionPanel. We can picture the relationships between these classes as follows:

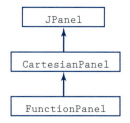

Since `CartesianPanel` already exists and we intend to define `FunctionPanel` as an extension of it, the only remaining unresolved design issue is how to take advantage of object-oriented design to facilitate future maintenance of this system. One obvious future enhancement is to add support for adding more functions. How can we design the system to make this as easy as possible?

As we saw in section 11.4, OOD provides an answer to this question. Each of the functions to be plotted (sine, cosine, tangent, ln, . . .) *is a* function. If instead of thinking of these functions as *operations* and view them as *objects,* we can build a class to represent each function. In terms of a class hierarchy, we can visualize this as follows:

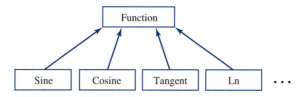

Perhaps you are wondering why we are doing it this way. Why don't we just use calls to the methods in Java's `Math` class? The answer is that this approach can take advantage of polymorphism. For the problem at hand, we must be able to determine the value of each function for a given *x*-value. Assuming that the name of the function the user has selected is stored in a `String` variable `functionName`, we could write:

```
if ( functionName.equals("Sine") )           // this works, BUT
   y = Math.sin(x);
else if ( functionName.equals("Cosine") )   // it is much more
   y = Math.cos(x);
else if ( functionName.equals("Tangent") )   // work to maintain
   y = Math.tan(x);
   .
   .
   .
```

But this is not easy to maintain; adding a new function requires adding another branch to this `if-else-if` structure and then recompiling the program.

By contrast, our O-O approach is to have each function class provide a polymorphic `valueAt()` method that, given an *x*-value, returns the value of the function for that *x*-value. This will allow us to write

```
Function myFunction
      = (Function) Class.forName(functionName).newInstance();
      . . .
y = myFunction.valueAt(x);
```

This requires no `if-else-if` structure, and adding a new function requires only defining a class for it and adding the name of the function to the `JComboBox` used in the GUI for function selection. This makes it easy to add an arbitrary function, thus simplifying maintenance of the application.

CODING—FUNCTION CLASSES. We begin with the function hierarchy. We define the ancestral `Function` class as shown in Figure 11.25. (Once again, to save space, our documentation is quite brief.)

FIGURE 11.25 CLASS Function

```
/** Function.java provides a class (abstract) that models arbitrary
 *  mathematical functions.
 *  Methods:  Compute the function's value at a given value x;
 *            string converter for output purposes
 */

abstract public class Function extends Object
{
 //-- Abstract method to compute function's value at x
 public abstract double valueAt(double x);
 //-- String converter -- for output
 public String toString()
 {
   return getClass().getName() + "(x)";
 }
}
```

By providing the `toString()` method as given, each subclass of `Function` will inherit a useful `toString()` behavior, provided that the name of that subclass is the name of the function. Additional methods can be added, as desired.

We will define just a few subclasses of `Function`, and leave others for the exercises. Our first subclass is the `Sine` class, which is given in Figure 11.26.

FIGURE 11.26 CLASS Sine

```
/** Sine.java provides a subclass of Function for the sine function.
 *  Method:  Compute the value of sine at x
 */

public class Sine extends Function
{
 //-- Method to compute Sine's value at x
 public double valueAt(double x) { return Math.sin(x); }
}
```

The `Cosine` class is similarly easy, as shown in Figure 11.27.

FIGURE 11.27 CLASS Cosine

```
/** Cosine.java provides a subclass of Function for the cosine function.
 *  Method:  Compute the value of cosine at x
 */

public class Cosine extends Function
{
 //-- Method to compute Cosine's value at x
 public double valueAt(double x) { return Math.cos(x); }
}
```

The body of the `valueAt()` method can, of course, be as complicated as we wish. For example, Java's `Math` class provides no base-10 logarithm function, but it does have a natural log function `log()`. We can use this to define a `Log10` class that provides the base-10 logarithm behavior as shown in Figure 11.28.

FIGURE 11.28   CLASS `Log10`

```
/** Log10.java provides a subclass of Function for the base-10 logarithm
 *   function.
 *   Method:    Compute the base-10 logarithm of x
 */
public class Log10 extends Function
{
 //-- Method to compute Log10's value at x
 public double valueAt(double x)
 {
   if (x > 0.0)
     return Math.log(x) / Math.log(10);
   else
     return Double.NEGATIVE_INFINITY;
 }
}
```

Each class can thus be as complex as needed to provide the behavior of a particular function. For example, to provide the behavior of the exponentiation function x^n, we need the value of the exponent n. We can have the class constructor use a dialog to get this value from the user, as shown in Figure 11.29.

FIGURE 11.29   CLASS `Power`

```
/** Power.java provides a subclass of Function for a power function.
 *   Attribute:  The exponent (myN) to be used
 *   Methods:    Input the exponent;    access the exponent myN;
 *               Compute x to the power myN
 */

import javax.swing.*;        // JOptionPane

public class Power extends Function
{

 //-- Power constructor
 public Power()
 {
   String nString = JOptionPane.showInputDialog("To compute x^n, enter n:")
   if (nString != null && nString != "")              // Cancel button
     myN = Double.parseDouble(nString);
 }
 //-- Method to compute Power's value at x and myN; i.e., x^myN
 public double valueAt(double x)
 {
   return Math.pow(x, myN);
 }

 //--- Accessor method ---
 public double getN() { return myN; }

 //--- Attribute variable ---
 private double myN;
}
```

Given this class, the statement

```
Function myFunction
    = (Function) Class.forName(functionName).newInstance();
```

where `functionName` is "Power", will invoke the `Power` constructor, which will display an input dialog to input the exponent; the constructor will then store this value in its attribute variable `myN`. The statement

```
y = myFunction.valueAt(x);
```

will then invoke the `valueAt()` method which will call `Maths`'s `pow()` function to calculate and return the value of x^{myN}.

THE `ColoredFunction` CLASS. To build in the capability of changing the color of a function, we use a wrapper class that encapsulates a `Function` and a `Color` into a single class. (This also makes it possible to modify the function plotter so that several functions can be plotted on the same set of axes using colors to distinguish them. This is left as an exercise.) Figure 11.30 shows the `ColoredFunction` class.

FIGURE 11.30   CLASS `ColoredFunction`

```
/** ColoredFunction.java provides a class to encapsulate a Function
 *   and a Color.
 *   Attributes: a Function and a Color
 *   Methods:  Construct a ColoredFunction from a Function and a Color;
 *             accessors; protected mutators
 */

import Function;
import java.awt.Color;
class ColoredFunction extends Object
{
  //--- ColoredFunction constructor ---
  public ColoredFunction(Function aFunction, Color aColor)
  {
    myFunction = aFunction;
    myColor = aColor;
  }

  //--- Accessor and mutator methods ---
  //---    To get/set myFunction:
  public Function getFunction() { return myFunction; }
  protected void setFunction(Function aFunction) { myFunction = aFunction; }

  //---    To get/set myColor:
  public Color getColor() { return myColor; }
  protected void setColor(Color aColor) { myColor = aColor; }

  //--- Attribute variables ---
  private Color myColor;
  private Function myFunction;
}
```

THE `FunctionPanel` **Class.** Having decided how to organize and implement the functions that are to be plotted, we turn now to the problem of actually drawing a function's graph. This will be accomplished using the `FunctionPanel` class. Its only attribute variable is the `Function` it draws:

```
class FunctionPanel extends CartesianPanel
{
 // ... methods ...
 private Function myFunction;
}
```

It provides a constructor, a mutator for this attribute variable, a `clear()` method to erase the function, and the `paintComponent()` method to draw its function. Figure 11.31 presents the complete class definition.

FIGURE 11.31   CLASS FunctionPanel

```
/** FunctionPanel.java provides a FunctonPanel class for plotting functions.
 *  Attribute: ColoredFunction object being plotted
 *  Methods:   default constructor;  paintComponent() to draw the function
 *             clear the function;  accessor;    mutator;
 */

import ann.gui.CartesianPanel;
import ColoredFunction;
import java.awt.*;              // Graphics, Color, ...

class FunctionPanel extends CartesianPanel
{
 //--- FunctionPanel constructor ---
 public FunctionPanel()
 {
    super();
    setBackground(Color.white);
    myColoredFunction = null;
 }

 //--- paintComponent method ---
 public void paintComponent(Graphics pen)
 {
   super.paintComponent(pen);

   if (myColoredFunction != null)
   {
     pen.setColor( myColoredFunction.getColor() );
     Function theFunction = myColoredFunction.getFunction();
     for (double x = minX(); x <= maxX(); x += deltaX() )
       pen.fillRect( xToColumn(x), yToRow( theFunction.valueAt(x) ), 2, 2);
   }
 }

 //--- Erase the function ---
 public void clear()
 {
   myColoredFunction = null;
   repaint();
 }

 //--- Mutator to set myFunction ---
 public void setFunction(ColoredFunction aFunction)
 {
   myColoredFunction = aFunction;
 }

 //--- Attribute variable ---
 private ColoredFunction myColoredFunction;
}
```

The most complex part of this class is the `paintComponent()` method. The first line

```
super.paintComponent(pen);
```

sends the `paintComponent()` message to its superclass (i.e., the `CartesianPanel` class), which paints the background. *Every definition of* `paintComponent()` *must begin with this statement, or the background of the component will not be painted.* Following this, our method sets the `Graphics` system's pen color, and then plots its `ColorFunction`.

The complications occur because the various drawing methods in Java's `Graph- ics` class draw in the screen's space of (integer) rows and columns, and treat the point (0,0) as the upper-left corner of the component:

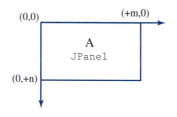

This *screen space* is different from the *user space* of (real) *x*- and *y*-values that comprise a Cartesian coordinate system:

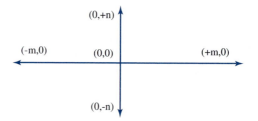

To hide the differences, we have built a `CartesianPanel` class that provides methods to map user-space (*x, y*) values into the graphics system's screen-space (*column, row*) values in a way that gracefully handles window resizing and similar events. Table 11.1 provides a partial list of the functionality provided by our `CartesianPanel` class. Unless specified otherwise, all argument types are `double`.

The class `FunctionPanel` is defined as an extension of `CartesianPanel`, and it thus inherits all of these methods. In particular, its `paintComponent()` method invokes `CartesianPanel`'s `paintComponent()` method with the statement

```
super.paintComponent();
```

TABLE 11.1   SOME `CartesianPanel` METHODS

`CartesianPanel` **Method**	**Description**
`CartesianPanel()`	Build a Cartesian coordinate system whose lower-left corner is $(-4, -4)$ and whose upper-right corner is $(4,4)$
`CartesianPanel(x1, y1, x2, y2)`	As in the preceding, but with lower-left corner $(x1, y1)$ and upper-right corner $(x2, y2)$
`xToColumn(x)`	Return the (`int`) screen column corresponding to x
`yToRow(y)`	Return the (`int`) screen row corresponding to y
`deltaX()` `deltaY()`	Return the (`double`) change in x for 1 screen column y for 1 screen row
`minX()` `minY()` `maxX()` `maxY()`	Return the (`double`) minimum x-value minimum y-value maximum x-value maximum y-value
`resetAxis(x1, y1, x2, y2)`	Change the axis so that its lower-left corner is $(x1, y1)$ and its upper-right corner is $(x2, y2)$
`resetAxis(p1, p2)`	Change the axis so that its lower-left corner is $p1$ and its upper-right corner is $p2$, which are both of type `Point`
`setAxisVisible(b)`	Show the axes if b (`boolean`) is true; otherwise hide it
`getAxisVisible()`	Return the visibility status (`boolean`) of the axes
`clear()`	Clear the grid of anything that has been drawn (except for the axes)
`setPenColor(c)`	Set the drawing color to c (of type `Color`)
`getPenColor()`	Return the current drawing `Color`
`paintComponent(pen)`	Paint the background, including the axes if the visibility status of the axes is true

to set the background color and draw the axes. It also uses some of these methods in its for loop that plots the function. For each point on the *x*-axis, `paintComponent()` uses the `Graphics` class `fillRect()` method to draw a 2-by-2 filled rectangle at user-coordinates (x, theFunction.valueAt(x)):

```
for (double x = minX(); x <= maxX(); x += deltaX() )
   pen.fillRect( xToColumn(x),
                 yToRow( theFunction.valueAt(x) ), 2, 2);
```

However, x and theFunction.valueAt(x) are *user-space* coordinates, and the arguments to fillRect() must be *screen-space* coordinates. As a result, these values must be mapped to the screen-space coordinates, using the mapping methods inherited from CartesianPanel:

```
for (double x = minX(); x <= maxX(); x += deltaX() )
   pen.fillRect( xToColumn(x),
                 yToRow( theFunction.valueAt(x) ), 2, 2);
```

Note also the use of minX(), maxX(), and deltaX() methods to control the repetition of the for loop.

THE FunctionPlotter CLASS. The sketches of our function-plotting GUI show text areas where the user will enter *x*- and *y*-values and a button labeled *Color*. These will be implemented with the Swing components JTextField and JButton, both of which fire ActionEvent events. This means that our FunctionPlotter class must implement the ActionListener interface and define the actionPerformed() method. Because it has a JComboBox, which fires ActionEvent events (and also ItemEvent events), we will handle the JComboBox events with the same actionPerformed() method.

We can thus start with the following skeleton class:

```
public class FunctionPlotter extends CloseableFrame
                  implements ActionListener
{
   public FunctionPlotter() {}
   public void actionPerformed(ActionEvent event) {}
   public static void main(String [] args) {}

   // ... details to be filled in ...
}
```

THE FunctionPlotter CONSTRUCTOR. As we have seen, building the GUI and initializing its attribute variables is the role of the constructor method. Here again is how we want our GUI to look. Accomplishing this requires a bit of thought.

Ignoring the title bar, we see that our GUI consists of 3 distinct panels.

❑ A *top panel* containing JLabel components "Function:", "X max:" and "Y max:", the JComboBox of functions, and JTextField components to store the maximum *x* and *y* values.

❑ A *grid panel* containing the axes and on which the functions will be plotted.

❑ A *bottom panel* containing JLabel components "X min:" and "Y min:", JTextField components to store the minimum *x* and *y* values, and a JButton by which the user can select the color in which a function's graph is drawn.

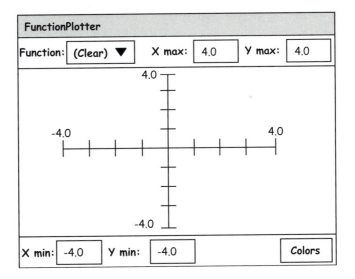

We will use `JPanel` components for the top and bottom panels, and a `Function-Panel` component (as described previously) for the grid panel.

Building the top and bottom panels takes a bit of work. In the top panel, we want the `JLabel` containing the string `"Function:"` and the `JComboBox` to be left-justified and the other components to be right-justified. But in the bottom panel, we want the `JButton` to be right-justified and the other components to be left-justified.

The easiest way to achieve this is to group the `JLabel` containing `"Function:"` and the `JComboBox` in its own `JPanel` and each set of `Jlabel` and `JTextBox` components into its own `JPanel`. That is, in the top panel, we build a "function-control" `JPanel` and add the components to it:

Then we build a "maximum" `JPanel` and add components to it:

Following this, we can build the top `JPanel` using a `BorderLayout` by adding the function-control `JPanel` at its left (west) side, and add the preceding panel at its right (east) side:

The bottom panel is similar:

We can thus add several following attribute variables to the `FunctionPlotter` class for these various components:

```
import java.awt.*;                    // BorderLayout, ...
import java.awt.event.*;              // ActionListener, ...
import javax.swing.*;                 // JLabel, JComboBox, ...
import ann.gui.CloseableFrame;
import FunctionPanel;

public class FunctionPlotter extends CloseableFrame
                             implements ActionListener
{
  public FunctionPlotter() {}
  public void actionPerformed(ActionEvent event) {}
  public static void main(String [] args) {}

  //—- Attribute variables —-
  private JLabel          myFunctionLabel,
                          myXLoLabel, myXHiLabel,
                          myYLoLabel, myYHiLabel;

  private JTextField      myXLoField, myXHiField,
                          myYLoField, myYHiField;

  private JComboBox       myFunctionComboBox;

  private JButton         myColorButton;

  private JPanel          myPanel,
                          myTopPanel, myBottomPanel,
                          myFunctionPanel,
                          myLoPointPanel, myHiPointPanel;

  private FunctionPanel myGrid;

  private Color           myPenColor;
}
```

THE `FunctionPlotter` CONSTRUCTOR. Once we have identified the attribute variables, the constructor must initialize these variables and build the graphical user interface as shown in Figure 11.32. This is a lengthy method and writing it is time-consuming, but it is not particularly difficult, once we have a design in mind to implement:

FIGURE 11.32 FunctionPlotter CONSTRUCTOR

```java
public FunctionPlotter()
{
 public FunctionPlotter()
 {
   myGrid = new FunctionPanel();

   myFunctionLabel = new JLabel("Function: ", SwingConstants.RIGHT);
   final String [] functionStrings = {"(Clear)", "Sine", "Cosine",
                                      "Log10", "Power"
                                      // add additional functions here
                                     };

   myFunctionComboBox = new JComboBox(functionStrings);
   myFunctionComboBox.setSelectedIndex(0);                    // (Clear)
   myFunctionComboBox.addActionListener(this);

   myFunctionPanel = new JPanel( new FlowLayout() );
   myFunctionPanel.add(myFunctionLabel);
   myFunctionPanel.add(myFunctionComboBox);
   myXHiLabel = new JLabel ("max X: ", SwingConstants.RIGHT);
   myXHiField = new JTextField(4);
   myXHiField.setText( Double.toString( myGrid.maxX() ) );
   myXHiField.addActionListener(this);
   myYHiLabel = new JLabel("max Y: ", SwingConstants.RIGHT);
   myYHiField = new JTextField(4);
   myYHiField.setText( Double.toString( myGrid.maxY() ) );
   myYHiField.addActionListener(this);

   myHiPointPanel = new JPanel( new FlowLayout() );
   myHiPointPanel.add(myXHiLabel); myHiPointPanel.add(myXHiField);
   myHiPointPanel.add(myYHiLabel); myHiPointPanel.add(myYHiField);

   myTopPanel = new JPanel( new BorderLayout() );
   myTopPanel.add(myFunctionPanel, BorderLayout.WEST);
   myTopPanel.add(myHiPointPanel, BorderLayout.EAST);

   myXLoLabel = new JLabel("min X: ", SwingConstants.RIGHT);
   myXLoField = new JTextField(4);
   myXLoField.setText( Double.toString( myGrid.minX() ) );
   myXLoField.addActionListener(this);
   myYLoLabel = new JLabel("min Y: ", SwingConstants.RIGHT);
   myYLoField = new JTextField(4);
   myYLoField.setText( Double.toString( myGrid.minY() ) );
   myYLoField.addActionListener(this);

   myLoPointPanel = new JPanel( new FlowLayout() );
   myLoPointPanel.add(myXLoLabel); myLoPointPanel.add(myXLoField);
   myLoPointPanel.add(myYLoLabel); myLoPointPanel.add(myYLoField);

   myColorButton = new JButton("Colors");
   myColorButton.addActionListener(this);
   myBottomPanel = new JPanel( new BorderLayout() );
   myBottomPanel.add(myLoPointPanel, BorderLayout.WEST);
   myBottomPanel.add(myColorButton, BorderLayout.EAST);

   myPanel = new JPanel( new BorderLayout() );
   myPanel.add(myTopPanel, BorderLayout.NORTH);
   myPanel.add(myGrid, BorderLayout.CENTER);
   myPanel.add(myBottomPanel, BorderLayout.SOUTH);
   setContentPane(myPanel);

   myPenColor = Color.black;
 }
```

THE `actionPerformed()` METHOD. Because the JButton, JComboBox, and various JTextField components fire ActionEvents, we implement the Ac-tionListener interface and define the `actionPerformed()` method to specify how to respond to such events.

Because we have multiple kinds of components that could be the source of the event, we will use the `instanceof` operator to determine which of the following actions the user performed:

- ❑ Clicked the JButton, in which case we use a JColorChooser dialog to let the user change the pen's color
- ❑ Pressed *Enter* in one of the JTextField components, in which case we read the value of each JTextField and update the axes in the CartesianPanel accordingly
- ❑ Selected an item from the menu in the JComboBox

Figure 11.33 implements this behavior.

FIGURE 11.33   METHOD `actionPerformed()`

```
public void actionPerformed(ActionEvent event)
{
  Object eventSource = event.getSource();
  if (eventSource instanceof JTextField)      // JTextField
  {
    String xMinString = myXLoField.getText(),
           yMinString = myYLoField.getText(),
           xMaxString = myXHiField.getText(),
           yMaxString = myYHiField.getText();
    double xMin = Double.parseDouble(xMinString),
           yMin = Double.parseDouble(yMinString),
           xMax = Double.parseDouble(xMaxString),
           yMax = Double.parseDouble(yMaxString);

    myGrid.resetAxis(xMin, yMin, xMax, yMax);
    repaint();
  }

  else if (eventSource instanceof JButton)    // Colors button
  {
    Color newColor
       = JColorChooser.showDialog(this, "Pick a color:", myPenColor);
    if (newColor != null)    // guard against "Cancel"
      myPenColor = newColor;
  }
```

```
else  // JComboBox
{
  String myFunctionString = (String) myFunctionComboBox.getSelectedItem();
  if ( myFunctionString.equals("(Clear)") )
    myGrid.clear();
  else  // it's a Function
  {
    try
    {
      Function theFunction
        = (Function) Class.forName(myFunctionString).newInstance();
      ColoredFunction theColoredFunction
        = new ColoredFunction(theFunction, myPenColor);
      myGrid.setFunction(theColoredFunction);
      repaint();
    }
    catch (Exception e)
    { System.err.println(e);}
  }
}
}
```

If the event source was a `JTextField`, we read the four `JTextField` values, use the `resetAxis()` message to ask the `FunctionPanel` to resize its axes, and then call `repaint()` to update the display. If the event source was the `Color` button, we use the Swing `JColorChooser` class to let the user select a color, and then send the `FunctionPanel` the `setPenColor()` message to modify its drawing color.

Otherwise, the `JComboBox` triggered the event. According to the `JComboBox` API documentation, we can send a `JComboBox` the `getSelectedItem()` message to find out which of its entries was selected. Since "`(Clear)`" is not a function, we first check for it and invoke the `CartesianPanel`'s `clear()` method if it was selected. Otherwise, a function must have been selected, so we:

a. Build an instance of that `Function`

b. Construct a `ColoredFunction` object from that `Function` object and the current pen color

c. Send the `FunctionPanel` the `setFunction()` message to set its `Colored-Function` attribute variable

d. Call `repaint()` to invoke the `paintComponent()` method in the `Function-Panel`, updating the display

THE `main()` METHOD. To complete our class, we need only add a `main()` method, which is given in Figure 11.34.

That's it! Our class is now ready to use.

FIGURE 11.34   METHOD `main()`

```
public static void main(String [] args)
{
  FunctionPlotter myGUI = new FunctionPlotter();
  myGUI.setSize(400,500);
  myGUI.setVisible(true);
}
```

TESTING. When we run our application, we get this initial view:

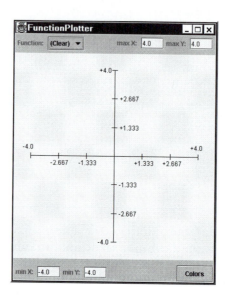

If we click on the JComboBox, the menu of functions is displayed:

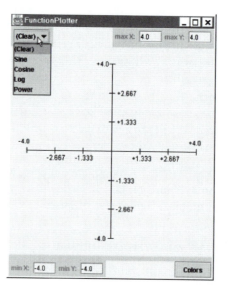

If we select the *Sine* function, our itemStateChanged() method builds an instance of and plots the Sine function:

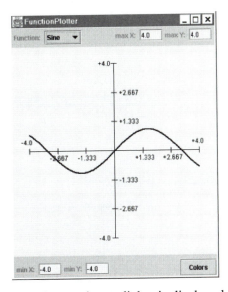

If we select the *Power* function, an input dialog is displayed in which the user can enter the exponent:

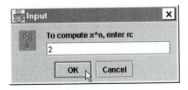

After the user clicks the OK button or presses the Enter key, the graph of the function ($y = x^2$ in this case) is plotted:

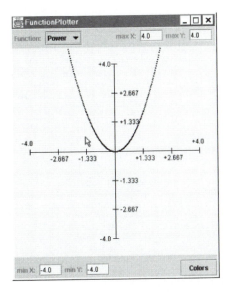

If we click on the *Color* button, our `actionPerformed()` method displays a `JColorChooser`:

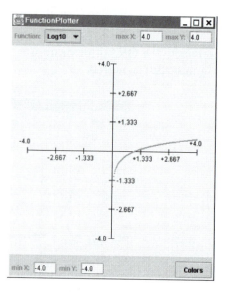

This allows the user to change the pen color. After this, the graphs will be drawn in whatever color was selected:

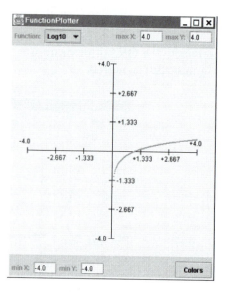

CHAPTER SUMMARY

KEY TERMS AND NOTES

abstract class	Java class hierarchy
abstract method	object-centered design (OCD)
ancestor classes	object-oriented design (OOD)
behavioral variance	parent class
child class	polymorphism
`Class` class	`protected`
class hierarchy	qualifying a method name
descendant classes	random integer
`extends` relationship	root
`getClass()` method	`subclass`
handle	`super`
I can do it myself principle	superclass
inheritance	transitive property
is-a relationship	

◎   When a class B extends another class A,

```
class B extends A
{ ... }
```

   B **is a** *specialization* **of** A; simply stated, every B object *is an* A object.

◎   A child class *inherits* the characteristics (attribute variables and methods) of its parent class.

◎   Inheritance is a very powerful technique that can be used to eliminate redundant coding effort.

◎   A handle for a class *C* can store a reference to any object whose class is a descendant of *C*.

◎   A message sent to an object of class *C* to use method *m*( ) is processed as follows:

   If there is a definition of *m*() in class *C*, then that definition is invoked;

   Otherwise, the parent of class *C* is searched for a definition of *m*( ),

   continuing on through the ancestors of *C*, until either a definition is found or a

   `NoSuchMethodException` is thrown.

◎   When a message is sent to an object to use method *m*( ), any messages that *m*( ) sends will also be sent to that same object.

◎   If an object receiving a message has a definition of the requested method, that definition is invoked. If the object does not have a definition, an inherited definition is invoked.

◎   Any time that an inherited method does not supply the desired behavior, a class should override that method with a definition that does supply the desired behavior.

◎ *Polymorphism* directly supports the "I can do it myself" principle of object-oriented programming, because when a message is sent to an object, polymorphism ensures that the right method—the one defined in that object's class—is invoked.

◎ In Java, every class (except `Object`) must be an extension of some other class. If a programmer does not specify an `extends` relationship for a class, then that class extends the `Object` class by default.

◎ Hierarchy design is a *bottom-up* process; implementing the design proceeds *top-down*.

◎ A child class constructor can invoke a constructor in its parent class by using the keyword `super`.

◎ If an attribute is declared as `protected`, then users of the class cannot access the attribute, but descendants of the class can.

◎ If a child class overrides a method `m()` inherited from its parent class and wishes to invoke the inherited method, the notation `super.m()` can be used.

◎ Java's `Class` class provides various operations for manipulating classes.

Documentation

REFERENCE The class `Object` is at the very top (root) of the Java class hierarchy. Thus, *all* classes inherit the methods in `Object`. The following table gives some of the more commonly used ones. See Java's API documentation for more.

■ **SOME** `Object` **METHODS** (`java.lang`)

Method	Description
`Object clone()`	Creates and returns a copy of the receiver
`boolean equals(Object obj)`	Returns true or false according to whether or not the receiver is equal to `obj`
`Class getClass()`	Returns an object of type `Class` that represents the runtime class of the receiver
`String toString()`	Returns a string representation of the receiver

Instances of the class `Class` represent classes (and interfaces) in a running Java application. They are constructed automatically by the Java Virtual Machine as classes are loaded. The following table lists only a few of the most useful methods in `Class`. See Java's API documentation for more.

■ **SOME Class METHODS (java.lang; EXTENDS Object)**

Method	Description
`static Class forName` `(String className)`	Returns the `Class` associated with the class (or interface) whose name is `className`.
`String getName()`	Returns the fully-qualified name of the class (or interface, array class, primitive type, or `void`) represented by the receiver
`Class getSuperclass()`	Returns the `Class` representing the superclass of the receiver
`boolean isArray()`	Returns true or false according to whether the receiver is an array class
`String toString()`	Returns a string representation of the receiver
`Object newInstance()`	Creates a new instance of the class represented by the receiver

■ **SOME Random METHODS (java.util; EXTENDS Object)**

Method	Description
`Random()`	Constructs a new random number generator
`Random(long seed)`	As above, but using a seed

`boolean nextBoolean(),`
`double nextDouble(),`
`flost nextFloat(),`
`double nextGaussian(),`
 	
`int nextInt(),`
`int nextInt(int n),`
`long nextLong()`
	Returns the next random
	  `boolean` value,
	  `double` value,
	  `float` value,
	  Gaussian (normally distributed)
	    `double` value,
	  `int` value,
	  `int` value in the range 1 through n,
	  `long` value

`void nextBytes((byte[] bytes)`	Generates random bytes and places them into a user-supplied `byte` array bytes

■ `CartesianPanel` **METHODS** (`ann.gui`)

Method	Description
`CartesianPanel()`	Build a Cartesian coordinate system with lower-left corner at $(-4,-4)$ and upper-right corner at $(4,4)$
`CartesianPanel(double x1, double y1, double x2, double y2)`	As above, but with lower-left corner at $(x1,y1)$, and upper-right corner at $(x2,y2)$
`double minX()`	Retrieve minimum x-value
`double minY()`	Retrieve minimum y-value
`double maxX()`	Retrieve maximum x-value
`double maxY()`	Retrieve maximum y-value
`double deltaX()`	Retrieve x-value for 1 screen column
`double deltaY()`	Retrieve y-value for 1 screen row
`int round(double x)`	Round x to nearest integer
`int xToColumn(double x)`	Map x to a screen column
`int yToRow(double y)`	Map y to a screen row
`void setAxisVisible(boolean b)`	Show the axes if b is true; hide otherwise
`boolean getAxisVisible()`	Return the visibility status of the axes
`void paintComponent(Graphics pen)`	Paint panel's background, including axes if visibility status of axes is true
`void clear()`	Erase all points and lines (but not the axes)
`void setPenColor(Color newColor)`	Change drawing color to `newColor`
`Color getPenColor()`	Return current drawing color
`void resetAxis(double x1, double y1, double x2, double y2)`	Change axes so lower-left corner is at $(x1, y1)$ and upper-right corner is at $(x2, y2)$
`void resetAxis(Point p1, Point p2)`	Change axes so lower-left corner is at $p1$ and upper-right corner is at $p2$

☞ PROGRAMMING POINTERS

PROGRAM STYLE AND DESIGN

1. *Every class inherits the attributes and methods of its ancestor classes.* In particular, every class inherits all of the attributes and methods of the Object class. This makes it possible to avoid a good deal of "reinventing the wheel;" reuse the characteristics of a class by extending it.

2. *A handle for a class can be used to refer to any object whose class is a descendant class.* For example, if class C is an extension of class B which is an extension of class A, and the handle x is declared by A x = new A();, then x can invoke any public method in A, any public method in B, and any public method in C.

3. *Suppose* obj *of type* C *is sent a message* obj.m(). *If* C *has a definition of method* m(), *that method will be invoked. Otherwise, the parent class of* C *will be searched for a definition of* m() *to invoke, continuing on through the ancestors of* C, *until either a definition of* m() *is found or a* NoSuchMethodException *is thrown.*

4. *Objected-oriented design (OOD) consists of the following steps:*

   a. *Identify the objects.*
      - ❏ *If an object cannot be directly represented using the existing type:*
        Design a class to do so.
      - ❏ *If two or more classes share common attributes:*
        Design a class hierarchy to store their common attributes.

   b. *Identify the operations.*

      If an operation cannot be performed using an existing operator or method:
      - ❏ *Define a method to do so.*
      - ❏ *Store that method within a class hierarchy so as to take advantage of inheritance.*
      - ❏ *Where necessary, have subclasses override inherited definitions.*

   c. *Organize the objects and operations into an algorithm.*

5. *Using inheritance merely to avoid some code writing is not acceptable. A class B should extend another class A only when the following are true:*
   - ❏ *Every B is an A; that is, B's are specialized A's.*
   - ❏ *All methods in A work appropriately in B.*

   Another useful test for deciding whether B can extend A:
   - ❏ *If all that is needed in some situation is an A, then a B can be used.*

6. *When it should be possible to send a message to a class but there is no clear way to define the corresponding method in that class, then either: (a) Define a generic method within the class that provides some default behavior and let subclasses override it when necessary or (b) Declare the method within the class as* abstract, *and leave it up to the subclasses to supply the specific behavior.*

7. *If an attribute can be stored in an attribute variable and retrieved using an accessor method, then do so in such a way as to exploit inheritance and avoid redundant coding.*

8. *When it is necessary to allow descendant classes to change the value of an attribute variable in an ancestor class, keep the attribute variable private (rather than declaring it pro-*

tected) and define a protected mutator method that checks new values and thus ensures the validity of changes to these attribute variables.

POTENTIAL PITFALLS

1. *Every class (except* `Object`*) must extend some other class.* If no `extends` clause is used in declaring a class, the default superclass is `Object`.

2. *A class that has at least one abstract method is an abstract class. Important features of an abstract class C are:*

   ❑ *There are no C objects (i.e., no instances of C).*
   ❑ *If an abstract method m() is declared but not defined in C, then m() must be defined in subclasses of C (or declared to be abstract).*
   ❑ *If an abstract method m() is defined in C, this definition serves as the default definition of m() in subclasses of C.*

3. *Because it invokes a constructor, the* `super()` *method can only be invoked in another constructor method. It must be the first statement in that method, so that the inherited attribute variables are initialized before any normal (non-inherited) attribute variables.*

4. *Private attribute variables (and methods) in a class cannot be accessed in descendant classes.* Either make them `protected`, or provide protected mutators in a parent class as described in Program Design and Style Guideline 8.

5. *To invoke an inherited method that is overridden in a subclass, one must qualify the method name with the prefix* `super`.

PROGRAMMING PROBLEMS

SECTION 11.2

1. Write a program to test the license classes and subclasses in Exercises 23 and 24.

2. Add three more subclasses from Exercise 14 to the license class hierarchy and extend the program in Problem 1 to test them.

3. Write a program to test the bank account classes and subclasses in Exercises 25 and 26.

4. Add three more subclasses from Exercise 15 to the bank account class hierarchy and extend the program in Problem 3 to test them.

For Problems 5–9, build and test a class hierarchy for the given collection of objects. Use attributes and methods that provide a simple, but realistic, model of the objects.

5. Geometric figures (Exercise 12).

6. Animals (Exercise 13).

7. Motorized vehicles (Exercise 20).

8. Computer equipment (Exercise 21).

9. Shoes (Exercise 22).

SECTION 11.3

10. Metamorphic rocks are formed when other rocks change—undergo a metamorphosis—because temperature, pressure, or fluids produce changes in texture and mineral structure. They are categorized as being *foliated* or *non-foliated*. In foliated rocks, certain minerals are aligned to produce lines or bands through the rock; non-foliated rocks do not have this layered look. Add a class `MetamorphicRock` to the `Rock` hierarchy to model metamorphic rocks.

11. Slate is a very fine-grained foliated metamorphic rock that resembles shale. It is often dark gray in color and produces a ringing sound when you strike it. Add a class `Slate` to the `Rock` hierarchy to model slate.

12. Marble is a non-foliated metamorphic rock whose dominant mineral is calcite (or dolomite). Its parent rock is limestone (or dolostone). Add a class `Marble` to the `Rock` hierarchy to model marble.

13. Quartzite is a non-foliated metamorphic rock made up of interlocking grains of quartz. Its parent rock is quartz sandstone. Add a class `Quartzite` to the `Rock` hierarchy to model quartzite.

For Problems 14–15, find information about the rock and add an appropriate class to the `Rock` hierarchy to model it.

14. Peat

15. Soapstone

16. Pumice

SECTION 11.4

17. Add the `Secretary` class to the employee hierarchy. Use a program like the payroll generator in Figure 11.24 to test your class.

18. Add the `Consultant` class to the employee hierarchy. Use a program like the payroll generator in Figure 11.24 to test your class.

19. Add a class to the employee hierarchy for a new category of employees who are paid on a contract basis. Each such employee is paid a specified amount for a certain task performed. For example, reviewers check documentation, advertising materials, and so on and are paid a specified amount for each document.

20. Add a class to the employee hierarchy for reviewers as described in Problem 19.

SECTION 11.5

For Problems 21–28, add the specified class to the collection of functions that can be plotted by the function-plotting program in this section.

21. A class `Tangent` for the trigonometric tangent function

22. A natural logarithm class `Ln`

23. An absolute value class `Abs`

24. A straight line class `Line` for a line $y = mx + b$, with slope m and y-intercept b

25. A class `Floor` for a function $floor(x)$ = greatest integer $\leq x$

26. A class `Ceiling` for a function $ceiling(x)$ = least integer $\geq x$

27. A class `Round` for a function that rounds x to the nearest integer

28. A class `Polynomial` for an arbitrary polynomial function

$$p(x) = a_0 + a_1x + a_2x^2 + \ldots + a_nx^n$$

where the coefficients $a_0, a_1, a_2, \ldots, a_n$ are real numbers

29. Modify the function-plotting program so that it can display several different function graphs simultanously with different colors.

DATA STRUCTURES

I've got a little list, I've got a little list. *Gilbert and Sullivan, The Mikado*

He's making a list, and checking it twice, gonna' find out who's naughty or nice . . .
Christmas Carol: Santa Claus Is Coming To Town

. . . is the sort of person who keeps a list of all of his lists. *V. Orehck III (fictitious)*

I think that I shall never see,
A poem lovely as a tree. *Joyce Kilmer*

Woodman, spare that tree! *George Pope Morris*

■ Chapter Contents

Chapter Objectives

- Study collection classes provided in Java—`ArrayList` and `LinkedList`, in particular
- Show how to build collection classes
- Study the important data structures stack and queue
- Learn about linked structures, both linked lists and binary trees
- Learn how to design and implement linked structures and use them to build other structures
- See how collection classes are used in graphical programming

In Chapter 9, we learned about Java's *array* mechanism for storing sequences of values. An array that can hold `capacity` values with a specified `type` can be created with a statement of the form

```
type [] anArray = new type [ capacity ];
```

A drawback to this mechanism is that once allocated, the capacity of the array is fixed and cannot be changed. This implies that to store a sequence of values in an array, we must know the maximum number of values there are in the sequence before we allocate the array. Otherwise:

- ❑ If the capacity of the array exceeds the number of values to be stored in it, memory will be wasted by the unused elements.
- ❑ If the capacity of the array is smaller than the number of values to be stored in it, the problem of array overflow will occur.

To circumvent this inconvenience, the Java class hierarchy provides a variety of **collection classes.** Like an array, each collection class can store a group of values. Unlike an array, however, a collection can grow and shrink as a program runs. In this chapter, we examine two of these collection classes: `ArrayList` and `LinkedList`. We will also build two other collections: a `Stack` class and a `Queue` class. To illustrate different ways of building collection classes, we will build a `Stack` class using a `LinkedList`, but build a `Queue` class "from scratch" as well as a `PointList` class, using a linked structure to store points in a plotting window. We will also describe a linked tree structure, focusing on binary search trees.

12.1   INTRODUCTORY EXAMPLE: COUNTING INTERNET ADDRESSES

The TCP (Transmission Control Protocol) and IP (Internet Protocol) communication protocols specify the rules computers use in exchanging messages across the Internet. One of the problems TCP/IP must solve is to uniquely identify every computer on the Internet. TCP/IP actually provides support for *two* different names for each computer:

- ❑ **A host name** that is meaningful to humans.
- ❑ **An IP address** that is meaningful to computers.

For example, at the time of this writing, `titan.ksc.nasa.gov` is the host name of a computer at the NASA Kennedy Space Center, whose IP address is `163.205.195.1`. A host name is made up of fields that represent specific parts of the Internet:

```
host.subdomain.subdomain.rootdomain
```

By contrast, an IP address is a 32-bit value, usually represented in *dotted-decimal notation* by separating the 32 bits into four 8-bit fields, expressing each field as a decimal integer, and separating the fields with a period:

```
163.205.195.1
```

PROBLEM

A **gateway** is a device used to interconnect two different computer networks, for example, a university network and the Internet. Mr. Nimda Krowten is the network administrator at I.O. University, and part of his job is to monitor connections through this gateway. Each time a connection is made through the gateway (for example, a student using the World Wide Web), the IP address of the student's computer is automatically logged in a file. Mr. Krowten has asked us to write a program that he can use to periodically check this file to see who has used the gateway and how many times they have used it.

Solution

The IP addresses will be read from the file and stored in a sequence of *address counters*. Each address counter will store an address and the number of times that address appeared in the file. As each address is read, we check to see if it is already in the sequence. If it is, we increment its count by 1; otherwise, we simply append a new address counter for that address to the end of our sequence. After all the addresses in the file have been read, each address counter is displayed, to show its distinct address and count.

Figures 12.1 and 12.2 use this approach to solve the problem. Figure 12.1 presents an `AddressCounter` class that we have implemented to store an IP address and its count.

FIGURE 12.1. CLASS AddressCounter

```
/** AddressCounter.java defines a class for storing an IP address and *
 *  its count. (See GatewayUsageCounter.java.)
 *  Attributes: maximum message length (static), address, and count
 *  Methods:    Construct an AddressCounter from a string representation of
 *              an address; equals() to compare addresses; count incrementer;
 *              accessors of address and count; to-string converter for output
 */

public class AddressCounter extends Object
{
/* AddressCounter constructor
 * Receive:       String anAddress
 * Postcondition: myAddress == anAddress && myCount == 1
 */
```

```
   public AddressCounter(String anAddress)
   {
     myAddress = anAddress;
     myCount = 1;
   }


 /* equals method
  * Receive:  Object anObject
  * Return:   true if this object is same as anObject
  */
  public boolean equals(Object anObject)
  {
    if (anObject instanceof AddressCounter)
    {
      AddressCounter otherCounter = (AddressCounter) anObject;
      return myAddress.equals( otherCounter.getAddress() );
    }
    else
      return false;
  }


 /* method to increment count
  * Postcondition:  myCount is incremented by 1.
  */
 public void incrementCount()
  {
    myCount++;
  }

 //--- Accessors ---
 /* count
  * Return: myCount */
  public int getCount()        { return myCount; }


 /* address
  * Return: myAddress */
  public String getAddress() { return myAddress; }


 /* String converter -- for output purposes
  * Return:  String representing an AddressCounter */
 public String toString()
  {
    String spaces = "";
    int spacesNeeded = MAX_ADDRESS_LENGTH - myAddress.length();
    for (int i = 0; i < spacesNeeded; i++)
      spaces += " ";
    return myAddress + spaces + ": " + myCount;
  }


 //--- Attribute variables ---
  private static int MAX_ADDRESS_LENGTH = 15;  // 12 digits + 3 dots
  private String      myAddress;
  private int         myCount;
 }
```

Figure 12.2 presents the `GatewayUsageCounter` class, which uses this `Address-Counter` class to count the occurrences of each IP address in the input file. Because we cannot anticipate how many IP addresses there are, we cannot store the sequence of address counters in an array. Instead, we use Java's `ArrayList` class which can be thought of as an array that can grow (and shrink) during program execution.

FIGURE 12.2.   CLASS `GatewayUsageCounter`

```java
/** GatewayUsageCounter.java counts IP Addresses using an ArrayList.
 *  Receive:           name of text file via args
 *  Input (from file): IP addresses
 *  Output:            table of distinct IP addresses and number of times
 *                     they appear in the file
 */

import java.util.ArrayList;
import java.io.*;
import ann.util.Controller;
import AddressCounter;


class GatewayUsageCounter extends Object
{
 public static void main(String [] args)
 {
   if (args.length < 1)
     Controller.fatal("GatewayUsageCounter.main()",
                     " usage: java GatewayUsageCounter <input-file>");

   try
   {
     BufferedReader in = new BufferedReader(
                           new FileReader( args[0] ) );
     String theAddress = null;
     ArrayList addressSequence = new ArrayList();
     AddressCounter anAddressCounter = null;
     int index;

     for (;;)
     {
        theAddress = in.readLine();
        if (theAddress == null)
          break;
        else if ( theAddress.equals("") )
          continue;
        else
        {
           anAddressCounter = new AddressCounter(theAddress);
           index = addressSequence.indexOf(anAddressCounter);
           if (index < 0)
              addressSequence.add(anAddressCounter);
           else
             ((AddressCounter)addressSequence.get(index)).incrementCount();
        }
     }
```

```
          System.out.println("\nGateway Accesses by IP Address\n\n"
                        + "-------------------------\n"
                        + "IP Address     : Accesses\n"
                        + "-------------------------");

     for (int i = 0; i < addressSequence.size(); i++)
        System.out.println( addressSequence.get(i) );
   }
   catch (Exception e) { System.err.println(e); }

    }
}
```

Sample Input file: `addressLog.txt`

```
128.159.4.20
123.111.222.333
123.111.222.333
100.1.4.31
34.56.78.90
120.120.120.120
123.111.222.333
123.111.222.333
77.66.55.44
100.1.4.31
101.202.303.404
101.202.303.404
123.111.222.333
128.159.4.20
```

Sample run:

```
C:\> java GatewayUsageCounter addressLog.txt

Gateway Accesses by IP Address

-------------------------
IP Address     : Accesses
-------------------------
128.159.4.20    : 2
123.111.222.333: 5
100.1.4.31      : 2
34.56.78.90     : 1
120.120.120.120: 1
77.66.55.44     : 1
101.202.303.404: 2
```

In the next section, we discuss Java's `ArrayList` class and the related `LinkedList` class in detail.

12.2   THE `ArrayList` AND `LinkedList` CLASSES

It is frequently necessary to store a collection of values in a single container. We have seen that Java *arrays* can be used to store sequences of values when the maximum number of values in the sequence is known in advance. However, it often happens that the number of values in the sequence cannot be anticipated; it can vary greatly from one data set to another. In such cases, one of Java's **collection classes,** which can grow and shrink, can be used to store the sequence.

As its name implies, a collection class is a class that can store a group of objects. Java provides three different kinds of collection classes, each with its own particular features that make it better suited for some collections than others:

- ❏ **Lists:** for storing collections of objects, some of which may be the same
- ❏ **Sets:** for storing collections of objects, with no duplicates
- ❏ **Maps:** for storing collections of pairs, each of which associates a *key* with an *object*

In Java, List, Set and Map are all *interfaces* that are implemented by other classes. The Java API documentation describes each of these collection interfaces in detail, as well as classes that implement them.

In this section, we will focus on implementations of the List interface. Some of the methods that must be defined to implement it are given in Table 12.1; see the Java API documentation for others. In the descriptions, the receiver refers to the object for which the method is invoked.

TABLE 12.1   SOME List METHODS

Method	Description
add(*obj*)	Append *obj* to receiver
add(*index*, *obj*)	Insert *obj* into receiver at position *index*
clear()	Remove all objects from receiver
contains(*obj*)	Return true if receiver contains *obj* and false otherwise
equals(obj)	Return true if receiver and *obj* are the same and false otherwise
get(*index*)	Return the object in receiver at position *index*
indexOf(*obj*)	Return the position of the first occurrence of *obj* in receiver (or −1 if not present)
isEmpty()	Return true if receiver contains no objects and false otherwise
listIterator()	Return a ListIterator for the elements of receiver
lastIndexOf(*obj*)	Return the position of the last occurrence of *obj* in receiver (or −1 if not present)
remove(*index*)	Remove and return the object at position *index* in receiver
remove(*obj*)	Remove the first occurrence of *obj* in receiver (if any), return true if *obj* did occur, false otherwise
set(*i*, *obj*)	Replace object in receiver at position *i* with *obj*; return the object that was there
size()	Return the number of objects that the receiver contains

`subList(i, j)`	Return the sublist of objects in the receiver from positions *i* to *j*
`toArray()`	Return an `Object` array representation of objects in the receiver

We will compare and contrast two implementations of the `List` interface: the `ArrayList` class and the `LinkedList` class.

The `ArrayList` Class

As its name suggests, `ArrayList` is a class that implements the `List` interface using an array. As such, it implements each of the `List` operations in Table 12.1, using an array of `Object`s to store the collection's values. It also adds additional operations that are described in the API documentation.

By using an `Object` array, an `ArrayList` can store *any* reference type, since all reference types are classes that (directly or indirectly) extend `Object`. The downside of this is that an `ArrayList` cannot *directly* store the primitive types (`int`, `char`, `double`, etc.), although it can *indirectly* store them by storing instances of their wrapper classes (`Integer`, `Character`, `Double`, etc.).

To illustrate, the program in Figure 12.2 uses an `ArrayList` named `addressSequence`. The statement

```
ArrayList addressSequence = new ArrayList();
```

defines `addressSequence` as a handle for an empty `ArrayList`, which we might visualize as follows:

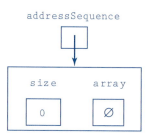

On the first pass through the input loop in Figure 12.2, we read an address (`128.159.4.20`), build an `AddressCounter` for it, and send this `ArrayList` the `indexOf()` message to search for that `AddressCounter`:

```
anAddressCounter = new AddressCounter(theAddress);
index = addressSequence.indexOf(anAddressCounter);
```

Since the `ArrayList` is empty, this method returns −1. The subsequent `if` statement:

```
if (index < 0)
    addressSequence.add(anAddressCounter);
```

```
else
    ((AddressCounter) addressSequence.get(index) ).incrementCount();
```

sends the `ArrayList` the `add()` message to append `anAddressCounter`. To do this, it first allocates an array of some (implementation-dependent) capacity *m*, makes the first element of the array refer to the `AddressCounter`, and then updates the *size* attribute of the `ArrayList`:

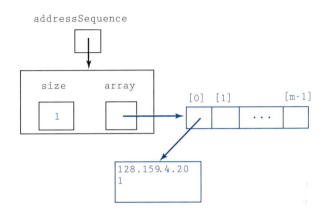

Note that in addition to its array, an `ArrayList` has two additional attributes:

❏ *size* attribute, which is the number of values currently in the `ArrayList`

❏ *capacity* attribute, which is the number of values the `ArrayList` *can* store (*m*)

The *capacity* need not be stored in an attribute variable because the array has a *length* attribute that provides this information.

On the second pass through the input loop, we read the second address (123.111.222.333), build an `AddressCounter` for it, and send `addressSequence` the `indexOf()` message to search for the newly read address. Since it is not there, `indexOf()` returns −1, and we again send the `add()` message to `addressSequence`. This time `add()` simply places the object to be added in the next available array location and then updates its *size* attribute:

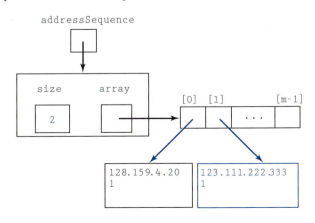

On the third pass through the input loop, we read the next address (123.111.222.333), build an AddressCounter for it, and send our ArrayList the indexOf() message to search for this address. Since addressSequence contains this address, indexOf() returns its index (1), and so the if statement sends the AddressCounter at index 1 the incrementCount() message:

```
if (index < 0)
   addressSequence.add(anAddressCounter);
else
   ((AddressCounter) addressSequence.get(index) ).incrementCount();
```

This actually involves several steps. The get() method in addressSequence is invoked to get the object at position index:

```
((AddressCounter) addressSequence.get(index) ).incrementCount();
```

We need to increment the counter in this object by 1. However, an ArrayList is an Object array, and an Object does not "understand" the incrementCount() message. Consequently, we must first *cast* this object to something that does have an incrementCount() method, namely an AddressCounter:

```
((AddressCounter) addressSequence.get(index) ).incrementCount();
```

Once this has been done, we can invoke the incrementCount() in the resulting AddressCounter to increment its *count* attribute (stored in myCount):

```
((AddressCounter) addressSequence.get(index) ).incrementCount();
```

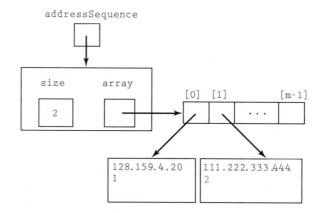

Note that the ArrayList's *size* attribute did not change since no new values were added to it.

Execution continues in this manner until all of the values in the input file have been read, adding new addresses to the `ArrayList`, and updating the count attribute of those already in the list. The final result is something like this:

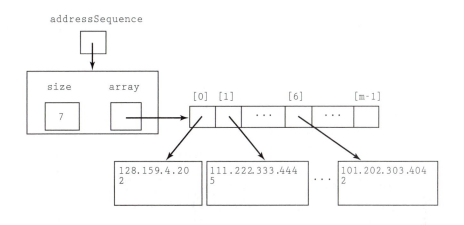

For a larger input file, the `AddressList`'s array may become full:

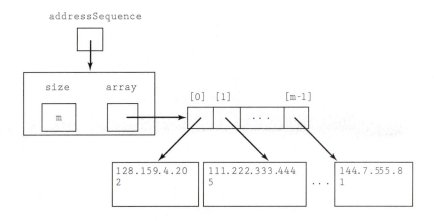

In this case, if the `add()` method is invoked to add a new object, the `ArrayList` will replace its array with a larger one:

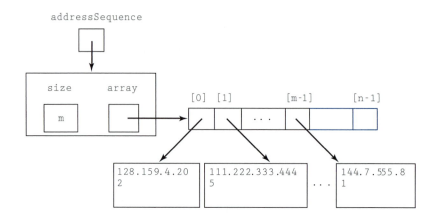

Accomplishing this is actually a 3-step process:

1. A new array of size $n > m$ is allocated
2. The values from the old array are copied into the new array
3. The old array is replaced by the new array

Because all of this is carried out "behind the scenes" by ArrayList's add() method, the details of how it is accomplished need not concern us here.

Once input is completed, execution moves on to the output loop:

```
for (int i = 0; i < addressSequence.size(); i++)
    System.out.println( addressSequence.get(i) );
```

The number of repetitions through the loop is determined by invoking the Ar-rayList's size() method. To actually output the entries in the ArrayList, we send it the get() message to retrieve the object at each index i and then pass this value to the println() method which, as we have seen, sends it the toString() message. Thanks to polymorphism, this invokes the toString() message in the Ad-dressCounter class, which formats and displays its *address* and *count* attributes.

An ArrayList Drawback. Although ArrayLists are easy to use to store sequences of values, they do have limitations. These arise from using an array to store the values. One limitation is that values can be efficiently added only at the *back* of the ArrayList. If there are empty components at the end of the array, the add() method simply adds a value at the *back* of the sequence:

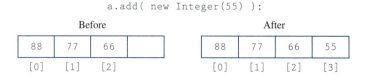

Appending a value to an `ArrayList` using `add()` does not require moving any values already in the list.[1]

The `ArrayList` class also implements another form of `List`'s `add()` method,

```
add(index, object)
```

which allows an `object` to be inserted at an arbitrary `index`. However, inserting and deleting values anywhere except at the end of an `ArrayList` requires extensive copying of values, which takes time. To illustrate this, if we use

```
a.add(0, new Integer(99) );
```

to insert a value at the front of an `ArrayList` named a, then all of the values in the array must be shifted one position to make room for the new value:

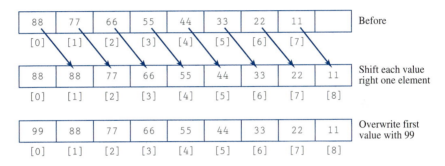

Similar shifts of values to make room for a new value are also required for insertions at other positions within the list. This means that if a problem requires that values be inserted anywhere except at the back of a sequence, an `ArrayList` is not the best container for storing that sequence.

A similar problem occurs if we remove any element other than the one at the end of an `ArrayList`, since all of the elements that follow it must be shifted one position to the left to close the gap. The following diagram illustrates this when the first element is removed:

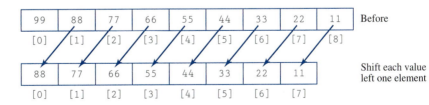

For problems where many such within-the-list insertions and deletions are required, Java provides the `LinkedList` class. This class allows values to be inserted or removed anywhere in a sequence without any of the copying that plagues `ArrayList`.

---

[1] In this and the next few diagrams, we present a simplified view of the `ArrayList`'s array: we show it storing actual values, rather than handles, to better illustrate the shifting behavior being described.

The LinkedList Class

To see how a LinkedList stores a sequence of values, suppose that aList is defined by

```
LinkedList aList = new LinkedList();
```

and consider the following sequence of add() operations:

```
aList.add( new Integer(88) );
aList.add( new Integer(77) );
aList.add( new Integer(66) );
```

We might picture the resulting object aList as follows:

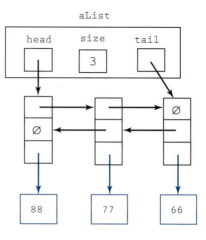

As the diagram indicates, a sequence of values is stored in a series of *linked* **nodes,** producing a container called a **linked list.** Each node contains three handles: one for the object being stored (shown in color), one to the node for the preceding object, and one to the node for the next object. The handle for the predecessor in the first node and the handle for the successor in the last node are both null (pictured as ⊘). If we think of a Node class having the (simplified) form

```
class Node
{
 // ... Node methods go here

 // --- Attribute variables ---
   private Node predecessor,
                successor;
   private Object value;
}
```

then a LinkedList class has a form something like the following:

```
class LinkedList implements List
{
```

```
// ... LinkedList methods go here

// --- Attribute variables ---
   private Node head, tail;
   private int size;
}
```

Linked lists of this form, whose nodes contain links to their successor and predecessor nodes, are called **doubly-linked lists.**

Although the designers of Java's `LinkedList` use a doubly-linked list for their class, other implementations are possible. One of these is a **singly-linked list,** consisting of the list's *size,*[2] plus a handle to the first node in the sequence. Each node contains a handle for the object being stored and one to its successor node. The final node in the sequence is marked by the `null` value:

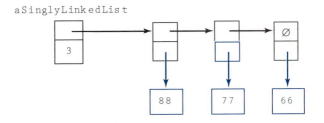

Another arrangement is a **circular-linked list,** which is similar to a singly-linked list, but contains a handle to the last node instead of the first node. In this approach, the final node's link is a handle back to the first node, providing easy access to both the last and first values in the sequence:

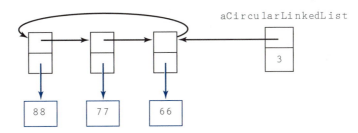

Regardless of its organization, a linked node implementation of the `List` interface allows insertion and deletion operations to be performed that do not require

---

[2] Technically, it isn't necessary to store the size attribute because a `size()` method could count the number of nodes. However, the size of a list is often needed, and such counting takes time. Maintaining a list's *size* in an attribute variable avoids this inefficiency.

the extensive copying that characterizes its `ArrayList` counterpart. Later we will see how this is carried out for Java's `LinkedList`s.

Using a `LinkedList`. Because both `ArrayList` and `LinkedList` implement the `List` interface and we used only `List` methods in Figure 12.2, we can in fact solve the same problem using a `LinkedList` with only minor modifications. Figure 12.3 presents such a solution.

FIGURE 12.3. CLASS `LinkedGatewayUsageCounter`

```
/** LinkedGatewayUsageCounter.java counts IP Addresses using a LinkedList.
 *   Receive:           name of text file via args
 *   Input (from file): IP addresses
 *   Output:            table of distinct IP addresses and number of times
 *                      they appear in the file
 */

import java.util.LinkedList;
import java.io.*;
import ann.util.Controller;
import AddressCounter;

class LinkedGatewayUsageCounter extends Object
{
 public static void main(String [] args)
 {
    if (args.length < 1)
      Controller.fatal("GatewayUsageCounter.main()",
                        " usage: java GatewayUsageCounter <input-file>");

    try
    {
      BufferedReader in = new BufferedReader(
                            new FileReader( args[0] ) );
      String theAddress = null;
      LinkedList addressSequence = new LinkedList();
      AddressCounter anAddressCounter = null;
      int index;

      for (;;)
      {
        theAddress = in.readLine();
        if (theAddress == null)
          break;
        else if ( theAddress.equals("") )
          continue;
        else
        {
          anAddressCounter = new AddressCounter(theAddress);
          index = addressSequence.indexOf(anAddressCounter);
          if (index < 0)
              addressSequence.add(anAddressCounter);
          else
            ((AddressCounter) addressSequence.get(index)).incrementCount()
        }
      }
    }
```

```
      System.out.println("\nGateway Accesses by IP Address\n\n"
                     + "-----------------------------\n"
                     + "IP Address      : Accesses\n"
                     + "-----------------------------");
         for (int i = 0; i < addressSequence.size(); i++)
           System.out.println( addressSequence.get(i) );
    }
    catch (Exception e) { System.err.println(e); }
    }
}
```

This program produces exactly the same output as that in Figure 12.2, but as we shall see, its use of memory is quite different.

The LinkedList Version. Figure 12.3 contains the statement:

```
      LinkedList addressSequence = new LinkedList();
```

which uses the LinkedList default constructor to build an empty linked list, which we can visualize as follows:

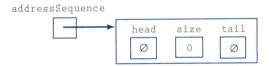

As shown in the diagram, the default class constructor simply sets its *head* and *tail* attributes to null and its *size* attribute to 0.

On the first pass through the input loop, we build an AddressCounter for the value 128.159.4.20, and send the LinkedList the indexOf() message to search for that AddressCounter:

```
      anAddressCounter = new AddressCounter(theAddress);
      index = addressSequence.indexOf(anAddressCounter);
```

Since the LinkedList is empty, this method returns −1. The subsequent if statement

```
   if (index < 0)
      addressSequence.add(anAddressCounter);
   else
      ((AddressCounter) addressSequence.get(index) ).incrementCount();
```

sends the LinkedList the add() message to append anAddressCounter:

```
      addressSequence.add(anAddressCounter);
```

To do this, the `add()` method allocates a new node, stores the reference of `Ad-dressCounter` in it, and updates the *size, head,* and *tail* attributes:

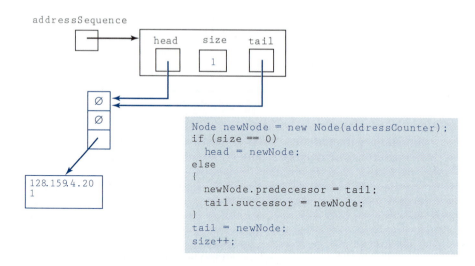

```
Node newNode = new Node(addressCounter);
if (size == 0)
    head = newNode;
else
{
    newNode.predecessor = tail;
    tail.successor = newNode;
}
tail = newNode;
size++;
```

On the second pass through the input loop, we read the address (`123.111.222.333`), build an `AddressCounter` for it, and send the `indexOf()` message to the `LinkedList` to search for the newly read address. Since it is not there, `index-Of()` again returns −1, and we again send the `add()` message to our `LinkedList`. This call to `add()` again creates a new node, stores the reference to `anAddress-Counter` in it, and then updates the various handles:

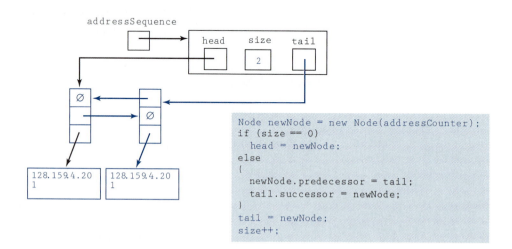

```
Node newNode = new Node(addressCounter);
if (size == 0)
    head = newNode;
else
{
    newNode.predecessor = tail;
    tail.successor = newNode;
}
tail = newNode;
size++;
```

On the third pass through the input loop, we read the address (`123.111.222.333`), build an `AddressCounter` for it, and send the `LinkedList` the indexOf() message to search for this address. Since the LinkedList already contains this address, indexOf() returns its index (1), so the else part of the if statement is executed to increment the counter in this object by 1:

```
if (index < 0)
    addressSequence.add(anAddressCounter);
else
    ((AddressCounter) addressSequence.get(index) ).incrementCount();
```

As with the earlier version in Figure 12.2, this involves several steps. We first send addressSequence the get() message to get the object at position index:

```
((AddressCounter) addressSequence.get(index) ).incrementCount();
```

Unlike an ArrayList, a LinkedList has no array behind the scenes that allows the value at a particular index to be accessed quickly. Instead, the get() method must perform the steps pictured in the following diagram:

1. Begin at the *head* node.
2. Iterate through index nodes to reach the correct node.
3. Return the reference of the object in that node:

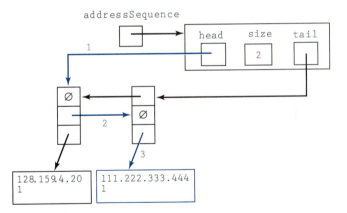

As before, we must then cast the Object returned by get() to an Address-Counter,

```
((AddressCounter) addressSequence.get(index) ).incrementCount();
```

and then send that object the incrementCount() message

```
((AddressCounter) addressSequence.get(index) ).incrementCount();
```

to update its *count* attribute:

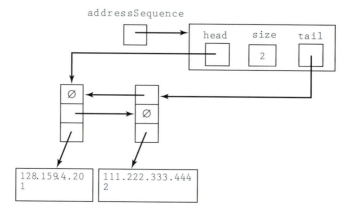

Execution continues in this fashion until all of the values in the input file have been read, adding new addresses to the `LinkedList`, and updating the *count* attribute of non-new addresses.

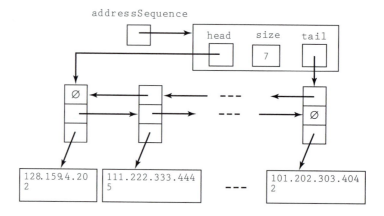

After this, execution continues with the output loop:

```
for (int i = 0; i < addressSequence.size(); i++)
    System.out.println( addressSequence.get(i) );
```

The number of repetitions is determined by `LinkedList`'s `size()` method. To actually output the entries in the `LinkedList`, we send it the `get()` message to retrieve the object at each index `i`. As we saw earlier, each call to `get()` starts at the first node and iterates `i` times to reach the node whose index is `i`. The following table illustrates the inefficiency of this approach:

For loop repetition #	i	Iterations within `get(i)`	Total iterations
1	0	0	0
2	1	1	1
3	2	2	3
4	3	3	6
5	4	4	10
6	5	5	15
7	6	6	21

Each call to `get()` passes over the same nodes as the previous call, because unlike an `ArrayList`, a `LinkedList` has no mechanism for directly accessing the object at a given index. Each access to the node at index `i` must first pass over all of the nodes at indexes 0 through $i - 1$.

Time Efficiency. When the same method in one class *A* takes more time than the same method in another class *B,* we say that *A*'s method is less **time-efficient** than *B*'s. For example, the `LinkedList` version of `get()` is less time-efficient than the `ArrayList` version. Consequently, the program in Figure 12.3 (the `LinkedList` version) is less time-efficient than the program in Figure 12.2 (the `ArrayList` version). Since the `ArrayList` and `LinkedList` classes implement many of the same methods (thus allowing either to be used to solve a problem), time-efficiency is an important consideration in choosing the right class for a given problem.

List Iterators. We can improve the time-efficiency of the program in Figure 12.3 by replacing its output loop with the following loop:

```
ListIterator it = addressSequence.listIterator();
while( it.hasNext() )
   System.out.println( it.next() );
```

This code fragment uses `List`'s `listIterator()` method . A call to this method returns an object called a `ListIterator` for the `List` to which it is sent. As its name suggests, a `ListIterator` is an object that *iterates* through the values in a `List`. The statement

```
ListIterator it = addressSequence.listIterator();
```

declares a `ListIterator` named `it`, and initializes `it` to refer to the node for the first object in our `LinkedList`.

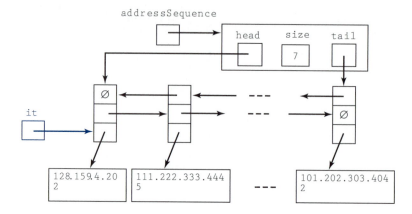

If we send it the message:

```
System.out.println( it.next() );
```

the next() method does three things:

1. It saves a handle to its current node's *object:*

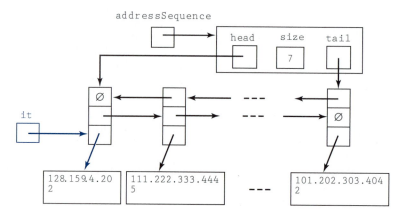

2. It advances the iterator to the next node using the *successor* attribute:

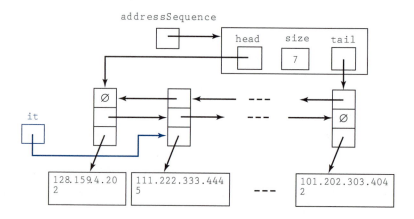

3. It returns the handle it saved in Step 1, effectively returning the object for that handle, so that it can be output

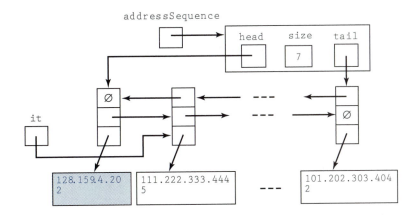

On the next pass through the loop, the call to `next()` will repeat this pattern but will return the second value in the list. The call after that will return the third value. Repeated calls to `next()` can thus be used to access each of the values in a `LinkedList` in turn.

To control such repetition, the `ListIterator` method `hasNext()` is provided:

```
ListIterator it = countList.listIterator();
while( it.hasNext() )
   System.out.println( it.next() );
```

This method returns `false` if the `ListIterator` is at the end of the list, and returns `true` otherwise.

An iterator thus provides an efficient way to access each of the values in a `List` in turn. See the API documentation for `ListIterator` in package `java.util` for additional `ListIterator` methods.

`LinkedList`'s `add()` Method. Recall that a weakness of the `ArrayList` class is that if

```
anArrayList.add(index, object);
```

is used to insert *object* anywhere other than at the end of the list, extensive copying is required to make room for the *object*. The worst case occurs when *object* is inserted at the beginning of the list,

```
anArrayList.add(0, object);
```

because *all* values in the list must be shifted.

Now, suppose we take the `LinkedList` from Figure 12.3 and invoke its `add()` method to add an `AddressCounter` object at the beginning of the list:

```
aLinkedList.add(0, new AddressCounter("101.2.303.4") );
```

Here, the add() operation builds a new node to store the AddressCounter, updates the *head* and *size* attributes, updates the various node handles, and is finished!

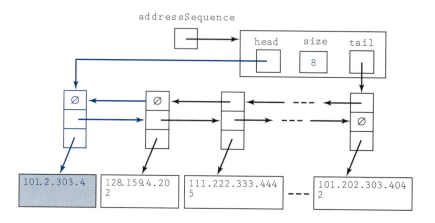

And this can be accomplished with just a few simple statements like the following:

```
Node newNode = new Node(addressCounter);
newNode.successor = head;
head.precedessor = newNode;
head = newNode;
size++;
```

Although it is a bit more complicated, the key point is that *no copying or shifting is required* to insert a new value into a LinkedList. As we have seen, the number of steps required to insert a new value into an ArrayList is proportional to the number of values in the list (since some fraction of those values must be shifted). By contrast, the number of steps required to insert a value into a LinkedList is constant and thus is independent of the size of the list. It is therefore more time-efficient than insertion for an ArrayList.

The same is true for removing a value from a list. The time to remove values from an ArrayList is proportional to the size of the list; but the time to remove a value from a LinkedList is constant; it does not depend on the size of the list.

Choosing the Proper List—Algorithm Efficiency

When we study the **time-efficiency** of algorithms in computer science, we do not concern ourselves with real (wall-clock) time, because that varies with the language in which the algorithm is encoded, the quality of the code, the quality of the compiler, the speed of the computer on which the code is executed, and various other factors. Instead, we study the number of *steps* an algorithm takes as a function of the size of the problem it solves. For example, the following method for the summation problem uses a for loop that iterates n times:

```
public static long summation(long n)
{
    long result = 0;
```

```
      for (int count = 1; count <= n; count++)
         result += count;
      return result;
   }
```

Because its for loop executes n times, we say that this version requires **linear time,** or **time proportional to** n, written **O(n),** to compute the sum of the first *n* positive integers. By contrast, here is another version that computes $1 + 2 + \cdots + n$ using a formula credited to Carl Friedrich Gauss, one of the greatest mathematicians of all time:

```
      long summation(long n)
      {
         return n * (n + 1) / 2;
      }
```

Because this second version computes the sum in 3 steps (1 addition, 1 multiplication, and 1 division) regardless of the value of n, we say that it does so in **constant time,** or **time proportional to 1,** expressed as **O(1).** Since it solves the same problem more quickly, this second method is *more time-efficient* than the first.

Time efficiency is a major consideration in deciding whether to use an `ArrayList` or a `LinkedList` to store a sequence needed to solve a given problem. To demonstrate this, we will consider the program in Figure 12.4.

FIGURE 12.4.   CLASS `ListTimer`

```
/** ListTimer.java times ArrayList and LinkedList operations.
 *  Output:  Time required to do these operations.
 */

import ann.util.Timer;
import java.util.*;         // LinkedList, ArrayList

class ListTimer extends Object
{
 public static void main(String [] args)
 {
   final int START = 10000,
             STEP = 10000,
             STOP = 10000000;
   Timer timer = new Timer();
   int i, j;
   Object obj = new Object();
   ArrayList anArrayList = new ArrayList();
   LinkedList aLinkedList = new LinkedList();

   for (i = 1; i <= START; i++)          // build initial lists
   {
     anArrayList.add(obj);
     aLinkedList.add(obj);
   }
                                         // print column headings
   System.out.println("Size    a.add() l.add() a.get(m)       "
             + "l.get(m)        a.add(0)        l.add(0)");
```

```
      for (i = START; i <= STOP; i += STEP)  // main loop
      {
        timer.start();
        anArrayList.add(obj);                  // append obj to an ArrayList
        timer.stop();

        System.out.print(i + "\t" + timer);  // display i and the time

        timer.reset();
        timer.start();
        aLinkedList.add(obj);                  // append obj to a LinkedList
        timer.stop();

        System.out.print("\t" + timer);      // display time

        int middleIndex = i / 2;
        timer.reset();
        timer.start();
        obj = anArrayList.get(middleIndex);  // access middle value in AL
        timer.stop();
        System.out.print("\t" + timer);

        timer.reset();
        timer.start();
        obj = aLinkedList.get(middleIndex);  // access middle value in LL
        timer.stop();
        System.out.print("\t\t" + timer);

        timer.reset();
        timer.start();
        anArrayList.add(0, obj);              // prepend value to an AL
        timer.stop();
        System.out.print("\t\t" + timer);

        timer.reset();
        timer.start();
        aLinkedList.add(0, obj);
        timer.stop();
        System.out.println("\t\t" + timer);  // prepend value to a LL

        for (j = 1; j <= STEP; j++)          // increase size of lists
        {
          anArrayList.add(obj);
          aLinkedList.add(obj);
        }
      }
    }
  }
}
```

Sample Run Fragment: (233MHz Pentium II)

Size	a.add()	l.add()	a.get(m)	l.get(m)	a.add(0)	l.add(0)
...						
1590000	0.0	0.0	0.0	0.22	0.11	0.0
1600000	0.0	0.0	0.0	0.22	0.11	0.0
1610000	0.0	0.0	0.0	0.22	0.11	0.0
1620000	0.0	0.0	0.0	0.22	0.11	0.0
1630000	0.0	0.0	0.0	0.22	0.11	0.0

1630000 0.0	0.0	0.0	0.22	0.11	0.0
1640000 0.0	0.0	0.0	0.22	0.11	0.0
1650000 0.0	0.0	0.0	0.22	0.11	0.0

The program begins by building an `ArrayList` and a `LinkedList`, each with 10,000 values. (Lists this large were needed to give nonzero times.) Our `Timer` class from the package `ann.util` is then used to measure the time required to perform various operations on the two lists, including:

- ❏ Append a value to the list using `add(obj)`
- ❏ Access the middle value in a list using `get(index)`
- ❏ Prepend a value to the list using `add(0, obj)`

The sample run provides several interesting observations. First, appending a value to either kind of list takes negligible time. This means that if a problem involves the manipulation of a sequence, but appending (or removing from the end) is the only sequence operation needed to solve the problem, then it makes no difference whether you store the sequence in an `ArrayList` or a `LinkedList`.

The second observation is that it is far more time-consuming to access the middle value in a `LinkedList` than in an `ArrayList`. The reason is that for an `ArrayList`, the `get(n)` operation can access the array value at index n in *constant* (i.e., O(1)) time, using the array subscript operation. By contrast, for a `LinkedList`, the `get(n)` operation must begin at the head node and follow n successor links to reach the appropriate node, making this a *linear* (i.e., O(n)) time operation. This implies that if a problem involves the manipulation of a sequence and involves a large number of accesses to values other than the first or last value in the sequence, then the `ArrayList` should be chosen to store the sequence, because those accesses will be much faster using a `LinkedList`.

The final observation is that it is far more time-consuming to insert values into an `ArrayList` than into a `LinkedList`. As we saw earlier, inserting into a `LinkedList` is a *constant* time (O(1)) operation, requiring the execution of only a handful of statements. By contrast, inserting into an `ArrayList` is a *linear* time (O(n)) operation, because it requires extensive copying to make room for the new value. This implies that if a problem involves the manipulation of a sequence and involves many insertions (or deletions) from anywhere other than the end of the sequence, then the `LinkedList` should be used to store the sequence, because insertions (or deletions) will be much more time-efficient than for an `ArrayList`.

Summary. If a problem involves many accesses to the interior of a sequence, then the sequence should be stored in an `ArrayList`. If a problem involves many insertions or deletions in a sequence from anywhere other than its end, then the sequence should be stored in a `LinkedList`. If neither of these is the case, then it does not matter which kind of `List` one uses.

Table 12.2 gives the various `List` operations, comparing their times for an `ArrayList` against those of a `LinkedList`.

TABLE 12.2   EFFICIENCY OF VARIOUS List OPERATIONS

List Method	Short Description	ArrayList Efficiency	LinkedList Efficiency
add(obj)	Append obj to list	O(1)	O(1)
add(i, obj)	Insert obj into the list at index i	O(n)	O(1)*
clear()	Remove all values from list	O(n)	O(n)
contains(obj)	Check if the list contains obj	O(n)	O(n)
equals(obj)	Compare the list to obj	O(n)	O(n)
get(i)	Find value in the list at index i	O(1)	O(n)
indexOf(obj)	Find index of first occurrence of obj in the list	O(n)	O(n)
isEmpty()	Check if the list is empty	O(1)	O(1)
lastIndexOf(obj)	Find index of last occurrence of obj in the list	O(n)	O(n)
remove(i)	Remove object from the list at index i	O(n)	O(1)*
remove(obj)	Remove the first occurrence of obj from the list	O(n)	O(1)*
set(i, obj)	Replace object at index i in the list with obj	O(1)	O(n)
size()	Return number of objects in the list	O(1)	O(1)
subList(i, j)	Return the sublist from index i up to but not including index j	O(n)	O(n)
toArray()	Return an array representation of the list	O(n)	O(n)

* While the time to perform insertion into a LinkedList is O(1), the time to find the value at index n where the insertion is to be performed is O(n). The ListIterator method add(obj) inserts in O(1) time, once O(n) time has been spent positioning the ListIterator. The same is true for deletion.

✔ Quick Quiz 12.2

1. A(n) _____ class is a class that can store a group of objects.
2. What are the three kinds of classes provided in Java that can store groups of objects?
3. An ArrayList is a class that implements the List interface using a(n) _____.

4. What are the three attributes in an `ArrayList`?

5. In a linked list, values are stored in _____ that are linked together.

6. What advantages do `LinkedLists` have over `ArrayLists`?

7. What advantages do `ArrayLists` have over `LinkedLists`?

8. Compare and contrast singly-linked lists and doubly-linked lists.

9. Compare and contrast singly-linked lists and circular-linked lists.

10. (True or false) Inserting values at the end of an `ArrayList` is more time-efficient than inserting them at the front.

11. (True or false) Inserting values at the end of a `LinkedList` is more time-efficient than inserting them at the front.

12. (True or false) An operation that requires O(1) time is a constant-time algorithm.

13. (True or false) An operation that requires O(n) time is a linear-time algorithm.

14. Accessing a value in an `ArrayList` is an O(_____) operation.

15. Accessing a value in a `LinkedList` is an O(_____) operation.

16. Inserting a value into an `ArrayList` is an O(_____) operation.

17. Inserting a value into a `LinkedList` is an O(_____) operation.

✏ EXERCISES 12.2

Exercises 1–10 assume the statements:

```
ArrayList animals = new ArrayList();          // 1
System.out.println(animals.size());           // 2
animals.add("cat");                           // 3
animals.add("horse");                         // 4
animals.add(1, "dog");                        // 5
System.out.println(animals.get(2));           // 6
animals.add("dog");                           // 7
animals.remove("dog");                        // 8
for (int i = 0; i < animals.size(); i++)      // 9.1
   System.out.print(animals.get(i) + " ");    // 9.2
System.out.println();                         // 9.3
```

For exercises that ask for a diagram, you are to draw a diagram like those in the text to picture the `ArrayList` that results when the specified statement is executed.

1. Give a diagram for Statement 1.

2. What output is produced by Statement 2?

3. Give a diagram for Statement 3.

4. Give a diagram for Statement 4.

5. Give a diagram for Statement 5.

6. What output is produced by Statement 6?

7. Give a diagram for Statement 7.

8. Give a diagram for Statement 8.

9. What output is produced by Statements 9.1 - 9.3?

10–18.   Proceed as in Exercises 1–9 but with `ArrayList` replaced by `LinkedList`.

19. Write statements to concatenate two `ArrayLists` to produce a new `ArrayList`.

20. Proceed as in Exercise 19 but with `ArrayList` replaced by `LinkedList`.

21. Suppose that `dubList` is an `ArrayList` that stores a sequence of `Double` objects. Write statements to calculate the average of the corresponding `double` values.

22. Proceed as in Exercise 21, but with `dubList` as a `LinkedList`.

23. For `dubList` as in Exercise 21, write statements to determine whether the `double` values are in ascending order.

24. Proceed as in Exercise 23, but with `dubList` as a `LinkedList`.

25. Suppose that `dubList1` and `dubList2` are `ArrayLists` as described in Exercise 21, but with values in ascending order. Write statements to merge these two lists to yield a list with the values in ascending order.

26. Proceed as in Exercise 25, but with `LinkedLists`.

12.3   EXAMPLE: A STACK APPLICATION AND CLASS

In this section, we study a problem that can be conveniently solved using a specialized structure called the **stack.** We will begin with the problem, then examine the stack and how it can be used to solve the problem, and then build a `Stack` class.

PROBLEM: DISPLAYING A NUMBER'S BINARY REPRESENTATION

We have seen that data values are stored in computer memory using a binary representation. In particular, positive integers are commonly stored using the base-2 representation described in the *Part of the Picture: Data Representation* section of Chapter 2. This means that the base-10 representation of an integer that appears in a program or in a data file must be converted to a base-2 representation. One algorithm for carrying out this conversion uses repeated division by 2, with the successive remainders giving the binary digits in the base-2 representation from right to left. For example, the following computation shows that the base-2 representation of 26 is 11010:

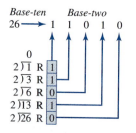

We can generalize this approach to determine the base-b representation for any value of b between 2 and 36 inclusive, simply by dividing by b instead of 2, and using the symbols a, b, . . ., z as base-b digits (in addition to 0–9) when $b > 10$. For example, the base-8 representation of 95 is 137_8, which we can compute as follows:

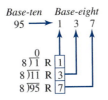

Similarly, the base-16 representation of 95 is $5f_{16}$, which we can compute as follows:

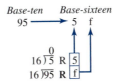

(The base-16 digits for ten, eleven, twelve, thirteen, fourteen, and fifteen are a, b, c, d, e, and f, respectively.) Our problem is to write a method that will output the base-*b* representation of a given base-10 number.

One of the difficulties in this problem is that the remainders are generated in the opposite order that they must be output. For example, in determining the binary representation of 26, the *first* remainder,

$$26 \% 2 = 0$$

is the *last* binary digit that we must display. Similarly, the *second* remainder we compute,

$$13 \% 2 = 1$$

produces the *next-to-the-last* binary digit that we must display. This pattern continues until we generate the final remainder,

$$1 \% 2 = 1$$

which produces the first binary digit that we must display.

The Stack Container

The preceding diagrams suggest one approach to solving this problem. What is needed is a special kind of list to store the remainders—a container into which values can be inserted and deleted, but where the delete operation always removes that value which was most recently inserted to the list. The values in such a list must, therefore, be maintained in **Last-In-First-Out (LIFO)** order; that is, the last item inserted is the first item to be removed. Such a list is called a **stack** (or a **push-down stack**) because it functions in the same manner as a spring-loaded stack of plates or trays used in a cafeteria:

Plates are added to the stack by *pushing* them onto the **top** of the stack. When a plate is removed from the top of the stack, the spring causes the next plate to *pop* up. For this reason, the operations to insert a value into and delete a value from a stack are commonly called **push** and **pop,** respectively. The most recently added value is called the **top** value. If the stack contains no plates, then it is described as **empty.** These properties of a stack in a cafeteria illustrate the four standard stack operations:

1. *isEmpty*(): returns true if there are no values in the stack and false otherwise
2. *top*( ):   returns a copy of the value at the top of the stack
3. *push*(*v*): adds a value *v* at the top of the stack
4. *pop*( ):   removes and returns the value at the top of the stack

A stack can be used to solve the base-conversion problem. To display the base-*b* representation of an integer in the usual left-to-right sequence, we must "stack up" the remainders generated during the repeated division by *b* by pushing them onto a stack. When the division process terminates, we can retrieve the remainders from this stack in the required "last-in-first-out" order by popping them from the stack.

If we have a stack class available, we can use the following algorithm to convert from base-10 to base-*b* and display the result:

BASE-CONVERSION ALGORITHM

/* This algorithm displays the representation of a base-10 number in any
    base from 2 through 36.
       Receive: *number,* an int;
                     base, the base to which we want to convert *number.*
    Precondition: *number* > 0 and 2 ≤ *base* ≤ 36.
       Return: the base-*base* representation of *number,* as a String.
*/

1. Create an empty stack to hold the remainders.
2. Repeat the following while *number* ≠ 0:
       a. Calculate the *remainder* that results when *number* is divided by *base.*
       b. Push *remainder* onto the stack of remainders.
       c. Replace *number* by the integer quotient of *number* divided by *base.*
3. Declare *result* as an empty String.
4. While the stack of remainders is not empty do the following:
       a. Remove the *remainder* from the top of the stack of remainders.

b. Convert *remainder* to its base-*base* equivalent.

c. Concatenate the base-*base* equivalent of *remainder* to *result*.

5. Return *result*.

The following diagram traces this algorithm for the integer 26 and base 2. Figure 12.6 presents a `DecimalConverter` class containing a `convertDecimal()` method that implements this algorithm.

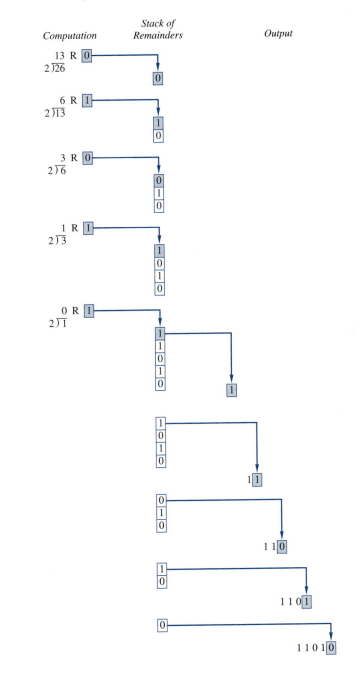

FIGURE 12.6.   CONVERTING DECIMAL NUMBERS

```java
/** DecimalConverter.java will convert a positive decimal to
 *    any positive base from 2 to 36 inclusive.
 *  Input:   Positive integers number and base
 *  Output: Prompts, representation of number in base entered
 */

import ann.easyio.*;              // Keyboard, Screen
import ann.util.Stack;

class DecimalConverter extends Object
{
 /** Convert a decimal value to a different base.
  *  Receive:      value, the int to be converted;
  *                base, the desired base.
  *  Precondition: value > 0 && base > 1 && base < 37.
  *  Return:       a String representation of value in base
  */
  public static String convertDecimal(int value, int base)
  {
    Stack myStack = new Stack();
    do
    {
      myStack.push( new Integer( value % base ) );
      value /= base;
    }
    while (value > 0);

    Integer nextIntegerRemainder;
    int nextIntRemainder;
    String resultString = "";
    while (! myStack.isEmpty() )
    {
      nextIntegerRemainder = (Integer) myStack.pop();
      nextIntRemainder = nextIntegerRemainder.intValue();
      resultString += baseDigit(nextIntRemainder);
    }

    return resultString;
  }

 /** Table look-up routine to convert a 0-35 value to 0-z.
  *  Receive:      value, an int
  *  Precondition: 0 <= value <= 35.
  *  Return:       the 0-z representation of value
  */
public static String baseDigit(int value)
  {
    String [] resultArray = {"0", "1", "2", "3", "4", "5",
                             "6", "7", "8", "9", "a", "b",
                             "c", "d", "e", "f", "g", "h",
                             "i", "j", "k", "l", "m", "n",
                             "o", "p", "q", "r", "s", "t",
                             "u", "v", "w", "x", "y", "z"};

    if ( value < resultArray.length )
      return resultArray[value];
    else
      return "error in base36(value): value must be less than "
             + resultArray.length;
  }
```

```java
public static void main(String [] args)
{
  Screen theScreen = new Screen();
  Keyboard theKeyboard = new Keyboard();
  int originalNumber, newBase;
  String convertedNumber;

  for (;;)
  {
    theScreen.print("\n\nTo convert a decimal number to a different base,
                    + "enter the number to be converted (-1 to quit): ")
    originalNumber = theKeyboard.readInt();

    if (originalNumber < 0) break;

    theScreen.print("Enter the base to which it is to be converted: ");
    newBase = theKeyboard.readInt();

    convertedNumber = convertDecimal(originalNumber, newBase);

    theScreen.println( "\n" + convertedNumber
                      + " is the base " + newBase
                      + " representation of "
                      + Integer.parseInt(convertedNumber, newBase) );
  }
 }
}
```

Sample Run:

```
To convert a decimal number to a different base,
enter the number to be converted (-1 to quit): 32
Enter the base to which it is to be converted: 2

100000 is the base-2 representation of 32

To convert a decimal number to a different base,
enter the number to be converted (-1 to quit): 32
Enter the base to which it is to be converted: 8

40 is the base-8 representation of 32


To convert a decimal number to a different base,
enter the number to be converted (-1 to quit): 32
Enter the base to which it is to be converted: 16

20 is the base-16 representation of 32


To convert a decimal number to a different base,
enter the number to be converted (-1 to quit): 255
Enter the base to which it is to be converted: 16

ff is the base-16 representation of 255
```

```
To convert a decimal number to a different base,
enter the number to be converted (-1 to quit): 255
Enter the base to which it is to be converted: 2

11111111 is the base-2 representation of 255

To convert a decimal number to a different base,
enter the number to be converted (-1 to quit): 577109
Enter the base to which it is to be converted: 36

cat is the base-36 representation of 577109

To convert a decimal number to a different base,
enter the number to be converted (-1 to quit): -1
```

Of course, for the preceding program to work, we need a `Stack` class. In the remainder of this section, we will build such a class.

Implementing a `Stack` Class

There are many different ways to build a `Stack` class. We present one approach here, and leave others for the exercises. We will use a `LinkedList` attribute variable within our `Stack` class to store the stack's values. This relationship between two classes—`Stack` and `LinkedList`—is commonly described as a ***has-a* relationship**— the `Stack` *has a* `LinkedList`—as opposed to the *is-a* relationship for the `extends` mechanism described in Chapter 11.

Figure 12.7 presents a `Stack` class implemented in this manner. Thanks to the existence of the `LinkedList` class, the various `Stack` operations are easy to implement.

FIGURE 12.7.   A SIMPLE `Stack` CLASS

```
/** Stack.java presents a Stack class whose integrity cannot be violated
 *   (unlike Java's Stack class). It is built using Java's standard LinkedList
 *   class.  It is contained in the package ann.util.
 *   Attribute:  A LinkedList to store the stack elements
 *   Methods:    Default constructor to construct an empty stack,
 *               isEmpty(), top(), pop(), push()
 */

package ann.util;

import java.util.LinkedList;
```

```java
public class Stack extends Object
{
/** Stack constructor
 *  Postcondition:  Empty stack is constructed.
 */
 public Stack()
 {
   myList = new LinkedList();
 }

/** Check if stack is empty
 *  Return:  true if stack is empty, and false otherwise
 */
 public boolean isEmpty()
 {
   return myList.size() == 0;
 }

/** Top operation
 *  Return:  Object at the top of the stack; null if stack is empty
 */
 public Object top()
 {
   if (myList.size() > 0)
     return myList.getLast();
   else
     return null;
 }

/** Push operation
 *  Receive:       Object value
 *  Postcondition: value has been added at the top of the stack
 */
 public void push(Object value)
 {
   myList.add(value);
 }

/** Pop operation
 *  Return:        Object at the top of the stack; null if stack is empty
 *  Postcondition: Value at the top of the stack has been removed.
 */
 public Object pop()
 {
   if (myList.size() > 0)
     return myList.removeLast();

   else
     return null;
 }

//--- Attribute variable
 private LinkedList myList;  // top of stack is at the back of myList
}
```

Although we have built our `Stack` using a `LinkedList`, we could just as well have used an `ArrayList`. A `Stack` always adds and removes values *at the end* of its list, and as we saw in Section 12.2, `LinkedList` and `ArrayList` are equally time-efficient for these operations.

Java's `Stack` Class. In the Java API, there is a `Stack` class in the package `java.util`. It *extends* Java's `Vector` class (which was described in Chapter 9 and is quite similar to the `ArrayList` class presented in this chapter). This is unfortunate because the set of methods that can *properly* be applied to a `Stack` are those we have just described: `isEmpty()`, `top()`, `push()`, and `pop()`. But `java.util.Stack` inherits all of `Vector`'s methods, which means that any message that can be sent to a `Vector` can also be sent to a `Stack`. However, many of the `Vector` methods are not appropriate for a `Stack`!

To illustrate, because a `java.util.Stack` inherits the properties of the `Vector` class, we can send a Java `Stack` the following messages:

`aStack.add(i, obj)` to insert *obj* into `aStack` at index *i*

`aStack.getElement(i)` to access the object in `aStack` at index *i*

`aStack.remove(i)` to remove the object in `aStack` at index *i*

However, *these are not valid stack operations!* A value should be added to a stack only by pushing it onto the stack's top; only the top object should be accessible; and only the top value in the stack should be removable. This is a clear violation of our **rule of thumb for using extends** from Section 11.2:

A class B should extend another class A if and only if

1. *B is a specialized version of A; and*

2. *All messages that can be sent to A can appropriately be sent to B.*

Since `Vector` contains operations that should not be used in a `Stack`, defining `Stack` as an extension of `Vector` is not an appropriate use of the `extends` mechanism. By contrast, the `Stack` class given in Figure 12.7 is a *safe design,* because only appropriate messages (i.e., `isEmpty()`, `top()`, `push()`, and `pop()`) can be sent to such a `Stack`.[3]

✔ Quick Quiz 12.3

1. Convert 1234 to a base-two number.
2. Convert 1234 to a base-eight number.
3. Convert 1234 to a base-sixteen number.
4. The last element added to a stack is the _____ one removed. This behavior is known as in maintaining the list in _____ order.
5. What are the four standard stack operations?
6. How does Java's `Stack` class violate the rule for one class extending another?

---

[3] The set of `Stack` operations is a *proper subset* of the set of `Vector` operations. Defining `Stack` as an extension of `Vector` results in a `Stack` whose set of operations is a *superset* of those for a `Vector`.

✍ EXERCISES 12.3

1. Convert 2748 to a base-two number.

2. Convert 2748 to a base-eight number.

3. Convert 2748 to a base-sixteen number.

Exercises 4–6 assume the following declarations

```
Stack s = new Stack();
Integer i = new Integer();
```

where `Stack` is the class described in this section. Draw a diagram of the `myList` attribute variable of `s` after the code segment is executed, or indicate why an error occurs.

4. ```
for (int k = 1; k <= 5; k++)
     s.push(new Integer(10*k));
```

5. ```
s.push(new Integer(10));
i = s.pop();
s.push(new Integer(22));
i = s.pop();
s.push(new Integer(33));
i = s.pop();
s.push(new Integer(44));
```

6. ```
s.push(new Integer(10));
s.push(new Integer(9));
s.push(new Integer(8));
s.push(new Integer(7));
i = s.pop();
```

7. Write a method `bottom()` for the `Stack` class that returns the bottom element of the stack.

8. Proceed as in Exercise 7, but design a method `element()` so that `element(n)` retrieves the nth stack element (counting from the top), if there is one.

## 12.4   EXAMPLE: BUILDING A Queue CLASS

In the preceding section, we examined the stack—a special kind of list in which values are always inserted and removed from the same end. In this section, we examine another special purpose list called a **queue,** in which values are always added at one end, called the **rear** or **tail,** and removed from the opposite end, called the **front** or **head.**

Queues abound in everyday life, because they provide a fair way to schedule things that are waiting for some kind of service. For example,

❏ a line of persons waiting to check out at a supermarket,

❏ a line of vehicles at a toll booth,

❏ a line of planes waiting to take off at an airport, and

❏ a line of persons waiting to purchase a ticket for a movie.
```

are all examples of queues. Arriving customers, vehicles, planes, and the like enter the line at the rear, and are removed from the line and served when they reach the front of the line, so that the first person to enter the queue is the first person served.

Because the first thing to enter the queue has been waiting the longest, it seems *fair* that it should be the first one served (People get irritated when others "cut ahead" of them in a line, because this *fairness principle* is violated.) Stated differently, whereas a stack exhibits Last-In-First-Out (LIFO) behavior; a queue exhibits **First-In-First-Out (FIFO)** behavior.

Queues in Computer Systems

In addition to lines of people, vehicles, and planes waiting for service, queues are also commonly used to model waiting lines that arise in the operation of computer systems. These queues are formed whenever more than one process requires a particular resource such as a printer, a disk drive, the central processing unit, and so on. As processes request a particular resource, they are placed in a queue to wait for service by that resource.

As one example, several personal computers may be sharing the same printer, and a **spool**[4] **queue** is used to schedule output requests in a first-come-first-served manner. If a print job is requested and the printer is free, it is immediately assigned to this job. While this output is being printed, other jobs may need the printer, and so they are placed in a spool queue to await their turns. When the output from the current job terminates, the printer is released from that job and is assigned to the first job in the spool queue.

Another important use of queues in computing systems is **input/output buffering.** As we noted in Chapter 10, transfer of information to and from a disk file can take thousands (or millions) of times as long as a typical CPU operation. Consequently, if the processing of a program must be suspended while data is transferred, program execution is slowed dramatically. As we described there, one common solution to this problem uses sections of main memory known as **buffers** and transfers data between the program and these buffers rather than directly between the program and the disk.

In particular, consider a problem in which data being processed by a program is to be read from a disk file. With a `BufferedReader` as described in Chapter 10, this information is transferred from the disk file to an input buffer in main memory while the central processing unit (CPU) is performing some other task. When data is required by the program, the next value stored in this buffer is retrieved. While this

---

[4] "Spool" is an acronym for **S**imultaneous **P**eripheral **O**peration **O**n-**L**ine.

value is being processed, additional data values can be transferred from the disk file to the buffer. Clearly, the buffer must be organized as a first-in-first-out structure, that is, as a queue. A queue-empty condition indicates that the input buffer is empty, and program execution is suspended while the operating system attempts to load more data into the buffer or signals the end of input.

Queue Operations

Just as there were four standard operations on a stack, there are four standard operations used to manipulate a queue:

1. *isEmpty*(): returns true if there are no values on the queue and false otherwise
2. *first*( ):   returns a copy of the value at the front of the queue
3. *add*( ):   adds a new value at the rear of the queue
4. *remove*( ): removes and returns the value at the front of the queue

We will now look at a `Queue` class where these operations are implemented.

Implementing a Queue Class

Like a stack, the queue is a list on which a restricted set of operations can be performed. The restriction is that values must be inserted at one end of the list and deleted from the other end.

Approach 1: A `LinkedList` Attribute Variable. We could take the same approach as we used for the `Stack` class and implement a `Queue` class using a `LinkedList` attribute variable to store the queue's elements:

```
public class Queue extends Object
{
 // ... Queue methods go here ...
 // --- Attribute variables ---
 private LinkedList myValues;
}
```

This would work well because insertions and deletions from either end of a `LinkedList` occur in constant (O(1)) time. We will leave this approach as an exercise, however, so that we can examine some alternative approaches.

Approach 2: An `ArrayList` Attribute Variable. We could take a slightly different approach and use an `ArrayList` attribute variable to store our queue's values:

```
public class Queue extends Object
{
 // ... Queue methods go here ...
 // --- Attribute variables ---
 private ArrayList myValues;
}
```

But this would be a poor choice because to add values at one end and remove them from the other would mean that we must either add or remove values at the beginning of the `ArrayList`, which would require shifting the list elements each time (an O(*n*) operation).

There is a way to get around this time-inefficient approach, however, by using two additional attribute variables:

```
public class Queue extends Object
{
  // ... Queue methods go here ...
  // --- Attribute variables ---
  private ArrayList myValues;
  private int myFront,  // index of value at front of queue
              myBack;   // index 1 past value at back of queue
}
```

A value is added to the queue at index `myBack`, and `myBack` is then incremented by 1. A value is retrieved or removed at index `myFront` and `myFront` is then incremented by 1. We think of the queue as being circular, so that when `myFront` or `myBack` reaches the end of the `ArrayList`, it is reset to 0. This approach works well and is left as an exercise.

Approach 3: Building a `Queue` From Scratch. Instead of using either of the two preceding approaches, we will build the class from the ground up by building a linked structure to store the queue elements. This will allow us to learn more about how to design and implement linked structures and how they can be used to build other structures.

Like `LinkedList`, our `Queue` class will contain three attribute variables: a handle `myHead` for the node containing the first value; a handle `myTail` for the node containing the last value; and an integer `mySize` to store the number of values in the `Queue`:

```
public class Queue extends Object
{
  // ... Queue methods go here ...
  // --- Attribute variables ---
  private SinglyLinkedNode myHead, myTail;
  private int              mySize;
}
```

Since a queue always adds at one end and removes from the other, doubly-linked nodes provide no benefit over singly-linked nodes. As a result, we will define a `SinglyLinkedNode` class, containing two attribute variables: `mySuccessor`, a handle for the successor node, and `myValue`, a handle for the node's (`Object`) value.

```
public class SinglyLinkedNode extends Object
{
  // ... SinglyLinkedNode methods go here ...
  // --- Attribute variables ---
  private SinglyLinkedNode mySuccessor;
  private Object           myValue;
}
```

We can then think of a `Queue` as having the following structure:

By using singly-linked nodes instead of doubly-linked nodes, this approach will be slightly more space-efficient and will be as time-efficient as using a `LinkedList` attribute variable to store the queue elements.

Figure 12.8 presents the complete declaration of a `SinglyLinkedNode` class that provides constructors, accessors, and mutators for the attribute variables `myValue` and `mySuccessor`. This class is contained in our `ann.util` package.

FIGURE 12.8   A `SinglyLinkedNode` CLASS

```
/** SinglyLinkedNode.java defines a class for singly linked nodes.
 *  Attributes:  myValue to store a queue element
 *               mySuccessor to refer to the next node
 *  Methods:     constructors -- build a node to store a particular
 *               object and a handle for the successor (default null);
 *               accessors and mutators
 */

package ann.util;

public class SinglyLinkedNode
{
 //--- Constructors ---
 /** Construct a node containing a given Object and having a given successor
  *  Receive:       Object value and SinglyLinkedNode successor
  *  Postcondition: myValue == value and mySuccessor == successor
  */
  public SinglyLinkedNode(Object value, SinglyLinkedNode successor)
  {
    myValue = value;
    mySuccessor = successor;
  }

 /** Construct a node containing a given Object
  *  Recieve:       Object value
  *  Postcondition: myValue == value and mySuccessor == null
  */
  public SinglyLinkedNode(Object value)
  {
    this(value, null);
  }
```

```
//--- Accessors and mutators---
/** Access value stored in a node
 *   Return: myValue */
public Object getValue()                  { return myValue; }

/** Access successor of a node
 *   Return: mySuccessor */
public SinglyLinkedNode getSuccessor() { return mySuccessor; }

/** Change value stored in a node
 *   Receive: newValue
 *   PostCondition:  myValue == newValue */
public void setValue(Object newValue)
{ myValue = newValue; }

/** Change successor of a node
 *   Receive: newSuccessor
 *   PostCondition:  mySuccessor == newSuccessor */
public void setSuccessor(SinglyLinkedNode newSuccessor)
{ mySuccessor = newSuccessor; }

//--- Attribute variables ---
private SinglyLinkedNode mySuccessor;
private Object           myValue;
}
```

Given this class for singly-linked nodes, we can proceed to define our `Queue` operations. (A complete definition of class `Queue` is given in Figure 12.9.) A `Queue` class invariant will help with remembering what must be true before and after each operation is executed.

Queue Invariant:
```
    mySize == 0 && myHead == null && myTail == null
|| mySize > 0  && myHead.getValue() is my oldest value
                && myTail.getValue() is my newest value
```

The `Queue` Constructor. The default constructor must initialize the attribute variables with values appropriate for an empty queue:

```
public Queue()
{
   myHead = myTail = null;
   mySize = 0;
}
```

Obviously, the invariant is satisfied.

The `isEmpty()` Method. Thanks to the `mySize` attribute, determining whether or not a `Queue` is empty is straightforward:

```
public boolean isEmpty()
{
   return mySize == 0;
}
```

The `first()` **Method.** Retrieving the value at the front of a `Queue` (without altering the `Queue`) is only slightly more complicated, because this operation has a precondition, namely that the `Queue` cannot be empty. We could throw an exception if this precondition is not met, but we will instead opt for the simpler approach of returning the `null` value.

If the precondition is met, then we can use the `SinglyLinkedList` accessor method `getValue()` to retrieve the return value:

```
public Object first()
{
   if ( isEmpty() )
     return null;
   else
     return myHead.getValue();
}
```

The `add()` **Method.** A method for appending a value to a `Queue` is a bit more complicated, because it must create a new `SinglyLinkedNode` for the value being added and then update the various attribute variables in the `Queue` as appropriate for this new node. The complication is that if the `Queue` is empty, then we must also update the `myHead` attribute variable:

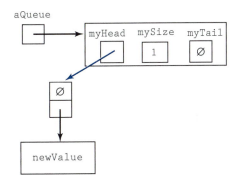

Otherwise, we must update the `mySuccessor` instance variable in the last node:

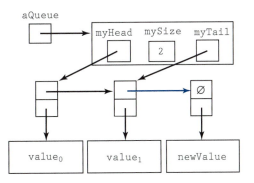

In either case, we must also update myTail to refer to the new node, and update mySize to indicate that we now have an additional value:

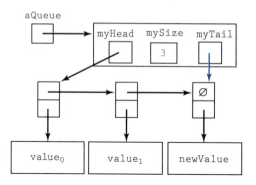

Although all of this may seem a bit complicated, coding it is actually not very difficult:

```
public void add(Object obj)
{
   SinglyLinkedNode newNode = new SinglyLinkedNode(obj);

   if ( isEmpty() )
     myHead = newNode;
   else
     myTail.setSuccessor(newNode);

   myTail = newNode;
   mySize++;
}
```

The remove() Method. A method to remove the front (oldest) value in a Queue is also complicated by the precondition that the Queue should not be empty. If it is empty, we will simply return null, as before. If the Queue is not empty, then we must save a handle to the first Object in the Queue,

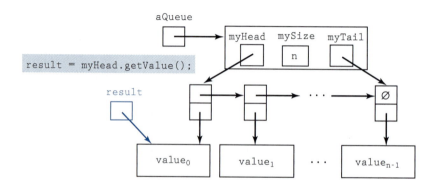

adjust myHead to refer to the second node,

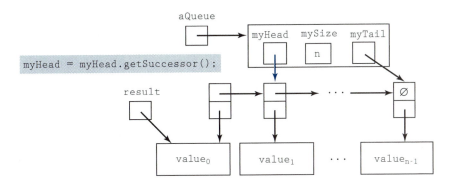

```
myHead = myHead.getSuccessor();
```

and update mySize:

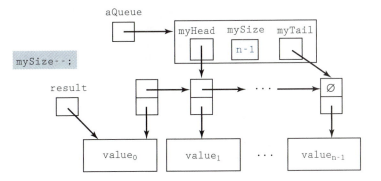

```
mySize--;
```

A small complication occurs if the queue has only one element before the preceding steps are applied. They produce the following scenario:

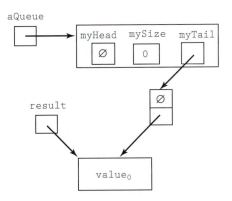

Note that the statement:

```
myHead = myHead.getSuccessor();
```

has correctly updated `myHead`; however, `myTail` has not been correctly updated. To satisfy the class invariant, it must be set to `null` in this situation:

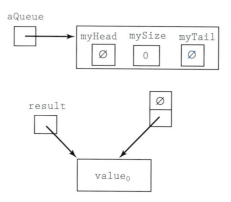

When we do this, there are now no handles to the obsolete node, and the Java system's *garbage collector* will reclaim the node.[5]

Finally, we can return `result`, and thus return a handle to the `Object` we just removed. Here is one way to encode the operation:

```
public Object remove()
{
  Object result = null;

  if ( !isEmpty() )
  {
    result = myHead.getValue();
    myHead = myHead.getSuccessor();
    mySize--;
  }

  if ( isEmpty() )
    myTail = null;

  return result;
}
```

Figure 12.9 provides a complete listing of the `Queue` class. We have added a few additional operations, namely

- ❏ `size()` to determine the length of a queue;
- ❏ `clear()` to empty a queue; and
- ❏ `toString()` to convert a queue to a `String` representation (for output/debugging purposes).

---

[5] Technically, we wouldn't have to set `myTail` to `null`. The next time we add a value to the queue, it will be reset to point to the new node. This will leave the old node with no references to it, at which point the garbage collector can reclaim it. We reset `myTail` here to be consistent with the class invariant.

FIGURE 12.9 A Queue CLASS

```java
/** Queue.java presents a Queue of linked nodes built "from scratch"  whose
 *  integrity cannot be violated (unlike Java's Queue class).  It is
 *  contained in the package ann.util.
 *  Attribute: SinglyLinkedNodes to store references to the head and tail
 *             of the queuu and an int to store its size
 *  Methods:   Default constructor to construct an empty queue,
 *             isEmpty(), front(), add(), remove()
 */

package ann.util;

import ann.util.SinglyLinkedNode;

public class Queue extends Object
{
/** Queueconstructor
 *  Postcondition:  Empty stack is constructed.
 */
 public Queue()
 {
   myHead = myTail = null;
   mySize = 0;
 }

/** Check if queue is empty
 *  Return:  true if queue is empty, and false otherwise
 */
 public boolean isEmpty()
 {
   return mySize == 0;
 }

/** First operation
 *  Return:  Object at the front of the queue; null if queue is empty
 */
 public Object first()
 {
   if ( isEmpty() )
     return null;
   else
     return myHead.getValue();
 }

/** Add operation
 *  Receive:  Object value
 *  Postcondition:  value has been added at the back of the queue
 */
 public void add(Object obj)
 {
   SinglyLinkedNode newNode = new SinglyLinkedNode(obj);
   if ( isEmpty() )
     myHead = newNode;
   else
     myTail.setSuccessor(newNode);

   myTail = newNode;
   mySize++;
 }
```

```
/** Remove operation
 *   Return:  Object at the front of the queue; null if queue is empty
 *   Postcondition:  Value at the front of the queue has been removed.
 */
public Object remove()
{
   Object result = null;
   if ( !isEmpty() )
   {
      result = myHead.getValue();
      myHead = myHead.getSuccessor();
      mySize--;
   }
   if ( isEmpty() )
      myTail = null;

   return result;
}

/** Size accessor
 *   Return:  number of elements in the queue */
public int getSize() { return mySize; }
/** Clear accessor
 *   Postcondition:  All values have been removed from the queue. */
public void clear()
{
   myHead = myTail = null;
   mySize = 0;
}

//--- String conversion for output purposes ---
public String toString()
{
   String result = "";
   for (SinglyLinkedNode current = myHead;
        current != null;
        current = current.getSuccessor() )
      result += (" " + current.getValue().toString() );

   return result;
}

//--- Attribute variables ---
private SinglyLinkedNode myHead, myTail;
private int  mySize;
}
```

The simple program in Figure 12.10 tests our queue class. It adds some values to the queue, displays the queue, and then removes them one at a time, displaying the value removed and the queue on each repetition.

FIGURE 12.10   A Queue CLASS TESTER

```java
// QueueTest.java -- a driver program to test the Queue class

import ann.util.Queue;

class QueueTest extends Object
{
  public static void main(String [] args)
  {
    Queue q = new Queue();

    for (int i = 0; i <= 100; i += 11)
      q.add( new Integer(i) );

    System.out.println( q );

    while ( !q.isEmpty() )
    {
      System.out.println( q.remove() );
      System.out.println( q );
    }
  }
}
```

Sample Run:

```
 0 11 22 33 44 55 66 77 88 99
0
 11 22 33 44 55 66 77 88 99
11
 22 33 44 55 66 77 88 99
22
 33 44 55 66 77 88 99
33
 44 55 66 77 88 99
44
 55 66 77 88 99
55
 66 77 88 99
66
 77 88 99
77
 88 99
88
 99
99
```

✔ Quick Quiz 12.4

1. Explain how a queue differs from a stack.
2. The last element added to a queue is the _____ one removed.
3. A stack exhibits LIFO behavior; a queue exhibits _____ behavior.
5. A(n) _____ queue is used to schedule output requests.
6. Queues are used to organize sections of main memory called _____ used to hold input/output data being transferred between a program and disk.
7. What are the four standard queue operations?

✍ **EXERCISES 12.4**

Exercises 1–3 assume the following declarations

```
Queue q = new Queue();
Integer i = new Integer();
```

where `Queue` is the class described in this section. Draw a diagram of the `Queue` (like those in the text) that results from the code segment being executed, or indicate why an error occurs.

1. ```
   for (int k = 1; k <= 5; k++)
       q.add(new Integer(10*k));
   ```

2. ```
   q.add(new Integer(10));
   i = q.remove();
   q.add(new Integer(22));
   i = q.remove();
   q.add(new Integer(33));
   i = q.remove();
   q.add(new Integer(44));
   ```

3. ```
   q.add(new Integer(10))
   q.add(new Integer(9));
   q.add(new Integer(8));
   q.add(new Integer(7));
   i = q.remove();
   ```

4. Write method `back()` for the `Queue` class that returns the last element of the queue.

5. Proceed as in Exercise 4, but design a method `element()` so that `element(n)` retrieves the nth queue element (counting from the front), if there is one.

12.5   AN INTRODUCTION TO TREES

In the preceding sections we have seen how lists can be implemented by linking together structures called nodes. We have seen that the main advantage of linked lists over array-based lists is that values can be inserted at any point in the list without having to move list elements to make room for the new element and items can be deleted without moving list elements to close the gaps.

We have also seen that the primary weakness of linked lists is that the elements cannot be accessed directly (except those at the ends of the list). If an array has n elements and these are ordered, then as we saw in Section 9.4, the direct access property of an array makes it possible to use binary search to locate a value in the list in $\log_2 n$ time as opposed to the $O(n)$ time required for linear search. Unfortunately, the binary search technique provides no such improvement over linear search for a linked list because the elements of such a list cannot be accessed directly. To access the middle element of a linked list, as required by binary search, one half of that list must be traversed, due to the linear nature of the links that connect the list's nodes. As a result, the time to perform a binary search of a linked list far exceeds the time required for a linear search, for all but small lists.

This raises an interesting question: Is it possible to organize a linked structure in some other way (other than with links from a node to its successor and predecessor)
   ```

so that its elements can be searched more quickly than is possible in a linearly-linked structure? Such a structure would ideally provide for easy insertion/deletion as in linked lists, but permit the access of individual elements in less than $O(n)$ time.

To see what would be needed to make it possible to search a list in a binary-search-like manner, consider the following ordered list of integers:

$$13, 28, 35, 49, 62, 66, 80$$

The first step in a binary search requires examining the middle element in the list. Direct access to this element is possible if we maintain a link to the node storing it:

13   28   35   (49)   62   66   80

For the next step, one of the two sublists, the left half or the right half, must be searched and both must therefore be accessible from this node. This is possible if we maintain two links, one to each of these sublists. Since these sublists are searched in the same manner, these links should refer to nodes containing the middle elements in these sublists:

13   (28)   35   (49)   62   (66)   80

By the same reasoning, in the next step, links from each of these "second-level" nodes are needed to access the middle elements in their sublists:

(13)   (28)   (35)   (49)   (62)   (66)   (80)

The resulting structure is usually drawn so that it has a treelike shape:

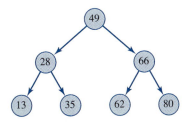

This structure is called a *binary search tree* and is a special kind of *binary tree*, which is a special instance of a more general structure called a *tree*.

Tree Terminology and Examples

A **tree** consists of a finite collection of **nodes** linked together in such a way that if the tree is not empty, then one of the nodes, called the **root,** has no incoming links, but every other node in the tree can be reached from the root by following a unique sequence of consecutive links.

Trees derive their names from the treelike diagrams that are used to picture them. For example,

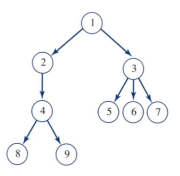

shows a tree having nine vertices in which the node labeled 1 is the root. As this diagram indicates, trees are usually drawn upside down, with the root at the top and the **leaves**—that is, nodes with no outgoing links—at the bottom. Nodes that are directly accessible from a given node (by using only one link) are called the **children** of that node, and a node is said to be the **parent** of its children. For example, in the preceding tree, node 3 is the parent of nodes 5, 6, and 7, and these nodes are the children of node 3 and are called **siblings.**

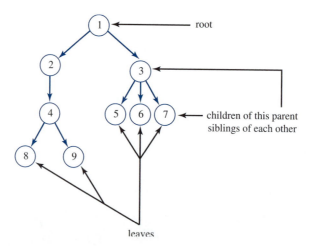

Applications of trees are many and varied. For example, a **genealogical tree** such as the following is a convenient way to picture a person's descendants:

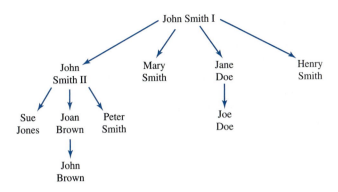

Game trees like the following, which shows the various configurations possible in the Towers of Hanoi problem with two disks (see Section 8.6), are used to analyze games and puzzles.

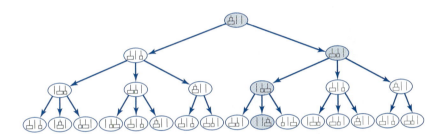

Parse trees constructed during the compilation of a program are used to check the program's syntax. For example, the following is a parse tree for the expression 2 * (3 + 4),

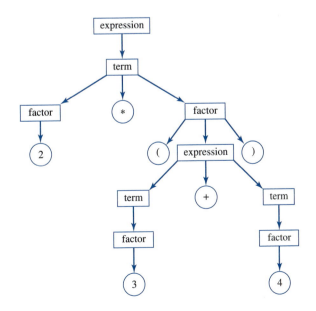

Examples of Binary Trees

Binary trees are trees in which each node has at most two children. Such trees are especially useful in modeling processes in which some experiment or test with two possible outcomes (for example, off or on, 0 or 1, false or true, down or up, yes or no) is performed repeatedly. For example, the following binary tree might be used to represent the possible outcomes of flipping a coin three times:

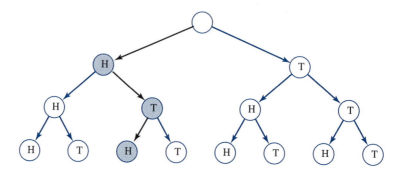

Each path from the root to one of the leaf nodes corresponds to a particular outcome, such as HTH (a head followed by a tail followed by another head), as highlighted in the diagram.

Similarly, a binary tree can be used in coding problems such as in encoding and decoding messages transmitted in Morse code, a scheme in which characters are represented as sequences of dots and dashes, as shown in the following table:

A	· —	M	— —	Y	— · — —		
B	— · · ·	N	— ·	Z	— — · ·		
C	— · — ·	O	— — —	1	· — — — —		
D	— · ·	P	· — — ·	2	· · — — —		
E	·	Q	— — · —	3	· · · — —		
F	· · — ·	R	· — ·	4	· · · · —		
G	— — ·	S	· · ·	5	· · · · ·		
H	· · · ·	T	—	6	— · · · ·		
I	· ·	U	· · —	7	— — · · ·		
J	· — — —	V	· · · —	8	— — — · ·		
K	— · —	W	· — —	9	— — — — ·		
L	· — · ·	X	— · · —	0	— — — — —		

In this case, the nodes in a binary tree are used to represent the characters, and each link from a node to its children is labeled with a dot or a dash, according to whether it leads to a left child or to a right child, respectively. Thus, part of the tree for Morse code is

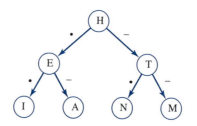

The sequence of dots and dashes labeling a path from the root to a particular node corresponds to the Morse code for that character; for example, ·· is the code for I, and —· is the code for N.

Decision-making processes can be modeled as a series of "yes-or-no" questions, and a binary tree can thus be used to model that process. Each non-leaf node is used to store a question, and if an affirmative answer to a question leads to another question, then the two nodes are connected with a link labeled "yes". Similarly, if a negative answer to a question leads to another question, then the two nodes are connected with a link labeled "no". Since there are only two choices for each question, the resulting structure is a binary tree with decisions at its leaf nodes. The problem of choosing a single choice from among many choices is solved simply by descending through the tree until a leaf node (i.e., a decision) is reached.

For problems in some areas, solutions can be obtained by designing decision trees that mimic the choices experts would make in solving these problems. For example, programs to help a person prepare their income tax returns have some of the expertise of a tax accountant encoded within them. Similarly, programs that lead a person through the steps of writing a will have some of the expertise of an estate lawyer encoded within them. Programs that control a robot that welds automobile components on an assembly line are based on the knowledge of an expert welder. In general, programs that exhibit expertise in some area through the use of a knowledge base are called **expert systems,** and the study of such systems is one of the branches of artificial intelligence.

Implementing Binary Trees

A binary tree can be represented by a multiply linked structure in which each node has two links, one connecting the node to its left child and the other connecting it to its right child. Such nodes can be represented in Java by a `BinaryTreeNode` class that has three attribute variables:

```
public class BinaryTreeNode
{
 //-- Methods go here

 // Attribute variables
 private BinaryTreeNode myLeftChild,
                        myRightChild;
 private Object         myValue;
}
```

The two handles `myLeftChild` and `myRightChild` refer to the left and right child, respectively, or are null if the node does not have a left or right child:

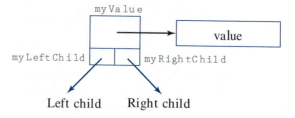

A leaf node is thus characterized by myLeftChild and myRightChild both being null:

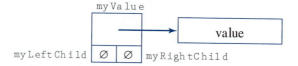

One of the attribute variables in a BinaryTree class would be a handle myRoot that refers to the node that is the root of the tree; and for convenience, we would probably also add an attribute variable mySize that keeps track of the number of nodes in the tree:

```
public class BinaryTree extends Object
{
// methods go here

// attribute variables
private BinaryTreeNode myRoot;
private int            mySize;
}
```

Given such a class, the binary tree

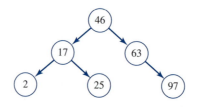

can be represented as the following linked structure:

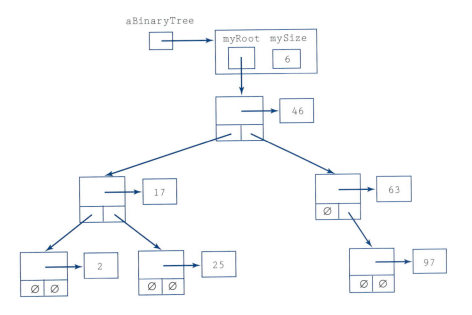

Binary Search Trees

In the preceding binary tree, the value in each node is greater than the value in its left child (if there is one) and less than the value in its right child (if there is one). A binary tree having this property is called a **binary search tree (BST)** because, as we noted at the beginning of this section, it can be searched using an algorithm much like the binary search algorithm for lists:

SEARCH ALGORITHM FOR A BST

1. Initialize a handle *currentNode* to the node containing the root.
2. Repeatedly do the following:

    If the *item* being sought is:

      Less than the value referred to by *currentNode*.myValue

        Set *currentNode* = *currentNode*.myLeftChild;

      Greater than the value referred to by currNode.myValue

        Set *currentNode* = *currentNode*.myRightChild;

    Else

      Terminate repetition because *item* has been found.

To illustrate, suppose we wish to search the preceding BST for 25. We begin at the root, and since 25 is less than the value 46 in this root, we know that the desired value is located to the left of the root; that is, it must be in the left **subtree,** whose root is 17:

Now we continue the search by comparing 25 with the value in the root of this sub-tree. Since 25 > 17, we know that the right subtree should be searched:

(25)

Examining the value in the root of this one-node subtree locates the value 25.
    Similarly, to search for the value 55, after comparing 55 with the value in the root, we are led to search its right subtree:

Now, because 55 < 63, if the desired value is in the tree, it will be in the left subtree. However, since this left subtree is empty, we conclude that the value 55 is not in the tree.

Tree Traversals

Another important operation is **traversal,** that is, moving through a binary tree, visiting each node exactly once. And suppose for now that the order in which the nodes are visited is not relevant. What is important is that we visit each node, not missing any, and that the information in each node is processed exactly once.
    One simple recursive scheme is to traverse the binary tree as follows:

1. Visit the root and process its contents.
2. Traverse the left subtree.
3. Traverse the right subtree.

To illustrate this algorithm, let us consider the following binary tree:

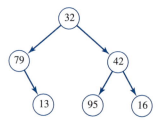

If we simply display a node's contents when we visit it, we begin by displaying the value 32 in the root of the binary tree. Next we must traverse the left subtree; after this traversal is finished, we then must traverse the right subtree; and when this traversal is completed, we will have traversed the entire binary tree.

(I)

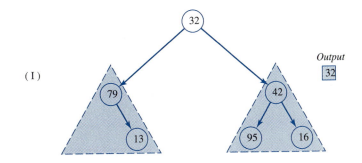

Output
32

Thus the problem has been reduced to the traversal of two smaller binary trees. We consider the left subtree and visit its root. Next we must traverse its left subtree and then its right subtree.

(II)

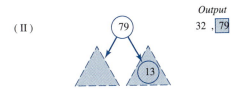

Output
32 , 79

The left subtree is empty, and we need do nothing. So we turn to traversing the right subtree. We visit its root and then must traverse its left subtree followed by its right subtree:

(III)

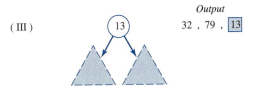

Output
32 , 79 , 13

As both subtrees are empty, no action is required to traverse them. Consequently, traversal of the binary tree in diagram III is complete, and since this was the right subtree of the tree in diagram II, traversal of this tree is also complete.

This means that we have finished traversing the left subtree of the root in the original binary tree in diagram I, and we finally are ready to begin traversing the right subtree. This traversal proceeds in a similar manner. We first visit its root, displaying the value 42 stored in it, then traverse its left subtree, and then its right subtree:

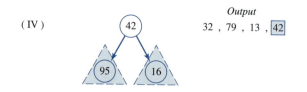

(IV)

Output

32 , 79 , 13 , 42

The left subtree consists of a single node with empty left and right subtrees and is traversed as described earlier for a one-node binary tree:

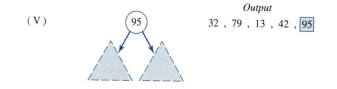

(V)

Output

32 , 79 , 13 , 42 , 95

The right subtree is traversed in the same way:

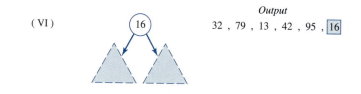

(VI)

Output

32 , 79 , 13 , 42 , 95 , 16

This completes the traversal of the binary tree in diagram IV and thus completes the traversal of the original tree in diagram I.

As this example demonstrates, traversing a binary tree recursively requires three basic steps, which we shall denote N, L, and R:

N: Visit a node.
L: Traverse the left subtree of a node.
R: Traverse the right subtree of a node.

We performed these steps in the order listed here, but in fact, there are six different orders in which they can be carried out: LNR, NLR, LRN, NRL, RNL, and RLN. For example, the ordering LNR corresponds to the following recursive traversal algorithm:

If the binary tree is empty then   // anchor
    Do nothing.
Else do the following: // inductive step

L: Traverse the left subtree.

N: Visit the root.

R: Traverse the right subtree.

For the preceding binary tree, this LNR traversal visits the nodes in the order 79, 13, 32, 95, 42, 16.

The first three orders, in which the left subtree is traversed before the right, are the most important of the six traversals and are commonly called by other names:

LNR ↔ Inorder
NLR ↔ Preorder
LRN ↔ Postorder

To see why these names are appropriate, consider the following **expression tree**, a binary tree used to represent the arithmetic expression

$$A - B * C + D$$

by representing each operand as a child of a parent node representing the corresponding operator:

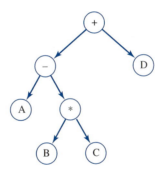

An **inorder** traversal of this expression tree produces the **infix** expression

$$A - B * C + D$$

A **preorder** traversal gives the **prefix** expression, in which an operator is written before its operands:

$$+ - A * B C D$$

And a **postorder** traversal yields the **postfix** expression—also called **Reverse Polish Notation** (RPN)—in which an operator is written after its operands:

$$A B C * - D +$$

It should be noted that an *inorder traversal visits the nodes in a BST in ascending order.* The reason is that in a binary search tree, for each node, the value in the left child is less than the value in that node, which, in turn, is less than the value in the right child. This means that for each node, all of the values in the left subtree are smaller than the value in this node, which is less than all values in its right subtree. Because an inorder traversal is an LNR traversal, it follows that it must visit the nodes in ascending order.

Constructing BSTs

A binary search tree can be built by repeatedly inserting elements into a BST that is initially empty (myRoot is null). The method used to determine where an element is to be inserted is similar to that used to search the tree. We simply maintain a handle *parentNode* that refers to the parent of the node currently being examined as we descend the tree, looking for a place to insert the item. That is, in the search algorithm, we set *parentNode = currentNode* before we change *currentNode* to its left or right child. If the value being inserted is not found in the BST, *currentNode* will eventually become null and *parentNode* will indicate the parent of a new node that will contain the value.

For example, the following sequence of diagrams indicates how 35 would be inserted into the binary search tree given earlier:

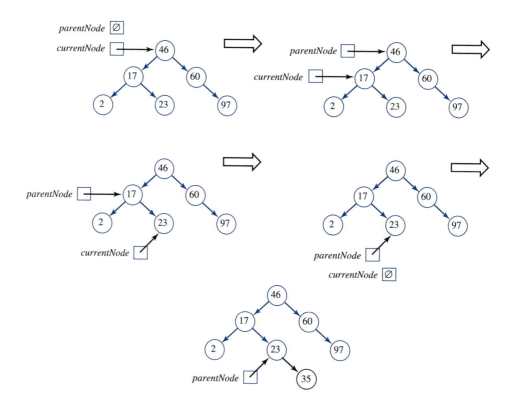

This completes our introduction to trees, and binary search trees in particular. Developing a BST class is not a difficult task and we will leave the details as exercises.

✔ Quick Quiz 12.5

1. A node that has no incoming links but from which every other node in the tree can be reached by following a unique sequence of consecutive links is called a(n) _____.

2. Nodes with no outgoing links are called _____ .

3. Nodes that are directly accessible from a given node (by using only one link) are called the _____ of that node, which is said to be the _____ of these nodes.

4. Binary trees are trees in which each node has _____ .

Questions 5–7 refer to the following binary search tree:

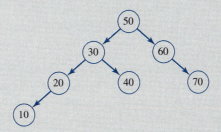

5. Which node is the root?

6. List all the leaves.

7. Draw the BST that results if 45, 55, and 65 are inserted.

For Questions 8–10, draw the BST that results when the Java keywords are inserted in the order given, starting with an empty BST.

8. `if, do, for, case, switch, while, else`

9. `do, case, else, if, switch, while, for`

10. `while, switch, for, else, if, do, case`

Questions 11–13 refer to the following binary search tree:

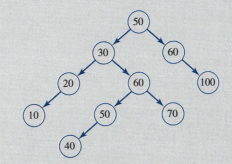

11. Perform an inorder traversal of this BST.

12. Perform a preorder traversal of this BST.

13. Perform a postorder traversal of this BST.

EXERCISES 12.5

For each of the lists of letters in Exercises 1–5, draw the BST that results when the letters are inserted in the order given, starting with an empty BST.

1. A, C, R, E, S

2. R, A, C, E, S

3. C, A, R, E, S

4. S, C, A, R, E

5. C, O, R, N, F, L, A, K, E, S

For each of the lists of Java keywords in Exercises 6–10, draw the binary search tree that is constructed when the words are inserted in the order given, starting with an empty BST.

6. `new, final, short, if, main, break, float`

7. `break, long, return, char, else, switch, float`

8. `double, float, long, class, public, int, new`

9. `while, static, public, private, extends, case`

10. `break, long, if, short, else, case, void, do, return, while, for, switch, double, true`

11–15.   Perform inorder, preorder, and postorder traversals of the trees in Exercises 6–10 and show the sequence of words that results in each case.

12.6 GRAPHICAL/INTERNET JAVA: A `PolygonSketcher` CLASS

As another illustration of the usefulness of container classes to store data, we will build a graphical application in which a user can use the mouse to sketch closed geometric figures called polygons. The basic idea of the application is to listen for mouse-clicks, and on each mouse-click, draw a line from the point of the previous click to where the mouse cursor is currently pointing:

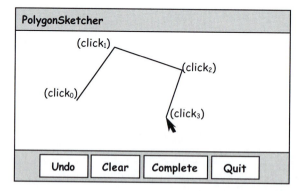

If the user *drags* the mouse (i.e., moves the mouse while holding down its button), the application should draw a line that moves with the mouse, creating a graphical effect called "rubber-banding."

For convenience, the application will provide an "Undo" button that allows the user to undo the last line segment drawn:

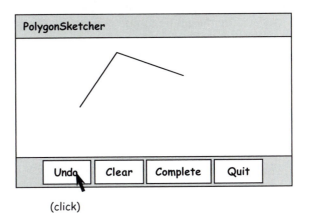

(click)

Repeated clicking of this button should undo any number of lines. The application will also have a "Clear" button that completely erases the current sketch. In addition, it will provide a "Complete" button that draws from the point of the most recent mouse-click back to the point of the first mouse-click, forming a closed polygon:

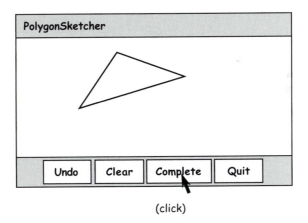

(click)

Also, although it isn't strictly necessary, the application will also provide a "Quit" button.

Design

As we begin to think about what classes will need to be built, it should be evident that we will need a class that actually constructs our application's GUI, listens for the user to click its buttons, and so on. We will call this the `PolygonSketcher` class.

As we have seen on several occasions, when doing "custom graphics" with Java's Swing components, each component that draws graphics should be designed as a separate class (usually extending `JPanel`) that confines all of its drawing to its `paintComponent()` method. This means that a separate class will be needed to draw the lines specified by the user's mouse and button clicks. We will call this a `SketchPanel`.

In our `SketchPanel` class there are a variety of ways to draw the lines that connect the points where the user clicks. Consequently, we will first examine the other features of our application to see if any of them suggests the best way to proceed.

To support the "repeated undo" feature, we will have to store each point at which the user clicks the mouse. Because an undo operation will require removing the last point we stored, we need a structure that has a last-in-first-out (LIFO) behavior. However, to support our "complete" feature, we also need access to the *first* point at which the user clicked the mouse. This means that a stack is not the proper data structure to use. A queue comes close, but it does not allow both push and pop operations at the back of the list.

None of the data structures we have studied provide all of the capabilities we need, and so we will create a new `PointList` class that does. Like a stack, a `PointList` will allow points to be pushed and popped in LIFO fashion at one end of the list, and in addition, will allow access to the value at the other end. If our `SketchPanel` class keeps track of the user's mouse-clicks in a `PointList` attribute variable, its `paintComponent()` method can draw what the user has specified simply by connecting the points. We will begin our project by building this class.

Coding

The `PointList` Class. Before building the `PointList` class, we must determine how to represent the mouse-click points within the class. There are several ways to do this, and to help us select one we will look at the methods Java provides for drawing connected lines and see if this leads us in a particular direction. The `drawPolyLine()` method from the `java.awt.Graphics` package appears to be exactly what we need. Java's API documentation states that it draws a sequence of connected lines defined by arrays of *x* and *y* coordinates of points; it has 3 parameters:

❑ An `int` array containing the sequence of *x* coordinates of the points
❑ An `int` array containing the sequence of *y* coordinates of the points
❑ The total number of points

This suggests that our `PointList` class should have an attribute variable for each of these—an `int` array `myX` for the *x* coordinates, another `myY` for the *y* coordinates, and an `int` variable `myPointCount` for the number of points. It will also need to provide accessor methods for these three instance variables. Figure 12.11 presents a `PointList` class that uses this approach:

FIGURE 12.11   A `PointList` CLASS

```java
/** PointList.java defines a data structure to store (x,y) points.
 *  Attributes: separate int arrays for x and y coordinates;
 *              number of points
 *  Methods:    Default constructor; add a point to end of the list;
 *              remove a point from the end of the list; retrieve
 *              each coordinate of point at end / front of the the list;
 *              accessors
 */

import java.awt.Point;

class PointList extends Object
{
 /** PointList constructor
  *  Postcondition:  myX and myY are int arrays with capacity DEFAULT_SIXE;
  *                  myPointCount == 0.
  */
  public PointList()
  {
    myX = new int [DEFAULT_SIZE];
    myY = new int [DEFAULT_SIZE];
    myPointCount = 0;
  }
//--- Push operations ---
/* Push a Point
 * Receive:        Point p
 * Postcondition: Coordinates of p have been added to myX and myY arrays.
 */
  public void pushPoint(Point p)
  {
    pushPoint(p.x, p.y);
  }

/* Push a point with coordinates x and y
 * Receive:        ints x and y
 * Postcondition: x has been added to array myX, y to array myY.
 */
  public void pushPoint(int x, int y)
  {
    if (myPointCount >= myX.length)          // arrays are full
    {
      int newCapacity = myX.length * 2;      // create bigger ones
      int [] tempX = new int [newCapacity];
      int [] tempY = new int [newCapacity];

      for (int i = 0; i < myPointCount; i++)  // put my values in them
      {
        tempX[i] = myX[i];
        tempY[i] = myY[i];
      }
      myX = tempX;                           // replace old arrays
      myY = tempY;                           //  with them
    }

    myX[myPointCount] = x;
    myY[myPointCount] = y;
    myPointCount++;
  }
```

```
    /* Pop operation
     * Postcondition: Point at end of Pointlist (last one added) has been
     *                        removed.
     */
    public Point popPoint()
    {
      Point result = null;
      if (myPointCount > 0)
      {
        myPointCount--;
        result = new Point(myX[myPointCount], myY[myPointCount]);
      }
      return result;
    }


//-- Retrieve coordinate of last node
/* Get x coordinate of last node
 * Return: int at the end of array myX or -1 if there is none */
 public int lastX()
 {
  if (myPointCount > 0)
   return myX[myPointCount-1];
  else
   return -1;
 }


/* Get y coordinate of last node
 * Return: int at the end of array myY  or -1 if there is none  */
 public int lastY()
 {
  if (myPointCount > 0)
   return myY[myPointCount-1];
  else
   return -1;
 }


//-- Retrieve coordinate of first node
/* Get x coordinate of first node
 * Return: int at the beginning of array myX or -1 if there is none */
 public int firstX()
 {
  if (myPointCount > 0)
   return myX[0];
  else
   return -1;
 }

/* Get y coordinate of first node
 * Return:  int at the beginning of array myY or -1 if there is none */
 public int firstY()
 {
  if (myPointCount > 0)
   return myY[0];
  else
   return -1;
 }
```

```
//--- Accessors ---
/* X coordinates
 * Return: myX */
 public int [] xCoordinates() { return myX; }

/* Y coordinates
 * Return: myXY */
 public int [] yCoordinates() { return myY; }

/* Number of points
 * Return: myPointCount */
 public int pointCount()        { return myPointCount; }

/* Clear the polygon
 * Postcondition: Point list is empty. */
 public void clear()             { myPointCount = 0; }

/* String converter -- for output purposes
 * Return: String representation of polygon */
 public String toString()
 {
   String result = "";
   for (int i = 0; i < myPointCount; i++)
     result += " (" + myX[i] + "," + myY[i] + ")";

   return result;
 }

//--- Attribute constant and variables ---
 private final static int DEFAULT_SIZE = 8;

 private int [] myX;
 private int [] myY;
 private int myPointCount;
}
```

The only part of the preceding class declaration that may not be self-evident is the code in the pushPoint() method that handles the condition when the arrays of coordinates are full. The solution used here is to "resize" the arrays as follows:

1. Allocate two new arrays that are twice as large as the old ones.
2. Copy all of the values from the old arrays into the new arrays.
3. Reset myX and myY to be handles for the new arrays.

Of course, this is an implementation detail. The PointList methods can be used without the user being aware that this is going on behind the scenes.

The SketchPanel Class. Now that the PointList class is implemented, we can build the SketchPanel class that uses it. The new feature in this class is that it must "listen" for mouse events. As we saw in Chapter 7, there are two different listener interfaces for mouse events:

- ❑ `MouseListener` listens for mouse button events, and handles them with the methods:
  - ❑ `mousePressed()`   The mouse button was pressed
  - ❑ `mouseReleased()`   The mouse button was released
  - ❑ `mouseClicked()`   The mouse button was pressed or released
  - ❑ `mouseEntered()`   The mouse was moved into a region
  - ❑ `mouseExited()`   The mouse was moved out of a region
- ❑ `MouseMotionListener` listens for mouse movements and handles them with the methods:
  - ❑ `mouseDragged()`   The mouse was moved with a button pressed
  - ❑ `mouseMoved()`   The mouse was moved with no button pressed

In our polygon sketcher, we must store a point's coordinates in the `PointList` whenever the user presses the mouse button. This means that we must implement the `MouseListener` interface and override the `mousePressed()` method to perform this action. To achieve the rubber-banding effect when the user drags the mouse, we must undraw the last line (by popping the `PointList`) and draw a new line to the new mouse coordinates (by pushing the new coordinates onto the `PointList`). For this, we must implement the `MouseMotionListener` interface and override the `mouseDragged()` method. Once the user has clicked the mouse, specifying a line to be drawn, the `paintComponent()` method will draw the line using the `drawPolyLine()` method from Java's Graphics class.

Figure 12.12 presents the `SketchPanel` class, which provides these capabilities. Anticipating the actions for the buttons in our GUI, we have also included methods to handle clicks on the buttons it will have:

- ❑ `eraseLastLine()` for the *Undo* button
- ❑ `eraseAllLines()` for the *Clear* button
- ❑ `completePolygon()` for the *Complete* button

FIGURE 12.12   A `SketchPanel` CLASS

```
/** SketchPanel.java records mouse-clicks in a PointList and draws the
 *   polygon determined by these points.
 *   Attributes: a PointList; (static) constants that specify background
 *               and foreground colors and height and width of the window
 *   Methods: constructors -- default, specify dimensions, or dimensions and
 *            colors; mousePressed() and mouseDragged();  paintComponent();
 *            eraseLastLine(); eraseAllLines(); completePolygon()
 */

import java.awt.*;               // Color, Graphics, ...
import java.awt.event.*;         // MouseEvent, MouseListener, ...
import javax.swing.*;            // JPanel, JButton, ...
import PointList;
```

```java
class SketchPanel extends     JPanel
                    implements MouseListener, MouseMotionListener
{
 //--- Constructors
 /** Default constructor
  *  Postcondition: SketchPanel is constructed with default width and height,
  *                 default background and foreground colors.
  */
  public SketchPanel()
  {
   this(DEFAULT_WIDTH, DEFAULT_HEIGHT,
        DEFAULT_BACKGROUND, DEFAULT_FOREGROUND);
  }

  /** Explicit-value constructor -- size
   *  Receive:       integers width and height
   *  Postcondition: SketchPanel is constructed with specified width and
   *                 height, but with default background and foreground
   *                 colors.
   */
  public SketchPanel(int width, int height)
  {
    this(width, height, DEFAULT_BACKGROUND, DEFAULT_FOREGROUND);
  }

 /** Explicit-value constructor -- size and color
  *  Receive:       integers width and height, Colors bg and fg
  *  Postcondition: SketchPanel is constructed with specified width and
  *                 height, background color bg, and foreground color fg.
  */
  public SketchPanel(int width, int height, Color bg, Color fg)
  {
    myLine = new PointList();
    addMouseListener(this);
    addMouseMotionListener(this);
    setSize(width, height);
    setForeground(fg);
    setBackground(bg);
  }

 //--- Override mousePressed() ---
  public void mousePressed(MouseEvent event)
  {
    int x = event.getX();        // get x
    int y = event.getY();        //   and y coordinates of mouse cursor
    myLine.pushPoint(x, y);      // add them to the PointList
    repaint();                   // update
  }

 //--- Override mouseDragged() ---
  public void mouseDragged(MouseEvent event)
  {
    if (myLine.pointCount() > 1)  // if a line exists to be 'erased'
      eraseLastLine();            // erase it
                                  // replace it
    int x = event.getX();         // get x
    int y = event.getY();         //   and y coordinates of mouse cursor
    myLine.pushPoint(x, y);       // add them to the PointList
    repaint();                    // update
  }
```

```java
//--- stub MouseListener and MouseMotionListener methods
public void mouseReleased(MouseEvent event)
{}
public void mouseMoved(MouseEvent e)
{}
public void mouseEntered(MouseEvent e)
{}
public void mouseExited(MouseEvent e)
{}
public void mouseClicked(MouseEvent e)
{}

//--- paintComponent() to draw a line
public void paintComponent(Graphics pen)
{
    super.paintComponent(pen);

    if (myLine.pointCount() > 1)
        pen.drawPolyline(myLine.xCoordinates(),
                         myLine.yCoordinates(),
                         myLine.pointCount() );
}

//--- Erase last line drawn
public void eraseLastLine()
{
    if (myLine.pointCount() > 0)
    {
        Point p = myLine.popPoint();
        repaint();
    }
}
//--- Erase all lines
public void eraseAllLines()
{
    if (myLine.pointCount() > 0)
    {
        myLine.clear();
        repaint();
    }
}

//--- Complete the polygon
public void completePolygon()
{
    if (myLine.pointCount() > 2)
    {
        int x = myLine.firstX();      // get first point
        int y = myLine.firstY();
        myLine.pushPoint(x, y);       // close polygon by adding it to PointList
        repaint();                    // update
    }
}
```

```
//--- Attribute variable and constants ---
  private PointList  myLine;

  private static final Color DEFAULT_FOREGROUND = Color.black;
  private static final Color DEFAULT_BACKGROUND = Color.white;
  private static final int   DEFAULT_HEIGHT = 300;
  private static final int   DEFAULT_WIDTH = 400;
}
```

To implement the `MouseListener` and `MouseMotionListener` interfaces, we must implement *all* of the mouse-handling methods, not just the two we need. As a result, the `SketchPanel` class contains five "stub" methods that do nothing.[6]

Each call to `repaint()` redraws the screen, which (among other things) invokes the `paintComponent()` method. If there is a line to be drawn, this method simply uses the `drawPolyline()` method to draw the sequence of connected lines specified by the `PointList`'s *x*-coordinate array, its *y*-coordinate array, and its point count.

The `PolygonSketcher` Class. Our final class is the `PolygonSketcher` class, which builds the graphical user interface—including a central `SketchPanel`—and then listens for clicks on its buttons. Upon receiving such events, its `actionPerformed()` method sends the appropriate messages to the `SketchPanel`, as can be seen in Figure 12.13.

FIGURE 12.13   A `PolygonSketcher` CLASS

```
/** PolygonSketcher.java provides a GUI for sketching polygons.
 *  Attributes: (static) constants for default dimensons and colors;
 *              undo, clear, complete, and quit buttons; a sketch panel;
 *              a control panel.
 *  Methods: constructors -- default, specify dimensions, or dimensions and
 *           colors; actionPerformed(); main()
 */

import ann.gui.CloseableFrame;
import java.awt.*;              // Color, Graphics, ...
import java.awt.event.*;        // ActionEvent, ActionListener, ...
import javax.swing.*;           // JPanel, JButton, ...
import SketchPanel;

public class PolygonSketcher extends    CloseableFrame
                             implements ActionListener
{
 //--- Constructors
 //--- Default
  public PolygonSketcher()
  {
   this(DEFAULT_WIDTH, DEFAULT_HEIGHT,
        DEFAULT_BACKGROUND, DEFAULT_FOREGROUND);
  }
```

---

[6] If an application that implements `MouseListener` (or `MouseMotionListener`) has no class it must extend, it can extend the abstract `MouseAdapter` (or `MouseMotionAdapter`) class. This class provides a stub for each mouse method. The application then inherits the stubs, so that it need only override the particular methods it needs.

```
//--- Specify dimensions
 public PolygonSketcher(int width, int height)
 {
    this(width, height, DEFAULT_BACKGROUND, DEFAULT_FOREGROUND);
 }

//--- Specify dimensions and foreground and background colors
 public PolygonSketcher(int width, int height, Color fg, Color bg)
 {
    setSize(width, height);
    mySketchPanel = new SketchPanel(width, height-100, fg, bg);

    myControlPanel = new JPanel(new FlowLayout());
    myControlPanel.setSize(width, 100);
    myUndoButton = new JButton("Undo");
    myUndoButton.addActionListener(this);
    myControlPanel.add(myUndoButton);

    myClearButton = new JButton("Clear");
    myClearButton.addActionListener(this);
    myControlPanel.add(myClearButton);

    myCompleteButton = new JButton("Complete");
    myCompleteButton.addActionListener(this);
    myControlPanel.add(myCompleteButton);

    myQuitButton = new JButton("Quit");
    myQuitButton.addActionListener(this);
    myControlPanel.add(myQuitButton);

    getContentPane().add(mySketchPanel, BorderLayout.CENTER);
    getContentPane().add(myControlPanel, BorderLayout.SOUTH);
 }

//--- Override actionPerformed()
 public void actionPerformed(ActionEvent event)
 {
    Object eventSource = event.getSource();
    if (eventSource instanceof JButton)
    {
      JButton buttonPressed = (JButton) eventSource;

      if (buttonPressed.equals(myUndoButton))
        mySketchPanel.eraseLastLine();
      else if (buttonPressed.equals(myClearButton))
        mySketchPanel.eraseAllLines();
      else if (buttonPressed.equals(myCompleteButton))
        mySketchPanel.completePolygon();
      else if (buttonPressed.equals(myQuitButton))
        System.exit(0);
      else
        System.err.println("PolygonSketcher.actionPerformed():"
                           + " unexpected event: " + event);
    }
 }
```

```
//--- main() method
public static void main(String [] args)
  {
    PolygonSketcher sketcher = new PolygonSketcher(400, 400,
                                              Color.yellow, Color.blue);
    sketcher.setVisible(true);
  }


//--- Attribute constants and variables
  private static final int   DEFAULT_WIDTH  = 400;
  private static final int   DEFAULT_HEIGHT = 400;
  private static final Color DEFAULT_BACKGROUND = Color.white;
  private static final Color DEFAULT_FOREGROUND = Color.black;

  private JButton            myUndoButton, myClearButton,
                             myCompleteButton, myQuitButton;
  private SketchPanel        mySketchPanel;
  private JPanel             myControlPanel;
}
```

Testing

Once we have built our application, we must test it thoroughly. On startup, our application appears as follows:

Drawing a line is as easy as clicking two different places:

Drawing more complex figures is equally easy:

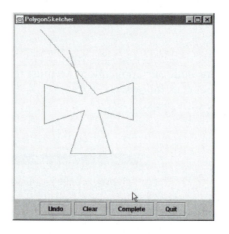

The *Undo* button makes it easy to fix one or more mistakes:

After the preceding correction is made, the *Complete* button makes it easy to finish the figure:

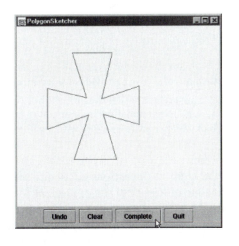

We can either continue with this sketch or use the *Clear* button to start over.

PART OF THE PICTURE: DATA STRUCTURES

In this chapter, we have seen that Java provides standard classes such as `ArrayList` and `LinkedList`, and that they can be used to solve a variety of problems involving collections of values. These are two of a variety of new structures for storing data provided by Java. By providing standard ways to efficiently store and manipulate collections of values, these **data structures** can greatly simplify the solutions to many problems.

As we saw, different data structures have different uses. For example, although both `ArrayList` and `LinkedList` can be used to store a sequence of values, `ArrayList` should be used if direct access to values within the sequence is needed—`ArrayList` can perform such actions in $O(1)$ time, compared to $O(n)$ for `LinkedList`—and `LinkedList` should be used if many insertions and deletions must be performed within the sequence and not just at the end. Both `LinkedList` and `ArrayList` provide these operations via `add()` and `remove()` methods, but the times required by the `ArrayList` versions of these operations are proportional to the number of values in the list, whereas the times for their `LinkedList` counterparts are independent of the number of values in the sequence. We have also seen how to implement other data structures: a `Stack` that provides LIFO access and a `Queue` that provides FIFO access. Our `Stack` implementation illustrated how to build a data structure as a wrapper for another data structure (i.e., `LinkedList`), while our `Queue` implementation illustrated how to build a linked data structure from scratch. In Section 12.5 we outlined how to implement a binary search tree, a linked structure in which binary search can be carried out efficiently (in O(log$_2$n) time on the average). In the preceding section, we illustrated how to build a dynamic array-based data structure from the ground up.

Java provides other collection interfaces and classes for data storage, including the following:

❑ The `Set` interface, which the `HashSet` and `TreeSet` classes implement. Like a mathematical set, `Set` provides for a collection of values without duplicates.

❑ The `Map` interface, which the `HashMap`, `TreeMap`, and `HashTable` classes implement. Like a mathematical mapping, `Map` creates a collection of (*key, value*) pairs, each of which associates a key with a value.

Deciding which collection (if any) is most appropriate for a particular problem depends on the kinds of operations needed to solve the problem as well as a knowledge of the time efficiency of the operations for a given collection. Such details are given in the Java API documentation for each class.

Java also provides the useful `Collections` class. It contains a number of class utility methods that can be used to manipulate collections, including methods to find the maximum value in a collection, find the minimum value in a collection, sort a collection, and many others. These methods implement operations that can be applied to any collection subclass.

The collection classes in `java.util` provide "off-the-shelf" data structures and operations that can be used to solve a wide variety of problems. Knowledge of these classes and their methods can save a great deal of work. Such knowledge can be acquired through study of the API and practice using the classes and methods.

CHAPTER SUMMARY

KEY TERMS AND NOTES

`ArrayList` class	dotted-decimal notation
back of a queue	doubly-linked list
binary search tree	expert system
binary tree	First-In-First-Out (FIFO)
buffer	front of a queue
children	gateway
circular-linked list	head of a queue
collection class	host name
constant time	infix

inorder
input/output buffer
Internet Protocol (IP)
IP address
Last-In-First-Out (LIFO)
leaf node
linear time
linked list
`LinkedList` class
list iterators
node
$O(1)$
$O(n)$
parent node
pop
postfix
postorder

prefix
preorder
push
push-down stack
queue
rear of a queue
Reverse Polish Notation (RPN)
siblings
singly-linked list
spool queue
stack
TCP/IP
time-efficient
top of a stack
Transmission Control Protocol (TCP)
traversal
tree

◎ Collection classes store groups of values.

◎ Two useful collection classes provided in Java are `ArrayList` and `LinkedList`. These are classes that can be used to implement the `List` interface.

◎ A stack has LIFO (Last-In-First-Out) behavior. A queue has FIFO (First-In-First-Out) behavior.

◎ A *tree* consists of a finite collection of nodes linked together in such a way that if the tree is not empty, then one of the nodes, called the *root*, has no incoming links, but every other node in the tree can be reached from the root by following a unique sequence of consecutive links.

◎ A *binary tree* is a tree in which each node has at most two children.

◎ In a *binary search tree*, the value in a left child is less than the value in its parent which is in turn less than the value in its right child (if there is one).

◎ Inorder traversal visits the nodes in a BST in ascending order.

◎ When doing custom graphics with Java's Swing components, each component that draws graphics should be designed as a separate class (usually extending `JPanel`) that confines all of its drawing to its `paintComponent()` method.

Documentation

■ **SOME METHODS IN** `List` **INTERFACE (**`java.util`**)**

Method	Description
`boolean add(Object obj)`	Appends `obj` at the end of the receiver. (For `Collections` in general, returns true if the collection changes as a result of this call; false if it does not permit duplicates and already contains the specified element. Lists typically allow duplications, in which case `add()` will return true.)
`void add(int index, Object obj)`	Insert `obj` at the position `index`
`boolean addAll(Collection c)`	Like `add()` above, but appends all the elements of `c`
`void addAll(int index, Collection c)`	Like the second form of `add()` above, but inserts all the elements of `c`
`void clear()`	Removes all elements from the list
`boolean contains(Object obj)`	Returns true or false according to whether the list contains `obj`
`boolean containsAll( Collection c)`	Returns true or false according to whether the list contains all the elements of collection `c`
`boolean equals(Object obj)`	Returns true if `obj` is also a list, both lists have the same size, and all corresponding pairs of elements in the two lists are equal; false otherwise
`Object get(int index)`	Returns the element at position `index` in the receiver
`int indexOf(Object obj)`	Returns the index of the first occurrence of `obj` in the receiver, −1 if not found. Search uses `equal()` to test for equality.
`boolean isEmpty()`	Returns true or false according to whether receiver is empty
`int lastIndexOf(Object obj)`	Like `indexOf()`, but searches for last occurrence
`ListIterator ListIterator()`	Returns a `ListIterator` for the elements of the list
`ListIterator listIterator( int index)`	Returns a `ListIterator` for the elements of list, starting at position `index`

`Object remove(int index)`	Removes and returns the element at location `index` in the list; subsequent elements are shifted to the left (reducing their indices by 1)
`boolean remove(Object obj)`	Removes the first occurrence of `obj` in the list, -1 if not found. Search uses `equal()` to test for equality. Element shifting occurs as above
`boolean retainAll(Collection c)`	Retains only the elements in the list that are in the collection `c`; returns true if this changes the list and false otherwise
`Object set(int index,` `            Object obj)`	Replaces the element at position `index` in the list with `obj`; returns the element that was at that position
`int size()`	Returns number of elements in the receiver
`List subList(int from, int to)`	Returns sublist of elements in list from position `from` up to but not including position `to`
`Object[] toArray()`	Returns an array containing all elements of the receiver in the same order
`Object[] toArray(Object[]arr)`	As above, but the (run-time) type of the returned array is that of `arr`

■ SOME `ArrayList` METHODS (`java.util`; IMPLEMENTS `List`; EXTENDS `AbstractList`)

Method	Description
`ArrayList()`	Constructs an empty list
`ArrayList(int initialCap)`	As in the preceding, but with the specified initial capacity
`ArrayList(Collection c)`	Constructs a list containing the elements of `c` in the order they are returned by `c`'s iterator
`Object clone()`	Returns a shallow copy of the list
`void ensureCapacity(` `            int minCapacity)`	Increases the capacity of the receiver (if necessary) so that it can hold at least `minCapacity` elements
`protected void removeRange(` `            int from, int to)`	Removes elements in receiver from position `from` up to but not including position `to`
`void trimToSize()`	Trims the capacity of the list to its current size.
The methods described for `List`	See `List`

■ **SOME** `LinkedList` **METHODS (**`java.util`**; IMPLEMENTS** `List`**; EXTENDS** `AbstractSequentialList`**)**

Method	Description
`LinkedList()`	Constructs an empty list
`LinkedList(Collection c)`	Constructs a list containing the elements of c in the order they are returned by c's iterator
`void addFirst(Object obj)`	Inserts obj at the beginning of the list
`void addLast(Object obj)`	Appends obj to the end of the list
`Object clone()`	Returns a shallow copy of the list
`Object getFirst()`	Returns the first element in this list
`Object getLast()`	Returns the last element in this list
`Object removeFirst()`	Removes and returns the first element in this list
`Object removeLast()`	Removes and returns the last element in this list
The methods described for `List`	See `List`

☞ **PROGRAMMING POINTERS**

PROGRAM STYLE AND DESIGN

1. *If a problem solution involves a dynamic list for which there are frequent insertions and/or deletions at points other than at the end of the list, then a linked list may be a more time-efficient way to store and process that list than an array-based implementation.* In an array-based list, the values are stored in consecutive memory locations. This means that when values are inserted into or deleted from an array-based list of n values, an average of $n/2$ of the values will have to be shifted to make room for the new value. The time required to shift these values makes insertion (and deletion) a time-expensive ($O(n)$) operation on an array-based list. By contrast, inserting a value and removing a value at a given point in a linked list are constant-time ($O(1)$) operations

2. *If a problem solution involves many accesses to the interior values of a list (i.e. all but the first and last values), then an array-based list may be a more time-efficient way to store and process that list.* In a linked list, all interior values must be accessed sequentially. For example, a node in a single-linked list can only be accessed from the node preceding it, which can only be accessed from the node preceding it, which . . ., which can only be accessed from the first node. An average of $n/2$ accesses are thus required to access an interior node in a linked list of length n, making this an $O(n)$ operation. By contrast, the interior values of an array-based list can be accessed directly (in $O(1)$ time).

3. *If a problem solution requires that values stored more recently will be needed before the values stored less recently, then a stack is the appropriate structure for storing these val-*

ues. Stacks are LIFO (last-in-first-out) lists, since the operation to remove a value will always retrieve the value that was inserted most recently.

4. *If a problem solution requires that values will be needed in the order in which they were stored, then a queue is the appropriate structure for storing these values.* Queues are FIFO (first-in-first-out) lists, since the operation to remove a value from the queue will always retrieve the value that was inserted least recently.

5. *If a problem solution requires fast access to arbitrary elements but also requires that the collection be allowed to grow and shrink due to frequent insertions and deletions, then a binary search tree (BST) may be the appropriate structure to use.* BSTs are linked structures and thus can grow and shrink without excessive memory waste. And they can be searched in a binary-search manner, which (except when the tree becomes lopsided) is more efficient ($O(\log_2 n)$) than a linear search ($O(n)$).

6. A *class B should extend another class A if and only if*

   i. *B is a specialized version of A; and*

   ii. *All messages that can be sent to A can appropriately be sent to B.*

WATCH OUT

POTENTIAL PITFALLS

1. *Java's* Stack *class extends the* Vector *class, which means that it inherits all of* Vector's *methods, so that any message that can be sent to a* Vector *can also be sent to a* Stack. However, many of the Vector methods are not appropriate for a stack!

2. *Java's* Queue *class extends the* Vector *class, which means that it inherits all of* Vector's *methods, so that any message that can be sent to a* Vector *can also be sent to a* Queue. However, many of the Vector methods are not appropriate for a queue!

3. *Pay attention to special cases in processing linked lists, and be careful not to lose access to nodes.* In particular, remember the following *programming proverbs:*

   ❑ *Don't take a long walk off a short linked list.* An error will result if an attempt is made to access a node via a handle that became null because the end of the list was reached. For example, the following attempt to locate objectSought in a linked list like those considered in Section 12.4 will produce an error if objectSought is not found:

   ```
   currentNode = myHead;
   while (!(currentNode.getValue()).equals(objectSought))
      currentNode = currentNode.getSuccessor();
   ```

   ❑ *You can't get water from an empty well.* Don't try to access elements in an empty list; this case usually requires special consideration. For example, if myHead is null, then initializing currentNode to myHead and attempting to send it the getValue() or message is an error because it refers to no node. In the same manner, trying to pop an element from an empty stack, or delete an element from an empty queue produces an error. To avoid such errors, such operations should be guarded with an if statement; for example,

   ```
   if (!aStack.isEmpty())
      obj = aStack.pop();
   else
      // .. take some remedial action ...
   ```

   will only perform the pop operation if there are values to be popped from aStack.

❑ *Don't burn bridges before you cross them.* Be careful to change links in the correct order, or you may lose access to a node or to many nodes! For example, in the following attempt to insert a new node at the beginning of a linked list,

```
SinglyLinkedNode newNode = new SinglyLinkedNode(obj);
myHead = newNode;
newNode.setSuccessor(myHead);
```

the statements are not in correct order. As soon as the second statement is executed, myHead refers to the new node, and access to the remaining nodes in the list is lost. The third statement then simply sets the link handle in the new node to refer to itself:

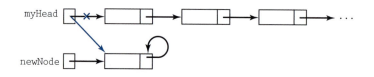

The correct sequence is to first connect the new node to the list and then reset myHead:

```
SinglyLinkedNode newNode = new SinglyLinkedNode(obj);
newNode.setSuccessor(myHead);
myHead = newNode;
```

4. *Attention to special cases like those in the preceding Potential Problem is also necessary in processing other linked structures such as binary trees.*

PROGRAMMING PROBLEMS

SECTION 12.2

1. A limited number of tickets for the Hoops championship basketball game go on sale tomorrow, and ticket orders are to be filled in the order in which they are received. Write a program that a box-office cashier can use to enter the names and addresses of the persons ordering tickets together with the number of tickets requested, and stores this information in a list. The program should then produce a sequence of mailing labels (names, addresses, and number of tickets) for orders that can be filled. Check that no one receives more than four tickets and that multiple requests from the same person are disallowed.

2. A *polynomial of degree n* has the form

$$a_0 + a_1x + a_2x^2 + \cdots + a_nx^n$$

where $a_0, a_1, \ldots, a_n$ are numeric constants called the *coefficients* of the polynomial and $a_n \neq 0$. For example,

$$1 + 3x - 7x^3 + 5x^4$$

is a polynomial of degree 4 with integer coefficients $1, 3, 0, -7$, and 5. One common implementation of a polynomial stores the degree of the polynomial and the list of coefficients.

   (a) Develop and test a `Polynomial` class whose attribute variables are an integer for the degree and an `ArrayList` for the list of coefficients. Provide methods that can be used for input, output (using the usual mathematical format with x^n written as x ↑ n or x^n), and addition.

   (b) Using O( ) notation, determine the time-efficiency of the addition method.

3. (a) Modify the polynomial class in Problem 2 so that it also provides for multiplication.

   (b) Using O( ) notation, determine the time-efficiency of the multiplication method.

4. The representation of a polynomial in Problem 2 is not efficient for *sparse* polynomials, that is, polynomials that have few nonzero coefficients. For example, an `ArrayList` of size 1000 would be required to store the coefficients of $1 + x^{999}$ (1 in position 0, zeros in positions 1 through 998, and 1 in position 999). Develop and test a polynomial class that provides the same operations as in Problem 2 but that uses a linked list in which each node stores a nonzero coefficient and the corresponding exponent. For example, for $1 + x^{999}$. the first node would store coefficient 1 and the exponent 0, and the second node would store the coefficient 1 and the exponent 999.

5. Add a multiplication operation to the polynomial class in Problem 4.

6. The Cawker City Candy Company maintains two warehouses, one in Chicago and one in Detroit, each of which stocks at most twenty-five different items. Write a program that first reads the product numbers of items stored in the Chicago warehouse and stores them in a linked list `Chicago`, and then repeats this for the items stored in the Detroit warehouse, storing these product numbers in a linked list `Detroit`. The program should then find and display the intersection of these two lists of numbers, that is, the collection of product numbers common to both lists. Do not assume that the lists have the same number of elements.

7. Repeat Problem 6, but find and display the union of the two lists, that is, the collection of product numbers that are elements of at least one of the lists.

8. The number of elements in an ordered list may grow so large that searching the list, always beginning with the first node, is not efficient. One way to improve efficiency is to use a list of several smaller linked lists. Write a program to read several lines of uppercase text and to produce a text concordance, which is a list of all distinct words in the text. Store distinct words beginning with A alphabetically ordered in one linked list, those beginning with B in another, and so on. After all the text lines have been read, print a list of all these words in alphabetical order. (You might use an `ArrayList` of size 26, each of whose elements is a `LinkedList`.)

9. Modify the program of Problem 8 so that the concordance also includes the frequency with which each word occurs in the text.

10. In addition to the words in a section of text, a concordance usually stores the numbers of selected pages on which there is a significant use of the word. Modify the program of Problem 8 so that the line numbers of the first ten or fewer references to a word are stored along with the word itself. The program should display each word together with its references in ascending order.

11. Proceed as in Exercise 10, but modify the data structure used for the text concordance so that the numbers of *all* lines in which a word appears are stored.

12. In Chapter 9 we represented matrices by two-dimensional arrays. But for a sparse matrix, that is, one with only a few nonzero entries, this is not an efficient representation. Imitating the construction in Problem 8, develop and test a representation for a sparse matrix by using an `ArrayList` of *row-lists,* each of which is a linked list for a row in the matrix that stores only the nonzero entries in that row and the columns in which they appear. In testing it, display matrices in the usual table format with all entries (including 0's) displayed.

13. Extend the class of Problem 12 to calculate the sum of two sparse matrices (see Exercise 20 in Section 9.4).

14. Extend the class of Exercise 13 to calculate the product of two sparse matrices (see Section 9.4).

SECTION 12.3

15. Design, build, and test a `Stack` class like that in the text but that uses an `ArrayList` instead of a `LinkedList`.

16. Design, build, and test a `Stack` class from scratch like we did for the `Queue` class in Approach 3 in Section 12.4.

17. Write a program that reads a string, one character at a time, and determines whether the string contains balanced parentheses, that is, for each left parenthesis (if there are any) there is exactly one matching right parenthesis later in the string. (Hint, store the left parentheses in a stack.)

18. The problem in Problem 17 can be solved without using a stack; in fact, a simple integer variable can be used. Describe how and write a program that uses your method to solve the problem.

19. For a given integer $n > 1$, the smallest integer $d > 1$ that divides n is a prime factor. We can find the *prime factorization* of n if we find d and then replace n by the quotient of n divided by d, repeating this until n becomes 1. Write a program that determines the prime factorization of n in this manner but that displays the prime factors in descending order. For example, for $n = 3960$, your program should produce

$$11 * 5 * 3 * 3 * 2 * 2 * 2$$

20. A program is to be written to find a path from one point in a maze to another.
    a. Describe how a two-dimensional array could be used to model the maze.
    b. Describe how a stack could be used in an algorithm for finding a path.
    c. Write the program.

SECTION 12.4

21. Design, build, and test a `Queue` class using a `LinkedList` as described in Approach 1 in the text.

22. Design, build, and test a `Queue` class using an `ArrayList` as described in Approach 2 in the text.

23. Write a program that generates a random sequence of letters and/or digits, displays them to the user one at a time for a second or so, and then asks the user to reproduce the sequence. Use a queue to store the sequence of characters.

24. Write a "quiz-tutor" program, perhaps on a topic from one of the earlier chapters, or some other topic about which you are knowledgeable. The program should read a question and its answer from a file, display the question, and accept an answer from the user. If the answer is correct, the program should go on to the next question. If it is not correct, store the question in a list. When the file of questions is exhausted, the questions that were missed should be displayed again (in their original order). Keep a count of the correct answers and display the final count. Also, display the correct answer when necessary in the second round of questioning.

25. Write a program that reads a string of characters, pushing each character onto a stack as it is read and simultaneously adding it to a queue. When the end of the string is encountered, the program should use the basic stack and queue operations to determine if the string is a *palindrome* (a string that reads the same from left to right as from right to left).

25. In text-editing and word-processing applications, one formatting convention sometimes used to indicate that a piece of text is a footnote or an endnote is to mark it with some special delimiters such as { and }. When the text is formatted for output, these notes are not printed as normal text but are stored in a queue for later output. Write a program that reads a document containing endnotes indicated in this manner, collects them in a queue, and displays them at the end of the document.

26. Suppose that jobs entering a computer system are assigned a job number and a priority from 0 through 9. The numbers of jobs awaiting execution by the system are kept in a *priority queue*. A job entered into this queue is placed ahead of all jobs of lower priority but after all those of equal or higher priority. Develop a priority queue class that has the same operations as a queue but with a modified add operation. Use your class in a program that reads one of the letters R (remove), A (add), or L (list). For R, remove a job from the priority queue and display the job number; for A, read a job number and priority and then add it to the priority queue in the manner just described; and for L, list all the job numbers in the queue.

27. (Project) Suppose that a certain airport has one runway, that each airplane takes `landingTime` minutes to land and `takeOffTime` minutes to take off, and that on the average, `takeOffRate` planes take off and `landingRate` planes land each hour. Assume that the planes arrive at random instants of time. (Delays make the assumption of randomness quite reasonable.) There are two types of queues: a queue of airplanes waiting to land and a queue of airplanes waiting to take off. Because it is more expensive to keep a plane airborne than to have one waiting on the ground, we assume that the airplanes in the landing queue have priority over those in the takeoff queue.

Write a program to simulate this airport's operation. You might assume a simulated clock that advances in one-minute intervals. For each minute, generate two random numbers: If the first is less than `landingRate` / 60, a "landing arrival" has occurred and is added to the landing queue; and if the second is less than `takeOffRate` / 60, a "takeoff arrival" has occurred and is added to the takeoff queue. Next, check whether the runway is free. If it is, first check whether the landing queue is nonempty, and if so, allow the first airplane to land; otherwise, consider the takeoff queue. Have the program calculate the average queue length and the average time that an airplane spends in a queue. You might also investigate the effect of varying arrival and departure rates to simulate the prime and slack times of day, or what happens if the amount of time to land or take off is increased or decreased.

SECTION 12.5

28. Build and test a BST class as described in the text. It should have a constructor, insert, search, and inorder traversal operations.

29. Add preorder and postorder traversal operations to the BST class in Problem 28.

30. Add a delete operation to the BST class in Problem 28. Deleting a leaf node or a node that has only one child is easy—simply reset the appropriate link in its parent node. For a node that has two children, find its inorder successor x—that is, the node that would be visited after this one in an inorder traversal. Replace the data in the node to be deleted with the value in x. Then delete x (which will have 0 or 1 children).

SECTION 12.6

31. Develop and test a simple rectangle-sketching GUI application. (See Java's API documentation for the method `drawRectangle()` in `java.awt.Graphics`.)

32. Extend the GUI application to include other geometric figures—e.g., ovals, circles, lines, squares, triangles. Let the user select the figure from a menu.

33. Modify the polygon-sketching GUI application so the user can specify the number of sides the polygon is to have, lets the user click on that many points, and which will then draw the polygon.

ADVANCED TOPICS

Truth is stranger than fiction because fiction has to have a rational thread running through it in order to be believable, whereas reality may be totally irrational. *Sydney J. Harris*

Human life is a continuous thread which each of us spins to his own pattern, rich and complex in meaning. *Henri Estienne*

Multithreading is as easy as walking and chewing gum at the same time. *V. Orehck III (fictitious)*

A doctor can bury his mistakes; an architect can only advise his clients to plant vines. *Frank Lloyd Wright*

Consciously or unconsciously, every one of us does render some service or other. If we cultivate the habit of doing this service deliberately, our desire for service will steadily grow stronger, making not only our own happiness, but that of the world at large. *Ghandi*

Chapter Contents

Chapter Objectives

- Study the use of threads in Java to construct multithreaded programs
- Learn about Java's built-in support for programs that communicate across a network
- See an example of how threads are used in animations
- (Optional) Investigate the TCP/IP communications architecture

The sequence of operations that a program performs as it is executing is sometimes described as that program's *thread of execution*. Our programs up to this point have all been *single-threaded programs,* meaning that they could only execute one operation at a time. In this chapter, we study *multithreaded programs,* which can execute multiple operations simultaneously.

13.1   INTRODUCTORY EXAMPLE: SORTING A LIST

In Chapter 12, we saw how Java's `ArrayList` and `LinkedList` classes implement the `List` interface. These are examples of the collection classes Java provides. Java also provides a class named `Collections` in the package `java.util` that provides a variety of methods that operate on collection classes. One example is a `sort()` method that, given any `List` of objects that can be compared, arranges those objects in ascending order. Our introductory example is to use our `Timer` class from `ann.util` to measure the times required to sort an `ArrayList` containing 100000 values in two different ways.

Design

Our first procedure will be quite simple. It will simply build an `ArrayList` of n random `Integer` values and then measure the amount of time required to sort the list.

The second approach is a bit more complicated. It will build *two* `ArrayList` objects, each containing $n/2$ randomly generated `Integer` objects. It then measures the time required to

- a. Sort the first `ArrayList` using a `Sorter` object that runs as a separate thread
- b. Sort the second `ArrayList` normally
- c. Merge the two sorted `ArrayLists` with $n/2$ objects into a single sorted `ArrayList` of length n.

On a computer with a single CPU (i.e., a **uniprocessor**), the first method should be slightly faster than the second method. This is because there is some overhead involved in creating threads, and with just one CPU, Steps a and b cannot be performed concurrently.

However, on a computer with multiple CPUs (i.e., a **multiprocessor**), the second method should be faster than the first, because the thread that performs Step (a) can run on one CPU while our program performs Step (b) on a different CPU.

Time measurements can vary significantly from execution to execution. For this reason we will have our main method compute the average time for each method over 10 trials.

Coding And Testing

Figure 13.1 presents the `Sorter` class that runs in its own thread.

FIGURE 13.1   SORTING A LIST WITH A SEPARATE THREAD

```
/** ListSorter.java sorts a List in a separate thread.
 *  Attribute: a List
 *  Methods:   construct a ListSorter from a List; run()
 */

import java.util.*;                   // Collections
```

```
class ListSorter extends Thread
{
/** Constructor
 *  Receive:        List aList
 *  Postconditin:  myList == aList
 */
 public ListSorter(List aList)
 {
   myList = aList;
 }

//--- run() method ---
 public void run()
 {
   Collections.sort(myList);
 }

//--- Attribute variable ---
 private List myList;
}
```

This class is quite simple: it merely receives the `List` to be sorted when it is constructed, and its `run()` method uses the `Collections` class method `sort()` to sort that `List`. However, because the `ListSorter` class is defined as an extension of class `Thread`, a `ListSorter` object will have *its own thread of execution*, distinct from that of the program that creates it.

Figure 13.2 presents the `SortTimer` class and some sample execution times.

FIGURE 13.2 THE `SortTimer` CLASS

```
/** SortTimer.java times single-threaded vs. multithreaded sorting.
 *  Attributes:   A random number and a timer
 *  Static constant:  ARRAY_SIZE
 *  Public method:    main()
 *  Private methods:  generateRandomList();
 *                    timeSingleThreadSort(); timeTwoThreadSort()
 */

import ann.util.Timer;
import java.util.*;        // ArrayList, Collections, Random, ...
import ListSorter;

class SortTimer extends Object
{
 final static int ARRAY_SIZE = 100000;

//--- main() method ---
 public static void main(String [] args)
 {
   double totalTime = 0.0;
   timeSingleThreadSort();                        // skip startup-outlier

   for (int i = 1; i <= 10; i++)
     totalTime += timeSingleThreadSort();
   System.out.println("1-thread average: " + totalTime / 10 + "\n");
   totalTime = 0.0;
   for (int i = 1; i <= 10; i++)
     totalTime += timeTwoThreadSort();
    System.out.println("2-thread average: " + totalTime / 10);
 }
```

```
/** Random List Generator
 *  Receive: int size
 *  Return:  ArrayList containing size random integers
 */
private static ArrayList generateRandomList(int size)
{
  ArrayList result = new ArrayList(size);
  for (int i = 0; i < size; i++)
    result.add( new Integer( myRandom.nextInt() ) );

  return result;
}

/** Time a single-thread sorter
 *  Return: time required to sort myList using a single thread
 *  Uses Timer class from ann.util
 */
private static double timeSingleThreadSort()
{
  ArrayList myList = generateRandomList(ARRAY_SIZE);

  myTimer.reset();
  Collections.sort(myList);
  myTimer.stop();

  System.out.println("SingleThreadSort took " + myTimer + " secs");
  return myTimer.getTime();
}

/** Time a two-thread sorter
 *  Return: time required to sort list1 and list2 using separate threads
 *          and then merge the results
 *  Uses Timer class from ann.util
 */
private static double timeTwoThreadSort()
{
  final int SIZE = ARRAY_SIZE / 2;
  ArrayList list1 = generateRandomList(SIZE),
            list2 = generateRandomList(SIZE),
            list3 = new ArrayList(ARRAY_SIZE);

  int i = 0, j = 0;
  myTimer.reset();
  myTimer.start();

  ListSorter secondSorter = new ListSorter(list1);
  secondSorter.start();

  Collections.sort(list2);

  try{ secondSorter.join(); }
  catch(Exception e) { System.err.println(e); }

  // merge sorted lists
  do
  {
    if ( ( (Integer)list1.get(i) ).compareTo( list2.get(j) ) < 0 )
      list3.add( list1.get(i++) );
    else
      list3.add( list2.get(j++) );
  }
  while (i < SIZE && j < SIZE);
```

```
   if (i < j)
     list3.addAll( list1.subList(i, SIZE-1) );
   else
     list3.addAll( list2.subList(j, SIZE-1) );

   myTimer.stop();

   System.out.println("TwoThreadSort took " + myTimer + " secs");
   return myTimer.getTime();
 }

//--- Attribute variables
 private static Random myRandom = new Random();
 private static Timer  myTimer = new Timer();
}
```

Sample Run (Pentium-II 233-MHz uniprocessor):

```
SingleThreadSort took 3.46 secs
SingleThreadSort took 2.36 secs
SingleThreadSort took 2.2 secs
SingleThreadSort took 2.19 secs
SingleThreadSort took 2.25 secs
SingleThreadSort took 2.25 secs
SingleThreadSort took 2.25 secs
SingleThreadSort took 2.25 secs
SingleThreadSort took 2.3 secs
SingleThreadSort took 2.25 secs
1-thread average: 2.255

TwoThreadSort took 2.26 secs
TwoThreadSort took 2.25 secs
TwoThreadSort took 2.75 secs
TwoThreadSort took 2.25 secs
TwoThreadSort took 2.26 secs
TwoThreadSort took 2.31 secs
TwoThreadSort took 2.31 secs
TwoThreadSort took 2.31 secs
TwoThreadSort took 2.3 secs
TwoThreadSort took 2.25 secs
2-thread average: 2.325
```

Sample Run (Sun Ultra-2 300-MHz multiprocessor):

```
SingleThreadSort took 1.466 secs
SingleThreadSort took 1.419 secs
SingleThreadSort took 1.574 secs
SingleThreadSort took 1.605 secs
SingleThreadSort took 1.543 secs
SingleThreadSort took 1.529 secs
SingleThreadSort took 1.394 secs
SingleThreadSort took 1.749 secs
SingleThreadSort took 1.843 secs
SingleThreadSort took 1.788 secs
SingleThreadSort took 1.535 secs
SingleThreadSort took 1.796 secs
1-thread average: 1.6356000000000002
```

```
TwoThreadSort took 1.587 secs
TwoThreadSort took 1.026 secs
TwoThreadSort took 1.233 secs
TwoThreadSort took 1.15 secs
TwoThreadSort took 1.272 secs
TwoThreadSort took 1.051 secs
TwoThreadSort took 1.1 secs
TwoThreadSort took 1.258 secs
TwoThreadSort took 1.124 secs
TwoThreadSort took 1.056 secs
2-thread average: 1.1857
```

The executions in Figure 13.2 confirm what we would expect.

1. On the Pentium-II uniprocessor, the single-threaded sort took less time than the two-threaded sort. This is what we would expect, because on a uniprocessor, the two threads must share the same CPU, preventing them from running simultaneously. The two-thread method must do everything the single-thread method does, and more—for example, create the threads—and thus takes longer on a uniprocessor.

2. On the Sun multiprocessor, the two-thread sort is faster than the single-thread sort. Again, this is what we would expect, given that the multiprocessor's two CPUs allow the two threads to run simultaneously. Using two threads is nearly 30% faster than using one thread.

13.2   TOPIC: MULTITHREADING

When a program runs, it executes a series of operations. For sequential statements, all of the statements in the sequence are performed:

```
{
    statement₁ ;
    statement₂ ;
    ... ;
    statementₙ ;
}
```

In a selection structure, some statements are performed, while others are skipped:

```
{
    statement₁ ;
    if ( condition )
        statement₂ ;
    else
        statement₃ ;
    statement₄ ;
}
```

In a loop, the statements within the loop may be repeated over and over:

```
for (;;)
{
    statement₁ ;

    if ( condition ) break;

    statement₂ ;
}
```

Regardless of which kind of execution takes place. executing such a series of operations is called a **thread of execution,** or more simply, a **thread;** the diagrams to the right of the code segments are intended to suggest this. As these examples indicate, a thread will move through sequential statements one after another. By contrast, when a thread reaches an `if` statement, it "skips", bypassing either the true section, or the false section, as determined by the `if` statement's condition. Finally, when a thread of execution reaches a loop statement, it "spins", repeating that loop's statements over and over until the exit condition for the loop is met.

Multithreading

The programs we have seen until now have all been **single-threaded programs,** meaning that each has a single thread of execution. As we just saw, this thread may move in a straight line through sequential statements, skip over statements in a selective execution statement, or spin through statements in a loop statement.

One of the things that distinguishes Java from other languages is its built-in support for writing **multithreaded programs.** As the name implies, a multithreaded program has more than one execution thread. There are two general situations in which multithreading is advantageous:

1. **Speedup Through Parallel Processing.** If a problem can be divided into n pieces, each of which can be solved independently, and an n-CPU multiprocessor is available, then the problem can be solved faster (than by a single-threaded program) by creating n threads and having each thread solve one piece of the problem. The application in Section 13.1 illustrates this benefit.

2. **Separating Input From Processing.** Most input operations are **blocking operations,** meaning that a thread performing input *suspends* or *blocks* until the input has completed. If an application involves extensive processing that can be done independently of its input, then handling the input and the processing in separate threads allows the processing thread to continue execution while the input thread is blocked. Sections 13.3 and 13.4 illustrate this benefit.

The CD Player application available on most personal computers uses this approach to play compact disks on the machine's CD drive. The application uses two threads: one to play the CD, and one to listen for mouse-clicks on the CD Player's GUI. If this were tried with one thread, listening for input at the GUI would make the thread block, preventing it from playing the CD.

Multithreading in Java

Java provides two different ways of building a multithreaded application.

1. **Extend the `Thread` Class.** The general pattern of a multithreaded program with this approach is as follows:

   a. Define a class that extends Java's `Thread` class and contains a `run()` method that does what you want to have happen in a separate thread; for example:

   ```
   class ListSorter extends Thread
   {
     // ...
     public void run() { ... }
     // statements that the thread is to execute
   }
   ```

   b. Have the normal thread create an instance of the class defined in (a). Because this class extends class `Thread` it inherits everything it needs to run as a distinct thread; for example:

   ```
   ListSorter secondSorter = new ListSorter(list1);
   ```

   c. Make this thread begin running by sending it the `start()` message; for example:

   ```
   secondSorter.start();
   ```

   At this point, a second thread, distinct from the program's normal thread begins execution. Graphically, we can visualize what happens as follows:

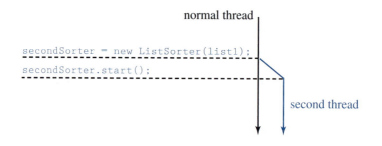

   On a multiprocessor, the second thread can run at the same time as the normal thread, providing for parallel processing, as we saw in Section 13.1. On a uniprocessor, the second thread can continue processing while the "normal" thread blocks for input, as we'll see in section 13.3.

2. **Implement the `Runnable` Interface.** Java only permits a class to extend one other class. This means that if a class needs to extend some non-`Thread` class *and* run as a distinct thread, the preceding approach cannot be used. For such circumstances, Java provides the `Runnable` interface that a class can implement, as opposed to extending `Thread`. The general pattern of a multithreaded program with this approach is as follows:

a. Define a class that implements Java's `Runnable` interface, containing a `run()` method that does what you want to have happen in a separate thread; for example:

```
class ListSorter extends Whatever
                 implements Runnable
{
  // ...
  public void run() { ... }
  // statements that the thread is to execute
}
```

b. Have the normal class create an instance of the class defined in (a); for example:

```
ListSorter secondSorter = new ListSorter(list1);
```

c. Also have the class create a new instance of the `Thread` class, initialized with the object created in Step (b); for example:

```
Thread secondThread = new Thread(secondSorter);
```

d. Send the new `Thread` object created in Step (c) the `start()` message; for example:

```
secondThread.start();
```

This approach is slightly more complicated than the first approach, and it is only provided for situations where a class we want to run as a separate thread must also extend some non-`Thread` class. Other than that, it produces the same multithreaded behavior as the first approach.

Synchronizing Accesses To Shared Data

One of the capabilities provided by threads is that different threads can share the same data. For example, a banking application might use an `Account` class:

```
class Account
{
  public Account(double startingBalance)
  { myBalance = startingBalance; }

  public void debit(double amount)
  { myBalance -= amount; }

  public void credit(double amount)
  { myBalance += amount; }

  private myBalance;
}
```

and there might be multiple `Transaction` threads that want to access an `Account` by sending it `debit()` and `credit()` messages:

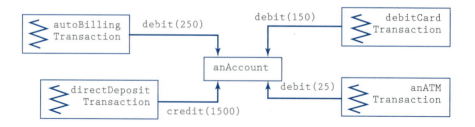

Just as an *atom* was originally a particle that could not be divided into smaller particles, an **atomic operation** is an operation that cannot be divided into "smaller" operations. In our banking scenario, the `debit()` and `credit()` methods are *not* atomic, which can lead to problems. To illustrate, suppose that `myBalance` is 500, and that a `credit(100)` and a `debit(100)` message are received and processed at about the same time:

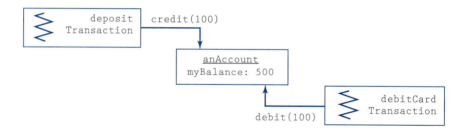

If our `debit()` and `credit()` operations were atomic, then `myBalance` would always be 500 following the execution of these transactions. However, our `debit()` and `credit()` operations are not atomic, because beneath the surface (at the byte-code level), each method consists of multiple operations:

```
credit(amount)              debit(amount)
{                           {
  myBalance += amount;        myBalance -= amount;
  a) temp = myBalance         a) temp = myBalance
  b) add amount to temp       b) sub amount from temp
  c) myBalance = temp         c) myBalance = temp
}                           }
```

To see the problem, let's trace what happens to `myBalance` when one thread uses `credit(100)` and another thread uses `debit(100)` to access `myBalance` at nearly the same time. Suppose that the `credit()` message is received a fraction of a second before the `debit()` message, so that `credit()`'s operation a) is performed, then `debit()`'s operation a) is performed, then `credit()`'s operation b) is performed, then `debit()`'s operation b) is performed, and so on. Table 13.2 traces the execution:

TABLE 13.2   TRACING CONCURRENT EXECUTION

Time-Step	credit(100)	temp$_{credit}$	my-Balance	debit(100)	temp$_{debit}$
1	temp = myBalance	500	500	—	—
1.5	—	500	500	temp = myBalance	500
2	add 100 to temp	600	500	—	500
2.5	—	600	500	sub 100 from temp	400
3	myBalance = temp	600	600	—	400
3.5	—	600	400	myBalance = temp	400

We just lost $100 from our account! Such errors can occur any time two threads access shared data at the same time, unless those accesses occur in an atomic fashion. The problem then is that `debit()` and `credit()` are not atomic operations—the operations they perform can be *interleaved* when performed by separate threads. In fact, one can make no assumptions about how they are interleaved—any random interleaving pattern is possible.

Making Methods Atomic. Fortunately, making methods atomic is easy in Java. All we need to do is use the keyword `synchronized` to declare each method that accesses the critical information (i.e., `myBalance`), as follows:

```
class Account
{
  public Account(double startingBalance)
  { myBalance = startingBalance; }

  synchronized public void debit(double amount)
  { myBalance -= amount; }

  synchronized public void credit(double amount)
  { myBalance += amount; }

  private myBalance;
}
```

We haven't mentioned it before, but Java associates a **lock** with every object. When a thread *T* sends a synchronized message to an object and no other thread is executing a synchronized method of that object, Java *locks* the object's lock and then lets the method begin execution:

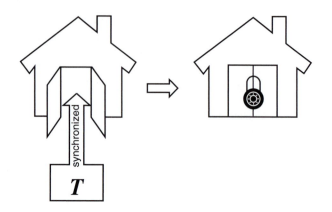

If another thread *T'* subsequently sends that object a synchronized message, then because the object's lock is *locked,* Java suspends thread *T'* until the synchronized method of *T* terminates:[1]

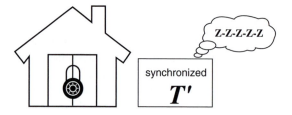

Once the method being executed by *T* terminates, Java wakes thread *T'* and lets it proceed with the execution of its synchronized method.

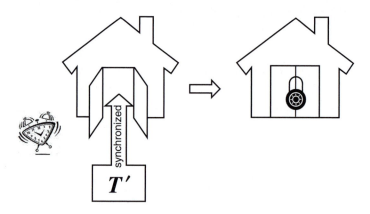

----

[1] Or until thread *T* executes a `wait()` call within the synchronized method it is executing, in which case *T* suspends and gives up the lock to another thread waiting to execute a synchronized method. *T* remains suspended until another thread executes a `notify()` call within a synchronized method of that object.

By synchronizing each mutator method in our `Account` class, we can ensure that all accesses to the shared data occur atomically. In our banking scenario, if we have the same situation as before but `debit()` and `credit()` are synchronized, then when the `credit()` method is invoked a fraction of a second before `debit()`, the `Account` is locked and `debit()` is blocked until `credit()` finishes, as shown in Table 13.3.

TABLE 13.3   SYNCHRONIZED EXECUTION OF `credit()` AND `debit()`

Time-step	credit(100)	temp$_{credit}$	my-Balance	debit(100)	temp$_{debit}$
1	temp = myBalance	500	500	—	—
2	add 100 to temp	600	500	—	—
3	myBalance = temp	600	600	—	—
4	—	600	600	temp = myBalance	600
5	—	600	600	sub 100 from temp	500
6	—	600	500	myBalance = temp	500

If a class properly synchronizes all of its methods, such a class is described as **thread-safe.** As you might gather, writing thread-safe classes is not trivial, and a complete discussion is beyond the scope of this introductory text.[2] But the basic rule of thumb is as follows:

> *If an instance of a class can be mutated by different threads, declare all mutator methods of that class as* `synchronized`.[3]

✔ Quick Quiz 13.2

1. Execution of a series of operations is called a(n) _____ of execution.
2. A(n) _____ program has more than one execution thread.
3. (True or false) Most input operations are blocking operations.
4. What are the two ways provided in Java for building a multithreaded application?
5. (True or false) Different threads cannot share data.
6. An operation that cannot be divided into smaller operations is called a(n) _____ operation.
7. A class that properly synchronizes all of its methods is said to be _____.

---

[2] See *Programming With Threads,* by Kleiman, Shah, and Smaalders (Sunsoft/Prentice Hall, 1996).

[3] Two additional rules of thumb are:

❑ *If a thread fails a precondition within a synchronized method* m$_1$() *and that precondition could be met by a thread executing another synchronized method* m$_2$(), *then* m$_1$() *can use* wait() *to suspend its thread until that precondition is satisfied by another thread executing* m$_2$().

❑ *If a synchronized method mutates an object, then it should call* notify() *to wake up any threads that might be waiting for a precondition that its mutation might have satisfied.*

13.3   TOPIC: CLIENT-SERVER NETWORKING

In addition to its support for graphics and threads, another exciting feature of Java is its built-in support for programs to communicate across a network. While there are several different models for network communication, one of the most popular is the **client-server** model. In this model, there are two kinds of programs:

❑ *Server programs* that wait for other programs (called clients) to contact them and request their service, which they then perform on behalf of the client; and

❑ *Client programs* that contact servers to ask them to perform a service.

A World-Wide-Web browser (e.g., Netscape Navigator and Internet Explorer) is an example of a client program. Each link on a web page specifies a file on a computer. When you click on a link, your browser-client contacts a server program on that computer, requesting that link's file. The server retrieves the file, and sends it to the browser-client, which then displays the file. Similarly, if you use a modern e-mail program, the odds are that it is an e-mail client program. When you run a mail-client, it contacts your mail-server to see if you have any mail. If you do, the mail-server transmits your mail to the mail-client, which then displays it.[4]

Sockets

Just as two people in different houses can communicate if each has a telephone, a client program can communicate with a server program if each has a socket. Like a telephone, a **socket** is a *communication endpoint* by which a program can send and receive information. To receive requests from clients, a server creates a `Server-Socket` and then waits for clients to connect to it. To contact to a server, a client creates a `Socket` to connect to that server's `ServerSocket`:

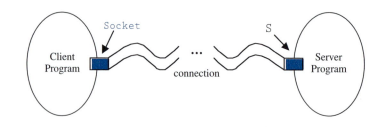

---

[4] With a **POP-mailer,** the server downloads all of the messages to the client, deletes them (by default), and closes the connection. With an **IMAP-mailer,** the server downloads only message headers to the client. Individual messages are then downloaded as requested by the client, but messages are not deleted from the server unless requested by the client. IMAP is convenient if you read your mail from many different machines; POP is convenient if you have a slow connection or pay for your connection by the minute. Also, whereas POP transmits your password in plain text, IMAP encrypts it, making IMAP the more secure system.

Once the connection is established, the client can communicate with the server, and vice versa.

Socket Details. In order for sockets to connect with others, every socket must be distinct from every other socket. The problem is that there are thousands (millions?) of socket-using programs around the Internet, and there many be hundreds of socket-using programs on any given computer. The name of the computer housing the program to whose socket we wish to connect is thus not sufficient by itself to distinguish one socket from another.

To resolve this difficulty, Java requires a socket to have a special integer value called a **port,** that is similar to an apartment or room number. Just as the address

> *Joan Smith*
> *1234 Main Street,* Apt. 16
> Anytown, MI

uniquely identifies where Joan lives, the pair

> *(computerName, portNumber)*

uniquely identifies the socket a program is using on computer *computerName.* Each socket on a given computer must thus have its own unique port to distinguish it from all of the other sockets on that computer.

The key point is that every socket is uniquely identified by two pieces of information:

- ❏ The name of the computer where the socket is located (e.g., *cs.calvin.edu*)
- ❏ The particular port associated with that socket

TCP/IP Services. As described in the Part of the Picture section following the next section, the TCP/IP communications architecture defines a number of standard services. Because each service is standardized, a server for a TCP/IP service uses a specific standard port number. Table 13.1 presents a few of these services, and the port numbers for servers of those services:

TABLE 13.1   SOME STANDARD TCP/IP SERVICES

Service	Description	Port
echo	echo by replying with whatever is sent	7
daytime	reply with local day and time	13
ftp	file transfer protocol	20 and 21
telnet	terminal-based remote login service	23
smtp	simple mail transfer protocol (e-mail)	25
http	hypertext transport protocol (www)	80
pop3	post office protocol (e-mail)	110
imap	internet message access protocol (e-mail)	143

Most of these services handle the day-to-day activities of the Internet. A few services (e.g., *echo*) are provided to allow client-server implementers to test the communication code of their clients.

Example: A Daytime Client

To illustrate how a `Socket` uses a port, Figure 13.3 presents a client for the *daytime* service, which provides the day and time at a given computer:

FIGURE 13.3   A TCP DAYTIME CLIENT

```
/** DaytimeClient.java provides a client for TCP's daytime service.
 *  Attribute: Constant DAYTIME_PORT
 *  Methods:  main(), getTimeFrom()
 */

import java.net.*;       // Socket, ...
import java.io.*;        // BufferedReader, ...


class DaytimeClient extends Object
{
//--- main() method ---
 public static void main(String [] args)
 {
  if (args.length != 1)
  {
    System.err.println("Usage: java DaytimeClient <remoteHost>");
    System.exit(1);
  }

  DaytimeClient myClient = new DaytimeClient();
  System.out.println( myClient.getTimeFrom(args[0]) );
 }

/** Get time from server
 * Receive: String remoteHost
 * Return:  String representing time and date obtained from remoteHost
 *          or execution terminates due to an exception
 */
 public String getTimeFrom(String remoteHost)
 {
  String timeOfDay = null;
  try
  {
   Socket mySocket = new Socket(remoteHost, DAYTIME_PORT);
   BufferedReader myReader = new BufferedReader(
                      new InputStreamReader(
                        mySocket.getInputStream() ));
   timeOfDay = myReader.readLine();
   myReader.close();
  }
  catch (Exception e)
  {
    System.err.println(e);
  }
```

```
    return timeOfDay;
  }

//--- Attribute variable ---
  private int DAYTIME_PORT = 13;
}
```

Sample Run:

```
C:\> java DaytimeClient atomictime.net

Fri Jun  9 15:23:33 2000
```

Client Socket Initialization. A Java `Socket` connects to another socket (usually a `ServerSocket`) when it is initialized. This means that the information needed to uniquely identify the remote socket must be passed to the `Socket` constructor, namely, the Internet name of the remote host and the port of the socket on that host to which we want to connect. Since the daytime service is standardized on port 13, we accomplish this in Figure 13.3 with

```
    Socket mySocket = new Socket(remoteHost, DAYTIME_PORT);
```

where `DAYTIME_PORT` is 13 and `remoteHost` is `args[0]`. Reading the name of the remote computer from the command-line makes it easy to find the day and time on any Internet computer that runs the daytime service. Thus, when we invoke this program,

```
    C:\> java DaytimeClient atomictime.net
```

the `Socket` constructor builds a connection between our `DaytimeClient` program and the daytime server waiting for a client to connect to port 13 at *atomictime.net*.[5]

Reading from a Socket. A connected `Socket` is of little use unless we can read from it whatever information the server sends to our client. Since reading is an input operation, and Java uses the `InputStream` class to perform input, Java's `Socket` class provides a `getInputStream()` method that, sent to a `Socket` object, returns an `InputStream` representation of that `Socket`. The program in Figure 13.3 uses this, wrapping the `InputStream` in an `InputStreamReader` and then wrapping that `InputStreamReader` in a `BufferedReader`,[6] as discussed in Chapter 10:

```
    BufferedReader myReader = new BufferedReader(
                                  new InputStreamReader(
                                      mySocket.getInputStream() ));
```

---

[5] *atomictime.net* is an Internet computer that reads the time from an atomic clock.

[6] To communicate information in binary format, a client and server can use a `DataInputStream` instead.

This allows us to read from the wrapped socket using the `readLine()` method:

```
timeOfDay = myReader.readLine();
```

A daytime server transmits its information via one line of text, and so a call to `read-Line()` is sufficient for our client. All that remains is to output `timeOfDay` in the usual manner.

Some services, however, generate multiple lines of text. In this case, the client can read the response from the server using a normal input loop:

```
String aLine = null, serverResponse = "";
for (;;)
{
  aLine = myReader.readLine();
  if (aLine == null) break;
  serverResponse += aLine;
}
```

Similar to other input loops, this loop accumulates the lines it reads from `myReader` in the variable referred to by `serverResponse`. But since `myReader` is a wrapper for a `Socket` connected to a socket on some other computer, `aLine` equals null when the remote server signals it is finished by closing its socket (see below).

As we saw in Chapter 10, these operations throw `IOExceptions`. As a result, a try-catch block must be used to read from a socket.

Writing to a `Socket`. While our `DaytimeClient` need not write to a `Socket`, the clients in other client-server applications must. To do so is as easy as reading from a `Socket`. We send the `Socket` the `getOutputStream()` message, and wrap the result in a `PrintWriter`:

```
PrintWriter myWriter = new PrintWriter(
                    mySocket.getOutputStream(),
                    true);            // enable auto-flush
```

We can then transmit information via the usual `print()` and `println()` methods:

```
myWriter.println("You are the " + count + " visitor to our server.");
```

ServerSockets

Java provides separate `Socket` and `ServerSocket` classes because the behavior of a socket on the server side of the connection is different from that on the client side. Whereas a client creates a socket that immediately connects to a specified socket, a server creates a socket whose role is to wait for clients to connect to it. As a result, the initialization steps are slightly different for a `ServerSocket`.

`ServerSocket` Initialization. When a client socket is initialized, we must specify the *remoteHost* and *port* to which we wish to connect:

```
Socket aSocket = new Socket( remoteHost, port );
```

By contrast, a `ServerSocket` is created by a server to await subsequent connection requests from client sockets. Since there is no remote host to be specified, we need only specify the `port` when we create a `ServerSocket`:

```
ServerSocket aServerSocket = new ServerSocket( port );
```

From the Java API documentation we find that if a port value of 0 is given, then `aServerSocket` will be given any free port. In this situation, the `getLocalPort()` message can be used to determine the particular port associated with the socket:

```
System.out.println( aServerSocket.getLocalPort() );
```

Note also that the standard TCP/IP ports listed in Table 13.1 are reserved for *official* servers of TCP/IP services. We thus cannot run our own servers on these ports unless we have sufficient privilege to replace the official servers with our own. Generally, only system administrators have such privileges. A good rule of thumb is for *unofficial servers to use port numbers above 1000.*

Accepting a Connection. The `ServerSocket` constructor builds and initializes a `ServerSocket` object. To get that object to actually listen for incoming connections is a separate step that is accomplished by sending it the `accept()` message:

```
Socket aSocket = aServerSocket.accept();
```

The effect of the `accept()` message is two-fold:

1. The server sending the `accept()` message blocks,

until some client socket requests a connection to the `ServerSocket`:

2. The `accept()` method builds and returns a `Socket` (distinct from the `ServerSocket`) that is the actual end-point for the connection back to the client:

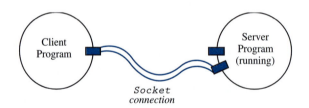

Creating and returning a separate `Socket` for the connection to the client frees the `ServerSocket` to handle additional connection requests. This is especially useful for a multithreaded server, as we shall see at the end of this section.

Reading From and Writing to a `ServerSocket`. We can read from (or write to) a `ServerSocket` in exactly the same way as one would read from (or write to) a `Socket`:

a. Build a `BufferedReader` (or `PrintWriter`) as a wrapper for the `ServerSocket`.

b. Then use `readLine()` (or `println()`) to communicate with the client.

Closing a Socket. When either a client or a server wants to terminate communication through a socket, it can send that socket the `close()` message to close the connection:

```
myReader.close();
```

Closing a socket is more than just good style; many clients and/or servers use the closure of the connection to determine when to terminate. If the socket is not closed, such programs can become *zombie processes*.

Example: A Daytime Server

To illustrate the use of these ideas, we will build a server for the daytime service. As indicated previously, such a service provides the local day and time of the computer on which the server is running. To do so, our server will behave as follows:

1. Build a `ServerSocket` that will listen for connections on port 1013.

2. Repeat the following:

a. Use `accept()` to accept a connection request.

b. Build a `PrintWriter` for the `Socket` returned by `accept()`.

c. Get the current day and time (using Java's `GregorianCalendar` class).

d. Write the current day and time to our `PrintWriter`.

e. Close the `PrintWriter` (and thus the `Socket`).

Note that since an official daytime server is likely to be using port 13, we will instead use port 1013 for our daytime server. Figure 13.4 presents the `DaytimeServer` class:

FIGURE 13.4   A DAYTIME SERVER

```
/** DaytimeServer.java defines a daytime server running on port 1013.
 *   Attributes:  MY_PORT (constant); a ServerSocket
 *   Methods:     Default constructor; run(); main()
 */

import java.net.*;        // Socket, ServerSocket, ...
import java.io.*;         // PrintWriter, BufferedOutputStream, ...
import java.util.*;       // GregorianCalendar, Date, ...

class DaytimeServer extends Object
{
 public final int MY_PORT = 1013;

/** Constructor ---
 *   Postcondition:  mySocket is a ServerSocket with port MY_PORT]
 *                 || execution terminates due to an exception.
 */
 public DaytimeServer()
 {
  try
  {
    myServerSocket = new ServerSocket(MY_PORT);
  }
  catch (Exception e)
  {
    System.err.println(e);
    System.exit(1);
  }
 }

//--- run() method ---
 public void run()
 {
  try
  {
    System.out.println("DaytimeServer: " + myServerSocket);
    for (;;)
    {
      Socket sessionSocket = myServerSocket.accept();
      PrintWriter myWriter = new PrintWriter(
                          sessionSocket.getOutputStream() );
      Date dayAndTime = new GregorianCalendar().getTime();
      myWriter.println(dayAndTime);
      myWriter.close();
    }
  }
  catch (Exception e)
  {
    System.err.println(e);
    System.exit(1);
  }
 }
//--- main() method ---
 public static void main(String [] args)
 {
   DaytimeServer myServer = new DaytimeServer();
   myServer.run();
 }

//--- Attribute variable ---
 private ServerSocket myServerSocket;
}
```

For feedback purposes (i.e., so that we can tell when our server is ready to use), we have added the output statement

```
System.out.println("DaytimeServer: " + myServerSocket);
```

to the server's `run()` method. If we run our `DaytimeServer` in an MS-DOS (or Unix) shell:

```
C:\> java DaytimeServer
```

we eventually[7] get a feedback message like

```
DaytimeServer: ServerSocket[addr=0.0.0.0/0.0.0.0,port=0,
localport=1013]
```

letting us know that our server is up and running.

If we now modify the `DaytimeClient` from Figure 13.3 to connect to port 1013 instead of port 13 and run it in an MS-DOS (or Unix) shell on a computer connected via a network to the one running our `DaytimeServer`, we can use it to test our `DaytimeServer`:

```
C:\> java DaytimeClient pcadams.calvin.edu
Fri Jun 9 16:45:55 EST 2000
```

Multithreaded Servers

The server program in Figure 13.4 is a **single-threaded server,** because the same thread accepts connect requests and processes those requests:

```
for (;;)
{
   Socket sessionSocket = myServerSocket.accept();

   PrintWriter myWriter = new PrintWriter(
                       sessionSocket.getOutputStream() );
   Date dayAndTime = new GregorianCalendar().getTime();
   myWriter.println(dayAndTime);
   myWriter.close();
}
```

More generally, we can think of the behavior of a server's *processing loop* as follows:

```
for (;;)
{
   Socket sessionSocket = myServerSocket.accept();

   // provide service using sessionSocket
}
```

A single-threaded server is adequate for simple fast services (like *daytime*), because the server can quickly return to the top of its processing loop to accept the next connection request.

---

[7] On a 233-MHz Pentium-II, this took anywhere from 5 to 45 seconds; so be patient!

If, however, a server's service cannot be performed quickly, then the time to perform the service delays the server's ability to accept another request. This is a potential problem, because if multiple clients try to connect to the server and the server is busy serving a client, the `ServerSocket` places the clients' connection requests in a *fixed-length queue*.[8] Over time, a *backlog* of client requests can build up in the queue. If the queue becomes completely filled, then any subsequent client requests will be lost. In summary, if servicing a client takes an extended period of time, connection requests may be lost before the server is able to accept them.

This problem can be addressed by using a **multithreaded server,** whose processing loop has the form

```
for (;;)
{
   Socket sessionSocket = myServerSocket.accept();

   // create a new thread to provide service using sessionSocket
   // start the thread
}
```

Rather than serving each client *itself,* each iteration of the processing loop in a multithreaded server simply accepts a connection request, and then creates a **handler thread** to provide the service for that client. Since the handler thread and the server thread can run at the same time, the server thread immediately returns to the top of the processing loop to handle the next connection request. We can visualize the resulting behavior as follows:

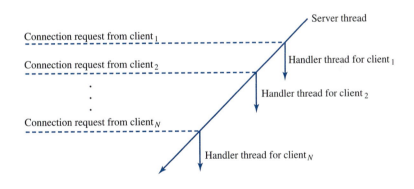

By using a separate thread to provide its service and then immediately returning to its `accept()` method, a multithreaded server reduces the likelihood of its `Server-Socket`'s queue becoming full and connection requests being lost.

Example: A Multithreaded Echo Server

To illustrate the multithreaded approach, we will build a multithreaded server for the *echo* service. Such a server does nothing but read lines of text that the client sends to it and echo each line back to the client, until the client closes the socket. Since the

---

[8] The default queue length is 50 requests.

client may send an arbitrary number of lines, this could be a time-consuming process, making it a good candidate for multithreading.

The EchoServer Class. As described above, our `EchoServer` class will simply build its `ServerSocket` and then enter a processing loop that repeatedly:

a. Invokes `accept()` to accept a connection request

b. Creates a new `EchoHandler` thread to handle that request

Figure 13.5 presents an implementation of a multithreaded server for the echo service:

FIGURE 13.5   A MULTITHREADED ECHO SERVER

```
/** EchoServer.java defines a multithreaded echo server.
 *   Attribute: a ServerSocket
 *   Methods:   constructor; socket accessor(); run(); stop(); main()
 */

import java.net.*;        // Socket, ServerSocket, ...
import EchoHandler;

class EchoServer extends Object
{
/** Constructor ---
 *   Receive:       String[] args
 *   Postcondition: mySocket is a ServerSocket with port specifed by args[0]
 *                  || execution terminates due to an exception.
 */
 public EchoServer(String [] args)
 {
  if (args.length != 1)
  { System.err.println("Usage: java EchoServer <port>");
    System.exit(1);
  }

  try
  {
    int port = Integer.parseInt(args[0]);
    myServerSocket = new ServerSocket(port);
  }
  catch (Exception e)
  {
    System.err.println(e);
    System.exit(1);
  }
 }

//--- run() method ---
 public void run()
 {
  try
  {
    System.out.println("\nEchoServer.run(): " + myServerSocket);
    for (;;)
    {
      Socket sessionSocket = myServerSocket.accept();
      EchoHandler sessionHandler = new EchoHandler(sessionSocket);
      sessionHandler.start();
    }
  }
```

```
    catch (Exception e)
    {
      System.err.println(e);
      System.exit(1);
    }
  }

//--- Serversocket accessor ---
 public ServerSocket getServerSocket() { return myServerSocket; }

//--- stop() method ---
 public void stop()
 {
    try
    {
      myServerSocket.close();
      System.exit(0);
    }
    catch (Exception e)
    {
      System.err.println(e);
      System.exit(1);
    }
  }

//--- main() method ---
 public static void main(String [] args)
 {
    EchoServer myServer = new EchoServer(args);
    myServer.run();
  }

//--- Attribute variable ---
 private ServerSocket myServerSocket;
}
```

Sample Run:

```
C:\> java EchoServer 1007

EchoServer.run(): ServerSocket[addr=0.0.0.0/0.0.0.0,port=0,localport=1007]
```

Note that since `EchoServer` is not an official echo server, we have written it to accept its port (1007) via a command-line argument. This makes it easy for different people to run and experiment with their own echo servers, each on a different port.

It is worth mentioning that we could have placed all of the functionality in the main method. However, placing the initialization code in a constructor and the processing loop in a `run()` method makes it possible for other applications (e.g., a *GUIechoServer*) to create an `EchoServer` object, and then activate it by sending it the `run()` message. Similarly, adding an accessor method for the `ServerSocket` and a `stop()` method to shut it down make for a well-rounded class that can be reused by other applications.

Within the `run()` method, the statements

```
        EchoHandler sessionHandler = new EchoHandler(sessionSocket);
        sessionHandler.start();
```

create a new `EchoHandler` object and start it running. Figure 13.6 presents the definition of our `EchoHandler` class. As described in Section 13.2, this class extends the `Thread` class, and so most of its functionality is placed in its `run()` method:

FIGURE 13.6   AN ECHO-HANDLER THREAD

```java
/** EchoHandler.java defines a thread to handle echo sessions.
 *  Attributes: a Socket, a PrintWriter, a BufferedReader
 *  Methods:    constructor; run(); Socket accessor
 *  See EchoServer.java
 */

import java.io.*;    // PrintWriter, BufferedReader, ...
import java.net.*;   // Socket, ...

class EchoHandler extends Thread
{
/** Constructor ---
 *  Receive:       Socket aSocket
 *  Postcondition: mySocket == aSocket && myWriter is a Printwriter
 *                 && myReader is a BufferedReader
 *                 || execution terminates due to an exception
 */
 public EchoHandler(Socket aSocket)
 {
   try
   {
     mySocket = aSocket;
     myWriter = new PrintWriter(
                 aSocket.getOutputStream(), true);
     myReader = new BufferedReader(
                 new InputStreamReader(
                  aSocket.getInputStream() ));
   }
   catch (Exception e)
   {
     System.err.println(e);
     System.exit(1);
   }
 }

//--- run method() ---
 public void run()
 {
   try
   {
     String aLine = null;
     for (;;)
     {
       aLine = myReader.readLine();      // read aLine from the client

       if (aLine == null) break;         // check for closed socket

       myWriter.println( aLine );        // echo aLine back to them
     }
     mySocket.close();
   }
   catch (Exception e)
   {
     System.err.println(e);
   }
 }
```

```
//--- Socket accessor ---
 public Socket getSocket() { return mySocket; }

//--- Attribute variables ---
 private Socket         mySocket;
 private PrintWriter    myWriter;
 private BufferedReader myReader;
}
```

Because this echo handler needs to read from and write to the `Socket`, we build `BufferedReader` and `PrintWriter` objects in its constructor. Since those objects are built from the `Socket`, the constructor must receive the `Socket` via a parameter.

The `run()` method in this class is invoked (indirectly) when we send an `EchoHandler` object the `start()` message. Accordingly, `run()` is where we place the loop to handle a session of reading text from the socket and echoing it back to the socket for the client to read.

Finally, we supply an accessor for our `Socket` object, just in case some user of the class wishes to use it to access the client's port number, host computer, or other information.

Figure 13.7 presents an echo client that reads values the user types at the keyboard, writes them to the `Socket`, and reads and displays the server's response:

FIGURE 13.7   AN ECHO CLIENT

```
/** EchoClient.java defines an echo client.
 *  Attributes: Name of remost host; remote port number;
 *              a Printwriter and BufferedReader to read from and write
 *              to the socket; a BufferedReader for keyboard input.
 *  Methods:    Constructor; run(); getLineFromUser(); accessors of
 *              port name and number; main()
 */
import java.net.*;      // Socket, ...
import java.io.*;       // BufferedReader, ...

class EchoClient extends Object
{
/** Constructor ---
 *  Receive:       String remostHost and int remotePort
 *  Postcondition: myRemoteHost == remostHost && myRemotePort == remotePort
 *                 && myWriter is a Printwriter
 *                 && myReader and myKeyboard are BufferedReaders
 *                 || execution terminates due to an exception
 */
 public EchoClient(String remoteHost, int remotePort)
 {
   try
   {
     myRemoteHost = remoteHost;
     myRemotePort = remotePort;
     Socket aSocket = new Socket(remoteHost, remotePort);
     myReader = new BufferedReader(
               new InputStreamReader(
                aSocket.getInputStream() ));
     myWriter = new PrintWriter(
                aSocket.getOutputStream(),
                true);
     myKeyboard = new BufferedReader(
                 new InputStreamReader(
                   System.in));
   }
```

```
      catch (Exception e)
      {
        System.err.println(e);
        System.exit(1);
      }
  }

  //--- run method() ---
   public void run()
   {
    try
    {
      String lineFromUser = null,
             lineFromServer = null;
      for (;;)
      {
        lineFromUser = getLineFromUser();

        if ( lineFromUser.equals("quit") ) break;
        myWriter.println(lineFromUser);
        lineFromServer = myReader.readLine();
        System.out.println(lineFromServer);
      }
      myWriter.close();
      myReader.close();
      myKeyboard.close();
    }

    catch (Exception e)
    {
      System.err.println(e);
      System.exit(1);
    }
  }

  /** Input
   *   Return: String entered by the user
   *            or execution terminates due to an exception
   */
   public String getLineFromUser()
   {
     String result = null;
     try { result = myKeyboard.readLine(); }
     catch (Exception e) { System.err.println(e); System.exit(1); }
     return result;
   }

  //--- Accessors
  /** remoteHost
   *   Return: myRemostHost */
   public String getRemoteHost() { return myRemoteHost; }

  /** remotePort
   *   Return: myRemotePort */
   public int    getRemotePort() { return myRemotePort; }


  //--- main method() ---
   public static void main(String [] args)
   {
    if (args.length != 2)
    { System.err.println("Usage: java EchoClient <remoteHost> <port>");
      System.exit(1);
    }
```

```
    String remoteHost = args[0];
    int remotePort = Integer.parseInt(args[1]);
    System.out.println("\nWelcome to the Echo client!\n"
                     + "Enter text and watch it echo back!\n"
                     + "Enter 'quit' to quit...\n\n");
    EchoClient myClient = new EchoClient(remoteHost, remotePort);
    myClient.run();
  }

//--- Attribute variables ---
  private String         myRemoteHost;
  private int            myRemotePort;
  private PrintWriter    myWriter;
  private BufferedReader myReader,
                         myKeyboard;

}
```

Sample Run:

```
C:\> java EchoClient pcadams 1007

Welcome to the Echo client!
Enter text and watch it echo back!
Enter 'quit' to quit...


Tasting, tasting, 1-2-3
Tasting, tasting, 1-2-3

Yodel-odel-eh-he-hooooo
Yodel-odel-eh-he-hooooo

blah!
blah!

quit
```

As with the `EchoServer`, this `EchoClient` would be simpler if we packed its functionality into its main method. However, the approach used here makes the code reusable by allowing other applications (e.g., a `GUIEchoClient`). In particular, an extension of this class can override the `getLineFromUser()` method to get input from another source, such as a `JTextField`.

Using Multithreading Wisely. Our discussion of multithreaded servers would be incomplete if we neglected to mention that creating a new thread is itself fairly time-consuming. As a result, multithreading should not be used indiscriminately. Our rule of thumb is as follows:

> *If providing a server's service takes less time than creating a thread,*
> *then a single-threaded server should be used; otherwise, a multithreaded server*
> *should be used.*

A class like the `Timer` class (in our package `ann.util`) can be used to measure the lengths of time for a server's service and thread creation on a particular system.

Summary

A client uses a `Socket` to connect to a server. To create a `Socket`, a client must specify the name of the computer where the server is running, and the port associated with that server.

To read from a `Socket`, send it the `getInputStream()` message and wrap the resulting `InputStream` in an `InputStreamReader` and a `BufferedReader`. Then use the `readLine()` method to read from the `Socket` via its `BufferedReader` wrapper. The `readLine()` method returns `null` when the connection is *closed*.

To write to a `Socket`, send it the `getOutputStream()` message and "wrap" the resulting `OutputStream` in a `PrintWriter`. Use the `print()` and `println()` methods to write to the `Socket` via its `PrintWriter` wrapper.

A server uses a `ServerSocket` to receive connection requests. The `Server-Socket` constructor requires only a port number. Sending a `ServerSocket` the `accept()` message causes the server to block until a client requests a connection, at which point the `accept()` method returns a `Socket` connected to the client's `Socket`. The server can then use this `Socket` (as described earlier) to interact with the client and provide its server.

A single-threaded server uses a processing loop to accept connection requests and provide service within the same thread. This works well if the server's service does not take long to perform, since such a server cannot accept additional requests until the service is completed.

A multithreaded server also accepts connection requests via a processing loop, but creates a new handler thread to service each client. A handler thread must be passed the `Socket` returned by `accept()` to interact with its client. The handler thread must close the `Socket` when its service is completed. This approach works well if the server's service is time-consuming, since the server thread can accept the next request while a handler thread is serving a client.

✔ Quick Quiz 13.3

1. A popular model for network communication is the _____ model.
2. A(n) _____ is a communication endpoint by which a program can send and receive information.
3. What two pieces of information are needed to uniquely identify a socket?
4. Name three TCP/IP services used for e-mail transfers.
5. _____ is a TCP/IP service for transferring files.
6. _____ is a TCP/IP service for transporting hypertext.
7. Java provides a(n) _____ class for creating sockets that wait for clients to connect to them.
8. What is a potential problem with single-threaded servers?
9. How does a multithreaded server solve the problem in Question 8?

13.4 GRAPHICAL/INTERNET JAVA: MOON ANIMATION

The moon has long been an object of romance and mystery. From the earliest times, the changing *phases* (full moon, new moon, and so on) of our moon have inspired reactions ranging from scientific curiosity to poetry. In this section, we will build an application whose graphical user interface displays an animation of the moon passing through its 28-day cycle of phases.

Design

GUI Design. There are many ways one might design a GUI application to present the phases of the moon. For simplicity, our GUI will present a stationary moon and use animation to show how its appearance changes as time passes. To let the user control the rate of animation, we will use a GUI control called a **slider,** whose setting will determine how fast the animation runs. To stop and start the animation we will use buttons similar to those on a video cassette recorder. For example, a "pause" button (‖) can be used to stop the animation and study a particular phase of the moon:

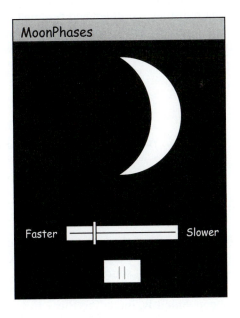

When the pause button is pressed, we will hide the slider, change the text of the button to be something like a "play" button, make "forward" and "backward" buttons appear, and display a label showing the current phase of the moon:

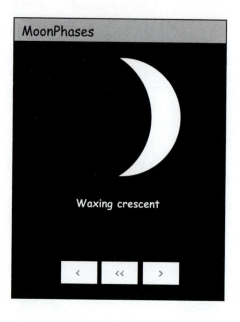

Pressing the forward (<) and backward (>) buttons will produce adjacent phases. If the user presses the play button (<<), we will hide the label and the backward and forward buttons, redisplay the slider, and resume the animation.

Our GUI thus has just two states that we will call *running* (the first view) and *paused* (the second view). This gives us the following state diagram for its behavior:

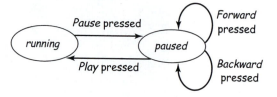

Animation Design. Since the moon runs through its cycle every 28 days, we will use a sequence of 28 images of the moon over successive days. Such images are freely available from a variety of sources, including the Internet.[9]

The `java.awt` package provides classes and methods to manipulate graphical images conveniently, including the `Image` class for storing images, and the `Graphics` method `drawImage()` for drawing images within a particular graphics context.

---

[9] Our thanks to those who provided the source of our images at *http://tycho.usno.navy.mil/vphase.html.*

To load the images into our program, we will use two `java.awt` classes:

- ❑ Java's `Toolkit` class provides a `getImage()` class method that, given the name of a file containing a graphics image, reads and returns an `Image` object representing the image.[10]
- ❑ Java's `MediaTracker` class provides a convenient way to prevent images (or other media) from being displayed until all of the images have been loaded.

Since each image has the same type, we will store them in an `Image` array, and then iterate through the array in a circular fashion, displaying each image in turn:

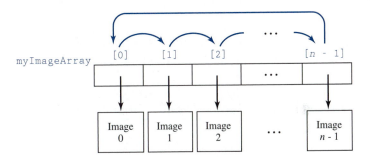

This is easily accomplished by having our `paintComponent()` method execute

```
pen.drawImage( myImageArray[myIndex], ... );
```

and then varying the value of `myIndex`, using the controls in our GUI.

Application Design. Our application must be able to do two things at once:

- ❑ Listen for user-generated events at the application's graphical user interface
- ❑ Animate the moon by cycling through and drawing each image in the `Image` array

Since listening for events is a blocking action, we can't listen for events *and* run our animation with the same thread. Instead, we will use the normal thread to build and listen for events at the graphical user interface, and then use a separate thread to animate the moon. This second thread will thus have to build, cycle through, and draw each image in the `Image` array.

Two threads of execution imply two separate classes, so we will define a class named `MoonPhases` to build and listen for GUI events, and a class named `MoonAnimator` to perform the animation. Because it must draw graphical images, the `MoonAnimator` class must extend some graphical (i.e., Swing or AWT) class such as `JPanel`. The `MoonPhases` class will then have a `MoonAnimator` as part of its GUI and extend the `CloseableFrame` class (as we have done in several previous graphics examples).

---

[10] The `Applet` class provides its own `getImage()` method, so classes that extend it need not use `Toolkit`.

If `MoonAnimator` extends `JPanel`, then it cannot extend `Thread`. As a result, it will have to implement the `Runnable` interface, as described in Section 13.2. We can visualize the resulting structure as follows (where the dashed arrow indicates the "implements" relationship):

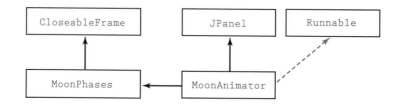

Coding: The `MoonAnimator` Class

Figure 13.8 presents our `MoonAnimator` class:

FIGURE 13.8   CLASS `MoonAnimator`

```
/** MoonAnimator.java carries out the animation of the moon phases.
 *   Attributes: current state, index in Image array, and sleep interval;
 *               Image array; a MediaTracker; a Thread; a ToolKit; an array
 *               of phase labels; Constants NUM_IMAGES, RUNNING, PAUSED
 *   Methods: Constructor; phaseOfImageIndex() to retrieve phase labels;
 *            forward(), backward(), and pause() controls; isPaused(),
 *            isRunning(), waitIfPaused(), go(), run(); accessor and mutator
 *            for the sleep interval; getPhase(); paintComponent().
 */

import java.awt.*;                    // Graphics, MediaTracker, ...
import javax.swing.JPanel;

class MoonAnimator extends JPanel
                   implements Runnable
{
  public final static int NUM_IMAGES   = 28,
                          RUNNING       = 0,
                          PAUSED        = 1;
                          DEFAULT_DELAY = 0;    // milliseconds

//----Constructors
/** First constructor
 *   Receive:      int delay and boolean running
 *   Postcondition: myImageArray and aTracker are initalized using moon-phase
 *      images, myPhaseArray with appropriate captions for these images;
 *      mySleepInterval == initialDelay; myIndex == 0;
 *      myState == RUNNING if running is true, and PAUSED otherwise;
 *      myThread has been created and has started executing.
 */
public MoonAnimator(int delay, boolean running)
{
  setBackground(Color.black);

  MediaTracker aTracker = new MediaTracker(this);
  myImageArray = new Image [NUM_IMAGES];
  myPhaseArray = new String [NUM_IMAGES];
  myToolkit = Toolkit.getDefaultToolkit();

  for (int i = 0; i < NUM_IMAGES; i++)
  {
```

```
     try { aTracker.waitForAll(); }
     catch (Exception e) { System.err.println(e); }

     mySleepInterval = delay;
     myIndex = 0;
     myState = (running) ? RUNNING : PAUSED;
     myThread = new Thread(this);
     myThread.start();
  }

 /** Second constructor
  *  Receive: int delay
  *  Produces same result as first constructor with running = true.
  */
 public MoonAnimator(int delay)    { this(delay, true); }

 /**  Third constructor
  *   Receive: boolean running
  *   Produces same result as first constructor with delay = DEFAULT_DELAY.
  */
 public MoonAnimator(boolean running) { this(DEFAULT_DELAY, running); }

 /** Get label for a phase
  * Receive: int index
  * Return: a caption (String) for index-th moon phase
  */
 private String phaseOfImageIndex(int index)
 {
    switch (index)
    {
      case 0:             return "Waning new moon";
      case 1:             return "New moon";
      case 2:             return "Waxing new moon";
      case 3: case 4:
      case 5: case 6:     return "Waxing crescent";
      case 7: case 8:     return "First quarter";
      case 9: case 10:
      case 11: case 12:   return "Waxing gibbous";
      case 13: case 14:   return "Waxing full";
      case 15:            return "Full moon";
      case 16: case 17:   return "Waning full moon";
      case 18: case 19:
      case 20: case 21:   return "Waning gibbous";
      case 22: case 23:   return "Third quarter";
      case 24: case 25:
      case 26: case 27:   return "Waning crescent";
      default:            return "mapImageToPhase(): Invalid index";
    }
 }

 /** Back up to next phase
  * Postcondition: In PAUSED state, myIndex == index of previous phase.
  */
 public synchronized void backward()
 {
   if (myState == PAUSED)
   {
     myIndex = myIndex - 1;
     if (myIndex < 0)                          // wrap-around, since %
       myIndex = myImageArray.length - 1;  // won't for negatives
     repaint();
   }
 }
```

```java
/** Detect if paused
 * Return: true if in PAUSED state and false otherwise
 */
public synchronized boolean isPaused()
{
  return myState == PAUSED;
}

/** Detect if running
 * Return: true if in RUNNING state and false otherwise
 */
public synchronized boolean isRunning()
{
  return myState == RUNNING;
}

/** Pause the animation
 * Postcondition: myState == PAUSED   */
public synchronized void pause()
{
  myState = PAUSED;
}

/** Switch from paused to running
 * Postcondition: myState switches from PAUSED to RUNNING and
 *    waiting thread is awakened.
 */
public synchronized void go()
{
  myState = RUNNING;
  notify();                // wake up waiting thread
}


//--- run() method ---
public void run()
{
  for (;;)
  {
    try
    {
      if (mySleepInterval > 0)
        myThread.sleep(mySleepInterval);
    }
    catch (InterruptedException e) {}
    waitIfPaused();

    myIndex = (myIndex + 1) % NUM_IMAGES;

    repaint();
  }
}

/** Block thread
 * Postcondition: Thread is blocked while myState == PAUSED.
 */
private synchronized void waitIfPaused()
{
  try
  {
    while (myState == PAUSED)
      wait();
  }
```

```
      catch (Exception e) {}
   }

//--- Nutators and accessors ---
/* Mutator for sleep interval
 * Receive:        newInterval
 * Postcondition: mySleepInterval == newTerval.   */
 public synchronized void setSleepInterval(int newInterval)
 {
    if (newInterval >= 0 && myState == RUNNING)
      mySleepInterval = newInterval;
 }

/* Accessor for sleep interval
 * Return: mySleepInterval */
 public synchronized int getSleepInterval() { return mySleepInterval; }

/* Access caption for current phase
 * Return: caption (String) corresponding to phase # myIndex */
 public synchronized String getPhase()
 {
    return myPhaseArray[myIndex];
 }

//--- paintComponent() method ---
 public void paintComponent(Graphics pen)
 {
    super.paintComponent(pen);
    pen.drawImage( myImageArray[myIndex], 0, 0,
                 getWidth(), getHeight(), this );
 }

//--- Attribute variables ---
 private int          myState,
                      myIndex,
                      mySleepInterval;
 private Image []     myImageArray;
 private MediaTracker myTracker;
 private Thread       myThread;
 private Toolkit      myToolkit;
 private String []    myPhaseArray;
}
```

Controlling Animation Speed. When animating a sequence of images, the smoothness of the animation depends on the number of images displayed each second. As this number increases, the animation becomes smoother. As the number of images per second decreases, the human eye finds it easier to see each separate image, until the discrete basis for the animation becomes evident.

Our GUI will provide a slider control that lets the user control the speed of the animation. One way that this can be done is to introduce a *delay* between the drawing of successive images. More precisely, a thread can "go to sleep" for a given period of time if it receives the `sleep()` message from the `Thread` class. Our `MoonAnimator` class uses this approach by:

❑ Providing an instance variable `mySleepInterval` to store the delay (in milliseconds)

❑ Having its constructors provide a parameter for the delay, which is then used to set `mySleepInterval`

❑ Providing accessor and mutator methods for `mySleepInterval`

❏ Having its `run()` method use `sleep()` to cause the thread to sleep for `mySleep-Interval` milliseconds on every repetition of its main processing loop

Note that because each of our threads will need to access `mySleepInterval`—the GUI thread to set it and the animation thread to read it—its accessor and mutator methods should be *synchronized*, as described in section 13.2.

Getting the Images. In our constructor, the code to initialize the `Image` array looks like this:

```
for (int i = 0; i < NUM_IMAGES; i++)
{
  myImageArray[i] = myToolkit.getImage("phases/m" + i + ".gif");
  aTracker.addImage(myImageArray[i], i);
  myPhaseArray[i] = phaseOfImageIndex(i);
}

try { aTracker.waitForAll(); }
catch (Exception e) { System.err.println(e); }
```

This loop presupposes that the 28 moon images are stored in a folder named `phases`, in separate files with the names `m0.gif, m1.gif, ..., m27.gif`.

You may wonder why the `MediaTracker` object `aTracker` is needed. The problem is that each call to `getImage()` is *nonblocking,* meaning that execution does not block while the image is loading. If we were to omit the use of the `MediaTracker`, the constructor could easily finish execution and the animator thread begin running and try to display the partially-loaded images. The result would be an ugly, flickering partial image of the moon at the outset, until all of the images were loaded. The `MediaTracker` class provides a convenient way to avoid such flicker. The call

```
aTracker.addImage(myImageArray[i], i);
```

adds the current image to the `MediaTracker`. When execution leaves the loop, the call

```
aTracker.waitForAll();
```

prevents the animation thread from continuing until all of the images have finished loading.

To indicate what phase of the image the animator is currently displaying, we maintain a parallel array named `myPhaseArray` such that `myPhaseArray[i]` gives the description of the phase whose image is in `myImageArray[i]`. To initialize this array, we have written a simple utility method `phaseOfImageIndex()` that given an `i` in the range 0 to 27, returns the `String` describing the image in the image file `mi.gif`. Our constructor then uses this method to initialize `myPhaseArray` in the same loop used to initialize `myImageArray`.

Self-Starting. With `myImageArray` and `myPhaseArray` initialized, the remaining code in the first constructor initializes the various instance variables needed by the class:

```
mySleepInterval = delay;
myIndex = 0;
myState = (running? RUNNING : PAUSED);
myThread = new Thread(this);
myThread.start();
```

The first statement initializes `mySleepInterval` to the value the constructor receives via its parameter. The second initializes `myIndex` to 0, so that when the `paintComponent()` method draws `myImageArray[myIndex]` (see below), the first image drawn will be that stored in `myImageArray[0]`. The third sets `myState` to RUNNING if the value of the parameter `running` is true and sets `myState` to PAUSED otherwise. At startup, `running` will be true (because the second constructor will be invoked—see Figure 13.9), wich means the moon will be initially animated rather than paused.

The initialization of `myThread` is a bit trickier. Because the `MoonAnimator` object needs to be able to put *itself* to sleep, it needs a handle for *its own* execution `Thread`. Since `MoonAnimator` implements the `Runnable` interface, `this` refers to a `Runnable` object, and the statement:

```
myThread = new Thread(this);
```

creates a new thread for this `MoonAnimator` object and makes `myThread` a handle for it. The statement

```
myThread.start();
```

then starts this new thread executing. Because these statements are at the end of the constructor, whenever any other class creates a `MoonAnimator` object, that object will initialize itself, create a new thread, and start itself running!

When this thread is started, the `paintComponent()` method is invoked to paint it on the screen, and then its `run()` method is invoked to generate its behavior. We will examine each of these methods in turn.

Drawing An Image. As we have seen before, the `paintComponent()` method is used to draw graphically within a Swing component. Our method is as follows:

```
public void paintComponent(Graphics pen)
{
  super.paintComponent(pen);
  pen.drawImage( myImageArray[myIndex], 0, 0,
                 getWidth(), getHeight(), this );
}
```

To draw an image, we use the `Graphics` method `drawImage()` of which there are several versions (see Java's API documentation). This version takes the `Image` to be drawn as its first argument, the coordinates within the Swing component as the second and third arguments, the *x*- and *y*- dimensions to which it is to be scaled as its fourth and fifth arguments, and finally the object (`this` one) responsible for the image. By passing `getWidth()` as the *x*-dimension and `getHeight()` as the *y*-dimension, the `Image` will be scaled to fill the `JPanel` that `MoonAnimator` is extending.

Defining Thread Behavior. As we saw earlier in this chapter, the `run()` method specifies the behavior for a `Thread`. Our `run()` method is as follows:

```
public void run()
{
  for (;;)
  {
    try
    {
      if (mySleepInterval>0)
        myThread.sleep(mySleepInterval);
    }
    catch (InterruptedException e) {}

    waitIfPaused();

    myIndex = (myIndex + 1) % NUM_IMAGES;

    repaint();
  }
}
```

This method consists of an infinite loop that puts the current `MoonAnimator` object to sleep for the specified (nonzero) sleep interval, checks to see if a `pause()` message has been received (see below), increments `myIndex` (with wraparound from 27 to 0), and then calls `repaint()` to update the display. Since `repaint()` calls `paintComponent()` which displays the `Image` referred to by `myImageArray[myIndex]`, the effect is that the next `Image` is displayed on each repetition of the loop. Each repetition thus displays one image. The time-delay between images will increase if `mySleepInterval` is increased.

Pausing Execution. To get our GUI thread to pause the animation when the user presses the pause button, the `MoonAnimator` class provides a `pause()` method:

```
public synchronized void pause()
{
  myState = PAUSED;
}
```

Note that because it provides a different thread with access to `myState`, this method must be `synchronized`.

On each repetition of its loop, the `run()` method calls the utility method `waitIfPaused()`:

```
private synchronized void waitIfPaused()
{
  try
  {
    while (myState == PAUSED)
      wait();
  }
```

```
      catch (Exception e) {}
   }
```

This method checks to see if the user has sent the `pause()` message to change the attribute variable `myState`, and if so, invokes the `wait()` method from class `Object`. This suspends the `MoonAnimator`'s thread until another thread invokes the following `go()` method:

```
   public synchronized void go()
   {
     if (myState == PAUSED)
     {
       myState = RUNNING;
       notify();                        // wake up waiting thread
     }                                  //
   }
```

More precisely, the `go()` message changes `myState` back to the *running* state, and then sends the `notify()` message, which wakes up any threads that were suspended via `wait()`, in particular, the `MoonAnimator` thread. It then resumes execution and rechecks to make sure that in the meantime no other thread has changed `myState` back to *paused*. If none has, `waitIfPaused()` terminates, returning control to the `run()` method, which resumes the animation.

Behind The Scenes. If all of this seems rather complicated, it is. In fact, it's even more complicated than the preceding explanation indicates. Every Java `Object` has a built-in attribute called a **monitor** that is used to provide the synchronization of synchronized methods. Recall that only one thread can execute any synchronized method at any given time. To enforce this, Java requires that a class *own the monitor* before it can execute a synchronized method. To prevent more than one class from owning the monitor at once, Java associates a **lock** with the class containing the synchronized methods.

When a thread tries to execute a synchronized method, Java first checks the lock for that method's class. If it is unlocked, Java gives ownership of the monitor to that thread, locks the lock, and allows the thread to continue. But if the lock is locked, the thread is suspended and placed in a list of threads waiting to own the monitor. We will call this list the **lock list.**

Whenever a thread finishes executing a synchronized method, it relinquishes ownership of the class monitor. Java then checks the lock list, to see if there are any threads waiting. If so, Java chooses one, gives it ownership of the monitor, and wakes it up, at which point it begins executing the synchronized method it was trying to invoke. If the lock list is empty, Java unlocks the monitor's lock.

How do `wait()` and `notify()` fit? If a thread is executing a synchronized method that invokes `wait()`, the thread relinquishes ownership of the monitor and Java *suspends the thread indefinitely*, placing it in a separate list of threads waiting to be *notified*. We'll call this list the **waiting list.** Such threads remain in the waiting list until some other `Thread` sends a synchronized message that invokes `notify()` or `notifyAll()`. The `notify()` method moves one waiting thread to the lock list, to re-acquire ownership of the monitor. The `notifyAll()` method moves all wait-ing threads to the lock list. We can visualize the situation as follows:

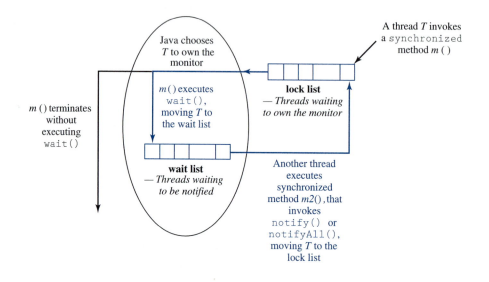

We use this mechanism to pause and resume the animation. When the `run()` method in the `MoonAnimator` thread executes `waitIfPaused()`, this is a syn-chronized method, so `MoonAnimator` must first acquire ownership of the class monitor. When this happens, if `myState` equals RUNNING, the while loop's condi-tion is false, and so `waitIfPaused()` terminates, returning control to its caller (i.e., `run()`). But if `myState` equals PAUSED, the while loop's condition is true and `wait()` is invoked:

```
private synchronized void waitIfPaused()
{
  try
  {
    while (myState == PAUSED)
      wait();
  }
  catch (Exception e) {}
}
```

This causes the thread to enter the list of threads waiting to be notified. It remains there (asleep) until the `MoonPhases` thread invokes the `go()` method:

```
public synchronized void go()
{
  if (myState == PAUSED)
  {
    myState = RUNNING;
    notify();                          // wake up waiting thread
  }                                    //
}
```

When `myState` equals `PAUSED`, the `go()` method invokes `notify()`, which awakens the `MoonAnimator` thread and moves it to the list of threads waiting to own the monitor. When the `MoonPhases` thread's execution of `go()` terminates, `Moon-Phases` relinquishes ownership of the monitor. Since `MoonAnimator` is the only thread waiting, it acquires ownership, at which point its `run()` method resumes execution immediately following its call to `waitIfPaused()`. Since `go()` sets `my-State` to `RUNNING`, the animation resumes. We can picture the behavior as follows:

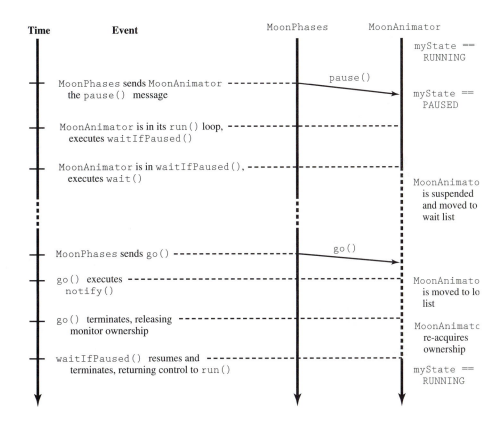

This `wait()`-`notify()` mechanism can be used in any situation where it is necessary to suspend a thread that has acquired ownership of a monitor. The accepted technique is to use an instance variable to store the thread's state (e.g., `myState`), invoke a synchronized method (e.g., `waitIfPaused()`) in the thread's `run()` method to check the value of this variable, and have that synchronized method invoke `wait()` as determined by the value of the instance variable. Of course if we ever want the thread to resume execution, the class must provide a complementary synchronized method (e.g., `go()`) that invokes the `notify()` method.

The Remaining Methods. Compared to `go()` and `waitIfPaused()`, the remaining methods are quite straightforward; most of them simply provide accessors or mutators for the instance variables. Of particular interest are the `forward()` and `backward()` methods, that change `myIndex`. The `forward()` method advances `myIndex` to its next value,

```
public synchronized void forward()
{
  if (myState == PAUSED)
  {
    myIndex = (myIndex + 1) % myImageArray.length;
    repaint();
  }
}
```

using the modulus operator (%) to cause the value 28 to wrap around to 0. The `backward()` method must perform the opposite operation:

```
public synchronized void backward()
{
  if (myState == PAUSED)
  {
    myIndex = myIndex - 1;
    if (myIndex < 0)                        // wrap-around, since %
      myIndex = myImageArray.length - 1;  // won't for negatives
    repaint();
  }
}
```

Since the modulus operator will not make the index value −1 wrap around to 27, we must explicitly check for this situation and make it happen. Because these methods allow different threads to access `myIndex`, they must be synchronized.

Coding: The `MoonPhases` Class

Compared to the `MoonAnimator` class, the `MoonPhases` class is straightforward, as shown in Figure 13.9.

FIGURE 13.9   CLASS `MoonPhases`

```
/** MoonPhases.java builds and listens for GUI events.
 * Attributes:  Check if animation paused;  a MoonAnimator object;
 *              JPanels for bottom, moon, control buttons, and slider;
 *              JLabels for the slider; back, pause/go,
 *              and forward JButtons; a JSlider; constant INITIAL_DELAY.
 * Methods: Constructor; actionPerformed(); stateChanged();
 *          enterRunningState() and enterPausedState(); main()
 */

import MoonAnimator;
import ann.gui.CloseableFrame;
import java.awt.*;              // Color, BorderLayout, ...
import java.awt.event.*;        // ActionListener, ActionEvent, ...
import javax.swing.*;           // JPanel, JSlider, ...
import javax.swing.event.*;     // ChangeListener, ...
```

```java
class MoonPhases extends CloseableFrame
                 implements ActionListener, ChangeListener
{
 final int INITIAL_DELAY = 100;    // msecs delay between frames

//--- Constructor ---
 public MoonPhases()
 {
   setBackground(Color.black);

   myAnimator = new MoonAnimator(INITIAL_DELAY);

   myLabel = new JLabel(" ", SwingConstants.CENTER);
   myLabel.setForeground(Color.white);
   myLabel.setBackground(Color.black);

   myFasterLabel = new JLabel("Faster");
   myFasterLabel.setForeground(Color.white);
   mySlider = new JSlider(0, 1000, INITIAL_DELAY);
   mySlider.setBackground(Color.white);
   mySlider.addChangeListener(this);
   mySlowerLabel = new JLabel("Slower");
   mySlowerLabel.setForeground(Color.white);

   mySliderPanel = new JPanel( new FlowLayout() );
   mySliderPanel.add(myFasterLabel);
   mySliderPanel.add(mySlider);
   mySliderPanel.add(mySlowerLabel);
   mySliderPanel.setBackground(Color.black);

   myBackButton = new JButton(">");
   myBackButton.addActionListener(this);
   myBackButton.setBackground(Color.white);
   myBackButton.setForeground(Color.red);
   myPauseGoButton = new JButton("||");
   myPauseGoButton.addActionListener(this);
   myPauseGoButton.setBackground(Color.white);
   myPauseGoButton.setForeground(Color.red);
   myForwardButton = new JButton("<");
   myForwardButton.addActionListener(this);
   myForwardButton.setBackground(Color.white);
   myForwardButton.setForeground(Color.red);

   myControlPanel = new JPanel( new FlowLayout() );
   myControlPanel.add(myForwardButton);
   myControlPanel.add(myPauseGoButton);
   myControlPanel.add(myBackButton);
   myControlPanel.setBackground(Color.black);

   myBottomPanel = new JPanel( new GridLayout(3,1) );
   myBottomPanel.add(myLabel);
   myBottomPanel.add(mySliderPanel);
   myBottomPanel.add(myControlPanel);
   myBottomPanel.setBackground(Color.black);

   myMoonPanel = new JPanel( new BorderLayout() );
   myMoonPanel.add(myAnimator, BorderLayout.CENTER);
   myMoonPanel.add(myBottomPanel, BorderLayout.SOUTH);

   setContentPane(myMoonPanel);
   enterRunningState();
 }
```

```
//--- actionPerformed() method ---
public void actionPerformed(ActionEvent event)
{
  Object eventSource = event.getSource();
  if (eventSource instanceof JButton)
  {
    JButton buttonPressed = (JButton) eventSource;
    if ( buttonPressed.equals(myPauseGoButton) )
    {
      if (myStatePaused)
        enterRunningState();
      else
        enterPausedState();
      myStatePaused = !myStatePaused;
    }
    else if ( myStatePaused
             && buttonPressed.equals(myBackButton) )
      myAnimator.backward();
    else if ( myStatePaused
             && buttonPressed.equals(myForwardButton) )
      myAnimator.forward();
  }
  else
    System.err.println("actionPerformed(): unknown event "
                       + eventSource);
}

//--- Implementation of ChangeListener interface's stateChanged() method --
public void stateChanged(ChangeEvent event)
{
  myAnimator.setSleepInterval( mySlider.getValue() );
}

//--- enterRunningState() method ---
private void enterRunningState()
{
  myPauseGoButton.setText("||");
  myForwardButton.setVisible(false);
  myBackButton.setVisible(false);
  myLabel.setText("");
  mySliderPanel.setVisible(true);
  myAnimator.go();
}

//--- enterPausedState() method ---
private void enterPausedState()
{
  myPauseGoButton.setText("<<");
  myBackButton.setVisible(true);
  myForwardButton.setVisible(true);
  myLabel.setText( myAnimator.getPhase() );
  mySliderPanel.setVisible(false);
  myAnimator.pause();
}

//--- main() method ---
public static void main(String [] args)
{
  MoonPhases myGUI = new MoonPhases();
  myGUI.setSize(300, 450);
  myGUI.setVisible(true);
}
```

```
//--- Attribute variables ---
private boolean            myStatePaused;
private MoonAnimator       myAnimator;
private JPanel             myBottomPanel, myMoonPanel, myControlPanel,
                             mySliderPanel;
private JLabel             myLabel, myFasterLabel, mySlowerLabel;
private JButton            myBackButton, myPauseGoButton,
                             myForwardButton;
private JSlider            mySlider;
}
```

In this class, the only new feature is our use of a slider control. We create a `JSlider` in the constructor with the statement

```
mySlider = new JSlider(0, 1000, INITIAL_DELAY);
```

which builds a `JSlider` with minimum value 0, maximum value 1000, and initial value `INITIAL_DELAY` (100). Since a `JSlider` fires `ChangeEvent` events, our class can listen for such events by implementing the `ChangeListener` interface. The statement

```
mySlider.addChangeListener(this);
```

makes this class the `ChangeListener` for the `JSlider`.

To implement the `ChangeListener` interface, this class must define the `state-Changed()` method, which is straightforward:

```
public void stateChanged(ChangeEvent event)
{
  myAnimator.setSleepInterval( mySlider.getValue() );
}
```

It simply sends a `getValue()` message to the `JSlider` to retrieve its value, and then passes this value to the `MoonAnimator` via its `setSleepInterval()` message. As we saw previously, this changes the value read by the `MoonAnimator` to see how long to delay between drawing successive images. Our `stateChanged()` method is this simple because the `JSlider` is the only control that fires `ChangeEvent` events.

By contrast, the `actionPerformed()` method must determine which of the three buttons was pressed, and vary its behavior accordingly:

```
public void actionPerformed(ActionEvent event)
{
  Object eventSource = event.getSource();
  if (eventSource instanceof JButton)
  {
    JButton buttonPressed = (JButton) eventSource;
    if ( buttonPressed.equals(myPauseGoButton) )
    {
      if (myStatePaused)
        enterRunningState();
      else
        enterPausedState();
      myStatePaused = !myStatePaused;
    }
```

```
            else if ( myStatePaused
                     && buttonPressed.equals(myBackButton) )
           myAnimator.backward();
            else if ( myStatePaused
                     && buttonPressed.equals(myForwardButton) )
           myAnimator.forward();
      }
      else
        System.err.println("actionPerformed(): unknown event "
                              + eventSource);
   }
```

Because the MoonAnimator provides a method for the action of each button, all that the actionPerformed() method needs to do when handling a given button-press is identify the button and then send the corresponding message to the MoonAnimator.

To implement our two states, we define an enterPausedState() method that modifies the GUI as required for its *paused* state:

```
   private void enterPausedState()
   {
      myPauseGoButton.setText("<<");
      myBackButton.setVisible(true);
      myForwardButton.setVisible(true);
      myLabel.setText( myAnimator.getPhase() );
      mySliderPanel.setVisible(false);
      myAnimator.pause();
   }
```

Its last action is to send a pause() message to the MoonAnimator, which changes MoonAnimator.myState to PAUSED, which will in turn cause it to execute wait() when its run() method next executes waitIfPaused().

Similarly, we define an enterRunningState() method that updates the GUI as needed for its *running* state:

```
   private void enterRunningState()
   {
      myPauseGoButton.setText("||");
      myForwardButton.setVisible(false);
      myBackButton.setVisible(false);
      myLabel.setText("");
      mySliderPanel.setVisible(true);
      myAnimator.go();
   }
```

Its last action is to send the MoonAnimator the go() message which, as we saw previously, causes its (paused) thread to resume execution by invoking notify().

Note that none of these methods are synchronized, since our MoonPhases thread is (presumably) the only thread that will ever invoke them.

Testing

When compiled and executed, the `MoonPhases` class starts the animation of the moon's phases. The slider can be used to adjust the speed at which the animation occurs.

Clicking the "pause" button generates a transition to the paused state, changing the GUI's appearance as follows:

Clicking the "back" button shows the preceding phase:

And clicking the "forward" button twice takes us back to the next phase:

Clicking the "play" button takes us back to the running state, resuming the animation:

PART OF THE PICTURE: THE TCP/IP COMMUNICATIONS ARCHITECTURE

by William Stallings

The key to the success of distributed applications is that all the terminals and computers in the community "speak" the same language. This is the role of the underlying interconnection software. This software must ensure that all the devices transmit messages in such a way that they can be understood by the other computers and terminals in the community. With the introduction of the Systems Network Architecture (SNA) by IBM in the 1970s, this concept became a reality. However, SNA worked only with IBM equipment. Soon other vendors followed with their own proprietary communications architectures to tie together their equipment. Such an approach may be good business for the vendor, but it is bad business for the customer. Happily, that situation has changed radically with the adoption of standards for interconnection software.

TCP/IP ARCHITECTURE AND OPERATION

When communication is desired among computers from different vendors, the software development effort can be a nightmare. Different vendors use different data formats and data exchange protocols. Even within one vendor's product line, different model computers may communicate in unique ways.

As the use of computer communications and computer networking proliferates, a one-at-a-time special-purpose approach to communications software development is too costly to be acceptable. The only alternative is for computer vendors to adopt and implement a common set of conventions. For this to happen, standards are needed.

However, no single standard will suffice. Any distributed application, such as electronic mail or client/server interaction, requires a complex set of communications functions for proper operation. Many of these functions, such as reliability mechanisms, are common across many or even all applications. Thus, the communications task is best viewed as consisting of a modular architecture, in which the various elements of the architecture perform the various required functions. Hence, before one can develop standards, there should be a structure, or protocol architecture, that defines the communications tasks.

Two protocol architectures have served as the basis for the development of interoperable communications standards: the TCP/IP protocol suite and the OSI (Open Systems Interconnection) reference model. TCP/IP is the most widely used interoperable architecture, and has won the "protocol wars." Although some useful standards have been developed in the context of OSI, TCP/IP is now the universal interoperable protocol architecture. No product should be considered as part of a business information system that does not support TCP/IP.

TCP/IP LAYERS

The communication task using TCP/IP can be organized into five relatively independent layers: physical, network access, internet, transport, and application.

The **physical layer** covers the physical interface between a data transmission device (e.g., workstation, computer) and a transmission medium or network. This layer is concerned with specifying the characteristics of the transmission medium, the nature of the signals, the data rate, and related matters.

The **network access layer** is concerned with the exchange of data between an end system and the network to which it is attached. The sending computer must provide the network with the address of the destination computer, so that the network may route the data to the appropriate destination. The sending computer may wish to invoke certain services, such as priority, that might be provided by the network. The specific software used at this layer depends on the type of network to be used; different standards have been developed for circuit-switching, packet-switching (e.g., X.25), local area networks (e.g., Ethernet), and others. Thus it makes sense to separate those functions having to do with network access into a separate layer. By doing this, the remainder of the communications software, above the network access layer, need not be concerned about the specifics of the network to be used. The same higher-layer software should function properly regardless of the particular network to which the computer is attached.

The network access layer is concerned with access to and routing data across a network for two end systems attached to the same network. In those cases where two devices are attached to different networks, procedures are needed to allow data to traverse multiple interconnected networks. This is the function of the **internet layer.** The internet protocol (IP) is used at this layer to provide the routing function across multiple networks. This protocol is implemented not only in the end systems but also in routers. A router is a processor that connects two networks and whose primary function is to relay data from one network to the other on its route from the source to the destination end system.

Regardless of the nature of the applications that are exchanging data, there is usually a requirement that data be exchanged reliably. That is, we would like to be assured that all of the data arrive at the destination application and that the data arrive in the same order in which they were sent. As we shall see, the mechanisms for providing reliability are essentially independent of the nature of the applications. Thus, it makes sense to collect those mechanisms in a common layer shared by all applications; this is referred to as the **host-to-host layer,** or **transport layer.** The transmission control protocol (TCP) is the most commonly-used protocol to provide this functionality.

Finally, the **application layer** contains the logic needed to support the various user applications. For each different type of application, such as file transfer, a separate module is needed that is peculiar to that application.

OPERATION OF TCP/IP

Figure 13.10 indicates how these protocols are configured for communications. To make clear that the total communications facility may consist of multiple networks, the constituent networks are usually referred to as subnetworks. Some sort of network access protocol, such as the Ethernet logic, is used to connect a computer to a subnetwork. This protocol enables the host to send data across the subnetwork to another host or, in the case of a host on another subnetwork, to a router. IP is

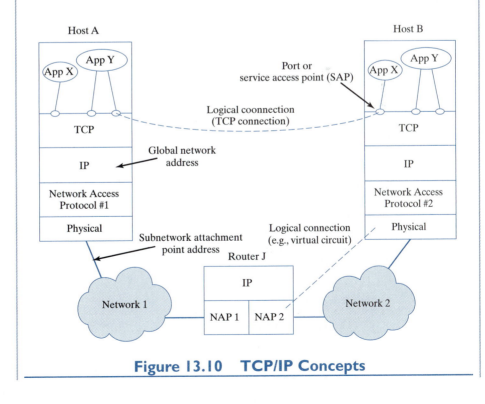

Figure 13.10   TCP/IP Concepts

implemented in all of the end systems and the routers. It acts as a relay to move a block of data from one host, through one or more routers, to another host. TCP is implemented only in the end systems; it keeps track of the blocks of data to assure that all are delivered reliably to the appropriate application.

For successful communication, every entity in the overall system must have a unique address. Actually, two levels of addressing are needed. Each host on a sub-network must have a unique global internet address; this allows the data to be delivered to the proper host. This address is used by IP for routing and delivery. Each application within a host must have an address that is unique within the host; this allows the host-to-host protocol (TCP) to deliver data to the proper process. These latter addresses are known as ports.

Let us trace a simple operation. Suppose that an application, associated with port 1 at host A, wishes to send a message to another application, associated with port 2 at host B. The application at A hands the message down to TCP with instructions to send it to host B, port 2. TCP hands the message down to IP with instructions to send it to host B. Note that IP need not be told the identity of the destination port. All it needs to know is that the data is intended for host B. Next, IP hands the message down to the network access layer (e.g., Ethernet logic) with instructions to send it to router J (the first hop on the way to B).

To control this operation, control information as well as user data must be transmitted, as suggested in Figure 13.11. Let us say that the sending process generates a block of data and passes this to TCP. TCP may break this block into smaller pieces to make it more manageable. To each of these pieces, TCP appends control information known as the TCP header, forming a TCP segment. The control information is to be used by the peer TCP protocol entity at host B. Examples of fields that are part of this header include:

❑ **Destination port:** When the TCP entity at B receives the segment, it must know to whom the data are to be delivered.

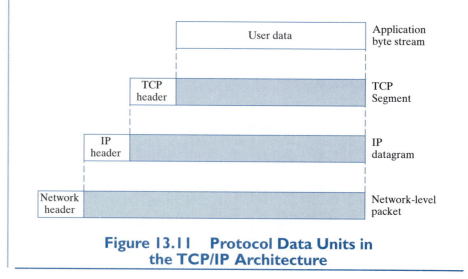

Figure 13.11   Protocol Data Units in the TCP/IP Architecture

❑ **Sequence number:** TCP numbers the segments that it sends to a particular destination port sequentially, so that if they arrive out of order, the TCP entity at B can reorder them.

❑ **Checksum:** The sending TCP includes a code that is a function of the contents of the remainder of the segment. The receiving TCP performs the same calculation and compares the result with the incoming code. A discrepancy results if there has been some error in transmission.

Next, TCP hands each segment over to IP, with instructions to transmit it to B. These segments must be transmitted across one or more subnetworks and relayed through one or more intermediate routers. This operation, too, requires the use of control information. Thus IP appends a header of control information to each segment to form an IP datagram. An example of an item stored in the IP header is the destination host address (in this example, B).

Finally, each IP datagram is presented to the network access layer for transmission across the first subnetwork in its journey to the destination. The network access layer appends its own header, creating a packet, or frame. The packet is transmitted across the subnetwork to router J. The packet header contains the information that the subnetwork needs to transfer the data across the subnetwork. Examples of items that may be contained in this header include:

❑ **Destination subnetwork address:** The subnetwork must know to which attached device the packet is to be delivered.

❑ **Facilities requests:** The network access protocol might request the use of certain subnetwork facilities, such as priority.

At router J, the packet header is stripped off and the IP header examined. On the basis of the destination address information in the IP header, the IP module in the router directs the datagram out across subnetwork 2 to B. To do this, the datagram is again augmented with a network access header.

When the data are received at B, the reverse process occurs. At each layer, the corresponding header is removed, and the remainder is passed on to the next higher layer, until the original user data are delivered to the destination application.

A SIMPLE EXAMPLE

Figure 13.12 puts all of these concepts together, showing the interaction between modules to transfer one block of data. For simplicity, the example shows two systems connected to the same network, so that no router is involved. Let us say that the file transfer module in computer X is transferring a file one record at a time to computer Y. At X, each record is handed over to TCP. We can picture this action as being in the form of a command or procedure call. The arguments of this procedure call include the destination computer address, the destination port, and the record. TCP appends the destination port and other control information to the record to create a TCP segment. This is then handed down to IP by another procedure call. In this case, the arguments for the command are the destination

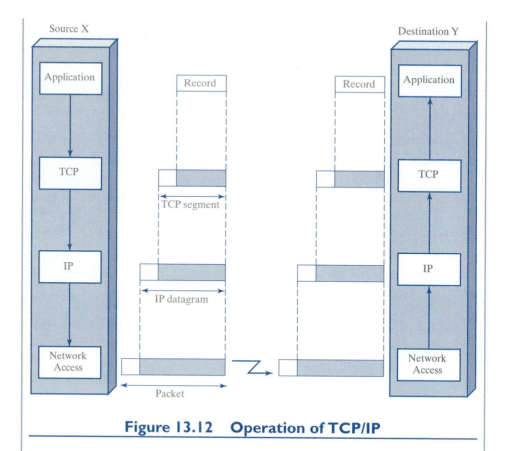

Figure 13.12   Operation of TCP/IP

computer address and the TCP segment. The resulting IP datagram is handed down to the network access layer, which constructs a network-level packet.

The network accepts the packet from X and delivers it to Y. The network access module in Y receives the packet, strips off the header, and transfers the enclosed transport PDU to Y's IP module, which strips off the IP header and passes the resulting TCP segment to TCP. TCP examines the segment header and, on the basis of the destination port field in the header, delivers the enclosed record to the appropriate application, in this case the file transfer module in Y.

TCP AND UDP

For most applications running as part of the TCP/IP protocol architecture, the transport layer protocol is TCP. TCP provides a reliable connection for the transfer of data between applications.

Figure 13.13a shows the header format for TCP, which is a minimum of 20 octets, or 160 bits. The Source Port and Destination Port fields identify the applications at the source and destination systems that are using this connection. The Sequence Number, Acknowledgment Number, and Window fields provide flow control and error control. In essence, each segment is sequentially numbered and must be acknowledged by the receiver so that the sender knows that the segment was suc-

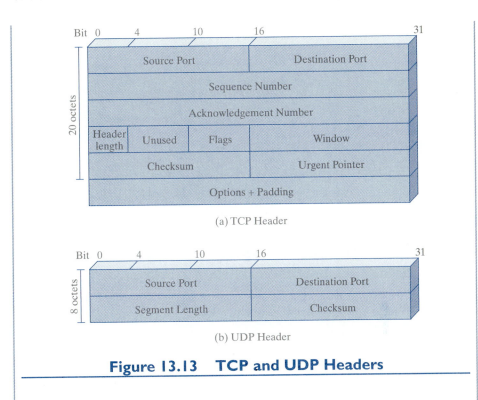

(a) TCP Header

(b) UDP Header

Figure 13.13   TCP and UDP Headers

cessfully received. The Windows field is passed from one side to the other to indicate how many data the other side may send before receiving additional permission. Finally, the checksum is a 16-bit frame check sequence used to detect errors in the TCP segment.

In addition to TCP, there is one other transport-level protocol that is in common use as part of the TCP/IP protocol suite: the user datagram protocol (UDP). UDP provides a connectionless service for application-level procedures. UDP does not guarantee delivery, preservation of sequence, or protection against duplication. UDP enables procedures to send messages to other procedures with a minimum of protocol mechanism. Some transaction-oriented applications make use of UDP; one example is SNMP (Simple Network Management Protocol), the standard network management protocol for TCP/IP networks. Because it is connectionless, UDP has very little to do. Essentially, it adds a port addressing capability to IP. This is best seen by examining the UDP header, shown in Figure 13.13b.

IP AND IPV6

For decades, the keystone of the TCP/IP protocol architecture has been the Internet Protocol (IP). Figure 13.14a shows the IP header format, which is a minimum of 20 octets, or 160 bits. The header includes 32-bit source and destination addresses. The Header Checksum field is used to detect errors in the header to avoid misdelivery. The Protocol field indicates whether TCP, UDP, or some other higher-layer protocol is using IP. The Flags and Fragment Offset fields are used in the fragmentation and reassembly process.

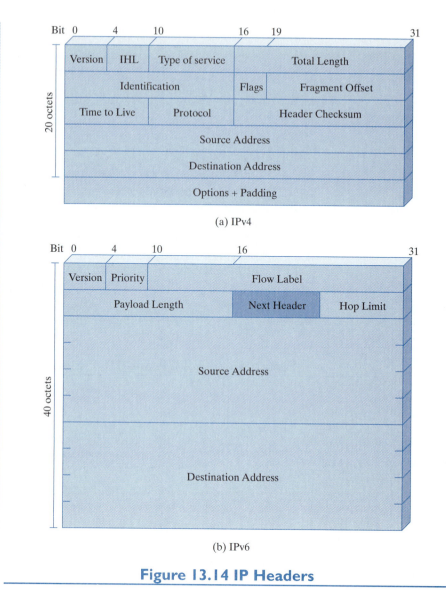

(a) IPv4

(b) IPv6

Figure 13.14 IP Headers

In 1995, the Internet Engineering Task Force (IETF), which develops protocol standards for the Internet, issued a specification for a next-generation IP, known then as IPng. This specification was turned into a standard in 1996 known as IPv6. IPv6 provides a number of functional enhancements over the existing IP, designed to accommodate the higher speeds of today's networks and the mix of data streams, including graphic and video, that are becoming more prevalent. But the driving force behind the development of the new protocol was the need for more addresses. The current IP uses a 32-bit address to specify a source or destination.

With the explosive growth of the Internet and of private networks attached to the Internet, this address length became insufficient to accommodate all of the systems needing addresses. As Figure 13.14b shows, IPv6 includes 128-bit source and destination address fields.

Ultimately, all of the installations using TCP/IP are expected to migrate from the current IP to IPv6, but this process will take many years if not decades.

TCP/IP APPLICATIONS

A number of applications have been standardized to operate on top of TCP. We mention three of the most common here.

The **simple mail transfer protocol (SMTP)** provides a basic electronic mail facility. It provides a mechanism for transferring messages among separate hosts. Features of SMTP include mailing lists, return receipts, and forwarding. The SMTP protocol does not specify the way in which messages are to be created; some local editing or native electronic mail facility is required. Once a message is created, SMTP accepts the message, and makes use of TCP to send it to an SMTP module on another host. The target SMTP module will make use of a local electronic mail package to store the incoming message in a user's mailbox.

The **file transfer protocol (FTP)** is used to send files from one system to another under user command. Both text and binary files are accommodated, and the protocol provides features for controlling user access. When a user wishes to engage in file transfer, FTP sets up a TCP connection to the target system for the exchange of control messages. These allow user ID and password to be transmitted, and allow the user to specify the file and file actions desired. Once a file transfer is approved, a second TCP connection is set up for the data transfer. The file is transferred over the data connection, without the overhead of any headers or control information at the application level. When the transfer is complete, the control connection is used to signal completion and to accept new file transfer commands.

TELNET provides a remote logon capability, which enables a user at a terminal or personal computer to logon to a remote computer and function as if directly connected to that computer. The protocol was designed to work with simple scroll-mode terminals. TELNET is actually implemented in two modules: User TELNET interacts with the terminal I/O module to communicate with a local terminal. It converts the characteristics of real terminals to the network standard and vice versa. Server TELNET interacts with an application, acting as a surrogate terminal handler so that remote terminals appear as local to the application. Terminal traffic between User and Server TELNET is carried on a TCP connection.

TO PROBE FURTHER

The topics in this section are covered in detail in Data and Computer Communications, Fifth Edition, by William Stallings (Prentice Hall, 1997). Links to web sites with further information can be found at http://www.shore.net/,ws/DCC5e.

13.5　THE END?

We have reached the end of our study of Java. However, we have not reached the end of Java or its capabilities. In fact, we have covered only a fraction of Java's extensive class library, and there is far more to Computer Science than just programming. As Winston Churchill once said,

> "Now is not the end.
> It is not even the beginning of the end.
> But it is perhaps, the end of the beginning."

We hope you have enjoyed this introduction to computing using Java, and that with this foundation, you can begin to write your own interesting applets and applications.

For more information on Java programming, here are some books to take you further:

- ❑ *Core Java* (multiple volumes), by Cornell and Horstmann, Prentice Hall/Sunsoft.
- ❑ *Core Java Foundation Classes,* by Topley, Prentice Hall.
- ❑ *Core Java Networking,* by Niemeyer, Prentice Hall.
- ❑ *Concurrent Programming in Java,* by Lea, Addison-Wesley.
- ❑ *Concurrent Programming: The Java Programming Language,* by Hartley, Oxford.
- ❑ *Graphic Java, Mastering the JFC* (multiple volumes), by Geary, Prentice Hall/Sunsoft.
- ❑ *Java Database Programming,* by Jepson, Wiley.
- ❑ *Thinking In Java,* by Eckel, Prentice Hall.

CHAPTER SUMMARY

KEY TERMS AND NOTES

atomic operation	single-threaded program
blocking operation	single-threaded server
client program	`sleep()` method
client-server	slider
handler thread	socket
lock list	`start()` method
monitor	`synchronized`
multiprocessor	TCP/IP
multithreaded program	`Thread` class
multithreaded server	thread of execution
`notify()` method	thread-safe
port	uniprocessor
`run()` method	`wait()` method
`Runnable` interface	waiting list
server program	zombie process

◎ A *single-threaded* program has a single thread of execution; a *multithreaded* program has more than one execution thread. One thing that distinguishes Java from other languages is its built-in support for writing multithreaded programs.

◎ On a uniprocessor, a single-threaded program may take less time than a mutiply-threaded one. On a multiprocessor, a multithreaded program should take less time than a single-threaded one.

◎ Java provides two different ways to build a multithreaded application:

   ❏ Normal approach: Extend the `Thread` class with another class that contains a `run()` method that does what is to happen in a separate thread, and then have the normal thread create an instance of this class. Execution of the thread is initiated by sending it the `start()` message.

   ❏ When the class must extend some other class: Implement Java's `Runnable` interface with a class containing a `run()` method as above. Then have the normal class create an instance of this class and have the class create an instance of the `Thread` class. Send this new `Thread` object the `start()` message.

◎ Non-atomic operations can be *interleaved* in any random patten whatsoever when performed by separate threads. When they are accessing shared data, this can result in unintended changes to the data.

◎ Methods can be declared to be `synchronized` to make them atomic so that no other method can access critical data while this method is. Java associates a **lock** with every object and sending a synchronized message to an object when no other thread is executing a synchronized method of that object locks the object's *lock* and then lets the method begin execution.

◎ If an instance of a class can be mutated by different threads, then all mutator methods of that class should be declared as `synchronized`.

◎ A client uses a `Socket` to connect to a server. To create a `Socket`, two pieces of information are required:

   ❏ The name of the computer where the socket is located (e.g., *cs.calvin.edu*)

   ❏ The port associated with that socket

◎ To read from a `Socket`, send it the `getInputStream()` message and wrap the resulting `InputStream` in an `InputStreamReader` and a `BufferedReader`. Then use the `readLine()` method to read from the `Socket`; it will return `null` when the connection is *closed*.

◎ To write to a `Socket`, send it the `getOutputStream()` message and wrap the resulting `OutputStream` in a `PrintWriter`. Then use the `print()` and `println()` methods to write to the `Socket`.

◎ A server receives connection requests via a `ServerSocket`. Its constructor requires only a port number. The `accept()` method causes a `ServerSocket` to block until a client requests a connection, at which point it returns a `Socket` connected to the client's `Socket`.

◎ A single-threaded server accepts connection requests and provides service within the same thread.

◎ A multithreaded server accepts connection requests, but creates a new handler thread to service each client. A handler thread must be passed to the `Socket` returned by `accept()` to interact with its client. The handler thread must close the `Socket` when its service is completed.

Documentation

■ The following table gives some of the methods for the classes that are new to this chapter: `Thread`, `Socket`, and `JSlider`. For others, see the Java API documentation.

SOME `Thread` METHODS (`java.lang`; EXTENDS `Object`)

Method	Description
`Thread(Runnable obj)`	Constructs a new execution thread for *obj*
`static Thread currentThread()`	Returns a reference to the currently executing thread object
`String getName()`	Returns this thread's name
`void interrupt()`	Interrupts this thread
`static boolean interrupted()` `boolean isInterrupted()`	Tests whether the current thread has been interrupted
`boolean isAlive()`	Tests if this thread is alive
`void run()`	If this thread was constructed using a separate `Runnable` object, then that object's `run()` method is called; otherwise, this method does nothing and returns
`static void sleep(long ms, int ns)`	Causes the currently executing thread to sleep (cease execution) for `ms` milliseconds plus `ns` nanoseconds (optional)
`void start()`	Causes this thread to begin execution
`String toString()`	Returns a string representation of this thread
`static void yield()`	Causes the currently executing thread object to temporarily pause and allow other threads to execute
Inherited from `Object`:	
`void notify()`	Wakes up a thread that is waiting on this object's monitor
`void notifyAll()`	Wakes up all threads waiting on this object's monitor
`void wait()` `void wait(long ms)`	Causes current thread to wait until: another thread invokes the `notify()`

`void wait(long ms, int ns))`	method or the `notifyAll()` method for this object; or, in the last forms, until some other thread interrupts the current thread or `ms` milliseconds plus `ns` nanoseconds have elapsed

■ SOME `Socket` METHODS (`java.lang`; EXTENDS `Object`)

Method	Description
`Socket(String host,int port)`	Creates a stream socket and connects it to the specified `port` number on the named `host`
`void close()`	Closes this socket

`InetAddress getInetAddress()`	Returns the address to which the socket is connected. The following methods can be used to convert this `InetAddress` object:
	`byte[] getAddress()`
	`String getHostAddress()`
	`String getHostName()`
	`String toString()`

`int getLocalPort()`	Returns the local port to which this socket is bound
`int getPort()`	Returns the remote port to which this socket is bound
`String toString()`	Returns a `String` representation of this socket

■ SOME `JSlider` METHODS (`java.lang`; EXTENDS `JComponent`)

Method	Description

`JSlider()`
`JSlider(int orient)`
`JSlider(int min, int max)`
`JSlider(int min, int max,int val)`
`JSlider(int orient,`
`        int min, int max, int val)`
	Creates a slider with:
	orientation *orient*, which is one of
	    `HORIZONTAL` (default) or `VERTICAL`
	range *min* to *max* (default 0 and 100)
	initial value *val* (default 50)

`void addChangeListener(`
`            ChangeListener 1)`
	Adds *1* to the slider; `ChangeListener` is an interface whose only method is:
	    `void stateChanged(ChangeEvent e)`
	`ChangeEvent` has only a constructor:
	    `ChangeEvent(Object obj)`

`void setExtent(int ext)` `int getExtent()`	Sets / returns the range of values for the slider

`void setMajorTickSpacing(int n)`
`void setMinorTickSpacing(int n)`
`int getMajorTickSpacing()`
`int getMinorTickSpacing()`
	Sets / returns the major / minor tick spacing for slider

`void setMaximum(int max)`
`void setMinimum(int min)`
`int getMaximum()`
`int getMinimum()`
	Sets / returns the maximum / minimum values for the slider

`void setOrientation (int orient)` `int getOrientation()`	Sets / returns the slider's orientation (`HORIZONTAL` or `VERTICAL`)
`void setValue(int val)` `int getValue()`	Sets / returns the slider's value
`void removeChangeListener(` `                ChangeListener l)`	Remove *l* from the slider

☞ PROGRAMMING POINTERS

PROGRAM STYLE AND DESIGN

1. *Multithreading can speed up execution by:*
   - ❑ *Processing independent tasks in parallel (on different processors)*
   - ❑ *Separating input from processing*

2. *Multithreading can be implemented in Java by*
   - ❑ *Extending the* `Thread` *class*
   - ❑ *Implementing the* `Runnable` *interface*

   The first method is simpler, but the second is needed when a class must extend some other class besides `Thread`.

3. *Multithreading should not be used indiscriminately, because creating threads is fairly time-consuming.*
   - ❑ *A single-threaded server works well if the server's service does not take long to perform.*
   - ❑ *A multithreaded server works well if the server's service is time-consuming. The server thread can accept the next request while a handler thread is serving a client.*

POTENTIAL PITFALLS

1. *Two threads that access shared data can interfere with each other's operations if they access that data at the same time.* To prevent this from happening, *synchronized* methods should be used to access the shared data. If an instance of a class can be mutated by different threads, declare all mutator methods of that class as `synchronized`.

2. *Creating a socket requires the name of the computer where the server is running and the port associated with the server.*

3. *In a single-threaded server, a backlog of requests may result if they cannot be served quickly enough.* Such servers use a processing loop to accept connection requests and provide service within the same thread and cannot move on to other requests until the current one is served.

PROGRAMMING PROBLEMS

SECTION 13.3

1. Build a single-threaded echo server that echoes just one line of text back to a client.

2. Build a multi-threaded daytime server.

3. Build a single-threaded random string server whose constructor reads a sequence of strings from a file into an array. When contacted by a client, your server should randomly select one of the strings and send it to the client. Use your server to randomly serve quotations from a famous person (e.g., Benjamin Franklin, Oscar Wilde, Mark Twain, Homer Simpson, . . .).

4. Proceed as in Problem 3, but use a multi-threaded server.

5. One of the simplest encryption schemes is the *Caesar-cipher* scheme, which consists of replacing each letter in the alphabet by the letter that appears k positions later in the alphabet for some integer k. (The alphabet is thought of as being arranged in a circle, with A following Z.) In the original Caesar cipher, k was 3, so that each occurrence of A in a message was replaced by D, each B by E, . . . , each Y by B, and each Z by C. Build a Caesar-cipher server that, upon receiving a text string from a client, encodes it using the Caesar-cipher and returns the encoded text to the client.

6. Decoding a message encrypted with the Caeser-cipher method (see Problem 5) is straightforward: Simply replace each character by the character k positions earlier in the alphabet. Build a Caesar-decipher server that, upon receiving a Caeser-cipher-encrypted text string, returns the decoded text to the client.

A UNICODE CHARACTER SET

At the time of this writing, Version 3.0 of the Unicode Standard has been released. It contains codes for 49,194 different characters and languages from many of the world's major locales—Africa, the Americas, Asia, Europe, India, the Middle East, and the Pacific Islands. Some of the recent languages added are Braille, Canadian Aboriginal Syllabics, Cherokee, Ethiopian, Khmer, Myanmar, Mongolian, Sinhala, and Syriac, In addition, it includes punctuation marks, mathematical symbols, technical symbols, geometric shapes, and dingbats.

Unicode uses 2 bytes for each numeric code so that $2^{16} = 65536$ characters can be represented. This means that there are 16,132 unused codes that can be used for other characters. For the latest information about standard Unicode, consult the website for the Unicode Consortium at http://www.unicode.org.

One of the most commonly used codes for characters is ASCII (American Standard Code for Information Interchange), which uses one byte for each character. The following table gives the codes for the 128 standard ASCII characters. The corresponding Unicode representations are obtained simply by widening the ASCII representation by adding eight 0s at the left. For example, the ASCII representation of 'A' is 65 = 01000001, and the Unicode representation is 65 = 0000000001000001 .

ASCII Codes of Characters

Decimal	Octal	Character
0	000	NUL (Null)
1	001	SOH (Start of heading)
2	002	STX (Start of text)
3	003	ETX (End of text)
4	004	EOT (End of transmission)
5	005	ENQ (Enquiry)
6	006	ACK (Acknowledge)
7	007	BEL (Ring bell)
8	010	BS (Backspace)
9	011	HT (Horizontal tab)
10	012	LF (Line feed)
11	013	VT (Vertical tab)
12	014	FF (Form feed)
13	015	CR (Carriage return)
14	016	SO (Shift out)
15	017	SI (Shift in)
16	020	DLE (Date link escape)
17	021	DC1 (Device control 1)
18	022	DC2 (Device control 2)
19	023	DC3 (Device control 3)
20	024	DC4 (Device control 4)
21	025	NAK (Negative ACK)
22	026	SYN (Synchronous)
23	027	ETB (EOT block)
24	030	CAN (Cancel)
25	031	EM (End of medium)
26	032	SUB (Substitute)
27	033	ESC (Escape)
28	034	FS (File separator)
29	035	GS (Group separator)
30	036	RS (Record separator)
31	037	US (Unit separator)
32	040	SP (Space)
33	041	!
34	042	"
35	043	#
36	044	$
37	045	%
38	046	&
39	047	' (Single quote)
40	050	(
41	051	)
42	052	*
43	053	+

Decimal	Octal	Character
44	054	, (Comma)
45	055	- (Hyphen)
46	056	. (Period)
47	057	/
48	060	0
49	061	1
50	062	2
51	063	3
52	064	4
53	065	5
54	066	6
55	067	7
56	070	8
57	071	9
58	072	:
59	073	;
60	074	<
61	075	=
62	076	>
63	077	?
64	100	@
65	101	A
66	102	B
67	103	C
68	104	D
69	105	E
70	106	F
71	107	G
72	110	H
73	111	I
74	112	J
75	113	K
76	114	L
77	115	M
78	116	N
79	117	O
80	120	P
81	121	Q
82	122	R
83	123	S
84	124	T
85	125	U
86	126	V
87	127	W

ASCII Codes of Characters

Decimal	Octal	Character
88	130	X
89	131	Y
90	132	Z
91	133	[
92	134	\
93	135	]
94	136	^
95	137	_ (Underscore)
96	140	`
97	141	a
98	142	b
99	143	c
100	144	d
101	145	e
102	146	f
103	147	g
104	150	h
105	151	i
106	152	j
107	153	k

Decimal	Octal	Character
108	154	l
109	155	m
110	156	n
111	157	o
112	160	p
113	161	q
114	162	r
115	163	s
116	164	t
117	165	u
118	166	v
119	167	w
120	170	x
121	171	y
122	172	z
123	173	{
124	174	|
125	175	}
126	176	~
127	177	DEL

B JAVA KEYWORDS

abstract	Default	if	private	throw
boolean	do	implements	protected	throws
break	double	import	public	transient
byte	else	instanceof	return	try
case	extends	int	short	void
catch	final	interface	static	volatile
char	finally	long	super	while
class	float	native	switch	
const	for	new	synchronized	
continue	goto	package	this	

The following table lists the operators available in Java, ordered by their precedence levels, from highest to lowest—higher precedence operators are applied before lower precedence operators. Operators in the same horizontal band of the table have equal precedence. The table also gives each operator's associativity—in an expression containing operators of equal precedence, associativity determines which is applied first—, and a brief description.

Operator	Associativity	Arity	Description
( )	left		parentheses
[ ]	left	binary	subscript (array index)
.	left	binary	member selection
++	right	unary	increment
- -	right	unary	decrement
+	right	unary	plus(sign)
-	right	unary	minus (sign)
!	right	unary	logical negation
~	right	unary	bitwise complement
( )	right	binary	type conversion (cast)
*	left	binary	multiplication
/	left	binary	division
%	left	binary	modulus (remainder)
+	left	binary	addition
-	left	binary	subtraction
<<	left	binary	bit-shift left
>>	left	binary	bit-shift right with sign extension
>>>	left	binary	bit-shift right with zero extension
<	left	binary	less than
<=	left	binary	less than or equal
>	left	binary	greater than
>=	left	binary	greater than or equal
instanceof	left	binary	type comparison
==	left	binary	equality
!=	left	binary	inequality

Operator	Associativity	Arity	Description
&	left	binary	bitwise and
^	left	binary	bitwise exclusive or
|	left	binary	bitwise or
&&	left	binary	logical AND
||	left	binary	logical OR
? :	left	ternary	conditional expression
=	right	binary	assignment
+=	right	binary	addition-assignment shortcut
-=	right	binary	subtraction-assignment shortcut
*=	right	binary	multiplication-assignment shortcut
/=	right	binary	division-assignment shortcut
%=	right	binary	modulus-assignment shortcut
&=	right	binary	bitwise-and-assignment shortcut
|=	right	binary	bitwise-or-assignment shortcut
^=	right	binary	bitwise-xor-assignment shortcut
<<=	right	binary	bitshift-left-assignment shortcut
>>=	right	binary	bitshift-right-assignment shortcut (sign extension)
>>>=	right	binary	bitshift-right-assignment shortcut (zero extension)

D JAVA PACKAGES AND CLASSES

The following packages are included in the `ann` package provided on the CD packaged with this text and on the book's website (`www/prenhall.com/adams` or `cs.calvin.edu/java/1e`):

Package	*Classes*
ann.easyio	Keyboard, Screen
ann.gui	CartesianCanvas, CartesianPanel, CloseableFrame
ann.math	DoubleArrays. Matrix, polynomial.Polynomial
ann.util	Controller, Timer

The following packages are provided in the Java 2 Platform Standard Edition v1.3 (`http://java.sun.com/products/jdk/1.3/docs/api/`):

java.applet
java.awt
java.awt.color
java.awt.datatransfer
java.awt.dnd
java.awt.event
java.awt.font
java.awt.geom
java.awt.im
java.awt.im.spi
java.awt.image
java.awt.image.renderable
java.awt.print
java.beans
java.beans.beancontext
java.io
java.lang
java.lang.ref
java.lang.reflect
java.math
java.net
java.rmi
java.rmi.activation
java.rmi.dgc
java.rmi.registry
java.rmi.server
java.security

java.security.acl
java.security.cert
java.security.interfaces
java.security.spec
java.sql
java.text
java.util
java.util.jar
java.util.zip
javax.accessibility
javax.naming
javax.naming.directory
javax.naming.event
javax.naming.ldap
javax.naming.spi
javax.rmi
javax.rmi.CORBA
javax.sound.midi
javax.sound.midi.spi
javax.sound.sampled
javax.sound.sampled.spi
javax.swing
javax.swing.border
javax.swing.colorchooser
javax.swing.event
javax.swing.filechooser
javax.swing.plaf

javax.swing.plaf.basic
javax.swing.plaf.metal
javax.swing.plaf.multi
javax.swing.table
javax.swing.text
javax.swing.text.html
javax.swing.text.html.parser
javax.swing.text.rtf
javax.swing.tree
javax.swing.undo
javax.transaction
org.omg.CORBA
org.omg.CORBA_2_3
org.omg.CORBA_2_3.portable
org.omg.CORBA.DynAny-
    Package
org.omg.CORBA.ORBPack-
    age
org.omg.CORBA.portable
org.omg.CORBA.TypeCode-
    Package
org.omg.CosNaming
org.omg.CosNaming.Naming-
    ContextPackage
org.omg.SendingContext
org.omg.stub.java.rmi

The following is a listing of all the classes and interfaces in these packages:

AbstractAction
AbstractBase
AbstractBorder
AbstractButton
AbstractCellEditor

AbstractCollection
AbstractColorChooserPanel
AbstractDocument
AbstractDocument.Attribute-
    Context

AbstractDocument.Content
AbstractDocument.Element-
    Edit
AbstractLayoutCache

897

CannotProceed
CannotProceedException
CannotProceedHelper
CannotProceedHolder
CannotRedoException
CannotUndoException
Canvas
CardLayout
Caret
CaretEvent
CaretListener
CellEditor
CellEditorListener
CellRendererPane
Certificate
Certificate
Certificate.CertificateRep
CertificateEncodingException
CertificateException
CertificateExpiredException
CertificateFactory
CertificateFactorySpi
CertificateNotYetValidException
CertificateParsingException
ChangedCharSetException
ChangeEvent
ChangeListener
Character
Character.Subset
Character.UnicodeBlock
CharacterIterator
CharArrayReader
CharArrayWriter
CharConversionException
CharHolder
CharSeqHelper
CharSeqHolder
Checkbox
CheckboxGroup
CheckboxMenuItem
CheckedInputStream
CheckedOutputStream
Checksum
Choice
ChoiceFormat
Class
ClassCastException
ClassCircularityError
ClassDesc
ClassFormatError
ClassLoader
ClassNotFoundException
Clip
Clipboard
ClipboardOwner
Clob

Cloneable
CloneNotSupportedException
CMMException
CodeSource
CollationElementIterator
CollationKey
Collator
Collection
Collections
Color
ColorChooserComponentFactory
ColorChooserUI
ColorConvertOp
ColorModel
ColorSelectionModel
ColorSpace
ColorUIResource
ComboBoxEditor
ComboBoxModel
ComboBoxUI
ComboPopup
COMM_FAILURE
CommunicationException
Comparable
Comparator
Compiler
CompletionStatus
CompletionStatusHelper
Component
ComponentAdapter
ComponentColorModel
ComponentEvent
ComponentInputMap
ComponentInputMapUIResource
ComponentListener
ComponentOrientation
ComponentSampleModel
ComponentUI
ComponentView
Composite
CompositeContext
CompositeName
CompositeView
CompoundBorder
CompoundEdit
CompoundName
ConcurrentModificationException
ConfigurationException
ConnectException
ConnectException
ConnectIOException
Connection
Constructor
Container

ContainerAdapter
ContainerEvent
ContainerListener
ContentHandler
ContentHandlerFactory
ContentModel
Context
Context
ContextIdentifierHelper
ContextIdSeqHelper
ContextList
ContextNotEmptyException
ContextualRenderedImageFactory
Control
ControlFactory
ControllerEventListener
ConvolveOp
CRC32
CRL
CRLException
CropImageFilter
CSS
CSS.Attribute
CTX_RESTRICT_SCOPE
CubicCurve2D
CubicCurve2D.Double
CubicCurve2D.Float
Current
CurrentHelper
CurrentHolder
CurrentOperations
Cursor
Customizer
CustomMarshal
CustomValue
DATA_CONVERSION
DatabaseMetaData
DataBuffer
DataBufferByte
DataBufferInt
DataBufferShort
DataBufferUShort
DataFlavor
DataFormatException
DatagramPacket
DatagramSocket
DatagramSocketImpl
DatagramSocketImplFactory
DataInput
DataInputStream
DataInputStream
DataLine
DataLine.Info
DataOutput
DataOutputStream
DataOutputStream

InputMethodRequests
InputStream
InputStreamReader
InputSubset
InputVerifier
Insets
InsetsUIResource
InstantiationError
InstantiationException
Instrument
InsufficientResourcesException
Integer
INTERNAL
InternalError
InternalFrameAdapter
InternalFrameEvent
InternalFrameListener
InternalFrameUI
InterruptedException
InterruptedIOException
InterruptedNamingException
INTF_REPOS
IntHolder
IntrospectionException
Introspector
INV_FLAG
INV_IDENT
INV_OBJREF
INV_POLICY
Invalid
INVALID_TRANSACTION
InvalidAlgorithmParame-
  terException
InvalidAttributeIdentifierEx-
  ception
InvalidAttributesException
InvalidAttributeValueExcep-
  tion
InvalidClassException
InvalidDnDOperationExcep-
  tion
InvalidKeyException
InvalidKeySpecException
InvalidMidiDataException
InvalidName
InvalidNameException
InvalidNameHelper
InvalidNameHolder
InvalidObjectException
InvalidParameterException
InvalidParameterSpecExcep-
  tion
InvalidSearchControlsExcep-
  tion
InvalidSearchFilterException
InvalidSeq

InvalidTransactionException
InvalidValue
InvocationEvent
InvocationHandler
InvocationTargetException
InvokeHandler
IOException
IRObject
IRObjectOperations
IstringHelper
ItemEvent
ItemListener
ItemSelectable
Iterator
JApplet
JarEntry
JarException
JarFile
JarInputStream
JarOutputStream
JarURLConnection
JButton
JCheckBox
JCheckBoxMenuItem
JColorChooser
JComboBox
JComboBox.KeySelection-
  Manager
JComponent
JDesktopPane
JDialog
JEditorPane
JFileChooser
JFrame
JInternalFrame
JInternalFrame.JDesktopIcon
JLabel
JLayeredPane
JList
JMenu
JMenuBar
JMenuItem
JobAttributes
JobAttributes.DefaultSelec-
  tionType
JobAttributes.DestinationType
JobAttributes.DialogType
JobAttributes.MultipleDocu-
  mentHandlingType
JobAttributes.SidesType
JOptionPane
JPanel
JPasswordField
JPopupMenu
JPopupMenu.Separator
JProgressBar
JRadioButton

JRadioButtonMenuItem
JRootPane
JScrollBar
JScrollPane
JSeparator
JSlider
JSplitPane
JTabbedPane
JTable
JTableHeader
JTextArea
JTextComponent
JTextComponent.KeyBinding
JTextField
JTextPane
JToggleButton
JToggleButton.ToggleButton-
  Model
JToolBar
JToolBar.Separator
JToolTip
JTree
JTree.DynamicUtilTreeNode
JTree.EmptySelectionModel
JViewport
JWindow
Kernel
Key
KeyAdapter
KeyEvent
KeyException
KeyFactory
KeyFactorySpi
KeyListener
KeyManagementException
Keymap
KeyPair
KeyPairGenerator
KeyPairGeneratorSpi
KeySpec
KeyStore
KeyStoreException
KeyStoreSpi
KeyStroke
Label
LabelUI
LabelView
LastOwnerException
LayeredHighlighter
LayeredHighlighter.Layer-
  Painter
LayoutManager
LayoutManager2
LayoutQueue
LdapContext
LdapReferralException
Lease

MulticastSocket
MultiColorChooserUI
MultiComboBoxUI
MultiDesktopIconUI
MultiDesktopPaneUI
MultiFileChooserUI
MultiInternalFrameUI
MultiLabelUI
MultiListUI
MultiLookAndFeel
MultiMenuBarUI
MultiMenuItemUI
MultiOptionPaneUI
MultiPanelUI
MultiPixelPackedSampleModel
MultipleMaster
MultiPopupMenuUI
MultiProgressBarUI
MultiScrollBarUI
MultiScrollPaneUI
MultiSeparatorUI
MultiSliderUI
MultiSplitPaneUI
MultiTabbedPaneUI
MultiTableHeaderUI
MultiTableUI
MultiTextUI
MultiToolBarUI
MultiToolTipUI
MultiTreeUI
MultiViewportUI
MutableAttributeSet
MutableComboBoxModel
MutableTreeNode
Name
NameAlreadyBoundException
NameClassPair
NameComponent
NameComponentHelper
NameComponentHolder
NamedValue
NameHelper
NameHolder
NameNotFoundException
NameParser
NamespaceChangeListener
NameValuePair
NameValuePairHelper
Naming
NamingContext
NamingContextHelper
NamingContextHolder
NamingEnumeration
NamingEvent
NamingException

NamingExceptionEvent
NamingListener
NamingManager
NamingSecurityException
NegativeArraySizeException
NetPermission
NO_IMPLEMENT
NO_MEMORY
NO_PERMISSION
NO_RESOURCES
NO_RESPONSE
NoClassDefFoundError
NoInitialContextException
NoninvertibleTransformException
NoPermissionException
NoRouteToHostException
NoSuchAlgorithmException
NoSuchAttributeException
NoSuchElementException
NoSuchFieldError
NoSuchFieldException
NoSuchMethodError
NoSuchMethodException
NoSuchObjectException
NoSuchProviderException
NotActiveException
NotAvailable
NotBoundException
NotContextException
NotEmpty
NotEmptyHelper
NotEmptyHolder
NotFound
NotFoundHelper
NotFoundHolder
NotFoundReason
NotFoundReasonHelper
NotFoundReasonHolder
NotOwnerException
NotSerializableException
NullPointerException
Number
NumberFormat
NumberFormatException
NVList
OBJ_ADAPTER
Object
OBJECT_NOT_EXIST
ObjectChangeListener
ObjectFactory
ObjectFactoryBuilder
ObjectHelper
ObjectHolder
ObjectImpl
ObjectInput
ObjectInputStream

ObjectInputStream.GetField
ObjectInputValidation
ObjectOutput
ObjectOutputStream
ObjectOutputStream.PutField
ObjectStreamClass
ObjectStreamConstants
ObjectStreamException
ObjectStreamField
ObjectView
ObjID
Observable
Observer
OctetSeqHelper
OctetSeqHolder
OMGVMCID
OpenType
Operation
OperationDescription
OperationDescriptionHelper
OperationMode
OperationModeHelper
OperationNotSupportedException
Option
OptionalDataException
OptionPaneUI
ORB
OutOfMemoryError
OutputStream
OutputStreamWriter
OverlayLayout
Owner
Package
PackedColorModel
Pageable
PageAttributes
PageAttributes.ColorType
PageAttributes.MediaType
PageAttributes.OrientationRequestedType
PageAttributes.OriginType
PageAttributes.PrintQualityType
PageFormat
Paint
PaintContext
PaintEvent
PanControl
Panel
PanelUI
Paper
ParagraphView
ParameterBlock
ParameterDescription
ParameterDescriptionHelper
ParameterDescriptor

ParameterMode
ParameterModeHelper
ParDescriptionSeqHelper
ParseException
ParsePosition
Parser
ParserDelegator
PartialResultException
PasswordAuthentication
PasswordView
Patch
PathIterator
Permission
PermissionCollection
Permissions
PERSIST_STORE
PhantomReference
PipedInputStream
PipedOutputStream
PipedReader
PipedWriter
PixelGrabber
PixelInterleavedSampleModel
PKCS8EncodedKeySpec
PlainDocument
PlainView
Point
Point2D
Point2D.Double
Point2D.Float
Policy
PolicyError
PolicyHelper
PolicyHolder
PolicyListHelper
PolicyListHolder
PolicyOperations
PolicyTypeHelper
Polygon
PopupMenu
PopupMenuEvent
PopupMenuListener
PopupMenuUI
Port
Port.Info
PortableRemoteObject
PortableRemoteObjectDele-
   gate
Position
Position.Bias
PreparedStatement
Principal
PrincipalHolder
Printable
PrinterAbortException
PrinterException
PrinterGraphics

PrinterIOException
PrinterJob
PrintGraphics
PrintJob
PrintStream
PrintWriter
PRIVATE_MEMBER
PrivateKey
PrivilegedAction
PrivilegedActionException
PrivilegedExceptionAction
Process
ProfileDataException
ProgressBarUI
ProgressMonitor
ProgressMonitorInputStream
Properties
PropertyChangeEvent
PropertyChangeListener
PropertyChangeSupport
PropertyDescriptor
PropertyEditor
PropertyEditorManager
PropertyEditorSupport
PropertyPermission
PropertyResourceBundle
PropertyVetoException
ProtectionDomain
ProtocolException
Provider
ProviderException
Proxy
PUBLIC_MEMBER
PublicKey
PushbackInputStream
PushbackReader
QuadCurve2D
QuadCurve2D.Double
QuadCurve2D.Float
Random
RandomAccessFile
Raster
RasterFormatException
RasterOp
Reader
Receiver
Rectangle
Rectangle2D
Rectangle2D.Double
Rectangle2D.Float
RectangularShape
Ref
RefAddr
Reference
Referenceable
ReferenceQueue
ReferralException

ReflectPermission
Registry
RegistryHandler
RemarshalException
Remote
RemoteCall
RemoteException
RemoteObject
RemoteRef
RemoteServer
RemoteStub
RenderableImage
RenderableImageOp
RenderableImageProducer
RenderContext
RenderedImage
RenderedImageFactory
Renderer
RenderingHints
RenderingHints.Key
RepaintManager
ReplicateScaleFilter
Repository
RepositoryIdHelper
Request
RescaleOp
Resolver
ResolveResult
ResourceBundle
ResponseHandler
ResultSet
ResultSetMetaData
ReverbControl
ReverbControl.ReverbType
RGBImageFilter
RMIClassLoader
RMIClientSocketFactory
RMIFailureHandler
RMISecurityException
RMISecurityManager
RMIServerSocketFactory
RMISocketFactory
Robot
RootPaneContainer
RootPaneUI
RoundRectangle2D
RoundRectangle2D.Double
RoundRectangle2D.Float
RowMapper
RSAKey
RSAKeyGenParameterSpec
RSAPrivateCrtKey
RSAPrivateCrtKeySpec
RSAPrivateKey
RSAPrivateKeySpec
RSAPublicKey
RSAPublicKeySpec

RTFEditorKit
RuleBasedCollator
Runnable
RuntimeException
RunTimeOperations
RuntimePermission
Sample
SampleModel
SampleRateControl
SchemaViolationException
Scrollable
Scrollbar
ScrollBarUI
ScrollPane
ScrollPaneConstants
ScrollPaneLayout
ScrollPaneLayout.UIResource
ScrollPaneUI
SearchControls
SearchResult
SecureClassLoader
SecureRandom
SecureRandomSpi
Security
SecurityException
SecurityManager
SecurityPermission
Segment
SeparatorUI
Sequence
SequenceInputStream
SequenceProvider
Sequencer
Sequencer.SyncMode
Serializable
SerializablePermission
ServantObject
ServerCloneException
ServerError
ServerException
ServerNotActiveException
ServerRef
ServerRequest
ServerRuntimeException
ServerSocket
ServiceDetail
ServiceDetailHelper
ServiceInformation
ServiceInformationHelper
ServiceInformationHolder
ServiceUnavailableException
Set
SetOverrideType
SetOverrideTypeHelper
Shape
ShapeGraphicAttribute
Short

ShortEvent
ShortHolder
ShortLookupTable
ShortSeqHelper
ShortSeqHolder
Signature
SignatureException
SignatureSpi
SignedObject
Signer
SimpleAttributeSet
SimpleBeanInfo
SimpleDateFormat
SimpleTimeZone
SinglePixelPackedSample-
    Model
SingleSelectionModel
SizeLimitExceededException
SizeRequirements
SizeSequence
Skeleton
SkeletonMismatchException
SkeletonNotFoundException
SliderUI
Socket
SocketException
SocketImpl
SocketImplFactory
SocketOptions
SocketPermission
SocketSecurityException
SoftBevelBorder
SoftReference
SortedMap
SortedSet
Soundbank
SoundbankProvider
SourceDataLine
SplitPaneUI
SQLData
SQLException
SQLInput
SQLOutput
SQLPermission
SQLWarning
Stack
StackOverflowError
StateEdit
StateEditable
StateFactory
Statement
Streamable
StreamableValue
StreamCorruptedException
StreamGenerator
StreamingPolicy
StreamParser

StreamTokenizer
StrictMath
String
StringBuffer
StringBufferInputStream
StringCharacterIterator
StringContent
StringHolder
StringIndexOutOfBoundsEx-
    ception
StringReader
StringRefAddr
StringSelection
StringTokenizer
StringValueHelper
StringWriter
Stroke
Struct
StructMember
StructMemberHelper
Stub
StubDelegate
StubNotFoundException
Style
StyleConstants
StyleConstants.CharacterCon-
    stants
StyleConstants.ColorCon-
    stants
StyleConstants.FontConstants
StyleConstants.ParagraphCon-
    stants
StyleContext
StyledDocument
StyledEditorKit
StyledEditorKit.AlignmentAc-
    tion
StyledEditorKit.BoldAction
StyledEditorKit.FontFamily-
    Action
StyledEditorKit.FontSizeAc-
    tion
StyledEditorKit.Fore-
    groundAction
StyledEditorKit.ItalicAction
StyledEditorKit.StyledTextAc-
    tion
StyledEditorKit.UnderlineAc-
    tion
StyleSheet
StyleSheet.BoxPainter
StyleSheet.ListPainter
SwingConstants
SwingPropertyChangeSupport
SwingUtilities
SyncFailedException
Synthesizer

ValueHandler
ValueHelper
ValueMember
ValueMemberHelper
VariableHeightLayoutCache
Vector
VerifyError
VersionSpecHelper
VetoableChangeListener
VetoableChangeSupport
View
ViewFactory
ViewportLayout
ViewportUI
VirtualMachineError
Visibility
VisibilityHelper
VM_ABSTRACT
VM_CUSTOM

VM_NONE
VM_TRUNCATABLE
VMID
VoiceStatus
Void
WCharSeqHelper
WCharSeqHolder
WeakHashMap
WeakReference
Window
WindowAdapter
WindowConstants
WindowEvent
WindowListener
WrappedPlainView
WritableRaster
WritableRenderedImage
WriteAbortedException
Writer

WrongTransaction
WStringValueHelper
X509Certificate
X509CRL
X509CRLEntry
X509EncodedKeySpec
X509Extension
ZipEntry
ZipException
ZipFile
ZipInputStream
ZipOutputStream
ZoneView
_BindingIteratorImplBase
_BindingIteratorStub
_IDLTypeStub
_NamingContextImplBase
_NamingContextStub
_PolicyStub

We noted in several places that a binary scheme having only the two binary digits 0 and 1 is used to represent information in a computer. The Part of the Picture: Data Representation section in Chapter 2 describes how these binary digits, called *bits*, are organized into groups of 8 called *bytes*, and bytes in turn are grouped together into *words*. Common word sizes are 16 bits (= 2 bytes) and 32 bits (= 4 bytes). Each byte or word has an *address* that can be used to access it, making it possible to store information in and retrieve information from that byte or word. In this appendix we describe the binary number system and how numbers can be converted from one base to another..

The number system that we are accustomed to using is a **decimal** or **base-10** number system, which uses the digits 0, 1, 2, 3, 4, 5, 6, 7, 8, and 9. The significance of these digits in a numeral depends on the positions that they occupy in that numeral. For example, in the numeral

$$485$$

the digit 4 is interpreted as

$$4 \text{ hundreds}$$

and the digit 8 as

$$8 \text{ tens}$$

and the digit 5 as

$$5 \text{ ones}$$

Thus, the numeral 485 represents the number four-hundred eighty-five and can be written in **expanded form** as

$$(4 \times 100) + (8 \times 10) + (5 \times 1)$$

or

$$(4 \times 10^2) + (8 \times 10^1) + (5 \times 10^0)$$

The digits that appear in the various positions of a decimal (base-10) numeral thus are coefficients of powers of 10.

Similar positional number systems can be devised using numbers other than 10 as a base. The **binary** number system uses 2 as the base and has only two digits, 0 and 1. As in a decimal system, the significance of the bits in a binary numeral is determined by their positions in that numeral. For example, the binary numeral

$$101$$

can be written in expanded form (using decimal notation) as

$$(1 \times 2^2) + (0 \times 2^1) + (1 \times 2^0)$$

that is, the binary numeral 101 has the decimal value

$$4 + 0 + 1 = 5$$

Similarly, the binary numeral 111010 has the decimal value

$$(1 \times 2^5) + (1 \times 2^4) + (1 \times 2^3) + (0 \times 2^2) + (1 \times 2^1) + (0 \times 2^0)$$

$$= 32 + 16 + 8 + 0 + 2 + 0$$
$$= 58$$

When necessary, to avoid confusion about which base is being used, it is customary to write the base as a subscript for nondecimal numerals. Using this convention, we could indicate that 5 and 58 have the binary representations just given by writing

$$5 = 101_2$$

and

$$58 = 111010_2$$

Two other nondecimal numeration systems are important in the consideration of computer systems: **octal** and **hexadecimal.** The octal system is a base-8 system and uses the eight digits $0, 1, 2, 3, 4, 5, 6,$ and $7.$ In an octal numeral such as

$$1703_8$$

the digits are coefficients of powers of 8; this numeral is therefore an abbreviation for the expanded form

$$(1 \times 8^3) + (7 \times 8^2) + (0 \times 8^1) + (3 \times 8^0)$$

and thus has the decimal value

$$512 + 448 + 0 + 3 = 963$$

A hexadecimal system uses a base of 16 and the digits $0, 1, 2, 3, 4, 5, 6, 7, 8, 9, A\ (10), B\ (11),$ $C\ (12), D\ (13), E\ (14),$ and $F\ (15).$ The hexadecimal numeral

$$5E4_{16}$$

has the expanded form

$$(5 \times 16^2) + (14 \times 16^1) + (4 \times 16^0)$$

which has the decimal value

$$1280 + 224 + 4 = 1508$$

Table E.1 shows the decimal, binary, octal, and hexadecimal representations for the first 31 non-negative integers.

TABLE E.I   NUMERIC REPRESENTATION

Decimal	Binary	Octal	Hexadecimal
0	0	0	0
1	1	1	1
2	10	2	2
3	11	3	3
4	100	4	4
5	101	5	5
6	110	6	6
7	111	7	7
8	1000	10	8
9	1001	11	9
10	1010	12	A
11	1011	13	B

12	1100	14	C
13	1101	15	D
14	1110	16	E
15	1111	17	F
16	10000	20	10
17	10001	21	11
18	10010	22	12
19	10011	23	13
20	10100	24	14
21	10101	25	15
22	10110	26	16
23	10111	27	17
24	11000	30	18
25	11001	31	19
26	11010	32	1A
27	11011	33	1B
28	11100	34	1C
29	11101	35	1D
30	11110	36	1E
31	11111	37	1F

In the decimal representation of real numbers, digits to the left of the decimal point are co-efficients of nonnegative powers of 10, and those to the right are coefficients of negative powers of 10. For example, the decimal numeral 56.317 can be written in expanded form as

$$(5 \times 10^1) + (6 \times 10^0) + (3 \times 10^{-1}) + (1 \times 10^{-2}) + (7 \times 10^{-3})$$

or, equivalently, as

$$(5 \times 10) + (6 \times 1) + \left(3 \times \frac{1}{10}\right) + \left(1 \times \frac{1}{100}\right) + \left(7 \times \frac{1}{1000}\right)$$

Digits in the binary representation of a real number are coefficients of powers of two. Those to the left of the binary point are coefficients of nonnegative powers of two, and those to the right are coefficients of negative powers of two. For example, the expanded form of 110.101_2 is

$$(1 \times 2^2) + (1 \times 2^1) + (0 \times 2^0) + (1 \times 2^{-1}) + (0 \times 2^{-2}) + (1 \times 2^{-3})$$

and thus has the decimal value

$$4 + 2 + 0 + \tfrac{1}{2} + 0 + \tfrac{1}{8} = 6.625$$

Similarly, in octal representation, digits to the left of the octal point are coefficients of non-negative powers of eight, and those to the right are coefficients of negative powers of eight. And in hexadecimal representation, digits to the left of the octal point are coefficients of non-negative powers of sixteen, and those to the right are coefficients of negative powers of six-teen. Thus, the expanded form of 102.34_8 is

$$(1 \times 8^2) + (0 \times 8^1) + (2 \times 8^0) + (3 \times 8^{-1}) + (4 \times 8^{-2})$$

which has the decimal value

$$64 + 0 + 2 + \tfrac{3}{8} + \tfrac{4}{64} = 66.4375$$

The expanded form of $1AB.C8_8$ is

$$(1 \times 16^2) + (10 \times 16^1) + (11 \times 16^0) + (12 \times 16^{-1}) + (8 \times 16^{-2})$$

whose decimal value is

$$256 + 160 + 11 + \frac{12}{16} + \frac{8}{256} = 417.78125$$

✍ EXERCISE E

Convert each of the binary numerals in Exercises 1-6 to base ten.

1. 1001   **4.** 111111111111111 (fifteen 1s)

2. 110010   **5.** 1.1

3. 1000000   **6.** 1010.10101

Convert each of the octal numerals in Exercises 7-12 to base ten.

7. 23   **9.** 2705   **11.** 10000

8. 77777   **10.** 7.2   **12.** 123.45

Convert each of the hexadecimal numerals in Exercises 13-18 to base ten.

13. 12   **15.** 1AB   **17.** ABC

14. FFF   **16.** 8.C   **18.** AB.CD

19-24. Converting from octal representation to binary representation is easy, as we need only replace each octal digit with its three-bit binary equivalent. For example, to convert 617_8 to binary, replace 6 with 110, 1 with 001, and 7 with 111, to obtain 110001111_2. Convert each of the octal numerals in Exercises 7-12 to binary numerals.

25-30. Imitating the conversion scheme in exercises 19-24, convert each of the hexadecimal numerals in Exercises 13-18 to binary numerals.

31-36. To convert a binary numeral to octal, place the digits in groups of three, starting from the binary point, or from the right end if there is no binary point, and replace each group with the corresponding octal digit. For example, $10101111_2 = 010\ 101\ 111_2 = 257_8$. Convert each of the binary numerals in Exercises 1-6 to octal numerals.

37-42. Imitating the conversion scheme in Exercises 31-36, convert each of the binary numerals in Exercises 1-6 to hexadecimal numerals.

One method for finding the base-b representation of a whole number given in base-ten notation is to divide the number repeatedly by b until a quotient of zero results. The successive remainders are the digits from right to left of the base-b representation. For example, the binary representation of 26 is 11010_2, as the following computation shows:

$$0\ R\ 1$$
$$2 \div 1R1$$
$$2 \div 3R0$$
$$2 \div 6R0$$
$$2 \div 13R0$$
$$2 \div 26$$

Convert each of the base-ten numerals in Exercises 43-46 to (a) binary, (b) octal, and (c) hexadecimal:

43. 27   **45.** 99

44. 314   **46.** 5280

To convert a decimal fraction to its base-b equivalent, repeatedly multiply the fractional part of the number by b. The integer parts are the digits from left to right of the base-b representation. For example, the decimal numeral 0.6875 corresponds to the binary numeral 0.1011_2, as the following computation shows:

$$
\begin{array}{r|l}
 & .6875 \\
 & \times\ \ 2 \\
\hline
1 & .375 \\
 & \times\ \ 2 \\
\hline
0 & .75 \\
 & \times\ \ 2 \\
\hline
1 & .5 \\
 & \times 2 \\
\hline
1 & .0 \\
\end{array}
$$

Convert each of the base-ten numerals in Exercises 47-51 to (a) binary, (b) octal, and (c) hexadecimal:

47. 0.5   **50.** 16.0625

48. 0.25   **51.** 8.828125

49. 0.625

Even though the base-ten representation of a fraction may terminate, its representation in some other base need not terminate. For example, the following computation shows that the binary representation of 0.7 is $(0.10110011001100110011001100110\ldots)_2$, where the block of bits 0110 is repeated indefinitely. This representation is commonly written as 0.1_2.

$$
\begin{array}{r|l}
 & .7 \\
 & \times\ 2 \\
\hline
1 & .4 \\
 & \times\ 2 \\
\hline
0 & .8 \\
 & \times\ 2 \\
\hline
1 & .6 \\
 & \times\ 2 \\
\hline
1 & .2 \\
 & \times\ 2 \\
\hline
0 & .4 \\
\end{array}
$$

Convert each of the base-ten numerals in Exercises 52-55 to (a) binary, (b) octal, and (c) hexadecimal:

52. 0.3   **54.** 0.05

53. 0.6   **55.** $0. = 0.33333 \cdots = 1/3$

Exercises 56-67 assume the two's-complement representation of integers described in the section Part of the Picture: Data Representation in Chapter 2.

Find the decimal value of each of the 32-bit integers in Exercises 56-61, assuming two's complement representation.

56.   00000000000000000000000001000000
57.   11111111111111111111111111111110
58.   11111111111111111111111110111111
59.   00000000000000000000000011111111
60.   11111111111111111111111100000000
61.   11111111111111111100000000000001

Find the 32-bit two's complement representation of each of the integers in Exercises 62-67.

62. 255	**64.** –255	**66.** –34567$_8$	
63. 1K	**65.** –256	**67.** –3ABC$_{16}$	

Assuming the IEEE floating point representation of real numbers described in the section Part of the Picture: Data Representation in Chapter 2, indicate how each of the real numbers in Exercises 68-73 would be stored.

68. 0.375	**70.** 0.03125	**72.** 0.1
69. 37.375	**71.** 63.84375	**73.** 0.01

F ANSWERS TO QUICK QUIZZES

Quick Quiz 1.1

1. software engineering
2. FORTRAN, COBOL, LISP
3. E, A, C, D, F, H, I, J, B, G

Quick Quiz 1.2

1. program
2. objects, messages
3. classes, blueprints or patterns
4. A collection of statements to solve a problem
   A collection of object interactions that solve a problem
5. comment
6. comment
7. import
8. package
9. variables, methods
10. main() method
11. concatenation

Quick Quiz 1.3

1. `JApplet` (or `Applet`)
2. graphical user interface
3. Abstract Windowing Toolkit
4. Java Foundation Classes
5. false
6. false
7. true
8. `extends JApplet` (or extends `Applet`)
9. Embed it in a web page and:
   i. Open it with a web browser; or
   ii. Use Java's appletviewer

10. HTML

11. server, client

Quick Quiz 1.4

1. Design
   Coding
   Testing, execution, and debugging
   Maintenance

2. State program's behavior
   Identify the objects
   Identify the operations
   Arrange operations in an algorithm

3. objects

4. operations

5. variables

6. constants

7. primitive

8. *, /

9. debugging

10. syntax errors and logic errors

Quick Quiz 2.2

1. primitive, reference

2. `byte`, `short`, `int`, `long`

3. `float`, `double`

4. `boolean`, `char`

5. 0 for numeric types, `false` for boolean type, and `null` for reference types

6. false

7. literal

8. not legal — identifiers must begin with a letter or underscore

9. legal

10. not legal — identifiers may contain only letters, digits, and underscores

11. not legal — same reason as 10

12. `int distanceTraveled;`

```
13. unsigned idNumber;
    float salary;
    char employeeCode;
```

```
14. int distanceTraveled = 0;
```

```
15. unsigned idNumber = 9999;
    float salary = 0;
    char employeeCode = ' ';
```

```
16. const int gravity = 32;
```

```
17. const double EARTH = 1.5E10,
                  MARS = 1.2E12;
```

Quick Quiz 2.3

1. multiline comment: enclosed between /* and */
   inline comment: extend from // to end of a line

2. class

3. objects (or instances)

4. attributes (or state)

5. behavior

6. main

7. package

8. import

9. message

Quick Quiz 2.4

1. false

2. false

3. API (or Application Programmer's Interface)

4. lang

5. util

6. packages

7. Object

8. inherits

Quick Quiz 2.4

1. GUI (or graphical user interface)

2. transition

3. widget

4. input-dialog

5. message-dialog

6. An icon, a prompt string sent to the method, a text field where the user can enter a response, and buttons labeled *Ok* and *Cancel*

7. An information icon, a `String` sent to it, and a button labeled *OK*

Quick Quiz 3.2

1. primitive   **2.** reference   **3.** reference

4. primitive   **5.** primitive   **6.** primitive

7. reference   **8.** reference   **9.** primitive

10. reference   **11.** primitive   **12.** primitive

13. literal

14. `void`

15. true

16. reference

17. false

18. `new`

19. handle

20. An information icon, a `String` sent to it, and a button labeled *OK*

Quick Quiz 3.3

1. `float` (4 bytes = 32 bits), double (8 bytes = 64 bits)

2. `byte` (1 byte = 8 bits), `short` (2 bytes = 16 bits), `int` (4 bytes = 32 bits), `long` (8 bytes = 64 bits)

3. true

4. false

5. true

6. promotion

7. Instance methods are invoked by sending a message of the form `obj.method()` to an object (i.e., instance) `obj`. Static methods are invoked by sending a message of the form `C.method()` to a class C.

8. integer   **9.** neither   **10.** real   **11.** real

12. neither   **13.** real   **14.** integer   **15.** neither

16. 0

17. 2.6

18. 2

19. 5

20. 8

21. 3

22. 2

23. 36.0

24. 3.0

25. 8.0

26. 2.0

27. 3.0

28. 11.0

29. 1

30. 7.0

31. 5.1

32. 8.0

33. 10.0

34. 3.0

35. 32.0

36. 4

37. 13

38. 96

39. 1

40. `10 + 5 * B - 4 * A * C`

41. `Math.sqrt(A + 3 * pow(B, 2))`

Quick Quiz 3.4

1. valid

2. not valid — variable must be to left of assignment operator

3. valid

4. not valid — variable must be to left of assignment operator

5. valid

6. not valid — can't assign a string to an integer variable

7. valid

8. valid

9. valid

10. valid

11. valid

12. valid

13. not valid — ++ can only be used with integers

14. valid

15. valid

16. `xValue`: 3.5

17. `xValue`: 6.1

18. not valid — type of right side (`double`) is not compatible with variable on left side (`int`)

19. `xValue: 5.0`

20. `jobId: 1`

21. `jobId: 5`
    `intFive1: 6`

22. `jobId: 6`
    `intFive2: 6`

23. `intEight: 64`

24. `intEight: 8`

25. `intEight: 32`

26. `distance = rate * time;`

27. `c = Math.sqrt(a*a + b*b);`

28. `++x;`
    `x++;`
    `x += 1;`
    `x = x + 1;`

Quick Quiz 3.5

1. `false, true`

2. `<, >, ==, <=, >=, !=`

3. `!, &&, ||`

4. `false`   **5.** `true`

6. `false`   **7.** `false`

8. `true`

9. `true`

10. `true`

11. `true`

12. not valid — should be written `0 <= count && count <= 5`

13. `false`

14. `true`

15. not valid — right side should be written `1 <= sum && sum <= 10`

16. `true`

17. `x != 0`

18. `-10 < x && x < 10`

19. `(x > 0 && y > 0) || (x < 0 && y < 0)`
    or more simply,
    `x * y > 0`

Quick Quiz 3.6

1. single quotes

2. double quotes

3. escape sequence

4. false

5. true

6. true

7. true

8. `assert('0' <= c && c <= '9');`

9. `assert(Character.isdigit(c));`

10. `c = Character.toLowerCase(c);`

11. `"listen"`   **12.** `"enlist"`   **13.** `"listen dear"`

14. `'s'`   **15.** `'e'`   **15.** 4

Quick Quiz 4.2

1. method

2. parameters

3. `double`

4. false

5. class (or static), instance

6. (i)   values the method receives
 (ii)   values input to the method
 (iii)   restrictions or limitations on these values (precondition)
 (iv)   value the method returns
 (v)   values the method outputs
 (vi)   effects produced by the method (postcondition)

7. `void`

8. no statements

9. argument

10. 6

11. true

12. false

13.
```
#include <cmath>
double func(double x)
{
    return x*x + sqrt(x);
}
```

14.
```
int average(int num1, int num2)
{
     return (num1 + num2) / 2;
}
```

15. The value of an argument is copied to the corresponding parameter. For a reference parameter, this means that the address of the value referred to by the argument is copied to the corresponding argument, so that both refer to the same value. Changing the value of the parameter changes the value of the corresponding argument. This does not happen for primitive types.

Quick Quiz 5.2

1. 6

2. 5

3. 6

4. 10

5. 10

6. 10

7. excellent

8. excellent

9. good

10. fair

11. bad

12.
```
if (number < 0 || number > 100)
     theScreen.println("Out of range");
```

13.
```
if (x <= 1.5)
     n = 1;
else if (x <= 2.5)
     n = 2;
else
     n = 3;
```

Quick Quiz 5.3

1.
```
Hello
Hello
Hello
Hello
Hello
```

2.
```
HelloHelloHello
```

3. Hello
Hello
Hello

4. 1 2
2 3
3 4
4 5
5 6
6 7

5. 36
25
16
9
4
1

6. Hello

7. No output

8. 1
3
5
7
9

9. 25

10. A pretest loop checks the termination condition at the top of the loop; a posttest loop checks it at the bottom.

11. false

12. true

13. 1
2
4
8
16
32
64

14. (a)   0   (b) no output produced
1
2
3
4

15. (a)   0   (b) 0
1
2
3
4

Quick Quiz 6.3

1. class

2. operations

3. data

4. false

5. I-can-do-it-myself

6. encapsulation

7. To prevent direct access to the attribute variables from outside the class declaration.

8. private

9. invariant

10. `public`

11. `static`

12. Objects share a class constant rather than having their own copy of it, as is the case with an instance constant. Class constants are accessed by sending messages to the class rather than to an instance of that class (i.e., object).

Quick Quiz 6.4

1. instance methods

2. constructors

3. accessors

4. mutators

5. converters

6. utilities

7. `Student()`

8. Default-value constructor: Initializes the attribute variables to default values
Explicit-value constructor: Initializes the attribute variables to user-supplied values

9. postcondition

10. true

11. address

12. handle

13. interface

Quick Quiz 7.3

1. `198`

2. 198
197
default

3. default

4. default

5. -2

6. -2
default

7. 123

8. 456

9. no output produced

10. error — x must be an integer type

Quick Quiz 7.5

1. events

2. event

3. true

4. event-delegation

5. fire

6. i. Define the event source(s)
   ii. Define the event listener(s)
   iii. Register a listener with each source, to handle the events generated by that source

7. headings (or prototypes)

8. Definitions for the methods whose headings are in the interface

9. A compilation error will result.

10. layout manager

11. panes, content pane

12. When the *Enter* key is pressed in that `JTextField` object.

Quick Quiz 8.5

1. counting, sentinel, query-controlled

2. counting (or counter-controlled) loops, `for`

3. initialization expression, loop condition, step expression, loop body

4. false

5. end-of-data flag, sentinel

6. true

7. query

8. `if-break` (or `if-return`)

9. pretest

10. posttest

11. posttest

12. pretest

13.
```
2i = 0
2i = 2
2i = 4
2i = 6
2i = 8
2i = 10
2i = 12
2i = 14
2i = 16
2i = 18
```

14. 1   3   5   7   9   11

15.
```
11
22
1
33
2
1
```

16.
```
0 0 0
1 1 2
2 2 8
18
```

17.
```
4
5
6
```

18.
```
3
2
1
0
-1
* * * * *
```

19.
```
0 1
1 2
2 5
3 10
4 17
```

20. 4 12
   3 5
   2 0
   1 -3

Quick Quiz 8.6

1. recursion

2. i. An anchor or base case that specifies the method's value for one or more values of the parameter(s).
   ii. An inductive or recursive step that defines the method's value for the current values of the parameter(s) in terms of previously defined method and/or parameter values.

3. 15

4. 0

5. 120

6. Infinite recursion results.

Quick Quiz 9.2

1. true

2. true

3. true

4. true

5. false

6. 5

7. 1

8. false

9. xValue[0]:   0.0
   xValue[1]:   0.5
   xValue[2]:   1.0
   xValue[3]:   1.5
   xValue[4]:   2.0

10. number[0]:   0
    number[1]:   3
    number[2]:   4
    number[3]:   7
    number[4]:   8

11. number[0]:   1
    number[1]:   2
    number[2]:   4
    number[3]:   8
    number[4]:   16

12. `number[0]:`   144
    `number[1]:`   72
    `number[2]:`   36
    `number[3]:`   18
    `number[4]:`   9

13. `value[0], number[0]:`   1
    `value[1], number[1]:`   0
    `value[2], number[2]:`   5
    `value[3], number[3]:`   7
    `value[4], number[4]:`   9

14. `value[0]:`   1
    `value[1]:`   3
    `value[2]:`   5
    `value[3]:`   7
    `value[4]:`   9
    `number[0]:`   1
    `number[1]:`   0
    `number[2]:`   5
    `number[3]:`   7
    `number[4]:`   9

15. `false`

16. `shallow`

Quick Quiz 9.3

1. It makes a number of passes through the list or a part of the list, and on each pass selects one item (e.g., the smallest one) to be correctly positioned.

2. It repeatedly inserts a new element into a list of already sorted elements so that the resulting list is still sorted.

3. true

4. It chooses some element called a *pivot* and then performs a sequence of exchanges so that all elements that are less than this pivot are to its left and all elements that are greater than the pivot are to its right. This correctly positions the pivot and divides the (sub)list into two smaller sublists, each of which may then be sorted independently.

5. pivot

Quick Quiz 9.4

1. two-dimensional

2. three-dimensional

3. square

4. 82

5. 33

6. −1

7. 33

8. 12

9. 1, 2, 3, 4

10. 95

11. 999

12. 29

13. 1326

14. 1326

15. $m \times n$ matrix

16. 2, 2

17. $\begin{bmatrix} 3 & 6 \\ 7 & 12 \end{bmatrix}$

18. $\begin{bmatrix} 1 & 0 & 2 \\ -1 & 0 & 0 \\ 10 & 0 & 14 \end{bmatrix}$

Quick Quiz 10.4

1. streams

2. `in`

3. `out`

4. `err`

5. *Readers* and *Writers* support `char` (16-bit Unicode) input and output. *InputStreams* and *OutputStreams* support `byte` (8-bit) input and output.

6. false

7. input buffer

8. output buffer

9. `Exception`

10. throw

11. try

12. catch

13. A text file is a container for Unicode character values stored on a secondary memory device. A binary file is a container for byte values stored on a secondary memory device.

Quick Quiz 11.1

1. abstract

2. abstract

3. Precede its declaration with the keyword `abstract`.

4. subclass or child class

5. superclass or parent class

6. true

7. `super(a, b);`

Quick Quiz 11.2

1. subclass or child class

2. superclass or parent class

3. descendant

4. ancestor

5. inherits

6. D

7. override

8. Class `X` is searched for a definition of `m2()`. Since none is found, its parent class `Y` is searched. Since none is found there, `Y`'s parent class `Z` is searched and the definition of `m2()` there is invoked.

9. `super.m1()`

10. `Object`

11. polymorphism

12. true

Quick Quiz 12.2

1. collection

2. lists, sets, and maps

3. array

4. an `Object` array, size, and capacity

5. nodes

6. It allows values to be inserted or removed anywhere in a sequence without copying. Also, it can grow or shrink as necessary.

7. Each element can be accessed directly.

8. Singly-linked lists have a single link to the successor node. Doubly-linked lists have two links per node: one to the successor and one to the predecessor.

9. In a singly-linked list, a handle is maintained to the first node, and the link in the last node is null. In a circularly-linked list, a handle to the last node is maintained, and the link in the last node refers to the first node in the list.

10. false

11. false

12. true

13. true

14. 1

15. n

16. n

17. 1

Quick Quiz 12.3

1. 10011010010

2. 2322

3. 4d2

4. first, LIFO (last-in-first-out)

5. *isEmpty*( ), *top*( ), *push*( ), and *pop*( )

6. Java's `Stack` class extends `Vector`, but a `Stack` is not a `Vector`, since `Vector` has many non-stack operations.

Quick Quiz 12.4

1. In a stack, items are added and removed at the same end. In a queue, items are added at one end and removed at the other.

2. last

3. FIFO (first-in-first-out)

4. spool

5. buffers

6. *isEmpty*( ), *first*( ), *add*( ), and *remove*( )

Quick Quiz 12.5

1. root

2. leaves

3. children, parent

4. at most two children

5. 50

6. 10, 40, 70

7.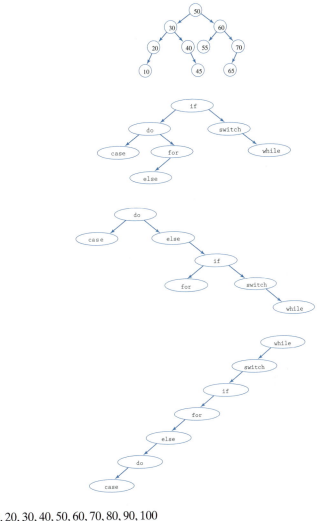

8.

9.

10.

11. 10, 20, 30, 40, 50, 60, 70, 80, 90, 100

12. 80, 30, 20, 10, 60, 50, 40, 70, 90, 100

13. 10, 20, 40, 50, 70, 60, 30, 100, 90, 80

Quick Quiz 13.2

1. thread

2. multithreaded

3. true

4. i. Extend the `Thread` class
ii. Implement the `Runnable` interface

5. false

6. atomic

7. thread-safe

Quick Quiz 13.3

1. client-server

2. socket

3. i. The name of the computer where the socket is located
ii. The port associated with that socket

4. smtp, pop3, imap

5. ftp

6. http

7. If servicing a client takes an extended period of time, connection requests may be lost before the server is able to accept them.

8. It accepts a connection request, then creates a handler thread to provide the service for that client, and the server thread can immediately return to the top of the processing loop to handle the next connection request.